VERSE BY VERSE
THE Four Gospels

VERSE BY VERSE
THE Four Gospels

D. KELLY OGDEN
ANDREW C. SKINNER

DESERET BOOK

SALT LAKE CITY, UTAH

Jesus with the Woman at the Well (page 133), *Jesus Clears the Temple* (page 115), *Peter's Denial* (page 618), and *The Burial* (page 667), by Carl Heinrich Bloch, © Det Nationalhistoriske Museum pa Frederiksborg, Hillerod, Denmark; used by permission. *Boy Jesus in the Temple* (page 69), by Grant Romney Clawson; *John the Baptist Baptizing Jesus* (page 87), *Calling of the Fishermen* (page 148), *Christ Ordaining the Apostles* (page 159), *Sermon on the Mount* (page 171), *Jesus Praying in Gethsemane* (page 600), and *The Second Coming* (page 521), by Harry Anderson; *Jesus Blessing Jairus's Daughter* (page 255), by Greg Olsen; *Mary and Martha* (page 387) and *Be Not Afraid* (page 310), by Del Parson; © Intellectual Reserve, Inc.; used by permission. *The Mount of Transfiguration* (page 338), by Gary Smith, © 1985 Brigham Young University; used by permission.

Illustration on page 718 adapted and used by permission of Leen Ritmeyer, Ritmeyer Archaeological Design, Harrogate, North Yorkshire, England. Illustration on page 717 by James Christiansen, © Intellectual Reserve, Inc.; used by permission. All other illustrations were created by Michael Parker.

Photos of the Model City of ancient Jerusalem (pages 261, 418, 441, 613, 624, 739, 741, 742, 743) used by permission. Photo page 490 courtesy MuseumSurplus.com. All other photos © D. Kelly Ogden.

© 2006 D. Kelly Ogden and Andrew C. Skinner

All rights reserved. No part of this book may be reproduced in any form or by any means without permission in writing from the publisher, Deseret Book Company, at permissions@deseretbook.com or P. O. Box 30178, Salt Lake City, Utah 84130. This work is not an official publication of The Church of Jesus Christ of Latter-day Saints. The views expressed herein are the responsibility of the authors and do not necessarily represent the position of the Church or of Deseret Book Company.

DESERET BOOK is a registered trademark of Deseret Book Company.

Visit us at DeseretBook.com

Library of Congress Cataloging-in-Publication Data
Ogden, D. Kelly (Daniel Kelly), 1947–
   Verse by verse, the four Gospels / D. Kelly Ogden, Andrew C. Skinner.
     p. cm.
   Includes bibliographical references and indexes.
   ISBN-10 1-59038-583-7 (hardbound : alk. paper)
   ISBN-13 978-1-59038-583-8 (hardbound : alk. paper)
   1. Bible. N.T. Gospels—Commentaries. 2. Church of Jesus Christ of Latter-day Saints—Doctrines. 3. Mormon Church—Doctrines.
I. Skinner, Andrew C., 1951- II. Title.
BS2555.53.O43 2006
226'.07—dc22   2006000932

Printed in the United States of America
Publishers Printing, Salt Lake City, UT

10 9 8 7 6 5 4

CONTENTS

Preface vii
Introduction 1

Part I. Before Jesus Came to Earth
 1 The Foreordained Messiah 11

Part II. Preparation for the Messiah
 2 Divinely Appointed Foundations 27
 3 The Birth and Childhood of Jesus 49
 4 The Ministry of John the Baptist 72

Part III. The Ministry of the Messiah
 5 An Early Galilean Ministry 107
 6 The Early Judean Ministry 114
 7 A Second Galilean Ministry 129
 8 The North Galilean Ministry 321
 9 The Perean and Later Judean Ministry 373
 10 The Atonement and the Resurrection 458

Appendixes
 1 Maps
  The Holy Land at the Time of Jesus 713
  Journeys from Nazareth to Bethlehem,
   Bethlehem to Egypt, and Egypt to Nazareth 714
  The Galilean Ministry 715
  New Testament Jerusalem 716
  The Last Week of Jesus' Life 717
  The Temple Mount 718
  The Inner Temple 719
 2 The World of the New Testament 720
 3 The Temple at the Time of Jesus 733
  Description of the Temple Built by Herod 735
  The Courts of the Temple 739

Contents

4 Religious and Political Groups, Occupations, and Institutions
    Chief Priests 745
    Elders 746
    Herodians 746
    Lawyers 746
    Pharisees 747
    Priests, Levites, and High Priests 748
    Publicans 750
    Rabbis 751
    Sadducees 752
    Samaritans 753
    Sanhedrin 753
    Scribes 754
    Synagogue 755
    Temple Police 756
    Zealots 756

5 Roman Government and Military System
    Caesar 758
    Legates, Prefects, and Procurators 759
    Cohorts, Centuries, and Legions 759
    Client Kings, Ethnarchs, and Tetrarchs 760

6 Israelite Feasts, Festivals, and Holy Days
    Dedication 763
    Passover 764
    Pentecost 765
    Tabernacles 765

7 Cultural and Religious Practices
    Betrothal 768
    The Challenge of Jesus' Date of Birth 770
    Circumcision 773
    Fishing on the Sea of Galilee 774
    Money 777
    Time 778
    Weights and Measures 779

Sources 781
Scripture Index 795
Subject Index 827

PREFACE

For two decades, from the mid-1970s to the mid-1990s, we periodically lived, learned, and taught in the Holy Land—walking where Jesus walked and teaching where Jesus taught. Working as teachers and administrators in the Brigham Young University Jerusalem Center, we were privileged to take thousands of students to study, on location, the teachings of the prophets and of Jesus Christ.

In March 1994, when Elder Richard G. Scott set apart Brother D. Kelly Ogden to a Church calling, Elder Scott told him, "You are one of the few who has ever had opportunity to study the life of the Savior as you have. Teach and testify of him!" Brother Ogden notes: "I accepted that as a commission to gather together helpful information gleaned from my studies and learning, including my personal experiences involving the life and teachings of Jesus, into a single volume. In this effort I heartily endorse the plea of the great Renaissance and Reformation figure Erasmus when he said: 'Make Christ the only goal of your life.' By doing that, we will automatically desire to emulate and glorify our Father in Heaven and have his Spirit to be with us.

"My purpose is the same as Nephi's: I labor diligently to write, to persuade my children, and also my brethren, to believe in Christ, and to be reconciled to God, so that they will 'know to what source they may look for a remission of their sins' (2 Nephi 25:26) and learn how to come unto him and be saved (1 Nephi 15:14). Any true study of the Savior's life has as its ultimate objective to learn of him, to love him, and become like him."

St. Augustine of Hippo (a fifth-century Catholic theologian) described feelings about Jesus with which countless numbers of Christians have resonated: "Our hearts are restless until they rest in thee." With that in mind Brother Andrew C. Skinner observes: "When I am not immersed in studying the Savior's life and ministry I feel restless, like I am not quite doing the things that matter most. Thus, it was with both satisfaction and discomfiture that I, along with my family, attended a fireside while living in Jerusalem and heard Sister Marjorie Hinckley say, 'Being in Jerusalem has made me realize that I do not think about the Savior enough.' President and Sister Hinckley had come to the Holy Land for a brief tour on their way home from an area conference in the Far East. 'Oh,' she continued, 'I think about him when I say my prayers at night before going to bed, and I think about him when I say my prayers getting up in the morning. But I do not think about him enough.' If this was true for the wife of the Lord's prophet, I know it is true for me. May the following pages motivate all of us to be consumed by thoughts of the Master."

We acknowledge the help of many people over the decades of our experience in the land of Jesus and during the years of preparation of this volume: Connie Lankford Brace, secretary to the dean of Religious Education, and student assistants Cory Niepraschk, Michael Howard, and Rachel Kimball Wilcox. We thank Thomas Child for the maps and Michael Parker for the drawings, along with all the other artists whose paintings are included in this book. We also express sincere gratitude to our Deseret Book editor, Suzanne Brady; designer, Shauna Gibby; typesetter, Tonya-Rae Facemyer; and others for their assistance in producing this volume that will help Latter-day Saints come to better know their Savior.

INTRODUCTION

As we launch into our study of the life and teachings of the Lord Jesus Christ, we might appropriately ask why we should study the Holy Bible in the first place, especially since we have additional volumes of modern scripture that often surpass the biblical record in clarity and power.

There are good reasons to study the Bible, which is our great connection with the rest of the Christian world. It is the most widely read book in the history of the world. It is also the most influential book in history. More copies of the Bible have been distributed throughout the earth than any other book. It has been translated more times into more languages than any other book. Millions of people have been named after biblical characters, and names of many cities and other places come from the Bible. Some of the greatest music, the greatest literature, and the greatest works of art are based on biblical characters and stories. Countless people have found hope, comfort, and guidance from the Bible during times of trouble and uncertainty.

Meaningful comments about this great book are attributed to a number of renowned people (the following are found on the pages indicated in Federer, *America's God and Country*):

George Washington, a founding father of the United States of America, declared that "it is impossible to rightly govern the world without God and the Bible" (660).

Immanuel Kant, an eighteenth-century German philosopher, claimed that "the existence of the Bible, as a book for

The Four Gospels

the people, is the greatest benefit which the human race has ever experienced. Every attempt to belittle it is a crime against humanity" (342).

Alfred, Lord Tennyson, English poet-laureate, remarked that "Bible reading is an education in itself" (581).

Patrick Henry, American patriot, observed in the late 1700s: "The Bible is worth all other books which have ever been printed" (289).

Daniel Webster, American statesman, predicted that "if we abide by the principles taught in the Bible, our country will go on prospering . . . but if we and our posterity neglect its instructions and authority, no man can tell how sudden a catastrophe may overwhelm us and bury all our glory in profound obscurity" (668–69).

Theodore Roosevelt, twenty-sixth president of the United States, proclaimed that "a thorough knowledge of the Bible is worth more than a college education" (540).

So why should we study the Bible? Because, as the eighth Article of Faith says, we believe the Bible to be the word of God and there are words in the Bible that teach us about God and guide us back to him.

Having established the value of studying the Holy Bible, we might also ask why we should study the King James Version of the Bible. There are some practical reasons: It is the largest selling version of the Bible in the world; therefore, it is more available. It was the most commonly used Bible at the time of the Restoration, all latter-day prophets have concurred with its use, and it has been used throughout our dispensation in all Church publications. The language of the other standard works is similar to the language of the King James Version. The Joseph Smith Translation revisions are also in harmony with the tone and expression of the King James Version. In addition, the King James Version has superior literary quality. Many authorities consider it to be *the* masterpiece of the English language.

A higher reason for studying the King James Version of

2

Introduction

the Bible is that its translators believed in the divine Sonship and the divine mission of Jesus Christ. Their renderings strengthen rather than destroy faith (some other versions have subtle changes that raise doubts).

In 1992, the First Presidency of the Church (Ezra Taft Benson, Gordon B. Hinckley, and Thomas S. Monson) issued a statement regarding the King James Version:

"The Lord has revealed clearly the doctrines of the gospel in these latter days. The most reliable way to measure the accuracy of any biblical passage is not by comparing different texts, but by comparison with the Book of Mormon and modern-day revelations.

"While other Bible versions may be easier to read than the King James Version, in doctrinal matters latter-day revelation supports the King James Version in preference to other English translations. All of the Presidents of the Church, beginning with the Prophet Joseph Smith, have supported the King James Version by encouraging its continued use in the Church. In light of all the above, it is the English language Bible used by The Church of Jesus Christ of Latter-day Saints.

"The LDS edition of the Bible (1979) contains the King James Version supplemented and clarified by footnotes, study aids, and cross-references to the Book of Mormon, the Doctrine and Covenants, and the Pearl of Great Price. These four books are the standard works of the Church. We encourage all members to have their own copies of the complete standard works and to use them prayerfully in regular personal and family study, and in Church meetings and assignments" (*Ensign*, August 1992, 80).

The Latter-day Saint edition of the King James Bible is the best English Bible in the world. Not one word of the currently used King James text has been changed, but numerous study helps have been added. The purpose of the creation of a Latter-day Saint edition of the King James Bible in the 1970s was, according to President Spencer W. Kimball, "to assist in improving doctrinal scholarship throughout the Church"

(*Ensign,* October 1979, 9). The basic charge, as noted by Elder Thomas S. Monson, who chaired the publication committee, was to "help people understand the Bible" (*Ensign,* October 1979, 12). Elder Boyd K. Packer, in the October 1982 general conference, pointed out that this new and unusual edition of the Bible was additional fulfillment of Ezekiel's prophecy of two sticks (records) testifying of each other in the latter days. Elder Packer predicted that succeeding generations would be able to develop gospel scholarship far beyond that which their forefathers could achieve (see *Ensign,* November 1982, 51).

Numerous prestigious awards have been presented to the Church in the United States and in Great Britain recognizing the unique contribution of the LDS edition of the Bible. One citation came in October 1982 from the Laymen's National Bible Committee: "Presented to The Church of Jesus Christ of Latter-day Saints in appreciation of outstanding service to the Bible cause through the publication of its own new edition of the King James version, which features interpretive chapter headings, a simplified footnote system, and the linking of references to all other LDS scriptures, thereby greatly enhancing the study of the Bible by its membership" (Monson, *Ensign,* December 1985, 48).

Unique features of the LDS edition of the King James Bible essential to our study include the following:

Pagination is standard in all editions, regardless of the size of the print.

Running heads at the top of each page indicate what is on each page.

Chapter headings, prepared by Elder Bruce R. McConkie, often contain valuable interpretive commentaries. Examples of particularly helpful chapter headings in the New Testament are Matthew 22 and John 8; 14; 21.

Footnotes are given in a particularly helpful format, and each verse is independently footnoted. Examples of important footnotes are Matthew 16:18a and Luke 17:21c. Examples of

INTRODUCTION

interesting footnotes are Matthew 1:16e; 5:3a; John 4:26a; 19:31c.

Cross-references, approximately 28,000 of them, involving all the standard works, contain easily recognized abbreviations. Important examples include Matthew 22:30c and John 1:18a.

The *Topical Guide* is an alphabetical index and concordance of topics for all of the standard works. It is nearly 600 pages long with 750 major subheadings and a total of nearly 3,500 topics, citing about 50,000 verses. The Topical Guide has its own cross-referencing system. An important example is the 58 categories of information about Jesus Christ: 18 pages of small print, single-spaced, listing thousands of references on the subject. It is, said President Boyd K. Packer, "The most comprehensive compilation of scriptural information on the mission and teachings of the Lord Jesus Christ that has ever been assembled in the history of the world" (*Ensign,* November 2005, 72).

Joseph Smith Translation (JST) excerpts provide more than six hundred major changes Joseph Smith made in his inspired revision. Short ones (usually, those fewer than eight words) are at the foot of the page; longer ones are in the Appendix at the end of the Bible. Verse numbers are not always the same in the Joseph Smith Translation and the King James Version. Words Joseph Smith added are in italics in the Joseph Smith Translation, and we have retained those italics in quoting from the Joseph Smith Translation. Examples of important entries in the Prophet's translation are Matthew 4:1b; 4:11a; 16:24d; 26:26b; Mark 10:27a; Luke 4:5a; 11:5a; 14:30a; 23:34c; John 4:24a; 9:32a; 19:17c; 20:1d; 20:17a. Examples of particularly interesting entries are Matthew 22:14b; 27:33a; Luke 2:46c; John 1:42a. Examples of important Joseph Smith Translation entries that are *not* included in our LDS edition are Matthew 7:23 (JST Matthew 7:33) "*Ye* never knew *me*" and Matthew 25:12 (JST Matthew 25:11) "*Ye* know *me* not."

Hebrew and Greek language notes (HEB and GR) give alternate translations or explanations to clarify the English translation of the original Hebrew or Greek term. Examples are Matthew 9:2a; 22:3a; Luke 15:16b; John 4:26a.

Alternate renderings (OR) explain archaic or difficult passages. Examples are Mark 2:1a; 3:31b; 6:25c; Luke 2:49a; 3:17a; 9:29b.

IE (Latin *id est,* "that is") explains idioms and difficult constructions. Examples are Matthew 5:3b; 14:25a; Luke 23:50a; John 15:22b.

The *Bible Dictionary* contains 1,285 entries, internally cross-referenced, including glossary of some King James Version vocabulary; for example, *by and by* and *anon* mean "immediately"; *corn* means "grain"; *prevent* means "come before, precede"; see also *bottles, lawyer, meet,* and others. Latter-day Saint content includes such topics as "Aaronic Priesthood"; "Dispensations"; "Dove, Sign of"; "Ephraim, Stick of"; "Family"; "Joseph Smith Translation"; "Melchizedek Priesthood"; and "War in Heaven." Topics in the Cambridge Bible Dictionary used by Latter-day Saints before 1979 have been made consistent with latter-day revelation. For example, the Cambridge Bible Dictionary entry "Sacrifice" read: "No Divine command can be quoted for the institution of sacrifice." That definition was changed in the LDS edition of the Bible to conform with revealed instruction in Moses 5:4–8. Under the heading "John," the former edition of the dictionary stated: "His death occurred somewhere near A.D. 100." That statement was changed to reflect latter-day revelation that John was translated.

Maps and Gazetteer help readers visualize historical events in their geographical context. Instead of the four two-tone maps in the Cambridge Bible before 1979, twenty-two full-color maps were included to show the physical setting and location of Bible stories and teachings. In 1999 these maps were replaced with fourteen maps created by the Church, with accompanying descriptions, references, and index of place-names, and thirty-two full-color photographs, also with

Introduction

descriptions and references. References to Bible maps in this book are to the 1999 printing or later.

Italicized words in the text of the King James Bible are not there in the Hebrew or Greek text; in most cases they were supplied by the translators to give the passage more sense in English. That stylistic device has been retained in the LDS edition.

SUGGESTIONS FOR GETTING THE MOST FROM YOUR STUDY OF THE SCRIPTURES AND OF THIS COMPANION VOLUME

1. Study the scriptures—the Lord's words—first and foremost. Use this supplementary text as a tool to help you understand the primary source of knowledge and inspiration. Use more than one of your five physical senses. We learn the most through our eyes, but sometimes it is good to read aloud also (using our ears). It is a good idea to have a fine-point pen or a colored pencil to mark certain passages, make notes in the margins, and cross-reference related scriptures. Involve more of your physical senses, and you'll learn more. It is likewise helpful to teach a new concept, idea, or doctrine to someone else; talking about it with another person reinforces it in your own mind.

2. It has been suggested that when we want to talk with God, we pray; when we want him to talk to us, we study the scriptures. Write down your impressions while studying his words. Occasionally while you are deeply involved in reading and pondering the scriptures, the Lord will reveal something to your mind, maybe even unrelated to what you are reading on the page, but something that will improve your life, enhance some relationship, or resolve some problem or conflict. But sometimes we seem to say to the Lord, "Don't bother me right now; I'm studying the scriptures!" Let the

The Four Gospels

Lord speak to you personally; allow his words to influence your thoughts and feelings.

3. Although we often impose schedules and quotas on ourselves for getting our scripture study "done," it can be counterproductive to try to read a certain number of chapters or a certain number of pages. Our scripture study should not be a race to see how quickly we can finish a book. The effort to push on, to stay on a fixed schedule, to reach a certain quantity of reading, can inhibit the Spirit from working on your mind and heart as you stop to ponder, to meditate on a doctrine or idea. That is the very moment revelation will often come. *[margin note: I needed this!]*

4. Do not be bothered by repetition. Repetition in the scriptures is not accidental; it is purposeful. Repetition is one of the Lord's main methods of instruction (for instance, in his Holy House). If the Lord is repeating something, it's for good reason. In a similar way, we repeat some points in this study companion (for example, the doctrine of the Divine Sonship of Jesus Christ) to emphasize key doctrines of salvation.

5. If you have a Temple recommend, go to the Temple frequently and regularly. All that is taught there (which is too sacred to be discussed elsewhere or published to the world) will greatly enhance your understanding of the scriptures. The scriptures and the Temple go hand in hand and richly complement each other.

To learn about the rewards of studying the Lord's words, take a few minutes to read and reflect on these four passages: 1 Nephi 11:1; Doctrine and Covenants 76:19; 138:1–2; and Joseph Smith–History 1:12. *[margin notes: He will show us things; eyes will be opened]*

To learn about the promises for serious and consistent searching of the Lord's words, read and reflect on these two passages: Joseph Smith–Matthew 1:37; 1 Nephi 15:24.

[handwritten notes: "If you trust in the Lord's words you will not be deceived. He will guide you to him"; "The adversary will have no power over you."]

PART I

BEFORE JESUS CAME TO EARTH

CHAPTER 1

THE FOREORDAINED MESSIAH

The Savior's ministry began long before he came to earth, long before this earth was populated with children of our Heavenly Father, who had been born as spirit sons and daughters of Elohim in the premortal existence. The First Presidency of The Church of Jesus Christ of Latter-day Saints stated: "All men and women are in the similitude of the universal Father and Mother, and are literally the sons and daughters of Deity" (*Messages of the First Presidency*, 4:203). And yet as noble as that heritage is, there was one who far transcended all the rest, who through the eons of a premortal existence stood "like unto God" (Abraham 3:24). This was the firstborn spirit child of all the Father's creations—the birthright Son—whom we know as our Savior.

THE FIRSTBORN

In 1833 the Savior himself testified of his position as the Firstborn: "And now, verily I say unto you, I was in the beginning with the Father, and am the Firstborn" (D&C 93:21). The doctrine of the Savior's status as firstborn was reemphasized by an official pronouncement of the First Presidency and Quorum of the Twelve in 1916: "Among the spirit children of Elohim the firstborn was and is Jehovah or Jesus Christ to whom all others are juniors" ("The Father and the Son: A Doctrinal Exposition," in *Messages of the First Presidency*, 5:33).

Not only is the term *Firstborn* a declaration of Jesus' birth status but it is also a significant name-title, one so important that the Savior's most faithful followers in mortality will share it throughout the eternities. Elder Bruce R. McConkie stated that just as The Church of Jesus Christ is the name of the Savior's earthly Church, "so *The Church of the Firstborn* is his heavenly church, albeit its members are limited to exalted beings, for whom the family unit continues and who gain an inheritance in the highest heaven of the celestial world. (Heb. 12:22–23; D&C 93:22.)" (*Promised Messiah*, 47).

PREMORTAL GODHOOD

Because Jesus Christ was the firstborn of our heavenly parents, he was our elder brother in that existence. He too possessed a spirit body that had a definite birth or time of organization just like every other spirit child of God (McConkie, *Promised Messiah*, 165). Unlike us, however, Jesus was himself a God in our premortal realm.

President Joseph Fielding Smith stated emphatically that Jesus Christ was "a God before he was born into this world" (*Doctrines of Salvation*, 1:32). He was like his Father. Using the analogy of family organization and family roles found in Old Testament culture, we may say that Jesus, as the Firstborn, possessed all the rights, interests, and inheritance of the Father. He was the Birthright Son. He was in premortality the inheritor and rightful heir of all the Father possessed. He was the Father's agent and executor, the "Word," or "messenger of salvation" (D&C 93:8). Thus, John's introduction to his Gospel should be taken literally: "In the beginning was the Word, and the Word was with God, and the Word was God. The same was in the beginning with God. All things were made by him; and without him was not any thing made that was made" (John 1:1–3).

AN EXPERIENCED CREATOR

As John testifies, Jesus was a God, a powerful and experienced creator in premortality. To Joseph Smith it was revealed that ancient prophets knew far more about Christ's sweeping and magnificent creative role than traditional Christianity ever fathomed possible. In the book of Moses we read:

"And behold, the glory of the Lord was upon Moses, so that Moses stood in the presence of God, and talked with him face to face. And the Lord God said unto Moses: For mine own purpose have I made these things. Here is wisdom and it remaineth in me.

"And by the word of my power, have I created them, which is mine Only Begotten Son, who is full of grace and truth.

"And worlds without number have I created; and I also created them for mine own purpose; and by the Son I created them, which is mine Only Begotten" (Moses 1:31–33).

Elder James E. Talmage noted that "the Father operated in the work of creation through the Son, who thus became the executive through whom the will, commandment, or word of the Father was put into effect. It is with incisive appropriateness therefore, that the Son, Jesus Christ, is designated by the apostle John as the Word; or as declared by the Father 'the word of my power' [Moses 1:32]" (*Jesus the Christ*, 31).

Like Moses, the Prophet Joseph Smith bore a powerful witness of the Savior's mighty acts of creation: "He is the Only Begotten of the Father . . . [and] by him, and through him, and of him, the worlds are and were created, and the inhabitants thereof are begotten sons and daughters unto God" (D&C 76:23–24).

The Prophet Joseph Smith also learned that the Creation is still going on: "For behold, there are many worlds that have passed away by the word of my power. And there are many that now stand, and innumerable are they unto man; but all things are numbered unto me, for they are mine and I know them" (Moses 1:35). Such power and wisdom are beyond the grasp of mortals. The written declarations of prophets about the creation of millions of earths by Jesus Christ is testimony enough of Jesus' stature before his birth into mortality as the Messiah. But such testimony is given great visual impact when one stands outdoors on a clear, cloudless night to gaze into the star-filled heavens with the realization that the vast expanse of the visible universe is only a small part of the Savior's realm.

Astronomers tell us that our solar system is located in a spiral arm of the Milky Way Galaxy, a flat disc-shaped cluster of stars approximately 100,000 light years across at its widest point. A light year is the distance light travels in one year. Moving at the speed of 186,000 miles per second, a beam of light traverses 5.7 trillion miles in 365 days. The size of our galaxy in miles, then, is a staggering 5.7 trillion times 100,000. Our galaxy is estimated to contain at least 200 billion stars, half of which likely possess solar systems similar to our own. The next closest galaxy is Andromeda, a star system much like our own Milky Way, approximately 2.2 million light years away from us. Furthermore, our best telescopes can probe outward into space to a distance of over 10 billion light years and view over 50 billion galaxies, each of which possesses billions of stars. And these galaxies are only the ones we can detect with the present state of our technology. Truly, the observation made by Enoch the seer is one of the grandest understatements of all time: "And were it possible that man could number the particles of the earth, yea, millions of earths like this, it would not be a beginning to the number of thy creations; and thy curtains are stretched out still" (Moses 7:30). Such are the sweeping and incomprehensible powers of Jesus the Creator.

Undoubtedly, this is why several passages in the Book of Mormon speak of Jesus Christ as creator of the heavens, the earth, and all things upon it: "And he shall be called Jesus Christ, the Son of God, the Father of heaven and earth, the Creator of all things from the beginning" (Mosiah 3:8). Some passages even speak explicitly of Jesus Christ as the creator of humankind (Mosiah 26:23; Alma 5:15; Ether 3:16). It is important to keep in mind, however, that there are two aspects of the Creation in which the Savior did not participate as primal Maker, or Organizer: the procreation of spirit children and the creation of the physical body of man. Elder Bruce R. McConkie taught this concept with clarity:

"In the ultimate and final sense of the word, the Father is the Creator of all things. That he used the Son and others to perform many of the creative acts, delegating to them his creative powers, does not make these others creators in their own right, independent of him. He is the source of all creative power, and he simply chooses others to act for him in many of his creative enterprises. But there are two creative events that are his and his alone. First, he is the Father of all spirits, Christ's included; none were fathered or created by anyone else. Second, he is the Creator of the physical body of man. Though Jehovah and Michael and many of the noble and great ones played their assigned roles in the various creative events, yet when it came time to place man on earth, the Lord God himself performed the creative acts. 'I, God, created man in mine own image, in the image of mine Only Begotten created I him; male and female created I them' (Moses 2:27)" (*New Witness for the Articles of Faith*, 63).

Still, even excluding the creation of man, the number and kind of creations which have come into existence as a result of the Savior's power are mind-boggling. And what is more, these creations are maintained and renewed on a continual basis by that very same power inherent in the Savior (see D&C 88:7–13).

Truly, Jesus was and is an experienced creator whose Godhood and greatness were clearly demonstrated in premortality. The premortal Jesus was, as Abinadi declared, "the very Eternal Father of heaven and earth" (Mosiah 15:4).

THE GREAT JEHOVAH

Before he came to earth as Jesus of Nazareth, our Savior was known as the great Jehovah, the God of ancient Israel, the divine Being graphically described in the pages of the Old Testament who gave laws to his covenant people and sustained them in the promised land. Jesus testified to the Nephites that he and Jehovah were one and the same being.

"Behold, I say unto you that the law is fulfilled that was given unto Moses.

"Behold, I am he that gave the law, and I am he who covenanted with my people Israel; therefore, the law in me is fulfilled, for I have come to fulfil the law; therefore it hath an end" (3 Nephi 15:4–5).

No greater witness can be invoked than this testimony from the resurrected Savior himself. He was Jehovah and every law by which the universe was framed, as well as those laws given to the people of Israel, issued forth from him (D&C 88:42). No law is above him or greater than he, for he is the law (3 Nephi 15:9).

The Savior used the phrase "I am" in connection with his self-identification as the great Jehovah who guided the prophet Moses. This is no accident, since Jehovah was known in ancient times by the name-title I AM (Exodus 3:13–15).

I AM is the English rendering of a first-person singular future-tense form of the Hebrew verb *hayah* ("to be," "to exist"). This divine name is referred to as the Tetragrammaton (Greek: "four letters") and connotes continual or eternal existence, something like "I was, I am, and I will be"—all encompassed in one word. Significantly, the expression I AM is a name-title the mortal Jesus of Nazareth used to testify of his divinity, both before and after his resurrection.

DIVINE INVESTITURE OF AUTHORITY

As we read the testimonies of the Gospel authors, it is important to remember that Jesus possessed the right to act as spokesman for God the Father. He was commissioned to speak as though he were himself God the Father. Jesus said many times in mortality, as well as after his resurrection, that he and his Father were one, not in personage or physical form but in purpose, intention, and thoughts (John 10:30; 14:10; 17:22). Even more than that, Jesus told the Nephites, "I am in the Father, and the Father in me, and the Father and I are one" (3 Nephi 11:27; compare 3 Nephi 9:15; 19:23; 28:10). This is true of Jesus and the Father in premortal life as well as during and after the Savior's mortal sojourn. In other words, God the Father and his firstborn spirit Son, whether acting as the premortal Jehovah or later as the resurrected Lord, were so unified in mind and will that what one thought, said, and did, the other one thought, said, and did—exactly.

This concept has been described by modern prophets as the principle of divine investiture of authority. That is, God the Father invested, or placed, in his Son his very own power, authority, and voice. The earliest use of the term "divine investiture of authority" is found in the 1916 statement entitled "The Father and the Son: A Doctrinal Exposition by the First Presidency and the Twelve." This most significant document sets forth the distinct ways in which Christ is rightfully known as the Father, which include his role as creator of the heavens and earth, his actions in making eternal life possible for his followers, and his power through the principle of divine investiture of authority. "In all His dealings with the human family," the Brethren declared, "Jesus the Son has represented and yet represents Elohim His Father in power and authority. This is true of Christ in His preexistent, antemortal, or unembodied state, in the which he was known as Jehovah; also during His embodiment in the flesh; and during His labors as a disembodied spirit in the realm of the dead;

and since that period in His resurrected state" (quoted in Talmage, *Articles of Faith*, 470–71). Thus, God the Father, whom we reverently call Elohim, has authorized Jesus Christ "to speak in the first person as though he were the original or primal Father" (McConkie, *Promised Messiah*, 63).

It wasn't simply exalted status, superior knowledge, or intense power and influence that made Jesus God in our premortal existence. If that were so, Lucifer would have tried, and in fact did try to stake a fair claim on such authority, for he possessed a lofty and exalted position among the Father's spirit children (D&C 76:25). Another ingredient was requisite for Godhood. One had to be endowed and invested with the power and authority to speak and act as God the Father, as Jesus shows us. To speak and act in the place of God the Father was not an honor that could be taken unto oneself, as the arrogance of Satan shows us.

President Joseph Fielding Smith taught the following:

"All revelation since the fall has come through Jesus Christ, who is the Jehovah of the Old Testament. In all of the scriptures, where God is mentioned and where he has appeared, it was Jehovah who talked with Abraham, with Noah, Enoch, Moses and all the prophets. He is the God of Israel, the Holy One of Israel; the one who led that nation out of Egyptian bondage, and who gave and fulfilled the Law of Moses. *The Father [Elohim] has never dealt with man directly and personally since the fall, and he has never appeared except to introduce and bear record of the Son*" (*Doctrines of Salvation*, 1:27; emphasis added).

THE CHOSEN REDEEMER

One cannot talk about the premortal stature of Jesus without examining his redemptive powers and actions. In addition to his position as God, Jesus was chosen and anointed in premortality to be our Redeemer and Savior. Peter, the chief apostle, taught this lesson in a very poignant way to the Saints of his day:

"Forasmuch as ye know that ye were not redeemed with corruptible things, as silver and gold . . .

"But with the precious blood of Christ, as of a lamb without blemish and without spot:

"Who verily was foreordained before the foundation of the world" (1 Peter 1:18–20).

The premortal Savior was the chief proponent of the Father's plan of salvation. A hallmark of the Savior's personality in premortality as well as mortality was humility: He humbly offered to be our Redeemer, to put into effect the Father's plan, to sacrifice his own comfort and lofty position to do his Father's will and yet to give the honor and glory to the Father.

THE ATONEMENT IN PREMORTAL LIFE

All the holy prophets since the world began have testified of the redeeming ministry of that second member of the Godhead who would come to earth as the Messiah (Jacob 4:4; Mosiah 3:5–13; 13:33). The testimonies of some of these seers are preserved in Restoration scripture to allow us to see more clearly the grandeur, majesty, and sweeping significance of Jesus' atoning power in a truly eternal context. They learned that the Atonement already operated on our behalf in our first estate, allowing each and every one of our Heavenly Father's children to be born into mortality innocent—with a clean slate, as it were.

To Moses it was revealed that "Enoch saw the day of the coming of the Son of Man, even in the flesh; and his soul rejoiced, saying: The Righteous is lifted up, and the Lamb is *slain from the foundation of the world*" (Moses 7:47; emphasis added).

The Savior's sacrifice, though not made in actuality until

he had taken a physical body in mortality, was regarded in our premortal existence as having already been accomplished. That is why, for example, in the opening scenes of mortal life on this earth, immediately after the fall of Adam and Eve, God could say to our primal patriarch, "Adam: Behold I have forgiven thee thy transgression in the Garden of Eden" (Moses 6:53). That is, Adam's transgression had already been paid for by the time our first parents embarked on their sojourn in mortality. How could this have been accomplished unless the Atonement was already in operation long before it took place in the flesh? This realization gives new meaning to Moses 6:54: "Hence came the saying abroad among the people, that the Son of God hath atoned for original guilt."

An important implication of the idea of the premortal operation of the Atonement is that sins were committed and mistakes were made in premortality. We know that one-third of the hosts of heaven rebelled against God and were cast out, evidence of the operation of moral agency as well as its consequences in our first estate. That such was the case is made explicit in a statement by Elder Orson Pratt, who, when writing about the nature of sin in our premortal existence, said: "Among the two-thirds [of God's spirit children] who remained, it is highly probable, that, there were many who were not valiant . . . , but whose sins were of such a nature that they could be forgiven through faith in the future sufferings of the Only Begotten of the Father, and through their sincere repentance and reformation. We see no impropriety in Jesus offering himself as an acceptable offering and sacrifice before the Father to atone for the sins of His brethren, committed, not only in the second, but also in the first estate" (*The Seer*, no. 4, 1:54; spelling standardized).

In premortality the atonement of Jesus Christ operated in our behalf so that each of us could begin our second estate with a fresh start, free from the blemishes, mistakes, and sins committed in premortality, free of the disabling and crippling spiritual baggage brought from a former life. As was revealed to the Prophet Joseph Smith, "Every spirit of man was innocent in the beginning; and God having redeemed man from the fall, men became again, in their infant state, innocent before God" (D&C 93:38).

Could it be that Satan and his followers were finally cast out of heaven because they ultimately refused to accept the efficacy of the Savior's atonement as it operated in premortality? Without the acceptance of the Atonement in our premortal phase of existence, any chance to be rendered innocent in our infant mortal condition would be eliminated.

THE REDEEMER OF ALL CREATION

With this sweeping perspective of the activities, powers, and roles of the premortal Savior, Amulek's discussion of the Atonement takes on added meaning: "For it shall not be a human sacrifice; but it must be an infinite and eternal sacrifice" (Alma 34:10). The Atonement was made by God himself, just as King Benjamin testified it would be (Mosiah 3:5–8). It was not an action of a mere human. But this is not all. The atonement of Christ is also infinite in scope.

Perhaps more stunning than Jesus' role as Creator of innumerable worlds is his corollary role as Redeemer of all that he has created. We do not know how many creations, how many worlds and galaxies, came into being before (or after) this earth was brought into existence through the power of God's Only Begotten Son, but we do know that his atonement operates for each and every one of the Father's innumerable creations.

The doctrine of the all-encompassing nature of the Atonement was taught by the Prophet Joseph Smith in majestic poetry when he gave a special rendering of Doctrine and Covenants 76:23–24 (verses 19–20 in the poetic version):

> And I heard a great voice, bearing record from heav'n,

He's the Saviour, and only begotten of God—
By him, of him, and through him, the worlds
   were all made,
Even all that career in the heavens so broad.

Whose inhabitants, too, from the first to the
   last,
Are sav'd by the very same Saviour of ours;
And, of course, are begotten God's daughters
   and sons,
By the very same truths, and the very same
   pow'rs.
   (*Times and Seasons,* 4:81–85; McConkie and
     Ostler, *Revelations of the Restoration,* 543)

The inhabitants of the millions of earths like the one on which we reside are all saved and redeemed by the same atonement of Jesus Christ that occurred in actuality on this world.

THE CONDESCENSION OF GOD

Given this brief glimpse at the premortal Godly stature of the Being known in mortality as Jesus of Nazareth, we can begin to appreciate more fully the concept spoken of in the Book of Mormon as the condescension of God. The ancient prophet Nephi was tutored in detail regarding this doctrine. An angel stood before him, "and he said unto me: Knowest thou the condescension of God?" (1 Nephi 11:16). Nephi responded that he knew that God loves his children but he did not know the meaning of all things. He was then shown many symbols and scenes pertaining to the plan of salvation, especially the mortal birth of the Son of God. And the angel said to Nephi again, "Look and behold the condescension of God!" (1 Nephi 11:26). Nephi then saw in vision scenes from the earthly ministry of the Savior. He who not only was "the

Lamb of God, yea, even the Son of the Eternal Father" was also God himself (1 Nephi 11:21; 13:40).

Thus, the condescension of God occurred on two levels. First, God the Father condescended to voluntarily associate himself with our fallen world by siring a Son to live as a mortal. Second, it was a condescension of almost incomprehensible magnitude for God the Son, the great Jehovah, the Eternal God, the Creator of all things from the beginning, to leave his throne of radiant glory and enter human history in the small town of Bethlehem as a helpless baby who had to learn to crawl and walk, who cut his first tooth, who stubbed his toes and bruised his shins, and who suffered the effects of cold, heat, hunger, thirst, and pain of every kind. As Elder Bruce R. McConkie said:

"The One [the Father] whose might and omnipotence we can scarcely glimpse and cannot begin to comprehend, this Holy Being to whom we, by comparison, are as the dust of the earth, this Almighty Personage, in his love, mercy, and grace, condescended to step down from his Almighty throne, to step down to a lesser and benighted state, as it were, and become the Father of a Son 'after the manner of the flesh.' . . . [And] the Creator [the Son] of all things from the beginning [did also] step down from his high state of exaltation and be, for a moment, like one of the creatures of his creating" (*Promised Messiah*, 467).

CONCLUSION

Because of the veil of forgetfulness as well as the relentless influence of a fallen world, mortals can scarcely comprehend the true stature of the premortal Jesus. Aside from discussions of his actual atoning sacrifice in mortality, some of the most powerful statements in the standard works speak to the nature of the premortal Jesus and describe his towering greatness and glory. By virtue of his position as Jehovah, and predicated upon the doctrine of divine investiture of authority, every name and every power that were the Father's (save one, procreation) also belonged to Jesus in the premortal realms. Even before he entered mortality as the Messiah of our redemption, all the names that Isaiah grandly pronounced would be his were already his: "Wonderful, Counsellor, The mighty God, The everlasting Father, The Prince of Peace" (Isaiah 9:6). He is also the Star arisen out of Jacob, and the Sceptre come out of Israel (Numbers 24:17). He is the Well Beloved and Chosen One of the Father (Helaman 5:47; Moses 4:2; 7:39). He is the Anointed One (Acts 10:38; D&C 109:53) and the Bridegroom (Matthew 25:1–13; D&C 133:10, 19). He was the hope of Israel in ancient times, and he is the hope of Israel today. After all is said and done, King Benjamin (Mosiah 3:5–8) and Abinadi (Mosiah 15:1) were right: God himself came down among us!

PART II

PREPARATION FOR THE MESSIAH

CHAPTER 2

DIVINELY APPOINTED FOUNDATIONS

Matthew 1:1; Mark 1:1 The word *gospel* comes from old English *godspel* ("god story"), the Bible translators' equivalent for the Greek word *euaggelion,* meaning "good tidings" or "good news." The four Gospels, or the good news written by the four authors, are testimonies, not histories or biographies. There is no substitute for these records written by the Savior's contemporaries. Three of the four (Matthew, Mark, and Luke) are often called *Synoptic* Gospels, because they are written from the same point of view—with parallel accounts, sometimes with the exact same wording, of teachings, parables, miracles, and events in Jesus' life. John's testimony, on the other hand, is less concerned with reporting the stories and experiences (for example, there are no parables in John) than in recording the deep doctrines of the Savior. The four testimonies are quite selective in their focus; they do not detail daily journeys and teachings and events through the three-year period of his ministry. In fact, if we laid out the various episodes recounted on a timeline, we would only have what Jesus said and did on possibly thirty or thirty-one days of his whole ministry (Matthews, *Behold the Messiah,* 22; for more on the authors of the Gospels and their accounts, see Bible Dictionary, "Gospels," 683).

The final third of each of the Synoptic Gospels deals with the last week of Jesus' ministry; half of John's record treats the final week—events leading to and including the atoning sacrifice and the resurrection. There were 156 weeks (three years) in Jesus' ministry, and the writers of these four testimonies

FOUR TESTIMONIES OF JESUS CHRIST

	Authors	Probable Audience	Purpose	Dominant Features	Examples of Unique Material
MATTHEW (LEVI)	Was tax collector (used parchment and ink, accustomed to making notes)	Pharisaic Jews in a Hellenistic world	Persuade Jews that Jesus is the promised Messiah, the Davidic King	Cited OT prophecies (almost 100 quotes); emphasized Jesus' royal, Davidic lineage	Visit of wise men, star in the east (2:1-12)
MARK	Papias (2d century) said Mark was Peter's scribe in Rome; was wealthy and educated; got his information from Peter (1 Pet. 5:13)	Romans (a Gentile audience); short and to the point, which suggests Roman preference	Emphasize *doings* rather than *sayings* of the Lord; testify to Romans (in short, no-nonsense facts and essentials); show that Jesus is God and on earth; He is here (don't look to Zeus, Jupiter)	A third of it is the Passion story; miracles of Jesus; geographical and cultural explanations (for non-Jewish readers)	A young man wearing a sheet (14:51-52)
LUKE	Was a physician (Col. 4:14) and a missionary (2 Tim. 4:11); educated; knew art of writing, dealt with sophisticated audiences	Theophilus (educated and prominent Greek audience), Gentiles	Provide polished literary account of Jesus' ministry as Savior of Jews *and* Gentiles; provide an accurate witness (history); show that Jesus is Savior of *all* mankind	More stories about women; favorable to Gentiles; dwells on Jesus' teachings and doings; detail in Jesus' life; importance of Temple	Visits of Gabriel (ch. 1); visits of shepherds (2:8-18); Jesus at Temple, age 12 (2:41-52); the 70 (10:1-24); Jesus sweating blood (22:44); discussion with thief on cross (23:39-43); Christ eating food after resurrection (24:42-43)
JOHN	In the fishing business with his brother; they were known as "sons of thunder" (e.g., Luke 9:51-56 may give some perspective)	Written to Saints who had a basic knowledge of Christ	Emphasize and testify of Christ's divine nature as Only Begotten in the flesh; teach Christ as great, spiritual, divine teacher	Jesus as Light, Life, Way for all men (presented in in-depth, doctrinal fashion); note what is not contained: 40 days in wilderness, Transfiguration, casting out spirits	Water to wine (2:1-11); Nicodemus (3:1-10); woman at well (4:1-42); Bread of Life (6:27-71); Lazarus raised (11:1-56); washing of feet (13:1-16); Holy Ghost discourse (14, 15, 16); promise of John tarrying on

dedicated more than a third of what they wrote to the last week of Jesus' mortal life and especially his last twenty-four hours.

The first verse of Mark's testimony attests, from the very beginning, that Jesus Christ (his name in Hebrew and Greek means literally "Anointed Savior") was the *Son of God*. Nephi learned this same doctrinal fact six hundred years earlier: "His name shall be Jesus Christ, the Son of God" (2 Nephi 25:19; cf. Mosiah 15:2).

The original condition of these four testimonies is described by Nephi, as he saw the book that would come forth from the Jews: "It contained the fulness of the gospel of the Lord, of whom the twelve apostles bear record. . . . Wherefore, these things go forth from the Jews in purity unto the Gentiles, according to the truth which is in God" (1 Nephi 13:24–25). The book, containing so many plain and precious things, was even entitled "the book of the Lamb of God" (1 Nephi 13:28), and Nephi testified that these "records of the prophets and of the twelve apostles of the Lamb are true" (1 Nephi 13:39).

Luke 1:1–4 Was Luke one of the first to write an account of Jesus' life? No, there were many writers before Luke (JST Luke 1:1). Matthew 1:18 says, "Now the birth of Jesus Christ was on this wise." The Joseph Smith Translation of the same verse reads: "Now, *as it is written*, the birth of Jesus Christ was on this wise," which clearly indicates that other written records existed before Matthew wrote and also before Luke wrote. It was important for the Savior and his apostles to keep records of the most important teachings and events. (Compare, for example, explicit instructions to the Lord's people to keep careful records in other eras: Moses 2:1; Alma 37:2; 3 Nephi 23:13; D&C 21:1; 72:6; 85:1.) Apparently Luke was not one of the original writers, not one of the eyewitnesses "from the very first" (he was a later convert, likely through Paul), so he must have received his knowledge and witness from those original witnesses, especially from Peter, and some details of Jesus' birth possibly from Jesus' mother, Mary.

29

Luke 1:4 Luke wrote this account to his friend or brother Theophilus (his Gospel being volume one of his two-volume history of the Church—Luke and Acts; in Acts 1:1 he refers to the "former treatise have I made"). This is Luke's testimony of the Savior's life and ministry to confirm or certify the things he had been taught.

John 1:1–5 Joseph Smith Translation v. 1: It is probably not coincidental that the first words are the same as those that begin Moses' account in Genesis (1:1). Being a good Jew, John used Genesis as a literary model: "In the beginning was the *gospel preached through the Son. And the gospel was the word, and the word was with the Son, and the Son was with God, and the Son was of God.*" This passage teaches that the Son was in the beginning with the Father (see D&C 93:21); that the gospel has been on earth from the beginning; and that the Father and the Son are two separate Beings. They have been carrying out their divine work together from the beginning.

John 1:3 Jesus Christ created all things, under the direction of the Father. Additional witness that Jesus created this earth, as well as worlds without number, is given in 3 Nephi 9:15; Hebrews 1:1–3; Doctrine and Covenants 76:22–24; Abraham 3:11–12; and Moses 1:31–33; 7:30.

That Jehovah and Jesus are the same person is evident in Joseph Smith Translation Exodus 6:3; 3 Nephi 15:1–5; and Doctrine and Covenants 110:1–4. Peter testified that Jehovah/Jesus was prepared, chosen, and foreordained before the foundation of the world (1 Peter 1:20).

John 1:4–5 As Christ has said, he is the life of the world and he is the light of the world (Mosiah 16:9; 3 Nephi 9:18; 11:11). He is the light of the sun, moon, and stars, and from him emanates the light that fills the immensity of space (D&C 88:7–13). Joseph Smith's translation of John 1:4 indicates that *the gospel was the life* and that the gospel was the light of men. The gospel, of course, comes from Christ. That light, Jesus Christ and his gospel, are the light for all humankind to follow, for the world is full of darkness—meaning that the world suffers from an absence of the light.

THE GENEALOGIES

Matthew 1:2–17 Ancestry was crucial to the Jews in authenticating a person's credibility and legitimacy. There is no recorded accusation against Jesus based on ineligibility of lineage (sources on Herod, on the other hand, frequently note the illegitimacy of his lineage).

The genealogy of Christ that Matthew presents is often considered that of Joseph, and the genealogy in Luke 3 that of Mary; or, Matthew gives a legal descent whereas Luke gives a natural descent through actual parentage (Bible Dictionary, "Genealogy," 678). Elder James E. Talmage wrote: "The all important fact to be remembered is that the Child promised by Gabriel to Mary, the virginal bride of Joseph, would be born in the royal line. A personal genealogy of Joseph was essentially that of Mary also, for they were cousins. Joseph is named as son of Jacob by Matthew, and as son of Heli by Luke; but Jacob and Heli were brothers, and it appears that one of the two was the father of Joseph and the other the father of Mary and therefore father-in-law to Joseph. That Mary was of Davidic descent is plainly set forth in many scriptures [see Topical Guide, "Jesus Christ, Davidic Descent of," 245]; for since Jesus was to be born of Mary, yet was not begotten by Joseph, . . . the blood of David's posterity was given to the body of Jesus through Mary alone. Our Lord, though repeatedly addressed as Son of David, never repudiated the title but accepted it as rightly applied to Himself" (*Jesus the Christ*, 81–82).

Why include Joseph's genealogy when he was not Jesus' father? Because "Joseph, as the adoptive father, would have been the legal ancestor through whom Jesus' royal lineage would have been traced" (Strobel, *Case for Christ*, 47).

Several names in these genealogical lists reflect a change

from the Hebrew spelling to the Greek form. In the following examples notice how the Hebrew ending changes to an "s" ending in the Greek form. The Hellenized (Greek) spelling is seen all through the New Testament:

Hebrew	*Greek*
Judah	Judas
Uriah	Urias
Hezekiah	Ezekias
Manasseh	Manasses
Josiah	Josias

Others	
Elijah	Elias
Jonah	Jonas
Zechariah	Zacharias
Jeremiah	Jeremias
Messiah	Messias

Matthew 1:16 Greek *Christos* and Hebrew *Mashiah* both mean the "Anointed One." Anciently, every prophet, priest, and king was anointed to his respective labor. Now comes One who, in a spiritual sense, is the Prophet, Priest, and King all in one Person. (For an excellent treatment of this theme, see Seely and Seely, in *Jesus Christ, Son of God, Savior*, 248–69.)

In a political and also a genealogical sense, Jesus was born in the royal Davidic line through his mortal mother, and as Elder James E. Talmage explained, "Had Judah been a free and independent nation, ruled by her rightful sovereign, Joseph the carpenter [Jesus' adoptive father] would have been her crowned king; and his lawful successor to the throne would have been Jesus of Nazareth, the King of the Jews" (*Jesus the Christ*, 82).

Matthew 1:17 There were fourteen generations from Abraham to David, fourteen generations from David to the Babylonian exile, and fourteen generations from the Babylonian exile to Christ. The significance of fourteen is that it is the double of seven, which in the scriptures is the number signifying completion, wholeness, or perfection. Hebrew writers valued order, systematic arrangement, and symmetry in all things. By using the number fourteen, Matthew emphasized Jesus' perfection and messiahship as well as his direct descent from King David. The name David, as spelled in Hebrew, has the numerical equivalent of fourteen: *daleth* (the fourth letter of the Hebrew alphabet) carries the numerical value of four; *vav* (the sixth letter of the Hebrew alphabet) carries the numerical value of six; so the name David (Hebrew *daleth, vav, daleth:* 4 + 6 + 4) totals fourteen. (Sometimes, as here, genealogies might be telescoped or condensed to match a desired number of which an author is particularly fond.)

Luke 3:23–38 Jesus began his consecrated work of the ministry at age thirty, which was according to the old law (Numbers 4:3, 47). Compare commentary from the Mishnah: "At five years old one is ready for the scripture, at ten years for the Mishnah, at thirteen for the commandments, at fifteen for Talmud, at eighteen for marriage, at twenty for pursuit of righteousness, at thirty for full strength" (*Pirke Aboth,* V.24).

Jesus' genealogy is given back to Adam, who was a son of God (Moses 6:22, 68), "*who was formed* of God, *and the first man upon the earth*" (JST Luke 3:45).

ANNUNCIATION TO ZACHARIAS (IN THE TEMPLE AT JERUSALEM)

Luke 1:5–25 Luke is very interested in the Temple. His first volume (his Gospel) opens (Luke 1:5–25) and closes (Luke 24:53) in the Temple. His second volume (Acts of the Apostles) shows the disciples as faithful worshippers in the Temple (Acts 2:46; 3:1; 5:12).

Zacharias was a priest in one of the priesthood courses or groups (Abia) that King David had organized to function in the Temple. "Zacharias belonged to the course of priests named after

Abijah (later known as Abia). This was the eighth of twenty-four courses established by David [still functioning] after the return from Babylon [ca. 538 B.C.; 1 Chron. 24:10]. Each course was appointed to serve a week in its turn at the temple. Because of the great number of priests, the honor came to relatively few, and seldom came twice to the same person" (Matthews, *Burning Light*, 18). Zacharias and his wife, Elisabeth, were direct descendants of Aaron, of the tribe of Levi. Elisabeth even carried the same name as Aaron's wife, Elisheba (Exodus 6:23).

Joseph Smith taught that the Aaronic Priesthood continued without interruption from Aaron to Zacharias: "The Levitical Priesthood is forever hereditary—fixed on the head of Aaron and his sons forever, and was in active operation down to Zacharias the father of John. Zacharias would have had no child had not God given him a son. He sent his angel to declare unto Zacharias that his wife Elisabeth should bear him a son, whose name was to be called John. The keys of the Aaronic Priesthood were committed unto him" (*Teachings of the Prophet Joseph Smith*, 319).

Had Zacharias not had a son, he would have had no one upon whom to confer the keys of the Aaronic Priesthood. John later had the privilege of conferring those keys on Joseph Smith (D&C 13).

Up to and during the meridian of time, the priesthood was perpetuated by lineage, from father to son. Today conferral of priesthood is determined by personal worthiness rather than lineage.

Luke 1:6–7 Zacharias and Elisabeth were righteous and kept the commandments and the ordinances. They were old and childless. How hard it must have been for Elisabeth to be the daughter of an Aaronic priest, knowing the premium placed on lineage and yet having no child herself.

Luke 1:8–11 Zacharias was a righteous priesthood holder and Temple worker, and because he functioned under the Aaronic Priesthood, he had the right to the ministering of angels (D&C 13). While Zacharias was performing his week-long service, having the rare opportunity to burn incense in the Holy Place (see Appendix 3, 743) and apparently while imploring the Father in Heaven for a son on whom to confer the priesthood, an angel appeared.

Joseph Smith applied the concept of "wrestling for a blessing" to Zacharias, who had no children. He "knew that the promise of God must fail, consequently he went into the Temple to wrestle with God according to the order of the priesthood to obtain a promise of a son" (Smith, *Words of Joseph Smith*, 235; compare Genesis 32:22–30).

Luke 1:12 It seems that we humans are usually afraid when a visitor from another world—or from our own spirit world—appears (the words "fear not" are found at least seventy-five times in scripture). Why are we fearful? Is it because we are naturally afraid of the unknown? Or because we feel spiritually unprepared and unworthy of contact with the heavenly world?

Luke 1:13 Four great revelatory messages are given in one verse of scripture:

> Fear not, Zacharias [the angel knew his name];
> Your prayer has been heard and is now answered;
> Your wife is going to have a son;
> You are to name him John. (See also D&C 27:7)

Luke 1:14–17 The angel declared to Zacharias that he and many others would rejoice because of John's birth, for he would be great and a deeply spiritual person (see D&C 84:27). Also, for a time he would be a Nazarite (Numbers 6:2–8), keeping an ancient "Word of Wisdom." (For the difference between a Nazarite and a Nazarene, see Bible Dictionary, "Nazarene" and "Nazarite," 737.) John would convert many people to the true God, and as an Elias (forerunner), he would go before the Lord to prepare the way for His coming into the world (Matthew 11:14).

The Prophet Joseph Smith explained the following about the spirit of Elias: "The spirit of Elias is to prepare the way for a greater revelation of God, which is the Priesthood of Elias, or the Priesthood that Aaron was ordained unto. And when God sends a man into the world to prepare for a greater work, holding the keys of the power of Elias, it was called the doctrine of Elias, even from the early ages of the world.

"John's mission was limited to preaching and baptizing; but what he did was legal; and when Jesus Christ came to any of John's disciples, He baptized them with fire and the Holy Ghost.

"We find the Apostles endowed with greater power than John: their office was more under the spirit and power of Elijah than Elias.

"In the case of Philip when he went down to Samaria, when he was under the spirit of Elias, he baptized both men and women. When Peter and John heard of it, they went down and laid hands upon them, and they received the Holy Ghost. This shows the distinction between the two powers. . . .

"What I want to impress upon your minds is the difference of power in the different parts of the Priesthood, so that when any man comes among you, saying, 'I have the spirit of Elias,' you can know whether he be true or false; for any man that comes, having the spirit and power of Elias, he will not transcend his bounds.

"John did not transcend his bounds, but faithfully performed that part belonging to his office. . . .

"That person who holds the keys of Elias hath a preparatory work" (*Teachings of the Prophet Joseph Smith*, 335–36; see further discussion about "Elias" in the commentary on John 1:19–28; Matthew 17:10–13).

Luke 1:18–20 Zacharias and Elisabeth must have wondered if they could receive some evidence or spiritual confirmation that this birth would really happen (after all, they were both old). Their asking how they could be sure was similar to the inquiries of Abraham (Genesis 15:8), Gideon (Judges 6:17), and Hezekiah (2 Kings 20:8).

Gabriel had come from God's presence to announce this happy, miraculous news. Why Gabriel? We do not know.

Because Zacharias did not immediately believe this exciting news, he was given a confirmatory sign. The sign was that he would be dumb, unable to speak, until after his son was born (cf. Daniel 10:15; Mosiah 27:19). The comment in Luke 1:62, "and they made signs to his father, how he would have him called," may suggest that Zacharias was also deaf.

Luke 1:21–23 The people perceived that Zacharias had seen a vision. We wonder if his countenance still reflected the glory or radiance of the heavenly being—compare the glory in the countenance of Moses (Exodus 34:29–30; 2 Corinthians 3:7; Moses 1:2, 11; 7:3), Abinadi (Mosiah 13:5), and Nephi and Lehi (Helaman 5:36). Zacharias finished his seven days' ministration in the Temple (Leviticus 8:33) and returned home.

ELISABETH'S SECLUSION (IN JUDEA)

Luke 1:24–25 Elisabeth "hid herself five months" upon becoming pregnant. Scripture does not tell us why, but scripture does teach that some sacred moments, events, and miracles are not for public exhibition. We do know that not having children was looked upon as a reproach—recall Sarah, Rebekah, and Rachel (Genesis 11:30; 16:2; 25:21; 29:31; 30:23). Now Elisabeth was going to have a child in her advanced age.

ANNUNCIATION TO MARY (IN NAZARETH)

Luke 1:26–38 Gabriel was Noah, the great prophet of the Flood. Elder Joseph Fielding Smith wrote: "Joseph Smith

Village of Nazareth, 1869

revealed that Gabriel was Noah; Luke declared that it was the angel Gabriel who appeared to Zacharias and Mary; and the Lord has declared that Elias appeared to Zacharias and Joseph Smith. Therefore, Elias is Noah" (*Answers to Gospel Questions,* 3:141; see also D&C 27:7; Smith, *History of the Church,* 3:386; Smith, *Teachings of the Prophet Joseph Smith,* 157). Gabriel was an alternate or heavenly name for the prophet Noah; *Gabriel* means literally "man of God."

Luke 1:27 How can a virgin have a child? Mary was not yet married to Joseph, only betrothed to him, having made a formal, binding contract for marriage (see Appendix 7, 768). "In the Law . . . betrothal was a far more binding step than is our custom of engagement before marriage, and the penalty for fornication with one person while betrothed to another was death for both guilty parties" (Albright and Mann, *Matthew,* 7). The normal length of time for betrothal was one month to one year, typically a year. During that period the families considered the young couple to be married (see Brown, *Mary and Elisabeth,* 43).

The Old Testament, the New Testament, and the Book of

Mormon all confirm that the young woman was a virgin—never having known intimately a mortal man (1 Nephi 11:13, 15; Alma 7:10). The names of the young couple were, in their Aramaic/Hebrew language, Yosef and Miriam. Miriam, or Mary—as her name comes down to us from Hebrew, through Greek, into English—is the only woman known prophetically by name in extant scripture (Mosiah 3:8; Alma 7:10; see also Brown, *Mary and Elisabeth*, 6).

Luke 1:28–33 The Joseph Smith Translation of verse 28 reads: "And the angel came in unto her and said, Hail, *thou virgin, who* art highly favored *of the Lord*. The Lord is with thee, *for thou art chosen and* blessed among women."

"Hail" is a greeting translated in the Latin Vulgate Version of the Bible as *Ave*, which is the source of the famous expression, *Ave Maria*. Though she was afraid at first, Mary was "highly favoured" and had "found favour with God." Her son would be called "JESUS" and the "Son of the Highest"—the "Highest" referring to God the Father, the first member of the Godhead. "The birth of the child, Jesus, was miraculous, his mother being his only earthly parent" (Bible Dictionary, "Joseph," 717). There is no question about his divine

Modern Nazareth, with Latin Church of the Annunciation (center)

Parentage. The First Presidency of the Church (Joseph F. Smith, Anthon H. Lund, and Charles W. Penrose) and the Twelve declared: "God the Eternal Father, whom we designate by the exalted name-title 'Elohim,' is the literal Parent of our Lord and Savior Jesus Christ" (*Messages of the First Presidency*, 5:26). Jesus would be a King and his kingdom would have no end, just as Isaiah had prophesied (Isaiah 9:7). Because Jesus was a descendant of Israel's greatest king, as a "son of David" he would inherit the throne of his father David. "The throne of his father David" (v. 32) refers to an eternal kingdom, not to a temporal, political kingdom.

Luke 1:34–35 How can such a thing happen—seemingly contrary to nature? The Holy Ghost would transfigure her, the "power of the Highest" would overshadow her, and she would give birth to the *Son of God* (Alma 7:10; 1 Nephi 11:18–20; 2 Nephi 25:19; emphasis added). Again, there is no question who the Child's Father was.

Elder Bruce R. McConkie testified: "God the Father is a perfected, glorified, holy Man, an immortal Personage. And Christ was born into the world as the literal Son of this Holy Being; he was born in the same personal, real, and literal sense that any mortal son is born to a mortal father. There is nothing figurative about his paternity; . . . he is the Son of God, and that designation means what it says" (*Mormon Doctrine*, 742).

President Ezra Taft Benson declared: "The Church of Jesus Christ of Latter-day Saints proclaims that Jesus Christ is the Son of God in the most literal sense. The body in which He performed His mission in the flesh was sired by that same Holy Being we worship as God, our Eternal Father. Jesus was not the son of Joseph, nor was He begotten by the Holy Ghost. He is the Son of the Eternal Father!" (*Come unto Christ*, 4).

Luke 1:36–38 Another miraculous thing was happening simultaneously with Mary's relative, Elisabeth—having a child in her old age. "For with God nothing shall be impossible."

The exact relationship of Mary and Elisabeth is not known; see footnote a to Luke 1:36. The Greek word here simply means "kin." John Wycliffe, the father of the English Bible, popularized the idea that "cousin" was meant. John the Baptist was, without question, a relative of Jesus on his mother's side.

ANNUNCIATION TO JOSEPH (IN NAZARETH)

Matthew 1:18–24 Mary was espoused or betrothed to Joseph (see Appendix 7, 768). She was the purest and most righteous young woman in all the land of the Jews, and she was in every respect worthy of the unusual blessings coming to her. Before she and Joseph were married, Mary was pregnant, as Alma 7:10 explains, by *the power of* the Holy Ghost.

Matthew 1:20 "Joseph pondered and prayed. Was Mary with child by the power of the Holy Ghost or in some other way? As to the true father of the unborn child, Mary knew; Elisabeth knew; Zacharias knew. They all gained their testimonies by revelation" (McConkie, *Mortal Messiah*, 1:332–33).

Joseph was a noble and great man, chosen before this world was for a unique assignment on earth. He was close enough to the Spirit to be in a position to receive revelation, and an angel of the Lord came to clarify things for a perplexed Joseph and to reassure him. He was consequently obedient to the divine instructions.

This verse also contains another note about the Holy Ghost's role in preparing Mary for the divine Conception. Elder Melvin J. Ballard wrote: "'And the Holy Ghost came upon her . . . and she came into the presence of the highest.' No man or woman can live in mortality and survive the presence of the Highest except by the sustaining power of the Holy Ghost. So it came upon her to prepare her for admittance into the divine presence, and the power of the Highest, who is the Father, was present, and overshadowed her, and the holy Child that was born of her was called the Son of God.

"Men who deny this, or who think that it degrades our Father, have no true conception of the sacredness of the most marvelous power with which God has endowed mortal men—the power of creation. Even though that power may be abused and may become a mere harp of pleasure to the wicked, nevertheless it is the most sacred and holy and divine function with which God has endowed man. Made holy, it is retained by the Father of us all, and in his exercise of that great and marvelous creative power and function, he did not debase himself, degrade himself, nor debauch his daughter. Thus Christ became the literal Son of a divine Father, and no one else was worthy to be his father" (*Sermons and Missionary Services,* 167).

Elder Harold B. Lee gave a specific caution to those who teach about the divine Conception:

"*Teachers should not speculate on the manner of Christ's birth.*

"We are very much concerned that some of our Church teachers seem to be obsessed of the idea of teaching doctrine which cannot be substantiated and making comments beyond what the Lord has actually said.

"You asked about . . . the birth of the Savior. Never have I talked about sexual intercourse between Deity and the mother of the Savior. If teachers were wise in speaking of this matter about which the Lord has said but very little, they would rest their discussion on this subject with merely the words which are recorded on this subject in Luke 1:34–35: 'Then said Mary unto the angel, How shall this be, seeing I know not a man? And the angel answered and said unto her, The Holy Ghost shall come upon thee, and the power of the Highest shall overshadow thee: therefore also that holy thing which shall be born of thee shall be called the Son of God.'

"Remember that the being who was brought about by [Mary's] conception was a divine personage. We need not question His method to accomplish His purposes. . . . Let the Lord rest His case with this declaration and wait until He sees fit to tell us more" (*Teachings of Harold B. Lee*, 13–14).

A good illustration of Elder Lee's counsel to write of this sacred subject with caution and propriety is the following statement from Elder Robert E. Wells in general conference of October 1995, describing the importance of our belief in the literal divine Sonship of Jesus Christ:

"The divine Sonship of Jesus Christ . . . is central to understanding the entire plan of salvation. He is the First Begotten Son of the Father in the premortal existence and the Only Begotten Son of the Father on earth. God the Eternal Father is the literal parent of our Lord and Savior Jesus Christ and of His other spirit children. . . .

"The 'divine Sonship' also refers to the designation 'Only Begotten Son in the flesh.' Ancient and modern scriptures use the title 'Only Begotten Son' to emphasize the divine nature of Jesus Christ. This title signifies that Jesus' physical body was the offspring of a mortal mother and of an immortal Eternal Father, which verity is crucial to the Atonement, a supreme act that could not have been accomplished by an ordinary man. Christ had power to lay down His life and power to take it again because He had inherited immortality from His Heavenly Father. From Mary, His mother, Christ inherited mortality, or the power to die.

"This infinite atonement of Christ and Christ's divine Sonship go together hand in hand to form the single most important doctrine of all Christianity" (*Ensign*, November 1995, 65).

Matthew 1:21 *Yeshua* (pronounced Ye-SHU-a; the first vowel is a short "e," as in the word "*e*verlasting"), his name in his own language, Aramaic, means salvation or Savior. He it is who would indeed save all people, upon repentance, from their sins.

His role as Savior and Redeemer was plainly prophesied by Lehi and Nephi, who saw him:

"Yea, even six hundred years from the time that my father left Jerusalem, a prophet would the Lord God raise up among the Jews—even a Messiah, or, in other words, a Savior of the world.

"And he also spake concerning the prophets, how great a number had testified of these things, concerning this Messiah, of whom he had spoken, or this Redeemer of the world" (1 Nephi 10:4–5; see also 1 Nephi 13:40).

Matthew 1:22–23 All this is fulfillment of prophecy; it was all known centuries earlier. Matthew's delight was to prove that Jesus was the Messiah (cf. 2 Nephi 11:4, 6). Matthew saw the great connection between the Old Testament and the New Testament (he uses the word "fulfill" at least twelve times). He saw Jesus as the fulfillment of all Old Testament prophecies of the Messiah (he gives us nearly fifty quotations, most of them messianic, from the Old Testament; see Topical Guide, "Jesus Christ, Prophecies about," 252). Isaiah had prophesied that a virgin would have a child (Isaiah 7:14). Emmanuel (or better, Immanuel; see Bible Dictionary, "Immanuel," 706) means literally "God [is] with us," fulfilling prophecy that God himself would come down, or condescend, to dwell among mortals (Isaiah 8:8, 10). Mary's foreordained role as mortal mother of God's own Son was plainly prophesied not only by Isaiah but also by Nephi (1 Nephi 11:13–21), King Benjamin (Mosiah 3:8), and Alma (7:10).

Matthew 1:24 The angelic messages came in dreams (though the JST changes "dreams" to "visions"). Joseph obeyed. Joseph's gift was the ability to receive revelation through dreams or visions. Joseph's "dreams" are mentioned five times in the first two chapters of Matthew. Revelatory dreams or visions are real; they teach valuable lessons and prepare, warn, and counsel individuals today (see Bible Dictionary, "Dreams," 659).

Divinely Appointed Foundations

MARY VISITS ELISABETH (IN JUDEA)

Luke 1:39–56 Who would believe that a local teenage girl was going to have a baby and that God was the baby's father? Rumors, accusations, and judgmental remarks would abound (cf. John 8:41). Mary needed understanding and solace during this biggest trial (and blessing) of her life. Upon visiting her relative a hundred miles away, Mary confirmed what the angel had told her (Luke 1:36)—that Elisabeth, too, had become the subject of a miracle. She and Zacharias had been able to conceive and have a son in their old age.

Luke 1:42–45 Elisabeth received a personal witness that Mary was carrying God's Son, who was the Lord Jehovah. And John, inside her own body, physically responded to the presence of the Lord. John's spirit was already in his body, and he was, as Luke 1:15 notes, "filled with the Holy Ghost, even from his mother's womb." Elisabeth bore testimony that the angel's message would all be fulfilled.

Luke 1:46–55 Mary responded with her own testimonial, which speaks volumes about the nobility and righteousness of her heart: "My soul doth magnify the Lord, and my spirit hath rejoiced in God my Saviour." How marvelous if each of us could likewise exclaim in purity and honesty: My soul doth magnify the Lord.

Mary also prophesied that she would be honored and revered (but not worshipped) by all future generations. She testified of the great things God had done to her and for all Israel. Her song of praise is generally known in the Christian world as the "Magnificat" because the Latin Vulgate translation begins with the word *Magnificat*, which means "magnifies" or "glorifies." Mary's song of praise includes many references to the psalms and the prophets that she must have known well (see references in footnotes to Luke 1:46–55). Her exultation is remarkably similar to that of another woman's song of praise after finding out that she, who had been barren, would bear a son—Hannah, mother of the prophet Samuel (1 Samuel 2:1–10). Both psalms of rejoicing contain majestic messianic imagery. Compare Nephi's elevated praise of the future Messiah: "Wherefore, my soul delighteth to prophesy concerning him, for I have seen his day, and my heart doth magnify his holy name" (2 Nephi 25:13).

"There is only one Christ," Elder McConkie wrote, "and there is only one Mary. Each was noble and great in preexistence, and each was foreordained to the ministry he or she performed. We cannot but think that the Father would choose the greatest female spirit to be the mother of his Son, even as he chose the male spirit like unto him to be the Savior" (*Mortal Messiah*, 1:326–27, n. 4).

Luke 1:56 Mary stayed with Elisabeth about three months—a time to talk and ponder and wonder.

BIRTH OF JOHN THE BAPTIST (IN JUDEA)

Luke 1:57–58 A new prophet had come into the eastern world, making it a time of rejoicing. It had been a long time—four hundred years—since the prophet Malachi.

NAMING OF JOHN (IN JUDEA)

Luke 1:59–66 On circumcision, see Appendix 7 (773). The name of Zacharias and Elisabeth's son was to be John, as prophesied. Elisabeth knew it, and Zacharias knew it. John was set apart at the age of eight days to the noble calling of forerunner and preparator of the Lord's coming. A forerunner was one who in ancient times ran before the chariot of the king and cleared the path and prepared the way for the royal one to follow. John was sent to prepare the way before the most Royal One.

"John, whom God raised up, [was] filled with the Holy Ghost from his mother's womb. For he was baptized while he was yet in his childhood [at eight years], and was ordained by the angel of God at the time he was eight days old unto this power, to overthrow the kingdom of the Jews, and to make straight the way of the Lord before the face of his people, to prepare them for the coming of the Lord" (D&C 84:27–28).

As part of his preparations for the coming of the Lord, John would indeed "overthrow the kingdom of the Jews," that is, begin to displace the less fruitful religious establishment of Judaism at the time in favor of a refreshing restoration of the divine truths of the gospel of Jesus Christ.

A writing table

Luke 1:63 A "writing table" or tablet was a small wooden board covered with wax, such as that which Ezekiel called a "stick" (see Ezekiel 37:16; footnote a).

Luke 1:64–66 Another miracle happened: the righteous Temple worker could speak again. The miraculous episode circulated, and all wondered what kind of child this would be.

ZACHARIAS'S PROPHETIC PSALM (IN JUDEA)

Luke 1:67–80 Zacharias, filled with the Spirit, uttered a psalm or hymn known in the Christian world as the *Benedictus* ("Blessed be") because that is the beginning word in this passage in the Latin Vulgate translation of the Bible. Zacharias prophesied using the prophetic future tense (past tense verbs, as if future events were already accomplished): the Lord God of Israel (Jehovah/Jesus) hath visited and redeemed his people. He has raised up a *horn* of salvation, meaning a *power* of salvation, through this descendant of David (cf. 2 Samuel 22:3; Psalm 18:2)—all of which had been prophesied since the world began. He had come to show mercy, remembering the holy Abrahamic covenant.

Hannah's psalm or hymn of praise (see Luke 1:46–55) mentions the messianic symbol of the horn (1 Samuel 2:1).

Luke 1:76–79 Zacharias told his son that he, John, would be called the prophet of the Highest (as Jesus would be called the Son of the Highest); he would prepare the way for the Lord's own ministry; he would give knowledge of salvation—that is, knowledge of *Yeshua* (Jesus)—which salvation comes through having sins remitted and through his mercy. The *dayspring* had come to give *light* to them that sit in darkness, as the dawn (dayspring) brings light to the dark world each morning, and to them that are in the shadow of death, to guide their feet (as his word does) into the way of peace. See also commentary on Matthew 4:16.

Luke 1:80 Luke reported that John, as a youth growing up, "was in the deserts till the day of his shewing [pronounced SHOW-ing] unto Israel." It is unlikely, however, that such a comment means that he lived his entire youth and all of his ministry in the desert. Elder McConkie wrote: "The idea that our Lord's forerunner was a Nazarite for life, had never cut his hair or married, and that he lived always in the deserts is speculation that cannot be true. . . . That he was married, had children, and lived as normal a life as his ministerial assignments permitted, we cannot doubt" (*Mortal Messiah,* 1:385).

CHAPTER 3

THE BIRTH AND CHILDHOOD OF JESUS

Luke 2:1–5 Joseph and Mary went from Nazareth to Bethlehem to be taxed because Caesar Augustus decreed a taxation of some kind, or *enrollment* for taxation, throughout *his empire* (JST). "The obligation on all persons to be enrolled at their domiciles of origin, which made it necessary for Joseph to return to Bethlehem, has been illustrated from an edict of AD 104, in which C. Vibius Maximus, Roman prefect of Egypt, gives notice as follows: 'The enrolment by household being at hand, it is necessary to notify all who for any cause whatsoever are away from their administrative divisions to return home in order to comply with the customary ordinance

Journeying through the desolate Judean wilderness

of enrolment' (A. Deissmann, *Light from the Ancient East*, 270ff., as cited in Bruce, *New Testament Documents*, 86–87). Apparently, in 9/10 BC, Augustus began to require yearly registration of all possessions including land, clothes, sheep, and slaves [see Schurer, *History of the Jewish People in the Age of Jesus Christ*, 400 ff.]. The taxpayer himself had to personally submit the necessary data. Moreover, lands had to be registered in the communities in which they were located. This point is extremely important in relation to the birth of Jesus as it demonstrates Joseph must have owned land in the Bethlehem area. Otherwise, it would not have been necessary for him and Mary to make the journey from Galilee to Judea" (Martin, *Jesus the Messiah—The Gospels in Context*, 42).

Luke 2:2 The enrollment occurred when Cyrenius was governor of Syria. Judea was neighbor to the province of Syria, and Cyrenius, or Quirinius, was the Roman governor (consul or legate) of the province of Syria. Though there is some uncertainty about the dating of the census or enrollment that Luke mentions, the service of Roman consul Publius Sulpicius Quirinius as governor or legate of Syria during the initial years of the first millennium after Christ is confirmed also by the Jewish historian Josephus. The New International Version *Learning Bible* contains on page 1971 the following note on Luke 2:2: "A distinguished military leader who may have begun serving as governor of Syria around 12 B.C. Herod the Great made him governor of Judea in 6 B.C. The census he conducted was for tax purposes. He would conduct another census in A.D. 6 [Acts 5:37]. Quirinius died in A.D. 21."

Luke is a careful writer. Of all the New Testament writers, Luke is the only one who names a Roman emperor. Three emperors, Augustus, Tiberius, and Claudius, are mentioned by name in his two volumes (Luke and Acts), and the emperor Nero is mentioned not by name but as the Caesar to whom Paul appealed (Acts 25:12). After Julius Caesar, "Caesar" became the official title of the emperor in Rome, much as

"Pharaoh" was the title of the king in Egypt—and the title "Caesar" has transferred to other languages, such as the German "Kaiser" and the Russian "Czar." "Names of note in the Jewish and Gentile world of his day appear in Luke's pages; in addition to the emperors, we meet the Roman governors Quirinius, Pilate, Sergius Paulus, Gallio, Felix, and Festus; Herod the Great and some of his descendants—Herod Antipas the tetrarch of Galilee, the vassal-kings Herod Agrippa I and II, Berenice and Drusilla; leading members of the Jewish priestly caste such as Annas, Caiaphas, and Ananias; Gamaliel, the greatest contemporary Rabbi and Pharisaic leader. A writer who thus relates his story to the wider context of world history is courting trouble if he is not careful; he affords his critical readers so many opportunities for testing his accuracy.... The historical trustworthiness of Luke has indeed been acknowledged by many biblical critics" (Bruce, *New Testament Documents,* 81–82, 91).

Luke 2:3–4 By Jewish custom, which the Romans countenanced, adults returned to their ancestral hometowns to be enrolled or registered for the tax (perhaps as landowners, as suggested in commentary on Luke 2:1–5, above). Both Joseph and Mary were of the royal Davidic line, so they made their way to Bethlehem of Judah, King David's hometown, for the Messiah must be born in Bethlehem, in the land of Jerusalem (Micah 5:2; Alma 7:10).

They would probably have made the journey from Nazareth to Bethlehem by one of two routes. One would have taken them south across the Jezreel Valley, then through the hills of Samaria into Judea. This is the more direct route in straight-line distance, but there are two reasons it probably was not the way Joseph and Mary went: it is physically demanding, with a circuitous trek through the hills, and it took the traveler directly through Samaritan country, and "the Jews [had] no dealings with the Samaritans" (John 4:9; see Appendix 4, 753).

The other possible route is the one Joseph and Mary more

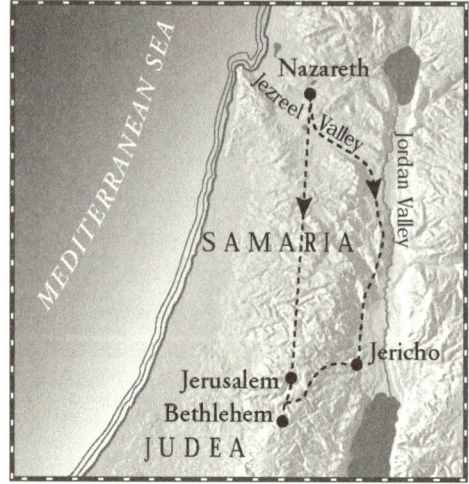

Two possible routes of the journey of Joseph and Mary to Bethlehem

likely traveled. It would have taken them southeast across the Jezreel Valley, connecting with the Jordan Valley, continuing level or slightly down in elevation all the way to Jericho, then up through the Judean desert to Jerusalem and Bethlehem.

To discover for himself what the possible routes would have been like, Brother Ogden walked both of them. Each route is about ninety-two miles long. Normal walking pace, even with a camel or donkey, is three miles per hour, so a traveler can usually cover between seventeen and twenty-four miles each day. Each route took about thirty hours to walk—seventeen to twenty miles a day for five days.

At that rate, the journey would have taken Joseph and Mary at least four to five days. Perhaps the journey was even longer because of Mary's condition, she being heavy with child and needing to travel even fewer miles per day to accommodate the physical strain. It would have been a wearying journey for anyone but especially for a pregnant woman soon to give birth. We wonder where Joseph and Mary stayed each night, where and with whom they camped along the way. It was early spring, which can still be very chilly at night in the hill-country; however, in the Jordan Valley—which is below

The Birth and Childhood of Jesus

sea level (Bible Map 14)—the temperatures could have been mild and pleasant.

The last leg of the eastern route would have been the hardest of all. Jericho is the lowest town on the globe, and Jerusalem and Bethlehem are situated right in the top of the hills. From Jericho through the desert to Bethlehem is an uphill hike of 3,300 feet. How exhausted Mary must have been. How anxious Joseph must have been to find a comfortable room at an inn. Desperate to find adequate shelter, they may have resorted at last to a limestone cave used for a stable. Bethlehem's Church of the Nativity, the oldest church in Christendom, is built over just such a cave. It is venerated by Christians the world over as the spot where Jesus was born (on Jesus' birth in a cave, see Brown, *Mary and Elisabeth,* 53).

"Bethlehem of Judea" is the usual rendering, to distinguish it from a Bethlehem in Galilee just west of Nazareth in the territory of Zebulun (Joshua 19:10, 15) but also to emphasize the Messiah's provenance from the prophesied tribal territory of Judah. Though Bethlehem figures in few biblical stories, the name is immortalized as the birthplace of two outstanding personalities in world history: King David and his descendant Jesus Christ.

The prophetic word had gone forth centuries before (recorded at least by Micah) that the Messiah would be born a "son of David," or descendant of David, in Bethlehem. Matthew, of course, took up Micah's prophecy to lend scriptural credibility to the divine and messianic origins of Jesus. In the citation of Micah, Matthew adds (apparently from 2 Samuel 5:2) "out of thee shall come a Governor [Greek, *leader*] that shall rule my people Israel" (Matthew 2:6). The Greek verb translated "rule" in this passage means to shepherd, tend, protect, or nurture.

In Matthew's account, "the chief priests and scribes of the people" (2:4) summoned by Herod are the ones who advised the king where Christ was to be born. It was generally known that the little Judean town, otherwise insignificant in the

Roman period, would perpetuate the glory of the Davidic dynasty by serving as birthplace of the Messiah. "Hath not the scripture said, That Christ cometh of the seed of David, and out of the town of Bethlehem, where David was?" (John 7:42).

Matthew also records that Herod issued his infamous extermination order that infants under the age of two in the vicinity of Bethlehem be slaughtered so that he would have no contender for his throne. Herod "sent forth, and slew all the children that were in Bethlehem, and in all the coasts thereof, from two years old and under, according to the time which he had diligently enquired of the wise men" (Matthew 2:16).

After the birth and infancy of Jesus in Bethlehem, we find no further narrative mention of the town in the New Testament.

BIRTH OF JESUS (IN BETHLEHEM)

Luke 2:6–7 Luke does not say the birth of Jesus occurred on the very night of their arrival in Bethlehem, though it seems to have been soon after that because they were anxious

Modern Bethlehem, as seen from Shepherds' Fields

about Mary's condition. We wonder how long it was before April 5 (according to a Latter-day Saint understanding of when "Christmas Eve" really was; D&C 20:1) that they began their journey southward from Galilee to Judea (see Appendix 7, 770).

Luke 2:7 When her "days were accomplished that she should be delivered," Mary "brought forth" her firstborn son. The Spanish text says *dio a luz,* "brought to light"—that is a pleasant expression, and it is true. She brought forth the Light of the world. She wrapped him in "swaddling clothes," meaning clothes that were wrapped tightly around the infant. They were apparently in some structure for stabling animals, likely one of the many limestone caves in the vicinity, where there was a manger—a feeding trough—in which to lay him. They had found no vacancy in the local *inns* (JST).

ANNUNCIATION TO THE SHEPHERDS (IN FIELDS AROUND BETHLEHEM)

Luke 2:8–20 Shepherds were out in the fields virtually all year long, even at night, watching over their flocks. Some authorities propose that the flocks destined for sacrifice on the great altar of the Temple were kept year round in the fields near Bethlehem.

Luke 2:9 An angel of the Lord appeared to the shepherds, with the accompanying *glory of the Lord* shining around them—and they were afraid. The shepherds were going to be, in part, a fulfillment of the law of witnesses—multiple witnesses, of various kinds, to the greatest birth in the history of the world.

Shepherds watched over the birth of lambs. Now they were instructed to search out the Firstborn Lamb, who would, within a few years, be sacrificed for the people.

Luke 2:10–11 "Fear not: for, behold, I bring you good tidings of great joy." *Good tidings* in Renaissance English is *gospel,* and it brings joy. The message and the joy will be for all people.

"City of David" always refers to Jerusalem, except in this passage. Luke calls Bethlehem the city of David, which is also appropriate because the great king had been born there. Now his descendant, the King of kings, is born in the same town. These two royal births give Bethlehem, an otherwise insignificant town, an immortal fame.

Were the shepherds surprised to hear of a *Savior* born in the nearby town? Perhaps not greatly surprised, because such an event had been announced and anticipated for centuries. This Savior would be the Christ, the Messiah, the Anointed One. Were the shepherds surprised to hear that the long-awaited *Messiah* had finally come? Very happy news indeed, but maybe not so surprising. This Savior or Christ would be "the *Lord.*" This term, though, may have surprised these and many other Jews. "The Lord" was *Jehovah*—the Creator of the earth and of all things, the God who established the covenant with the ancient patriarchs and who gave the Torah to Moses on Mount Sinai, He who was worshipped for a thousand years in his House, the great Temple, five miles to the north in Jerusalem. This same great, worshipped Being is now born as a Babe in this nearby town? That is a surprising announcement indeed. (We are not sure how many Jews at the time had made the connection—how many equated the Christ, or Messiah, who would become mortal in order to provide salvation, with their God, the Lord Jehovah.)

Luke 2:12 The sign, or evidence, of the angel's message was simple: the shepherds would find the infant wrapped in swaddling clothes, lying not in the clean linen of home or hospital but in the animals' feeding trough. The Greatest of all would enter mortality in the humblest circumstances imaginable: "Jesus, once of humble birth" (*Hymns,* 1985, no. 196).

Luke 2:13 The one angel was joined by many. Where else in all the vast universe would the heavenly hosts—the sons and daughters of our Father—have wanted to be than right there in those shepherds' fields around Bethlehem when the Father's Firstborn, the Savior of us all, was born into the world?

Luke 2:14 The heavenly host praised God and exulted in the glory that would come to the Highest. On earth, peace was coming and "good will toward men." "Glory to God in the highest" is in Latin *Gloria in Excelsis Deo*.

In October 1980, Brother Ogden "took a group of Jerusalem Study Abroad students for an Arab dinner in Manger Square in Bethlehem. Following the shishkabob we listened to a political speech by the spirited mayor of Bethlehem, Elias Freij. He came down pretty hard on the United States, reciting grievances about life under military occupation, taxation without representation, having all office and home phones tapped, and so on. I was personally saddened by his reminder that none of us as free citizens of the United States could understand what his whole life had been like, being controlled first by British, then by Jordanians, now by Israelis. He was bitter. He said he wants some of the 'peace on earth' spoken of by a Man from his town two thousand years ago. I reflected on the words of Henry Wadsworth Longfellow: 'And in despair I bowed my head: "There is no peace on earth," I said, "for hate is strong and mocks the song of peace on earth, good will to men. [And since that's the prevailing condition there:] Then pealed the bells more loud and deep: 'God is not dead, nor doth he sleep; the wrong shall fail, the right prevail, with peace on earth, good will to men'" (*Hymns*, 1985, 214).

"Two decades later, in August 2001, I ventured to make another of many trips to Israel. While in Jerusalem, for the first time in many years I feared to go into Bethlehem. The turmoil and tension were thick and fierce in the land of Jerusalem right then (including Bethlehem), inhibiting any traveler from daring to visit there. It's pathetic, I thought, that the peace proclaimed at his Birth still hasn't managed to get a strong foothold in that land. There will only be peace—ultimately—when the Prince of peace and his gospel of peace reign supreme in the hearts of all peoples there and everywhere. True peace will not be won by armaments and fighting, nor at the negotiating table, but by accepting the Lord Jesus Christ as the real God of the land and honoring and obeying him. Maybe that can only happen with a *second* coming into the world, with even more glory and with power" (Ogden, journal).

Luke 2:15–18 The shepherds were excited to go and see. They quickly followed the angel's directions and found Mary, Joseph, and the Baby Jesus. They saw and believed, and they broadcast far and wide what they had learned from the angelic visitors from heaven. Those who heard their testimony marveled at the things they heard.

Luke 2:19, 51 Mary, on the other hand, did not publicize but maintained a respectful shroud of silence over these sacred events, keeping them quietly guarded in her heart to reflect on them again and again.

NAMING OF JESUS (IN BETHLEHEM)

Matthew 1:25 Until Mary had given birth to Jesus, Joseph "knew her not." Jesus was *her* firstborn son (but not Joseph's, because Joseph was not his literal father). Having been specifically instructed what to name the boy, Joseph called him *YESHUA,* or in English, JESUS. The role and ministry that Joseph was called upon to perform shows us that there is great honor in being a stepparent. And the life of Jesus in this regard shows that there is no dishonor in being raised by a stepparent. In fact, there is great honor and blessing regarding this relationship.

Luke 2:21 Jesus was circumcised at eight days, according to the sign of the covenant he had given to Abraham and his descendants (see Appendix 7, 773). He also officially received his name, *YESHUA* (meaning "Savior" or "salvation"), the name given him long before his conception and birth into mortality (2 Nephi 25:19).

PRESENTATION IN THE TEMPLE (IN JERUSALEM)

Luke 2:22–39 The "days of purification" meant forty days in isolation. We do not know all the reasons for such a period. Why did he have to be taken to the Temple at Jerusalem to be presented to the Lord (especially since he *was* the Lord)? The Mosaic law stipulated that every "male that openeth the womb," that is, every firstborn male, would be dedicated to the Lord's service (Exodus 13:2; see also Bible Dictionary, "Firstborn," 675). When Mary had fulfilled the forty-day ritual of purification after giving birth, Jesus was taken to the Temple in Jerusalem for the ceremonial redemption of the firstborn. Not every male of every tribe was needed for the Temple service, of course, so a sacrifice could be offered to satisfy the requirement of the Law. The poor who could not afford a larger animal for the sacrificial offering could give a pair of turtledoves or two young pigeons (as provided in Leviticus 1:14; 5:7; 12:8). There, before entering the grounds of the Holy Place, Mary would have been immersed and ritually cleansed in a *mikvah* (on the ritual immersion bath, or *mikvah*, see commentary on Matthew 9:14–17).

Luke 2:25–32 Simeon, a righteous Temple worker, had received a witness through the Holy Ghost that he would have the privilege of seeing the Anointed One before he passed from this life. Guided by the Spirit, he recognized the Child when his mother and guardian brought him in according to Mosaic stipulations. Simeon took the Child in his arms, blessed God, and exulted in the privilege of seeing "salvation" with his own eyes. The Hebrew word for "salvation" in this passage is *Yeshua*. He came as the Light of the world, to enlighten Gentile as well as Jew.

Luke 2:33 "Joseph and his mother"—notice that Joseph is not designated as Jesus' father, and quite correctly so. He was Jesus' earthly guardian but not his father.

Luke 2:34 Simeon, the old Temple worker, blessed *them*, meaning that Joseph and Mary received a blessing from his hands also. And to Mary, Jesus' mother, he prophesied that the Child was appointed for the fall of many in Israel; that is, he would serve as a stumbling block or rock of offense in bringing many people down, but he would also help many to rise again—rise above their sinful and fallen condition and be raised up through his loving kindness and expiatory forgiveness. The Savior would help many to rise from the deadly consequences of the Fall and raise their bodies and their souls to immortality and eternal life. But for those who would not believe in that fall and the rising again, Christ would be a sign (an evidence, a testimony) against which they would fight.

Luke 2:35 And—continuing the prophecy to Mary—"a *spear* shall pierce through *him* [Christ] *to the wounding of thine* [Mary's] own soul also" (JST Luke 2:35), which constituted a clear foreshadowing of what the Son and his mother would both suffer at Golgotha.

Luke 2:36–38 Another witness of the Redeemer came forward—a very old prophetess and Temple worker of the tribe of Asher named Anna (Hebrew, *Hannah;* cf. 1 Samuel 1:2). The Bible gives the title "prophetess" to six women: Miriam (Exodus 15:20), Deborah (Judges 4:4), Huldah (2 Kings 22:14; 2 Chronicles 34:22), Noadiah (Nehemiah 6:14), Isaiah's wife (Isaiah 8:3), and Anna (Luke 2:36–37). In addition, Philip the evangelist had four daughters who "did prophesy" (Acts 21:9). As Alma teaches, God "imparteth his word by angels unto men, yea, not only men but women also" (Alma 32:23). Of Deborah, for example, Daniel Ludlow wrote: "The reference to Deborah as a prophetess does not mean she held the priesthood office or calling of a prophet.

Her gift of prophecy would have been essentially the same that is available to every worthy person who has received the gift of the Holy Ghost [cf. Numbers 11:29]" (*Companion to Your Study of the Old Testament,* 210). Joseph Smith said: "Every man who has come into this Church; and every woman, for that matter, who has received the testimony of the Spirit of the Lord, is a prophet or a prophetess; that every man should be a prophet, because every man in the Church should have the testimony of Jesus which is the spirit of prophecy" (quoted by Joseph F. Smith Jr., Conference Report, April 1918, 159).

Anna's husband had died after seven years of marriage, leaving her a widow for eighty-four years (or else she was now eighty-four years of age), and she had dedicated herself wholly to fasting, praying, and Temple service. Anna bore testimony of this little Anointed One to all who "looked for redemption in Jerusalem."

VISIT OF THE WISE MEN (IN JERUSALEM AND BETHLEHEM)

Matthew 2:1–12 Wise men came from the east. We do not know who they were or where they were from, for we do not pretend to know where all the colonies of God's faithful followers could have been. A large colony of Jews had resided in Babylon for centuries, since the Babylonian exile. The term by which they are referenced in the Greek version of Matthew 2:1, *magi,* is a Persian word and suggests a region of the Babylonian Empire conquered by the Persians. Perhaps from among them came this group of wise seekers for the Messiah. "That they were privileged to search out the Son of God and give him gifts, and that they were spiritually sensitive and knowledgeable, suggests that they were actually prophets on a divine errand" (Bible Dictionary, "Wise Men of the East," 789; see also "Magi," 727).

Matthew 2:2 The wise men inquired as to the whereabouts

of him who was born to be the *Messiah* of the Jews (JST Matthew 3:2). They had seen his star in the east (cf. Helaman 14:5; 3 Nephi 1:13, 21), and they had come to worship him. Alfred Edersheim, an authority on Jewish tradition, wrote, citing rabbinic literature, "The star shall shine forth from the East, and this is the star of the Messiah" (*Jesus the Messiah*, 212; see also the prophecy in Numbers 24:17).

Matthew 2:3 This was the wrong thing to say to Herod the Great (the great murderer). Herod was insanely jealous and suspicious of anyone who might dethrone or displace him.

Matthew 2:4–6 Herod inquired of the Jewish leaders and scholars exactly where this Messiah was supposed to be born. They knew. The prophecies were specific: in Bethlehem of Judah, as recorded in Micah 5:2. To illustrate the importance of this prophecy, we relate the following experience in the Holy Land:

Early in 1990 Brother Ogden noticed an advertisement in the *Jerusalem Post* for a seminar on Christ, sponsored by an agency of the Israeli government, to be held in March of that year for several days in a hotel on the shore of the Dead Sea. "I thought it advisable," he wrote, "that someone from among the Latter-day Saints should be present to hear what Jews were saying these days about Jesus.

"Patrons of the Seminar were free to ask questions. At one point during the many hours of lectures and panel discussions, a man posed the following question: 'Is it not true that our scripture [Micah 5:2] says the Messiah would be born in Bethlehem?' No response was forthcoming, so the interrogator continued, 'Well, if we don't believe the Messiah has come, and he is yet to be born in Bethlehem, what's he going to be—an Arab Palestinian?' (Bethlehem is an all-Arab town today.) Professor Shmuel Safrai finally responded: 'The scripture is not important from a Jewish historical point of view; it's only important if you believe Jesus is the Messiah'" (Ogden, journal).

Herod the king knew something of the prophecies

The Birth and Childhood of Jesus

concerning the coming of the Messiah. He asked: "*Where is the place that is written of by the prophets, in which Christ should be born? For he greatly feared, yet he believed not the prophets*" (JST Matthew 3:4). Joseph Smith's translation of Matthew also renders Micah's passage in significantly different terms: "*It is written by the prophets, that he should be born* in Bethlehem of Judea . . . And thou Bethlehem, *which lieth* in the land of Judea, *in thee shall be born a prince* . . . out of thee shall come *the Messiah,* who shall *save* my people Israel" (JST Matthew 3:5–6).

Matthew 2:7–8 Herod, upon learning what he could from the wise men, deviously remarked that when they discovered His whereabouts, he would like to go "and worship him also."

Matthew 2:9–10 The wise men again followed the star; it guided them and stood over the spot where the *young child* was now housed, demonstrating in some miraculous way the very location of the Holy Child they sought.

Matthew 2:11–12 It was some time after Jesus' birth now—he was a "young child," and the family was living in a house in Bethlehem. They had apparently decided to remain in Bethlehem until additional instructions were given to them. The gifts the wise men presented to Jesus, especially the gold, would soon be helpful to a poor couple on the road in a foreign country. (Incidentally, it is the number of gifts given—three—that gives us the traditional number of wise men.) Perhaps the gold was representative of royalty, the frankincense symbolic of priesthood (as it was used in the Temple with certain offerings; Exodus 30:34–36), and the myrrh a foreshadowing of his death and burial (as one of the precious spices used in preparing his body for the sepulchre; see commentary on Matthew 27:57–61).

The wise men were warned in a dream to flee the country immediately, and an angel warned Joseph to flee also—to go to Egypt and stay there until he received further instructions.

FLIGHT TO EGYPT

Matthew 2:13–15 God knew that Herod would try to kill the young Messiah. The text is always careful to differentiate between Joseph and the Child and his mother. Mary is always called his mother, but Joseph is not generally called his father. The journey in a southwesterly direction, at night, would be fraught with dangers, though less dangerous than remaining in Herodian territory. With Jesus' temporary residence in the land of Egypt, Matthew, as he enjoyed doing, found direct fulfillment in prophecy: "Out of Egypt have I called my son" (some translations capitalize "son"). The prophecy is from Hosea 11:1. Besides its application to the Israelite exodus from Egypt, Matthew adapted the verse to this new sense. The ancient Israelites living for a time in and then coming out of Egypt thus became a type of the Son of God living for a time in and then coming out of Egypt.

SLAUGHTER OF THE INFANTS (IN BETHLEHEM)

Matthew 2:16–18 Feeling deceived by his visitors from the east, Herod issued his infamous extermination order—the execution of children two years and under in Bethlehem and environs. Another prophecy was thus fulfilled, this time from Jeremiah, about lamentation over the deaths of children.

The context of Jeremiah's prophecy is the period of the Babylonian captivity. After Jeremiah's forty years of warning the inhabitants of Judah, he described the pathetic picture of Judahites being carried away captive from the Babylonian military government position at Ramah, five miles north of Jerusalem: "The word that came to Jeremiah from the Lord, after that Nebuzaradan the captain of the guard had let him go from Ramah, when he had taken him being bound in chains among all that were carried away captive of Jerusalem and Judah, which were carried away captive unto Babylon" (Jeremiah 40:1). The Lord encouraged Jeremiah to "refrain [his] voice from weeping, and [his] eyes from tears: for . . . they shall come again from the land of the enemy. . . . Thy children shall come again to their own border" (Jeremiah 31:16–17).

In commenting on the phrase about weeping in Ramah, Edward Robinson (a renowned theologian from New York City who spent many months in the mid-1800s exploring the Holy Land) wrote: "Eusebius and Jerome [early Christian church fathers] assume a Ramah near Bethlehem, in order to afford an explanation of the language of Matthew. This, however, is quite unnecessary. In the original passage of Jeremiah, Rachel, the ancestress of the tribe of Benjamin, is poetically introduced as bewailing the departure of her descendants into exile, from Ramah of Benjamin, their place of rendezvous" (*Biblical Researches*, 4:273).

Matthew, who made constant reference to former-day prophecies that he saw fulfilled in the life and labors of Jesus, extracted this poetic picture of Jeremiah and accommodated the sense of it to a new event or circumstance. This may appear to be a form of falsification or text tampering to the modern mind uninitiated in Hebrew writing style and figures of speech, but this is an acceptable and typical Semitic literary device. And it is a proper approach to scripture interpretation to this day. Elder Dallin H. Oaks noted that "a scripture is not limited to what it meant when it was written but may also include what that scripture means to a reader today" (*Ensign*, January 1995, 8).

There are hundreds of cases in which New Testament authors saw fulfillment of Old Testament passages in the words and works of Jesus. Matthew alone makes reference to nearly ninety passages from ten Old Testament books. Many things in the Old Testament were regarded as types of things to come.

FROM EGYPT TO NAZARETH

Matthew 2:19–23 For a brief time there was another Joseph in Egypt, nearly two millennia after the son of Jacob/Israel. Once Herod had died, the angel returned to advise Jesus' guardian that it was safe to return to the land of Israel (one name of the country in the days of Jesus). The southern part of the nation, the province of Judea, was now ruled by one of Herod's sons, Archelaus, who was as vicious a tyrant as his father, so the family was warned to avoid that province and return to Nazareth in Galilee—for yet another prophecy must be fulfilled: "He shall be called a Nazarene" (v. 23).

The phrase "Jesus of Nazareth" occurs seventeen times in the Gospels and Acts. We have no specific reference in extant biblical literature to prophets declaring that the Messiah would be a Nazarene, unless it is an allusion to Isaiah 11:1. Isaiah prophesied that a "Branch" (*netzer*) would grow out of the root of Jesse—that is, from the Davidic line—and thus Jesus would be a Nazarene (*notzri*). Both Hebrew words come from the same root.

An early church father, Jerome, wrote in his commentary on Isaiah: "What all the churchmen seek and do not find in the Prophets, that is, where it stands written: He will be called a Nazarene (Mt. 2:23), scholars of the Hebrews are of the opinion that it is taken from this passage (Is. 11:1)" (as cited in Pixner, *With Jesus through Galilee*, 14).

Luke 2:39–40 Luke, who recorded nothing about the sojourn in Egypt, recorded that the family returned to "their own city Nazareth." Jesus grew and became strong in spirit, filled with wisdom, and the grace of the Father was upon him.

"Lorenzo Snow taught that 'Jesus was a god before he came into the world and yet his knowledge was taken from him. He did not know his former greatness, neither do we know what greatness we had attained to before we came here' (Office Journal of Lorenzo Snow, 8 October 1900, 181–82).

"But President Snow also taught that during the Savior's life 'it was revealed unto Him who He was, and for what purpose He was in the world. The glory and power He possessed *before* He came into the world was made known unto Him' (in Conference Report, April 1901, 3; emphasis added). Just as the Savior came to understand exactly who He was, so may we" (Dew, *No Doubt about It*, 37).

Elder McConkie explained that Jesus had a normal boyhood:

"He was as much the product of the mother who bare him as were her other children. As a babe he began to grow, normally and naturally, and there was nothing supernatural about it. He learned to crawl, to walk, to run. He spoke his first word, cut his first tooth, took his first step—the same as other children do. He learned to speak; he played with toys like those of his brothers and sisters; and he played with them and with the neighbor children. He went to sleep at night and he awoke with the morning light. . . .

"He learned to speak, to read, to write; he memorized passages of scripture, and he pondered their deep and hidden meanings. He was taught in the home by Mary, then by Joseph, as was the custom of the day. Jewish traditions and the provisions of the Torah were discussed daily in his presence. He learned the Shema, reverenced the Mezuzah, and participated in prayers, morning, noon, and night. Beginning at five or six he went to school, and certainly continued to do so until he came a son of the law at twelve years of age" (*Mortal Messiah*, 1:368–69).

PASSOVER VISIT TO THE TEMPLE (IN JERUSALEM)

Luke 2:41–50 Passover was one of the three great pilgrimage festivals (see Appendix 6, 764). Jews from all over the land and from the whole Mediterranean world went up to

Jerusalem to remember their ancient deliverance from Egypt and to anticipate the long-hoped-for arrival of the greatest Deliverer, the Messiah. Jewish tradition held that he would come at Passover time.

Jesus went with his parents at age twelve. "At the age of 12 a Jewish boy was taken to Jerusalem . . . and tested by the doctors of the law in the temple as to his knowledge of the duties and privileges to which by circumcision he had been admitted. In passing this test he was regarded as freely and intelligently 'taking upon himself the yoke of the law,' or 'of the kingdom of God,' and henceforth he was bound to fulfill all the precepts of the ceremonial law. Thus Jesus was at the temple at age 12" (Bible Dictionary, "Education," 660).

On the return trip Joseph and Mary discovered Jesus was missing, supposing he was with relatives or friends among the throng traveling northward to Galilee. If they were traveling via Samaria they could nearly have reached the ancient site of Shiloh, or if via the Jordan Valley, they could have reached Jericho. They had to go back a day's journey (possibly twenty to twenty-five miles) to search for him in Jerusalem, and still they did not find him for three days (the total of three days may have consisted of the day's journey toward Galilee, the day's journey back to Jerusalem, and a day's search for Jesus in the Holy City). Finally they located him in the midst of teachers and leaders of the Jews in the Temple, who were listening to *him and asking him* questions (JST), astonished at his understanding and answers.

It would be amazing in modern times to see a twelve-year-old boy sitting for three days and discussing weighty issues of religious import, but this was an unusual twelve-year-old indeed—he was *teaching* the older men, instructing them in eternal verities that their accumulated years of training and experience could not match.

Joseph and Mary were surprised at the sight, and his mother offered a mild rebuke, asking, essentially, why her son had treated his parents in that way, failing to consider that they

The Birth and Childhood of Jesus

Boy Jesus in the Temple, by Grant Romney Clawson

would have been searching for him for days and grieving over him. Jesus' response must have surprised them (with a pointed correction regarding his paternity): "How is it that ye sought me? wist ye not that I must be about my Father's business?" His Father's business was not carpentry or stone work or other such mortal occupations, but his Father was the Eternal God of heaven, and his work was to immortalize and exalt the Father's children. It is apparent that at this young age Jesus already knew who he was and that he understood at least something of what his life's work entailed.

During the morning of the day he was martyred, the Prophet Joseph Smith taught: "When still a boy [Jesus] had all the intelligence necessary to enable Him to rule and govern the kingdom of the Jews, and could reason with the wisest and most profound doctors of law and divinity, and make their theories and practice to appear like folly compared with the wisdom He possessed; but He was a boy only, and lacked physical strength even to defend His own person" (*Teachings of the Prophet Joseph Smith*, 392).

THE RETURN TO NAZARETH

Luke 2:51–52 Jesus went down from Jerusalem with his mortal parents to Nazareth (traveling any direction from Jerusalem is going down from the spiritual center). The fulness of the time of his ministry had not yet come, so he continued under their guardianship and was subject to them, even as he would be, during his ministry, subject to the will of his Father in heaven.

Of the thirty years before his ministry began, Jesus probably spent at least twenty-six years in Nazareth and environs. (After approximately two years in Bethlehem and a time in Egypt, he probably lived a minimum of twenty-six years in Nazareth and vicinity before starting his ministry at age thirty.) Though he was "subject unto" his parents, yet we wonder about his activities and work during those early years: Who were his friends? What did he do? Where did he travel? Elder McConkie wrote: "We cannot believe that he was silent all those years. He spoke at twelve; was his tongue then tied until he was thirty?" (*Mortal Messiah,* 1:379).

Luke reports on the eighteen years in one sentence: Jesus grew intellectually (wisdom), physically (stature), spiritually (favor with God), and socially (with his fellow man).

Modern revelation adds that Jesus, in his mortal condition, did grow gradually—all the graces and skills and understanding were not automatically endowed on him in his youth: "And he received not of the fulness at first, but continued from grace to grace, until he received a fulness" (D&C 93:13).

Joseph Smith Translation Matthew 3:24–26 provides significant details about Jesus' preparatory time of youth:

"And it came to pass that Jesus grew up with his brethren, and waxed strong, and waited upon the Lord for the time of his ministry to come.

The Birth and Childhood of Jesus

"*And he served under his father, and he spake not as other men, neither could he be taught; for he needed not that any man should teach him.*

"*And after many years, the hour of his ministry drew nigh.*"

CHAPTER 4

THE MINISTRY OF JOHN THE BAPTIST

Matthew 3:3; John 1:23 Long before John's prophetic ministry began, Isaiah foretold John's foreordained mission of preparing the way for the Messiah, laying the groundwork, and getting disciples ready for their Master. John taught, testified, and baptized believers so Jesus would have a congregation awaiting the Messiah when he began his ministry.

Isaiah's prophecy of John (Isaiah 40:3) was originally a synonymous parallelism (two lines saying essentially the same thing—a very common literary device in the Old Testament):

> A voice is crying,
> In the wilderness prepare ye the way of the Lord,
> make straight in the desert a highway for our God.

Making his paths straight means that one is "in the paths of righteousness; . . . in the path which leads to the kingdom of God" (Alma 7:19).

Lehi also prophesied of John, his preparatory labors, and his baptizing the Lamb of God, who would take away the sins of the world (1 Nephi 10:7–10). Isaiah, Lehi, Nephi (1 Nephi 11:27; 2 Nephi 31:4), and Malachi (3:1) all wrote about the Baptist's preparatory work. Just as with Jesus' mission to earth, the prophetic mission of John was also known long in advance.

The Ministry of John the Baptist

Mark 1:1–3 The words "my messenger" in verse 2 are in Hebrew *malachi*, which is also the name of the prophet who pronounced the prophecy of the messenger who would prepare the way for the Messiah (cf. Malachi 3:1; Isaiah 40:3). Jesus himself explained that the messenger was John the Baptist (Matthew 11:10).

Luke 3:4–6 The Joseph Smith Translation adds five new verses here (JST Luke 3:5–9; Bible Appendix, 805). Verse 5 suggests that the topography of the earth will still experience some drastic changes, with great upheavals of nature (cf. Helaman 14:23; D&C 109:74).

A garment of camel's hair

Matthew 3:4; Mark 1:6 John the Baptist was clothed in a garment woven of camel's hair. His diet in the Judean wilderness included locusts and wild honey. Although some define locusts as the pods of the carob tree (also called the locust tree; see illustration with the commentary on Luke 15:11–32), it is more likely that John actually ate the small insect. The Greek word used in Matthew's text is also used in the book of Revelation and definitely refers to the insects. Locusts were allowed as food by Mosaic law: "These may ye eat of every flying creeping thing that goeth upon all four . . . even these of them ye may eat; the locust after his kind" (Leviticus 11:21–22). Natives of the Near East and Africa even today eat locusts; some consider them a delicacy.

John also ate wild honey. The context of some biblical passages and some rabbinic sources indicates that honey may be the thick, heavy syrup of dates or of grapes (Genesis 43:11; Ezekiel 27:17). However, the honey (*dvash*) of the Hebrew Bible may also be the product of bees. In fact, the Greek term (*meli*) used in Matthew 3:4 means bee honey, and the honeycomb that was given to Jesus to eat after his resurrection (Luke 24:42) was a honeycomb from a beehive.

THE BEGINNING OF JOHN'S MINISTRY (WILDERNESS OF JUDEA)

Matthew 3:1 Robert J. Matthews wrote: "The work of John is spoken of by Isaiah (40:3–5; compare Matthew 3:1–3) and Malachi (3:1; compare Luke 7:27), and Lehi (1 Nephi 10:7–10), and Nephi (1 Nephi 11:27; 2 Nephi 31:4, 8). . . . The term *forerunner* is descriptive. Forerunners anciently would run before the chariot of the king and clear the path of rocks or other obstacles, and loudly proclaim the coming of the ruler. This practice is referred to in 1 Samuel 8:11, 1 Kings 1:5, and Isaiah 62:10. Both Saul and Rehoboam kept 'runners' for this purpose" (*Behold the Messiah*, 44, 46).

In English we call him John the Baptist. Primary children sing, "Jesus came to John the Baptist, in Judea long ago" (*Children's Songbook*, 100). Was there any other ministry in connection with a river for John? Yes, at the Susquehanna River in Pennsylvania in 1829. He announced himself as "the one who is known in the New Testament as John the Baptist" (D&C 13,

The Ministry of John the Baptist

Baptizing in the Jordan River

headnote). If he had used his mortal name, he might have said, Shalom. Ani Yohanan ben Zechariah Ha Cohen . . . [Hello. I am John, son of Zechariah the priest]—and Joseph Smith might still have wondered who he was. Thus the wording "the one who is known in the New Testament as John the Baptist."

John the Baptist came first to prepare the way for the Messiah, and he helped train and teach future apostles, for example, John and Andrew and possibly others (Bible Dictionary, "John the Baptist," 714). In our day he came to restore the Aaronic Priesthood, acting under the direction of Peter, James, and John, who held the keys of the Priesthood of Melchizedek (Joseph Smith–History 1:72).

Matthew 3:2 The first word from the lips of John the Baptist, as recorded in the New Testament, is "Repent." That is also the first word of Jesus to the multitudes (Matthew 4:17), and it is the main message of all the prophets. The single most important thing we do in this world, to fulfill the purpose of the Savior's mission, is to repent of our sins. All else is made possible if we repent. Why repent? "For the kingdom of heaven is at hand"—the message of all the standard works (see references in footnote a to Matthew 3:2; on the usage of "kingdom of heaven" and "kingdom of God," see also commentary on Luke 17:20–22). The Hebrew verb *lashuv*, translated "to repent," also means "to return," and that is the basic idea of repenting: correcting our course in order to return to our Father in Heaven (the concept "repent and return" appears quite a few times in scripture; e.g., Alma 34:34; 3 Nephi 10:6; 16:13; D&C 109:21).

Mark 1:4; see also Luke 3:3; D&C 107:20 John preached "the baptism of repentance." That phrase is fascinating, as are others that are similar, such as the "gospel of repentance" (D&C 13:1; Joseph Smith–History 1:69). Perhaps the most essential doctrine of all is repentance. The Lord himself has commanded, "Say nothing but repentance unto this generation" (D&C 6:9). This one principle is so vital that it towers above all others in primacy and urgency. "The thing which will be of the most worth unto you will be to declare repentance unto this people" (D&C 15:6; 16:6). Our message constitutes the gospel, or "good news," of repentance. And the culmination of our faith and repentance is the simple, beautiful ordinance of baptism. But that brief act of total immersion in water never has and never will take away anyone's sins. It is not the baptismal water that cleanses sin; it is the faith and the repentance that precede the baptism that remove the stain and the pain from us—faith in the Savior's atoning sacrifice and the genuine repentance to fulfill our part of making the Atonement work for us personally. The baptism is but a climax of the process that washes away (baptism of water) and burns out (baptism of fire) all that is unclean and undesirable in us. Therefore, the phrase "baptism of repentance" indicates that baptism is the fulfillment, or the concluding act, of all our prior efforts to repent and return to God. The brief action of going down into and coming back up out of the waters of baptism is a manifestation of humility and submission on the part of a person to do exactly what the Lord requires. The ordinance is short in time and eternal in significance. But does the process end there?

The Ministry of John the Baptist

Sometimes we may look with envy on the new convert stepping out of the baptismal font; we feel almost jealous of the fact that there goes the cleanest, purest person on earth. How would it be, we wonder, if we could be baptized again and be freed from all our sins? The fact is, we can be freed from all our sins on a regular basis. If we go to sacrament meeting each week, the most sacred public meeting we have in the Church, and we go there having thoroughly repented of all our sins, and we worthily eat that little piece of bread and drink that little cup of water, renewing the covenants we made at baptism, we may leave that meeting totally free of sin. We can literally be clean and pure as we walk out of sacrament meeting each week. We experience again and again the baptism of repentance.

Luke 3:1–3 John the Baptist began his ministry "in the fifteenth year of the reign of Tiberius Caesar, Pontius Pilate being governor of Judea, and Herod [Antipas] being tetrarch of Galilee, and his brother Philip tetrarch of Ituraea and of the region of Trachonitis."

When Herod the Great died, his son Philip was granted control of the lands north and east of Galilee, including the slopes of Mount Hermon and the Lebanese Beq'a. This area comprised Iturea and Trachonitis. Important towns were Caesarea Philippi, at the foot of Mount Hermon, and Bethsaida, at the northeast shore of the Sea of Galilee. South of Iturea were regions called Ulatha and Gaulanitis (today's Golan); south of Trachonitis were Batanea and Auranitis (see Appendix 1, 715).

Abilene was a region named after its capital city, Abila (not to be confused with Abila, a city of the Decapolis farther south), which was situated about twenty miles northwest of Damascus. The governor of Abilene, Lysanias, is mentioned not only by Luke but on an inscription at Abila dating from the reign of Tiberius (Thompson, *Bible and Archaeology*, 389).

Luke 3:2 Annas and his son-in-law, Joseph Caiaphas (John 18:13), were two members of an influential priestly family who virtually monopolized the office of high priest for thirty-five years (Galbraith, Ogden, and Skinner, *Jerusalem, the Eternal City*, 174).

John 1:6–14 In the Gospel of John the name John always refers to John the Baptist. Though we do not refer to John the Baptist as an apostle, he is one who was sent, which is the meaning of the Greek *apostolos*. His mission was to bear witness of the Light, so that all men would turn to that Light for salvation. Interestingly, John the apostle, who quotes John the Baptist extensively in the prologue to his Gospel (John 1), never refers to himself by name in his Gospel.

John 1:9–11 Jesus is the one true Light, and he gives light to every soul born into this world so that each person knows how to differentiate between good and evil (Moroni 7:16; cf. D&C 84:46). He came into the world, even the One who made the world, and the world did not recognize their Creator. He came as a Jew, and his own people, the Jews, generally did not receive him (3 Nephi 9:16).

John 1:12–13 Upon those who did receive him (such as Peter, James, John, Mary, Martha, Lazarus, and many others), he bestowed the powers, rights, and privileges of citizenship in the kingdom—to be sons and daughters of God forever (3 Nephi 9:17; D&C 11:30; 25:1; 39:4). God the Father is the father of our spirits. Through our spiritual conversion in this life, God the Son—Jesus Christ—becomes the father of our spiritual rebirth, and we are born into the family of Christ (Mosiah 5:5–8).

The Joseph Smith Translation indicates that Jesus Christ was born not through the normal human process ("not of blood, nor of the will of the flesh, nor of the will of man"—meaning, not through two mortal parents) but of God, with divine paternity of his mortal body.

John 1:14 As prophesied, God's own Son became mortal and lived among us. John the apostle testified that he beheld the Savior's glory, as at the Transfiguration (Matthew 17:2); Peter also testified of that glorious occasion (2 Peter 1:16; see also D&C 93:11). John bore witness that Jesus was the Only

Begotten of the Father. The Son reflected the glory of the Father (Hebrews 1:3).

Jesus is said to be full of grace—possessing that quality which is the essence of his personality—because of his atoning act, which is pure mercy extended to all mortals and which alone allows us to dwell in God's presence (2 Nephi 2:8; Alma 5:33; 7:12; 26:37). In addition, Jesus "continued from grace to grace" in mortality "until he received a fulness" of grace (D&C 93:13) and thus became exactly like the Father, who is also full of grace and truth (D&C 66:12). Jesus is full of truth in that as Jehovah he gave the laws that frame the universe as well as govern Israel (3 Nephi 15:5); he is at the heart of things as they were, are, and are to come (D&C 93:24); and he is the fountain of all righteousness (Ether 12:28).

Matthew 3:5–6; Mark 1:5 In the New Testament, there seems to be constant intentional juxtaposition of Jerusalem and the rest of Judea. Jerusalem was the capital, the chief and holy city, and merited preferential status and singular mention alongside all other places. Thus we see, "there went out unto him all the land of Judea, and they of Jerusalem" (Mark 1:5), "a great multitude of people out of all Judea and Jerusalem" (Luke 6:17), and "Ye shall be witnesses unto me both in Jerusalem, and in all Judea" (Acts 1:8).

Jerusalem was synonymous with leadership. The headquarters of the early Christian Church were in the same place where centuries earlier God had chosen to place his name, where the Holy Temple had epitomized Judaic life for a millennium. Like some of the old prophets, Jesus performed his most important work in Jerusalem and gave his life there. And though nearly all the members of the Quorum of the Twelve Apostles were originally from Galilee, they clearly understood, too, that the center place of Zion, where the law and the word must go forth, was Jerusalem.

WARNING TO PHARISEES AND SADDUCEES (AT BETHABARA)

Matthew 3:7; Luke 3:7 John the Baptist and Jesus both referred to their religious antagonists as vipers (see also Matthew 12:34; 23:33). The Palestine viper (*Vipera palaestina*) is the most dangerous and poisonous of all snakes in the land of Israel. Though frightening, the tongue of the viper is harmless. It serves as a smell-taste organ that darts in and out of the mouth, gathering air particles that are deciphered inside the brain. The front fangs are the potent weapon; they are sunk into a victim, and the poison is secreted from glands to the wound. The venom destroys red corpuscles, causing hemorrhage that if not immediately and properly cared for can result in death.

A viper

Some years ago, a thirty-eight-year-old male Brigham Young University student, large and sturdy, was working in the banana fields of an Israeli kibbutz (a collective farming settlement) near the Sea of Galilee. One day he tried to save a snake from students who had uncovered it and intended to kill it. When he picked it up with his fingers to remove it from danger, the viper somehow elongated itself, swung around, and sank its fangs into his forefinger.

Immediately after the bite, kibbutz personnel rushed him to a nearby hospital where he remained for three days of observation. They released him, but after he spent a few hours at the school in Jerusalem, the pain in his finger was still so intense that he was rushed in the middle of the night to the emergency room of a Jerusalem hospital. The student remained in the hospital for twelve more days. Doctors tried every kind of painkiller to ease his periodic agony. Now and then his whole body writhed with pain from his finger. The finger increased to double its normal size, and the tissue inside turned a deep black color. It seemed possible that his finger might have to be amputated, or even his hand, or more.

Finally, the student was released from the Jerusalem hospital to fly back to the United States with his student group, and there he was admitted to another medical center. Several months passed before he recovered completely from the venomous fangs that had sunk just a fraction of an inch into his finger. Had this student been smaller or had a weaker body, the poison would likely have killed him.

That was the only encounter with vipers in many years by BYU students, who spent thousands of hours in banana fields and throughout the varied terrain of the Holy Land. Everyone involved learned some vivid lessons about the viper from just that one incident. No wonder John and Jesus used the viper in their denunciation of hypocrites.

The Palestine viper bites only when it is trodden on. Some Sadducees, Pharisees, scribes, and lawyers apparently felt that they were being trodden on. And there was venom in their mouths. While they were lashing out, intending to strike deathblows to their would-be victims, John and Jesus issued warnings to beware of their poison.

Matthew 3:8–9; Luke 3:8 Our fruits, or good works, are part of the process of showing true, sincere repentance—the only way to eventually enter into the rest of the Lord, which is the fulness of his glory (D&C 84:24; cf. Moroni 7:3). And do not claim, says the Lord, any exclusive prerogative or preferential status because of covenant lineage ("We have Abraham [as] our father"). Covenant blessings are granted for righteousness and obedience, not because of favored ancestry. God is able "of these stony Gentiles . . . to raise up children unto Abraham," thus teaching the doctrine of adoption into the covenant people of the Lord (Smith, *Teachings of the Prophet Joseph Smith*, 319; see also Bible Dictionary, "Adoption," 604).

Joseph Smith's translation of Matthew 3:8–9 (JST Matthew 3:34–36) contains several additions (see Bible Appendix, 802).

John and Jesus advised their antagonists that they had no cloak for their sins. "To atone" in Hebrew literally means to cover or cloak, and those who reject the Savior will have no access to the Atonement. They will have no cover.

John 1:19–28 Some Jewish leaders among the Pharisees (v. 24) sent priests and Levites down from Jerusalem to ask John the Baptist who he was (see Appendix 4, 748). John did not deny his prophetic calling, but he denied being the promised Messiah. They wanted to know if he were Elias (Elijah; Malachi 4:5) or "that prophet"; that is, the prophet of whom Moses had prophesied, who was actually the Messiah (Deuteronomy 18:15, 18). John called on the words of Esaias (the Greek form of the Hebrew name Isaiah) to describe his mission (v. 23). They responded by asking why, if he wasn't the Messiah or Elijah or "that prophet," he was baptizing. The Baptist humbly explained that the Messiah, though coming after him, stands before him in greatness and importance.

John the Baptist "confessed, and denied not *that he was Elias*," meaning one who would help prepare the way before someone greater, "but confessed, *saying;* I am not the Christ. And they asked him, saying; *How then art thou Elias? And he said, I am not that Elias who was to restore all things*" (JST John 1:21–22). John made a quick disclaimer that he was, indeed, a forerunner and preparer, but not the great restorer, who would actually come in the last days to restore all things (see further in commentary on JST Matthew 17:10–13).

John 1:28 "Beyond Jordan" (Greek, *Perea*) is the name of a region on the east bank of the Jordan River (see Appendix 1, 713). The place-name Bethabara appears in most manuscripts (as in the King James Version), while Bethany appears in others (as in the Revised Standard Version). There is no other available literary or archaeological evidence of a Bethany near the Jordan River opposite Jericho. We hold that Bethabara was the correct name of the site of John's baptizing. Nephi recorded a prophecy from his father, Lehi, that John would "baptize in Bethabara, beyond Jordan" (1 Nephi 10:9). Bethabara is near the natural fording place east of Jericho entering Perea (see more in the commentary on John 3:23–36). In Hebrew, *Bethabara*, or *Beth-avara*, means "place of crossing." At such an important juncture along a major east-west travel route, John could have taught people traveling from the regions of Judea, Perea, Galilee, Decapolis, and Phoenicia.

"They came unto John, and said unto him, Rabbi, he that was with thee beyond Jordan, to whom thou barest witness, behold, the same baptizeth, and all men come to him" (John 3:26). Just across the Jordan opposite Jericho is where the closing scenes of the ministries of the great prophets Moses and Elijah occurred, a fitting location for the opening scenes of the ministries of the great Forerunner and the Messiah.

CALL TO REPENTANCE (AT BETHABARA)

Matthew 3:10; Luke 3:9 Trees represent people. The root of the tree is the essential core, the source and supplier for the body of the tree, which should bear the fruit. The fruit represents "works of righteousness" (Alma 5:36). "If the root be holy, so are the branches" (Romans 11:16), but if the root system becomes corrupted, absorbing poisonous elements from its environment, then "the axe is laid unto the root of the trees: every tree therefore which bringeth not forth good fruit is hewn down, and cast into the fire" (Luke 3:9). The fire into which the wicked "trees" are cast is the fire of hell—remorse, regret—which is unquenchable, not able to be put out (Alma 5:52; cf. Jacob 5:46; 3 Nephi 14:19; D&C 97:7).

Matthew 3:11–12 Joseph Smith's translation of these two verses (JST Matthew 3:38–40) adds to the meaning of John the Baptist's teachings (Bible Appendix, 802).

Mark 1:7; John 1:27 John understood his role and his place. There was no vying for superiority. He knew that Jesus was greater than he and that Jesus was the long-promised Messiah. His humility is demonstrated in his expression that he felt unworthy to even unloose the latchet of Jesus' sandals.

Mark 1:8 There are two baptisms: of water and of the Spirit. Baptism of water is only half a baptism (Smith, *Teachings of the Prophet Joseph Smith,* 314). The water baptism is administered under the authority of the Aaronic Priesthood, but the greater priesthood is required for the baptism of fire—the gift of the Holy Ghost. That greater priesthood is the Priesthood after the Order of the Son of God (D&C 107:3)—the same who came after John.

Luke 3:10–11 What are we supposed to do to show genuine righteousness? If we have more material wealth than others, we demonstrate unselfishness and charity by sharing what we have. References in footnote b to Luke 3:11 contain poignant reminders to be charitable (cf. Mosiah 4:16–21).

Luke 3:12–13 Publicans (tax collectors; see Appendix 4, 750) sought baptism also, and they specifically asked the Baptist what they should do. The answer was simple: Be honest in your dealings with your fellowman, and don't demand of the taxpayers more than is proper. The Joseph Smith Translation (Luke 3:19–20) adds two verses here by way of explanation (see Bible Appendix, 806).

Luke 3:14 Roman soldiers wanted to know what was

Winnowing—separating the wheat from the chaff

expected of them. John told them, in effect, not to be violent, not to falsely accuse in order to extort, and to be content with their wages.

Luke 3:15–18 As the people listened to John's teachings, they wondered if he were the long-awaited Messiah. John answered that one far greater than he was coming, that he (John) baptized with water but he who was coming would baptize with fire, which is the symbol of the Holy Ghost (cf. Helaman 5:45). The prophet then employed imagery from agriculture to explain that his mission was to harvest the field, separating the wheat (righteous disciples) from the chaff (rebellious ones who would reject him). In harvesting grain, after the threshing came the winnowing, which separated the grain from the husks. With a winnowing fork (sometimes called a "fan"), the threshed mixture was tossed into the air, and the afternoon and evening breeze coming off the Mediterranean Sea during harvest time would carry the lighter husks (the chaff) to settle in their own pile while the heavier grain fell into a pile immediately below the winnower. Any stones or impurities could be further sifted out with a sieve (Luke 22:31), and then the grain was ready to be used or transported to storage.

The separation of the grain from the chaff is a scene similar to that in which John the Baptist described the coming Messiah as one "whose fan [winnowing fork] is in his hand, and he will burn up the chaff with unquenchable fire" (Matthew 3:12; also Luke 3:17; Mosiah 7:30). The Messiah will come with fan in hand to purge the threshing floor and gather his wheat into the garner. The word translated "garner" means a storehouse or barn used as a granary. When will the Savior's "wheat" finally be gathered? (see D&C 101:64–65).

BAPTISM OF JESUS (AT BETHABARA)

Matthew 3:13–17; Mark 1:9–11; Luke 3:21–22; John 1:32–34; 1 Nephi 10:7–10. Jesus walked from Galilee to the place of John's baptizing in the Jordan River. He began at Nazareth (says Mark 1:9), so he walked a distance of eighty to ninety miles, possibly walking south along the eastern side of the Jordan Valley into Perea, opposite Jericho.

Matthew 3:14–15 John remonstrated, "I have need to be baptized of thee, and comest thou to me?" Jesus replied affirmatively, "Suffer *me to be baptized of thee,* for thus it becometh us to fulfill all righteousness" (JST Matthew 3:43). It was important that they perform every righteous ordinance for salvation. Baptism was a law given to God's covenant people from the beginning; it was a law that all must keep. The first man, Adam, asked the Lord, "Why is it that men must repent and be baptized in water?" (Moses 6:53). The Lord answered, "Ye must be born again into the kingdom of heaven, of water . . . for by the water ye keep the commandment" (Moses 6:59–60). *"And John went down into the water and baptized him"* (JST Matthew 3:44).

Nephi explained the meaning of the phrase "to fulfill all righteousness." Even the Lamb of God, the Sinless One, submitted to the simple, saving ordinance of baptism for the following reasons: "He showeth unto the children of men

The Ministry of John the Baptist

John the Baptist Baptizing Jesus, by Harry Anderson

that, according to the flesh he humbleth himself before the Father, and witnesseth unto the Father that he would be obedient unto him in keeping his commandments. . . .

"And again, it showeth unto the children of men the straitness of the path, and the narrowness of the gate, by which they should enter, he having set the example before them. . . .

"Wherefore [the Savior says], follow me, and do the things which ye have seen me do" (2 Nephi 31:5–12).

In sum, Jesus was baptized to fulfill all righteousness, to signal that he was consecrated to God, to enter the narrow gate of the celestial kingdom, to be obedient, to receive power from on high, and to set the example for all of God's children.

A dove resting on barbed wire in front of Skull Hill, Jerusalem

Matthew 3:16 Upon being baptized Jesus "went up straightway out of the water," suggesting total immersion as the proper method of baptism (see also 3 Nephi 19:11–12).

Jesus was baptized at a spot more than a thousand feet below sea level, the lowest spot on earth where anyone could be baptized in fresh water. He not only descended to our condition; he descended (quite literally) below all things.

As he came up out of the water, "the heavens were opened unto him, and he saw the Spirit of God descending like a dove." Or, as Luke recorded, "the Holy Ghost descended in a bodily shape like a dove upon him" (Luke 3:22)—that is, the Holy Ghost, having a bodily shape, descended as a dove descends, and rested upon Jesus, "and John bare record, saying, I saw the Spirit descending from heaven like a dove, and it abode upon him" (John 1:32; also 1 Nephi 11:27). John saw the Holy Ghost descending; his spiritual eyes were opened to see pure, refined matter (D&C 131:7–8).

According to the Prophet Joseph Smith, the dove is the sign of the Holy Ghost's presence and was instituted before this world was populated (*Teachings of the Prophet Joseph*

The Ministry of John the Baptist

Smith, 275–76). Thus, an actual dove was also present at Jesus' baptism. "The sign of the dove, as an emblem for the Holy Ghost, was a pre-appointed signal by which John knew he was to recognize that he had baptized the Son of God" (Bible Dictionary, "John the Baptist," 714). "The personage of the Holy Ghost descended upon Christ with the grace of a dove, which imagery is chosen because the dove was present—it being the visible or outward sign of the presence of the Holy Ghost" (McConkie and Ostler, *Revelations of the Restoration*, 673).

Matthew 3:17 The voice of the Father was heard from heaven. Therefore, all three Beings in the Godhead were present. Where in all the universe would the other Two have wanted to be when the Son was baptized?

The voice of the Father is heard on rare and sacred occasions in this telestial world. For example, his voice was heard at the Transfiguration (Matthew 17:5), in announcing his Son to the Nephites (3 Nephi 11:7), and in presenting his Son to Joseph Smith (Joseph Smith–History 1:17). When the Father does come, he comes to say one specific thing: "This is my Son." Why does he testify of this one, single fact? Because that is the most important thing he could say, the most needed testimony he could bear. The Jews do not believe God, Elohim, would have a Son (their Shema proclaims: "Hear, O Israel, the Lord our God is one"; Deuteronomy 6:4). The Muslims (many hundreds of millions of them on the earth now) do not believe God, Allah, would have a Son who would come to live with the rest of us groveling humans in this world (the Qur'an declares: "Far is it removed from his transcendent majesty that he should have a son"; Sura IV:171, in *Meaning of the Glorious Koran*). Neither do many Christians these days believe that God the Father literally had a Son in this world. It is a unique and powerful witness of the divinity of that Son that his own Father bears solemn testimony of that fact at each momentous occasion in the Old World and in the New World, in ancient times as well as in modern times.

TEMPTATION OF JESUS (IN THE WILDERNESS OF JUDEA AND AT JERUSALEM'S TEMPLE MOUNT)

Matthew 4:1–11; Mark 1:12–13; Luke 4:1–13 After his baptism, as preparation for the commencement of his ministry, Jesus experienced temptations from his adversary and ours. Why did Jesus need to experience temptations? Just as with his baptism, Jesus experienced temptations in this world "to fulfill all righteousness"—that is, to pass through every kind of human experience, as Alma said, so "that he may know according to the flesh how to succor his people according to their infirmities" (Alma 7:12). Paul also understood the reason why Jesus experienced temptations during his sojourn in mortality: "For in that he himself hath suffered being tempted, he is able to succour them that are tempted" (Hebrews 2:18). "For we have not an high priest which cannot be touched with the feeling of our infirmities; but was in all points tempted like as we are, yet without sin" (Hebrews 4:15).

C. S. Lewis eloquently described the virtue and the rationale behind the temptations of Jesus, applicable to this present setting in the Judean desert and on other occasions during his ministry, especially in the Garden of Gethsemane, when he suffered (for the first time) for sins:

"No man knows how bad he is till he has tried very hard to be good. A silly idea is current that good people do not know what temptation means. This is an obvious lie. Only those who try to resist temptation know how strong it is. After all, you find out the strength of [an] army by fighting against it, not by giving in. You find out the strength of a wind by trying to walk against it, not by lying down. A man who gives in to temptation after five minutes simply does not know what it would have been like an hour later. That is why bad people, in one sense, know very little about badness. They have lived a sheltered life by always giving in. We never find out the strength of the evil impulse inside us until we try to fight it: and Christ, because He was the only man who never yielded to temptation, is also the only man who knows to the full what temptation means" (*Mere Christianity,* 126).

None of us will ever be able to shake our fist at heaven and exclaim: "But you don't understand what I'm going through!" Actually, our Savior does. None of us will ever teach Jesus anything about pain, or suffering, or anguish, or injustice, or affliction, or temptation. He understands perfectly our every distress and malady and tribulation and trial, and he expects each of us to eventually gain the same understanding. Elder Neal A. Maxwell wrote: "How can you and I really expect to glide naively through life, as if to say, 'Lord, give me experience, but not grief, not sorrow, not pain, not opposition, not betrayal, and certainly not to be forsaken. Keep from me, Lord, all those experiences which made Thee what Thou art! Then let me come and dwell with Thee and fully share Thy joy!'" (*Ensign,* May 1991, 88).

Matthew 4:1 After Jesus' baptism—the glorious spiritual celebration involving the entire Godhead—the Holy Ghost led Jesus westward up into the Judean desert (Luke 4:1), not to be immediately tempted of the devil (as Matthew's text tells us) but, as the Joseph Smith Translation tells us, to continue to be *with God* (JST Matthew 4:1), to commune with his Father, and to be filled with the Spirit to launch his ministry.

Matthew 4:2 Forty days and forty nights of fasting—nearly six weeks—is a long time. Forty is a curious number in biblical scripture.

Joseph's father, Jacob, was embalmed for forty days (Genesis 50:3). The twelve spies were gone for forty days (Numbers 13:25; 14:34). Goliath presented himself to the Israelites for forty days (1 Samuel 17:16). Nineveh was to be overthrown after forty days (Jonah 3:4). Jesus returned after his resurrection to give instruction for forty days (Acts 1:3).

Rain and flood waters came upon the earth forty days and forty nights (Genesis 7:4, 12). Moses was on Mount Sinai forty days and forty nights (Exodus 24:18; 34:28; Deuteronomy 9:9, 11, 18, 25; 10:10). Elijah went fasting to Horeb for forty days and forty nights (1 Kings 19:8). Jesus fasted forty days and forty nights (Matthew 4:2; Mark 1:13; Luke 4:2).

Isaac married at forty years of age (Genesis 25:20). Esau married at forty (Genesis 26:34). Moses was a shepherd for forty years (Acts 7:30). Israelites remained in the wilderness forty years (Numbers 14:33–34; 32:13; Deuteronomy 8:2; 29:5; Joshua 5:6). Caleb was forty when sent to scout out the land (Joshua 14:7). The land had rest for forty years (Judges 3:11; 5:31). The land was in quietness forty years (Judges 8:28). The land was in the hands of Philistines for forty years (Judges 13:1). Eli judged forty years (1 Samuel 4:18). Ishbosheth was forty when he started his reign (2 Kings 2:10). Saul reigned forty years (Acts 13:21). David reigned forty years (1 Kings 2:11). Solomon reigned forty years (1 Kings 11:42). Jehoash reigned forty years (2 Kings 12:1). Egyptian cities would be desolate forty years (Ezekiel 29:11–12).

In some cases the number forty appears to mean exactly that amount, or duration, of time. In other cases it seems to be simply figurative for a long period of time.

Whether or not Jesus fasted for literally forty days and nights (though we assume he did), and whether or not he was transfigured during that time (as was Moses during his communing with God for the same length of time; Exodus 34:28; Deuteronomy 9:9; Moses 1:1, 11), upon finishing this lengthy fast, Jesus' physical body was, of course, immensely hungry. King Benjamin, in his prophetic preview of the Lord's ministry, noted that "he shall suffer temptations, and pain of body, hunger, thirst, and fatigue, even more than man can suffer" (Mosiah 3:7). After that long time and in that physically weakened condition, and after he *"had communed with God,"* he *"was left to be tempted of the devil"* (JST Matthew 4:2).

Joseph Smith Translation Mark 1:11 says he "was there in the wilderness forty days, *Satan seeking to tempt him;* and was with the wild beasts; and the angels ministered unto him."

What wild beasts were in the Judean desert? Lions and bears were wild beasts known in the biblical period. Lions were last seen there in the days of the Crusaders, and the last Syrian bear was spotted in the middle of the twentieth century (see Ogden and Chadwick, *Holy Land,* 53).

Matthew 4:3 The first of three temptations appealed to the physical appetite. Mention of bread would have sounded so good in these circumstances. The tempter was subtle: Not only did he tempt Jesus to misuse his divine power but he cast doubt on that power with his first word, "if." Satan seems to be saying that if Jesus is really God's Son, he should demonstrate his power by satisfying his hunger in a miraculous way. Significantly, the last temptation Jesus experienced, which came as he hung on the cross, was also framed around the word "if": "If thou be the Son of God, come down from the cross" (Matthew 27:40). The temptation was more than a call

The southwest corner of the retaining wall of the Temple Mount, considered by some to be the "pinnacle of the temple"

for self-preservation. It was an attempt to appeal to vanity and power. It seems significant that Matthew emphasizes the "if" temptations, for he was writing to the Jews to show that Jesus was the Davidic Messiah—not concerned with geographical conquest and personal power but conquest of sin, death, and the natural man.

Matthew 4:4 Jesus replied with words he had revealed through Moses centuries before (Deuteronomy 8:3), and his response was direct and to the point: Put the needs of the spirit before the needs of the body. The body may be nourished temporarily by bread, but the spirit is nourished and sustained by God's words of eternal life.

Matthew 4:5 The devil did not take the Savior anywhere. Joseph Smith's corrected text says that Jesus was taken up by the Spirit to Jerusalem, the holy city (depending on exactly where they were in the Judean desert, Jerusalem was about ten to fifteen miles westward in the top of the hill country). The *Spirit* set him on the pinnacle of the Temple (JST Matthew 4:5; the Greek word for "pinnacle" means "little wing" or top corner, tower, or rampart). The pinnacle, or highest point, is assumed to be either the southwest or the southeast corner of the Temple Mount. If the former, it could have been an impressive spectacle seen by many in the city. If the latter, it was appropriately the highest man-made elevation ever achieved anciently in the Holy Land. Of the whole length of the retaining walls of the Temple Mount, the southeast corner is the highest point—211 feet, or 64 meters. The distance from the top of Herod's portico to the bottom of the Kidron Valley was more than four hundred feet (see Appendix 1, 718).

Matthew 4:6–7 While Jesus was in an exhilarating position high above the city and the esplanade of the Holy Mount, Satan came a second time to again cast doubt and to again tempt Jesus to misuse his divine power. The devil can also quote scripture for his purposes. He quoted what was written in the poetic literature (Psalm 91:11–12), but Jesus responded with something written in the Torah (the writings of Moses):

"Thou shalt not tempt the Lord thy God" (Deuteronomy 6:16). Jesus knew perfectly well who he was, and he was not even going to listen to such blatant and beguiling impropriety.

Matthew 4:8–9 The Joseph Smith Translation makes clear by repetition (*"And* again") that Jesus was *"in the Spirit,"* and the Spirit, not the devil, escorted him to an "exceeding high mountain," and showed him "all the kingdoms of the world" and their glory. The view of all the kingdoms of the world must have been seen while in the Spirit—a spiritual vision (cf. Moses 1:11)—because few kingdoms of the world are visible from the vantage point overlooking the Jordan Valley.

High mountains are, of course, defined in terms of ancient Jewish geographic mentality, not in comparison with the American Rockies and Andes or European Alps. The mountains are "high" compared to the surrounding terrain. For instance, when the scripture says that Jesus was taken to "an exceeding high mountain," the summit of the fault escarpment above the Jordan Rift Valley floor near Jericho is acceptable as an exceedingly high mountain from a Judean's point of view (see Bible Map 14a).

Mountaintops are typical locations for spiritual encounters, being close to God and above the contaminating influences on the earth below, for example, Enoch on Mount Simeon (Moses 7:2–3), the brother of Jared on Mount Shelem (Ether 3:1; 4:1), Abraham on Mount Moriah (Genesis 22:2), Moses on a mountain in Sinai (Exodus 3; Moses 1:42), Nephi on an unnamed high mountain (1 Nephi 11:1; 18:3), Jesus and his apostles on the Mount of Transfiguration (Matthew 17:1), Orson Hyde on the Mount of Olives (Smith, *History of the Church,* 4:459), and pioneer Saints on Ensign Peak overlooking the Valley of the Great Salt Lake (*Encyclopedia of Mormonism,* 2:456; *Encyclopedia of Latter-day Saint History,* 339).

Matthew 4:9 In the height of the spiritual moment, along comes the devil—not an unfamiliar occurrence. Satan, who really believes that he is the god of this world and that he has genuine power and glory (Luke 4:6), will not leave anyone to bask very long in the light and warmth of communion with Heaven. He arrived on the scene for a third time with an outlandish claim to Jesus: "All these things will I give thee, if thou wilt fall down and worship me"—again using the "if" clause.

God is the author or provider of light, life, truth, joy, and good. The adversary can only provide the opposites, because *he takes away.* He can provide darkness (the absence of light), death (the absence of life), falsehood (the absence of truth), misery (the absence of joy), and evil (the absence of good). The devil really provides nothing; he just sees to it that all who cooperate with him are devoid of the blessings that God does provide. The unrighteous may not be miserable according to their perspective, but they do not know real happiness.

Matthew 4:10 Jesus saw right through the devil's assertion, of course, for he himself is the true God of this world and has created the earth and all things in it. "I, the Lord, stretched out the heavens, and built the earth, my very handiwork; and all things therein are mine" (D&C 104:14). He told his adversary (the meaning of the Hebrew word *Satan*) to depart, and he cited, for the third time, his own words of scripture in responding to the temptation to pursue the glories of the world: the Lord God is the only true object of worship (Exodus 20:3; cf. Deuteronomy 6:13). We are commanded to serve him only and not the vanities of the world. "Great women and men," President Spencer W. Kimball said, "are always more anxious to serve than to have dominion" (*Ensign,* November 1979, 104).

Matthew 4:11 Having been commanded of Jesus Christ to leave, the devil left—but only for a season (Luke 4:13). Satan had tempted the Creator and Savior of the world with strong enticements to satisfy the desires of the flesh (bread after fasting), to misuse divine power (angelic protection against the hazards of mortality), and to pursue the fleeting glories of mortals (glories of earthly kingdoms). Jesus "suffered temptations but gave no heed to them" (D&C 20:22; see also Mosiah 15:5). The devil had no effect on Jesus because He was so full of the Spirit. He had gone into the wilderness to commune with the Infinite, to set aside the things of the flesh and prepare for his ministry through empowerment of the Holy Ghost. All mortals may, as we travel through this wilderness of life, follow his example and do the same: fill ourselves daily (especially with scripture study and prayer) so that when the temptations come—as they inevitably will—they will have no power to overcome us because we are, like our Exemplar, filled with the Spirit.

Another valuable lesson coming from these accounts of temptation is to be familiar with the scriptures. Having our heads and our hearts full of the words of the Lord, the doctrines of the kingdom, will always wield a power in us to rebuff any enticements to abandon our God and his ways. Jesus used the scriptures to thwart temptations; so can we. The word of God can safely and successfully guide us through all temptation (Helaman 3:29–30). Nowhere in sacred writ does the Lord encourage us merely to read the scriptures; he counsels us to search, to study, to ponder, and to treasure up the words of life (cf. Ether 3:21).

We might add, after examining these three temptations to which Jesus was subjected, that he undoubtedly suffered more than three temptations during his ministry. Alma wrote that "he shall go forth, suffering pains and afflictions and temptations of every kind" (Alma 7:11). Thus we conclude that temptation pursued Jesus throughout his mortal life, just as it does us.

The Joseph Smith Translation adds, at this point, a curious footnote to the temptations in the wilderness. "*Now Jesus knew* that John was cast into prison, *and he sent angels,* and, behold, *they* came and ministered unto him (John)" (JST Matthew 4:11). There is no doubt that angels may have come and ministered to Jesus also, but an additional lesson is taught: When we are filled with the Spirit, we think about blessing the lives of others and ministering unto them in their distress—as He did.

JOHN THE BAPTIST'S TESTIMONY (AT BETHABARA)

John 1:15–18 John the Baptist testified of the preeminence of the Chosen One. A more complete record of his testimony is contained in Doctrine and Covenants 93:6–18.

That the Savior only gradually learned who he was and what his mission was in this mortal sphere is explained by President Lorenzo Snow: "When Jesus lay in the manger, a helpless infant, He knew not that He was the Son of God, and that formerly He created the earth. When the edict of Herod was issued, He knew nothing of it; He had not power to save Himself; and His father and mother had to take Him and fly into Egypt to preserve Him from the effects of that edict. Well, He grew up to manhood, and during His progress it was revealed unto Him who He was, and for what purpose He was in the world. The glory and power He possessed before He came into the world was made known unto Him" (Conference Report, April 1901, 3).

Though we call the earlier code of conduct and ritual observances by which Israelites lived the law of Moses, it was not Moses' law—it was the law of Jesus Christ given *through* Moses (JST John 1:17) for that people at that time. But the higher law of grace and the fulness of truth came through Jesus Christ himself, personally delivered to his people in the meridian of time (and were actually a restoration of what had been on the earth in the beginning).

John 1:18 The first phrase of this verse, "No man hath

The Ministry of John the Baptist

seen God at any time," has caused considerable doctrinal confusion through the centuries. Anyone who has given even a cursory reading to the Old Testament of the Bible knows that this statement is not true—if it is referring to God-Jehovah. We know for example, that Abraham saw God (Jehovah) on several occasions (Genesis 12:7; 17:1; 18:1); Jacob saw God (Genesis 32:30); Moses, Aaron, and seventy leaders of Israel saw God (Exodus 24:9–10; 33:11); and Isaiah and Amos saw God (Isaiah 6:1; Amos 9:1).

The Joseph Smith Translation (John 1:19) resolves the doctrinal problem by completing the statement in reference to God the Father: "No man hath seen God at any time *except he hath borne record of the Son; for except it is through him no man can be saved.*" In other words, no human has ever seen God the Father in this telestial world except when he has come to earth to testify of his Son. That is the truth. Whenever the Father comes to earth, he comes to say one specific thing: "This is my Son." Whenever he comes to this telestial world, he introduces his Son, and his Son takes over, because the Son is the Creator and Lord of this world.

Other scriptural renderings of this truth help us to see the intent of the statement from various angles:

"Not that any man hath seen the Father save he which is of God, he hath seen the Father" (John 6:46).

"No man hath seen God at any time, *except them who believe*" (JST 1 John 4:12).

"For no man has seen God at any time in the flesh, except quickened by the Spirit of God" (D&C 67:11).

No man, in the natural, mortal condition, could stand the glory of God's presence; he must be changed/quickened/transfigured to at least a terrestrial level (Moses 1:11): "For without this no man can see the face of God, even the Father, and live" (D&C 84:22).

John 1:29–31 John the Baptist testified of Christ. The Old Testament prophets sometimes referred to the Messiah as the Lion of Judah, coming in strength and roaring in the wilderness of the world (Hosea 5:14; 11:10); this New Testament prophet now refers to him as the Lamb of God, coming in meekness and gently sharing his gospel of compassion.

Twice in John 1, John the Baptist announces Jesus: "Behold the Lamb of God" (vv. 29, 36). Not only were the people of Israel referred to as sheep but Jesus himself was also deemed a young and tender sheep, or lamb. Paul called him "our passover" who was "sacrificed for us," referring to the sacrificial lamb at Passover (1 Corinthians 5:7). Jesus as a lamb was fulfilling the symbolism of all the lambs slain on the great altar of the Temple over the centuries. He would be the lamb brought to the slaughter (Isaiah 53:7; Mosiah 14:7); he was the "offering for sin" (Isaiah 53:10; Mosiah 14:10); and he would be "cut off out of the land of the living" (Isaiah 53:8; Mosiah 14:8; Daniel 9:26).

Of all the New Testament writers, only John called Jesus the Lamb of God, twice quoting John the Baptist and twenty-eight times mentioning the Lamb in the book of Revelation. There the Lamb is personified: He was slain (5:12), his blood was able to cleanse (7:14), and he was worshipped (5:8). The Lamb felt wrath (6:16) and fought a war (17:14). He had a marriage supper (19:9) and was married to his bride (19:7; 21:9). He possessed a book of life (13:8; 21:27) and a song (15:3) and served as light for the city of God (21:23).

The Baptist testified that this mild Lamb would provide atonement and redemption by taking away the sin of the world (cf. 3 Nephi 11:11). The prophet repeated his message that the Lamb was "preferred before me"—Jesus was preeminent, and the disciples must now turn their full attention and devotion to him.

The Joseph Smith Translation corrects the first phrase of John 1:31—"And I knew him not"—to read *"and I knew him, and* that he should be made manifest to Israel" (JST John 1:30). John continued, "Therefore am I come baptizing with water."

JOHN'S DISCIPLES FOLLOW JESUS (FROM BETHABARA TO GALILEE)

John 1:35–51 John the Baptist testified of the Lamb, the Messiah, in the hearing of two disciples, at least one of whom would become an apostle and member of the Twelve. The two began following Jesus, and he stopped and asked them, "What seek ye?" They in turn (maybe embarrassed or startled, or perhaps interested or inspired) asked, "Where dwellest thou?" His response was an invitation, "Come and see."

John 1:39–42 "For it was about the tenth hour," or about 4 P.M., time to arrange overnight lodging. The disciples may have stayed the night with him.

Andrew found his brother, Simon Peter (both were sons of a man named Jonah; v. 42), and excitedly bore his testimony, "We have found the Messiah" (Greek, *Christ*). As Andrew introduced his brother to Jesus, the Savior's greeting was more significant, with deeper meaning, than a common, ordinary greeting: "Thou art Simon the Son of Jona: thou shalt be called Cephas, which is, by interpretation, *a seer, or* a stone. *And they were fishermen. And they straightway left all, and followed Jesus*" (JST John 1:42).

The name Peter comes from the Greek *petros,* which means "rock." The Aramaic equivalent is Cephas (*kepha*), which also means "rock."

Here we have identified the three main languages used in the land at the time of Jesus. His chief apostle was to be known not so much by his Hebrew name, Shimon (Greek, *Simon*), as by his new Greek name, Petros, and his Aramaic appellation, Cephas. The renaming foreshadowed the apostle's future role. In guiding the early Church as its chief prophet, seer, and revelator, Peter (Cephas) would provide strength and stability (which are the symbolic, scriptural attributes of rock) to the fledgling organization.

Jesus later promised the keys of the kingdom, the commission of leadership, to Peter the Rock at Caesarea Philippi, at the foot of the most massive rock formation in the country (Matthew 16:13–19).

John 1:43–44 The first three of the future Twelve Apostles—Peter, Andrew, and Philip (all Greek names)—were from the same hometown, Bethsaida, which was situated at the northeast corner of the Sea of Galilee, near where the Jordan River empties into the lake. Jesus invited Philip, "Follow me."

John 1:45 This narration is a classic example of "first contacting"—the word "findeth" appears in verses 41, 43, and 45. Finding is an essential element of true missionary work in all ages: first the relatives and then the friends. Andrew first sought out his own brother. Philip sought out his friend Nathanael. Philip bore his testimony to his friend: "We have found him, of whom Moses in the law [the Torah], and the prophets [such as Isaiah, Micah, Jeremiah, and Zechariah], did write, Jesus of Nazareth." He also called Jesus "the son of Joseph," which is what he understood at that point. He would later hear Jesus many times bear testimony of who his Father really was.

John 1:46 Nazareth was not an important town in Jesus' day. It is not mentioned in the Old Testament or by Josephus or the Talmud. "Nazarene" was even a derisive term, as evidenced by Nathanael's remark, "Can there any good thing come out of Nazareth?" Having been raised there, Jesus truly did descend below *all* things (D&C 122:8), even in matters of socioeconomic environment and status. Nazareth was a lowly place to grow up.

The answer to Nathanael's question has deep import for every one of God's children. We are all invited, as Nathanael was, to "come and see." Inviting all of us to listen, learn, and live the gospel, the Savior is inviting us to come and see if anything good has come out of Nazareth.

John 1:47–48 "Every man under his vine and under his fig tree" became a figurative and formulaic expression of living comfortably, safely, and securely. Just after Philip had

The Ministry of John the Baptist

Leaves and fruit of the fig tree

encouraged his friend Nathanael to come and meet Jesus, the following conversation ensued: "Jesus saw Nathanael coming to him, and saith of him, Behold an Israelite indeed, in whom is no guile [no deceit or craftiness]! Nathanael saith unto him, Whence knowest thou me? Jesus answered and said unto him, Before that Philip called thee, when thou wast under the fig tree, I saw thee."

The statement may be taken literally—Nathanael may have been meditating under a fig tree. Or the statement may be figurative—"under the fig tree" may mean that Nathanael was living comfortably and contentedly, having no reason to make any changes in his life. By meeting Jesus, however, the course of his life would change abruptly and dramatically. Some rabbinical sources suggest that "under a fig tree" is the proper place for personal scripture study and that the phrase may be idiomatic, synonymous with "in search of truth."

In modern revelation the Lord compared the character of the first bishop of the Church, Edward Partridge, to the character of this disciple of the mortal Jesus: "his heart is pure before me, for he is like unto Nathanael of old, in whom there is no guile" (D&C 41:11).

John 1:49 Though the account of this conversation may be fragmentary, it appears that Nathanael was touched by the seeric and intimate knowledge of Jesus about him personally, and he opened his mouth to utter dramatic witness of Jesus: "Thou art the Son of God; thou art the King of Israel."

John 1:50–51 Jesus' response took the course of the conversation a step higher, saying in essence that after just this brief insight and receiving such a powerful witness, Nathanael would "see greater things than these" (v. 50; see also Helaman 14:28; Ether 4:13). Just as with Nephi, because he was faithful in all things, the Lord showed him "great things" (1 Nephi 18:3)—his views were "glorious" (2 Nephi 1:24)—so Nathanael, as one of the twelve special witnesses in that ancient world, would be privileged to see "heaven open, and the angels of God ascending and descending upon the Son of man." When a person is true and faithful to a portion of the knowledge of God and to the covenants and ordinances of his kingdom, that person is always promised more (see Ether 4:13). The greater things will be revealed line upon line and the light will grow brighter and brighter until the heavens are opened and the Son of Man is eventually seen and known, along with his Father, the Man of Holiness.

Jesus used the name-title "Son of man" more than eighty times in the Gospels as a messianic title for himself, making it his most commonly used title (see Skinner and Marsh, *Scriptural Parables,* 154). "Son of Man" always appears in modern revelation with "Man" capitalized because it is a reference to the Father, who is a glorified, resurrected, exalted Man (the phrase "Son of Man" is always capitalized in the New International Version of the Bible, one of the best of the more recent scholarly translations of the English Bible). The Father is the "Man of Holiness" (Moses 6:57); his Son, therefore, is the Son of Man of Holiness. Jesus is actually the only man in history who was *not* a son of man, meaning a mortal man.

PART III

THE MINISTRY OF THE MESSIAH

CHAPTER 5

AN EARLY GALILEAN MINISTRY

John 2:1–11 "There was a marriage in Cana of Galilee," which happened "on the third day" (the Greek text) or on the "third day *of the week*" (JST John 2:1). So begins the story of Jesus' first recorded miracle, performed at a wedding feast in Cana.

John, the writer of the fourth Gospel (and Joseph Smith, the inspired reviser of the Bible text), "may have pointed to an ancient Jewish tradition, which is to perform weddings on Tuesday, the third day of the week, Sunday being the first (John 2:1). This tradition is based on Genesis 1:9–13, where the word 'good' (*tov*) is used twice for the third day of

Ruins of Cana of Galilee

creation instead of once only for the other days. Accordingly, important matters like weddings were decided, settled, or celebrated on the third day of the week to call for a double blessing from God" (Rousseau and Aviv, *Jesus and His World*, 38–39).

Jesus' second miracle of record was also performed at Cana—the healing of the son of a nobleman, or royal official, in Capernaum more than twenty miles away, showing that distance was no obstacle to his divine power. One of the Twelve Apostles, Nathanael, was from Cana.

The traditional site of Cana is along the Nazareth-Tiberias highway, a town now called in Arabic *Kfar Kanna,* literally the "village of Cana." Archaeology and toponymy (the study of place-names) tell us, on the other hand, that Cana was located about eight miles north of Nazareth across the Bet Netofa Valley. There is a hill (inaccessible by automobile) with ancient ruins called in Arabic *Kanna el-Jalil* (Cana of Galilee.)

Jesus' presence at a marriage celebration shows that he was no social recluse (as were some Essenes, for example; see Appendix 2, 726). He enjoyed the company and association of others in wholesome human activities. The marriage itself might have been that of one of Jesus' (half) brothers or sisters. His mother Mary seems to have had some hosting role and turned to Jesus for help.

Jesus himself was now more than thirty years of age and would probably have married, as was customary for Jewish men to do in their late teens: "At five years old one is ready for the scripture, at ten years for the Mishnah, at thirteen for the commandments, at fifteen for Talmud, at eighteen for marriage, at twenty for pursuit of righteousness, at thirty for full strength" (*Pirke Aboth*, V:24). Had Jesus not been married, we would undoubtedly read of accusation after accusation against him, because marriage was number one of the commandments God had given from the beginning to the meridian of time. As we have no record of objections to his teaching, it would appear that he had already complied with this most important commandment. (This point of view does not represent a doctrinal statement but is simply an observation about ancient Jewish culture.) Joseph Smith taught that the Savior obeyed all ordinances necessary for exaltation: "If a man gets a fullness of the priesthood of God he has to get it in the same way that Jesus Christ obtained it, and that was by keeping all the commandments and obeying all the ordinances of the house of the Lord" (*Teachings of the Prophet Joseph Smith*, 308). Robert J. Matthews reemphasizes the Prophet's point: "Jesus kept every commandment of His Father; He held the Melchizedek Priesthood and observed every ordinance of the priesthood pertaining to mortality, including all ordinances of the temple" (*Jesus Christ, Son of God, Savior*, 316).

Jesus' words in John 2:4 as rendered in the King James Version sound insensitive, even disrespectful, to our ears, but the Joseph Smith Translation records a more endearing response from Jesus, which also begins with the reverential term "Woman." Other uses of "Woman" in direct address are the following: Luke 13:12, when Jesus healed a woman with an eighteen-year infirmity; John 19:26, when Jesus spoke to his mother, Mary, from the cross; John 20:13, when angels spoke to Mary Magdalene at the tomb; and John 20:15, when Jesus spoke to Mary Magdalene at the tomb. It is clear in all these cases that the translated designation "Woman" is used in a kindly and respectful context and tone.

"What *wilt thou have me to do for* thee? *that will I do*" (JST John 2:4). From the beginning to the end of his ministry, the Savior was always attentive to the needs of his mother and solicitous of her. He asked her, just as he asked the brother of Jared, "What will ye that I should do . . ?" (Ether 2:23). It is the responsibility of humans to do all that humans can do—and then God does the rest. And even before God acts, he expects us to ask, to petition, and to suggest a solution (D&C 9:8).

John 2:6 "There were set there six water pots of stone, . . . containing two or three firkins apiece." Water pots in this

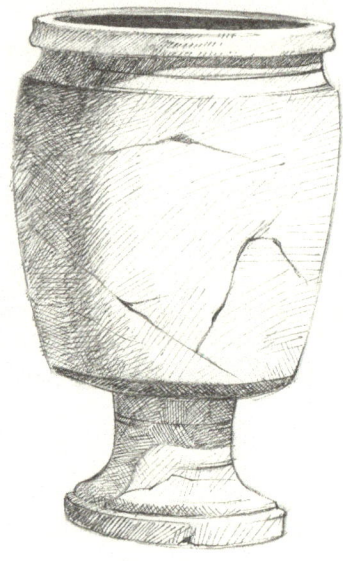

Stone water pot

case were also used for wine. A firkin was approximately nine gallons, so the six pots could have contained between a hundred and a hundred and fifty gallons, which would have supplied a large wedding celebration. Though pots were often made of clay, they were also made of stone. A pot made from porous clay or limestone allowed for evaporation, which cooled the liquid contents. Several stone pots from the Roman period are on permanent display in the Israel Museum in Jerusalem.

Vessels made from native stone were ceremonially clean and were used for holding water that was likewise ritually clean for use in washings and purifyings (for example, of hands and feet of guests). In fact, according to Jewish purification laws, stone vessels had special status because they could not become ritually impure.

Was the wine Jesus created really the intoxicating kind? A woman wrote to the editor of the *Biblical Archaeology Review* (September/October, 1985, 24), making the following

An Early Galilean Ministry

interesting point: "Jesus turned water into wine for the wedding guests in John 2:1–11. But the word 'wine' in the Bible can refer to non-alcoholic as well as alcoholic beverages—as can our word 'drink,' today. Had Jesus turned water into an intoxicant for the wedding guests, God would not have included Proverbs 20:1 in the Bible: 'Wine is a mocker, strong drink is raging: and whosoever is deceived thereby is not wise.' In Proverbs we have a definite reference to an intoxicant. God, being consistent with His own laws and principles—remember that He changes not . . .—would hardly write the foregoing line from Proverbs and then miraculously create an alcoholic wine at a wedding!"

The wine Jesus created for the wedding guests was likely new, fresh wine rather than something strong that would cause drunkenness, which was contrary to the Jews' own laws of physical health.

John 2:8–9 The governor of the feast was the "master of ceremonies," or the main host of the banquet, whoever that might have been.

John 2:11 The incident at the wedding feast is labeled the "beginning of miracles." Though it may be the first recorded miracle of his mortal ministry, it is certainly not Jesus' first miracle—the first was the creation of Earth. (And even that was not his first miracle, for he created worlds without number before he created this sphere; Moses 1:33.) One purpose of his miracles was to "manifest forth his glory," that his Father might be glorified, and that his disciples might believe in him, as stated here. He later healed a man born blind, "that the works of God should be made manifest in him" (John 9:3), and he raised his friend Lazarus from the dead "for the glory of God, that the Son of God might be glorified thereby" (John 11:4).

There is always purpose in using divine power. Having created or organized all the elements in the beginning of the creation of this world, Jesus could understandably reorganize and transform the chemical constituency of a few elements in some water pots in Cana of Galilee.

Though miracles do not create faith, they can certainly help to increase it (D&C 63:9–11). The Joseph Smith Translation changes "his disciples believed on him" to "*the faith of his disciples was strengthened in* him" (JST John 2:11).

VISIT TO CAPERNAUM

John 2:12 Jesus' family and followers went down to Capernaum on the northern shore of the Sea of Galilee. It was a twenty-mile journey *down* to the lake, from above sea level to below sea level (John 4:46–54). The traveling group included Jesus' mother, Mary; Joseph is not mentioned. In fact, we do not hear anything about Joseph in the rest of Jesus' ministry, suggesting that Joseph had possibly died by this time. (If Joseph had been in his twenties when Jesus was born, he would have been in his fifties by the time of Jesus' ministry and perhaps had passed away.) There is a further distinction between Jesus' "brethren" and his "disciples." His

Ruins of Capernaum, c. 1900

"brethren" meant his half brothers and sisters, children that Joseph and Mary had together after Jesus' birth. Some of their names are given in the Gospels: James (Jacob), Joses (Joseph), Simon, Judas (Judah), plus sisters. "The number of girls is not specified, but the Greek text makes it clear that there were more than two" (Bible Dictionary, "Brethren of the Lord," 627). The names are noted in Matthew 13:55–56 and Mark 6:3. Other references to Jesus' mother and brothers and sisters include Matthew 12:46; Mark 3:31; Luke 8:19; Acts 1:14; Galatians 1:19.

"They continued there not many days" because they were soon going up to Jerusalem.

CHAPTER 6

THE EARLY JUDEAN MINISTRY

John 2:13, 23–25 This was Jesus' first Passover during his ministry (see Appendix 6, 764). He came into the world at Passover time, and he would leave the world at Passover time. He was the Passover Lamb. This day was initiated centuries before by him; the day was his.

Even though the Passover was a time of messianic expectation and hope for deliverance, Jesus did not commit himself to the crowds, "because he knew all *things*" (JST John 2:24)—that is, the time for public broadcast of his Messiahship and for triumphal entries and acceptance of his proper royal and kingly titles was not yet. Besides, he did not need any mortal adulation or acclamation. He did not need the popularity of crowds. His own and his Father's testimony would stand as the prime witnesses for the coming three years. Neither did the Master need any explanation of men's motives, "for he knew what was in man."

FIRST CLEANSING OF THE TEMPLE (COURT OF GENTILES, JERUSALEM TEMPLE)

John 2:14–17 Oxen, sheep, and doves were sold in the Temple porticoes or colonnades for sacrificial purposes, and because all national currencies were converted into Temple coinage, the moneychangers were ever present. The law itself was holy, and the execution of the law was right, but motives

Jesus Clears the Temple, *by Carl Heinrich Bloch*

were still crucial: "Jesus went up to Jerusalem, and found in the temple those that sold oxen and sheep and doves, and the changers of money sitting: and when he had made a scourge [a whip] of small cords, he drove them all out of the temple, and the sheep, and the oxen; and poured out the changers' money, and overthrew the tables; and said unto them that sold doves, Take these things hence; make not my Father's house an house of merchandise."

Jesus left no doubt about who he was. The Temple was his Father's house, and he did not want to see it desecrated by greedy merchandisers, who seldom entertained a worthy thought about the sacredness of their sales. Annas and Caiaphas, who would become two of the chief persecutors of the Lord, could have been among the most furious over this daring act of Jesus, as they were likely prominent shareholders in the business of sacrificial animals.

Jesus was not always passively submissive; he sometimes expressed righteous wrath. When attacked himself, he controlled the response, but when his Father was shamed, then he did become wrathful, although that, too, was a perfectly controlled response. The Father deserved respect.

John W. Welch, Brigham Young University law professor and scripture scholar, observed: "For John, the cleansing [of the Father's house] occurs at the very beginning of Jesus' ministry . . . perhaps to show Jesus working at a clean temple throughout His ministry" (*Jesus Christ, Son of God, Savior,* 309).

As Matthew often does, John notes that the disciples found direct fulfillment of an Old Testament passage (Psalm 69:9) in Jesus' action.

SIGN OF JESUS' DEATH AND RESURRECTION (AT THE JERUSALEM TEMPLE)

John 2:18–22 Jesus routinely used in his teaching things from his immediate environment, often referring to something appropriate to the place where he taught. On this occasion, when in the Temple at Jerusalem, he made figurative use of the Temple. "Jesus answered and said unto them, Destroy this temple, and in three days I will raise it up. Then said the Jews, Forty and six years was this temple in building, and wilt thou rear it up in three days? But he spake of the temple of his body."

According to the testimony of John, all this was said near the beginning of Jesus' ministry, which would make this declaration his first recorded prophecy of his death and resurrection. Jesus knew from the commencement of his ministry what the outcome would be.

Evidently the Jews understood his figurative language, perceiving, at least in part, that he referred not to Herod's forty-six-year Temple-building project but to his own body, which he claimed he had the power to raise up again after its death. At his later hearing before the chief priests, one of the false witnesses testified, "This fellow said, I am able to destroy the temple of God, and to build it in three days" (Matthew 26:61). At the cross, "they that passed by reviled him, wagging their heads, and saying, Thou that destroyest the temple, and buildest it in three days, save thyself" (Matthew 27:39–40). The following is preserved from a conversation after Jesus' death: "Now the next day, that followed the day of preparation, the chief priests and Pharisees came together unto Pilate, saying, Sir, we remember that that deceiver said, while he was yet alive, *After three days I will rise again.* Command therefore that the sepulchre be made sure until the third day" (Matthew 27:62–64; emphasis added; see also vv. 65–66).

NICODEMUS (AT JERUSALEM)

John 3:1–10 Nicodemus, a Jew with a Greek name, was a Pharisee and a member of the ruling body called the Sanhedrin. The Sanhedrin consisted of Sadducees, Pharisees, and scribes, who were variously called "chief priests," "elders," or "rulers" (see Appendix 4, 753). We hear of Nicodemus on three occasions: this nighttime interview; later as he defended Jesus' right to a fair trial before the law (John 7:50–51); and in preparing, with Joseph of Arimathea, Jesus' body for burial (John 19:38–40).

John 3:2 Nicodemus was apparently concerned about his status and standing before his fellow "rulers of the Jews," and before the people themselves—as evidenced by this secretive, nighttime visit with Jesus—but he also seems to have been an honest seeker for truth, and it appears that he was impressed with something Jesus had done or something he had taught. He addressed Jesus respectfully, calling him Rabbi, meaning "Great One," or "Master" (see Appendix 4, 751). Nicodemus's first assertion was a statement of truth: "We [he and other members of the Sanhedrin?] know that thou art a teacher come from God: for no man can do these miracles that thou doest, except God be with him." Nicodemus was right. Righteous performance of miracles is one sign of a true priesthood holder, a servant truly sent from God (3 Nephi 8:1). Peter later testified that Jesus was "approved of God among you by miracles and wonders and signs" (Acts 2:22), and Paul bore his witness, as did Nicodemus, that Jesus "went about doing good, and healing . . . for God was with him" (Acts 10:38).

John 3:3 Every human who lives on the earth has been born physically, but for each to become a citizen in the kingdom of God, it is requisite that each also be born spiritually. We must be born not only here below but also from above.

John 3:4–7 Nicodemus, apparently feigning ignorance of Jesus' meaning, asked if it is possible to reenter a mother's womb and be born a second time. Jesus made his teaching unmistakably clear: unless a person is born of water and of the Spirit, it is not possible to enter the kingdom of God, meaning the celestial kingdom (see also Smith, *Answers to Gospel Questions,* 5:147). Enoch, citing the teachings of Adam, elaborated on the doctrine: "As ye were born into the world by water, and blood, and the spirit, . . . even so ye must be born again into the kingdom of heaven, of water, and of the Spirit, and be cleansed by blood . . . ; for by the water ye keep the commandment; by the Spirit ye are justified and by the blood ye are sanctified" (Moses 6:59–60).

Whoever is born of the flesh, Jesus taught, is flesh or mortal, but whoever is born of the Spirit becomes a spiritual being and rises above the things of the flesh. Being spiritually reborn is a must. A recent official Church publication teaches: "To be able to receive the blessing of eternal life, we need to be 'spiritually minded' and conquer our unrighteous desires. We need to change. More accurately, we need to *be changed,* or converted, through the power of the Savior's Atonement and through the power of the Holy Ghost. This process is called conversion.

"Conversion includes a change in behavior, but it goes beyond behavior; it is a change in our very nature. It is such a significant change that the Lord and His prophets refer to it as a rebirth, a change of heart, and a baptism of fire. . . .

"Conversion is a process, not an event. You become converted as a result of your righteous efforts to follow the Savior" (*True to the Faith,* 40–41).

John 3:8 "Wind" and "spirit" are the same word in both Hebrew and Greek. Here is a clever word play: both wind and spirit can be felt but not seen. Though not visible, their effect is undeniable.

John 3:9–10 Nicodemus, again feigning incredulity, wondered how all this could be. Jesus responded with a mild rebuke: "Art thou a master [leader and teacher] of Israel, and knowest not these things?" His answer suggests that these principles were known and taught in Old Testament times and Nicodemus should have been well acquainted with them.

MESSIANIC WITNESS TO NICODEMUS (AT JERUSALEM)

John 3:11–21 Here we have recorded the testimony of Jesus to a member of the Sanhedrin. That ruling body in matters of Jewish law had thus far generally rejected the witness of the greatest Master of Israel, though the witness presented to Nicodemus this night took root and grew, as later passages in John's Gospel demonstrate (John 7:45–53; 19:39–42).

John 3:12 Jesus' powerful question could be paraphrased in other words. It was as if he were saying, If you do not grasp the simple, basic doctrines, how can you understand the deep and profound? If you cannot digest the milk, how can you deal with the meat?'

John 3:13 No man had yet ascended back to heaven after mortality. Through four thousand years of mortals dying and remaining dead, no physical body had yet resurrected to immortality, but the Son of Man (Son of Man of Holiness, Son of the Father in Heaven; Moses 6:57) was about to do just that. Jesus was condescending, and then he would be ascending. He followed up the doctrine with a practical example, or type, that his people would understand from their history.

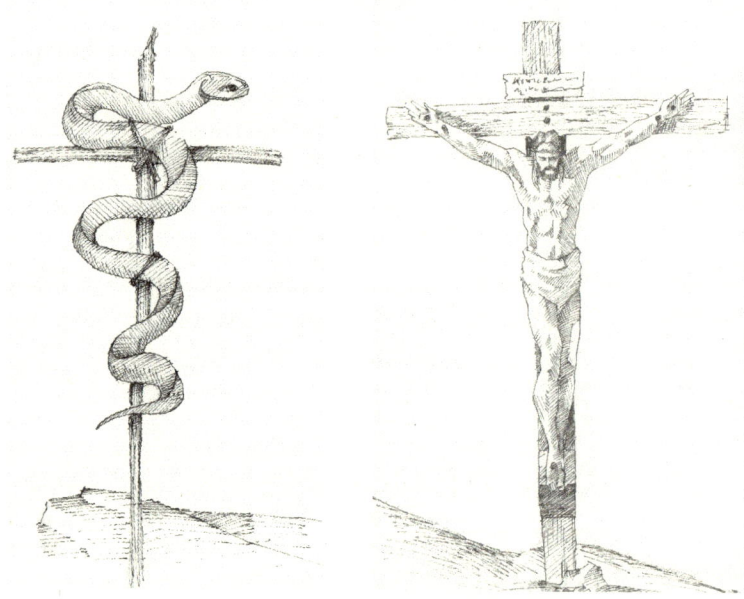

A serpent on a pole and Christ on the cross

John 3:14–15 "Jesus taught from the scriptures. He read from them, quoted them, and explained them to his hearers. On numerous occasions he quoted Isaiah, Moses, or the Psalms, or cited events from the book of Kings. Jesus often reminded his audience of events recorded in the Old Testament, and used the Old Testament to cite a precedent in actions of David, or Moses, or Abraham. He also used the Old Testament to teach doctrine, such as the laws governing marriage and divorce, the doctrine of the resurrection, and particularly his own Messiahship" (Matthews, *Behold the Messiah,* 222).

Now Jesus cited an example from the travels and travails of Moses in Sinai. "As Moses lifted up the serpent in the wilderness, even so must the Son of man be lifted up: that whosoever believeth in him should not perish, but have eternal life" (see Alma 33:19–20; Helaman 8:13–15). As Israel had looked to the serpent on a pole in order to live, so they were now encouraged to look to their Redeemer, who would be lifted up and would live. The serpent was a symbol of Christ.

From the very beginning, however, there was a perversion of the true symbol. Satan usurped the image to also represent himself. "The great dragon was cast out, that old serpent, called the Devil, and Satan, which deceiveth the whole world" (Revelation 12:9; 20:2). "The serpent beguiled Eve through his subtilty" (2 Corinthians 11:3).

Moses' serpent on a pole was able to heal; and the Savior lifted up on the cross was able to heal. The snake's healing power persisted in the mythologies of Near Eastern religions, even down to the Graeco-Roman Asclepius, the god of healing and medicine. Centers for the healing arts were established throughout the Roman Empire, for example, the Asclepieum at Pergamum and the Asklepeion on the island of Cos (where Hippocrates practiced for years). The symbol of Asclepius was a serpent wrapped around a pole. Today that is the symbol of the American Medical Association. (For a fuller treatment of the serpent as a dual symbol, see Skinner, "Serpent Symbols and Salvation," 42–55).

The parallel of the serpent with God penetrated other ancient cultures as well. For example, the ancient American god Quetzalcoatl, whose name means "feathered serpent," reputedly lived in Coatzacoalcos ("sanctuary of the serpent").

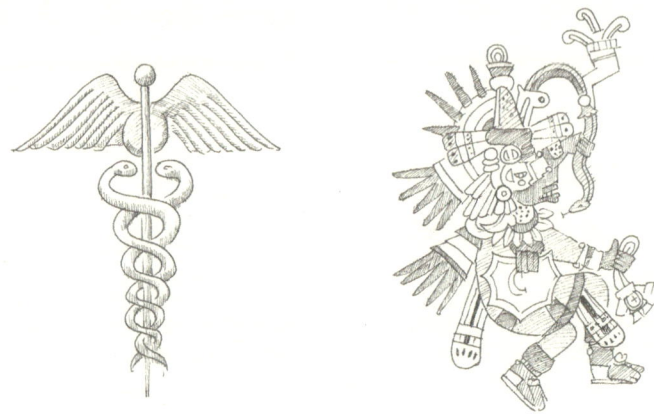

Symbol of medical association and of Quetzalcoatl

Ancient Mesoamericans associated the serpent with fertility, wisdom, and power. In ancient Near Eastern Baalism, the serpent's role was to stimulate moisture and, hence, fertility.

Moses is one of the greatest testators of the Messiah. He is famous for that unique type he raised up in the wilderness. To rescue his people he crafted the bronze serpent and lifted it up so the people could look upon it and be healed from the deadly plague. It was easy to look (1 Nephi 17:41), therefore "many did look and live" (Alma 33:19).

"But," Alma sadly commented, "few understood the meaning of those things, and this because of the hardness of their hearts . . . there were many who were so hardened that they would not look, therefore they perished." Imagine! A simple matter of glancing up to the symbol of the Savior, and they refused. Why? "Now the reason they would not look is because they did not believe that it would heal them" (Alma 33:20). There it is—exactly the same reason why many people stubbornly refuse to look to the Master Healer today: They do not really believe that he will heal them. They do not believe that he is real, or that he lived and suffered for every soul, or that he *can* heal them. If people will look to him, they can be healed and live. "I, the Lord, will feel after them . . . and I will heal them" (D&C 112:13; cf. 3 Nephi 9:13). He suffered not only for our sins but also for our sicknesses. With faith in him, we can be made whole.

Some of us refuse to look to him because we adopt the unbelieving attitude of Laman and Lemuel: "The Lord maketh no such thing known unto us" (1 Nephi 15:9). We think that he may heal others but would not heal us.

John 3:16–17 Elder Bruce R. McConkie identified John 3:16 as "perhaps the most famous and powerful single verse of scripture ever uttered. It summarizes the whole plan of salvation, tying together the Father, the Son, his atoning sacrifice, that belief in him which presupposes righteous works, and ultimate eternal exaltation for the faithful" (*Doctrinal New Testament Commentary*, 1:144).

The Father so loved the world (meaning the inhabitants of the world, his children; cf. Ether 12:33), that he gave his most precious gift, his Beloved Son. Here and in many other passages of scripture Jesus is called the Father's "only begotten Son." Of course Jesus is not the only child of the Father—all mortal beings are children of the Father—but Jesus is the only child the Father ever had *in the flesh,* here in mortality. Jesus is the Firstborn of all the Father's children in the spirit and the *only* begotten in the flesh (Greek, *monogenes,* "only begotten"; see also Luke 1:34–35; John 1:13). Jesus Christ is the only person ever born into mortality of whose physical body God our Father in Heaven is the biological father (see *Encyclopedia of Mormonism*, 2:729, 740).

After having given the greatest gift of his Son, the Father provides a sequel, the next greatest gift: everlasting life—his kind of life—for all his children (cf. Helaman 14:8). Whoever believes the Son will believe the Father, and love and obey them both. All we have to do is look to them and live. The Father did not send his Son to the inhabitants of the world to condemn them but to save them. The Savior taught, "The Son of Man is not come to destroy men's lives, but to save them" (Luke 9:56)—all because he loves them. John further testified, "In this was manifested the love of God toward us, because that God sent his only begotten Son into the world, that we might live through him" (1 John 4:9).

Centuries earlier, Nephi testified: "He doeth not anything save it be for the benefit of the world; for he loveth the world, even that he layeth down his own life that he may draw all men unto him" (2 Nephi 26:24).

John 3:18–21 John frequently includes in his account of Jesus' teaching the contrasting motif of light and darkness. While Jesus was in the Temple, for example, He testified, "I am the light of the world: he that followeth me shall not walk in darkness, but shall have the light of life" (John 8:12). John 9 contains the story of a man born blind who was healed—a man who spent his entire life in darkness until his eyes were opened and he saw the Light. The man born blind was taken before some Jewish leaders, who were still in the dark, and those spiritually blind "masters of Israel" refused to accept the Source of light (cf. Helaman 13:29).

Those who see the Light, accept the Light, and live by the Light are not condemned to remain in darkness but are redeemed and eventually will live in eternal light, in "everlasting burnings," away from all darkness.

Mortals in this fallen condition are by nature inclined to love darkness because we sin and thereby feel uncomfortable in the light, hesitant to turn to the light because our sinning will be exposed and we will then feel guilt and condemnation. Often "the guilty taketh the truth to be hard, for it cutteth them to the very center" (1 Nephi 16:2). But those who love truth will humble themselves and turn to the Light and gradually and eventually be "wrought in God"—forged or fashioned in his image. Lovers of truth and light are not flawless souls who never sin but are regular mortals who struggle and repent and overcome; they are "just men made perfect through Jesus the mediator of the new covenant, who wrought out this perfect atonement" (D&C 76:69).

Nicodemus, who went to Jesus in the dark—physically and spiritually—was now enlightened by the Light of the world, the Source of all light. From the few references we have of Nicodemus in the rest of the Gospel accounts he seems to have continued in his desire to follow the Light.

JESUS' EARLY MINISTRY IN JUDEA

John 3:22, 26; 4:1 Jesus himself baptized people into his Church and kingdom (see further in JST John 4:1–4). What a spirit would have been felt in such baptismal services where the Creator and Redeemer of this world was personally performing the sacred ordinance!

JOHN'S MINISTRY AND TESTIMONY (AT AENON NEAR SALIM)

John 3:23–36 There are three possibilities for the place where John was baptizing.

The sixth-century Medeba Map, an east-oriented, mosaic map that is our oldest cartographic representation of the Holy Land, shows Aenon on the eastern side of the Jordan River opposite Jericho, near Bethabara where John was baptizing (John 1:28; the town of Medeba, where the unique map was found, is in today's nation of Jordan).

Eusebius preserved a tradition (in the early church father's listing of biblical place-names called the *Onomastikon*, 40:1) of Aenon being about seven miles south of Beth-shan (in the Roman period called Scythopolis), which is about twenty miles south of the Sea of Galilee. There is a nearby site called Salem, now Tel Shalem.

Still another possible location for Aenon was near Neapolis (modern Nablus, or ancient Shechem), not far from where Eusebius noted that another Salim/Salem was located (*Onomastikon*, 160:13; cf. Genesis 33:18). *Aenon* means

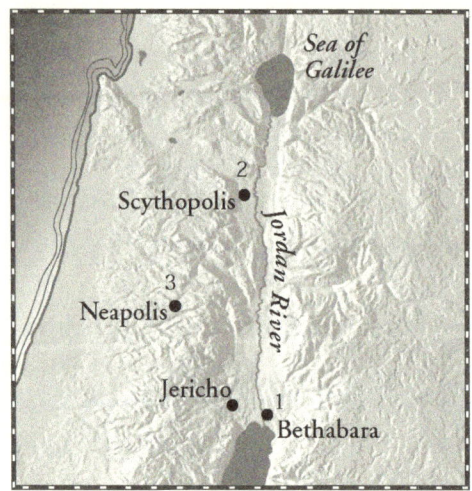

Three possibilities for the location of John's baptizing

"springs" in Hebrew, and there are many of them around that country.

There seems to be no way at present to identify with certainty which of the three sites is alluded to in this particular passage, but it does appear possible that John baptized in more than one location in the land of the Jews.

John 3:25 Baptism was an ordinance of purification, and the Jews had numerous rituals of purification. Some Jewish religious groups extended and exceeded the original laws Jehovah had given them and were meticulous to the extreme in their ceremonial washings and cleansings (see, for example, Mark 7:1–4). Thus the question arose about the purpose and meaning of the immersions that John and Jesus performed.

John 3:26 Some Jews came to John, addressing him respectfully (whether honestly or sarcastically) as "Rabbi," saying that "he that was with thee beyond Jordan [over in Perea], to whom thou barest witness, behold, the same baptizeth, and all men come to him," and, as the Joseph Smith Translation notes, *"he receiveth of all people who come unto him"* (JST John 3:27).

John 3:27–36 John testified further of Jesus that no one could understand anything unless a spiritual witness came from heaven. (We must have the Spirit to understand spiritual things; 1 Corinthians 2:11, 14.) John pointed out that Jesus Christ must increase but he (John) must decrease.

That statement is one of the noblest and most selfless remarks in all of scripture. Here is a man, called the Baptist, who has hundreds, possibly thousands of followers, from all over the country. The people are applauding his labors and acknowledging his role as a great prophet. But there is no inappropriate pride, no contention for superiority, no envy of this newcomer, no jealousy. John is totally loyal to his Savior—a supreme example of humility.

John explained that he was just a man and that He who comes from above is above all. John was testifying of what he had seen and heard—what he knew—and few seemed to be listening. Those who receive his witness certify that God is real. The One the Father has sent delivers the Father's message. The Father did not give him merely a portion of his Spirit, for the Son has a fulness ("God giveth *him* not the Spirit by measure, *for he dwelleth in him, even the fulness*"; JST John 3:34). "The Father loveth the Son, and hath given all things into his hand."

JST John 3:36 "*And* he *who* believeth on the Son hath everlasting life; *and shall receive of his fulness. But* he *who* believeth not the Son, shall not *receive of his fulness; for* the wrath of God *is upon* him."

HEROD ANTIPAS REPROVED BY JOHN (IN JUDEA OR PEREA?)

Matthew 14:3–5; Mark 6:17–20; Luke 3:19–20 Herod Antipas imprisoned John the Baptist because the prophet condemned the ruler's adulterous and illegal relationship with Herodias, his half brother Philip's former wife (see further at Matthew 14:3–12). Herodias was responsible for John's arrest. What Antipas had done in marrying her directly contravened ancient Israelite law (Leviticus 20:21). Although wanting to be rid of John, Antipas hesitated to harm him because of the prophet's popularity among the people and because he knew John was a holy man, so he protected him.

The New Testament itself cites no specific place for the imprisonment and execution of the Baptist. For that information, we have to rely on the accuracy of the historical report of Josephus, who wrote, "John, because of Herod's suspicions, was brought in chains to Machaerus . . . and there put to death" (*Antiquities* [Loeb] XVIII.119; see also Bible Dictionary, "Machaerus," 727).

Machaerus sits at the edge of the Transjordanian mountains overlooking the Dead Sea, near the southern border of Perea (see Appendix 1, 713). The Hasmonean king Alexander Jannaeus had reared the fortress, but Roman forces destroyed it. Herod the Great rebuilt it, along with Masada on the other side of the Dead Sea.

JOHN IMPRISONED AND VISITED BY ANGELS (AT MACHAERUS, IN PEREA)

JST Matthew 4:11 "*And now Jesus knew* that John was cast into prison, *and he sent angels,* and, behold, *they* came and ministered unto him (John)."

CHAPTER 7

A SECOND GALILEAN MINISTRY

Matthew 4:12; Mark 1:14; Luke 4:14; John 4:1–4 Jesus left Judea and returned to Galilee with the power of the Spirit. He had obtained the Spirit through fasting and prayer, and he had retained the Spirit through overcoming temptation. His fame now went before him. Of Jesus, the Joseph Smith Translation (John 4:2–4) adds:

"They sought more diligently some means that they might put him to death; for many received John as a prophet, but they believed not on Jesus.

"Now the Lord knew this, though *he* himself baptized not *so many as* his disciples;

"For he suffered them for an example, preferring one another."

This last sentence may mean that Jesus did not put the spotlight on himself (as we would say) but acknowledged his local leaders, allowing them the opportunity to perform ordinances and render service.

WOMAN AT THE WELL (AT SYCHAR, IN SAMARIA)

John 4:4–42 Jesus journeyed back and forth between Galilee and Judea, sometimes walking through Samaria, which is surprising considering the Judeans' derisive attitude toward Samaritans. The Jews regarded them as genealogical halfbreeds and historical enemies and adversaries: "The Jews have

Sychar and Jacob's Well in the hill country of Samaria, between Mount Gerizim (left) and Mount Ebal (right)

no dealings with the Samaritans" (John 4:9; see Bible Dictionary, "Samaritans," 768). One of the Jews' ultimate curses was to pronounce someone a Samaritan: "Say we not well that thou art a Samaritan, and hast a devil?" (John 8:48).

But Jesus did not avoid Samaritans. In fact, he once stayed for several days in Samaritan villages and taught the people. Just as the story of Jonah taught former-day Israelites that salvation was for all of God's children, that all must have a chance to hear and repent, so Jesus pointedly illustrated God's concern for all peoples despite others' prejudices. He immortalized the Samaritan people by his parable about a man (a Jew) assaulted along the Jericho road: "A certain Samaritan, as he journeyed, came where he was: and when he saw him, he had compassion on him" (Luke 10:33). The only one of the ten lepers Jesus healed who came back to express gratitude was a Samaritan (Luke 17:16).

The first recorded instance in the New Testament Gospels of Jesus openly declaring to anyone that he was the Messiah was to a Samaritan woman at Jacob's Well. The woman in

A Second Galilean Ministry

Drawing water from Jacob's Well, 1869

great excitement called the townspeople, who eagerly listened to Jesus. "Many of the Samaritans of that city believed on him," saying, "We have heard him ourselves, and know that this is indeed the Christ, the Saviour of the world" (John 4:39, 42). Here were the fruits of one conversion—many more.

John 4:5–6 John is the only Gospel writer to record a journey north from Jerusalem to Galilee directly through Samaria, where Jesus stopped at Jacob's Well.

Upon returning from his twenty-year residence in Mesopotamia, the Old Testament patriarch Jacob settled on a parcel of ground he purchased east of the city of Shechem (Genesis 33:18–19). Though there is no mention in the Old Testament of a well dug by or for Jacob, it is believed that Jacob did dig a well and that this well, situated east of the ancient city and at the foot of "this mountain" (Mount Gerizim; John 4:20), is the well mentioned by John. If so, by Jesus' day it had already been used for a millennium. The place-name Sychar is a corruption of the ancient name Shechem, or perhaps the village Jesus visited was another village a short distance away, at the ruins of what Arabs today call Khirbet Askar.

John's account notes that Jesus was wearied from the journey and sat down at the well. (Jesus did get tired, as prophesied by King Benjamin; see Mosiah 3:7.) It was the sixth hour—twelve noon—of the second day into his journey to Galilee, since Shechem is forty miles north of Jerusalem. Desiring to teach among the Samaritans, he had, in the first place, chosen this route to Galilee instead of the route through the Jordan valley. In addition, he sent the disciples to buy food, again so he could have opportunity to initiate a conversation with a Samaritan, knowing that his friends might have spoiled the opportunity since "the Jews have no dealings with the Samaritans" (John 4:9).

How did the woman recognize Jesus as a Jew? Perhaps some physical feature distinguished the two peoples or they wore distinctive clothing or spoke in a different dialect or accent.

For centuries, the Jews and Samaritans had drawn water from cisterns—underground water storage chambers—and from wells, such as Jacob's Well. Jesus told a Samaritan woman about the source of "living water," that is, ever-flowing or perennial water. Just as he intimated at the foot of Mount Hermon that he was the Rock of Salvation and at Capernaum, where mills for grinding wheat to make bread were produced, that he was the Bread of Life, so at Jacob's Well he described himself as the Living Water, a source from which any person could draw spiritual water and quench spiritual thirst: "The water that I shall give him shall be in him a well of water springing up into everlasting life."

John 4:7 C. Wilfred Griggs, archaeologist and Brigham Young University professor of ancient scripture, wrote: "Because this person was a woman, traditional avenues of educational and religious training were not open to her; because she was a Samaritan, her social status was that of an outcast in Jewish society; and because she had lived with five men before her present

A SECOND GALILEAN MINISTRY

Jesus with the Woman at the Well, *by Carl Heinrich Bloch*

male companion, her moral standing was considered the worst imaginable. We cannot easily think of a less likely candidate for spiritual conversion under normal circumstances than such a person, and her meeting with Jesus did not begin on an auspicious note" (in Jackson and Millet, *The Gospels*, 123–24).

John 4:10 "Living water" is a term full of meanings for ancient Israel. In the Near East water symbolizes life itself. Israel's prophets had repeatedly declared that the Lord was a fountain of living water (e.g., Jeremiah 2:13; Isaiah 8:6). Living water, or the "water of life," was also an important and powerful symbol in the Book of Mormon (see Alma 42:27).

John 4:11–12 The well today is more than one hundred feet deep, and most travelers do not carry a hundred-foot rope with them. The New International Version Study Bible noted: "When the present well was cleaned out in 1935, it was found to be 138 feet deep." Indeed, Jesus was greater than father Jacob who gave them the well.

John 4:13–15 There is a saying in the Near East, "From water comes all life." Water *is* life to citizens of the Near East, ancient and modern. Recent history has emphasized, even exaggerated, the importance of oil as a source of energy and as a political weapon, yet clearly the foremost issue in the Near East has always been and still is *water.*

The God of the Hebrews warned his people that, living as they were at the edge of the great deserts, they would have to be faithful to his commandments to be assured of a continuous supply of life-sustaining water. They knew that rain came not simply from the clouds but from heaven (Leviticus 26:3–4; Deuteronomy 11:10–17).

An effective and often used form of teaching in the ancient Near East was to illustrate something in human conduct with something in nature. Comparison was the heart of Semitic literary expression. Jesus compared the lifestyle he espoused to spiritual drink. Since water is so vital to body systems, it is an appropriate analogy to speak of drinking deeply from spiritual waters that satisfy the inner and eternal thirsts of man. "Whosoever drinketh of the water that I shall give him shall never thirst; but the water that I shall give him shall be in him a well of water springing up into everlasting life" (John 4:14). "He that believeth on me, . . . out of his belly shall flow rivers of living water" (John 7:38).

Cisterns and pools, artificial containers or reservoirs for storage of water from another source, are subject to stagnation and pollution. Wells, springs, and rivers, on the other hand, may be "living," that is, *flowing*—a continual supply of refreshing and life-giving water.

In modern revelation the Lord describes the living water, a reward for obedience, as a special endowment of knowledge, covenants, and ordinances: "Unto him that keepeth my commandments I will give the mysteries of my kingdom, and the same shall be in him a well of living water, springing up unto everlasting life" (D&C 63:23).

John 4:16–19 When Jesus revealed to the Samaritan woman privileged information concerning her past, her regard for him changed from "sir" to "prophet."

John 4:20–21 "This mountain" was Mount Gerizim, the holy mountain of the Samaritans and rival of the Jews' Mount Moriah in Jerusalem (see Appendix 1, 713).

True worship is not centered in a place but ultimately in a Person, even the everlasting Father.

John 4:22–23 The Samaritans did not have the true knowledge of God or proper practices for worship, the Savior said, though the Jews now did—for salvation is of the Jews. The word "salvation" in Hebrew is *Yeshua* (English, *Jesus*). Yeshua was a Jew, and salvation therefore sprang from the Jews. But, Jesus pointed out again, the time had come when true worshippers would worship the Father not so much in a certain place as in spirit and in truth.

John 4:24 The first phrase, "God is a Spirit," is perhaps better understood from the Joseph Smith Translation, as the Prophet rendered the teaching in perfect harmony with the surrounding text: "*For unto such hath God promised his Spirit. And they who worship him, must worship in spirit and in truth.*"

Yet even the King James Version translation of the Greek text is acceptable with proper understanding: "God is a spiritual Being" or "God *has* a spirit," just as Doctrine and Covenants 93:33 notes that "man is spirit." That isn't all he is, but man, too, has a spirit, and, in a sense, is a spiritual and eternal being. Stephen E. Robinson explains: "Actually John 4:24 should be translated 'God is Spirit' rather than 'God is *a* Spirit,' for there is no indefinite article (*a, an*) in the Greek language, and it is always a matter of subjective judgment as to when the translator should add one. The consensus among biblical scholars is that there should *not* be an indefinite article at John 4:24. C. H. Dodd insists that 'to translate [John 4:24]

"God is a Spirit" is the most gross perversion of the meaning'" (*Are Mormons Christians?* 80).

President Gordon B. Hinckley recounted an "occasion of more than 50 years ago when, as a missionary, I was speaking in an open-air meeting in Hyde Park, London. As I was presenting my message, a heckler interrupted to say, 'Why don't you stay with the doctrine of the Bible which says in John [4:24], "God is a Spirit"?'

"I opened my Bible to the verse he had quoted and read to him the entire verse: 'God is a Spirit: and they that worship him must worship him in spirit and in truth.'

"I said, 'Of course God is a spirit, and so are you, in the combination of spirit and body that makes of you a living being, and so am I.' . . .

"Jesus' declaration that God is a spirit no more denies that he has a body than does the statement that I am a spirit while also having a body" (*Ensign*, March 1998, 2).

John 4:25–26 The woman at the well expressed her understanding that the *Anointed One* was to come (Hebrew, *Mashiah;* Greek, *Christos*), and that when he had come he would teach all requisite things for salvation. Jesus then proclaimed, as the Greek text reads, "The One speaking to thee is I AM." In other words, Jesus said that he who was now talking with the woman was Jehovah, the great Creator of heaven and earth and he who gave the law to Moses on Mount Sinai. This is the first time in our present record that Jesus openly proclaimed himself to be the Messiah—and this proclamation was to a Samaritan woman at Jacob's Well. The next record of his testifying of the same truth is to his own people in his Holy House in Jerusalem (John 8:58).

John 4:27–30 The woman's estimation of Jesus had now progressed from "sir" to "prophet" to "Christ." Surely the only person who could properly and sincerely speak such things was the promised Messiah. Upon feeling this she naturally wanted to share her discovery with family and friends.

John 4:31–35 After Jesus' encounter with the Samaritan

A Second Galilean Ministry

woman at Jacob's Well, his disciples returned with food, and Jesus used the meal as a setting for a lesson, a teaching moment: "I have meat [food] to eat that ye know not of.... Say not ye, There are yet four months, and then cometh the harvest? Behold, I say unto you, Lift up your eyes, and look on the fields; for they are white already to harvest."

To this day, many of the fields along the road leading to Jacob's Well at ancient Shechem are planted with wheat. If there were yet four months to the harvest, Jesus must have journeyed through Samaria in late December or early January. Calling on his disciples to look out on the fields as they were ready to harvest was his way of suggesting that the harvest of humanity was ripe all around them, even among the Samaritans, and that they could thrust in their sickles and reap fruit leading to eternal life (John 4:36). The succeeding verses indicate that Jesus and his disciples did labor among the Samaritans, and many of them believed in him.

In all ages fields of labor are white (ripe), ready to harvest. In our own day the Lord has repeated: "For behold the field is white already to harvest; and lo, he that thrusteth in his sickle

A field that is "white already to harvest"

with his might, the same layeth up in store that he perisheth not, but bringeth salvation to his soul" (D&C 4:4).

John 4:37–38 The harvest is not the climax of a unilateral process. Rather, it is a team effort. "Herein is that saying true, one soweth, and another reapeth. I sent you to reap that whereon ye bestowed no labour: other men laboured, and ye are entered into their labors." There can be no boastful presumption of single-handedness in a harvest—many hands bring it to fruition. Even with the labor that human hands invest in the production process, in the end God is the One who puts the miracle together to consummate the harvest. Paul wrote, "I have planted, Apollos [his co-worker] watered; but God gave the increase" (1 Corinthians 3:6).

The King James Version reads, "other men laboured, and ye are entered into their labours" (v. 38), but the Joseph Smith Translation reads, "*the prophets have* labored and ye are entered into their labors" (JST John 4:40).

John 4:39–42 What a powerful lesson. Because of the testimony and actions of one person, many more received a witness of the truth. Here the pattern of missionary labors is disclosed. These Samaritans now gained their own personal witness that this Jew was indeed the long-anticipated Messiah, the Savior of the world. They recognized who he was, unlike his own in Nazareth, who rejected him (Luke 4).

JESUS RETURNS TO GALILEE AND PREACHES

Matthew 4:12, 17; Mark 1:14–15; Luke 4:14–15; John 4:43–45 Jesus continued on from Samaria into Galilee. He taught in the synagogues that the kingdom of God had arrived (footnote d to Matthew 4:17) and that all must repent. "Repent" is the first recorded word of the ministries of the Baptist and the Christ. It is the main message of any true ministry.

John 4:44–45 A prophet is not honored in his own country (see commentary on Luke 4:16–30). Jesus' countrymen of Galilee were impressed with what they saw Jesus do in Jerusalem at the feast, so they wanted to know more.

HEALING OF THE NOBLEMAN'S SON (AT CANA OF GALILEE)

John 4:46–54 The adverbs *up* and *down* may not register any particular importance to Westerners accustomed to driving vehicles in the modern world, but travel in the ancient world was arduous and fraught with danger. Elevation differences in the Holy Land were remembered with every footstep, and biblical writers referred constantly, even automatically, to those differences.

When Jesus was again in Cana of Galilee, a nobleman, or royal official (possibly of the court of Herod Antipas) from Capernaum came pleading for his dying son: "When [the nobleman] heard that Jesus was come out of Judea into Galilee, he went unto him, and besought him that he would come *down*, and heal his son. . . . The nobleman saith unto him, Sir, come *down* ere my child die." And later, "as he was now going *down*, his servants met him, and told him, saying, Thy son liveth" (John 4:47–51; emphasis added). Cana lies a few miles north of Nazareth at an elevation of about seven hundred feet *above* sea level; Capernaum is situated along the northern shore of the Sea of Galilee, at nearly seven hundred feet *below* sea level.

John 4:47–50 Jesus apparently tested the sick son's father by stating, as regards the natural tendency of humans, "Except ye see signs and wonders, ye will not believe." But this was a noble man, and his faith would not be deterred. The man's faith, combined with Jesus' power, would make his son whole. "Go thy way; thy son liveth," Jesus promised, and the man believed.

John 4:51–53 Upon hearing that his son was recovering, the nobleman inquired about the timing of his improvement and realized it was the very time that Jesus had reassured him. He and all his house were converted.

John 4:54 This was Jesus' second miracle (as recorded in our present New Testament). This one proved that distance was no obstacle to his miraculous, healing power. Jesus merely pronounced the word in Cana, and a boy twenty-five miles away in Capernaum was healed. And so it continues to be: The Savior, though physically distant from us, can still heal us.

JESUS REJECTED AT NAZARETH (AT NAZARETH OF GALILEE)

Luke 4:16–30 This scene constitutes the most detailed description from antiquity of a synagogue service (see Appendix 4, 755). As was his custom, Jesus attended the synagogue on the Sabbath day. He quoted a familiar messianic prophecy from the scroll of Isaiah (61:1–2), closed it up, returned it to the minister or attendant, and then sat down to give commentary. The commentary was pure and simple: the scripture was being fulfilled by him.

Knowing what their reaction would be as they incredulously puzzled over who this hometown boy was claiming to be, Jesus gave them to understand that their disbelief would obstruct any miracles on their behalf, and he expressed the axiom, No prophet is accepted in his own country. After he angered the people by saying that other prophets in the northern regions of the land, namely Elijah and Elisha, had also been unable to invoke miraculous blessings on their own unbelieving people, the pious synagogue attendees of Nazareth led Jesus out to a nearby hill and tried to cast him off to his death. He escaped and went down to continue his ministry at Capernaum.

Mark added, "A prophet is not without honour, but in his

own country, and among his own kin, and in his own house" (Mark 6:4). The verse indicates that some of Jesus' own relatives and family members did not accept at that time his claim to divinity. "For neither did his brethren believe in him" (John 7:5).

Luke 4:18–19 The words that Jesus had given to Isaiah over seven centuries earlier, and which now He cited, contained prophecies with dramatic messianic implications:

"The Spirit of the Lord is upon me, because he hath anointed me [Hebrew, *Mashiah,* and Greek, *Christos,* both mean 'Anointed One']

"To preach the gospel to the poor [he preached to the poor in spirit; Matthew 5:3; 3 Nephi 12:3];

"He hath sent me to heal the broken-hearted [he healed not only the physically sick and maimed but also those who were emotionally broken and wounded, the broken-hearted],

"To preach deliverance to the captives [spiritually captive souls in this world and in the spirit world; 1 Peter 3:19; D&C 138:8, 31],

"And recovering of sight to the blind [both the physically and spiritually blind],

"To set at liberty them that are bruised [he would offer to liberate those who were physically, spiritually, and emotionally bruised],

"To preach the acceptable year of the Lord [the acceptable year or the acceptable day of the Lord is the time salvation is offered to the souls of men; D&C 93:51; 138:31]."

Luke 4:23 "Physician, heal thyself." The hometown people seem to be saying, Master Healer, start here on home terrain, and heal yourself, and then let us see some of those miraculous healings we've heard about from Capernaum. They apparently thought there was something wrong in Jesus that needed correcting rather than in themselves.

Luke 4:25–26 Jesus referred to a historical episode in the days of Elijah the prophet (*Elias* is the Greek form of *Elijah*) recorded in 1 Kings 17:1–10. The condition described as the "heaven was shut up" is the precursor to most famines. Other causes, such as prolonged military sieges, diseases, or pestilence brought on by insects, especially locusts, could result in famine, but the usual cause in Bible lands was drought—heaven (not the sky, but *heaven*) was shut. Elijah made it clear that heaven could be opened again through humble faithfulness. Meanwhile, he was cared for by a widow outside of Israel, a Gentile with greater faith than the widows of Israel.

Luke 4:27 Jesus reminded his townspeople of another historical episode involving Elijah's successor, Elisha, who cleansed a Syrian army officer who had more faith than did Elisha's fellow Israelites (2 Kings 5:1–14).

Luke 4:30 Jesus had the ability to disappear, to pass unnoticed through a crowd of people. Compare also Jesus in the Temple (John 8:59).

Matthew 4:13–16 The land of Zebulun is Nazareth and vicinity. The land of Naphtali is the region around the Sea of Galilee.

Matthew referred to Isaiah 9:1–2, a messianic prophecy (using future perfect tense verbs as if the prophecy had already been fulfilled): the people who walked in the darkness of apostasy, those who lived in the land of the shadow of death (where the ancient armies of the Near East marched through), have seen the great Light, the Messiah. Jesus is the literal fulfillment of the prophecy.

Isaiah's description of "people that walked in darkness" and "dwell in the shadow of death" suggests their living in the darkness of sin and apostasy. There is also physical significance to the image. The Galilee is covered with dark volcanic basalt spewed all over the region by several now-extinct volcanoes on the Golan east of the lake, and the black stone casts a dark shadow across the land.

The people that dwell in the shadow of death are all mortals who live on this earth. We live with the shadow of death hanging over us, and it is a dark thing to us, able to be dispelled only by the Light of life.

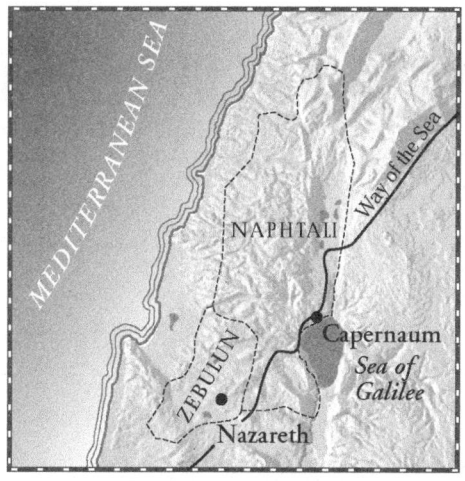

The regions of Zebulun and Naphtali in Galilee and the Way of the Sea (Via Maris)

Matthew 4:15 "Galilee of the Gentiles." When the region of Galilee first appeared in historical records (in the annals of Pharaoh Thutmose III), it was not Jewish but a conglomeration of Amorites and Canaanites. Perhaps this is the rationale behind the expression "Galilee of the gentiles" or "Galilee of the nations" (Isaiah 9:1; Greek, *Galilaia ton ethnon*).

REMOVAL TO CAPERNAUM

Matthew 4:13 Jesus left Nazareth and went down to live in Capernaum, on the northern shore of the Sea of Galilee. He probably took his family with him—that is, Mary and her children by Joseph. Joseph himself had likely died, as there is no more mention in the Gospels of him alive.

Luke 4:31–32 The people at Capernaum were astonished at Jesus' doctrine because he spoke authoritatively. He was the ultimate source. "His word was with power" because he was filled with the Spirit. The Holy Ghost can endow mortals with power while speaking of the Word (cf. Micah 3:8; Luke 24:49; Acts 1:8; 1 Nephi 2:14; 2 Nephi 33:1–2; Words of Mormon 1:17).

Aerial view of Capernaum

CASTING OUT AN UNCLEAN SPIRIT (AT CAPERNAUM)

Mark 1:21–28; Luke 4:33–37 Jesus performed basically four categories of miracles: healing the sick (the most common), subduing the elements, casting out devils, and raising the dead (the most unusual and dramatic); in fact, Jesus' greatest miracle of all was raising *himself* from the dead, not to live as a mortal again for a time but to living immortality (see Hunter, Conference Report, April 1986, 18). We have already seen an example of healing (the nobleman's son) and power over the elements (water to wine); now comes the first recorded episode of casting out an unclean spirit.

The setting was the synagogue at Capernaum. As Jesus taught, the people were astounded at his doctrine, not so much because it was extraordinarily different but because he taught as one who had authority himself, not having to constantly cite the rabbis of old for authority, as the scribes did (see commentary on Matthew 7:29).

One man in the synagogue was possessed of an evil, or

A Second Galilean Ministry

unclean, spirit, and that spirit cried out: "Let us alone; what have we to do with thee, Jesus thou Son of God? art thou come to destroy us?" before the final casting out (see commentary on Matthew 8:29). Even the devils themselves know who the Savior is and can testify of him. Jesus silenced the evil spirit and cast him out. Before, the people were impressed with Jesus' teaching; now they were impressed with his miraculous power—even spirits from the other realm obey him. His fame went before him.

Joseph Smith recorded the first miracle in the restored Church, casting out an evil spirit, as follows: "Amongst those who attended our meetings regularly, was Newel Knight, son of Joseph Knight. . . . We had got into the habit of praying much at our meetings, and Newel had said that he would try . . . but when we again met together, he rather excused himself. I tried to prevail upon him. . . . He replied . . . he would wait until he could get into the woods by himself, and there he would pray. Accordingly, he deferred praying until next morning, when he retired into the woods; where, according to his own account afterwards, he made several attempts to pray, but could scarcely do so. . . . He began to feel uneasy, and continued to feel worse both in mind and body, until, upon reaching his own house, his appearance was such as to alarm his wife very much. He requested her to go and bring me to him. I went and found him suffering very much in his mind, and his body acted upon in a very strange manner; his visage and limbs distorted and twisted in every shape and appearance possible to imagine; and finally he was caught up off the floor of the apartment, and tossed about most fearfully.

"His situation was soon made known to his neighbors and relatives, and in a short time as many as eight or nine grown persons had got together to witness the scene. After he had thus suffered for a time, I succeeded in getting hold of him by the hand, when almost immediately he spoke to me, and with great earnestness requested me to cast the devil out of him,

THE MIRACLES OF JESUS

	Matthew	Mark	Luke	John
RAISING THE DEAD				
1. Son of the widow of Nain			7:11–17	
2. Daughter of Jairus	9:18–26	5:22–43	8:41–56	
3. Lazarus				11:1–46
CASTING OUT DEVILS				
1. Unclean spirit		1:21–28	4:31–37	
2. Blind and dumb demoniac	12:22–23			
3. Two demoniacs (or one)	8:28–34	5:1–20	8:26–39	
4. Dumb demoniac	9:32–34			
5. Demoniac—disciples fail	17:14–21	9:14–29	9:37–43	
6. A dumb devil			11:14–26	
ASSERTING POWER OVER THE ELEMENTS				
1. Water to wine				2:1–11
2. Jesus leaves unseen			4:28–30	8:59
3. Catch of fish			5:1–11	
4. Storm stilled	8:23–27	4:35–41	8:22–25	
5. Five thousand fed	14:15–21	6:33–44	9:10–17	6:1–14
6. Jesus walks on the sea	14:23–33	6:47–52		6:15–21
7. Four thousand fed	15:29–38	8:1–9		
8. Tribute money in the fish	17:24–27			
9. Barren fig tree cursed	21:18–21	11:12–21	13:6–9	
10. Great haul of fish				21:6–14

	Matthew	Mark	Luke	John
HEALING THE SICK				
1. Nobleman's son				4:46–54
2. Peter's wife's mother	8:14–15	1:29–31	4:38–39	
3. Multitudes	8:16–17	1:32–34	4:40–41	
4. A leper	8:1–4	1:40–45	5:12–15	
5. One sick with palsy	9:2–8	2:1–12	5:17–26	
6. Infirmity of 38 years				5:1–16
7. Man with withered hand	12:9–13	3:1–5	6:6–10	
8. Centurion's servant	8:5–13		7:2–10	
9. Woman with issue of blood	9:20–22	5:25–34	8:43–48	
10. Two blind men	9:27–31			
11. Healed—touch of garment	14:34–36	6:53–56		
12. Daughter of Greek woman	15:21–28	7:25–30		
13. Deaf with speech problem		7:32–37		
14. Blind man		8:22–26		
15. Man born blind				9:1–41
16. Ten lepers			17:11–19	
17. Bartimaeus, blind beggar	20:29–34	10:46–52	18:35–43	
18. Ear of Malchus restored			22:50–51	

Calling of the Fishermen, *by Harry Anderson*

saying that he knew he was in him, and that he also knew that I could cast him out.

"I replied, 'If you know that I can, it shall be done;' and then almost unconsciously I rebuked the devil, and commanded him in the name of Jesus Christ to depart from him; when immediately Newel spoke out and said that he saw the devil leave him and vanish from his sight. This was the first miracle which was done in the Church, or by any member of it; and it was done not by man, nor by the power of man, but it was done by God, and by the power of godliness" (*History of the Church,* 1:82).

FISHERMEN CALLED TO BE FISHERS OF MEN (AT THE SEA OF GALILEE)

Matthew 4:18–22; Mark 1:16–20 Jesus called his first two apostles from among the rugged fishermen working the lake in Galilee. They were the brothers Simon Peter and

Andrew, sons of a man named Jonah (Matthew 16:17). When Jesus caught their attention, they were casting a net into the lake (see Appendix 7, 774). Jesus chose these future leaders while they were working.

Jesus changed the fishermen's life in a single sentence: "*I am he of whom it is written by the prophets;* follow me, and I will make you fishers of men" (JST Matthew 4:18).

The Savior had dramatic and immediate impact on the souls of these men: they left their nets and their business and committed their lives into his hands (Luke 18:28; cf. Luke 5:11, 28). They left what was apparently a lucrative business; Peter owned a boat (Luke 5:3), nets and other equipment, and a home in Capernaum (Luke 4:38).

Matthew 4:21–22 Two other brothers were then called: James (Hebrew, *Ya'akov;* English, *Jacob;* Smith, *Teachings of the Prophet Joseph Smith,* 349) and John, sons of a man named Zebedee. The sons of Jonah and the sons of Zebedee (and likely both fathers) were all fishermen. They were all sent to earth to Galilee to learn how to work hard and to be available for the momentous call to serve as fishers of men.

PROCLAMATION OF THE GOSPEL IN GALILEE: THE FIRST TOUR

Matthew 4:23–24 Jesus traveled throughout the region of Galilee, teaching in the synagogues. He must have had some credentials that opened the way for use of all the local synagogues as a locale for preaching. He didn't just promulgate the old law, however. He taught "the gospel of the kingdom," and he healed people who suffered from all kinds of sicknesses and diseases, at least those who *"believed on his name"* (JST Matthew 4:22).

His fame went throughout all Syria, meaning the regions north and northeast of the Holy Land.

Verse 24 describes the ailments of those healed: divers

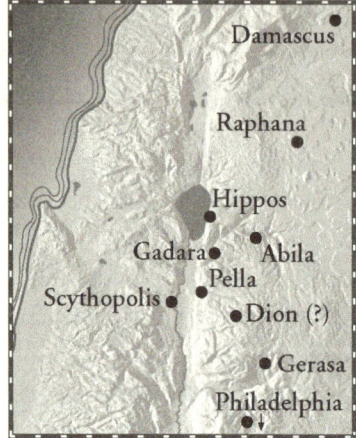
The ten cities of the Decapolis

(various, diverse) diseases and torments, those possessed with devils and those with mental illness, and those with some form of paralysis (palsy); compare King Benjamin's list of Jesus' miraculous healings given over a century before His coming into mortality (Mosiah 3:5–6).

Matthew 4:25 Multitudes of people gathered to Jesus from all parts of the Levant, the eastern Mediterranean coastal lands:

Galilee—his own home region

Decapolis—an association of ten Greek cities (*deca*, "ten," and *polis*, "city") to the east and southeast of Galilee, cities with a predominantly Greek or Hellenistic culture. Although his brief mission was reserved generally only for the Jews, Jesus did travel and perform miracles among the Greeks, some of whom became disciples. The ten cities included Damascus, Raphana, Dion, Hippos (Hebrew, *Susita*), Gadara, Scythopolis (formerly called Beth-shean), Pella, Gerasa (today's Jerash), Philadelphia (today's Amman), and Abila or Canatha.

Jerusalem—the Jewish capital of the land

Judea—the heart of the Jewish homeland

Perea—the words "beyond Jordan" are in Greek *Perea*. Because all place-names in this verse are regional names (besides Jerusalem), it follows that "beyond Jordan" is also a regional name. Both Galilee and Perea were provinces ruled by Herod Antipas. Antipas incarcerated John the Baptist and put him to death in the prison-fortress of Machaerus in southern Perea.

Mark 1:35–39; Luke 4:42–44 Jesus sometimes began his day by rising early and finding a solitary place to pray. That would be a happy habit for us to develop. Elsewhere Jesus said, "The works which ye have seen me do that shall ye also do" (3 Nephi 27:21).

Rising early in the morning seems to be a habit developed by many of the noble and great ones. "Abraham rose up early in the morning" (Genesis 22:3); "Moses rose up early in the morning" (Exodus 34:4); and Job "rose up early in the morning" (Job 1:5); and again, Jesus rose up early in the morning because the scripture notes that "all the people came early in the morning to him in the temple" (Luke 21:38); Mary Magdalene, Mary the mother of James, and Salome came to Jesus' sepulchre "very early in the morning" (Mark 16:2; Luke 24:1). In our day the Lord has given us these words of temporal wisdom: "Cease to sleep longer than is needful; retire to thy bed early, that ye may not be weary; arise early, that your bodies and your minds may be invigorated" (D&C 88:124). Elder Boyd K. Packer wrote: "I have learned that the best time to wrestle with major problems is early in the morning. Our minds are then fresh and alert. The blackboards of our minds have been erased by a good night's sleep. The accumulated distractions of the day are not in our way. Our bodies have been rested also. That is the time to think something through carefully and to receive personal revelation. . . . I heard President Harold B. Lee begin many a statement about matters involving revelation with an expression something like this: 'In the early hours of the morning, while I was pondering upon that subject . . . ' He made it a practice to work in the fresh, alert hours of the early morning on the problems that required revelation. . . . I counsel our children to do their critical studying in the early hours of the morning when they're

Reenactment of a scene from the life of Jesus (Genesis Project, 1978), filmed near Magdala on the western shore of the Sea of Galilee

fresh and alert, rather than to fight physical weariness and mental exhaustion at night. I've learned the power of the dictum, 'Early to bed, early to rise.' When I'm under pressure, you won't find me burning the midnight oil. I'd much rather be in bed early and getting up in the wee hours of the morning, when I can be close to Him who guides this work" (*Teach Ye Diligently*, 204–5).

During his three-year mission, Jesus repeatedly and deliberately set aside hours of solitude in which he prayed to Heavenly Father and rejuvenated his spirit. "And when it was day, he departed and went into a desert place" (Luke 4:42). "And he withdrew himself into the wilderness, and prayed" (Luke 5:16). "And he withdrew himself into a mountain to pray, and continued all night in prayer to God" (Luke 6:12). Compare also Matthew 14:23; 17:1; 26:36; John 6:15. Although he was incessantly pressed upon by multitudes and many times forced to go without food and sleep, in key moments he would find solitude and commune with his Father in preparation for more spiritual labor.

A SECOND GALILEAN MINISTRY

Jesus did not attempt to accomplish his great purposes alone. Frequently he turned to the Twelve and the Seventy, preparing them and delegating to them part of the responsibility. "And he took them, and went aside privately into a desert place" (Luke 9:10). He also prepared leaders among the leaders: "He took Peter and John and James, and went up into a mountain to pray" (Luke 9:28).

As his fame increased, people everywhere sought him. And he went to them. That is why he came to earth, to teach and influence as many as possible. That is also one of the reasons we came here.

DISCOURSE FROM A BOAT
(ON THE SEA OF GALILEE)

Luke 5:1–3 The crowd pressed upon Jesus at the Sea of Galilee, here called by its alternate name, the lake of Gennesaret. *Gennesaret* is the Greek adaptation of the Old Testament name *Chinnereth* (Numbers 34:11); it is therefore

A first-century boat is visible in a mosaic found on the western shore of the Sea of Galilee

related to modern *Kinneret*, the name Israelis use for the lake today.

Two ships were anchored just offshore, one of them belonging to Simon Peter. Jesus entered Peter's boat, thrust it out from the shore a little, and sat down to teach the people gathered on the shore.

PETER CALLED TO CATCH MEN; HIS HEART TOUCHED (AT THE SEA OF GALILEE)

Luke 5:4–11 More than once Jesus instructed his fishermen disciples to cast their nets into a different spot from where they were fishing, and they were provided an overabundance of fish, "and their net brake" (Luke 5:6). Commercial fishing was and still is sometimes done at night (see Appendix 7, 774). The fish school nearer the surface of the lake at night and remain deeper during the warmth of the day, making miraculous catches of fish during the day all the more unusual (Luke 5:5–6; John 21:3–6). Incidentally, the word *draught* in verse 4 is a Renaissance English word that describes a sweeping motion with a net for "drawing out" a catch of fish.

Luke 5:7–9 It was an almost humorous scene: both ships filled with an overwhelming haul of fish, and both beginning to sink. But Peter recognized the miraculous power that Jesus had over all living things and was humbled by it, and he felt unworthy even to be in His presence.

Luke 5:10–11 Peter and his partners in their fishing business, James and John, were called to "catch men" and bring them into the "gospel net." They forsook all and followed him. (This is Luke's parallel account to Matthew 4:18–22; Mark 1:16–20.)

Jesus called his first disciples while they were working. Notice the contrast: "Satan selects his disciples when they are idle; Jesus selected his when they were busy at their work" (Longden, Conference Report, April 1966, 39).

HEALING OF THE LEPER (IN GALILEE)

Matthew 8:2–4; Mark 1:40–45; Luke 5:12–15 Leprosy is an infectious disease, almost a living death, where the skin literally flakes off the bones. "It began with little specks on the eyelids, and on the palms of the hand, and gradually spread over different parts of the body, bleaching the hair white wherever it showed itself, crusting the affected parts with shining scales, and causing swellings and sores. From the skin it slowly ate its way through the tissues, to the bones and joints and even to the marrow, rotting the whole body piecemeal. The lungs, the organs of speech and hearing, and the eyes were attacked in turn, till, at last, consumption or dropsy brought welcome death" (Geikie, *Life and Words of Christ*, 390–91).

It was not necessarily communicable by touch; at least Jesus was not afraid to touch the leprous man, especially

Lepers in nineteenth-century Jerusalem

THE ORIGINAL TWELVE APOSTLES

Given Name	Other Names, Special Meanings	Personal Details
Simon Peter	*Shimon bar Yonah* (son of a man named Jonah); *Cephas* (Aramaic) or *Petros* (Greek) meaning "stone" or "rock" (see John 1:42). Along with James and John, the "First Presidency"; appeared together to Joseph Smith in 1829.	Brother of Andrew, from Bethsaida; independent householder in Capernaum, married, prosperous fishing business with Andrew, James, and John; impulsive, impetuous; his death prefigured; tradition—crucified upside down in Rome.
James	Hebrew *Ya'akov*. He and his brother John called *Boanerges,* "sons of thunder" (wanted to call down fire on Samaritans, wanted to be highest in the kingdom).	Son of Zebedee, brother of John (Matthew 4:21); first martyr apostle, beheaded by Herod Agrippa (see Acts 12).
John	Hebrew *Yohanan,* meaning "God is gracious (or merciful)." Called "the Beloved," "the Revelator."	Son of Zebedee, brother of James (Matthew 4:21); role in Last Supper and at Golgotha; wrote the Gospel; now translated being; only apostle mentioned by name in Book of Mormon.
Andrew	Greek *Andreas,* meaning "manly."	Son of Jonah; Peter's brother (Matthew 4:18).
Philip	Greek name meaning "lover of horses."	From Bethsaida, as were Peter, Andrew.
Nathanael	Hebrew name meaning "gift of God" (see meaning of *Matthew,* below). Otherwise called Bartholomew.	*Bar Tolmai:* son of a man named Tolmai; from Cana; Jesus said, "Behold an Israelite . . . in whom is no guile" (John 1:47).
Thomas	Greek *Didymus* means the same as his Aramaic name, *Thomas:* "twin" (see John 20:24).	"Doubting" Thomas? It was Thomas who said, "Let us also go, that we may die with him" (John 11:16).
Matthew	Also called Levi (priestly lineage?); Greek *Matthias* is short form of *Mattathias,* same as Hebrew *Mattithyah,* "gift of God."	Son of Alphæus (Mark 2:14); brother of James? former publican; wrote the Gospel.
James	Often called "the less" to distinguish him from the other James.	Son of Alphæus (Matthew 10:3; Mark 3:18; Luke 6:15; Acts 1:13); brother of Matthew?
Jude	Hebrew *Yehuda* or *Judah,* or Greek *Judas.* Also called Lebbæus and Thaddæus.	Sometimes called "not Iscariot" to distinguish him from the traitor Judas.
Simon	Called "the Canaanite" (Matthew 10:4) or *Zelotes,* "the Zealot" (Luke 6:15).	Apparently a former Zealot, advocate of violent overthrow of Roman rule.
Judas	Called Iscariot: Hebrew *ish Kerioth* means man from (the Judean village of) Kerioth (see Joshua 15:25).	The only Judean, other eleven from Galilee; treasurer of Quorum; betrayed Jesus; died by suicide.
Matthias	A follower before his call, later added to Quorum (Acts 1:21–26).	

A Second Galilean Ministry

because of his power over disease. He rewarded the leper's faith by cleansing him totally of his leprosy. Then he instructed him not to broadcast what had happened far and wide but to keep the sacred event quiet. One thing the former leper had to do, though, according to the Mosaic law, was show himself to the priest and offer the prescribed offering (Leviticus 13–14).

After performing a number of different miracles, such as healing this leper, raising the synagogue ruler's daughter (Luke 8:56), curing the blind man (Matthew 9:30), healing the deaf and speech-impaired man in the Decapolis (Mark 7:31–36) and another blind man, (Mark 8:26), and the Transfiguration (Matthew 17:9; Mark 9:9), Jesus cautioned those involved not to tell people what had happened and who he was. After Peter's dramatic witness of the divine Sonship at Caesarea Philippi, Jesus "charged his disciples that they should tell no man that he was Jesus the Christ" (Matthew 16:20); "he charged them that they should tell no man of him" (Mark 8:30). It was wise to wait until "his time had come" and not stir up excessive opposition prematurely.

Mark's account of this cleansing of the leper notes that the beneficiary could not contain his gratitude and adoration and "went out, and began to publish it much, and to blaze abroad the matter" (Mark 1:45), causing Jesus to have to be more cautious and concerned about accusatory and apprehensive enemies lurking in the cities.

Jesus performed this miraculous healing because he was "moved with compassion" (Mark 1:41). Matthew, Mark, and Luke, while recording the miracles of Jesus, frequently note that Jesus was filled with compassion for the physical, mental, emotional, and spiritual ailments of his people (Matthew 9:36; 14:14; 20:34; Mark 5:19; 6:34; Luke 7:13; see also Mosiah 15:9; 3 Nephi 17:6).

Though Jesus encouraged the recipients of his compassionate healing power to keep the miracles quiet, to maintain a low profile, yet all the more his fame spread abroad and more and more people came to be healed.

President Spencer W. Kimball commented on this "tell no man" phenomenon: "I have been impressed at the number of times the Lord said, 'Go thy way and tell no man.' And I have been led many times in my blessings—when I felt there was going to be special healing, and that they were such people as would go out and shout it from the housetops—to say, 'And when you are healed, tell no man who laid his hands upon your head.' I think that takes away from me the temptation to want to be spectacular, or to want praise, or to want credit, and from them the urge to publish a sacred, intimate miracle. That relieves me. It leaves me more humble and I am sure then I am in a better position to call down the blessings of the Lord again" (*Teachings of Spencer W. Kimball*, 234–35).

TWELVE CALLED AND ORDAINED (IN GALILEE)

Matthew 10:1–4; Mark 3:13–19; Luke 6:12–16 An effective leader surrounds himself with other strong, dynamic leaders. Jesus called, trained, empowered, and sent forth twelve men who would further the Father's work on earth. (He did the same among his people on the western hemisphere; 3 Nephi 12.) The Twelve were known as apostles (Hebrew, *tashlikhim;* Greek, *apostolos*), meaning "those who are sent forth." Even Christ is called an apostle (Hebrews 3:1) because he was sent forth by the Father. The apostles were sent out to do as the Master did: teach, cast out evil and unclean spirits, heal all kinds of sicknesses and diseases, and later perform sacred priesthood ordinances, including conferral of the gift of the Holy Ghost.

Before Jesus called the Twelve together as a quorum, to be ordained and formally begin their training, he "went out into a mountain to pray, and continued all night in prayer to God" (Luke 6:12). Then, by divine guidance and premortal knowledge, he selected the Twelve. Their names, with various

A SECOND GALILEAN MINISTRY

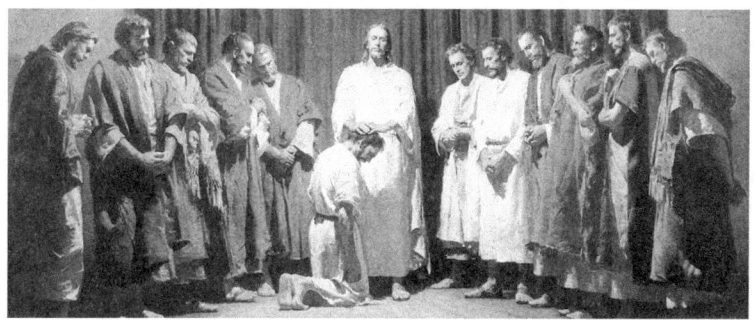

Christ Ordaining the Apostles, *by Harry Anderson*

interesting details, are listed in the Synoptic Gospels (Matthew 10:2–4; Mark 3:16–19; Luke 6:14–16) and in the book of Acts (1:13).

Mark 3:17 James and John, sons of Zebedee, were also surnamed by Jesus "sons of thunder" (Greek, *Boanerges,* with possible meanings of impetuosity or hot temper). James and John wanted to call down fire from heaven and destroy some Samaritans who failed to respond to Jesus (Luke 9:54). Alternatively, in a more positive vein, the label "sons of thunder" could refer to their propensity toward vigor, dynamism, and boldness.

Matthew 10:4; Mark 3:18 The term *Canaanite* appears twice in the New Testament, referring to an apostle named "Simon the Canaanite," otherwise called "Simon Zelotes" (Luke 6:15; Acts 1:13). The word *Canaanite,* or *Cananean* in this case, refers not to nationality or geographical origin but derives from the Aramaic word *qan'an,* meaning zealous. Simon may have been a Zealot, which was a group active in opposing Roman rule (see Appendix 4, 756).

Ten men named Simon are mentioned in the New Testament, so they are usually differentiated with a surname or other designation: Simon Peter (Matthew 4:18); Simon Zelotes (Matthew 10:4; Luke 6:15); Simon, half brother of Jesus (Matthew 13:55); Simon the leper (Matthew 26:6); Simon of Cyrene (Matthew 27:32); Simon, father of Judas

Iscariot (John 6:71); Simon the sorcerer (Acts 8:9); Simon the tanner (Acts 9:43; the name Simeon is the same as Simon; cf. Acts 15:14); Simeon, the Temple worker (Luke 2:25); and Simeon called Niger (Acts 13:1).

The two Simons among the Twelve have additional names to help distinguish them.

Luke 6:16 At least six men in the New Testament are known as Judah or Judas or Jude (all the same name); they are normally referred to with other distinguishing nomenclature or attributes: Judah, son of Jacob or Israel (Matthew 1:2; Hebrews 8:8); Judas Iscariot (Matthew 10:4); Judas, half brother of Jesus, brother of James, also called Jude (Matthew 13:55; Luke 6:16; Acts 1:13; Jude 1:1); Judas of Galilee, a political agitator (Acts 5:37; Judas of Damascus (Acts 9:11); Judas Barsabas (Acts 15:22, 27, 32).

Judas the betrayer was often designated by reference to his hometown. Iscariot derives from *ish Kerioth*, literally "man from Kerioth," a village in southern Judah (Joshua 15:25). All the apostles were from Galilee except one, this man named Judas from Kerioth in the tribal land of Judah.

Ironically, it was the original Judah (son of Jacob/Israel) who proposed selling his brother Joseph for the price of a slave (Genesis 37:26–28). Later, another man named Judah (Judas Iscariot) was responsible for selling Jesus for the price of a slave (Matthew 27:3, 9).

CHARGE TO THE TWELVE (IN GALILEE)

Matthew 10:5–42 In our day the Lord sent out the Twelve Apostles, "first unto the Gentiles and then unto the Jews" (D&C 107:35). In Jesus' day the reverse was true: Jesus charged his apostles not to go (yet) to the Gentiles, meaning the Greeks, Romans, Samaritans, and others but rather to dedicate their efforts first to the lost sheep of the house of

A Second Galilean Ministry

Israel. The message was simple: the kingdom of heaven has come.

Matthew 10:8–10 (cf. Mark 6:7–9; Luke 9:1–3) Jesus trained the Twelve and gave them specific instructions. They were to go two by two (cf. Luke 10:1; D&C 42:6) and show forth the power of God as they had seen him do, by healing the sick, cleansing the lepers, raising the dead, and casting out devils. The apostles had received the power; now it was their turn to give. And they would have sacred experiences that would allow them to say, "I know." And when they said "I know," it carried the weight of sacred testimony they could not openly talk about.

On the unique role of those called as special witnesses of Christ in all the world, Elder Boyd K. Packer wrote:

"We do not talk of those sacred interviews that qualify the servants of the Lord to bear a special witness of Him, for we have been commanded not to do so.

"But we are free, indeed, we are obliged, to bear that special witness. . . .

"Like all of my Brethren, I too come from among the ordinary people of the Church. I am the seventy-eighth man to be accepted by ordination into the Quorum of the Twelve Apostles in this dispensation.

"Compared to the others who have been called, I am nowhere near their equal, save it be, perhaps, in the certainty of the witness we share.

"I feel compelled . . . to certify to you that I know that the day of miracles has not ceased. I know that angels minister unto men.

"I am a witness to the truth that Jesus is the Christ, the Son of God, the Only Begotten of the Father; that He has a body of flesh and bone; that He knows those who are His servants here and that He is known of them" (*Ensign,* May 1980 65).

Shepherds' equipment is mentioned in connection with supplies normally taken on journeys but which the Lord commanded his apostles not to take on their missions. The staff (plural, staves) was a long stick used for a variety of purposes: maneuvering through the rocky hill country, controlling movement of sheep, and even using as a weapon when necessary. The scrip was a small leather bag used to carry food and other provisions. It was often distinguished from the purse, which carried money. Those sent on missions were discouraged from taking staff, scrip, shoes, bread, money, or two coats. Instead of providing for all their own needs, they were to trust in God for vital provisions.

The apostles, as they went out, were not to be concerned for their temporal needs; they were not to worry about where their next meal would come from, what they would wear, or where they would sleep; while they were in the service of the Lord, their temporal needs would be met by others. The Lord repeated the same instruction to his servants in the latter days, explaining also the means for provision: "Take no purse nor scrip, neither staves, neither two coats [symbolic of provision and security], for *the church shall give unto thee in the very hour what thou needest for food and for raiment, and for shoes and for money, and for scrip*" (D&C 24:18; emphasis added).

"For the workman is worthy of his meat" (elsewhere rendered, "the labourer is worthy of his hire"; Luke 10:7). Apostles, members of the Seventy, missionaries, or whoever is sent out must always be worthy of all that others provide for them temporally, so that they can dedicate full time to the Lord's service.

These instructions were given to missionaries, those in full-time service of the Lord. The regular members are taught, in some cases, quite the opposite: be concerned about temporal sustenance, clothing, housing, getting out of debt, getting an education, working to support the family, living providently, and building up the family's food storage. Full-time servants were not to be preoccupied with temporal matters, but full-time members were supposed to be concerned also with the temporal.

A Second Galilean Ministry

Staff, purse, and scrip

Matthew 10:11–15 (cf. Mark 6:10–13; Luke 9:4–6) Similar counsel is given in modern revelation: "And in whatsoever place ye shall enter, and they receive you not in my name, ye shall leave a cursing instead of a blessing, by casting off the dust of your feet against them as a testimony, and cleansing your feet by the wayside" (D&C 24:15; cf. 60:15; 75:20; 84:92). Testifying against anyone is a terrifying responsibility, and the ordinance of cursing should be applied only under the Lord's specific command through his authorized servants. "No curse should ever be decreed except by direct revelation from the Lord commanding such to be done" (McConkie, *Doctrinal New Testament Commentary*, 2:123).

Matthew 10:16 True followers of the Lord Jesus Christ, even his leaders, are humble and submissive—as sheep or lambs (Luke 10:3). But they are sent out into the midst of wolves. Wolves represent unworthy persons, those attempting to destroy the flock of God (his Church and its members). "Behold, I send you forth as sheep in the midst of wolves," Jesus told his apostles. All New Testament uses of the wolf are in a figurative context, carrying the deeper, underlying meaning of fierce apostates and antagonists determined to harm the sheep of his fold. "Beware of false prophets, which come to you in sheep's clothing, but inwardly they are ravening wolves" (Matthew 7:15). "He that is an hireling, and not the shepherd, whose own the sheep are not, seeth the wolf coming, and leaveth the sheep, and fleeth: and the wolf catcheth them, and scattereth the sheep" (John 10:12; cf. Alma 5:59). "For I know this, that after my departing shall grievous wolves enter in among you, not sparing the flock" (Acts 20:29).

To the serpent was attributed the characteristic of cunning, and since early history, doves have symbolized peace, purity, and innocence. True followers and leaders must be wise as serpents and harmless as doves. (The Prophet Joseph Smith changed this verse to read that the Lord wants us to be "wise *servants,* and *as* harmless as doves"; JST Matthew 10:14.)

Matthew 10:17–18 Warning: Watch out for crafty and deceitful men. The apostles would be delivered up to councils, like the Sanhedrin, and they would be ill treated in synagogues. They would encounter serious opposition and persecution, even to being arraigned before political rulers, on account of the apostles' taking upon themselves the Savior's name and power in order to bear witness before Israelites and Gentiles (*goyim,* pronounced go-YEEM, are the non-Jewish people throughout the world). Paul, for example, was given the specific commission "to bear my name before the Gentiles, and kings" (Acts 9:15).

Matthew 10:19–20; Mark 13:11; Luke 12:11–12 When the apostles found themselves before political rulers or religious leaders, they were not to be overanxious about how or what they should speak: "For it shall be given you in that same hour what ye shall speak" (Matthew 10:19). Extending the teaching to ourselves, does that mean that we should not prepare our talks or think in advance about what we might say in a testimony? Surely the Lord does not mean for us to be negligent in preparation; he wants us to be constantly preparing—allowing the solemnities of eternity to be ever flowing in us, to be regularly and consistently storing up and treasuring the word, so that when the moment comes, when the occasion calls for it, the Spirit can speak through us. If you have done your spiritual homework and treasured up the words of Christ, then "the Holy Ghost shall teach you in the same hour what ye ought to say" (Luke 12:12). Doctrine and Covenants 84:85 explains: "Neither take ye thought beforehand what ye shall say; but treasure up in your minds continually the words of life, and it shall be given you in the very hour that portion that shall be meted [given] unto every man." As the Lord long before said to Moses, "I will be with thy mouth, and teach thee what thou shalt say" (Exodus 4:12).

Elder Boyd K. Packer wrote, "On one occasion in a meeting I heard President Marion G. Romney say, 'I always know when I am speaking under the inspiration of the Holy Ghost because I always learn something from what I've said'" (*Teach Ye Diligently*, 357).

Matthew 10:21–23; Mark 13:12–13 The gospel message taught by the apostles would have the effect of causing divisiveness even among family members (see Matthew 10:34–36).

As they went forth representing the Lord Jesus, the apostles would be persecuted and hated by people in all the nations where they labored (see commentary on John 15:18–19). Nevertheless, they and all the souls who would soften their hearts and listen—learn the gospel and live it, enduring to the end—had the promise of salvation, meaning eternal life (3 Nephi 15:9).

"Ye shall not have gone over the cities of Israel, till the Son of man be come," possibly meaning that those sent out could scarcely be able to reach all the cities where the people of covenant Israel reside before the coming of the Son of Man in glory.

Matthew 10:24–25 The true disciple or servant is submissive and subservient to the Master and Lord. It is appropriate to try to become like the Master and Lord but not to attempt to rise above him. That is what Lucifer in all his pride desired to do—to rise *above* the throne of God (Isaiah 14:12–13; D&C 76:28; Moses 4:1).

If the Master of the house (the Savior) is subject to the meanest name-calling, how can those of his household expect to escape the same ill treatment?

Beelzebub is from Hebrew *Baalzebub*, a pagan god and an epithet for Satan (cf. 2 Kings 1:1–6), meaning literally "lord of the flies."

Matthew 10:26–28; Luke 12:2–5 There is no need to fear antagonists and persecutors, because in the end all will be exposed. Nothing will remain covered up or hidden: "All things which are hid must be revealed upon the house-tops" (Mormon 5:8; also 2 Nephi 27:11; 30:17); "the rebellious shall be pierced with much sorrow; for their iniquities shall be spoken upon the housetops, and their secret acts shall be revealed" (D&C 1:3). Whatever is done in darkness, in "secret," will be broadcast on the housetops (perhaps by sophisticated television and satellite systems or greater media yet to be invented or revealed—a day we are already seeing).

Because mortality is such a brief moment in all of our immortal life, do not be overly concerned about those who can kill the physical body ("fear not what man can do, for God shall be with you forever and ever"; D&C 122:9) but do be concerned about those who can injure the spirit and lead your soul down to hell.

Matthew 10:29–31; Luke 12:6–7 The King James Version of the Bible uses the English term "farthing" for the Greek *assarion*, a coin in circulation in the Roman empire at the time of Jesus (see also commentary on Matthew 5:25–26). Two sparrows were sold for a farthing (Matthew) and five sparrows for two farthings (Luke), but not even a single sparrow is captured or sold without God knowing it. The Father is aware of all things: nothing escapes his infinite notice. If God watches over his minor creations, then what of his crowning creation, his own children? "Fear not therefore; ye are of more value than many sparrows" (Luke 12:7). The very hairs of your heads are all numbered and accounted for.

Matthew 10:32–33; Luke 12:8–9 If we stand up and testify as the apostles did and defend the cause of Christ in this world, he will stand up, testify, defend us, and be our Advocate before the Father in the next world. But the reverse is also true: if we deny him here—refuse to take upon us his name, testify of him, and live his laws—he will deny our entry into the Father's presence.

Matthew 10:34–36; Luke 12:49–53 "I have a baptism to be baptized with," said Jesus, "and how am I straitened [Greek, "stressed or pressured"] till it be accomplished!" (Luke 12:50). Indeed, he came to immerse himself in the most arduous and painful of missions. Even though he came to proclaim the gospel of peace, his "baptism" or mission would involve personal temptation, pain, hunger, thirst, fatigue, suffering, and anguish (Mosiah 3:7). It would provide peace and joy for some, but for others animosity and divisiveness even to the point of separating family members as they react individually to the gospel.

Nobel Prize–winning Jewish writer Elie Wiesel once commented on a television broadcast, "We know when Messiah comes there will be peace; Jesus came, and there is no peace"

(Ogden, notes on Seminar on Christ). But Jesus himself declared that his divine message would bring not always peace but a sword. Quoting a teaching he had inspired Micah to record (Micah 7:6), he noted that "a man's foes shall be they of his own household" (Matthew 10:36; see also commentary on John 14:27).

The New International Version Study Bible has an interesting footnote to verse 34: "At first glance this saying sounds like a contradiction of Isa 9:6 ('Prince of Peace'), Lk 2:14 ('on earth peace to men') and Jn 14:27 ('Peace I leave with you'). It is true that Christ came to bring peace—peace between the believer and God, and peace among men. Yet the inevitable result of Christ's coming is conflict—between Christ and the anti-christ, between light and darkness, between Christ's children and the devil's children. This conflict can occur even between members of the same family (vv. 35–36)" (NIV Study Bible, 1457).

Matthew 10:37–39; Luke 14:25–27 The first and great commandments were to "have no other gods before me" (Exodus 20:4) and "love the Lord thy God with all thine heart, and with all thy soul, and with all thy might" (Deuteronomy 6:5; cf. 2 Nephi 25:29). From the beginning, top priority has always been given to love of God above all else and before all other persons. Now Jesus reconfirms that teaching, "He that loveth father or mother [or son or daughter] more than me is not worthy of me." Putting any other person or any other thing before God is idolatry (see Romans 1:25). Even in the most sacred of human relationships, the union of man and woman, it is important for the husband and for the wife to love the Lord first and foremost. If each one puts the Lord first, that marriage can succeed, and the union can remain eternally intact.

The parallel teaching in Luke 14:26 records Jesus' saying in hyperbolic form: "If any man come to me, and hate not his father, and mother, and wife, and children, and brethren, and sisters, [*or husband;* JST] yea, and his own life also [*or in other words, is afraid to lay down his life for my sake;* JST], he cannot be my disciple."

The word *hate* is not to be taken literally, of course (nowhere in all of scripture is there a command to hate any of our loved ones). Rather, this is an example of the ancient literary device called hyperbole, which intentionally exaggerates and strongly contrasts emotions to emphasize the importance of the top priority. "Jesus' original command to hate one's family was not meant to be taken literally but was an exaggeration used for effect. 'Hate' is simply an idiomatic way of saying 'love less'" (Stein, *Difficult Sayings in the Gospels,* 48). Matthew's wording sounds more reasonable to our modern-language ears: you just can't love someone else *more* than you love God; you must place your greatest affection on him.

To be worthy of God, we, like the apostles, must be willing to "take up our cross." The cross was a symbol of shame and ignominy, extreme suffering, and death. As Jesus willingly took up his cross to save others, so we symbolically take up our cross to help save others. We do what we have seen that he was willing to do. Jacob taught that "they who have endured the crosses of the world, and despised the shame of it, they shall inherit the kingdom of God" (2 Nephi 9:18; see also Jacob 1:8).

Later Matthew records, "If any man will come after me, let him deny himself, and take up his cross, and follow me" (Matthew 16:24), to which the Joseph Smith Translation appends, *"And now for a man to take up his cross, is to deny himself all ungodliness, and every worldly lust, and keep my commandments"* (JST Matthew 16:26; cf. Alma 39:9). Interestingly, the idea of "taking up the cross," relating to our willingness to follow Jesus' example in giving his life for others, as well as his dying by crucifixion, was known and spoken of centuries before crucifixion was invented by the Persians (sixth to fourth century before Christ).

"He *who seeketh to save* his life shall lose it: and he that loseth his life for my sake shall find it" (JST Matthew 10:34).

If we focus all our efforts on ourselves, we can never find lasting joy in life; if we lose ourselves in the service of others, we find ourselves in eventual possession of eternal life, the greatest of all the gifts of God (D&C 14:7). Missionaries are among our most vivid exemplars of this principle. When they dedicate themselves one hundred percent to the lives of others, forgetting their own interests and concentrating wholly on others, they invariably report that those are some of the happiest moments of their lives.

Matthew 10:40–42 Final instructions to the apostles, as recorded in this chapter by Matthew: If the people accept you, they accept me and they accept the Father. The same message is given in the latter days: "He that receiveth my servants receiveth me; and he that receiveth me receiveth my Father" (D&C 84:36–37). "Whether by mine own voice or by the voice of my servants, it is the same" (D&C 1:38).

Giving a cup of cold water as a sign of true discipleship (v. 42) reflects the value of water in a land bordering on great deserts. In modern times similar promises are given to those who help sustain the apostles and missionaries: "Whoso receiveth you receiveth me; and the same will feed you, and clothe you, and give you money. And he who feeds you, or clothes you, or gives you money, shall in nowise lose his reward" (D&C 84:89–90).

THE SERMON ON THE MOUNT (IN GALILEE)

Matthew 5–7; Luke 6:17–49; cf. 3 Nephi 12–14 Human expression cannot fully capture the meaning and significance of the Sermon on the Mount. A great and profound discourse, the Sermon on the Mount reflects truth as a multifaceted diamond reflects light. It signals the inauguration of a new dispensation of the gospel. It provides a window into the Savior's own personality and character and summarizes the

A Second Galilean Ministry

Sermon on the Mount, *by Harry Anderson*

essence of Christlike behavior. It describes the characteristics of those who will inhabit the celestial kingdom. It compares the old law with the new. It teaches *all* people how to live and how to pray, and yet it was addressed to a specific group of individuals and was one of the most significant training sessions ever presented to teach the newly called apostles how to fulfill their stewardships. It continues to testify of Jesus' divinity, godly wisdom, and unsurpassed teaching skills. Truly, it is a discourse given by God himself.

Jesus taught the Nephites the same eternal truths that he gave his disciples in the Old World. Like the Ten Commandments, the principles he has repeated to all peoples in all dispensations—to ancient Israelites in the Holy Land (Exodus 20; Deuteronomy 5) and in the New World (Mosiah 13) and to modern Israel in the Doctrine and Covenants (42)—are also timeless. Whether given on a mount (Matthew 5:1) or on a plain (Luke 6:17) or at the Temple (3 Nephi 11:1), these teachings constitute what Elder Harold B. Lee called "the constitution for a perfect life" (*Decisions for Successful Living*, 57). The main theme is "how to reach the kingdom of heaven" or "how to overcome the flesh." Elder Melvin J. Ballard said, "A man may receive the priesthood and all its privileges and blessings, but until he learns to overcome the flesh, his temper, his tongue, his disposition to indulge in the things God has forbidden, he cannot come into the celestial kingdom of God" (cited in Kimball, *Miracle of Forgiveness,* 168). These magnificent lessons teach us how to overcome the natural man and achieve that celestial glory.

Matthew 5:1–2 The opening verses of Matthew 5 discloses the setting for the Sermon. Great crowds had been following Jesus because of his spreading fame, owing to the many miracles he had performed. People from all over the Holy Land—Galilee, Decapolis, Jerusalem, and all of Judea—had become part of the entourage (Matthew 4:24–25). Matthew 5:1 is a continuation of the report in the previous verses, a fact sometimes obscured by the chapter break. Precisely because great crowds were following him, Jesus chose that time to instruct those responsible for leading the Church and teaching the unconverted multitude in the future. When arrangements suitable to his plan and purpose were in place, he instructed his disciples. In fact, as the Joseph Smith Translation indicates, the whole of the Sermon was not specifically intended for all disciples; rather, important portions were pointedly directed to the Twelve Apostles and other leaders (see JST Matthew 5:3–4; 6:25–39; 7:6–17).

Matthew 5:3–12; cf. 3 Nephi 12:1–12 The Sermon on the Mount was given to those who had already learned the basic principles of the gospel and made covenants; it was given not to the multitudes in general but to believers, particularly those with leadership responsibilities. The great sermon was given as a quiet, private talk, in what we might call a missionary preparation meeting. (Luke's account of the sermon on the plain apparently includes a wider compass of listeners; there Jesus found himself in the midst of a "company of his disciples, and a great multitude of people out of all Judea and Jerusalem, and from the sea coast of Tyre and Sidon"; Luke 6:17.)

Jesus began by pronouncing what in English have come

A Second Galilean Ministry

Sea of Galilee from the traditional Mount of Beatitudes

to be known as "The Beatitudes" (or, as a Primary child called them, "The Beautiful Attitudes"), which are, in effect, Jesus' character in words. The Beatitudes are both characteristics of and conditions enjoyed by the exalted—those who are or will be recipients of eternal life. The term "Beatitude" derives from the Latin *beatus*, which means "to be blessed" or "to be happy or fortunate," and is the equivalent of the Greek *makarioi* and the Hebrew *'ashre*. The latter is found in some of Israel's ancient psalms. "Blessed is the man that walketh not in the counsel of the ungodly, nor standeth in the way of sinners, nor sitteth in the seat of the scornful" (Psalm 1:1). In one sense, Jesus was adopting the language of ancient Israel's great lyric prophet-kings and inspired poets to teach his profound message, citing words that he had inspired them to record. Beatitudes, as a literary form, are also found in intertestamental and rabbinic literature, but Jesus gave them a fresh, new perspective.

The Lord gave at least four beatitudes to the Nephites before beginning the same, well-known collection in the New Testament:

"Blessed are ye if ye shall give heed unto the words of these twelve" (3 Nephi 12:1).

"Blessed are ye if ye shall believe in me and be baptized" (3 Nephi 12:1).

"More blessed are they who shall believe in your words because that ye shall testify that ye have seen me" (3 Nephi 12:2).

"Blessed are they who shall believe in your words, and come down into the depths of humility and be baptized, for they shall be visited with fire and with the Holy Ghost, and shall receive a remission of their sins" (3 Nephi 12:2).

These four "beatitudes" emphasize the first principles and the first ordinances of the gospel: have faith in the Lord Jesus Christ, repent, be baptized, and receive the gift of the Holy Ghost. They show that the Beatitudes were meant for disciples seeking the celestial kingdom.

"President Harold B. Lee . . . suggested that the Beatitudes represent a recipe for righteousness with incremental steps, beginning with 'the *poor in spirit* who come unto [Christ]' (3 Nephi 12:3; emphasis added). The next step in the celestial direction is to *mourn,* especially for our sins, for 'godly sorrow worketh repentance to salvation' (2 Corinthians 7:10). One then becomes *meek* and begins to *hunger and thirst for righteousness.* A natural sequel is a greater inclination to be *merciful,* and increased desire to become *pure in heart,* and a stronger desire to be a *peacemaker* (see 3 Nephi 12:5–9). But even the proper and inspired use of our moral agency has a price indicated in the next beatitude: 'And blessed are all they who are *persecuted* for my name's sake, for theirs is the kingdom of heaven' (3 Nephi 12:3–10; emphasis added). As we climb the steps outlined in the Beatitudes, we soon humbly recognize that our lives are on a higher plane than those who love the things of this world. And notwithstanding our attempts to share with them gospel truths that can also elevate their lives, many of them will begin to persecute us and scoff at our lifestyle and point mocking fingers at those who have partaken of the fruits of the gospel (see 1 Nephi 8:26–27).

"The Savior reserved a special blessing for those who would be reviled and persecuted and falsely accused for his sake: 'Ye shall have great joy and be exceedingly glad, for great shall be your reward in heaven; for so persecuted they the prophets who were before you' (3 Nephi 12:11–12)" (Condie, *Ensign*, September 1995, 19).

THE POOR IN SPIRIT

Matthew 5:3; Luke 6:20; cf. 3 Nephi 12:3 The first essential characteristic possessed by the blessed or exalted, according to the account as found in Matthew, is "poor in spirit." This expression is not found in either the Massoretic Text (the standardized Hebrew Bible, the Old Testament) or rabbinic literature. Presumably, it means those who are "poor in pride," those who are devoid of pride, or those who are "poor in the spirit of the world." This fits perfectly with the fuller accounts of this Beatitude in 3 Nephi and in the Joseph Smith Translation, wherein the poor in spirit are blessed or happy if they come unto Christ (3 Nephi 12:3; JST Matthew 5:5), on whom all of us are dependent. In fact, all of the Beatitudes may be read more profitably by inserting the phrase, "who come unto me," for in truth that is the implication in all of them (those who mourn who come unto me, the meek who come unto me, the peacemakers who come unto me, and so forth). We are dependent on Jesus for exaltation and lasting happiness.

Those who follow Him are often judged as "poor" or misguided in the world's estimation. Through another Book of Mormon prophet, Moroni, the Lord promises to those who will come unto him that he "will show unto them their weakness," explaining, "I give unto men weakness that they may be humble; and my grace is sufficient for all men that humble themselves before me; for if they humble themselves before me, and have faith in me, then will I make weak things become strong unto them" (Ether 12:27). The natural and expected reward of those who are poor in the spirit of the world and come unto Christ is nothing less than the riches of the kingdom of heaven.

We must be willing to be dependent on our Savior. Here in mortality we are nothing of ourselves (Mosiah 4:11). Recognizing our nothingness should lead not to hopelessness but to willing dependence on the only Person in the universe who can rescue us from our fallen condition. The nothingness we refer to here is our incapacity and helplessness to get ourselves out of this fallen, mortal condition; we are not suggesting that we are worthless—nothingness is not worthlessness—because we know each soul is worth a great deal in the sight of God.

The opposite of dependence is pride, which always drives us away from God; when we feel independent, we may think we don't need God. Doctrine and Covenants 56:18 tells us: "Blessed are the poor who are pure in heart, whose hearts are broken, and whose spirits are contrite, for they shall see the kingdom of God coming in power and great glory unto their deliverance."

An example of those who are poor or humble in spirit but pure in heart is the people who hearkened to King Benjamin: "They had viewed themselves in their own carnal state, even less than the dust of the earth. And they all cried aloud with one voice, saying: O have mercy, and apply the atoning blood of Christ that we may receive forgiveness of our sins, and our hearts may be purified; for we believe in Jesus Christ, the Son of God" (Mosiah 4:2).

Other examples of those with clean and pure hearts are the men we sustain as prophets, seers, and revelators who are on the earth today.

THOSE WHO MOURN

Matthew 5:4; cf. 3 Nephi 12:4 Those who mourn, who are trying to keep God's commandments, will eventually be comforted; their sorrow shall be turned into joy (John 16:20).

One sign of a true Saint is that he or she is "willing to mourn with those that mourn; yea, and comfort those that stand in need of comfort" (Mosiah 18:9).

Jesus' ministry perfectly illustrates this godly quality of character; we often read that he was "moved with compassion" (Matthew 9:36; 14:14; Mark 1:41; 6:34; cf. Matthew 15:32; 20:34; Mark 5:19; Luke 7:13). The English word *compassion* derives from Latin *com* ("with") plus *pati* ("to bear, to suffer"). Thus having compassion means to bear with or suffer with. (A synonym that derives from the Greek is "sympathy" (*sym*, "with," plus *pati*, from which we get *pathos*). Other related terms are *commiseration* ("to lament with, to have pity for") and *condolence* ("to feel pain with").

When the scriptures speak of Jesus' compassion, therefore, we can visualize him experiencing deep feeling for someone's pain and understanding that person's misery or suffering, combined with a desire to relieve it. Being moved with compassion is a spiritual consciousness of someone's personal tragedy and a feeling of selfless tenderness toward it.

In the Beatitudes, and in this great sermon and in his whole life, we learn of Jesus' character, the way he lived. He said, "I am the way," and this is the way he wants us to live—to be willing to feel for others' burdens and be willing to help carry them.

THE MEEK

Matthew 5:5; cf. 3 Nephi 12:5; Psalm 37:11; Alma 32:8; see also Matthew 23:6 Blessed are the meek. Meekness is the quality of character that may be defined as poise under pressure and patience in the face of provocation. "A meek man is defined as one who is not easily provoked or irritated and forbearing under injury or annoyance. Meekness is not synonymous with weakness" (Lee, *Decisions for Successful Living,* 60). "The meek and the humble are those who are teachable. They are willing to learn. They are willing to listen to the whisperings of the still, small voice for guidance in their lives. They place the wisdom of the Lord above their own wisdom" (Hinckley, *Stand a Little Taller,* 18). The Prophet Joseph Smith taught that we should cultivate a quiet, meek, and peaceable spirit (*Teachings of the Prophet Joseph Smith,* 316). Mildness, humbleness, and gentleness are meekness, and meekness is power under control.

An excellent example of meekness in the New Testament is John the Baptist. He was bold and rigorous in denouncing evil and hypocrisy, but at the same time he was humble and meek. Speaking of the Savior, the great prophet said, "He must increase, but I must decrease" (John 3:30).

As the Beatitudes indicate, the meek will inherit this celestialized earth (D&C 130:9). Thus, the meek are also those who have been baptized and living the celestial law (D&C 88:17–22).

HUNGER AND THIRST AFTER RIGHTEOUSNESS

Matthew 5:6; Luke 6:21; cf. 3 Nephi 12:6 "Blessed are they which do hunger and thirst after righteousness: for they shall be filled." Here the Nephite record adds with what we may be filled: "with the Holy Ghost" (3 Nephi 12:6). When we are spiritually hungry and thirsty, nothing is more desirable, rich, and satisfying than the Spirit of God.

The Holy Ghost is the great comforter and testator and is only one of Three who can really satisfy our emotional and mental hunger and quench our spiritual thirst (John 14:16–18, 26). He operates under the direction of Jesus

Christ (John 16:13–16). The Greek word used by Matthew that is translated "filled" originally meant to feed and fatten an animal. It carries the notion of eating till one is completely full and totally satisfied. Such is the Lord's promise to those who hunger and thirst after righteousness. He will feed us more than we can possibly imagine.

THE MERCIFUL

Matthew 5:7; cf. 3 Nephi 12:7 The law of the harvest is, that which we send out comes back to us. If we are merciful, compassionate, tolerant, and patient with the foibles or weaknesses of others, then that merciful treatment will be given us, too.

President Gordon B. Hinckley encouraged: "Let us be more merciful. Let us get the arrogance out of our lives, the conceit, the egotism. Let us be more compassionate, gentler, filled with forbearance and patience and a greater measure of respect one for another. In so doing, our very example will cause others to be more merciful, and we shall have greater claim upon the mercy of God who in His love will be generous toward us" (*Teachings of Gordon B. Hinckley,* 338).

THE PURE IN HEART

Matthew 5:8; cf. 3 Nephi 12:8 All those whose hearts are clean and pure have the promise that they shall see God. "It shall come to pass that every soul who forsaketh his sins and cometh unto me, and calleth on my name, and obeyeth my voice, and keepeth my commandments, shall see my face and know that I am" (D&C 93:1). Thus, the pure in heart are those who forsake their sins, call on the Savior's name, obey his voice, and keep his commandments—and then they can see God. That is a literal promise. Those who are pure, as he is pure, not only will see him but will remain and live with him forever. That promise is not solely for our postearth life, however. In the Doctrine and Covenants the Lord explains one way that God can be seen in this life:

"And inasmuch as my people build a house unto me in the name of the Lord, and do not suffer any unclean thing to come into it, that it be not defiled, my glory shall rest upon it;

"Yea, and my presence shall be there, for I will come into it, and all the pure in heart that shall come into it shall see God" (D&C 97:15–16).

To see God, according to Elder Royden G. Derrick, means to come to know God, discover him, visualize him, recognize him, and understand him (*Temples in the Last Days*, 80).

THE PEACEMAKERS

Matthew 5:9; cf. 3 Nephi 12:9 Those who eventually become the children of God (that is, those who become permanently part of the eternal family of God) are those who have learned to make peace. They have learned, for example, to get rid of pride and have stopped stirring up contention and spawning criticism in favor of more charitable relationships. They guide themselves and others to the Prince of Peace.

PERSECUTED FOR RIGHTEOUSNESS; PERSECUTED BY FALSE ACCUSERS

Matthew 5:10–12; Luke 6:22–23; cf. 3 Nephi 12:10–12 Peter wrote: "If ye suffer for righteousness' sake, happy are ye: and be not afraid of their terror, neither be troubled" (1 Peter 3:14). Being persecuted while bearing the name of Jesus Christ and while trying to be Christlike is nothing new. It has happened to many people greater than we throughout the ages. Paul wrote, "All that will live godly in

Christ Jesus shall suffer persecution" (2 Timothy 3:12). And we will be blessed for it. How great is our reward? "All that my Father hath shall be given unto [you]" (D&C 84:38). How do we endure the painful persecution? "He also gave them strength, that they should suffer no manner of afflictions, save it were swallowed up in the joy of Christ" (Alma 31:38).

Matthew 5:11 How shall we love our enemies? President Joseph F. Smith explained:

"Do you love these slanderers, these liars, these defamers, these persecutors of the innocent and of the unoffending—do you love them? [several voices, No, no.] I can scarcely blame you. . . . I want to tell you how I feel towards them. I love them so much that if I had it in my power to annihilate them from the earth I would not harm a hair of their heads—not one hair of their heads.

"I love them so well that if I could possibly make them better men, convert them from the error of their ways I would do it, God being my helper. I love them so much that I would not throw a straw in their way to prosperity and happiness, but so far as possible I would hedge up their headlong and downward course to destruction, and yet I detest and abominate their infamous actions and their wicked course. That is how I feel towards them, and that is how much I love them, and if this is not the love that Jesus desired us to have for our enemies, tell me what kind of love we should have for them?

"I do not love them so that I would take them into my bosom, or invite them to associate with my family, or that I would give my daughters to their embraces, nor my sons to their counsels. I do not love them so well that I would invite them to the councils of the Priesthood, and the ordinances of the House of God, to scoff and jeer at sacred things which they do not understand, nor would I share with them the inheritance that God, my Father, has given me in Zion; I do not love them well enough for this, and I do not believe that God ever designed that I should; but I love them so much that I would not hurt them, I would do them good, I would tell the truth about them, I would benefit them if it was in my power, and I would keep them to the utmost of my ability from doing them harm to themselves and to their neighbors.

"I love them that much; but I do not love them with that affection with which I love my wife, my brother, my sister or my friend. There is a difference between the love we should bear towards our enemies and that we should bear towards our friends" (*Journal of Discourses,* 23:284–85; paragraphing altered).

THE SALT OF THE EARTH

Matthew 5:13; Luke 14:34–35 (cf. 3 Nephi 12:13; 16:15; D&C 101:39–40) In an age before refrigerators, salt was the great preservative. In this memorable metaphor, Jesus calls his disciples salt: They would preserve his teachings and lifestyle among the peoples of the earth, but if they failed in their conscientious following of his example, they would be worthless in his kingdom and would be cast out, as useless salt is cast out.

Salt is plentiful. It is calculated that the evaporation of one cubic mile of seawater leaves about 140 million tons of salts, most of which would be sodium chloride, or common salt. It could also be extracted from the seawaters themselves but with care to remove impurities and poisonous elements in those waters, which are heavy with various minerals. Salt was mined in biblical times from the hills at the southern end of the Dead Sea.

Salt does not lose its savor with age. Rather, its savor is lost through mixture and contamination (see Asay, *Ensign,* May 1980, 42–44). The Lord's metaphor in this passage may be a warning to avoid any alteration of God-given teachings or admixture with the philosophies of men or the corrupting influences of those who love evil. The encouragement is for

A Second Galilean Ministry

Salt, the great preservative, was mined from the southern end of the Dead Sea or extracted from the water itself

disciples to maintain a pure and undefiled gospel and to season the world with their tasteful living. "Salt is good: but if the salt have lost his saltness, wherewith will ye season it [bring back its saltiness]? Have salt in yourselves, and have peace one with another" (Mark 9:50).

In Leviticus, the handbook for Levitical priests, the Lord commanded that "every oblation of thy meat offering shalt thou season with salt; neither shalt thou suffer the salt of the covenant of thy God to be lacking from thy meat offering" (Leviticus 2:13). Salt was a token of the covenant that the Lord had made with his people and was part of Israel's sacrificial system. That sacrificial system was a type, shadow, and symbol of the great and last sacrifice that Jesus himself would offer (see Hebrews 9–10). Salt ultimately points to the Savior.

Jesus perpetuated the symbol by labeling the people themselves as the possessors and promulgators of his covenant. As the salt would season the meat offering, so the disciples of the Lord Jesus Christ would season the world and preserve his truth in it.

The parallel passage in Luke was placed in a specific

context by the Prophet Joseph Smith: "*Then certain of them came to him, saying, Good Master, we have Moses and the prophets, and whosoever shall live by them, shall he not have life? And Jesus answered, saying, Ye know not Moses, neither the prophets; for if ye had known them, ye would have believed on me; for to this intent they were written. For I am sent that ye might have life. Therefore I will liken it unto salt* which is good; but if the salt *has* lost *its* savor, wherewith shall it be seasoned?" (JST Luke 14:35–37).

In modern revelation the Lord uses a play on words, referring to the Saints as *savor* and as *saviors,* meaning that real Saints can bring a unique savor, a higher quality, into the lives of other souls and even serve as saviors of those souls:

"When men are called unto mine everlasting gospel, and covenant with an everlasting covenant, they are accounted as the salt of the earth and the savor of men;

"They are called to be the savor of men; therefore, if that salt of the earth lose its savor, behold, it is thenceforth good for nothing only to be cast out and trodden under the feet of men" (D&C 101:39–40).

"For they were set to be a light unto the world, and to be the saviors of men;

"And inasmuch as they are not the saviors of men, they are as salt that has lost its savor, and is thenceforth good for nothing but to be cast out and trodden under foot of men" (D&C 103:9–10).

"YE ARE THE LIGHT OF THE WORLD"; LET YOUR LIGHT SHINE

Matthew 5:14–16; Luke 8:16; 11:33; cf. 3 Nephi 12:14–16 Just as the Savior gave unto us to be the salt of the earth—to preserve his word and his work in the world, so he gives unto us to be the light of this people. We are many lights now, a large city, and we cannot be hid. We are conspicuous

A Second Galilean Ministry

"A city that is set on an hill" in Samaria

lights in this world of darkness. As a candle or lamp is put up on a candlestick or lampstand (Hebrew, *menorah*), so we must set our light to shine throughout our communities and nations: "Let your light so shine before this people." Jesus Christ is our light, for he said, "I am the light which ye shall hold up" (3 Nephi 18:24). In other words, our objective is to let him, our Light, shine through us to the glory of the Father, not for our own glory.

So, as Jesus said, we are the light of the world but only in the sense that we allow him to shine through us. In the ultimate sense, *he* is the light of the world to illuminate the darkened minds and lives of those who live without God in the world. There is no switch to turn off the darkness, but we do have Him to turn on the light, which dispels the darkness. We may not be able to turn off all the darkness of sin in the world— the drunkenness, the pornography, the abuse, the immorality, the violence, the hate—but we can turn on the light of Christ, any time and any place, to help dispel the evil influences that surround us.

THE LAW FULFILLED

Matthew 5:17ff.; cf. 3 Nephi 12:17ff. The Savior now shifts to a crucial theme that he will teach and illustrate: "Think not that I am come to destroy the law or the prophets." The Law and the Prophets are two of the three major parts of the holy scriptures that the people then possessed. The Jews called them the *Torah* (the Law) and the *Nevi'im* (the Prophets). The other was called the *Ketuvim*, the Writings, or poetical works, such as Psalms, Proverbs, and Ecclesiastes.

Jesus was not destroying or canceling out all those sacred writings any more than a university professor is destroying basic arithmetic by teaching integral calculus (McConkie, *Doctrinal New Testament Commentary,* 1:219–20). He came not to abolish but to complete. As the Latter-day Saints would

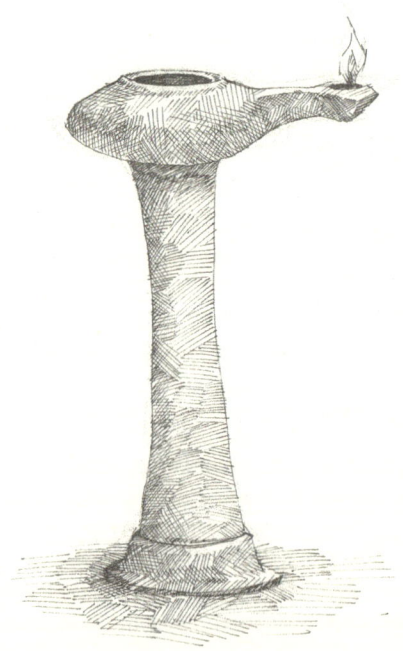

An oil lamp on a stand

say to other Christians—or to Jews, Muslims, or anyone else—we do not come to erase any truth you already have but to fulfill, to complete, to add to what you have with the fulness of the everlasting gospel. We would say, as the Lord said, "I do not bring it to destroy that which [you] have received, but to build it up" (D&C 10:52). And Joseph Smith added, "We don't ask any people to throw away any good they have got; we only ask them to come and get more" (*Teachings of the Prophet Joseph Smith*, 275).

Matthew 5:18–20; Luke 16:17; cf. 3 Nephi 12:18–20, 46–47 A "jot" is the smallest letter in the Hebrew alphabet (*yod*). In this case, "jot" is a transliteration of the Greek *iota* (equivalent of the Hebrew *yod*), which is the smallest letter in the Greek alphabet. A "tittle" is the English word representing Greek *keraia*, meaning "horn," or "projection," a small stroke or mark used to distinguish one letter from another. It could also represent a tiny decorative flourish that the calligrapher adds to a letter of a word in the Hebrew Bible as he writes it out by hand.

A scroll of the Torah

The first ten letters of the Hebrew alphabet are as follows, reading from right to left. The last of the ten letters (circled) is the *yod* (English *jot*):

ⓘ ט ח ז ו ה ד ג ב א

Tittles (circled) define the difference between a *beth* and a *kaph:*

ב כ

And between a *daleth* and a *resh:*

ד ר

Jesus was referring to two of the smallest things known to ancient Israelites to show that not even the minutest detail of the old law (and the prophetic writings) is negated or voided, but all is now accomplished and fulfilled in him. (The text of Matthew suggests future fulfillment; 3 Nephi 1:25 also indicates "the law was not yet fulfilled"; but 3 Nephi 12:18 uses the past perfect tense, meaning the law had now been fulfilled.) The purpose of the old law was to lead Israel to Christ, and his commandments are now before us, to save us. Keeping them is the only way any of us will enter into the kingdom of heaven.

Verse 19 is presented more clearly in Joseph Smith Translation Matthew 5:21 (see Bible Appendix, 802).

ANGER: "THOU SHALT NOT KILL"

Matthew 5:21ff.; cf. 3 Nephi 12:21ff. Specific examples are given of how the Savior came not to destroy but to fulfill. He did not do away with the old law, especially the basic commandments, but rather added higher laws. These examples illustrate a basic theme of the sermon: how to overcome the flesh—that is, how to learn to control the body. We came to earth not just to obtain a physical body but to learn to control it, to achieve self-mastery. The examples Jesus gave teach us that we must learn to control our emotions (especially anger), our sexual desires (any immoral thoughts and actions), our food intake (through fasting), and our tongue (our verbal communication).

Matthew 5:21–22; cf. 3 Nephi 12:21–22 Included in the old law was a commandment not to kill (the Hebrew verb *ratzakh* means to murder, to slay with premeditation; Exodus 20:13). That law, of course, still stands. But the higher law is to refrain from even getting angry. The Savior charges us not to allow the feelings of anger to get started that could lead to murder. Anger is a very strong emotion. It is beyond irritation, annoyance, disgust, or other such feelings (which are also contrary to the spirit of the gospel); it is a deep, passionate wrath or anger that could lead one to commit murder. Even Nephi, son of Lehi, a noble, righteous prophet, struggled with feelings of anger toward his enemies (his older brothers), and he knew that such intense feelings were wrong, sinful, and damaging to his own spirituality (2 Nephi 4:17–31, especially vv. 17–19, 27–29). Nephi knew that such intense anger was forbidden by the gospel of Jesus Christ, as is plainly expressed here in verse 22. Joseph Smith Translation Ephesians 4:26 asks the relevant question: "*Can ye be* angry, and *not sin?*"

"We have seen that anger against another can only result after we commit sin (think unrighteously), but there is something in the nature of anger itself and its consequences that is also sinful. *Anger itself is a sin* when sin is defined as anything that retards the growth or progress of an individual" (Kelly, *Ensign*, February 1980, 10).

"President Spencer W. Kimball, in his excellent book *The Miracle of Forgiveness*, tells us in effect that anger is 'a sin of thought' which, if not controlled, may be the forerunner of vicious and violent acts" (Christiansen, *Ensign*, June 1971, 37).

Elder Theodore M. Burton wrote: "Whenever you get red in the face, whenever you raise your voice, whenever you get 'hot under the collar,' or angry, rebellious, or negative in spirit, then know that the Spirit of God is leaving you and the spirit of Satan is beginning to take over. At times we may feel justified in arguing or fighting for truth by contentious words and actions. Do not be deceived" (*Ensign*, November 1974, 56).

An experience taught one sister missionary to avoid anger. She wrote: "I had one companion that I regret very much getting angry with. That was twenty-five years ago, when I knew nothing about it being a sin to criticize and even let something get to the point of anger. No one got along with this sister . . . we just walked to a different drumbeat. She was very philosophical in an emotional way. She was all heart. I was all head and hard work. She wanted to disobey the rule that we should be in at 1 P.M. every afternoon, to study and allow the people their siesta time until 3 P.M. I desperately needed that study time. I loved studying the scriptures and Spanish. She was bored with that and really didn't know the discussions. She loved talking to the people all day long. She would cry and get emotional at almost every door. It was so embarrassing to me. I refused to stay out with her. It made us both hard-hearted towards one another to the point that we wouldn't even walk down the same side of the street together. Now, when I look back on it with the maturity and gospel knowledge I have about anger and contention, I wish I had let her have her way now and then and not insisted so rigidly on obeying every rule. Keeping the Spirit would have been so much more important than having all that contention. . . . She wasn't asking that we break any covenants or commandments; she was just happier teaching than studying. . . . I could have loved her anyway. She wasn't asking me to go to movies or break those kinds of rules; she just wanted to rearrange the proselyting. I could have done that and lived with fewer regrets. I wish someone had taught me about anger back then. I thought I was justified. I wasn't." She spoke further about uncontrolled emotions: "Do I repent daily and frequently, especially of improper and unkind feelings such as anger, impatience, sarcasm, and cynicism? Do I understand that anger and irritation are wrong, even when I am in the right—that anger is an offense to the Spirit and is not the Lord's way of solving differences and frustrations?" (Ogden and Ogden, *President and the Preacher,* 152–53, 148).

"Anger, irritation, annoyance—all from below. My, how the devil loves to separate people: spouses from each other, children from parents, ward members from each other, brothers and sisters, etc. [BYU colleague] Catherine Thomas said that the reason we have abrasive people in our lives is so we can learn to develop divine love. This life is a laboratory for practicing divine love. And until we get the hang of it, we will have one irritating person after another come into our lives to give us plenty of practice" (Ogden and Ogden, *President and the Preacher,* 177).

The text of Matthew reads "Whosoever is angry with his brother without a cause . . ." The latter phrase is deleted in the purer rendition by the Savior as recorded among the Nephites (3 Nephi 12:22), because there is no cause, no justification, ever, to become really angry with a brother. The phrase was also deleted by the Prophet Joseph Smith in his inspired revision of the biblical text (JST Matthew 5:22). The Spanish Bible (Casiodoro de Reina, dating from half a century earlier than the English King James Version) also omits that phrase.

"Raca" is an Aramaic term that means an "empty" or "worthless" person. Labeling someone a *raca* or a fool or any other such term of denigration is forbidden by the Lord, because we simply do not tell another child of Heavenly Father that he or she is worthless or "good for nothing" (on the value of every soul, see D&C 18:10; Topical Guide, "Worth of Souls," 591). A person may be doing foolish things, yet he or she is not inherently a "fool" but a child of the God of heaven.

"The council" referred, in the Greek New Testament, to

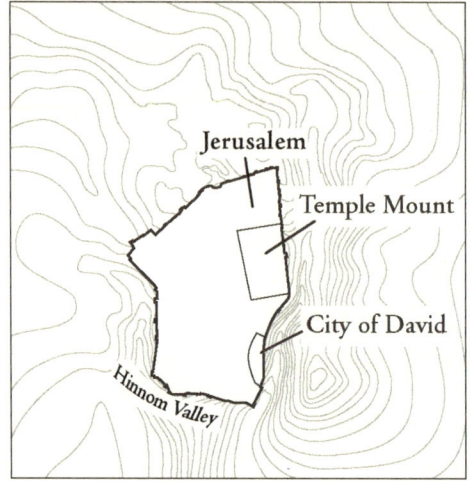

The Hinnom Valley (Gehenna, Hell) in Jerusalem

the Jewish Sanhedrin. A person charged with denunciation, castigation, or condemnation of a brother could be arraigned before that council. In a larger sense, one guilty of such sinful name-calling in a future day may be arraigned before a heavenly council, at the judgment bar of God.

"Hell fire" in Hebrew is *esh Gei Hinnom,* literally, "fire of the Hinnom Valley," or, in the Greek transliteration, *Gehenna.* The hell to which people are cast down or cast out, the place of punishment by ever-burning fire, is represented by the Greek word *Gehenna.* The Hinnom Valley was the border between the Israelite tribes of Judah and Benjamin (Joshua 15:8; 18:16). The valley lay to the southwest just outside the original Zion, the City of David. Centuries before the Roman period, the Hinnom Valley was used for burning the trash of the city and for the burning of incense (2 Chronicles 28:3). The valley was also the scene of the burning of children as sacrifices to idols (2 Kings 23:10; 2 Chronicles 33:6; Jeremiah 7:31); prophets warned of fiery judgments upon all those involved in such a repulsive practice.

The burning in that valley came to symbolize in the New Testament the devouring fire of judgment, representing the concept of hell as a place of continual burnings and eternal punishment. The book of Revelation (19:20; 20:10; 21:8) describes hell as a lake of fire and brimstone. (Brimstone is sulphur, a yellow-green, highly combustible element commonly found along the shores of the Dead Sea. The same substance is used today to make matches, gunpowder, and other products in the chemical and paper industries. When ignited, sulphur liquefies and produces a sharp, suffocating, burning vapor that in sufficient quantities can desolate and kill. Apparently, in those days, no harsher picture of the hellish fate of the wicked could be portrayed than that of being thrown into a lake of fire burning with brimstone.) The twelve occurrences of *Gehenna* in the New Testament are translated as "hell" or "hell fire." The most famous is Jesus' teaching here in the Sermon on the Mount and repeated among the Nephites (3 Nephi 12:22; see also Mormon 8:17).

Matthew 5:23–24; cf. 3 Nephi 12:23–24 If there are strained relations or friction between us and anyone else, before going to the Temple or to sacrament meeting and renewing our covenants with God, we should first be reconciled with that person—talk things over, work them out, resolve differences, forgive, and forget. "If thy brother shall trespass against thee, go and tell him his fault between thee and him alone: if he shall hear thee, thou hast gained thy brother" (Matthew 18:15). Then we can approach the Lord and his sacred things with full purpose of heart and, as he says, "I will receive you" (3 Nephi 12:24).

Matthew 5:25–26; Luke 12:58–59; cf. 3 Nephi 12:25–26 "Agree with thine adversary quickly" means "Quickly have kind thoughts for, or be disposed toward" (footnote a to Matthew 5:25). The adversary in this case means an opponent in a lawsuit. There would be far fewer lawsuits if people would be disposed to agreeing, or working things out, before going to court.

"Be reconciled to each other. Do not go to the courts of the Church nor to the courts of the land for litigation. Settle

Ancient coins

your own troubles and difficulties; . . . there is only one way in which a difficulty existing between man and man can be truly settled, and that is when they get together and settle it between them. The courts cannot settle troubles between me and my brother" (Smith, *Gospel Doctrine*, 257).

Roman, Greek, and Jewish coins were the three main kinds of money in circulation in the Holy Land during Jesus' lifetime (see Appendix 7, 777). Roman coinage consisted of the copper quadrans (Greek, *kodrantes*) and assarion, the bronze dupondius and sestertius, the silver denarius, and the gold aureus. The quadrans was the coin of least value: at the time of Jesus, it was worth 1/64 of a denarius. Jesus mentioned that if a man were sent to prison by his opponent in a lawsuit, he would not be released until he had paid "the uttermost farthing," that is, the last quadrans (see commentary on Matthew 10:29–31; see also Rousseau and Arav, *Jesus and His World*, 55–61).

ADULTERY, LUST

Matthew 5:27–30; cf. 3 Nephi 12:27–30 Included in the old law was a commandment not to commit adultery (Exodus 20:14, one of the basic Ten Commandments). That law, of course, still stands. But the higher law is for individuals never even to lust after another. If they do, they have already committed adultery in their hearts. We must not allow the lustful feelings to get started which could lead to adultery, and we will never have to worry about that great sin. As Alma encouraged his son, "Bridle all your passions, that ye may be filled with love" (Alma 38:12). If we are filled with genuine love, there is no room for lust. If we control the first tempting urges to accommodate physical desires, then we will not follow through and succumb to the serious sexual sin. Benjamin Franklin said, "It is easier to suppress the first desire, than to satisfy all that follow it" ("Way to Wealth," 28). The Savior reiterated the same commandment in our day, with added warnings of consequences for violating it:

"Verily I say unto you, as I have said before, he that looketh on a woman to lust after her, or if any shall commit adultery in their hearts, they shall not have the Spirit, but shall deny the faith and shall fear" (D&C 63:16).

Larry E. Dahl, a professor in Religious Education at Brigham Young University, wrote: "In the scriptures, the heart has to do with the core or essence of a person—his real intent and unfeigned desires. (See Proverbs 23:7.) If one would in fact commit adultery with the object of his lust if the opportunity were present, he is an adulterous person. Although taught in terms of a man lusting after a woman, the principle applies to all, male and female.

"But what if one really wouldn't commit the act of adultery, yet suffers real temptation? In a world saturated with immoral aural and visual stimuli, such thoughts and temptations can be daily fare.

"Although we cannot avoid all the stimuli, we can plead

with the Lord to help us control and channel our thoughts. We can consciously avoid compromising situations and forthrightly resist temptation. Rather than allowing improper thoughts to linger—and enhancing and savoring them—we can dismiss them with a prayer or an uplifting hymn or song, and deliberately channel our thoughts into positive paths.

"If we imagine ourselves involved in improper things, our thoughts may influence our heart's inclination and perhaps even our future behavior. Dr. Maxwell Maltz underscores the connection between our thoughts and our body's nervous system: 'Experimental and clinical psychologists have proved beyond a shadow of a doubt that the human nervous system cannot tell the difference between an "actual" experience and an experience *imagined vividly and in detail*'" (*Ensign*, February 1991, 8).

If your right eye or your right hand offends you (or causes you trouble), pluck it out or cut it off—not literally, of course, but Jesus uses hyperbole to emphasize how important it is that when we identify a weakness, we must get rid of that weakness rather than let it destroy our whole soul (cf. Matthew 18:8). The Joseph Smith Translation adds the Lord's own explanation of his figurative language:

"*And now this I speak, a parable concerning your sins; wherefore, cast them from you, that ye may not be hewn down and cast into the fire*" (JST Matthew 5:34; see also commentary on Matthew 18:8–9; Mark 9:43–48; cf. Helaman 14:18).

The Nephite version of this sermon renders that concept differently and more simply:

"Behold, I give unto you a commandment, that ye suffer none of these things to enter into your heart; for it is better that ye should deny yourselves of these things, wherein ye will take up your cross, than that ye should be cast into hell" (3 Nephi 12:29–30).

The Lord commands us to not allow the lusts of the flesh to enter into our heart. Though our physical bodies normally contain strong sexual desires—which are good, wholesome, and proper when used at the right time and under the right conditions for divinely approved purposes—it is better to deny ourselves any improper, lustful desires. That is, in a figurative sense, a way of "taking up our cross," denying ourselves certain forbidden pleasures to avoid being cast into hell and losing the opportunity to enjoy those sacred sexual powers forever. Moroni wrote: "Touch not the evil gift, nor the unclean thing . . . come unto Christ . . . and deny yourselves of all ungodliness" (Moroni 10:30, 32; also JST Matthew 16:26).

Elder Spencer W. Kimball taught: "Many acknowledge the vice of physical adultery, but still rationalize that anything short of that heinous sin may *not* be condemned too harshly; however, the Lord has said many times: 'Ye have heard that it was said by them of old times, Thou shalt not commit adultery:

"'But I say unto you, That whosoever looketh on a woman to lust after her hath committed adultery with her already in his heart.' (Matthew 5:27–28.)

"And to paraphrase and give the modern version: 'And she that looketh upon a man to lust after him shall deny the faith, and shall not have the Spirit; and if she repents not she shall be cast out [or excommunicated]' (D&C 42:23). The commands of the Lord apply to women with equal force as to their husbands, and those scriptures come with the same sharpness and exactness to both sexes, for he has but a single standard of morality. It is not always the man who is the aggressor. Often it is the pursuing, coveting woman, and note that for both, *all* is lost if there is not true, sustained, and real repentance.

"Home-breaking is sin, and any thought, act, or association which will tend to destroy another's home is a grievous transgression" (Conference Report, Oct. 1962, 58).

Matthew 5:29–30 Elder Bruce R. McConkie explained: "If thy right eye offend thee, pluck it out and cast it from thee—that is, if a situation or circumstance exists which might lead to sin, avoid it, lest continued association therewith lead to sin. If thy neighbor's wife is unduly attractive to you, stay away from her. If you have an urge to gamble, don't associate with gamblers or go where gambling is found. If you love money and the riches of men, consecrate your properties to the Welfare Plan, and ask your bishop to recommend you for a mission. . . . If you have an urge to steal, lock yourself in your closet until it passes. If the smell of coffee is enticing, don't go where it is being prepared" (*Doctrinal New Testament Commentary,* 1:225).

In other words, if you know you have a certain weakness, "cut it out," get rid of that weakness as quickly as possible, so that it does not destroy your whole soul.

Most of us love our eyes, and we would be extremely reluctant to lose one or both of them or to cut off one of our hands. It is the same problem with some of our sins. Maybe we like them too much. The Savior warns us to rid ourselves, at all cost, of those weaknesses and sinful inclinations that are obstacles to our peace and our progress toward exaltation (for more on weaknesses being overcome and actually becoming our strengths, see Ether 12:23–37).

DIVORCE

Matthew 5:31–32; Luke 16:18; cf. 3 Nephi 12:31–32
The old law permitted the option of divorce when a marriage partner was unfaithful and committed a sexual transgression with another person. A writing of divorcement was issued (Deuteronomy 24:1). Divorce is "permitted under some circumstances because of the hardness of the people's hearts, but as explained by Jesus, 'from the beginning it was not so'" (Bible Dictionary, "Divorce," 658). At the time of Jesus and in the modern Church of Jesus Christ divorce is likewise countenanced. But the higher law of God makes no allowance for divorce. In celestial realms there is no such thing as making an eternally binding covenant and then breaking it. The higher

law of celestial marriage is now available and encouraged, though the full penalties for marriage failure are not currently exacted, due to human shortcomings.

President Gordon B. Hinckley wrote: "There may be now and again a legitimate cause for divorce. I am not one to say that it is never justified. But I say without hesitation that this plague among us, which seems to be growing everywhere, is not of God, but rather is the work of the adversary of righteousness and peace and truth" (*Ensign,* May 1991, 74; see also commentary on Matthew 19:3–12; Faust, *Ensign,* May 1993, 35–37).

SWEARING AN OATH: HONESTY

Matthew 5:33–37; cf. 3 Nephi 12:33–37 In the old law was a commandment not to "forswear thyself" but follow through on all oaths to the Lord (Leviticus 19:12; Numbers 30:2; Deuteronomy 23:21). Not to "forswear thyself" means to not break your oath or perjure yourself (footnote a to Matthew 5:33). The higher law advised against swearing by heaven, or by the earth, or by our head, and so on. It is best to keep our communication plain and simple. Oaths, vows, and covenants of eternal import are made between a person and the Father or the Lord, in sacred ways and in sacred places.

Verse 35 singles out Jerusalem, giving it a noble epithet: "the city of the great King" (cf. Psalm 48:2). Indeed, the greatest events in history took place in Jerusalem: the atoning sacrifice and resurrection of the Lord Jesus. His dwelling place for centuries was in Jerusalem. His meeting place was there. His glory filled his house. He manifested himself to his servants, the prophets. For a millennium, he was worshipped in Jerusalem. His people "looked for redemption in Jerusalem" (Luke 2:38). From Melchizedek to Malachi, the Messiah was anticipated and announced there.

Jesus clearly knew the importance Jerusalem would have in his mission. "When the time was come that he should be received up, he stedfastly set his face to go to Jerusalem" (Luke 9:51), for as he noted, "it cannot be that a prophet perish out of Jerusalem" (Luke 13:33).

Jesus wept over the city as he recalled its past and foresaw its future. He left no doubt concerning the immediate future of Jerusalem. His were vivid prophetic pronouncements about succeeding generations being trodden down (Luke 21:24).

What was it all for? Why would Jesus and Jerusalem both suffer indignities and anguish and death? Their end was but a beginning. Jesus and Jerusalem would both be resurrected and live again, but to do so, both must be buried and brought forth anew. Jerusalem would eventually become, in an immortal and eternal sense, "the city of the great King."

EVIL FORCE OR GENEROUS SERVICE

Matthew 5:38–42; cf. 3 Nephi 12:38–42 In the old law was the notion of an eye for an eye and a tooth for a tooth (Exodus 21:24; Leviticus 24:20). The higher law of the gospel of Jesus Christ stipulates forbearance in striking back when we are harmed or deprived in any way. "Ye shall not resist evil" is, in the Greek text, an injunction against setting ourselves against the evil one; in other words, we are not to return evil for evil but submit, with forbearance and not vengeance, to any injustice against us. This is not *passive* submission to injury but *pacific*, or meek, response to it.

The Joseph Smith Translation of Luke 6:29–30 gives the proper sense of the teaching: "Unto him who smiteth thee on the cheek, offer also the other; *or, in other words, it is better to offer the other, than to revile again. . . . For it is better that thou suffer thine enemy to take these things, than to contend with him.*" Go the extra mile to be "submissive, meek, humble, patient, full of love" (Mosiah 3:19). Being willing to live the gospel makes us willing to go beyond what the law requires.

"The Lord requires sacrifice, meaning something above and beyond the minimum. The Master spoke of the 'second mile' and told us to go there. . . . Why? Because he wants to bless us. So he put all the blessings in the second mile" (Rector, *Ensign,* May 1979, 30).

President Joseph F. Smith taught: "It is extremely hurtful for any man holding the Priesthood, and enjoying the gift of the Holy Ghost, to harbor a spirit of envy, or malice, or retaliation, or intolerance toward or against his fellowmen. We ought to say in our hearts, let God judge between me and thee, but as for me, I will forgive. I want to say to you that Latter-Day Saints who harbor a feeling of unforgiveness in their souls are more guilty and more censurable than the one who has sinned against them. Go home and dismiss envy and hatred from your hearts; dismiss the feeling of unforgiveness; and cultivate in your souls that spirit of Christ which cried out upon the cross, 'Father, forgive them; for they know not what they do.' This is the spirit that Latter-Day Saints ought to possess all the day long. The man who has that spirit in his heart and keeps it there will never have any trouble with his neighbor" (*Gospel Doctrine,* 255–56).

LOVE ENEMIES

Matthew 5:43–47; Luke 6:27–36; cf. 3 Nephi 12:43–45 Included in the old law as understood by some of the ancients was the notion that we could love our friends but hate our enemies (cf. 4 Nephi 1:39). The group known as Essenes, for example, who lived during Jesus' mortal life in Jerusalem and in Qumran near the Dead Sea (see Appendix 2, 726) openly taught as a fundamental tenet of their brand of Judaism that one should love the children of light but hate the children of darkness (see Dead Sea Scrolls, *The Manual of*

Discipline, otherwise called *The Community Rule,* I:9–11, IX:21–23; Vermes, 62, 75). But the higher law of the gospel of Jesus Christ teaches us a better way to respond to opposition and persecution: "Love your enemies, bless them that curse you, do good to them that despitefully use you and persecute you."

Heavenly Father and the Savior are our example. An essential attribute of God is love. And we have a mortal example: Joseph Smith said, "I have no enemies but for the truth's sake. I have no desire but to do all men good. I feel to pray for all men" (*Teachings of the Prophet Joseph Smith,* 275).

Thus, in the Sermon on the Mount, Jesus commands his audience to love their enemies, bless those who hurl curses at them, and pray for those who despitefully use them. The reason? "That you may be the children of your Father which is in heaven" (Matthew 5:45).

After all, God the Father is kind and loving toward all his children, even those who forsake or ignore him. God the Father is patient and long-suffering. "He maketh his sun to rise on the evil and on the good" (Matthew 5:45), meaning that righteousness and wickedness cannot be immediately and constantly rewarded or punished. Such interference in the lives of men and women would thwart the plan of salvation and the purposes for which earth life was designed—to allow individuals to walk by faith and be tested. It is no accident that Jesus concludes this section of the Sermon by commanding his listeners to be perfect, as their Father in heaven is perfect (Matthew 5:48). Loving kindness and tolerant restraint are great hallmarks of God's perfection.

Matthew 5:46–47; cf. 3 Nephi 12:46–47 It is easy to love those who love us and salute or greet those who are friends; even publicans (signifying "sinners") do that. But the real challenge is to genuinely care for the abrasive, seemingly unlovable types: Learn to love them anyway; that is the higher law.

A SECOND GALILEAN MINISTRY

PERFECT AS YOUR FATHER

Matthew 5:48; cf. 3 Nephi 12:48 President Hugh B. Brown said, "We take seriously and literally the injunction of the Savior to be perfect" (Conference Report, Oct. 1966, 102). In fact, the Old Testament also teaches that we should be perfect (Deuteronomy 18:13). But what is the perfection that God expects of us here on the earth? We often think perfection is defined as "flawless" or "sinless." But there has been only One in the history of this world who was literally and in every way flawless and sinless. Yet the scriptures say that "Noah was a just man and perfect" (Genesis 6:9); Job was "perfect and upright" (Job 1:1); and Seth was "a perfect man" (D&C 107:43).

Apparently the scriptural definition of perfection is different from our usual one. In the Bible three Hebrew words and two Greek words are translated into King James English as "perfect." They are *shalem* (1 Kings 8:61; 15:14; 2 Kings 20:3), *tam* (Job 1:1), *tammim* (Genesis 6:9; 17:1; Deuteronomy 18:13), *teleios* (Matthew 5:48; 19:21; Ephesians 4:13; Colossians 4:12; James 3:2), and *artios* (2 Timothy 3:17). None of these five words means "flawless" or "sinless." They are otherwise rendered as "whole," "upright," "undefiled," "just," or "complete." A person who is whole, complete, upright, and so forth, is one who, upon sinning, as all mortals do, immediately and thoroughly repents and is again reconciled to God and becomes whole, complete, and upright once more. It is an ongoing process of repenting and improving throughout this life.

"We don't need to get a complex or get a feeling that you have to be perfect to be saved. You don't. There's only been one perfect person, and that's the Lord Jesus, but in order to be saved in the Kingdom of God and in order to pass the test of mortality, what you have to do is get on the straight and narrow path—thus charting a course leading to eternal life—and then, being on that path, pass out of this life in full fellowship. . . . If you're on that path and pressing forward, and you die, you'll never get off the path. There is no such thing as falling off the straight and narrow path in the life to come, and the reason is that this life is the time that is given to men to prepare for eternity. . . .

"You don't have to live a life that's truer than true. You don't have to have an excessive zeal that becomes fanatical and becomes unbalancing. What you have to do is stay in the mainstream of the Church and live as upright and decent people live in the Church—keeping the commandments, paying your tithing, serving in the organizations of the Church, loving the Lord, staying on the straight and narrow path. If you're on that path when death comes—because this is the time and the day appointed, this the probationary estate—you'll never fall off from it, and, for all practical purposes, your calling and election is made sure" (McConkie, "Probationary Test of Mortality," 8; paragraphing altered).

As 3 Nephi 12:48 indicates, the Father and the Son are our supreme examples of the perfection that we eventually and ultimately want to achieve. By becoming one with our Savior (that's the meaning of the word *at-one-ment*) we may eventually become perfect in him. Note the words of Moroni: "Come unto Christ, and be perfected in him, and deny yourselves of all ungodliness . . . that by his grace ye may be perfect in Christ" (Moroni 10:32).

ALMS: NOTORIETY OR GENEROSITY

Matthew 6:1–4; cf. 3 Nephi 13:1–4 Jesus spent a good deal of the next part of his sermon teaching about the nature of our Father in heaven by discussing private daily devotions. Do not, he said, make a public show of doing that which is better done in private—almsgiving, welfare relief, fasting, and personal prayer (Matthew 6:1–6), for "thy Father which seeth in secret shall reward thee openly" (Matthew 6:6).

A central message of several teachings in Matthew 6 is to be careful not to do good things just *to be seen of men*. Satan always sponsors his own imitation of righteous principles; for example, we should seek glory but not the glory of men. Our immediate and ultimate objective is to have our eye single to the glory of God. We should "do our alms," all our righteous acts, secretly and quietly.

PRAYER: HYPOCRISY OR REVERENCE

Matthew 6:5–15; Luke 11:2–4; cf. 3 Nephi 13:5–15; Alma 31:14–18 As with almsgiving, so with praying. No ostentation. Do not pray in order to parade your piety or else you are revealing your absence of the same. Those who "sound a trumpet" or give alms to be seen of men are "hypocrites," an epithet favored by Matthew to describe those Pharisees who sought prestige above all else.

As with other religious acts, prayer should be done privately and quietly. "Entering into thy closet" (v. 6; cf. Alma 33:7) may, indeed, mean your bedroom and its closet, or, as the New Testament Greek term connotes—your "places of privacy," whether in your house, your office, or your "wilderness" (Alma 34:26).

We are warned against "vain repetitions" (the Greek term here suggests speaking without thinking). There is nothing wrong with repetition itself. In fact, God teaches us more often than not through repetition. He continually teaches and reteaches, iterates and reiterates, all through the scriptures. And in the holiest classroom on earth, in the house of God, the main method used is repetition. "Vain" repetition is what we are encouraged to avoid.

Are the Latter-day Saints guilty of using vain repetitions? Consider the following standard cliches used in Latter-day Saints' prayers:

"We're thankful for this day."

"We're thankful for the building we have to meet in."

"We're grateful for all our many blessings."

"Bless those who aren't here this week that they'll be here next week."

"Bless the sick and afflicted."

"Bless us that no harm or accident will befall us."

"Bless us with all the blessings we stand in need of."

"Bless the missionaries that they'll be guided to the honest in heart."

"Bless us that we'll strive to incorporate these things into our daily lives."

"Take us all home in peace and safety."

Is there anything inherently wrong with any of these phrases? Absolutely not, *as long as voicing them is sincere, genuine, and heartfelt.* If we will, we can pray, even a long prayer, without multiplying words (3 Nephi 19:24). Heavenly Father knows what we are grateful for and what we need before we ever kneel down. He does not necessarily need to hear it, but we need to say it. We need to express ourselves to him verbally—frequently and regularly.

One day in Galilee Brother Ogden learned an unforgettable lesson about the power of sincere prayer. He wrote:

"When my daughter Sara was only four years old, I took her on an overnight campout and fishing trip with the Jerusalem Branch Boy Scouts to the northeastern corner of the Sea of Galilee, near the site of ancient Bethsaida, near where the Jordan River enters the lake and which from 1948 to 1967 was the border between Israel and Syria. While the boys were out fishing, pulling in some big catfish, maybe a St. Peter's fish or two, Sara and I went for a walk about a quarter of a mile west from the camp to find the precise place where the Jordan River flows into the lake.

"There were thickets of tall canes or reeds, and after some time fighting our way through the thick jungle of reeds and tangling undergrowth, knowing that they must be very close to the river, we found it simply impossible to move forward.

We were stuck in the middle of the tall thickets, about eight to ten feet high, unable to see in any direction and hardly able to move.

"I was carrying Sara on my shoulders and had by now grown tired, out of energy, and perplexed. Sara suggested, 'Daddy, why don't we pray?'

"So we folded our arms and prayed, asking Heavenly Father to help us find our way safely out of the thick tangle of vegetation.

"We forged on, back in the general direction toward the camp, until we came to a barbed-wire fence. Having maneuvered our way over the fence, we looked back. Hanging on the fence was the international triangular sign for a minefield. *We had just made our way through a minefield!*

"Needless to say, I am thankful for a daughter who suggested we pray and for a Father in Heaven who answered our prayer" (Ogden, journal).

The scriptures say this world is a field. These days it is a minefield. How do we avoid stepping in the wrong places, risking getting tangled up in the world's thick undergrowth or blown to bits by hidden weapons? We make sure we are staying morally clean, avoiding improper reading material, films, and videos, studying the scriptures, worshipping in the Temple, fasting, keeping the Sabbath Day holy, serving others, and especially praying—frequently and regularly. If we're not doing all those things, we can be sure that we will be stepping into dangerous situations. If we are doing all those things, then we will be "worthy to stand."

Matthew 6:9–13; cf. 3 Nephi 13:9–13 Jesus gave an example of how to pray to the Father: "after this manner," not that these exact words should be repeatedly uttered. Third Nephi 13:10 omits one phrase contained in the biblical text (Matthew 6:10), "Thy kingdom come," likely because it had come. "Give us this day our daily bread" (v. 11) was the life-long plea of a people dependent on the rain of heaven and the produce of the land, for bread is the basic substance of life.

One phrase in verse 13 is curious: "Lead us not into temptation." God does not, of course, lead anyone into temptation, but the sense may be "Don't bring us into the *control* or *power* of temptation" greater than we can bear. That is what the Hebrew rendering of the New Testament phrase means. Joseph Smith Translation Matthew 6:14 says, "And *suffer* us not *to be led* into temptation," or Joseph Smith Translation Luke 11:4, "*let us not be led unto* temptation."

Matthew 6:14–15; cf. 3 Nephi 13:14–15 Can we expect Heavenly Father to forgive us of all our sins if we are refusing to forgive others? To be forgiven, we must forgive (Mosiah 26:31; D&C 64:8–10). The Prophet Joseph Smith showed us how a mortal can do it; he once remarked that "all was well between him and the heavens; that he had no enmity against any one; and as the prayer of Jesus, or his pattern, so prayed Joseph—Father, forgive me my trespasses as I forgive those who trespass against me, for I freely forgive all men. If we would secure and cultivate the love of others, we must love others, even our enemies as well as friends" (*Teachings of the Prophet Joseph Smith,* 312–13).

A most poignant example of this kind of forgiving power in modern times is the experience of Corrie ten Boom during and after World War II.

"In modern history perhaps no more atrocious crime has been committed than the Holocaust, the systematic murder of millions of Jews, political prisoners, handicapped persons, and others by Hitler's Nazi regime. Corrie ten Boom, a Christian political prisoner, survived the concentration camp at Ravensbruck, but her beloved sister Betsie did not. After the war Corrie traveled the world preaching sermons of reconciliation, peace, and forgiveness. Then it happened. She was called upon to practice what she preached. She records in her autobiography, *The Hiding Place,* the defining moment of her Christian discipleship:

"'It was at a church service in Munich that I saw him, the former S.S. man who had stood guard at the shower room door in the processing center at Ravensbruck. He was the first of our actual jailers that I had seen since that time. And suddenly it was all there—the roomful of mocking men, the heaps of clothing, Betsie's pain-blanched face.

"'He came up to me as the church was emptying, beaming and bowing. "How grateful I am for your message, Fraulein," he said. "To think that, as you say, He has washed my sins away!"

"'His hand was thrust out to shake mine. And I, who had preached so often . . . the need to forgive, kept my hand at my side. Even as the angry, vengeful thoughts boiled through me, I saw the sin of them. Jesus Christ had died for this man; was I going to ask for more? Lord Jesus, I prayed, forgive me and help me to forgive him.

"'I tried to smile. I struggled to raise my hand. I could not. I felt nothing, not the slightest spark of warmth or charity. And so again I breathed a silent prayer. Jesus, I cannot forgive him. Give me Your forgiveness.

"'As I took his hand the most incredible thing happened. From my shoulder along my arm and through my hand a current seemed to pass from me to him, while into my heart sprang a love for this stranger that almost overwhelmed me.

"'And so I discovered that it is not on our own forgiveness any more than on our goodness that the world's healing hinges, but on His. When He tells us to love our enemies, He gives, along with the command, the love itself' (Corrie ten Boom, with John and Elizabeth Sherrill, *The Hiding Place* [New York: Bantam Books, 1971], p. 238)" (Sowell, "Along with the Command," 51–52).

FASTING: HYPOCRISY OR SIMPLICITY

Matthew 6:16–18; cf. 3 Nephi 13:16–18 As with prayer, so with fasting. No ostentation. Do not do it to parade your religious feelings or else you are revealing your absence of the same. As with other religious acts, fasting should be done privately and quietly. By your sad, distorted facial expressions do not suggest: "Oh, look, world, I've fasted now for twenty-*five* hours!" The Lord actually encourages us to "appear not unto men to fast" (v. 18). Quiet devotion brings open blessings.

Here are some suggestions for a great fast: Plan and prepare your schedule. Have a particular purpose. Start the fast with a private prayer. Keep the Spirit by using Saturday evening as part of your fasting period, and fast a full twenty-four hours, refraining from all food and drink, if possible. Plan specific activities: study the scriptures, write in your journal, and attend church meetings; maybe even participate in a *family* testimony meeting. Pay a full fast offering. Before concluding your fast, set aside twenty or thirty minutes to ponder and meditate. Ponder Moroni 7 or 10, or Mosiah 4, or Isaiah 53, or some other particularly powerful chapter of scripture. And finally, end your fast with a private prayer.

The combination of fasting and praying can cause humble followers of the Savior to "wax stronger and stronger in their humility, and firmer and firmer in the faith of Christ, unto the filling their souls with joy and consolation, yea, even to the purifying and the sanctification of their hearts, which sanctification cometh because of their yielding their hearts unto God" (Helaman 3:35).

TREASURE ON EARTH OR IN HEAVEN

Matthew 6:19–34; Luke 12:33–34; cf. 3 Nephi 13:19–34; Helaman 8:25 Whatever you consider your "treasure," that is where your heart will be. That is where your thoughts and affections will be placed. The Savior warns: Be careful about accumulating earthly treasures; they are all transitory and apt to be stolen. You will take none of them with you when you depart from this earth (Psalm 49:16–17;

1 Timothy 6:7; Alma 39:14). But do lay up treasure in heaven. Those are treasures that will endure forever.

Matthew 6:22–23; Luke 11:34–36; cf. 3 Nephi 13:22–23 The eye is the light of the body and the window to the soul. If our eye is single (and Joseph Smith later added to this phrase "single *to the glory of God*"; JST Matthew 6:22; see also D&C 4:5), that is, if we are dedicated to our Savior's glorious cause, then our whole body will be full of light (D&C 88:67). He is our light, so our whole life can be filled with his influence, and no darkness will persist in us. There is no life without Light.

Matthew 6:24; Luke 16:9–13; cf. 3 Nephi 13:24; Moroni 7:11 *Mammon* is an Aramaic term referring to worldly riches or wealth. It is true that we cannot have one foot in the kingdom and one foot still in the world. It is not possible to walk that way. No man can serve two masters. Service to God and the pursuit of worldly wealth are mutually exclusive enterprises for those called to the holy apostleship or full-time Church service. *La'avod* in Hebrew means to serve; it also means to work and to worship. It is certainly not possible to serve or worship two opposite lords at the same time. We must choose, just as the original Twelve and Seventy had to choose. We either prove ourselves a true child of God or we become a child of the devil (Alma 5:41). We must hold to the one, the Holy One, only.

"There is a line of demarcation, well defined, between the Lord's territory and the devil's. If you will stay on the Lord's side of the line you will be under his influence and will have no desire to do wrong; but if you cross to the devil's side of the line one inch, you are in the tempter's power, and if he is successful, you will not be able to think or even reason properly, because you will have lost the spirit of the Lord" (Smith, *Sharing the Gospel with Others*, 42–43).

If our objective is to serve God and flee mammon, why would Luke encourage us to make "friends of the mammon of unrighteousness"? (Luke 16:9). The Doctrine and

Covenants helps supply an answer. "This is wisdom, make unto yourselves friends with the mammon of unrighteousness, and they will not destroy you" (D&C 82:22). In other words, while reaching out to the world and trying to bring in as many as possible to the truth, be friendly and kindly disposed towards them in every righteous way.

President Joseph Fielding Smith explained further: "The commandment of the Lord that the saints should make themselves 'friends with the mammon of unrighteousness,' seems to be a hard saying when not properly understood. It is not intended that in making friends of the 'mammon of unrighteousness' that the brethren were to partake with them in their sins; to receive them to their bosoms, intermarry with them and otherwise come down to their level. They were to so live that peace with their enemies might be assured. They were to treat them kindly, be friendly with them as far as correct and virtuous principles would permit, but never to swear with them or drink and carouse with them. If they could allay prejudice and show a willingness to trade with and show a kindly spirit, it might help to turn them away from their bitterness. Judgment was to be left with the Lord" (*Church History and Modern Revelation,* 1:323).

The questions raised in Luke 16:10–12 may be answered in the following way:

If you anticipate receiving the true riches of eternity, it is wise to learn obedience and faithfulness with regard to things of this world. If you will become prudent in dealing with a small quantity, you may find yourself in eventual possession of great treasure. If you learn to handle a minor stewardship entrusted to you from someone else, you can be trusted with something of great value that will be your own.

Matthew 6:25–34; Luke 12:22–32; cf. 3 Nephi 13:25–34 Jesus changed the focus of his instruction, as well as his audience, for the concluding section of his great sermon (Matthew 6:25–7:27). He turned his attention to the Twelve and other leaders whose calling was to go out two by two to teach and testify (Luke 10:1)—and by extension today to all authorities and missionaries, anyone in full-time service to the kingdom. "Take no thought for" (v. 25) means "don't worry about" or "don't be overly anxious about." Those in full-time service to the Lord must not be burdened with the daily cares of food, drink, and clothing (cf. Alma 31:37–38). Others can help provide for their temporal needs so they can dedicate themselves completely to his work, without distractions. The Father promises that will happen:

"And, again, I say unto you, go ye into the world, and care not for the world; for the world will hate you, and will persecute you, and will turn you out of their synagogues.

"Nevertheless, ye shall go forth from house to house, teaching the people; and I will go before you.

"And your heavenly Father will provide for you, whatsoever things ye need for food, what ye shall eat; and for raiment, what ye shall wear or put on" (JST Matthew 6:25–27; cf. Alma 26:28).

Jesus' illustrations are refreshing. Look at the birds and the flowers, how the God of heaven cares for their needs (cf. D&C 84:81–82). Notice, he said, the ravens (crows, or birds in general, as in the other accounts; Luke 12:24); they do not plant, cultivate, and harvest the fields; they do not store up great quantities of supplies in barns; but God takes care of them. The lesson is one of faith and trust. Jesus encouraged his disciples to divest themselves of constant preoccupation with worldly survival, though he did not intend for people to abandon their mortal labors and wait for God to provide.

Consider the example of a young, newly married couple. The world suggests that before they start bringing babies into the world, they should wait until they have a house and a good, stable, full-time job, the car paid for, and all the clothes and amenities that the baby will need upon arrival and for the first months of his or her life. The Lord says that even though they don't have everything in place; they're not yet financially secure—and, in fact, are still struggling to finish school and working full time—and yes, the schedule is exhausting, still, they should not put off bringing children into the world. If we are faithful, we do what we can, and then we have confidence that God will take care of us. God wants his children to be submissive and dependent, to look to him and live. We work hard, do all we can, and God provides.

Can any of us add, just by thinking about it, even one cubit (about eighteen inches) to our height? A foot and a half is a significant addition to one's height, and it takes time. The answer must be no. We are quite dependent on God for our growth—but consider the lilies of the field; they grow without thinking about it.

"Consider the lilies how they grow" (Luke 12:27). Lilies are flowers that grow from a bulb, like iris, crocus, hyacinth, tulip, and narcissus. Though not a true lily, the common crown anemone was possibly the object of Jesus' superlative comparison to Solomon. By saying that the once-wise king in all his glory was not arrayed like one of the lilies, we are to understand that the flush of colorful spring flowers scattered over all the hills, valleys, and plains would produce in the eyes of the beholder genuine admiration and awe for the elegant beauty of one of God's simple creations. If God cares for the smallest works of his hands, surely he will care for and provide for humankind, his crowning creation.

God's own children are of greater value than all the flora and fauna; surely he will care for our needs, too. "How much more will he *provide for* you, *if ye are not* of little faith?" (JST Luke 12:30). Heavenly Father knows all our needs; he can provide (D&C 84:83). One of his divine efforts is "providence" for his children (Jacob 2:13; D&C 78:14; JS–H 1:75).

Our priority must be to seek "first the kingdom of God, and his righteousness; and all these things shall be added unto you" (Matthew 6:33). Joseph Smith, as was his prerogative as a prophet, later made significant additions to the teachings of verse 33: "*Wherefore, seek not the things of this world,* but seek ye first *to build up* the kingdom of God, *and to establish* his righteousness" (JST Matthew 6:38). We must "do many things of [our] own free will, and bring to pass much righteousness" and we shall "in nowise lose [our] reward" (D&C 58:27–28). "Whosoever will lose his life for my sake shall find it" (Matthew 16:25), the Savior has promised, and Luke reassures us, "Fear not little flock; for it is your Father's good pleasure to give you the kingdom" (Luke 12:32; cf. D&C 29:5).

Seek first the kingdom of God. He is always first; our fellowman is second; we are third. We get in trouble spiritually when we put ourselves in first place. God and his work and glory must always be our number one priority.

President Ezra Taft Benson said:

"Why did God put the first commandment first? Because He knew that if we truly loved Him we would want to keep all of His other commandments. . . .

"We must put God in the forefront of everything else in our lives. . . .

" . . . Our love of the Lord will govern the claims for our affection, the demands on our time, the interests we pursue, and the order of our priorities.

"We should put God ahead of *everyone else* in our lives" (Conference Report, April 1988, 3).

"Take therefore no thought for the morrow" (Matthew 6:34)—again, the idea is "don't worry about" or "don't be overly anxious about" the things of tomorrow. "Let the morrow take thought for the things of itself" (D&C 84:84). There is enough to be concerned about each day—one day at a time—without piling on all future concerns. That does not negate, however, the need to prepare for the future, but that is what we do when we live fully and properly each day. Daily, righteous living quietly and automatically provides for the morrow.

JUDGMENT: HYPOCRITICAL OR HELPFUL

Matthew 7:1–5; Luke 6:37–38, 41–42; cf. 3 Nephi 14:1–5 What followed next might well be summarized as a dialogue in which Jesus provided help to the Twelve on how to teach the people and overcome the challenges or objections they would present. This is made clear only in the Joseph Smith Translation: *"Now these are the words which Jesus taught his disciples that they should say unto the people"* (JST Matthew 7:1).

The Lord's people are commanded not to judge others. The danger in judging others is that we are never in possession of all the facts. We can never really know what is happening in others' lives, in their homes, with their families or friends. Tragic, stressful, or anxiety-producing events may bring out negative, evil, or hateful reactions and words. If we knew and understood the background causes of such undesirable behavior or unkind words, we might feel more compassion towards a person who perpetrated or spoke such things.

What blessings, joy, and peace come as we avoid unrighteously judging others. If we do misjudge others, we can repent. If others misjudge us, we can forgive.

A danger in judging others is that our inclination is to judge them by their *actions,* whereas we would like to be judged by our *intentions.* It is wise to leave judgment to the great Judge of us all. He is in possession of all the facts and the intentions, and he is just and merciful.

In one sense we are, and should be, constantly judging what is good for us and what is not. We must be careful to judge what to read and what not to read, what to watch on TV and in movie theaters and what not to watch, what music we should listen to and what would be damaging to our spiritual sensitivities, what we should wear and what we should not wear, what we should eat or drink and what we should not eat or drink, and what we should say and what we should avoid saying.

Knowing that we should and must judge in some ways, the Lord has clarified the command: "Judge not *unrighteously,* that ye be not judged: *but judge righteous judgment*" (JST Matthew 7:1–2). He has given us definitive guidelines on how to judge righteously. We may know with a perfect knowledge whether something is good for us or bad for us, as Moroni 7:14–18 teaches us.

An incentive to our judging righteously and compassionately is the warning that whatever measure of judgment we use on someone else, that same measure of judgment will be used on us (Matthew 7:2; see also Alma 41:14–15; Mormon 8:19–20; Moroni 7:18; D&C 1:10).

The good measure that is pressed down and shaken together, that men "give into your bosom" (Luke 6:38), means a measure of grain that is poured into one's lap; that is, the outer garment in the lap. If the good measure is pressed down, more can fit. If it is then shaken, even more can fit—until it is overflowing.

A "mote" is a tiny splinter; a "beam" is a large board used in construction. We are quick to notice the tiny weaknesses and flaws in others and yet slow to recognize large debilities in ourselves.

This message is cleverly rendered in the hymn "Let Each Man Learn to Know Himself":

> Let each man learn to know himself;
> To gain that knowledge let him labor,
> Improve those failings in himself
> Which he condemns so in his neighbor.
> How lenient our own faults we view,
> And conscience' voice adeptly smother,
> Yet, oh, how harshly we review
> The self-same failings in another!
>
> And if you meet an erring one
> Whose deeds are blamable and thoughtless,

Consider, ere you cast the stone,
If you yourself are pure and faultless.
Oh, list to that small voice within,
Whose whisperings oft make men confounded,
And trumpet not another's sin;
You'd blush deep if your own were sounded.

And in self-judgment if you find
Your deeds to others' are superior,
To you has Providence been kind,
As you should be to those inferior.
Example sheds a genial ray
Of light which men are apt to borrow,
So first improve yourself today
And then improve your friends tomorrow.
(*Hymns,* 1948, no. 91)

Jesus put these teachings in the context of his hypocritical antagonists:

"*And Jesus said unto his disciples, Beholdest thou the Scribes, and the Pharisees, and the Priests, and the Levites? They teach in their synagogues, but do not observe the law, nor the commandments; and all have gone out of the way, and are under sin.*

"*Go thou and say unto them, Why teach ye men the law and the commandments, when ye yourselves are the children of corruption?*

"*Say unto them,* Ye hypocrites, first cast out the beam out of thine own eye; and then shalt thou see clearly to cast out the mote out of thy brother's eye" (JST Matthew 7:6–8).

HOLY THINGS ARE LIKE PEARLS

Matthew 7:6; cf. 3 Nephi 14:6 "Give not that which is holy unto the dogs" is a behest that was given in a parallelism; the second phrase is "neither cast ye your pearls before swine." The parallel clearly defines the Israelites' regard for the dog.

A Second Galilean Ministry

To the Jews, pigs were the embodiment of impurity and ill repute

Unlike in modern Western society, the dog in Israelite culture was not "man's best friend" but an ill-respected scavenger. Jesus said, "It is not meet to take the children's bread, and to cast it to dogs" (Matthew 15:26), a hyperbolic statement of the priority of gospel dissemination and of the care with which the mysteries of the kingdom should be reserved for the spiritually attuned. Figuratively, then, dogs represent unworthy persons, or, as in a later case, persons who are not matured or prepared for sacred things (Matthew 15:21–28).

The delicate structure of pearls is implied in Jesus' warning not to cast pearls before swine, since, unlike other gems, pearls are relatively soft and trampling on them could destroy them. Our most precious and sacred gems of the gospel must be shared only with those who are prepared to receive them. The Lord later added another dimension to this admonition: "*And the mysteries of the kingdom* [for example, sacred teachings, covenants, and ordinances of the Temple] *ye shall keep within yourselves; for it is not meet to give that which is holy unto the dogs. . . . for the world cannot receive that which ye, yourselves, are not able to bear; wherefore ye shall not give your pearls unto them*" (JST Matthew 7:10–11; cf. D&C 41:6).

PRAYER: ASK, SEEK, KNOCK

Matthew 7:7–12; Luke 11:9–13; cf. 3 Nephi 14:7–12
Here is one of the most powerful promises ever given to humankind and the most often repeated. There are conditions to this promise, of course. We must ask in faith (James 1:6), we must seek persistently (Luke 11:5–10; 18:1–5), and we must knock with rigor. We must also ask, seek, and knock obediently and not improperly ("ask not amiss"; 2 Nephi 4:35; Helaman 10:5), else we have no promise from the great Benefactor (D&C 82:10). "His invitation, 'Ask, and ye shall receive' (3 Nephi 27:29) does not assure that you will get what you *want*. It does guarantee that, if worthy, you will get what you *need*, as judged by a Father that loves you perfectly" (Scott, *Ensign*, November 1995, 17).

At this point the Prophet Joseph Smith added four additional verses, placing the teachings in the context of Jesus' day and his people:

"*And then said his disciples unto him, they will say unto us, We ourselves are righteous, and need not that any man should teach us. God, we know, heard Moses and some of the prophets; but us he will not hear.*

"*And they will say, We have the law for our salvation, and that is sufficient for us.*

"*Then Jesus answered, and said unto his disciples, thus shall ye say unto them,*

"*What man among you, having a son, and he shall be standing out, and shall say, Father, open thy house that I may come in and sup with thee, will not say, Come in, my son; for mine is thine, and thine is mine?*" (JST Matthew 7:14–17).

Jesus seems to be giving a help session to the apostles to enable them to overcome the objections of their audience. This is very insightful. Nowhere except in the Joseph Smith Translation do we get the information that Jesus was so careful in helping his apostolic ministers craft their teaching points. And nowhere else do we receive such perceptive but disheartening information about the social and religious atmosphere in which the apostles had to carry out their ministry. The attitudes held in certain quarters of Judaism toward the doctrines of continuing revelation, salvation, and Jesus as Messiah indicate that Judaism was in much sadder condition than might be supposed from evidence in the other versions of the text of the Sermon on the Mount.

Matthew 7:12 The law and the prophets are summarized in one idea, known widely as the "golden rule": whatever you would like people to do to you, you do that to them. "The best and most clear indicator that we are progressing spiritually and coming unto Christ is the way we treat other people" (Ashton, *Ensign,* May 1992, 20).

THE WAY IS STRAIT AND NARROW

Matthew 7:13–14; Luke 13:23–24; cf. 3 Nephi 14:13–14; 1 Nephi 8:20; 2 Nephi 9:41; Jacob 6:11 Baptism is not the *door* to our heavenly mansion but the *gate* to the path that leads to the mansion. Relatively few are genuinely interested in entering the gate and walking that path (see also 1 Nephi 14:12; 2 Nephi 31:17–20; 3 Nephi 27:33; D&C 132:25).

The words *strait* and *narrow* mean about the same thing: constricted, tight. The juxtaposition of synonyms is a familiar ancient Hebrew literary technique (see *Encyclopedia of Mormonism,* 3:1419).

A modern use of the word *strait* is the Strait of Magellan (in Patagonia, at the southern tip of South America), which connects the Pacific and Atlantic Oceans. It is not a straight line between two points—one cannot see one ocean from the other. So with us: we cannot see the other side (of heaven), but if we persevere in the strait path, we will arrive there.

Note the scriptural difference between *strait* and *straight*; they are two different words. Our path is described as "strait"; the Lord's path is "straight" (Alma 7:9; 37:12; D&C 3:2). Jesus Christ is the only one who never had to make course corrections. (We thank Jared Halverson, seminary teacher and BYU Religious Education graduate student, for this insight.)

Our Savior's paths are always straight because "he cannot walk in crooked paths; neither doth he vary from that which he hath said; neither hath he a shadow of turning from the right to the left, or from that which is right to that which is wrong" (Alma 7:20).

FALSE PROPHETS KNOWN BY THEIR FRUITS

Matthew 7:15–20; Luke 6:43–44; cf. 3 Nephi 14:15–20 Jesus warned his listeners to beware of false prophets who are among the sheep (the members of the Church), but they are dangerous wolves in disguise (on the figurative use of wolves in the New Testament, see Matthew 10:16). How can we recognize them? "Ye shall know them by their fruits" (cf. Moroni 7:5). The words and works of men and women are compared to fruit, good works being good fruit, and evil works, bad fruit. Whether in the world of plant life or human life, God wants good produce, good fruit.

There grew in the land of Jesus a formidable abundance of thorns and thistles, and they could not escape the figurative eye of the prophets and the Savior. Thorns and thistles served only to afflict, distract, and annoy. They never symbolized anything good or positive.

The bramble (Luke 6:44) is a prickly, evergreen, vinelike shrub that produces an edible berry. It grows in all parts of the land, forming impenetrable thickets, especially along the riverbanks and by springs and swamps. Again using nature as a comparison, Jesus' point was "every tree is known by his own fruit" (Luke 6:44). No one gathers figs from thorns, and no

A Second Galilean Ministry

Thistles and thorns symbolized affliction, distraction, and annoyance

one gathers grapes from brambles. Likewise, all people are known by their "fruits"—their words and their works, their character and their thoughts, which determine their actions.

Trees have always been a significant feature of the landscape of the Holy Land. They have, therefore, figured prominently in the physical survival of the people and in the didactic imagery of their preachers and writers. There are more references to the fig tree in the New Testament than to any other tree, but also mentioned are the mustard tree (Luke 13:19), the sycamine (Luke 17:6), the sycomore (Luke 19:4), the palm (John 12:13), and the olive (Romans 11:17, 24).

Because of their essential role in providing food, material for buildings, shelter, occupational tools and implements, and shade, and for preventing deterioration of the landscape, trees in the biblical periods enjoyed respect and near reverence from the inhabitants of the land.

Trees were also among the favorite objects of biblical imagery and symbolism. Trees usually represent people. Comparing the characteristics of trees to the human experience was a familiar teaching approach among the Jewish sages for centuries. Following is an example from the most known and used part of the Mishnah (volumes of rabbinic writings). One rabbi used to say, "One whose wisdom is greater than his deeds what is he like? A tree whose branches are many and its roots few. And the wind comes and roots it up and overturns it on its face. . . . But one whose deeds exceed his wisdom what is he like? A tree whose branches are few and its roots many; so that even if all the winds that are in the world come and blow upon it they stir it not from its place" (*Pirke Aboth*, III:22, 92–93).

From Jesus and his disciples came many examples of trees as object lessons. Bad trees produce ill will, negativism, criticism, accusation, cynicism, and all kinds of destructive thinking and sinful behavior. Good trees produce good fruit. Joseph Smith was a good tree. The Book of Mormon is a good tree. The Church of Jesus Christ of Latter-day Saints is a good tree. Jesus Christ himself is the best tree of all—the Tree of Life. You can know the trees; that is, you can know the hearts and souls of people perfectly by what comes out of their minds and mouths. In a sense, we seldom speak or act truly impulsively; we say and do what we are.

DO THE WILL OF THE FATHER

Matthew 7:21–23; Luke 6:46; 13:25–30; cf. 3 Nephi 14:21–23 President John Taylor declared: "We are told that 'Many will say to me in that day, Lord, Lord, have we not prophesied in Thy name and in Thy name have cast out devils, and in Thy name done many wonderful works?' Yet to all such he will say; 'Depart from me, ye that work iniquity.' You say that means the outsiders? No, it does not. Do they do many wonderful works in the name of Jesus? No; if they do anything it is done in the name of themselves or of the devil. Sometimes they will do things in the name of God; but it is simply an act of blasphemy. This means you, Latter-day Saints, who heal the sick, cast out devils and do many wonderful things in the name of Jesus. And yet how many we see among this people of this class, that become careless, and treat lightly the ordinances of God's house and the Priesthood of the Son of God; yet they think they are going by and by, to slide into the kingdom of God; but I tell you unless they are righteous and keep their covenants they will never go there. Hear it, ye Latter-day Saints!" (quoted in Smith and Sjodahl, *Doctrine and Covenants Commentary,* 462–63).

To live eternally with our Father in Heaven, we must learn his will and do it. We must obey the Father and know the Son, too. Joseph Smith made an interesting change in the concept expressed in verse 23, "I never knew you" (cf. Mosiah 26:27). He reversed the pronouns to read: "Ye never knew me" (JST Matthew 7:33). In essence, the Savior was saying that his listeners knew that he was born in Bethlehem, that he carried on his ministry around the Sea of Galilee, chose Twelve Apostles, would die and be resurrected, and even that he would come in this last dispensation to restore his gospel and his Church to the earth—but his listeners *did not really know him*. They did not pay the price to become personally acquainted with him, to the point that they understood well his plan and purposes and were willing to sacrifice anything to accomplish his will.

A HOUSE BUILT ON A ROCK OR ON SAND

Matthew 7:24–27; Luke 6:47–49; cf. 3 Nephi 11:39–40; 14:24–27; 18:13 The parable that concludes Matthew's version of the great sermon is a classic illustration from nature. Whoever hears the words of life and obeys them is like a wise man who built his house (his life) upon a rock. Luke adds that the wise man even "digged deep, and laid the foundation on a rock" (Luke 6:48). The Greek text of Matthew 7:24 uses the definite article, *the* rock. And how do

A house built on a typical rocky hill in Judea

we define "the rock" in this case? It is the Lord Jesus Christ. He is the Rock of our salvation, the Stone of Israel. The image of rock or stone is commonly used in scripture to denote something firm, solid, and immovable. The Savior is our Rock, a sure foundation whereon if we build, we cannot fall.

"And now . . . remember, remember that it is upon the rock of our Redeemer, who is Christ, the Son of God, that ye must build your foundation; that when the devil shall send forth his mighty winds, yea, his shafts in the whirlwind, yea, when all his hail and his mighty storm shall beat upon you, it shall have no power over you to drag you down to the gulf of misery and endless wo, because of the rock upon which ye are built, which is a sure foundation, a foundation whereon if men build they cannot fall" (Helaman 5:12; see also 2 Nephi 28:28).

That is wonderful wording: if we found our lives on the Rock, they *cannot* collapse. If our lives are founded solidly on the Redeemer, when the mighty winds, whirlwind, hail, and storms—the temptations of life—beat down upon us, our lives cannot fall apart.

The rains come down from above, the floods come up

from below, the winds blow from the sides; that is the way temptations come (D&C 90:5). They come at us from above, from below, and from all sides, trying to weaken and destroy our house (our life), but again, the promise is sure: if our lives are centered in, or founded on, the Savior Jesus Christ, they *cannot* fall apart.

Elder Howard W. Hunter explained this teaching: "The words of the Master regarding the house without a foundation say to me that a man cannot have a shallow and reckless notion that he is sufficient to himself and can build his own life on any basis that happens to be easy and agreeable. As long as the weather is fair, his foolishness may not be evident; but one day there will come the floods, the muddy waters of some sudden passion, the rushing current of unforeseen temptation. If his character has no sure foundation in more than just lip service, his whole moral structure may collapse" (Conference Report, October 1967, 12–13).

TAUGHT HAVING AUTHORITY, NOT AS SCRIBES

Matthew 7:28–29; 8:1 People were astonished at Jesus' doctrine and his methodology. He taught as one having "authority *from God,* and not as *having authority from* the Scribes" (JST Matthew 7:37). In other words, his teachings and his delivery, his presentation, were remarkable because he did not just cite the great rabbis and scribes, as everyone else did (that is, "Rabbi so and so used to say," a typical formula in rabbinic writings). Jesus cited his Father. He was teaching the doctrine of the Father. No doctrine is more intellectually impressive or spiritually moving than the doctrine of the Father, which is carried into the people's hearts by the Spirit.

Because Jesus taught with authority, and because the clear and simple truth was accompanied by miraculous power, great multitudes soon followed him.

A milestone from Roman times along the Via Maris
(the International Highway, "the way of the sea") near Capernaum

HEALING OF THE CENTURION'S SERVANT (AT CAPERNAUM)

Matthew 8:5–13; Luke 7:1–10 Capernaum was situated on the northern shore of the Sea of Galilee and was a local crossroads near the International Highway (the *Via Maris,* the "Way of the Sea," which runs from Egypt on the southwest to Mesopotamia on the northeast). Roman soldiers were stationed there. One would assume that a centurion was an officer over one hundred men ("century" being one hundred), but Roman records at the time suggest that a centurion commanded about eighty others (Galbraith, Ogden, and Skinner, *Jerusalem, the Eternal City,* 153; Bible Dictionary, "Centurion," 632). Still, a centurion was an important officer in command of many. One of the subjects of this miracle was a humble man who was considerate of the Jews among whom he served. The elders of the Jews themselves were anxious for Jesus to respond to the plea of the centurion: "For he loveth our nation, and he hath built us a synagogue" (Luke 7:5). It is interesting that the leaders of the Jews would have enough confidence in Jesus' power to approach him about the matter. Jesus was willing to go to the centurion's home and heal the servant or son (Matthew 8:6, footnote a) of some sort of paralysis (palsy) that tormented him, but the centurion humbly countered that he was not worthy to have such a holy guest under his roof, not to mention the Jewish disinclination to enter the home of a Gentile. Jesus responded that he had not found such "great faith, no, not in Israel" (Matthew 8:10; cf. 3 Nephi 17:8; 19:35).

The Savior further taught (v. 11) that many would be exalted (sitting down in the kingdom of heaven with Abraham, Isaac, and Jacob; D&C 132:37) from the east (for example, Jewish converts in the Holy Land) and from the west (even from among the Romans and other Gentiles). On the other hand, the children of the wicked one (JST Matthew 8:12; cf. Alma 40:13) would be expelled into outer darkness, where there is no light and no glory.

Like the nobleman's son in the same town of Capernaum (John 4:46–54), Jesus showed that he did not need to be present for his divine power to raise someone from a bed of affliction.

WIDOW'S SON RESTORED (AT NAIN)

Luke 7:11–17 The day before his arrival at Nain, Jesus had been with his disciples in Capernaum. He had had a rigorous hike uphill of more than twenty miles to get to Nain "the day after." On one occasion Brother Ogden and some Brigham Young University students hiked the twenty-three miles. They were past exhaustion after ten hours of walking and were duly convinced that Jesus and his disciples must have been in good physical condition.

Nain was (and still is) a small village at the northern foot of Mount Moreh in the eastern Jezreel Valley. Jesus stopped a funeral procession there and raised a widow's only child from

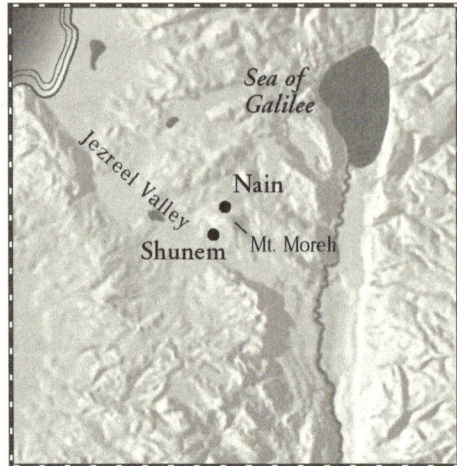

The Sea of Galilee, Nain, and Shunem

the dead, the very same thing the prophet Elisha had done centuries before at Shunem on the other side of that same mountain.

Both Elisha and Elijah paralleled and foreshadowed the ministry of Jesus Christ in specific and impressive ways, but especially in raising a widow's son from death to life (1 Kings 17:21–22; 2 Kings 4:32–35). The New Testament indicates that Christ was keenly aware of Elijah's and Elisha's missions and even identified with them (Luke 4:24–27). The lives and activities of those ancient prophets were similitudes of the God whom they served and pointed to him (for further discussion, see Skinner, *Ensign*, June 2002, 24–29).

The word "bier" in verse 14 refers to a wooden frame or platform used to carry a coffin or corpse to a burial place.

Many people accompanied Jesus as he journeyed (v. 11), and many people of the town walked with the burial party (v. 12). They all saw the miracle, and "there came a fear on all" (v. 16). The term "fear," rather than meaning fright and trembling, means reverence and awe—"they glorified God, saying, that a great prophet is risen up among us; and, that God hath visited his people" (v. 16). God had, indeed, visited his people. One of his divine titles is Immanuel, which means, literally, "God [is] with us" (Isaiah 7:14; Matthew 1:23). God himself had come down to be with his people and show them the way back Home. By seeing a man raised from the dead, the people had seen irrefutable evidence of divine power, and the word spread—not only through Galilee but a hundred miles away in Judea.

Some years ago, Brother Skinner took a group of students to the modern-day village of Nain to read and contemplate the Savior's great miracle, one of only three recorded occasions during which he restored life to a dead person (see also Mark 5:35–43; John 11:38–44). A lovely but worn church in Nain commemorates the Savior's miracle. Inside the church, a painting depicts the scene described in Luke. Brother Skinner writes: "We entered the church, and as we began singing 'I Am a Child of God,' the church door opened slightly and little children from the village poked their heads inside. The students beckoned the little visitors to enter and soon the small church, which had only benches arranged around its interior walls, was filled with little people who began to sit on our laps. It was a profound moment for all of us, as the painting of the Savior, who had demonstrated his love in a specific way in Nain, peered down at us.

"We found out that the young children didn't want money, though students tried to give them some. They wanted to be held and talked to and enjoy the kindness of the students. (They did, however, freely take what gum, candy, and pencils the students offered.)

"All of us learned a valuable lesson. Like the widow of Nain and her son, all of Heavenly Father's children have needs. Most often money is not what addresses those needs, that helps comfort, enrich, and enliven the soul. Rather, it is the gift that the Savior gave in Nain, the same gift which the students gave: time, attention, little kindnesses, and love. Nain became an important place in Jesus' day for the disciples as they witnessed events unfold. It became an important place in modern times for modern disciples as they witnessed other events unfold" (Skinner, journal).

THE MOTHER OF PETER'S WIFE IS HEALED (AT CAPERNAUM)

Matthew 8:14–15; Mark 1:29–31; Luke 4:38–39
Peter's mother-in-law was the beneficiary of Jesus' compassion and healing power. We have meager details of the apostles' wives, although 1 Corinthians 9:5 suggests that the wives of some apostles on occasion traveled with them in the ministry. Elder McConkie wrote, "Jesus' specially selected disciples were married men with wives and children and families of their own, as his specially called servants should be in all ages" (*Mortal Messiah*, 2:37). Peter's wife's mother was in their home in Capernaum when Jesus came, took hold of her hand, lifted her up, and healed her.

HEALING IN THE EVENING (AT CAPERNAUM)

Matthew 8:16–17; Mark 1:32–34; Luke 4:40–41
These verses in the Synoptic Gospels follow the healing of Peter's mother-in-law. That same day Jesus continued healing all evening long. Matthew, the apostle who loved to cite the Old Testament prophecies and show them fulfilled in Jesus, now quoted Isaiah, who wrote that the Messiah would take upon himself our infirmities and bear our sicknesses (cf. Isaiah 53:4; Mosiah 14:4; Alma 7:11). Even closer to the apostolic era, an angel from God told King Benjamin (ca. 124 B.C.) that the Lord Omnipotent was soon coming into the world to "go forth amongst men, working mighty miracles, such as healing the sick, raising the dead, causing the lame to walk, the blind to receive their sight, and the deaf to hear, and curing all manner of diseases. And he shall cast out devils, or the evil spirits

which dwell in the hearts of the children of men" (Mosiah 3:5–6; see also 1 Nephi 11:31). Matthew, Mark, and Luke here testify and verify the fulfillment of these prophecies. Many townspeople were gathered together watching these miraculous events (Mark 1:33). Devils, or evil spirits, came out of some of the sick people. The devils knew him and tried to speak, but Jesus would not allow testimony to come from them (Mark 1:34; Luke 4:41). Only the witness of the Spirit leads to true conversion and changes lives.

President Brigham Young explained for whom miracles are done: "Miracles, or these extraordinary manifestations of the power of God, are not for the unbeliever; they are to console the Saints, and to strengthen and confirm the faith of those who love, fear, and serve God, and not for outsiders" (*Journal of Discourses,* 12:97). Also, while we are examining many miracles Jesus performed, it would be appropriate to include a caution about us, in modern times, always expecting the miraculous in order to confirm our testimony. President Spencer W. Kimball counseled: "Even in our day, many people . . . expect if there be revelation it will come with awe-inspiring, earth-shaking display. . . . The burning bushes, the smoking mountains, the sheets of four-footed beasts, the Cumorahs, and the Kirtlands were realities; but they were the exceptions. The great volume of revelation came to Moses and to Joseph and comes to today's prophet in the less spectacular way—that of deep impressions, without spectacle or glamour or dramatic events. Always expecting the spectacular, many will miss entirely the constant flow of revealed communication" (Munich Germany Area Conference Report 1973, 76–77).

FOXES HAVE HOLES (AT CAPERNAUM)

Matthew 8:18–22; Luke 9:57–62 Disciples of Jesus were told that in following him they may not even have the security and comfort that animals have: the foxes burrow their holes and the birds build their nests, but the disciple, following the example of the Son of Man, may have to abandon permanence and embrace transience. The disciple may be called to forsake the stability of home and travel without purse or scrip to minister to the needs of others.

Responding to the command the Savior issues to all humankind, "Follow me," some express commitment and devotion but desire to pursue other pressing cares (such as burying a loved one or holding a farewell testimonial). Jesus' examples of the priority of devotion may seem unusually harsh to us. It is not that those other cares and concerns were to be left undone but that some things are more vital than others. This was Jesus' way of describing that when a man has set his plough on a straight course, when he has planted his life in a more spiritual furrow, he must not look back wistfully on the old life but persist and push ahead with full commitment to the new life he has adopted and never look back. "Lord, I would follow thee, but . . ." must be changed to "Lord, I will follow thee," especially if called to full-time service in the kingdom. That work takes precedence over all other things. Elder James E. Talmage wrote, for example, that "while it would be manifestly unfilial for a son to absent himself from his father's funeral under ordinary conditions, nevertheless, if that son had been set apart to service of importance transcending all personal or family obligations, his ministerial duty would of right take precedence" (*Jesus the Christ*, 285).

PEACE BE STILL
(ON THE SEA OF GALILEE)

Matthew 8:23–27; Mark 4:35–41; Luke 8:22–25 The physical setting of the Sea of Galilee lends itself to sudden storms or tempests. The lake sits in the Jordan Rift Valley at nearly seven hundred feet below sea level (see Bible Map 14).

A Second Galilean Ministry

Because of the hills on the west, north, and east, winds can whip down the western slopes and create formidable waves on the relatively small body of water. Seasoned fishermen in the middle of the lake can be frightened for their lives. Jesus, on this occasion, slept calmly while the tempest raged, until his friends awakened him, full of fear. (Why would they fear, with the very Creator of the wind and the rain in the boat with them?) He stood and rebuked the winds and the waves. Should it be surprising that the same God who organized the elements in the beginning, who exhibited his divine power by parting the waters of the Red Sea, and who caused the flow of the Jordan River to stop could control the elements on a small lake in Galilee?

The elements are part of the earth and the earth itself is a living entity and has a spirit, and the earth and all its elements respond obediently to their Creator. "By the power of his word man came upon the face of the earth, which earth was created by the power of his word. Wherefore, if God being able to speak and the world was, and to speak and man was created, O then, why not able to command the earth, or the workmanship of his hands upon the face of it, according to his will and pleasure?" (Jacob 4:9).

"What manner of man is this, that even the winds and the sea obey him!" (Matthew 8:27). What manner of man indeed. He is the Son of Man of Holiness, in whose hands all things move and have their being, under whose control all things function. "If he say unto the waters of the great deep—Be thou dried up—it is done" (Helaman 12:16). What wonder and awe and reverence all beings should feel as we contemplate the glories and powers of the Lord of the universe!

Elder Howard W. Hunter related the story of the woman who wrote the words to "Master, the Tempest Is Raging":

"Let me recall for you the story of Mary Ann Baker. Her beloved and only brother suffered from the same respiratory disease that had taken their parents' lives, and he left their home in Chicago to find a warmer climate in the southern part of the United States.

"For a time he seemed to be improving, but then a sudden turn in his health came and he died almost immediately. Mary Ann and her sister were heartbroken. It only added to their deep grief that neither their own health nor their personal finances allowed them to claim their brother's body or to finance its return to Chicago for burial.

"The Baker family had been raised as faithful Christians, but Mary's trust in a loving God broke under the strain of her brother's death and her own diminished circumstances. 'God does not care for me or mine,' said Mary Ann. . . . 'I have always tried to believe on Christ and give the Master a consecrated life,' she said, 'but this is more than I can bear. What have I done to deserve this? What have I left undone that God should wreak His vengeance upon me in this way?' (Ernest K. Emurian, *Living Stories of Famous Hymns,* Boston: W. A. Widdle Co., 1955, pp. 83–85.)

"I suppose we have all had occasion, individually or collectively, to cry out on some stormy sea, 'Master, carest thou not that we perish?' And so cried Mary Ann Baker.

"But as the days and the weeks went by, the God of life and love began to calm the winds and the waves of what this sweet young woman called 'her unsanctified heart.' Her faith not only returned but it flourished, and like Job of old, she learned new things, things 'too wonderful' to have known before her despair. On the Sea of Galilee, the stirring of the disciples' faith was ultimately more important than the stilling of the sea, and so it was with her.

"Later, as something of a personal testimonial and caring very much for the faith of others who would be tried by personal despair, she wrote the words of the hymn we have all sung, 'Master, the Tempest Is Raging.' May I share it with you?

> Master, the tempest is raging!
> The billows are tossing high!

> The sky is o'ershadowed with blackness.
> No shelter or help is nigh.
>
> Carest thou not that we perish?
> How canst thou lie asleep
> When each moment so madly is threatening
> A grave in the angry deep?
>
> Master, with anguish of spirit
> I bow in my grief today.
> The depths of my sad heart are troubled.
> Oh, waken and save, I pray!
>
> Torrents of sin and of anguish
> Sweep o'er my sinking soul,
> And I perish! I perish! dear Master,
> Oh, hasten and take control!

"Then this beautiful, moving refrain:

> The winds and the waves shall obey [thy] will;
> Peace, be still! Peace, be still!
> Whether the wrath of the storm-tossed sea
> Or demons or men or whatever it be,
> No waters can swallow the ship where lies
> The Master of ocean and earth and skies.
> They all shall sweetly obey [thy] will.
> Peace, be still! Peace, be still!
> They all shall sweetly obey [thy] will.
> Peace, peace be still!

"Too often, I fear, both in the living of life and in the singing of this hymn, we fail to emphasize the sweet peace of this concluding verse:

> Master, the terror is over.
> The elements sweetly rest.

Earth's sun in the calm lake is mirrored,
And heaven's within my breast.

Linger, Oh, blessed Redeemer!
Leave me alone no more,
And with joy I shall make the blest harbor
And rest on the blissful shore.
(*Hymns* [1985], no. 106)

"All of us have seen some sudden storms in our lives. A few of them, though temporary like these on the Sea of Galilee, can be violent and frightening and potentially destructive. As individuals, as families, as communities, as nations, even as a church, we have had sudden squalls arise which have made us ask one way or another, 'Master, carest thou not that we perish?' And one way or another we always hear in the stillness after the storm, 'Why are ye so fearful? how is it that ye have no faith?'" (Hunter, *Ensign,* November 1984, 33–34).

LEGION OF DEVILS ENTER INTO SWINE (PROBABLY AT GERGESA)

Matthew 8:28–34; Mark 5:1–20; Luke 8:26–40 Two discrepancies exist in the accounts of evil spirits being cast out in the Decapolis. Matthew indicates two men were possessed with devils; Mark and Luke mention only one. That difference is resolved by the change Joseph Smith made in the text of Matthew, reading "*a man*" rather than two (JST Matthew 8:29).

Matthew has the incident taking place in Gergesa, whereas Mark and Luke both cite Gadara as the location of the miracle. Other Greek manuscripts claim Gerasa was where the demons were expelled.

The facts that swine were being herded and the phrase "other side of the sea" logically indicate Gentile country in the Decapolis. When the devils possessed the large herd of

A Second Galilean Ministry

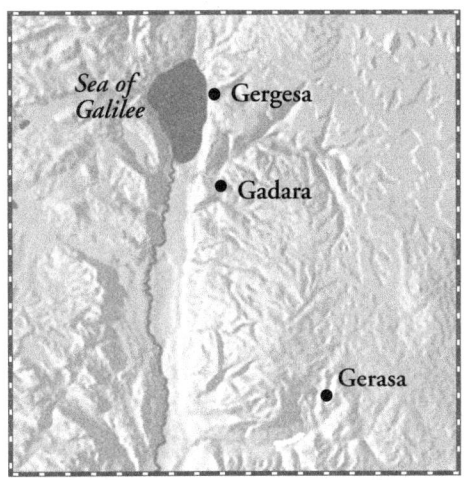

Possible locations of the swine incident: Gergesa, Gadara, Gerasa

two thousand swine (with Jesus' permission), the swine ran down a steep place and were drowned in the lake (Mark 5:13; Luke 8:33). That alone disqualifies Gerasa (Jerash) as a possible location, as it is more than thirty miles from the Sea of Galilee, in the hill country of Gilead. Of the other two possibilities, Gadara seems also to be rather far for a herd to stampede into the Sea of Galilee. Its slopes are several miles distant from the lake, with an intervening deep gorge and streambed of the Yarmuk River. Matthew's choice, Gergesa, now partially excavated and restored, is situated less than a mile from the eastern shore of the Sea of Galilee. It is the most likely site of this dramatic encounter between the forces of good and evil.

Elder Bruce R. McConkie wrote: "Some cavilers [those who find fault or object for frivolous reasons] exhibit a mocking concern as to whether Jesus commanded or merely permitted the devils to enter the swine. . . . They pretend to find in his act, whatever it was, an unwarranted destruction of the property of others. Surely it was an unethical if not an immoral act, they contend. If such it is assumed to be, so be it. But, realistically, who is to say that He who sends hail to beat down the ears of ripened corn, or storms to sink fish-filled boats, may not also send devils into swine to sweep them in a maddened surge to a watery grave?" (*Mortal Messiah*, 2:281). It seems that the Lord, just as later with the fig tree that he cursed (Matthew 21:18–22), felt that the significant lesson to be taught was worth the life of those animals.

Our Bible Dictionary ("Devil," 656) explains that "since the devil and his premortal angels have no physical body of flesh and bones, they often seek to possess the bodies of mortal beings [or even animals]. There are many such instances recorded in scripture (Matthew 9:32; 12:22; Mark 1:24; 5:7; Luke 8:30; Acts 19:15 . . .)." Elder LeGrand Richards noted, "It is so desirable to have a body that these evil spirits, who had forfeited the right to bodies of their own, were even willing to enter the bodies of swine" (*A Marvelous Work and a Wonder*, 293). Jesus used his power to cast out those evil spirits, and he gave that power to his true disciples.

The healing of those possessed by evil spirits teaches these truths:

"(1) That evil spirits, actual beings from Lucifer's realm, gain literal entrance into mortal bodies;

"(2) That they then have such power over those bodies as to control the physical acts performed, even to the framing of the very words spoken by the mouth of those so possessed;

"(3) That persons possessed by evil spirits are subjected to the severest mental and physical sufferings and to the basest sort of degradation—all symbolical of the eternal torment to be imposed upon those who fall under Satan's control in the world to come;

"(4) That devils remember Jesus from pre-existence, recognize him as the One who was then foreordained to be the Redeemer, and know that he came into mortality as the Son of God;

"(5) That the desire to gain bodies is so great among Lucifer's minions as to cause them, not only to steal the mortal tabernacles of men, but to enter the bodies of animals;

"(6) That the devils know their eventual destiny is to be cast out into an eternal hell from whence there is no return;

"(7) That rebellious and worldly people are not converted to the truth by observing miracles; and

"(8) That those cleansed from evil spirits can then be used on the Lord's errand to testify of his grace and goodness so that receptive persons may be led to believe in him" (McConkie, *Doctrinal New Testament Commentary,* 1:311).

"We cannot tell and do not know how it is that evil spirits—few or many—gain entrance into the bodies of mortal men. We do know that all things are governed by law, and that Satan is precluded from taking possession of [and destroying] the bodies of the prophets and other righteous people. Were it not so, the work of God would be thwarted—always and in all instances—for Lucifer leads the armies of hell against all men, and more especially against those who are instrumental in furthering the Lord's work.

"There must be circumstances of depression and sin and physical weakness that, within the restrictions of divine control, permit evil spirits to enter human bodies" (McConkie, *Mortal Messiah,* 2:282).

"We do not know how or under what circumstances such tenancy is permitted. That all things are governed and controlled by law, we do know; and we are left to suppose that in the day when the Incarnate Jehovah came among men, there must have been more persons who were susceptible to spirit possession than has been the case in other days" (McConkie, *Mortal Messiah,* 2:37).

Elder Joseph Fielding Smith also commented on evil spirits and their power then and now: "We all realize that there are diseases of the mind as well as of the organs and other parts of the human body, and it may be that at times mankind have ascribed many if not all of these to the possession or influence of evil spirits. The fact remains however, that the cases of spirit-possession as recorded in the New Testament, are true. It is also true that under some conditions Satan has bound the bodies of individuals by his power. This is not only true of such conditions in the days of our Savior and his apostles, but we have the evidence of such being true in this dispensation in which we now live. We must not discount the power of the adversary of all righteousness. There are scores of cases, fully attested in our own day of demon influence and possession. Cases which were not caused by derangement of the mind, but by actual overpowering of the individual and taking possession of his body. One of the most outstanding was the case where Satan and his cohorts endeavored to destroy the work of the Lord when it was opened in Great Britain. The story is recorded in the *Life of Heber C. Kimball*" (*Man: His Origin and Destiny*, 487).

"'Saturday evening,' says Heber C. Kimball, 'it was agreed that I should go forward and baptize, the next morning, in the river Ribble, which runs through Preston.

"'By this time the adversary of souls began to rage, and he felt determined to destroy us before we had fully established the kingdom of God in that land, and the next morning I witnessed a scene of satanic power and influence which I shall never forget.

"'Sunday, July 30th (1837), about daybreak, Elder Isaac Russell (who had been appointed to preach on the obelisk in Preston Square, that day), who slept with Elder Richards in Wilfred Street, came up to the third story, where Elder Hyde and myself were sleeping, and called out, 'Brother Kimball, I want you should get up and pray for me that I may be delivered from the evil spirits that are tormenting me to such a degree that I feel I cannot live long, unless I obtain relief.'

"'I had been sleeping on the back of the bed. I immediately arose, slipped off at the foot of the bed, and passed around to where he was. Elder Hyde threw his feet out, and sat up in the bed, and we laid hands on him, I being mouth, and prayed that the Lord would have mercy on him, and rebuked the devil.

"'While thus engaged, I was struck with great force by

some invisible power, and fell senseless on the floor. The first thing I recollected was being supported by Elders Hyde and Richards, who were praying for me; Elder Richards having followed Russell up to my room. Elder Hyde and Richards then assisted me to get on the bed, but my agony was so great I could not endure it, and I arose, bowed my knees and prayed. I then arose and sat up on the bed, when a vision was opened to our minds, and we could distinctly see the evil spirits, who foamed and gnashed their teeth at us. We gazed upon them about an hour and a half (by Willard's watch). We were not looking towards the window, but towards the wall. Space appeared before us, and we saw the devils coming in legions, with their leaders, who came within a few feet of us. They came towards us like armies rushing to battle. They appeared to be men of full stature, possessing every form and feature of men in the flesh, who were angry and desperate; and I shall never forget the vindictive malignity depicted on their countenances as they looked me in the eye; and any attempt to paint the scene which then presented itself, or portray their malice and enmity, would be vain. I perspired exceedingly, my clothes becoming as wet as if I had been taken out of the river. I felt excessive pain, and was in the greatest distress for some time. I cannot even look back on the scene without feelings of horror; yet by it I learned the power of the adversary, his enmity against the servants of God, and got some understanding of the invisible world. We distinctly heard those spirits talk and express their wrath and hellish designs against us. However, the Lord delivered us from them, and blessed us exceedingly that day.'

"Elder Hyde's supplemental description of that fearful scene is as follows, taken from a letter addressed to President Kimball:

"'Every circumstance that occurred at that scene of devils is just as fresh in my recollection at this moment as it was at the moment of its occurrence, and will ever remain so. After you were overcome by them and had fallen, their awful rush upon me with knives, threats, imprecations and hellish grins, amply convinced me that they were no friends of mine. While you were apparently senseless and lifeless on the floor and upon the bed (after we had laid you there), I stood between you and the devils and fought them and contended with them face to face, until they began to diminish in number and to retreat from the room. The last imp that left turned round to me as he was going out and said, as if to apologize, and appease my determined opposition to them, "I never said anything against you!" I replied to him thus: "It matters not to me whether you have or have not; you are a liar from the beginning! In the name of Jesus Christ, depart!" He immediately left, and the room was clear. That closed the scene of devils for that time.'

"Years later, narrating the experience of that awful morning to the Prophet Joseph, Heber asked him what it all meant, and whether there was anything wrong with him that he should have such a manifestation.

"'No, Brother Heber,' he replied, 'at that time you were nigh unto the Lord; there was only a veil between you and Him, but you could not see Him. When I heard of it, it gave me great joy, for I then knew that the work of God had taken root in that land. It was this that caused the devil to make a struggle to kill you.'

"Joseph then related some of his own experience, in many contests he had had with the evil one, and said: 'The nearer a person approaches the Lord, a greater power will be manifested by the adversary to prevent the accomplishment of His purposes'" (Whitney, *Life of Heber C. Kimball,* 129–32).

Joseph Smith taught: "The great principle of happiness consists in having a body. The devil has no body, and herein is his punishment. He is pleased when he can obtain the tabernacle of man, and when cast out by the Savior he asked to go into the herd of swine, showing that he would prefer a swine's body to having none.

"All beings who have bodies have power over those who

have not. *The devil has no power over us only as we permit him. The moment we revolt at anything which comes from God, the devil takes power*" (*Teachings of the Prophet Joseph Smith,* 181; emphasis added).

Regarding the power of Satan and his followers, someone might ask: Considering the fact that there now exist billions of evil spirits, plus eventually all the potentially billions of resurrected telestial beings who will still have evil dispositions (all of these from our world in addition to millions of other worlds, too), and since there is no disintegration or annihilation of bodies—could it be possible some time that under the leadership of malevolent personalities, such as Lucifer and Cain, they could rise up against the forces of good and shake the foundations of heaven (as depicted in the Star Wars films, the Star Trek series, and other such imaginative portrayals)?

The answer is no; it will never happen, because *they have no power.* Righteousness is power; purity is power; priesthood is power; there is power in the covenants and in the sacred ordinances; and the evil ones have no such powers. In the end the Lord will say to the wicked ones: "Depart from me, ye cursed, into everlasting fire, prepared for the devil and his angels. And now, behold, I say unto you, never at any time have I declared from mine own mouth that they should return, for where I am they cannot come, for *they have no power*" (D&C 29:28–29; emphasis added). On the other hand, the righteous will "have no end; therefore shall they be from everlasting to everlasting, because they continue; then shall they be above all, because all things are subject unto them. Then shall they be gods, because *they have all power*" (D&C 132:20; emphasis added).

We learn from the experience of Moses that Satan, the devil, the father of lies, can deceive and blind men, particularly those who will "not hearken to [the Lord's] voice" (Moses 4:4).

The devils cried out, "What have we to do with thee, Jesus, thou Son of God?" (Matthew 8:29). The evil spirits were once among all the spirits, with Heavenly Father and his Firstborn Son in the celestial realms. They know who Jesus is, and they know of his power.

"Art thou come hither to torment us before the time?" they continued (Matthew 8:29). Evil spirits are all aware that their days are numbered; they know their oppositional efforts will soon end, after the Millennium, when Satan and his angels will be cast out permanently (D&C 76:32–38). "The devil is come down unto you, having great wrath, because he knoweth that he hath but a short time" (Revelation 12:12).

"The whole city came out to meet Jesus" (Matthew 8:34) and implored that he leave their territory. They were terrified by such power (they were also probably not a little upset about the economic setback of having just lost two thousand of their animals, which is an example of caring more about the value of their possessions than about the worth of a soul; D&C 18:10, 15–16).

Luke 8:39 Unlike other occasions, this time Jesus told the recipient of the miracle to go back home and tell others what great things God had done for him. The man broadcast the extraordinary miracle throughout his hometown. There was apparently no problem publicizing the incident in a Gentile region outside the purview of the Jewish authorities (cf. Matthew 8:2–4).

PARALYTIC HEALED (AT CAPERNAUM)

Matthew 9:1–8; Mark 2:1–12; Luke 5:16–26 Capernaum was Jesus' "own city," where his mother and half brothers and sisters lived (Matthew 4:13). A bedridden man who had suffered a stroke or some sort of paralysis was brought before Jesus. Mark's and Luke's accounts note that four of his friends, wanting to devise some means to get the suffering man before Jesus, went up on the housetop and let the man down through the tiling (Greek, *keramos;* English,

A Second Galilean Ministry

ceramic; Luke 5:18–19). Jesus was moved by their faith and, rather than immediately healing him, spoke something infinitely more significant: "Man, thy sins are forgiven thee" (Luke 5:20). Of course some Jewish leaders present complained and criticized that such talk was blasphemous—only God can forgive sins, which was exactly the point: he was indeed forgiving the man's sins. In various dispensations the Lord has taught that great faith can bring forgiveness of one's sins (see also James 5:15); so can bearing a fervent testimony of the Savior (D&C 62:3; 84:61; 112:3) and dedicating oneself to preaching the gospel in missionary work (D&C 31:5; 36:1; 60:7). A special promise is given to all servants of the Lord, those who are committed to serving him with all their heart and soul, who thrust in their sickle with their might: Their sins are forgiven (D&C 31:5). When we throw ourselves wholeheartedly into the service of God and service to his children, our sins are taken away.

Jesus countered with the pointed question, "*Is it not easier to say,* Thy sins be forgiven thee, *than to say,* Arise and walk?" (JST Matthew 9:5). But just so they would know that he had power to do both, he raised the paralyzed man on the spot. The healed man and those who saw the miracle were amazed and praised and glorified God, and said, "We have seen strange [marvelous] things to day" (Luke 5:26).

It is interesting that as Jesus healed, he stirred a variety of reactions from people. Following are some examples: "We never saw it on this fashion" (after healing a paralytic; Mark 2:12); "What manner of man is this"? (after calming a storm; Mark 4:41); "they were astonished with a great astonishment" (after raising a girl from the dead; Mark 5:42); "Never man spake like this man" (after speaking of his Father's doctrine; John 7:46); "He hath done all things well" (after healing the deaf and dumb; Mark 7:37); "These are not the words of him that hath a devil" (after healing a blind man; John 10:21); "all things that John spake of this man were true" (after preaching to a multitude; John 10:41). Now we might ask ourselves:

how do we react to these miracles or to the miracles that Jesus continues to perform in modern times?

A FEAST AT THE HOUSE OF MATTHEW (AT CAPERNAUM)

Matthew 9:9–13; Mark 2:13–17; Luke 5:27–32 Capernaum was the last town in Herod Antipas's territory before one crossed the Jordan, about two miles to the east, into Herod Philip's territory. It would therefore have been a toll place, or a collection point of custom or tax. Matthew Levi, one of the *publicani,* or publicans, sat at receipt of custom, or at the tax office, and collected taxes, at the same time drawing reproach from some of his fellow Jews.

What a remarkable effect Jesus had on the hearts of men. In a single verse we are informed that the Savior saw Matthew Levi sitting at his job. He merely said to Matthew, "Follow me," and Matthew left his employment of going after taxes to pursue the noble work of going after souls. From tax collector to apostle of Jesus Christ—the Lord Omnipotent knew him and had foreordained him before he ever came to earth. In the middle of reporting a series of miracles that Jesus performed, Matthew stops and tells us about the one he personally considered the greatest: his own changed heart.

The phrase "publicans and sinners" expresses how the Jewish populace in general regarded those who worked as government tax collectors. Some Jewish leaders had adopted a "holier than thou" attitude (Isaiah 65:5) toward the outcasts of society, but much of Jesus' ministry was devoted to those very souls. As he perfectly observed: "They that be well need not a physician, but they that are sick" (Matthew 9:12), "for I am not come to call the righteous [especially the righteous in their own eyes], but sinners to repentance" (v. 13; cf. Moroni 8:8). Or as has been suggested in modern terms, the Church is not a country club for Saints but a hospital for sinners (see

Douglas, *Ensign,* April 1989, 15). More than a thousand years before his mortal ministry, in the days of Moses, the Savior taught, "I am the Lord that healeth thee" (Exodus 15:26); the Hebrew text actually reads, "I am your physician." He told his detractors to go and learn what the scripture means: "I desired mercy, and not sacrifice" (Hosea 6:6; Matthew 9:13). He admonished the scribes and Pharisees to follow his example in showing compassion. They were too focused on the rigid observance of the law and exacting justice; these "publicans and sinners" were the very people who needed the loving kindness of a merciful God. The Savior came to save; he "came into the world to save sinners" (1 Timothy 1:15).

JOHN'S DISCIPLES ASK ABOUT FASTING; PHARISEES ASK ABOUT BAPTISM (GALILEE)

Matthew 9:14-17; Mark 2:18-22; Luke 5:33-39
Some who had been following the teachings of John the Baptist inquired: "Why do we and the Pharisees fast oft, but thy disciples fast not?" (Matthew 9:14). Jesus' response is reminiscent of the teachings of Old Testament prophets, placing the Lord in the role of the Bridegroom of his bride, his people: "Thy Maker is thine husband" (Isaiah 54:5); "for I am married unto you" (Jeremiah 3:14). "Can the children of the bridechamber [the disciples of Jesus] mourn, as long as the bridegroom is with them? but the days will come," Jesus poignantly prophesied, "when the bridegroom shall be taken from them, and then shall they fast" (Matthew 9:15; cf. Acts 13:2).

Although these teachings almost make it sound as if Jesus' disciples did not fast during his ministry, it is likely that they did periodically fast; how else could they prove the efficacy of their Lord's instruction that certain evil spirits "goeth not out but by prayer and fasting"? (Matthew 17:21).

A mikvah at Qumran

In the Joseph Smith Translation, the Lord adds four dramatic verses:

"*Then said the Pharisees unto him, Why will ye not receive us with our baptism, seeing we keep the whole law?* [They had been practicing ritual immersions in their *mikvahs*, their immersion pools, for centuries.]

"*But Jesus said unto them, Ye keep not the law. If ye had kept the law, ye would have received me, for I am he who gave the law.*

"*I receive not you with your baptism, because it profiteth you nothing.*

"*For when that which is new is come, the old is ready to be put away*" (JST Matthew 9:18–21).

Jesus clearly proclaimed that he was the great Lawgiver and the promised Messiah. The Pharisees were well trained in the law and the prophets, so they should have recognized him and warmly welcomed him. Their strict observance of the old laws had become meaningless ritual, of no value to them. It was time to replace the old with the new.

Jesus continued to answer their question about accepting their baptism by illustrating his point. "No man putteth a piece of new cloth unto an old garment" (Matthew 9:16). He had not come to patch up Judaism. The gospel of Jesus Christ was to be a freshly made garment.

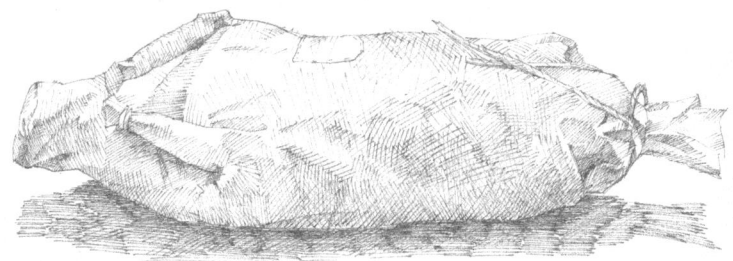

Goatskin "bottle"

"Neither do men put new wine into old bottles" (v. 17). In those days grape juice was drawn out of the vat and put into wineskins ("bottles" made from goatskins) or earthenware jars. New wine—grape juice—was put into new bottles, "else the new wine doth burst the [old] bottles, and the wine is spilled" (Mark 2:22). The gases coming from the fermenting juice as it turned into wine would expand and stretch the wineskin and cause it to burst if it was old and already stretched. Jesus' intent was to avoid packaging the fresh, new fruit of the vine (the gospel produced from the True Vine) in the old and already stretched skin of Judaism. With pointed insight into human nature, he explained that "no man . . . having drunk old wine straightway desireth new: for he saith, the old is better" (Luke 5:39). Many of the Jews of his day tragically preferred the old wine of Judaism to the refreshing new wine of the gospel of Jesus Christ.

A modern-day illustration of this teaching is the calling of a young man to restore the gospel and Church of Jesus Christ. Joseph Smith was a "new bottle" who could receive "new wine," free from the contamination of the philosophies and religious dogmas of men. In October general conference of 2002 President Gordon B. Hinckley said, "Why did both the

Father and the Son come to a boy, a mere lad? . . . The instrument in this work of God was a boy whose mind was not cluttered by the philosophies of men. That mind was fresh and without schooling in the traditions of the day" (*Ensign*, November 2002, 80).

JAIRUS'S DAUGHTER RAISED; VIRTUE (POWER) IS GONE OUT OF ME (AT CAPERNAUM)

Matthew 9:18–26; Mark 5:21–43; Luke 8:41–56 Two more examples of people with faith to be healed: a ruler of the local synagogue with a dying daughter and a woman who had suffered for twelve years from severe hemorrhaging.

The synagogue leader was named Ya'ir (from Hebrew to Greek to English: Jairus), and he had only one daughter, who was twelve years old (Luke 8:42). Although her condition was seemingly hopeless, the father demonstrated faith that if Jesus would just lay his hands on the girl, she would live.

"Come and lay thy hands on her . . . and she shall live"—"These are not only the words of faith of a father torn with grief," wrote Elder Howard W. Hunter, "but are also a reminder to us that whatever Jesus lays his hands upon lives. If Jesus lays his hands upon a marriage, it lives. If he is allowed to lay his hands on the family, it lives" (*Ensign*, November 1979, 65).

En route to the man's house the crowd pressed hard upon Jesus and his disciples, and a woman who had spent all her money on doctors' bills demonstrated her faith in Jesus by thinking that if she could only touch the hem of his garment she could be healed (the fringe, Hebrew *tzitzit*, which in some minds seemed connected to religious power, even priesthood power; cf. Matthew 23:5; see also Bible Dictionary, "Hem of Garment," 700). "Who touched me?" Jesus asked (Luke 8:45). He could have known that without asking, of course, but Jesus used every opportunity to teach. "Somebody hath touched me: for I perceive that virtue [power, or spiritual strength] is gone out of me" (v. 46; cf. Luke 6:19). He wanted all the people crowding around him to understand what had just happened. It was not the touch of the cloth of his garment that healed the woman, any more than the waters of the Jordan healed Naaman (2 Kings 5:14) or the clay or Siloam's water healed the blind man (John 9:6–7) or Paul's handkerchiefs healed people at Ephesus (Acts 19:12) or the anointing oil heals any of us. It was faith that made her whole. When any child of God is broken or feels that he is falling apart, faith in Jesus Christ can make him whole again.

While Jesus was still speaking to the woman of faith who had touched the hem of his garment, messengers arrived from the ruler's house, saying that the girl had died. Jesus quickly reminded the father to continue showing faith: "Fear not: believe only, and she shall be made whole" (Luke 8:50). In those days the Jews hired mourners who were trained in outward lamentation and "pounding of the breast" and other such forms of expressing the grief of losing a loved one in death. The professional mourners, who were making excessive noise in weeping and wailing (Matthew 9:23), were asked to withdraw so that the Spirit of the Lord could grace the quiet and sacred moment. Jesus ignored the ridicule of some scoffers and proceeded in with parents and the chief apostles. The Ruler of the universe had the power; the ruler of the synagogue had the faith. Priesthood power and faith brought the spirit and life back into the precious daughter. "Talitha cumi," Jesus spoke in Aramaic (the words are pronounced "Tah-LEE-thah COO-me"; Mark 5:41)—"Young girl, arise." The Savior's tenderness and affection are implicit in this episode.

Jesus encouraged those who witnessed the miracle to keep it quiet and sacred. They had exercised faith and had been rewarded. Others needed to do the same.

The Prophet Joseph Smith related an experience similar to those recorded in the Gospels: "Elder Jedediah M. Grant enquired of me the cause of my turning pale and losing strength last night while blessing children. I told him that I saw that Lucifer would exert his influence to destroy the children that I was blessing, and I strove with all the faith and spirit that I had to seal upon them a blessing that would secure their lives upon the earth; and so much virtue went out of me into the children, that I became weak, from which I have not yet recovered; and I referred to the case of the woman touching the hem of the garment of Jesus. . . . The virtue here referred to is the spirit of life; and a man who exercises great faith in administering to the sick, blessing little children, or confirming, is liable to become weakened" (*Teachings of the Prophet Joseph Smith*, 280–81).

A beautiful lesson comes from this episode in Jesus' ministry. Likely many people were touching Jesus that day, but there was only one person, we are told, who really touched the Savior, coming to him in such a way as to gain access to his healing power—his "virtue" that he is willing to pass from himself to others. In a sense, Jesus is thronged every day by a multitude of scholars and religious thinkers and adherents, but how many of us really "touch" him? (We thank Richard Davis for this thought-provoking insight.)

Following is a modern illustration of a woman being healed by her faith. A mother of two had contracted a rare blood disease. "Though not fatal, it prohibited her from having more children. In an administration at the hands of her husband, she received the promise that her body would heal itself. Yet all medical efforts proved painful, frustrating, and ineffectual. At a stake conference attended by a member of the Twelve, she experienced the impression that if her faith were great enough, she could be healed. She labored to increase her faith. Six months later another apostle, Elder Bruce R. McConkie, was sent to the stake in which they lived. Her children were ill that Sunday, and though she usually would have been the one to stay with them, she and her husband decided that she should attend the

Jesus Blessing Jairus's Daughter, *by Greg Olsen*

conference. "'I took a seat in the middle of the auditorium,' she wrote to Elder McConkie later, 'and watched as you shook hands with many before the meeting. I was delighted as I watched the smiles of many I recognized enjoying your touch and smile.

"'Throughout the meeting I found it difficult to concentrate, and as it came to a close, I could hardly remain seated. As the closing prayer was said, I felt very calm. Then,' she continued, 'the Spirit whispered to me, "You could go up on that stage and be healed by Brother

McConkie." I replied, "I don't want to bother him—look at all those people who want to talk to him. I'm just thrilled to be able to have heard him." Then the Spirit reminded me—"just touch the edge of his jacket"—as I recalled the story of the woman who had touched the hem of the Savior's garment. I'm sure I literally shook my head and said, "No. I can't possibly do that!" She and the Spirit continued their debate. Finally she went.

"'As I made my way through the crowd,' she wrote, 'I felt very anxious and wanted to turn around, but I edged forward until finally I was right behind you and you were engaged in conversation. I fixed my eyes upon your jacket edge and held my breath—you were so tall—I reached out and quickly touched with my index finger the hem of your jacket. Suddenly, you spun around and extended your hand to me. I shook it and tearfully uttered, "Thank you." You simply nodded and returned to your conversation, and I went to my car practically dancing!'

"When she entered her home, she announced to her husband that she was healed. They knelt together in a prayer of thanksgiving. The doctor was baffled. At the time of her writing she had become the mother of three more children. Her faith had made her whole" (McConkie, *Bruce R. McConkie Story*, 359–60).

TWO BLIND MEN HEALED (AT CAPERNAUM)

Matthew 9:27–31 Two blind men started following Jesus. He allowed them to follow him for a while, and then he asked them if they had faith to be healed. They affirmed that they did, and he touched their eyes—so they could participate physically in the miracle, too. This is the first recorded instance in the Gospels of the blind receiving their sight.

A Second Galilean Ministry

HEALS DEMONIAC: PRINCE OF DEVILS (AT CAPERNAUM)

Matthew 9:32–34; Luke 11:14–15 A dumb man (one unable to speak) was possessed of a devil, an evil spirit (cf. JST Luke 11:15). Jesus cast it out, and some marveled and saw the power of God and good, whereas others attributed the marvel to the power of the devil and evil. Beelzebub (literally, "Lord of the flies") is a name-title for Satan.

An angel from God taught King Benjamin that things like this would happen: "Even after all this they shall consider him a man, and say that he hath a devil" (Mosiah 3:9; cf. Helaman 13:26).

TEACHING TOUR IN CITIES OF APOSTLES (AT CAPERNAUM, BETHSAIDA, ETC.)

Matthew 11:1 Jesus taught the apostles and then proceeded to teach the people in the apostles' hometowns—a good missionary approach: teach the people with their friends and associates, others they know.

JOHN SENDS DISCIPLES TO JESUS (IN GALILEE)

Matthew 11:2–6; Luke 7:18–23 Two followers of John the Baptist were apparently having a difficult time shifting over to their new Master, so John sent them to watch Jesus and return and report to him what they had seen and heard. This was likely an object lesson to help those two disciples find their Savior. "While in prison, John sent two of his disciples to inquire of Jesus to reassure their faith. Many have thought this event reflected a lack of confidence in John's own mind. However, Jesus took the occasion to bear testimony of the great work John had done, emphasizing that he was unwavering and true" (Bible Dictionary, "John the Baptist," 714). After seeing for themselves the spiritually convincing miracles, they must have realized that Jesus surely was the promised Messiah. The Savior added that those who are not offended in him are blessed. Some seemed to be growing impatient that he was not going to be the great political deliverer that they expected. For some he would be, as Isaiah prophesied, "a stone of stumbling . . . a rock of offense" (Isaiah 8:14).

JOHN: NO GREATER PROPHET (IN GALILEE)

Matthew 11:7–19; Luke 7:24–35 Jesus asked, "What went ye out into the wilderness to see? A reed shaken with the wind?" (Matthew 11:7). No, they had gone to see a prophet, and one of the greatest prophets. ("Reed" is a general term for any tall, hard, hollow-stemmed grass or cane that grew along bodies of water in the Holy Land.)

Malachi prophesied, "Behold, I will send my messenger, and he shall prepare the way before me" (Malachi 3:1). The words "my messenger" in Hebrew are *malach-i;* the name of the prophet is one of his main messages (cf. "Isaiah," which in Hebrew is *yesha-yah,* meaning "Jehovah saves," one of that prophet's main messages, too). Malachi's prophecy finds fulfillment in more than one context, but here Jesus uses it to describe John the Baptist; in fact, John has fulfilled this prophecy twice—helping prepare the way before the Lord's first coming *and* his second coming.

"Among them that are born of women there hath not risen a greater than John the Baptist" (Matthew 11:11). This is a Semitic way of saying John the Baptist was one of the greatest prophets who ever lived. (Compare the superlative statement about Melchizedek: "There were many before him, and also there were many afterwards, but none were greater"; Alma 13:19).

The Prophet Joseph Smith, speaking in Nauvoo on January 29, 1843, answered the question: "How is it that John was considered one of the greatest prophets?"

"First. He was entrusted with a divine mission of preparing the way before the face of the Lord. Whoever had such a trust committed to him before or since? No man.

"Secondly. He was entrusted with the important mission, and it was required at his hands, to baptize the Son of Man. Whoever had the honor of doing that? Whoever had so great a privilege and glory? . . .

"Thirdly. John, at that time, was the only legal administrator in the affairs of the kingdom there was then on the earth, and holding the keys of power. The Jews had to obey his instructions or be damned, by their own law; and Christ Himself fulfilled all righteousness in becoming obedient to the law which he had given to Moses on the mount, and thereby magnified it and made it honorable, instead of destroying it. The son of Zacharias wrested the keys, the kingdom, the power, the glory from the Jews, by the holy anointing and decree of heaven, and these three reasons constitute him the greatest prophet born of a woman" (*Teachings of the Prophet Joseph Smith,* 275–76).

Then the Prophet Joseph Smith asked and answered a second question: "How was the least in the kingdom of heaven greater than he [John the Baptist]?" (Matthew 11:11).

"In reply I asked—Whom did Jesus have reference to as being the least? Jesus was looked upon as having the least claim in God's kingdom, and [seemingly] was least entitled to their credulity as a prophet; as though He had said—'He that is considered the least among you is greater than John—that is I myself'" (*Teachings of the Prophet Joseph Smith,* 276).

Note the significant changes Joseph Smith made in Matthew 11:13–15 (see Bible Appendix, 803).

See commentary on Matthew 17:10–13 for more about the Elias who *prepares* all things and the Elias who *restores* all things.

Matthew 11:16–19 This generation, the Jewish people in Galilee and Judea, were like children in the marketplace, which was a site of socializing and recreation. They complained: We have piped (played on a flute), but you would not dance; we sang you a funeral dirge, but you would not mourn. John the Baptist came declining invitations to eat and drink (strong drink)—living the strict life of his Nazarite vow—and they complained that he was possessed of a devil. Then Jesus came, socializing with the people, not living the austere life, and they complained that he was a glutton and a drunkard who associated with tax collectors and other sinners. These people could find fault with anyone.

"But wisdom is justified of her children"—that is, the wise will understand; they will discern and know him by his good works.

SECOND PASSOVER AT JERUSALEM (BRIEF TRIP TO JUDEA)

John 5:1 During his ministry, on the anniversary of his birth, Jesus always went up to Jerusalem to observe the Feast of the Passover. After all, he was the Passover Lamb. At the final Passover he would be offered up—sacrificed.

HEALING ON THE SABBATH (AT THE POOL OF BETHESDA, IN JERUSALEM)

John 5:2–16 The double pool called the Pool of Bethesda (or Bethzatha, possibly from the Aramaic word meaning "house of mercy") was situated just north of the Temple Mount gate through which sheep are supposed to have been brought into the Temple for sacrifice.

Five porticoes (colonnades or porches) surrounded the twin pools: four around the sides and one dividing them. Certain medicinal or curative properties were ascribed to the

A Second Galilean Ministry

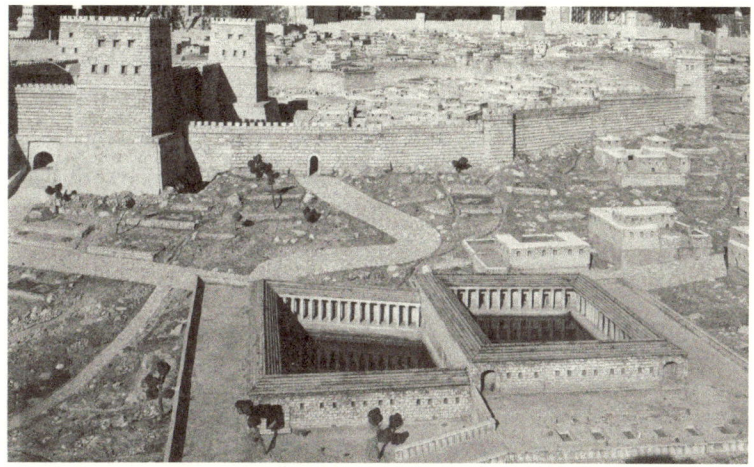

The Pool of Bethesda, Model City, Jerusalem

pool. A superstitious tradition had an angel coming down and "troubling" the waters, probably the result of a siphon-karst spring flowing into the pool, causing bubbling at the surface. At this pool, Jesus met an invalid man, lame or paralyzed for thirty-eight years. On the Sabbath day, he raised him up, completely healed.

Some Jews complained that the healed man was desecrating the Sabbath by carrying his bedding. The man replied simply: "He that made me whole, the same said unto me, Take up thy bed, and walk" (v. 11). These Jews then criticized Jesus for having done something unlawful on the Sabbath. But was it against Jewish law to heal on the Sabbath, to do something kind and compassionate and wonderful? No. According to most authorities on Jewish law, it was not unlawful to do such good on the Lord's day.

In July 1985 an article in *The Jerusalem Post* entitled "Chief rabbinate approved Sabbath rescue of Ethiopians" said:

"Ethiopian Jews were rescued on Shabbat with the full concurrence of the chief rabbinate, Sephardic Chief Rabbi Mordechai Eliahu revealed on Friday.

"Speaking to a session of the Rabbinical Council of

America . . . Eliahu said that when asked whether it was permissible to carry out the rescue mission also on the Sabbath, he replied that it was not only permissible, but a *mitzvah* (a good deed [or commandment]) to do so."

Verse 16 reports that certain Jews even wanted to kill Jesus because he had done this good deed. Intense feelings of envy, jealousy, and anger were building up in those who felt threatened by the Savior's goodness and his power.

Both Brother Ogden and Brother Skinner have seen this kind of intense feeling on a number of occasions in modern Jerusalem: Orthodox Jews endangering people's lives by throwing rocks at cars that drive by on main streets near their housing areas on the Sabbath. Not wanting their children growing up seeing people desecrating God's holy day by driving their cars, they want to force their own view of obeying a commandment (keeping the Sabbath holy) by disregarding another commandment ("thou shalt not kill").

In reality, the Sabbath is a great day for healing. When we go to Church each Sabbath, prepared to truly worship our Father and our Savior, we are healed. We partake of the sacrament, and we are whole again. We are healed through the atoning power of this same Master Healer, the Lord Jesus Christ.

DISCOURSE: WITNESS OF THE FATHER (AT JERUSALEM)

John 5:17–47 (see also 10:31–39; 19:7) Many in the modern, scholarly world question whether Jesus ever really claimed to be the Son of God. John leaves no doubt concerning the matter (though, of course, some scholars simply write off the entire Gospel of John as containing no authentic words of Jesus, as the "Jesus Seminar," a group of two hundred religious academics, did in the 1990s). Regardless of scholarly circumlocutions and polemics, however, all four Gospel writers, especially John, plainly and constantly reiterate that Jesus announced himself as the Son of God. In addition, Joseph Smith's translation of the Gospels—entitled Testimonies in that inspired revision of the Bible—contains at least forty declarations beyond those in the King James Version that Jesus is the Son of God. Jesus consistently testified that he was sent by his Father and that he spoke the words and did the works of the Father. Some of the Jews believed and accepted his witness, and others did not. Those who rejected his claims to divinity labeled as blasphemy Jesus' claim to have been sent from God or to actually be God and thus making himself "equal with God" (v. 18). Some might also have had a problem with Jesus' claim because they believed in one God only, so the claims to be God's Son would be blasphemous. For that capital offense, in the eyes of Jewish law, they sought to kill him.

Yet there are *numerous* testimonies of Jesus as the Son of God, not just those from Matthew, Mark, Luke, and John. The greatest of all testimonies is the Father's own testimony: "This is my Beloved Son," at Jesus' baptism (Matthew 3:17; D&C 93:15); at the Transfiguration (Matthew 17:5); at the appearance of the resurrected Christ to the Nephites (3 Nephi 11:7); and at Joseph Smith's First Vision (Joseph Smith–History 1:17). Additional testimonies by the Father include the vision of Moses (Moses 1:33; 2:1, 26); the vision of glories (D&C 76:20–23); and others (1 John 5:9–11; D&C 29:42; 49:5).

To all of the following, Jesus bore his own testimony that he is the Son of God: Adam (Moses 5:9); Moses (Moses 4:2); the Jews (Matthew 27:43; Luke 10:21–22; John 5:18–27; 10:36; 19:7); the apostles (John 20:21); a blind man (John 9:35–37); Caiaphas (Matthew 26:63–64); Nephites and Lamanites (3 Nephi 9:15; 20:31); Latter-day Saints in general (D&C 6:21; 10:57; 45:52; 50:27); Hyrum Smith (D&C 11:28); David Whitmer (D&C 14:9); Joseph Smith and Sidney Rigdon (D&C 35:2); Edward Partridge (D&C 36:8);

elders of the Church (D&C 42:1, 44); William W. Phelps (D&C 55:2); and four men who would later be called as apostles: Orson Hyde, Luke Johnson, Lyman Johnson, and William E. McLellin (D&C 68:6, 25).

Others testified that Jesus is the Son of God and the Only Begotten of the Father: Moses (Alma 33:18-19; Helaman 8:13-15); Isaiah and Jeremiah (Helaman 8:20); Zenos and Zenock (Alma 33:13-17; Helaman 8:19-20); the angel Gabriel (Luke 1:32, 35); John the Baptist (John 1:34; D&C 93:14); apostles (Matthew 14:33); Nathanael (John 1:49); Mark (Mark 1:1); Peter (Matthew 16:16; John 6:69; Acts 3:13, 26); Martha (John 11:27); John (John 1:14; 3:16, 35; 20:31; 1 John 3:8, 23; 4:10, 14-15; 5:5, 10-13); a Roman soldier (Matthew 27:54); an Ethiopian officer (Acts 8:37); Paul (Acts 9:20; Romans 1:4; 8:3, 32; 15:6; 2 Corinthians 1:19; Galatians 2:20; 4:4; Ephesians 4:13; Colossians 1:13; 1 Thessalonians 1:10; Hebrews 1:2; 4:14); Silas and Timothy (2 Corinthians 1:19); Nephi (1 Nephi 10:17; 11:7, 18, 21, 24; 13:40; 2 Nephi 25:12, 16, 19); Jacob (Jacob 4:5, 11); King Benjamin (Mosiah 3:8); Benjamin's people (Mosiah 4:2); Abinadi (Mosiah 15:2); Amulek (Alma 11:32-35; 34:2, 5); Alma the Elder and Alma the Younger (Alma 36:17-18); Alma the Younger (Alma 5:48; 6:8; 12:33-34; 13:5, 16; 33:14, 22); Samuel the Lamanite (Helaman 14:2, 8, 12); Mormon (Helaman 3:28; 3 Nephi 5:13, 26; Mormon 5:14; 7:5-7); Moroni (Ether 12:18); Joseph Smith (D&C 20:21); and Joseph Smith and Sidney Rigdon (D&C 76:20-25).

To some it is given to know Jesus Christ is the Son of God; to others it is given to believe on their words (D&C 46:13-14). Whoever denies Jesus, the Son, is a liar and is anti-Christ (1 John 2:21-22).

So, to conclude this listing of witnesses that Jesus is the Son of God, we ask the same questions Alma asked: "Now behold, my brethren, I would ask if ye have read the scriptures? If ye have, how can ye disbelieve on the Son of God?" (Alma 33:14).

John 5:21–27 The Son has life in himself, independent of all other powers in the universe. The Father gave the Son that privilege and power and also the authority to judge and to quicken, or resurrect, bodies to everlasting life. Those who hear and hearken to the voice of the Son will pass "from death unto life" (v. 24).

By exercising these powers Jesus was also doing what his Father had done before him. Joseph Smith taught:

"The Scriptures inform us that Jesus said, As the Father hath power in Himself, even so hath the Son power—to do what? Why, what the Father did. The answer is obvious—in a manner to lay down His body and take it up again. Jesus, what are you going to do? To lay down my life as my Father did, and take it up again. Do we believe it? If you do not believe it, you do not believe the Bible" (*Teachings of the Prophet Joseph Smith*, 346).

"As the Father hath power in Himself, so hath the Son power in Himself, to lay down His life and take it again, so He has a body of His own. The Son doeth what He hath seen the Father do: then the Father hath some day laid down His life and taken it again; so He has a body of His own" (*Teachings of the Prophet Joseph Smith*, 312).

John 5:28–29 The Prophet Joseph Smith wrote on February 16, 1832: "I resumed the translation of the Scriptures [what we call the Joseph Smith Translation]. From sundry revelations which had been received, it was apparent that many important points touching the salvation of man had been taken from the Bible, or lost before it was compiled. It appeared self-evident from what truths were left, that if God rewarded every one according to the deeds done in the body, the term 'Heaven,' as intended for the Saints' eternal home, must include more kingdoms than one. Accordingly, while translating St. John's Gospel [John 5:29], myself and Elder Rigdon saw the following vision" (D&C 76, heading).

The Prophet called the ensuing revelation "a transcript

from the records of the eternal world" (*Teachings of the Prophet Joseph Smith*, 11).

"For while we were doing the work of translation, which the Lord had appointed unto us, we came to the twenty-ninth verse of the fifth chapter of John, which was given unto us as follows–

"Speaking of the resurrection of the dead, concerning those who shall hear the voice of the Son of Man:

"And shall come forth; they who have done good, in the resurrection of the just; and they who have done evil, in the resurrection of the unjust.

"Now this caused us to marvel for it was given unto us of the Spirit.

"And while we meditated upon these things, the Lord touched the eyes of our understanding and they were opened, and the glory of the Lord shone round about" (D&C 76:15–19).

Then unfolded the grand panoramic vision of the kingdoms of glory, where the Prophet and his companion learned that there is a much broader spectrum of resurrected bodies and rewards and punishments than simply "the resurrection of life" and "the resurrection of damnation" (John 5:29; cf. Mosiah 16:11).

John 5:30 Jesus attests that he does nothing independent of the Father. He and the Father are one (John 10:30; D&C 50:43; 93:3), so his word, his work, and his will are identical to the Father's. He spoke the Father's words, accomplished the Father's work, and was always submissive to the Father's will.

John 5:31 Joseph Smith's translation of this verse reverses the statement: "*Therefore* if I bear witness of myself, *yet* my witness is true" (JST John 5:32). John 8:14 affirms the same verity: "Though I bear record of myself, yet my record is true."

John 5:32–38 The Savior is not alone in bearing witness of his divine mission. John the Baptist came as "a burning and a shining light" (v. 35) to testify of One greater than he.

"And he received not his testimony of man, but of God, and ye yourselves say that he is a prophet, therefore ye ought to receive his testimony" (JST John 5:35).

Yet Jesus has a greater witness than that of John the Baptist. The very works he does constitute an undeniable witness that he is from God. And the Father himself has borne witness of the Son. But the Jews whom Jesus addressed here had not merited hearing the Father's voice or seeing his Person, and because they refused to believe Jesus, the word of God was not in them.

John 5:39 Jesus rebuked and condemned the unbelieving Jews, saying, in a sense, that they searched the scriptures because in them *they thought* they had eternal life, but the scriptures testified of him. (The Greek text itself suggests the following translation, in modern terms: Just knowing the scriptures, you mistakenly think you have eternal life.) In truth, the rabbis taught that study of the words in scripture brought eternal life. Hillel said, "He who has acquired words of Torah has acquired for himself the life of the world to come" (*Pirke Aboth*, II:8, page 48). Jesus is contradicting the erroneous rabbinic notion, and saying, essentially, that if they really understood the words of life and had the accompanying Spirit with them, they would have recognized him of whom all the scriptures testify (cf. Jacob 7:19).

In verses 31 through 39 Jesus invoked those witnesses of his divinity that are also available to us in our day: the testimony of his own voice (recognized through personal revelation; v. 31); the testimony of a living prophet (which John was; v. 33); the works performed by Jesus (which same type of works we witness today in his Church; v. 36); the voice of the Father (heard again in our day; v. 37); and the testimony of the scriptures (v. 39).

John 5:40–44 In essence, Jesus said to the people that they were not willing to come to him, thereby securing the promise of eternal life. He knew them, that they did not have the love of God in them. He came in his Father's name and they rejected Him, though if someone came in his own name, they received him. How would they ever receive Him, they who were so adept at self-adulation, patting themselves on the back but uninterested in the real and lasting honor that comes from God?

John 5:45–47 Jesus assured his listeners that they did not need to worry about him accusing them before the Father, because their great mentor Moses would accuse them. If they really loved and understood Moses' words, they would see that he testified plainly of Jesus. But if they would not believe Moses' writings, how would they believe Jesus' words?

PROCLAMATION OF THE GOSPEL IN GALILEE: SECOND PREACHING TOUR

Matthew 9:35–38; Mark 6:6 Sheep, the sheepfold, and the shepherd were all used as symbols in the Gospels. Earth life was seen as a desert, and the children of God as scattered sheep wandering hungry and helpless, needing guidance from the Good Shepherd who desires to lead them over the trails and trials of life, to bring them all back into the safety of the fold. Without him they are "as sheep having no shepherd" (Matthew 9:36), "notwithstanding a shepherd hath called after you and is still calling after you, but ye will not hearken unto his voice!" (Alma 5:37).

Jesus continued his teaching and healing, moved with compassion for the sheep of his fold. As noted in footnote 36b, the Greek rendition of this passage indicates that his sheep were being harassed and scattered. There was great need both then and now not only for the Shepherd but for many undershepherds (Jacob 5:70) to help nourish and safely guide the sheep; or, to change the metaphor, there is need for many more laborers in the mission fields because the fields are ripe and the harvest is plentiful. Pray that the Lord of the harvest will send out many more laborers—not only the apostles and the seventy but elders and sisters and couples without number.

THIRD PREACHING TOUR (IN GALILEE)

Luke 8:1–3 Jesus appears to be making a fairly thorough circuit through the region of Galilee, teaching "in every city and village" (v. 1). His ordained apostles traveled with him. Many women also accompanied them to help care for the physical welfare of the traveling group. (Some of the women could have been wives of apostles; McConkie, *Mortal Messiah*, 3:31.) Among the women were some he had healed of various maladies, particularly casting out evil spirits. One notable example was Mary Magdalene, "out of whom went seven devils" (v. 2; see also Mark 16:9; Matthew 8:28–34). Of Mary Magdalene Elder McConkie wrote: "At some unrecorded time she was healed by Jesus from severe physical and mental maladies, and from her body the Master—of the seen and the unseen—cast out seven devils. Hers was no ordinary illness, and we cannot do other than suppose that she underwent some great spiritual test—a personal Gethsemane, a personal temptation in the wilderness for forty days, as it were—which she overcame and rose above—all preparatory to the great mission and work she was destined to perform. . . . Can we do other than rank Mary Magdalene with the Blessed Virgin . . . [and] with Mother Eve?" (*Mortal Messiah*, 2:205–6).

Two other women who had been healed of some sickness or of being possessed by evil spirits are also singled out: Joanna the wife of Chuza, Herod the tetrarch's steward (who was in charge of the ruler's household), and Susanna. Joanna is one of the women who later went to the sepulchre of Jesus to help prepare his body (Luke 24:10). Nothing further is known of Susanna.

SABBATH CONTROVERSIES AND THE WITHERED HAND (IN GALILEE)

Matthew 12:1–21; Mark 2:23–3:12; Luke 6:1–11
Corn is a British English word meaning grain, which is the meaning also of the Greek term. Passing through a field of grain and being hungry, Jesus and disciples rubbed grain in their hands, which some rabbis considered threshing, and blew the chaff away, which the same rabbis considered winnowing, causing Jesus and his disciples to desecrate the Sabbath—according to those Jewish leaders. What they had done was actually not against the law but specifically provided for: "When thou comest into the standing corn [Hebrew, "grain"] of thy neighbour, then thou mayest pluck the ears with thine hand; but thou shalt not move a sickle unto thy neighbor's standing corn" (Deuteronomy 23:25).

In fact, that is still the custom in modern Israel. After a day of walking the twenty miles from Cana to the Sea of Galilee, Brother Ogden wrote: "We were pleasantly surprised by some 'experimenting upon the word.' As we passed many ripened fields of wheat we thought we'd try what Jesus and the Twelve did when they were hungry and walking through that same general area one day. We snapped off an ear of grain, rubbed it vigorously in our palms, let the afternoon breeze carry off the chaff, and then feasted on what we'd never before realized were delicious little treats. We repeated the process several times, and were delighted with our newly discovered wheat snack" (Ogden, journal).

Anciently, Jesus illustrated the legitimacy of their action by recalling the eating of the Temple shewbread (pronounced "SHOW-bread"; Bible Dictionary, "Shewbread," 773) by David and his men (1 Samuel 21:4–6) and by pointing out that the Temple priests work hard when slaughtering and sacrificing animals on the Sabbath day. The priests properly did that because there is a higher law of worship—the purpose of the Sabbath is to honor and worship the Lord, not just to rest from work. And, in fact, the Hebrew verb *la'avod* means both to work and to worship. Thus, working and worshipping are the same verb in Hebrew: To properly worship the Lord requires spiritual work.

Citing a teaching recorded in Hosea (6:6) Jesus reminded his disputants that he, God, wants mercy—acts of love and kindness—more than sacrifices and other such ritual and mechanical observance of the law. If they understood the higher principle, they would not be so quick to condemn:

"*Wherefore the Sabbath was given unto man for a day of rest; and also that man should glorify God, and not that man should not eat;*

"*For the Son of Man made the Sabbath day,* therefore the Son of Man is Lord also of the Sabbath" (JST Mark 2:26–27).

Matthew 12:6, 8 Jesus plainly taught his followers and his critics who he is. The Creator and Lord of all the earth is greater than John the Baptist (Matthew 11:11), greater than Jacob (John 4:12), greater than Abraham (John 8:53), greater than Jonah (Matthew 12:41), greater than Solomon (Matthew 12:42), greater than the Temple (Matthew 12:6), and greater than the Sabbath (Matthew 12:8).

Matthew 12:10–13; Mark 3:1–5 Another Sabbath, another synagogue: Jesus encountered a man with a withered right hand (Luke 6:6). Again his opponents tried to find something wherewith to accuse him. Jesus' assailants produced a seemingly endless array of accusations against him. For example, he was accused of all of the following: being a Sabbath breaker (John 5:16); a gluttonous man and a winebibber (Matthew 11:19); having a devil in him (John 8:48); being a Samaritan (John 8:48); being a friend of publicans and sinners (Luke 7:34); being a sinner (John 9:24); deceiving the people (John 7:12); being a blasphemer (John 10:33); being crazy (John 10:20) and "beside himself" (Mark 3:21); perverting the nation (Luke 23:2); stirring up the people (Luke 23:5); and being a false witness (John 8:13).

On this occasion Jesus' enemies asked, "Is it lawful to heal on the sabbath days?" Jesus asked back to them: "Is it lawful on the sabbath days to do good, or to do evil? to save life, or to destroy it?" (Luke 6:9). And he posed a simple question from their experience with sheep—if one fell into a pit and the animal's life is in danger, would you lift it up and help it out? Then the clincher: "How much then is a man better than a sheep?" They had the answer to their question, but still Jesus pronounced in all plainness that of course it is lawful to do good on the Sabbath. He himself had given the law, and it provided for the rescue of an animal in peril, and even more so if a man—a child of God—needed rescuing, either temporally or spiritually. Jesus looked around on his accusers "with anger," Mark notes (3:5), "being grieved for the hardness of their hearts"; then he healed the withered hand.

Matthew 12:14–21; Mark 3:6–12 Some Pharisees and Herodians counseled together about how they could destroy Jesus (the Herodians were a political group among the Jews who favored Herodian rule over direct Roman rule; see Appendix 4, 746). Once again Jesus cautioned those who saw his miracles and heard his teachings not to broadcast them so as not to stir up his opponents to unrestrained vehemence and violence.

Early Christians saw in Jesus the fulfillment of Isaiah's visions of the suffering servant. Isaiah 42 begins with the prophet speaking messianically, describing him as the epitome of gentle tenderness, unwilling to harm even the weakest plant. "A bruised reed shall he not break, and the smoking flax shall he not quench" (Isaiah 42:3; Matthew 12:20). The reed is a type or symbol of humanity; and the Messiah, who finds many reeds bruised by the storms of life, is inclined to bind up and heal rather than to break and destroy.

The Greek word for flax was *linen*, which is one of the products prepared from the fibrous plant. Flax was grown in various parts of the ancient Near East, especially in Egypt. It was cultivated in the tropical climate of Jericho at the time of the Israelites' incursion into the land of Canaan (Joshua 2:6).

The "smoking flax" is a reference to the wick of an oil lamp. The gentleness of the Messiah would figuratively disallow his even putting out the smoking linen wick used in a lamp.

Mark notes that people were coming from all over the land to hear the One who said he was the long-awaited Messiah—not only from all of Galilee, but also from the Phoenician coastal cities of Tyre and Sidon, from Judea, from Perea ("beyond Jordan"), and even from Idumea, the southernmost part of the land.

Clearly the Gospel writers were impressed not only with the crowds that gathered around Jesus but also with the distances they had traveled to hear him. Those present at the Sea of Galilee from Idumea had journeyed at least one hundred fifty miles to listen to this new teacher who spoke as one having authority.

BEELZEBUB, BLASPHEMY, AND THE SIN AGAINST THE HOLY GHOST (IN GALILEE)

Matthew 12:22–37; Mark 3:20–30; Luke 6:45; 11:14–26; 12:10 Jesus' miraculous works generated serious differences of opinion and divisiveness about how the people regarded him. Some Jews couldn't help but believe, although certain Pharisees accused him of using satanic power to exorcise evil spirits. His response to their derisive thoughts was perfect: "Every kingdom divided against itself is brought to desolation . . . if Satan cast out Satan, he is divided against himself; how shall then his kingdom stand?" (Matthew 12:25–26). In effect, Jesus said to the Pharisees, If I am using the devil's power to cast out evil spirits, by whom are your followers doing it? If, on the other hand, I am doing those miraculous acts using God's power, that is a clear sign to you that the kingdom of God is come unto you. At this point the Joseph Smith Translation adds: "*For they* [true disciples of

Christ] *also cast out devils by the Spirit of God, for unto them is given power over devils, that they may cast them out*" (JST Matthew 12:23).

All manner of sins can be forgiven of men "*who receive me and repent*" (JST Matthew 12:26) but not the sin of blasphemy against the Holy Ghost. The Joseph Smith Translation of Mark 3:21–25 provides a fuller rendering of the context and meaning of Jesus' teaching (see Bible Appendix, 804).

Joseph Smith explained what it means to commit the sin against the Holy Ghost: "Jesus will save all except the sons of perdition. What must a man do to commit the unpardonable sin? He must receive the Holy Ghost, have the heavens opened unto him, and know God, and then sin against Him. After a man has sinned against the Holy Ghost, there is no repentance for him. He has got to say that the sun does not shine while he sees it; he has got to deny Jesus Christ when the heavens have been opened unto him, and to deny the plan of salvation with his eyes open to the truth of it" (*Teachings of the Prophet Joseph Smith*, 358).

President Spencer W. Kimball declared: "The eyes can be deceived, as can the other physical senses, but the testimony of the Holy Ghost is certain. The sin against the Holy Ghost requires such knowledge that it is manifestly impossible for the rank and file to commit such a sin" (*Teachings of Spencer W. Kimball*, 23).

Matthew 12:29; Luke 11:21–22 How could the Savior overcome Satan's kingdom without having already overcome Satan himself (the "strong man")? Satan ultimately will be bound (Revelation 20:2; 1 Nephi 22:26) and his "house" permanently spoiled and leveled.

Matthew 12:33–37; Luke 6:45 On trees and their good or bad fruit, see commentary on Matthew 7:15–20. On the "generation of vipers," see commentary on Matthew 3:7. "Out of the abundance of the heart the mouth speaketh" (Matthew 12:34). The Greek text means "out of what the heart is full of," that is what will come out of the mouth. If the treasury of the heart is full of kind, happy, positive things, those are what will undoubtedly proceed out of the mouth. The opposite is likewise true: If the heart is full of angry, dark, and hostile feelings, those are what will spew forth out of the mouth. The Lord warns that we are accountable for all our words: "every idle word [and gossipy, profane, accusatory, or destructive word] that men shall speak, they shall give account thereof in the day of judgment" (Matthew 12:36); our words will either exalt us or condemn us. If change is needed, now is the time. Now is the day of repentance and preparation to meet God, for every tongue shall confess him in the end; every mouth will admit that his judgment (even our own self-judgment) is just. See 2 Nephi 9:46; Mosiah 3:24–25; Alma 11:43; 12:14–15.

Luke 11:24–26 Jesus warned that once we have expelled an evil influence from our lives, it is vital to clean our "house"—our body and soul—and strengthen ourselves, so that the evil influence cannot return to exercise even greater control and dominion than at first. In other words, it is not enough to repent and cleanse ourselves; we must also strengthen ourselves (through prayer, scripture study, church and Temple service and worship, and keeping all commandments) so that Satan and his evil spirits can have no power over us. We must leave not only sinful behavior but also the environment that fostered sin.

PHARISEES ASK FOR A SIGN (IN GALILEE)

Matthew 12:38; Luke 11:16 Certain leaders of the Jews came flagrantly and flippantly requesting a sign, something that comes only by first showing faith and having a believing heart. "Behold, faith cometh not by signs, but signs follow those that believe. Yea, signs come by faith, not by the will of men, nor as they please, but by the will of God. Yea, signs come by faith, unto mighty works, for without faith no man pleaseth God; and . . . unto such he showeth no signs, only in wrath unto their condemnation" (D&C 63:9–11; cf. Alma 30:43).

SIGN OF JONAH (IN GALILEE)

Matthew 12:39–45; Luke 11:29–32 Jesus pointedly responded: "An evil and adulterous generation seeketh after a sign." Joseph Smith affirmed: "Whenever you see a man seeking after a sign, you may set it down that he is an adulterous man" (*Teachings of the Prophet Joseph Smith,* 157).

President Joseph F. Smith wrote concerning sign-seekers: "It is a wicked and adulterous generation that seeketh after a sign. Show me Latter-day Saints who have to feed upon miracles, signs and visions in order to keep them steadfast in the Church, and I will show you members of the Church who are not in good standing before God, and who are walking in slippery paths. It is not by marvelous manifestations unto us that we shall be established in the truth, but it is by humility and faithful obedience to the commandments and laws of God. When I as a boy first started out in the ministry, I would frequently go out and ask the Lord to show me some marvelous thing, in order that I might receive a testimony. But the Lord withheld marvels from me, and showed me the truth, line upon line, precept upon precept, here a little and there a little, until he made me to know the truth from the crown of my head to the soles of my feet, and until doubt and fear had been absolutely purged from me. He did not have to send an angel from the heavens to do this, nor did he have to speak with the trump of an archangel. By the whisperings of the still small voice of the Spirit of the living God, he gave to me the testimony I possess" (*Gospel Doctrine,* 7).

The book of Jonah records that a "great fish" swallowed Jonah (1:17). In Matthew's recounting of the experience, Jesus spoke of the prophet's staying three days and three nights in the belly of a *ketos,* that is, a "great fish." Because some have labeled the story of Jonah (Greek, *Jonas*) as scriptural fiction, as a fable, we should note that Jesus' mention of the prophet and his unique ordeal and the fact that the people of Nineveh "repented at the preaching of Jonas" (Matthew 12:41) give the whole episode historical credibility.

Jesus' purpose in alluding to Jonah was to give the scribes and Pharisees "a sign." The sign of the prophet Jonah—his three days and three nights in the belly of the great fish—was a type of things to come: "So shall the Son of man be three days and three nights in the heart of the earth" (Matthew 12:40). He was, of course, referring to his own death, burial, and resurrection—another specific witness that he knew his mortal end from the beginning.

"Three days and three nights" is an idiom covering any parts of three days and nights. "According to early Jewish time-reckoning, any part of a day counted as a full day" (William Lane Craig, as quoted in Strobel, *Case for Christ,* 217; see also Kloner, referring to the phrase "on the third day": "The counting of the days . . . follows Jewish custom, which included both the first and the last day in the count," *Biblical Archaeology Review,* September/October, 1999, 29). At his death Jesus did not remain in the earth three whole days and three whole nights, else his rising from the dead would have been on the *fourth* day, whereas the scriptures ten times mention his Resurrection "on the third day."

Referring to the Queen of Sheba, Matthew and Luke indicate that "she came from the uttermost parts of the earth to hear the wisdom of Solomon" (Matthew 12:42; Luke 11:31). The land of Sheba, or Seba—the land of the Sabeans—is thought to be the southwestern part of today's Arabian Peninsula, specifically the modern land of Yemen.

The men of Nineveh and the queen of Sheba rising up and condemning that generation of Jews was similar to Jesus proclaiming that the inhabitants of Tyre and Sidon, and even Sodom, would find more clemency in the day of judgment than the Jews of Galilee (Matthew 11:21–24), because the Galileans had a greater witness—a witness from the Savior in person—than did the Ninevites, Sabeans, Tyrians, Sidonians, or Sodomites. A greater witness than Jonah, Solomon, or any other mortal had personally ministered among them and had been rejected by most of them.

Matthew 12:43–45 The Joseph Smith Translation of this passage (JST Matthew 12:37–38) renders it in a different context than the parallel passage in Luke 11:24–26:

"*Then came some of the Scribes and said unto him, Master, it is written that, Every sin shall be forgiven; but ye say, Whosoever speaketh against the Holy Ghost shall not be forgiven. And they asked him, saying, How can these things be?*

"*And he said unto them,* When the unclean spirit is gone out of a man, he walketh through dry places, seeking rest and findeth none; *but when a man speaketh against the Holy Ghost, then he saith,* I will return into my house from whence I came out; and when he is come, he findeth him empty, swept and garnished; *for the good spirit leaveth him unto himself.*"

Another point that can be made about one's house being "empty, swept, and garnished," is that having "cleaned out" the evil from one's life, there is still a lighted "vacancy" sign in the window—just waiting for bad habits to return. Rather than leaving things empty, once the bad habit is gone, fill up the house with good habits, so that the evil things have nowhere to stay when they try to return. (We thank Jared Halverson, a seminary teacher and Religious Education graduate student, for this insight.)

Alma teaches the same principle in these clear and simple terms: "And thus we can plainly discern, that after a people have been once enlightened by the Spirit of God, and have had great knowledge of things pertaining to righteousness, and then have fallen away into sin and transgression, they become more hardened, and thus their state becomes worse than though they had never known these things" (Alma 24:30).

JESUS' MOTHER AND BRETHREN (IN GALILEE)

Matthew 12:46–50; Mark 3:31–35; Luke 8:19–21 A simple object lesson was taught as Jesus' mother and half brothers and sisters (see Matthew 13:55–56) desired to talk with him one day as he instructed the people. He gestured toward the crowds and said that they were his family. In fact, in a symbolic way, his true disciples become part of his eternal family. King Benjamin taught his people: "Because of the covenant which ye have made ye shall be called the children of Christ, his sons, and his daughters" (Mosiah 5:7).

PARABLES: FUTURE OF THE KINGDOM (IN GALILEE)

Matthew 13:1–53; Mark 4:1–34; Luke 8:4–18 Following are important reasons why the Savior taught with parables.

1. *Parables were part of the world in which Jesus grew up and lived as an adult.* The greatest teachers and rabbis of Jesus' era used parables, even some of the very same specific elements found in the parables presented by the Savior.

2. *Parables teach by analogies that are not easily forgotten.* The Greek word *parabole*, from which our English word *parable* derives, means to "set side by side or to compare one thing to another." Because parables compared or set principles of the gospel side by side with ordinary objects, common events, or familiar circumstances of life, they could be readily identified, understood, and remembered.

3. *Parables have a double use in communicating messages—they can simultaneously veil or unveil concepts, reveal or conceal meaning, according to each person's spiritual capacity and ability to receive.* Thus, the Savior could simultaneously teach

THE PARABLES OF JESUS

Parable(s)	Main Reference(s)
1. Two debtors	Luke 7:36–50
2. The sower (The four kinds of soil)	Matthew 13:3–23; Luke 8:5–15
3. The wheat and tares	Matthew 13:24–30, 36–43
4. Mustard seed and leaven	Matthew 13:31–33; Mark 4:30–32
5. Treasure hid in field, pearl of great price, the net	Matthew 13:44–48
6. The unmerciful servant and the debt	Matthew 18:23–35
7. The good Samaritan	Luke 10:25–37
8. The friend at midnight	Luke 11:5–13
9. The foolish rich man	Luke 12:13–21
10. The watchful servants	Luke 12:35–40
11. The faithful and wise steward	Luke 12:41–48
12. The unfruitful fig tree	Luke 13:6–9
13. The shut door	Luke 13:23–30
14. The wedding feast	Luke 14:7–11
15. The great supper	Luke 14:16–24
16. Building the tower, the king going to make war	Luke 14:25–33
17. The lost sheep, ten pieces of silver, prodigal son	Luke 15:3–32
18. The unjust steward	Luke 16:1–13
19. The rich man and Lazarus	Luke 16:19–31
20. The unprofitable servants	Luke 17:7–10
21. The importunate widow	Luke 18:1–8
22. The Pharisee and the publican	Luke 18:9–14
23. The laborers in the vineyard	Matthew 20:1–16
24. The two sons	Matthew 21:28–32
25. The wicked husbandmen	Matthew 21:33–46; Luke 20:9–18
26. The marriage of the king's son	Matthew 22:1–14
27. The faithful and the evil servant	Matthew 24:42–51
28. The ten virgins	Matthew 25:1–13
29. The talents (cf. pounds in Luke 19:11–27)	Matthew 25:14–30
30. The sheep and the goats	Matthew 25:31–46

truths to those ready to receive them and withhold truths from those unprepared to receive them.

The prophet Alma taught: "He that will harden his heart, the same receiveth the lesser portion of the word; and he that will not harden his heart, to him is given the greater portion of the word" (Alma 12:10).

The lesser portion of the word is what is on the printed page of the scriptures. The greater portion of the word is what comes from the Spirit while we are reading, "according to the heed and diligence" we give to the gospel. Pondering over the scriptures invites the Holy Ghost into our minds and hearts. That is why studying the scriptures with the Spirit is critical. The scriptures have the answers to all questions, not because they contain a comprehensive index to every dilemma facing the human family but because when the words of the Lord are read with the Spirit, the Holy Ghost can give us greater light and understanding than is possible to obtain on our own (see Moroni 7:15–18; D&C 88:6–13; John 1:9).

Elder Boyd K. Packer taught, "If [we] are acquainted with the revelations there is no question—personal or social or political or occupational—that need go unanswered. Therein is contained the fulness of the gospel. Therein we find the principles of truth that will resolve every confusion and every problem and every dilemma that will face the human family or any individual in it" ("Teach the Scriptures," 89).

4. *By teaching in parables, the Lord protects unprepared individuals from more truth than they can live—a merciful way to teach.* The parables can be read and understood on different levels. A "veiled" view of them would render only the lesser portion of what was meant. Individuals with veiled hearts listening to the Savior teach would have heard a few simple stories about common, familiar things. But those same individuals, listening with the Spirit, would have understood that each story was given to teach an eternal principle or truth. And if they were sensitive to the Spirit's promptings, they would have readily perceived that the parables have multiple

levels of meaning and may simultaneously reach people on more than one level, and even reach people living in different periods of time.

Before going further into the parables of Jesus, it would be wise to read "Parables" (Bible Dictionary, 740–41). There we are given additional definition, classification, examples, and cautions about studying the stories Jesus told. A few definitions of literary devices used by the ancient Israelites may also help:

A *hyperbole* is an intentional exaggeration to illustrate a point. Modern, colloquial examples include "I'm so hungry I could eat a horse"; "I wrote till my hand fell off." A scriptural example is "Say nothing but repentance unto this generation" (D&C 6:9; 11:9)—not literally, of course, because we do have other important things to say to this generation, but this commandment is rendered in this hyperbolic language to emphasize that of all the things we do declare, there is nothing more important we can preach than repentance. Another scriptural example is a camel passing through the eye of a needle (see commentary on Matthew 19:23–24). Other examples are pointed out in the commentary on Matthew 5:27–30; 7:6; 8:18–22; 13:31–32; 23:23–24; Luke 14:25–27.

A *simile* is an explicit comparison, a declaration that one thing is like another: "his face did shine as the sun" (Matthew 17:2); "[be] harmless as doves" (Matthew 10:16); "[the kingdom of God] is like a grain of mustard seed" (Luke 13:19).

A *metaphor* is an implicit comparison, a declaration that one thing is (or represents) another. Most metaphors are not meant to be taken literally (some would be strange and grotesque, even perverting true doctrine): "Ye are the salt of the earth" (Matthew 5:13); "This [bread] is my body . . . this [cup of wine] is my blood" (Matthew 26:26, 28); "I am the vine, ye are the branches" (John 15:5); and notice all the "I am" metaphors in the Gospel of John: I am . . . the living water (4:14), the bread of life (6:35), the light of the world

(8:12), the door (10:9), the true vine (15:1), and the good shepherd (10:11).

Many colorful metaphors teach us something about the Savior. He is the Stone, the Rock, the Branch, the Sower, the Husbandman, the True Vine, the Lord of the vineyard, the Lamb, the Sheep, and the Shepherd. Actually he is not *any* of those things—literally. But each comparison teaches us something about the Savior's character, something that we can emulate. But before we can emulate that quality of his character, we have to understand the image, the metaphor being used.

In the Gospels people are salt, plants, olive trees and fig trees, branches of the vine, grapes, grass, sheep, goats, and fish. Unworthy people are vipers, dogs, and wolves. Again, people are not literally any of those things, but we can learn something from each of the images, if we study them in their original context and come to understand them.

An *allegory* is an extended metaphor. Unlike a parable, an allegory can have every object or idea representing something. Every point can have its own meaning. The Gospel of John has no true parables but does contain two allegories, the good shepherd in chapter 10 and the true vine in chapter 15. The longest chapter in the Book of Mormon, Jacob 5, is a classic example of an allegory. The images continue to build on each other, each having meaning, leading to a climax or a conclusion.

A *parable* is an extended simile and metaphor. It is a short story that uses familiar characters, conditions, and customs to teach a single point or lesson. Unlike fables, which are imaginative, exaggerated, and improbable, created to amuse more than to teach, parables contain no fiction, nothing artificial—they are all true to life.

Jesus nearly always had only one main lesson he was teaching with each parable (except, for example, the parable of the prodigal son, which has at least two major themes). It is, therefore, unwise to overanalyze and attempt to find meaning in every detail (as with an allegory); pushing the analogy too far, in fact, is doctrinally dangerous.

Joseph Smith gave us his key to understanding a parable: "Enquire, what was the question which drew out the answer, or caused Jesus to utter the parable? . . . To ascertain its meaning, we must dig up the root and ascertain what it was that drew the saying out of Jesus" (*Teachings of the Prophet Joseph Smith,* 276–77).

A parable, then, generally has one interpretation but may have many applications—to people in ancient times and, in quite different circumstances, to people in modern times. "The only true interpretation is the meaning the parable conveyed, or was meant to convey, when first spoken," notes the Bible Dictionary, but "the application of a parable may vary in every age and circumstance" ("Parables," 741). We greatly value the interpretation and applications given by the Savior himself and by his spokesmen, the prophets, in both ancient and modern times.

DISCOURSE FROM A BOAT (ON THE SEA OF GALILEE)

Matthew 13:2; Mark 4:1 A boat just offshore served as Jesus' stage and pulpit to teach the multitude about the future growth of his kingdom. Joseph Smith discoursed at some length about the meaning and application of these parables in Matthew 13, which has more parables than any other chapter in all of scripture. The Prophet Joseph was a Seer, and he interpreted these parables from a totally different perspective than any other Bible commentator. The parables of Matthew 13 describe in great detail the history and destiny of the Church and kingdom of God from the days of Jesus Christ down through the Millennium. But no one in all of Christian history had ever seen it—until the eyes of the Prophet Joseph Smith were touched by the Spirit, and he was inspired by revelation from heaven to understand the ultimate meaning of the Savior's teachings (see Skinner and Marsh, *Scriptural Parables*, 65). The Prophet's unique commentary on the parables of Matthew 13 is recorded in *History of the Church*, 2:265–72.

THE PARABLE OF THE SOWER (ON THE SEA OF GALILEE)

Matthew 13:3–9, 18–23; Mark 4:3–9, 14–20; Luke 8:4–8, 11–15 "The seed is the word of God," says Luke (8:11; cf. Alma 32:28). Seeds may also represent the Lord's disciples. Matthew, in another context, wrote that Jesus said, "The good seed are the children of the kingdom" (13:38).

Whether seed is the word itself or the people who carry the word to all parts of the field (the world), the analogies Jesus made all apply. Some seeds, when sown in the earth, fall by the wayside, where fowls fly in and devour them. Some fall in rocky places, where they are shortlived because they do not sink roots for nourishment and go inactive. Some fall among thorns, where they are choked by the weeds of worldliness—the cares, riches, and lusts of the flesh. Some, however, fall on good ground, where they grow by absorbing the nutrients from sun, soil, and water.

An important inference is found in these scriptures: the seed itself seems always to be good; the soil in which the seed is planted is what makes the difference. Whether the seed (the word of God) will flourish and become productive depends on what ground it is planted in, whether we are barren, hard, briery, or fertile (cf. Alma 32:39). Furthermore, if we are fertile, the seed's growth depends on whether we will nourish it by giving it Living Water and exposing it to sufficient Light.

We have several helps given to us by the Lord and his prophets to understand the significant parables recorded in Matthew 13. The Prophet Joseph Smith taught:

Along the shore of the Sea of Galilee, seeds fall among stones or thorns or on good soil

"Listen to the explanation of the parable of the Sower: 'When any one heareth the word of the Kingdom, and understandeth it not, then cometh the wicked one, and catcheth away that which was sown in his heart.' Now mark the expression—that which was sown in his heart. This is he which receiveth seed by the way side. Men who have no principle of righteousness in themselves, and whose hearts are full of iniquity, and have no desire for the principles of truth, do not understand the word of truth when they hear it. The devil taketh away the word of truth out of their hearts, because there is no desire for righteousness in them. 'But he that receiveth seed in stony places, the same is he that heareth the word, and anon [immediately; Bible Dictionary, "Anon," 609] with joy receiveth it; yet hath he not root in himself, but dureth for a while: for when tribulation or persecution ariseth because of the word, by and by [immediately; Bible Dictionary, "By and by," 627], he is offended. He also that receiveth seed among the thorns, is he that heareth the word; and the care of this world, and the deceitfulness of riches choke the word, and he becometh unfruitful. But he that received seed into the good ground is he that heareth the word, and understandeth it, which also beareth fruit, and bringeth forth, some an hundred fold, some sixty, some thirty.' Thus the Savior himself explains unto His disciples the parable which He put forth, and left no mystery or darkness upon the minds of those who firmly believe on His words.

"We draw the conclusion, then, that the very reason why the multitude, or the world, as they were designated by the Savior, did not receive an explanation upon His parables, was because of unbelief. To you, He says, (speaking to His disciples,) it is given to know the mysteries of the Kingdom of God. And why? Because of the faith and confidence they had in Him. This parable was spoken to demonstrate the effects that are produced by the preaching of the word; and we believe that it has an allusion directly, to the commencement, or the setting up of the Kingdom in that age; therefore we shall continue to trace His sayings concerning this Kingdom from that time forth, even unto the end of the world" (*History of the Church,* 2:266–67).

A vivid comparison may be made between the parable of the sower and the dream of Lehi, as recorded in 1 Nephi 8. When someone hears the gospel but does not relate to it or respond to it, the devil can come and quickly alienate that person from wanting to hear any more (Matthew 13:19). Such an individual is more interested in what is happening in the great and spacious building (1 Nephi 8:26–27).

When someone joyfully receives the word and temporarily prospers, but then trials and opposition come, the person is offended, becomes weak, and slips away (Matthew 13:20–21). That is like tasting of the delicious fruit and then feeling ashamed and falling away (1 Nephi 8:28).

When someone receives the word, having one foot in the kingdom but the other foot still stepping in the thorny world (having his heart set on the things of this world; D&C 121:35), that person is choked by deceitful worldly wealth and pleasures (Matthew 13:22), which are parallel to becoming lost in the mists of darkness, wandering off and falling into forbidden paths (1 Nephi 8:23, 28).

When someone receives the seed into good ground and helps it to sprout and produce fruit—hearing, understanding, and enduring (JST Matthew 13:21)—that is comparable to holding fast to the rod (the word) and partaking of the fruit (1 Nephi 8:24, 30).

The Lord of the Vineyard clearly expects us to cultivate our good soil and be fruitful; he expects us to hold firmly to the rod, get to the tree, and continuously partake of the fruit that nourishes us and gives us life—eternal life (cf. Alma 32:42).

WHY PARABLES? (ON THE SEA OF GALILEE)

Matthew 13:10-17, 34-35; Mark 4:10-13; Luke 8:9-10; 10:23-24 Of these verses the Prophet Joseph Smith taught the following:

"'And the disciples came and said unto Him, Why speakest thou unto them in parables? [I would here remark, that the 'them' made use of in this interrogation, is a personal pronoun, and refers to the multitude.] He answered and said unto them, [that is unto the disciples,] because it is given unto *you* to know the mysteries of the Kingdom of Heaven, but to *them*, [that is, unbelievers,] it is not given; for whosoever hath, to him shall be given, and he shall have more abundance; but whosoever hath not, from him shall be taken away even that he hath.' [See also Alma 12:9-10; 26:22.]

"We understand from this saying, that those who had been previously looking for a Messiah to come, according to the testimony of the Prophets, and were then, at that time looking for a Messiah, but had not sufficient light, on account of their unbelief, to discern Him to be their Savior; and He being the true Messiah, consequently they must be disappointed, and lose even all the knowledge, or have taken away from them all the light, understanding, and faith which they had upon this subject; therefore he that will not receive the greater light, must have taken away from him all the light which he hath; and if the light which is in you become darkness, behold, how great is that darkness! . . .

"We again make remark here—for we find that the very principle upon which the disciples were accounted blessed, was because they were permitted to see with their eyes and hear with their ears—that the condemnation which rested upon the multitude that received not His saying, was because they were not willing to see with their eyes, and hear with their ears; not because they could not, and were not privileged to see and hear, but because their hearts were full of iniquity and abominations; 'as your fathers did, so do ye.' The prophet, foreseeing that they would thus harden their hearts, plainly declared it; and herein is the condemnation of the world; that light hath come into the world, and men choose darkness rather than light, because their deeds are evil. This is so plainly taught by the Savior, that a wayfaring man need not mistake it" (*History of the Church,* 2:265–66).

THE PARABLE OF THE CANDLE (ON THE SEA OF GALILEE)

Mark 4:21–25; Luke 8:16–18 On the candle that must be set on a candlestick or lampstand, see the commentary on Matthew 5:14–16. Nothing is hidden or kept secret (Matthew 10:26–28). On the measure that is meted [given] back to us, see the commentary on Matthew 7:1–5.

Mark 4:24–25 The Lord explained that "unto him that receiveth I will give more; and from them that shall say, We have enough, from them shall be taken away even that which they have" (2 Nephi 28:30). Those who continue to hear, or continue to receive (JST Mark 4:20) shall be given more; they continue to receive more and more light, and "that light groweth brighter and brighter until the perfect day" (D&C 50:24).

THE PARABLE OF THE TARES (ON THE SEA OF GALILEE)

Matthew 13:24–30, 36–43; cf. Mark 4:26–29 A favorite and effective way of teaching involved comparing phenomena in nature with the human experience: "I have also spoken by the prophets, and I have multiplied visions, and used similitudes, by the ministry of the prophets" (Hosea 12:10). A familiar oratorical and literary device of the rabbinic sages at the time of Jesus was to inquire, "To what shall we liken this?" or "What is he like?" (See the example from the rabbis at Matthew 7:15–20.) Jesus, too, adopted this rhetorical device often. "I will liken him unto a wise man . . . [or] a foolish man" (Matthew 7:24–27). "He is like a man which built an house" (Luke 6:48).

Sometimes, in asking such a question, Jesus gave many answers: "Unto what is the kingdom of God like? and

Fields of wheat growing in Galilee

whereunto shall I resemble it? It is like a grain of mustard seed. . . . Again he said, Whereunto shall I liken the kingdom of God? It is like leaven" (Luke 13:18–21). "The kingdom of heaven is like unto treasure hid in a field. . . . The kingdom of heaven is like unto a merchant man, seeking goodly pearls. . . . The kingdom of heaven is like unto a net, that was cast into the sea, and gathered of every kind" (Matthew 13:44–47).

The field was a familiar similitude, too: "The field is the world" (Matthew 13:38), and all the people planted in the good field are cultivated and nourished. Eventually comes the harvest. The good produce is gathered into the barn and used to fulfill the purpose of its creation, while the bad is cast off.

The most famous use of wheat in Jesus' teachings was that expressed in his parable of the wheat and the tares, recorded only in Matthew 13 and interpreted by the Lord more than eighteen hundred years later in Doctrine and Covenants 86:1–7. "The kingdom of heaven is likened unto a man which sowed good seed in his field: but while men slept, his enemy came and sowed tares among the wheat" (Matthew 13:24–25).

The word *tares* occurs in the New Testament only in this one parable. The Greek word *zizanion*, translated as "tares," is

Wheat and tares

said to come from a Semitic root and refers to weeds in grain. Most assume it is the somewhat poisonous bearded darnel, or weed grass. It resembles wheat in its early stages of growth, and the roots of the two are often intertwined (Matthew 13:29). The owner of the wheat field discouraged those who wanted to go in immediately to weed the crop "lest while ye gather up the tares, ye root up also the wheat with them. Let both grow together until the harvest: and in the time of harvest I will say to the reapers, Gather ye together first the tares, and bind them in bundles to burn them: but gather the wheat into my barn" (vv. 29–30). Notice that in Doctrine and Covenants 86 the order is reversed: first the wheat is gathered, and then the tares are burned (see also JST Matthew 13:29).

The apostles were the sowers of the good seed, but Satan sowed the bad seed (D&C 86:2–3). The tares did not grow naturally; they were deliberately planted. The tares represent apostates, flourishing together with the righteous (the wheat) in the Lord's kingdom. At the Judgment, however, they will be separated, as with the wheat and the chaff (D&C 86:7).

Of the parable of the wheat and tares the Prophet Joseph Smith taught: "Now we learn by this parable, not only the setting up of the Kingdom in the days of the Savior, which is represented by the good seed, which produced fruit, but also the corruptions of the Church, which are represented by the tares, which were sown by the enemy, which His disciples would fain have plucked up, or cleansed the Church of, if their views had been favored by the Savior. But He, knowing all things, says, Not so. As much as to say, your views are not correct, the Church is in its infancy, and if you take this rash step, you will destroy the wheat, or the Church, with the tares; therefore it is better to let them grow together until the harvest, or the end of the world, which means the destruction of the wicked, which is not yet fulfilled, as we shall show hereafter, in the Savior's explanation of the parable" (*History of the Church,* 2:267).

In addition to this explanation, the Lord himself gave the

meaning of the parable (see D&C 86:1-7; see also 101:65-66; JST Matthew 13:39-44, Bible Appendix, 803).

Mark 4:26-29 This passage from Mark describes in agricultural terminology the plan of God's work on earth. The sower is the Son of God, planting the children of God in the earth. He gives them nourishment, sending the Sun of Righteousness and the Water of Life to bring them to spiritual maturity. When the children of God are ripe, in righteous living or in rebellion, he sends his messengers to reap the harvest, that is, to cut off their mortality and bring them to the scales of judgment. The ultimate harvest is "the end of the world" (Matthew 13:39).

THE PARABLE OF THE MUSTARD SEED (ON THE SEA OF GALILEE)

Matthew 13:31-32; Mark 4:30-32; Luke 13:18-19 There is only partial consensus among botanists who have studied biblical plants as to which member of the mustard family represented in the land of Israel could be the "tree" Jesus referred to. The most likely candidate is *Brassica nigra,* from which the important condiment black mustard is derived. Although rabbinical writings label mustard as a field plant, it was also planted in gardens.

As with most Semites, Jesus loved a contrast, even a hyperbolic contrast, to teach a lesson. Though the villages of Bethlehem and Nazareth and even the land of Israel itself were all small and relatively insignificant, yet, as New Testament writers understood, out of them would come the Messiah, the King of all the earth. Thus the mustard seed is an apt analogy: It "is less than all the seeds that be in the earth" (Mark 4:31), "which a man took, and cast into his garden; and it grew, and waxed a great tree; and the fowls of the air lodged in the branches of it" (Luke 13:19).

Although the mustard seed is not really the smallest of all

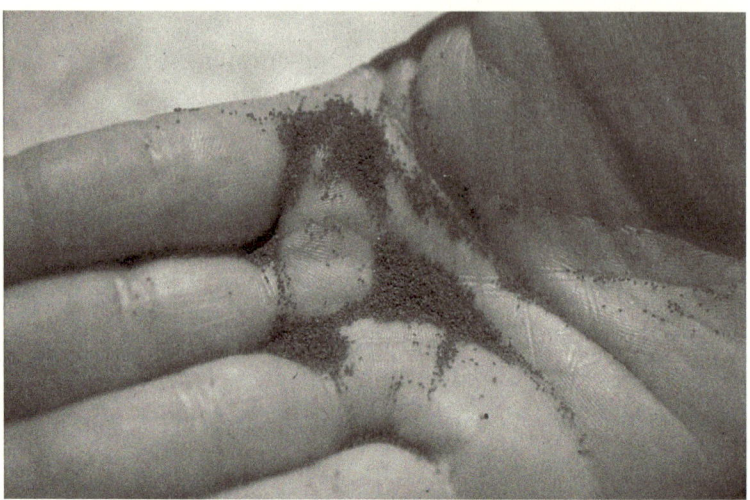
Tiny mustard seeds in the palm of a hand

seeds, proverbially or hyperbolically it denotes the strength and power inherent in even the smallest particle: "If ye have faith as a grain of mustard seed, ye shall say unto this mountain, Remove hence to yonder place; and it shall remove; and nothing shall be impossible unto you" (Matthew 17:20).

Jesus also taught that the kingdom he was establishing was like a mustard seed, "which indeed is the least of all seeds: but when it is grown, it is the greatest among herbs" (Matthew 13:32). That the glorious kingdom of God would begin in such a small and obscure way was a very un-Jewish teaching; that the kingdom would be even "the least" of all kingdoms was near heresy. Most Jews in the days of Jesus expected the Messiah to come and champion their cause, overthrow the Romans (as Judah the Maccabee had overthrown the Greeks), and reestablish a mighty kingdom of the Jews with the Anointed One ruling as King. Jesus, however, implanted a different concept of greatness growing out of something small.

The Prophet Joseph Smith placed the analogy of the mustard seed in the context of the latter days:

"And again, another parable put He forth unto them,

having an allusion to the Kingdom that should be set up, just previous to or at the time of the harvest. . . . Now we can discover plainly that this figure is given to represent the Church as it shall come forth in the last days. Behold, the Kingdom of Heaven is likened unto it. Now, what is like unto it?

"Let us take the Book of Mormon, which a man took and hid in his field, securing it by his faith, to spring up in the last days, or in due time; let us behold it coming forth out of the ground, which is indeed accounted the least of all seeds, but behold it branching forth, yea, even towering, with lofty branches, and God-like majesty, until it, like the mustard seed, becomes the greatest of all herbs. And it is truth, and it has sprouted and come forth out of the earth, and righteousness begins to look down from heaven, and God is sending down His powers, gifts and angels, to lodge in the branches thereof.

"The kingdom of heaven is like unto a mustard seed. Behold, then is not this the Kingdom of heaven that is raising its head in the last days in the majesty of its God, even the Church of the Latter-day Saints, like an impenetrable, immovable rock in the midst of the mighty deep. . . .

"The above clouds of darkness have long been beating like mountain waves upon the immovable rock of the Church of the Latter-day Saints; and notwithstanding all this, the mustard seed is still towering its lofty branches, higher and higher, and extending itself wider and wider; and the chariot wheels of the Kingdom are still rolling on, impelled by the mighty arm of Jehovah; and in spite of all opposition, will still roll on, until His words are all fulfilled" (*History of the Church*, 2:268, 270).

THE PARABLE OF THE LEAVEN (ON THE SEA OF GALILEE)

Matthew 13:33; Luke 13:20–21 The Prophet Joseph Smith taught: "'And another parable spake He unto them.

The Kingdom of heaven is like unto leaven which a woman took and hid in three measures of meal till the whole was leavened.' It may be understood that the Church of the Latter-day Saints has taken its rise from a little leaven that was put into three witnesses. Behold, how much this is like the parable! It is fast leavening the lump, and will soon leaven the whole" (*History of the Church*, 2:270).

Leaven is variously used in the scriptures as something good or bad (yeast and baking powder are two examples of leaven). In this case, leaven is good. Without the leaven, the Church would not rise to its potential for good. There are several sets of three that help the kingdom to rise in the last days: the Three Witnesses, as Joseph Smith indicated; the Godhead: Father, Son, and Holy Ghost; and three scriptural witnesses: the Bible, the Book of Mormon, and the Doctrine and Covenants (cf. 2 Nephi 11:3).

THE PARABLE OF A TREASURE IN A FIELD (ON THE SEA OF GALILEE)

Matthew 13:44 Joseph Smith explained: "To illustrate more clearly this gathering: We have another parable—'Again, the Kingdom of heaven is like a treasure hid in a field, the which, when a man hath found, he hideth, and for joy thereof, goeth and selleth all that he hath, and buyeth that field!' The Saints work after this pattern. See the Church of the Latter-day Saints, selling all that they have, and gathering themselves together unto a place that they may purchase for an inheritance [Zion, the New Jerusalem], that they may be together and bear each other's afflictions in the day of calamity" (*History of the Church*, 2:271–72).

Millions around the world are discovering the priceless worth of the true Church and gospel of Jesus Christ. It is worth sacrificing all else of lesser value to obtain and retain that which is of eternal value: an inheritance with the Saints in

Zion. In fact, the willingness to sacrifice all things is a prerequisite for those who desire to attain the riches of eternity, which is the gift of eternal life (see *Lectures on Faith,* 6:7; D&C 6:7; 38:39).

THE PARABLE OF THE PEARL OF GREAT PRICE (ON THE SEA OF GALILEE)

Matthew 13:45–46 Pearls are the only gem created by a living process and are found in the sea. Thus they were imported into the land of Israel. Pearls always represent richness and luxury and are listed with other precious commodities in several passages of scripture.

Jesus taught that it would be worth all else a person owns to search out and purchase one pearl of great price, meaning the kingdom of God. The delicate structure of pearls is implied in Jesus' warning not to cast pearls before swine, since, unlike other gems, pearls are relatively soft and trampling on them could destroy them.

The message, then, is the same as the treasure in a field: it is worth sacrificing all worldly things we may hold dear to secure the most precious gem of eternal life.

Joseph Smith gave this parable, or analogy, a specific context in the progress of the latter-day kingdom of God. One of the multiple definitions of the pearl of great price was the place for Zion: "'Again, the Kingdom of heaven is like unto a merchantman seeking goodly pearls, who, when he had found one pearl of great price, went and sold all that he had, and bought it.' The Saints again work after this example. See men traveling to find places for Zion and her stakes or remnants, who, when they find the place for Zion, or the pearl of great price, straightway sell that they have, and buy it" (*History of the Church,* 2:272).

THE PARABLE OF THE NET (ON THE SEA OF GALILEE)

Matthew 13:47–50 The Prophet Joseph Smith declared: "'Again, the Kingdom of heaven is like unto a net that was cast into the sea, and gathered of every kind, which when it was full they drew to shore, and sat down, and gathered the good into vessels, but cast the bad away.' For the work of this pattern, behold the seed of Joseph, spreading forth the Gospel net upon the face of the earth, gathering of every kind, that the good may be saved in vessels prepared for that purpose, and the angels will take care of the bad. So shall it be at the end of the world—the angels shall come forth and sever the wicked from among the just, and cast them into the furnace of fire, and there shall be wailing and gnashing of teeth" (*History of the Church*, 2:272).

THE PARABLE OF THE HOUSEHOLDER (ON THE SEA OF GALILEE)

Matthew 13:51–52 Joseph Smith taught: "'Then said He unto them, therefore every scribe which is instructed in the kingdom of heaven, is like unto a man that is an householder, which bringeth forth out of his treasure things that are new and old.' For the works of this example, see the Book of Mormon coming forth out of the treasure of the heart. Also the covenants given to the Latter-day Saints, also the translation of the Bible—thus bringing forth out of the heart things new and old" (*History of the Church*, 2:272).

Summarizing all the parables of Matthew 13, we see that the great latter-day Prophet of the Restoration, Joseph Smith, saw a broader scope of meaning in them. He saw the progress of the kingdom of God from its humble inception in Jesus' day through the great Apostasy, the Restoration in the latter days, and its growth into a large and influential body.

A Second Galilean Ministry

PARABLES OF MATTHEW 13 SEEN WITH GREATER VISION

The sower and the soils	Jesus and the apostles sowing the seeds of the gospel in the meridian of time
The wheat and the tares	The great Apostasy
The mustard seed	Restoration—the kingdom rolls forth to fill the earth
The leaven	Witnesses of the Book of Mormon and testimony by revelation raises sinners to become Saints
The treasure in a field	People gathering to the kingdom and working toward building Zion
The pearl of great price	Saints sacrificing to establish Zion in all places
The net	Gathering into the gospel net; separating good from bad at the Second Coming
The householder	Helping establish Zion: the Book of Mormon, covenants, and the Joseph Smith Translation of the Bible

Jesus the Messiah knew Joseph the Prophet. As Jesus delivered this sermon of parables just off the shore of the small lake of Galilee, we wonder if he might have thought about Joseph Smith. Consider how the latter-day Prophet might have been regarded if Jesus had prophesied (and had the apostles recorded it and later scribes retained it): Some of you will join my Church and endure trials, and others will not. My Church will prosper for a short season, and then because of apostasy it will be lost. In another eighteen hundred years my Father and I will visit a young farm boy in a village in a land far from here and talk with him. Through him I will commence my work once again. This obscure boy will be called Joseph Smith, and people all over the world will come to know him and praise his testimony of me. I, the Savior of the world, and he, the prophet to the world, will be companions in bringing about a great and marvelous work that will benefit all of humankind.

SECOND REJECTION AT NAZARETH

Matthew 13:53–58; Mark 6:1–6 Geographical and geological evidence suggests that forests were more plentiful in the Holy Land during the Roman period than in any succeeding time until our present century. Wood was available and was used in construction during Jesus' day. There are two occurrences in the New Testament of the word *carpenter*, both in reference to Joseph and Jesus. Matthew suggests that Jesus' mortal guardian, Joseph, was a carpenter, and Mark asks, "Is not this the carpenter, the son of Mary?" (6:3), suggesting that Jesus himself was a carpenter also.

But were they really carpenters? The Greek word in these two passages is *tekton,* meaning "artificer" or "craftsman." Though contemporary usage in the first century after Christ allows the connection with woodworking, there is little specific indication that Joseph and Jesus were carpenters, workers of wood. Matthew and Luke record only one reference to the processes of carpentry in Jesus' teachings: "Why beholdest thou the mote [speck or splinter] that is in thy brother's eye, but considerest not the beam [wooden beam used in constructing houses] that is in thine own eye?" (Matthew 7:3; Luke 6:41).

Joseph and Jesus could just as well have been artificers or craftsmen of stone, which was much more available and used in the building trades. Note that the imagery in Jesus' teachings frequently includes the use of stone in building (see, for example, Matthew 7:24–25; 16:18; Luke 14:28–30; 20:17–18).

In these passages we also have our most detailed list of the names of Jesus' family members. Joseph, father of the family, has possibly died by this time, but the mother, Mary, is very much present through all of Jesus' ministry and after his resurrection. Mary's other children include James (Hebrew, *Ya'akov;* Latin and English, *Jacob*), Joses (Joseph), Simon, and Judas (Hebrew, *Yehuda;* English, *Judah*). Joseph and Mary's daughters are also mentioned but not by name. After Jesus' birth, then, Joseph and Mary had at least six children.

The people of Nazareth wondered who Jesus was claiming to be; they knew his (step)father, mother, and brothers and sisters and could not accept his being anything more than a local, hometown boy. At this rejection in Nazareth, Jesus reminded them that "a prophet is not without honour, save in his own country, and in his own house" (Matthew 13:57; cf. Luke 4:24). Little faith yielded few miracles. "For if there be no faith among the children of men God can do no miracle among them" (Ether 12:12; cf. 3 Nephi 19:35), "for it is by faith that miracles are wrought" (Moroni 7:37).

HEROD'S FEAR OF JESUS (SOMEWHERE IN GALILEE?)

Matthew 14:1–2; Mark 6:14–16; Luke 9:7–9 Herod Antipas, son of Herod "the Great," was *tetrarch* of Galilee and Perea, meaning that he ruled over "the fourth" part of the country (see Appendix 5, 760). He murdered John the Baptist; now he was haunted by his foul deed and feared that Jesus might be the martyred prophet come back from the dead. Some even supposed that Jesus could be the fulfillment of the prophesied return of Elijah (Bible Dictionary, "Elias," 663; see Mark 6:15; Luke 9:8). Antipas wanted to arrange an interview with Jesus (Luke 9:9).

THE BAPTIST'S EARLIER DEATH RECOUNTED (AT MACHAERUS, IN PEREA)

Matthew 14:3–12; Mark 6:17–29 Herod Antipas had married Herodias, wife of his half brother Herod Philip. John the Baptist had condemned their adulterous and incestuous relationship. The relationship was adulterous because

Herodias had not lawfully divorced her first husband, and it was legally incestuous because the law stated: "Thou shalt not uncover the nakedness of thy brother's wife: it is thy brother's nakedness" (Leviticus 18:16; the warnings recorded in Leviticus 18:6–17 all deal with incestuous relationships; see also Leviticus 20:21).

The law of Moses prohibited such a relationship, and Herodias hated the prophet John the Baptist because of his open condemnation of their sin. On the occasion of Herod's birthday celebration, possibly held in the fortress-palace of Machaerus, east of the Dead Sea (see commentary on Matthew 14:3–5), Herodias's daughter Salome pleased the tetrarch with her dancing. (Salome is a Greek name from the Hebrew *Shalom*. Her name is not recorded in the Gospels but is noted by the historian Josephus in his *Antiquities* [Loeb] XVIII.136.) Antipas rashly promised the girl anything she wanted, and after consulting with her mother, she asked for the head of the prophet. The king balked at the notion of killing John, as he was widely regarded as a prophet and was popular among the people and Herod himself knew that the Baptist was "*a holy man, and one who feared God and observed to worship him;* and when he heard him he did many things *for him* [to protect him], and heard him gladly" (JST Mark 6:21), yet he bent to pressure, acquiesced to the request, and had the prophet beheaded. Disciples took the body and gave it a proper burial. This forerunner prophet thus became the first martyr in the early Christian Church.

PASSOVER: RETURN OF THE TWELVE (NEAR BETHSAIDA)

Matthew 14:13–15; Mark 6:30–32; Luke 9:10; John 6:1–4 Matthew tells us that upon hearing of the death of John, Jesus went to a desert place (JST Luke 9:10 changes "desert" to "solitary") to be alone, likely to think about and

A SECOND GALILEAN MINISTRY

mourn for his cousin. (All of us are commanded to mourn, to weep, for the passing of loved ones: "Thou shalt weep for the loss of them that die" [D&C 42:45].) Yet a great multitude would not let Jesus be alone, and in the midst of his own grief, Jesus was moved with compassion toward others—a powerful and constant theme in the Gospels (JST Mark 7:22–23). He healed the sick among the multitude. What an amazing lesson in service and self-sacrifice, as well as an insight into the fundamental nature of the Savior's personality. He was the personification of compassion. Even when he deserved to be alone after the death of a family member, Jesus forsook his own needs and desires and ministered to others.

The Gospel of John provides an interesting chronological detail about the timing of the feeding of the five thousand. John begins chapter 6 with the words "after these things," meaning the events that inaugurated the third year of Jesus' public ministry. During the third year, events crescendo, as the Gospel writers indicate. Regarding the first year of Jesus' ministry, eighteen events are reported in the Gospels; for the second year, twenty-seven; but for the third year, seventy-two events are recounted.

"Jesus went over the sea of Galilee, which is the sea of Tiberias" (John 6:1). The Sea of Galilee is alluded to more than forty times in the Gospels, either by "Galilee," "Tiberias," or "Gennesaret." Luke sometimes called it a "lake" (Greek, *limne*) rather than a "sea" (Greek, *thalassa*). Technically the small body of water, which is less than eight miles wide and about twelve miles long, is a lake, but the Hebrew term *yam* may be translated as either "lake" or "sea." The Sea of Galilee lies in the Rift Valley nearly seven hundred feet below sea level (see Bible Map 14), making it the lowest freshwater lake in the world. Most of Jesus' ministry occurred around its shores, especially to the north and northwest.

The words *desert* and *wilderness* are used interchangeably in English translations or versions of the Bible, in both the Old and the New Testaments. All Hebrew and Greek words

THREE-YEAR MINISTRY OF JESUS CHRIST

ADAPTED FROM GEORGE A. HORTON, JR.

Preparation (early life):

Birth/ presented in Temple in Egypt/ youth in Nazareth at Temple at 12/ grows to manhood baptized/ 40 days in wilderness meets Andrew, Simon, others first miracle/ in Capernaum

1st YEAR

Attends **Passover**/ cleanses Temple Nicodemus visits/ baptizes John imprisoned/ woman at well teaches in synagogue/ noble's son is rejected/ calls four disciples teaches/ casts out unclean spirit heals Peter's mother-in-law tours Galilee/ Sermon on Mount heals leper and man sick of palsy calls Matthew/ John's disciples

2d YEAR

Attends **Passover**/ heals at pool Jews seek to kill/ corn on Sabbath heals man/ teaches from ship night praying/ chooses Twelve heals many/ Sermon on Plain heals centurion's son/ widow's son praises John/ upbraids cities anointed by woman/ teaches heals/ accused by Pharisees sign seekers/ mother and brethren teaches from ship/ stills storm casts out devils/ Jairus's daughter heals woman, blind, and dumb teaching rejected/ heals sick sends out Twelve/ John beheaded Twelve return/ rests in solitude

3d YEAR

Attends **Passover**/ feeds 5,000 walks on sea/ Bread of Life heals many/ discourses on cleanliness in Tyre and Sidon/ heals Canaanite girl return to Galilee/ heals deaf man teaches and heals/ feeds 4,000 visits Magdala/ discourses on signs heals blind man/ Peter's confession tells of death/ Transfiguration heals boy/ gets tribute money discourses/ refused by Samaritans sends Seventy/ **Feast of Tabernacles** teaches in Temple/ woman in adultery bears record of self/ Seventy return the good Samaritan/ Mary and Martha teaches prayer/ casts out dumb devil discourses on cleanliness/ parables heals blind man/ the good shepherd Feast of Dedication/ escapes enemies beyond Jordan/ heals woman on Sabbath warned about Herod/ Lazarus is ill heals man of dropsy/ teaches sacrifice parables/ talks about offenses raises Lazarus/ priests plot his death in Ephraim/ journey to Jerusalem heals ten lepers/ talks about kingdom parables/ goes beyond Jordan (Perea) on marriage, divorce/ blesses children rich young ruler/ laborers in vineyard heals Bartimaeus/ sees Zacchaeus parable of pounds/ goes to Jerusalem many seek him/ goes to Bethany Triumphal Entry/ cleanses Temple teaches near Temple and on Mt. Olivet Upper Room/ **Passover**/ sacrament discourses/ Gethsemane/ suffering betrayal/ arrest/ Sanhedrin trial before Pilate/ Crucifixion burial/ in the tomb/ Resurrection

The Sea of Galilee is below sea level

that are used signify deserted or uninhabited places. The most frequently used Hebrew word is *midbar*, which is a tract for pasturing flocks.

The apostles were sent out on missions, and "when they were returned, . . . he took them, and went aside privately into a desert place belonging to the city called Bethsaida" (Luke 9:10); that is, a solitary or uninhabited place near Bethsaida. At that quiet place, out on the plain of Bethsaida, the apostles enjoyed a welcome rest from their labors and reported on their missionary work.

FEEDING THE FIVE THOUSAND (NEAR BETHSAIDA)

Matthew 14:16–21; Mark 6:33–44; Luke 9:11–17; John 6:5–14 One important event recorded by all four Gospel writers is the feeding of "five thousand men, beside women and children" (Matthew 14:21). People flocked to hear Jesus teach, and on this occasion the apostles became nervous, being outside the city in an uninhabited area, about how such multitudes would find sufficient food to eat. Andrew

Plain of Bethsaida, the site of the feeding of the five thousand: "a desert place" with "much grass"

underscored their predicament by informing Jesus that "there is a lad here, which hath five barley loaves, and two small fishes: but what are they among so many?" (John 6:9).

Andrew's information demonstrated the bewilderment the apostles felt; he emphasized that here were two *small* fishes and five *barley* loaves. All four Gospel writers recorded this incident, but John is the only one who specifically mentioned that the fishes were small (possibly sardines, which along with bread provide part of the basic diet of Galileans to this day) and noted what the loaves were made of. Barley was a staple grain for the poorer people, less favored than wheat. Fishes that were small and loaves that were made of barley would supply meager nourishment to few people.

But Jesus intended to test the apostles' faith (John 6:6), to teach them a lesson. When they suggested that he send the people away to get food, Jesus replied that they didn't need to leave, and he told the apostles to give them food. Jesus had them sit down in the grassy area, organized in companies of hundreds and fifties (Mark 6:40). He blessed the food; they all ate until they were full; then they gathered up the

A Second Galilean Ministry

Bread and fishes in mosaic at Church of the Multiplication

leftovers—twelve baskets full, considerably more than they had started with. Therein was an additional lesson. Though miraculous power could be used to supply their needs on any occasion—*do not waste;* nothing should be lost (John 6:12). When Jesus visited his disciples in ancient America after his Resurrection, he performed once again the same miracle: providing for their physical needs while he also gave them spiritual food (3 Nephi 20:3–7).

There are several reasons why Jesus fed the five thousand:

1. The people were hungry, and Jesus was supremely compassionate. He also knew that spiritual receptivity is linked to physical needs and senses.

2. The miracle of feeding the multitude with bread provided the important setting and object lesson for future teachings, particularly his discourse on the bread of life.

3. The miracle was a profound testimony of the Savior's power—that he has power over the elements of the earth because he was and is the Messiah. As Jehovah he created those elements. Jesus is still the Lord of the earth and Lord

over the elements, and the following real-life example, told by Elder Carlos C. Revillo, an Area Seventy, testifies of this fact:

"An experience my wife and I had several years ago illustrates the power of the Lord and how He can bless our lives if we rely on Him. My wife was in charge of catering food for a special banquet to be attended by numerous city leaders and many high-ranking national officials. The host of the event instructed my wife to prepare food for 350 people, emphasizing repeatedly the importance of the occasion and of the invited guests.

"On the night of the banquet, the guests began to arrive. Soon the 350 reserved seats were filled. My wife had made allowance for additional guests, but these 25 extra seats were soon filled also. More people streamed in, joining those who were already standing and lining up on all sides of the hall. There were approximately 1,000 people in the hall, and more were still coming in.

"My wife recalls what happened this way: 'At that moment, I just wished to melt and disappear. I approached the hostess, and she too had the same feeling of desperation. Though I was nervous, I tried to stay calm and began praying fervently and silently: 'Heavenly Father, please help me. I do not know what to do. Please don't forsake me.' Then my husband approached me and whispered, 'Don't be afraid. I will bless the food silently.'

"Instantly, my fears were gone. I had no doubt that I could rely on the Lord. The dinner began. Eleven waiters replenished the food on the tables without ceasing as the banquet proceeded. After the affair, when the guests were gone, all the tables were still filled with food. And there was still food left in the kitchen—five big baskets full of leftovers. All the guests and visitors had been fed and satisfied. Once home, I went immediately to my room and poured out my soul in gratitude to Heavenly Father. My whole body shook and trembled as I cried. My sincere prayer had been answered. The power of the priesthood had been manifest. Truly the Lord will not forsake us if we strive to be righteous" (*Ensign*, January 2004, 22–23).

JESUS WALKS ON THE WATER (ON THE SEA OF GALILEE)

Matthew 14:22–33; Mark 6:45–52; John 6:15–21
John notes that Jesus perceived the intentions of the people, how "they would come and take him by force, to make him a king." They were so inclined because, by popular tradition, the Messiah would come during Passover, and having witnessed so many healings and now the miraculous multiplication of loaves and fishes, they recognized that he must be their long-awaited Messiah. But it was not his time to become a king (that would happen at his second coming to earth). So "he departed again into a mountain himself alone."

Reference to a "mountain apart" usually signifies an occasion when Jesus wanted to get away from the crowds to spiritually rejuvenate himself, that is, to participate in some private communication (to "commune") with his Father. "When he had sent the multitudes away, he went up into a mountain apart to pray" (Matthew 14:23; see commentary on Mark 1:35–39; Luke 4:42–44).

Gospel writers recorded several instances when violent storms came up on the Sea of Galilee: "There arose a great tempest in the sea, insomuch that the ship was covered with the waves" (Matthew 8:24). "There arose a great storm of wind, and the waves beat into the ship" (Mark 4:37). "There came down a storm of wind on the lake; and they were filled with water, and were in jeopardy" (Luke 8:23; the JST says they were "filled with *fear,* and were in *danger*"). "The sea arose by reason of a great wind that blew" (John 6:18; Matthew 14:24; Mark 6:47–48).

The Sea of Galilee lies deep in the Rift Valley, nearly seven hundred feet below the level of the Mediterranean. It is

The Four Gospels

Be Not Afraid, *by Del Parson*

surrounded by hills that are above sea level on all sides except the south. Winds sweeping down the western slopes can stir up waves on the small lake with considerable ferocity. In wintertime the eastern winds, called the *sharkiyeh,* can whip up sometimes dangerous choppiness. Even mature and experienced fishermen can be struck with fear and panic if caught in a tempest in the middle of the lake.

Matthew 14:25–27 "When they had rowed about five and twenty or thirty furlongs" (three to four miles, right out in the middle of the lake), Jesus approached them on the water. It was during the fourth watch of the night, the watches being (first) from 6 to 9 P.M., (second) 9 P.M. to midnight, (third) midnight to 3 A.M., and (fourth) 3 to 6 A.M. The fourth watch is an eerie time of night to see a figure moving on the water. The apostles cried out in fear, supposing they had seen a ghost or spirit. Jesus calmed them with a reassuring, "It is I; be not afraid."

Matthew 14:28–33 Divine power could operate in others, too. Peter showed unusual faith in desiring to walk on the water. While he kept his eyes on Jesus, he stayed upon it, but when he noticed the boisterous winds and waves around him, he became afraid and started to sink. In this life, when our thoughts are wholly centered on Christ, we, too, can "walk on water." If we take our eyes off Jesus, however, we may be frightened by the boisterous winds and waves around us—the distractions of the world—and begin to sink. But "immediately Jesus stretched forth his hand, and caught him." When we start sinking, our Savior will help us, too. As long as we are trying to live true to our beliefs, his almighty hand will always be stretched out to help us back up again.

The apostles affirmed their conviction, "Of a truth thou art the Son of God," which is the first occurrence of the divine title in the Synoptic Gospels (Nathanael had thus testified earlier, as recorded in John 1:49).

DISCOURSE: BREAD OF LIFE (IN THE SYNAGOGUE AT CAPERNAUM)

John 6:22–71 The city of Tiberias, named for the Roman emperor at the time, was established by Herod Antipas about A.D. 18, replacing his former Galilean residence, Sepphoris. Tiberias was a Gentile city with no record of Jesus ever visiting or teaching there, though he may have passed through it when traveling south. The "sea of Tiberias" constitutes the only mention of the city in the New Testament, all in the Gospel of John (6:1, 23; 21:1). The city evidently had become prominent enough that the Sea of Galilee was sometimes called after the city.

Capernaum was a local crossroads by land but also a crossroads for those who sailed the lake. The town had a small port

Reconstructed remains of a Capernaum synagogue

facility. Jesus' disciples "entered into a ship, and went over the sea toward Capernaum" (John 6:17). "The people . . . also took shipping, and came to Capernaum, seeking for Jesus" (John 6:24).

The details of movement among the people, the apostles, and Jesus are key to understanding the background of one of Jesus' greatest discourses. Notice in verse 22 that some of the people who had witnessed the miraculous multiplication of loaves and fishes were at the shore near Bethsaida. They saw that there had been only one boat in which the apostles had sailed away and that Jesus had not accompanied the apostles in that boat. In verse 24 we are told that those people sailed to Capernaum also, seeking for Jesus. When they found him there (v. 25), they asked, in essence, How did you get here? They were baffled at how he had arrived there, because he had not embarked in the one boat they had watched sail away. Then Jesus leveled them with the pointed indictment: "Ye seek me, not because ye *desire to keep my sayings, neither because ye* saw the miracles, but because ye did eat of the loaves and were filled" (JST John 6:26). They wanted to keep following Jesus not so much because they wanted to live his teachings or had faith to continue witnessing miracles but because they anticipated free bread. They reasoned, If this man keeps feeding us like this, we won't even have to go back to work.

Then Jesus opened his masterful analogy of himself as the Bread of Life. He who was born in Bethlehem, literally "house of bread," now focused on his role as the living Bread, the staff of life who has power to give us eternal sustenance.

"I AM" is one of Jesus' descriptive name-titles from antiquity. He often used the phrase to introduce metaphors that taught something of his character and his purposes. John, especially, repeatedly records the symbolisms: I am, said Jesus, the living water (4:10), the living bread (6:51), the light of the world (8:12), the door (10:9), the true vine (15:1), the good shepherd (10:11), the resurrection and the life (11:25), the way, the truth, and the life (14:6).

At Jacob's well, where there was water to quench mortal thirst, the Savior drew the comparison to his being Living Water. This time, too, he gave a message appropriate to the place. At Capernaum, more grinding mills used for making bread have been found than at any other place in the country, leading some to believe that mills were manufactured in this Galilean town and exported to others. Where these mills were produced for making bread, Jesus taught of spiritual bread, the partaking of which could nourish one to eternal life.

John 6:37 "All that the Father giveth me shall come to me" (v. 37). With his perfect foreknowledge of all things, the Father knows those who are his; they are they who respond to the spiritual hunger and come unto him to partake of the bread of life (cf. Alma 5:34). They are "numbered among those whom the Father hath given me" (3 Nephi 15:24; 18:31). The invitation to come and eat is given to "all those whom my Father hath given me out of the world" (D&C 27:14; see also 50:41; 84:63; 3 Nephi 19:20). What the Father knows, the Son also knows. As Paul later wrote to

Basalt grinding mills found at Capernaum

Timothy, "The Lord knoweth them that are his" (2 Timothy 2:19).

John 6:38–40 Jesus came down to do his Father's will, not his own (cf. 3 Nephi 11:11; 27:13), and the Father's will was to save all those "he hath given me"—that of all those he should lose none. Later, when Jesus had finished the work his Father sent him to do, he would declare, "Those that thou gavest me I have kept, and none of them is lost" (John 17:4, 12; see also 18:9). True disciples of the Father in Heaven and the Lord Jesus Christ will likewise make that their purpose: to find the elect, those who will come up and eat and "feast upon that which perisheth not" (2 Nephi 9:51) and to work hard to see that none of them is lost but that the elect according to the covenant are all raised up again at the last day (John 6:39–40, 44, 54; see also 3 Nephi 15:1). In Joseph Smith's translation of John 6:40 the Lord adds: "I will raise [them] up *in the resurrection of the just* at the last day."

John 6:41–44 Some people supposed that Jesus was the son of Joseph. His mortal mother and stepfather were known;

therefore they were suspicious of his claim to have come "down from heaven."

Joseph Smith expanded the message and meaning of verse 44 (see Bible Appendix, 808).

John 6:48–58 Now Jesus gave an illustration the Jews knew well from their history (Exodus 16:31–35). "Your fathers did eat manna in the wilderness, and are dead. This is the bread which cometh down from heaven, that a man may eat thereof, and not die" (vv. 49–50).

The New International Version Study Bible observes: "A popular Jewish expectation was that when the Messiah came he would renew the sending of manna. The crowd probably reasoned that Jesus had done little compared to Moses. He had fed 5,000; Moses had fed a nation. He did it once; Moses did it for 40 years. He gave ordinary bread; Moses gave 'bread from heaven'" (footnote on John 6:31).

The Jews of course knew concerning "the manner of prophesying among the Jews" (2 Nephi 25:1); that is, they well knew the metaphorical expressions and figurative language their prophets were accustomed to using. Yet they feigned ignorance: "How can this man give us his flesh to eat?" (v. 52). Once again Jesus concealed his teachings in terms only the spiritually enlightened would understand. Using sacramental language, he taught: "Except ye eat the flesh of the Son of man, and drink his blood, ye have no life in you" (v. 53). Those who will partake in remembrance of his body and drink in remembrance of his blood may always have his Spirit to be with them (D&C 20:77, 79). "He that eateth my flesh, and drinketh my blood, dwelleth [Greek, "remains or abides"] in me, and I in him" (v. 56).

John 6:59 The great discourse on the bread of life was given in the synagogue at Capernaum. In fact, it was Jesus' last discourse there. The foundations of Capernaum's synagogue where he taught are still visible today.

John 6:60–62 Some disciples were offended by these "hard sayings," and they complained. Jesus responded with

Basalt foundation of first-century synagogue visible under a later limestone synagogue at Capernaum

another pointed question: "What and if ye shall see the Son of man ascend up where he was before?" (v. 62). Would they then believe? If they had such difficulty believing that he came down from God out of heaven, would they believe if they were to watch him ascend back up where he was before? How dramatic a miracle would it require for them to believe in him?

John 6:63–65 Jesus taught his followers to pay attention to spiritual things. Things of the flesh, worldly things, are so transitory. "The words that I speak unto you [the scriptures], they are spirit, and they are life" (v. 63). But there were some who would not believe him. With a perfect knowledge of all things, Jesus knew who would believe and who would not—those the Father had given him out of the world would be willing to give up anything, even all things, to follow him (John 6:37). He knew Judas, too, the one who would betray him (John 13:11). That is why he taught them: "No man can come unto me, except *he doeth the will* of my Father *who hath sent me*" (JST John 6:65).

John 6:66–69 At that point many of Jesus' disciples abandoned him, refusing to walk with him any more. Then he asked the Twelve the emotion-laden question, "Will ye also go away?"

In October 1983, Brother Ogden and Brother Skinner were in Galilee with apostle Mark E. Petersen during a tour with many hundreds of Latter-day Saints. Elder Petersen delivered a powerful talk on the Mount of Beatitudes. (That talk turned out to be his final great discourse because he died of cancer shortly after his return to Utah. Most of the Saints did not know that he was in great pain during those travels.)

While in the synagogue at Capernaum, Brother Ogden was leading the discussion of John 6, the discourse on the bread of life. After reviewing key verses, he arrived at that poignant question, "Will ye also go away?"

Brother Ogden afterward recorded: "At that point I glanced up and thought I saw some emotion in the face of Elder Petersen, one of the current Twelve, as he reflected on the gravity of the Savior's question. And I realized that the question is asked of every one of us also. With the traumas and vicissitudes of life, the Savior is watching each of us to see if we will go away, if we will waver and abandon him, or hold fast to him and his promises. Hopefully we will stand and say with Peter: 'Lord, to whom shall we go? thou hast the words of eternal life. And we believe and are sure that thou art that Christ, the Son of the living God' (vv. 68–69). By living up to that kind of testimony we cannot abandon our hope of salvation. As Elder Petersen demonstrated right to the end of his life, we must remain faithfully with Him" (Ogden, journal).

HEALINGS (IN GENNESARET)

Matthew 14:34–36; Mark 6:53–56 The Greek word *Gennesaret* is found twice in the New Testament as "the land of Gennesaret" in Matthew 14:34 and the parallel verse in Mark 6:53. The word is also found once as a name for the Sea of Galilee. *Gennesaret* is the Greek adaptation of the Old

Testament name *Chinnereth* (Numbers 34:11) and is therefore related to modern *Kinneret* (Hebrew, *kinnor*, "harp," because the lake is shaped like a harp). Gennesaret refers to the cultivated plain on the northwest side of the Sea of Galilee. There the people's faith was rewarded with wholeness, and their diseased bodies were healed.

TRADITIONS CAN DEFILE (IN GALILEE)

Matthew 15:1–20; Mark 7:1–23; Luke 6:39–40 Certain scribes and Pharisees had walked all the way from Jerusalem, a hundred miles, to investigate, antagonize, and criticize. "Why do thy disciples transgress the tradition of the elders?" (Matthew 15:2). Jesus altered the question and turned it back on them: "Why do ye also transgress the commandment of God by your tradition?" (Matthew 15:3). Many of the ceremonial washings the Jews carried out were not required by the law of Moses; they were simply Pharisaism—organized, institutionalized traditions. Jesus did not condemn the law (which he himself had given centuries earlier), but he did condemn their hypocrisy in not observing it and substituting instead the commandments of men. It was not the written, authorized, canonized law that was objectionable but the oral law—the traditions of the elders—that alienated the people from the Spirit and from their God (see further in Matthew 23).

Well did Isaiah prophesy of the hypocrites when he said, "This people honoureth me with their lips, but their heart is far from me" (Mark 7:6; Isaiah 29:13; 2 Nephi 27:25).

"Howbeit in vain do they worship me," continued Jesus, "teaching for doctrines the commandments of men. For laying aside the commandment of God, ye hold the tradition of men, as the washing of pots and cups: and many other such like things ye do," as the myriad rules of *kashrut*—kosher laws and today's rules for the Sabbath: refraining from using elevators or turning on light switches, etc.

"Full well ye reject the commandment of God, that ye may keep your own tradition" (Mark 7:7–9).

Mark 7:10–13 Jesus illustrated his point with an example from the old law, saying in essence that Moses had taught them to honor their father and mother, but they perverted the intent of the law by saying, "It is Corban, that is to say, a gift" and withholding this corban from their parents in favor of offering the thing to God. Hebrew *corban* (from *karav*, "to draw near [to God]") is the word used many times throughout the Old Testament, especially in the Mosaic law, for oblation or offering (Leviticus 1:2; Numbers 31:50). The practice Jesus condemns is the offering of something to God to avoid sharing with family, thereby trying to legally exempt themselves from giving help and honor to parents (cf. the Ten Commandments; Exodus 20:12).

You make, Jesus argued, "the word of God of none effect through your tradition . . . and many such like things do ye" (v. 13).

Mark 7:14–16 More than external, ritual cleansings, Jesus emphasized cleansing the inner vessel. "There is nothing from without a man, that entering into him can defile him, *which is food;* but the things which come out of him; those are they that defile the man, *that proceedeth forth out of the heart*" (JST Mark 7:15). This teaching of the Savior is of course not justification to ignore counsel like the Word of Wisdom and other such laws of God governing the care of our physical bodies. What enters into our bodies does matter, but Jesus is here referring to even higher laws, governing things that come out of man—things that can do infinitely more damage than the temporal substances that may be ingested into our bodies.

Mark 7:17–23 There is defilement or corrupting influence far worse than what enters into a man's mouth. What goes into the belly just goes back out as waste material and is disposed of and forgotten, but that which comes out of the mouth can do enormous damage; it comes from the heart, the proverbial command-center of character and behavior. From the heart come inclinations to blaspheme, steal, kill, lie, and commit sexual sins and all other violations of the basic laws of God.

"Lasciviousness" means looseness, lustfulness, immoral desires. "An evil eye" is one that focuses on worldly things and promotes the glory of Satan rather than the glory of God.

More important than ritual washings of the hands, Jesus taught, is the sincere, inner cleansing of the heart.

Matthew 15:13 Figuratively speaking, plants represent people. God has planted his children in the field (the world), and he expects each one to blossom where he or she is planted. The root of a plant is the organ that absorbs and stores what is supplied to the rest of the plant. It is also the means of anchorage. Those who have turned inward and refused God's nutrients, even openly rejecting them, will be uprooted and left without root or branch—that is, left without connection to ancestry or posterity, which is the ultimate expression of extinction (Malachi 4:1; Amos 2:9).

Matthew 15:14; Luke 6:39–40 The offended Pharisees were blind leaders of their blind followers. If the blind lead the blind, they both fall into the ditch of apostasy, sin, and rebellion (cf. Helaman 13:29). An evil eye or a blind eye will not serve to guide anyone to God; only those who have an eye single to the glory of God will help others find him.

CHAPTER 8

THE NORTH GALILEAN MINISTRY

CANAANITE DAUGHTER HEALED (ALONG THE COAST OF TYRE AND SIDON)

Matthew 15:21–28; Mark 7:24–30 Except for this visit to "the coasts of Tyre and Sidon," we have no record of Jesus ever laboring along the Gentile coast. His one recorded visit may have been prompted by the presence of Tyrians and Sidonians while he taught and healed in Galilee: "They about Tyre and Sidon, a great multitude, when they had heard what great things he did, came unto him" (Mark 3:8).

Canaan is the historical name of the ancient Egyptian province that included the geographical boundaries of most of modern Lebanon (ancient Phoenicia) and all of present-day Israel/Palestine. The "woman of Canaan" (Matthew 15:22) is identified as "a Greek, a Syrophenician by nation" (Mark 7:26). In Jesus' day, Phoenicia, the coastal region with the old cities Sidon, Sarepta, and Tyre, was part of the Roman province of Syria. There, seeking some seclusion and rest, he "would *that* no man *should come unto him*. But he could not deny them; for he had compassion upon all men" (JST Mark 7:22–23).

A Gentile woman, whose young daughter was harassed by an unclean spirit, or devil, insisted on Jesus' help. He tested her. "I am not sent but unto the lost sheep of the house of

Israel" (Matthew 15:24). "Let the children *of the kingdom* first be filled: for it is not meet to take the children's bread and to cast it unto the dogs" (JST Mark 7:26). Jesus' mission was to his own people; the Gentiles would generally receive the gospel message through the preaching of the apostles and Church members by the power of the Holy Ghost, after Jesus' departure (3 Nephi 15:22–23). Casting bread to the dogs was not intended to be a harsh malignment of non-Jewish people; "dogs" signifies those who are not yet matured, prepared, and worthy to receive the sacred things of the kingdom (see D&C 41:6; see also commentary on Matthew 7:6). Jesus continued to test her, but the woman persisted: "Yes, Lord: yet the dogs under the table eat of the children's crumbs" (Mark 7:28). With that, Jesus could not help but respond to the woman's faith, and he healed her daughter—again, not even being where the girl was. The woman's faith in his power made the child whole.

HEALS LAME, BLIND, AND DUMB (IN THE DECAPOLIS AND NEAR THE SEA OF GALILEE)

Matthew 15:29–31; Mark 7:31–37 Following his stay in the Phoenician coastal cities Jesus journeyed through the Decapolis, the region with a Hellenized or Greek cultural influence to the east and southeast of the Galilee. There, again in Gentile country, he rewarded those who had faith to be healed. Here is another example (as related in Mark) of Jesus physically touching parts of the recipient's body so the person, too, could participate in the miracle.

Regarding Jesus' injunction to "tell no man" about his miraculous healings, see commentary on Matthew 8:2–4.

FOUR THOUSAND FED (SOMEWHERE IN THE HILLS SURROUNDING THE SEA OF GALILEE)

Matthew 15:32–38; Mark 8:1–9 The scene of disciples lingering with Jesus, hungry for his teachings but having little temporal food, probably resonated with some familiarity among the apostles. Here they were again, as with the five thousand, in an uninhabited area outside the numerous towns that dotted the lakeshore (Matthew 14:16–21; John 6:5–14). The miracle of multiplication of loaves and fishes once more occurred, along with the subsequent lesson of taking up the remnants and not wasting. On this occasion Jesus fed "four thousand men, beside women and children" (Matthew 15:38). Again Jesus demonstrated his concern about mortals' spiritual and physical well-being.

PHARISEES AND SADDUCEES ASK A SIGN (AT MAGDALA)

Matthew 15:39–16:4; Mark 8:10–13; Luke 12:54–57 The town of Magdala, on the western shore of the Sea of Galilee, is mentioned once by this Hebrew name (*Migdol*, "tower"). The parallel passage in Mark mentions taking a ship to "the parts of Dalmanutha" (Mark 8:10). Dalmanutha must be the same site as Magdala, or nearby.

Pharisees and Sadducees, as curiosity-seekers, came requesting a sign from heaven. The ancients knew how to read the sky for probable weather conditions. After the long half-year of changeless summer sky, rain clouds begin to appear. Colors burst across earth's canopy in the morning or hang onto wide portions of the evening sky, portending various changes in the weather.

Jesus contrasted that ability to anticipate the weather with the inability to see God's signs: "When it is evening, ye say, It will be fair weather: for the sky is red. And in the morning, It will be foul weather to day: for the sky is red and lowring [threatening]. O ye hypocrites, ye can discern the face of the sky; but can ye not discern the signs of the times?" (Matthew 16:2–3).

The Mediterranean Sea is the focal point of the region's storm systems. Evaporation off the great sea has been measured in our modern day to average one hundred thousand tons of water per second! Winter winds pick up moisture from the sea and carry rain-laden clouds eastward over the land. When the clouds meet the mountains and hills running north and south through the coastal countries, they are forced to ascend. As they rise, they part with some of their water load in the form of rain. Once past the mountains, air currents descend, and with a warmer terrain in the Judean Desert and Rift Valley, little precipitation occurs, until the clouds move eastward to the hills of Transjordan and part with most of the remaining moisture.

Thus, once over the land, clouds dump their water load generously on the coastal lands and western slopes of the hill country, whereas the eastern slopes are left in what is known as a "rain shadow," or topographical desert. The general pattern in the Holy Land is rain and fertility in the northern and western regions, and dry desert lands to the east and south. Jerusalem, for example, averages twenty-two to twenty-five inches of rain per year, as much as or more than London, Athens, Vienna, or Paris. The peculiarity is the duration, Jerusalem receiving most of its annual rainfall in the two-month period from mid-January to mid-March.

Rain was an obsessive concern of the ancient inhabitants of the Holy Land. Egypt had the Nile, and Mesopotamia, the Tigris and Euphrates. Peoples of the eastern Mediterranean coastlands, however, had no assured water source. Actually, they *did* have a constant water source, for the Lord made it clear that the heavens were open to pour out all the moisture they needed, according to their obedience (Deuteronomy 11:11–15). If they kept his commandments, they received the rain in its due season. The land in which they lived was a testing ground of their obedience, and with his people's faithfulness, the Lord God was pleased to respond.

Jesus made use of the meteorological pattern to illustrate his teaching. "When ye see a cloud rise out of the west, straightway ye say, There cometh a shower; and so it is" (Luke 12:54).

Luke 12:55 The Eastern Mediterranean lands are encompassed on the east and on the south by great deserts. Barometric lows or depressions over northeast Africa can draw strong, dry winds off the eastern and southern deserts and over the Holy Land. The condition is known in Arabic as *khamsin* ("fifty," from the tradition that an average year has fifty days with *khamsin* conditions). A scientific name for the wind is *sirocco* (or *scirocco*), an Italian word that derives from the Arabic *sharkiyeh*, meaning "east wind." Whether from the east or the south, it is the same phenomenon—a wind that comes off the deserts carrying fine dust that impairs visibility, raises temperatures, and dissipates human energy. This weather condition occurs mostly during the unpredictable transitional periods of April to May and September to October and affects water sources, agriculture (and therefore the economy), and individuals' behavior.

Once again Jesus used phenomena in nature to emphasize his teaching: his people could tell that when clouds formed in the west, rain was going to fall, and that when the south wind began to blow, there would be a *khamsin*. "Ye can discern the face of the sky and of the earth; but how is it that ye do not discern this time?"

Matthew 16:4 On the wicked and adulterous generation seeking after a sign and the sign of the prophet Jonas, see commentary on Matthew 12:39–40.

LEAVEN OF PHARISEES AND SADDUCEES (EASTERN SIDE OF THE SEA OF GALILEE)

Matthew 16:5–12; Mark 8:14–21; cf. Luke 12:1 The disciples had forgotten to take bread with them, so Jesus created another teaching moment: "Beware ye of the leaven of the Pharisees [and of the Sadducees], which is hypocrisy" (Luke 12:1). The disciples thought he was chastising them for not remembering to bring food for such multitudes, but Jesus patiently reminded them that they did not need to supply food (nor could they have supplied such quantity) for so many people—they should remember the miracles. He was now referring not to bread but to the leaven, or corruption, of his adversaries. Leaven (from the Latin *levare*, "to raise"), is an ingredient in baking, such as yeast, that makes bread rise; likewise, good, spiritual leaven would cause the kingdom of God to rise (Matthew 13:33). Jesus warned his disciples, however, to be careful of bad leaven—the doctrine of the Pharisees and Sadducees, which is the doctrine of men, for it is hypocritical and fallacious. Paul later added: "Know ye not that a little leaven leaveneth the whole lump? Purge out therefore the old leaven, that ye may be a new lump" (1 Corinthians 5:6–7) to help the kingdom rise and be stable.

BLIND MAN HEALED BY STAGES (AT BETHSAIDA)

Mark 8:22–26 A former student of one of the authors in Jerusalem, a Canadian named Deborah Layton, read this episode of healing and then penned her reaction in the following clever verses:

> 'Twas on the road to Bethsaida (within a mile or so)

The North Galilean Ministry

That Jesus helped a man to see a long, long time ago.
He led the man forth from the town and put his hands upon his head
Then turned and spat into his eyes (I'm sure the poor man was surprised!)
I wish that I'd been there to hear just what was said.

Then Jesus asked that blind man to say what he could see . . .
He opened his eyes and looked—to find some men like walking trees.
So once again the Savior placed his hands upon those sightless eyes;
He completely healed that faithful one, and joyous were his cries.

He sent the man back to the town while he went on his way,
Counseling him to tell no man what had transpired that day.
I do not think it was provoked; it was just the Savior's way
That caused him to lend a healing hand to help the man that day.

I can believe the man was healed, tho' I don't understand the method.
I wonder if perhaps the slight delay was to cause the man to be tested.
His partial sight just might have been to see if his faith was whole;
It was, and so the man could see in Bethsaida long ago.

It shows that Jesus was humble, for he told him to tell no one.

It was not for his glory he performed this way,
It was the *Father's* will to be done.

We know that the Savior is loving and kind; it's
　　often been proved to me.
And I hope that he won't need to spit in *my* eyes
Just to help me to spiritually see.

TESTIMONY OF PETER (AT CAESAREA PHILIPPI)

Caesarea Philippi, at the source of the Hermon River at the foot of Mount Hermon

Matthew 16:13–20; Mark 8:27–30; Luke 9:18–21 At the southern foot of Mount Hermon and at the headwaters of one source of the Jordan River, thirty-five miles north of the Sea of Galilee, lies a town called in the Hellenistic period Panion or Panias. Herod the Great had erected there a white marble temple to the Greek god Pan (god of forests, meadows, mountain slopes, and caves). Inscribed niches still remain along the cliff face above the water source. When this town came under Herod Philip, he had it rebuilt, renaming it "Caesarea Philippi" ("Caesarea of Philip") to distinguish it from the Caesarea on the coast.

"When Jesus came into the coasts [the borders or boundaries] of Caesarea Philippi, he asked his disciples, saying, Whom do men say that I the Son of man am?" (Matthew 16:13). They reported the circulating rumors that he was perhaps John the Baptist or Elijah or Jeremiah or some other prophet come back to life. Then Peter responded with forceful affirmation, "Thou art the Christ, the Son of the living God" (v. 16). Jesus blessed Peter for listening to the voice of revelation from heaven. Peter had not received that witness from "flesh and blood"—from the voice of human reason—but from the Father.

Two interesting points may be made regarding the site of Caesarea Philippi. First, it is the only place in the country with a river flowing through the city. This is appropriate to what Jesus taught there: revelation must be continuous and flowing, like the river. Second, it provided a point of comparison for the Lord, because of the physical setting at the foot of a mountain of solid rock or bedrock. As Hebrew writers loved to do, Jesus used paronomasia, a word play, on Peter's name. Said Jesus, "Thou art Peter [Greek, *petros,* "a rock"], and upon this rock [Greek, *petra,* "rock mass"] I will build my church" (v. 18). Peter's Aramaic name, Cephas, also means "rock or stone" (John 1:42).

The context of the statement, which immediately follows the Lord's blessing of Peter for receiving revelation, indicates that the rock—*petra*—in this case signifies revelation. Joseph Smith explained, "Jesus in his teaching says, 'Upon this rock I will build my [church;] and the gates of hell shall not prevail against it.' What rock? Revelation" (*Teachings of the Prophet Joseph Smith,* 274; cf. 3 Nephi 11:39; 18:13).

In mentioning the rock, Jesus may also have gestured to himself, meaning that he was the Rock of Salvation, the Stone of Israel (Deuteronomy 32:4, 31; 1 Samuel 2:2; 2 Samuel 22:2; 1 Corinthians 10:4; D&C 50:44). Jesus may well have been saying that Peter would be a rock (as the president of the Church holding the keys of the kingdom), and upon the Rock of Salvation, who will give revelation, firmness, strength, and stability, the Savior would build his Church. Latter-day Saints believe, unlike the Catholic world, that Jesus was founding his Church not on Peter but on the rock of revelation, as declared by the Rock of our salvation.

Decades ago, Elder Orson F. Whitney, of the Quorum of the Twelve Apostles, became well acquainted with a renowned Catholic scholar, versed in law, literature, science, and philosophy, and conversant in a dozen languages. This erudite friend commented to the apostle one day: "You Mormons are all ignoramuses. You don't even know the strength of your own position. It is so strong that there is only one other position tenable in the whole Christian world, and that is the position of the Roman Catholic Church. The issue is between Mormonism and Catholicism. If you are right, we are wrong. If we are right, you are wrong. And that's all there is to it. These Protestant sects haven't a leg to stand on; for if we are right, we cut them off long ago as apostates; and if we are wrong, they are wrong with us, for they were part of us and came out of us. If we have the apostolic succession from St. Peter as we claim, there was no need of Joseph Smith and Mormonism; but if we have not that succession, such a man as Joseph Smith was necessary and Mormonism's position is the only consistent one. It is either the perpetuation of the gospel from ancient times, or the restoration of the gospel in latter days" (Conference Report, October 1924, 19–20).

The whole discussion of rock was particularly appropriate for the location to which the Savior and the apostles had journeyed, because Caesarea Philippi sits at the foot of Mount Hermon, the most massive rock formation in the country. It was not by coincidence that Jesus taught what he did at that location. The text seems to imply that he went there purposely, and he used the rock formation as a graphic visual aid.

The North Galilean Ministry

SEALING KEYS OF THE KINGDOM PROMISED (AT CAESAREA PHILIPPI)

Matthew 16:19 Speaking specifically to Peter, the Lord promised that he would receive the keys of the kingdom, and the sealing power—to seal on earth and in heaven. Those keys and powers Peter did receive just a week later, on the Mount of Transfiguration (Matthew 17:1). As the book of Acts opens (it being the second volume of Luke's two-volume history of the ancient Church), we see that Peter held the keys and served as the presiding authority in that part of the earth (Nephi was serving in that capacity in the western hemisphere; Helaman 10:7). Peter presided over choosing the new apostle to fill the vacancy in the Quorum of the Twelve (Acts 1:15) and at Pentecost (Acts 2:14); and Peter received the revelation to open the gospel to the Gentiles (Acts 10).

An epistle of the Prophet Joseph Smith, recorded in Doctrine and Covenants 128, elaborates on the meaning of the sealing power:

"Whatsoever you record on earth shall be recorded in heaven, and whatsoever you do not record on earth shall not be recorded in heaven . . .

"It may seem to some to be a very bold doctrine that we talk of—a power which records or binds on earth and binds in heaven. Nevertheless, in all ages of the world, whenever the Lord has given a dispensation of the priesthood to any man by actual revelation, or any set of men, this power has always been given. Hence, whatsoever those men did in authority, in the name of the Lord, and did it truly and faithfully, and kept a proper and faithful record of the same, it became a law on earth and in heaven, and could not be annulled, according to the decrees of the great Jehovah. This is a faithful saying. Who can hear it?"

[Then follows a citation of Matthew 16:18, 19]

"Now the great and grand secret of the whole matter, and the *summum bonum* [Latin, "the highest good"] of the whole subject that is lying before us, consists in obtaining the powers of the Holy Priesthood. . . .

" . . . This, therefore, is the sealing and binding power, and, in one sense of the word, the keys of the kingdom, which consist in the key of knowledge" (D&C 128:8–14).

Of the keys of the kingdom—the right of presidency—President Joseph F. Smith explained:

"It is necessary that every act performed under this authority shall be done at the proper time and place, in the proper way, and after the proper order. The power of directing these labors constitutes the *keys* of the Priesthood" (*Gospel Doctrine*, 136; see also D&C 7:7).

The first person on this earth to possess the keys of the priesthood was Adam. In fact, our first father holds the keys of presidency over *all* dispensations and eras of the gospel. He is the presiding high priest, under Christ's direction, over all the earth. Noah stands next to Adam in priesthood authority (Smith, *Teachings of the Prophet Joseph Smith*, 157). "After these two come all the heads of the different gospel dispensations, together with a host of other mighty prophets" (McConkie, *Mormon Doctrine*, 412). Not the least of these is Elijah, who held the keys of the sealing power in ancient Israel (D&C 27:9; 110:13–16), and Nephi the son of Helaman, who held the keys of the sealing power among the Nephites (Helaman 10:4–10).

Among the keys of authority and power bestowed upon Peter and other apostles and prophets, including Joseph Smith and each of his successors in The Church of Jesus Christ of Latter-day Saints, none are of greater or more far-reaching significance than those given by Elijah (Smith, *Doctrines of Salvation*, 3:126). This ancient prophet held the keys of the kingdom in his day. He held the keys of presidency and the keys of the sealing power that constitute the fulness of the Melchizedek Priesthood.

Matthew 16:20 Regarding the charge to tell no man that he was Jesus the Christ, see commentary on Matthew 8:2–4.

PROPHECY OF DEATH AND RESURRECTION (AT CAESAREA PHILIPPI)

Matthew 16:21; Mark 8:31; Luke 9:22 From the farthest point in his journey (Caesarea Philippi), Jesus turned his face resolutely toward Jerusalem, "for it cannot be that a prophet perish out of Jerusalem" (Luke 13:33). He began to foreshadow in plain detail his approaching harsh treatment at the hands of some Jewish elders, chief priests, and scribes, his death, and his resurrection on the third day. (Concerning "the third day," see commentary on Matthew 12:39–45.)

PETER REBUKED (AT CAESAREA PHILIPPI)

Matthew 16:22–23; Mark 8:32–33 What Jesus had just prophesied about his upcoming suffering and death was certainly not the traditional Jewish idea of the culminating mission of the great Anointed One, the Messiah. Peter the rock now became Peter the stumbling block as he took Jesus aside and began to "rebuke" him, suggesting that such a fate could not possibly happen to his beloved Redeemer. Jesus' sensitive feelings appear to have been wounded at Peter's lack of understanding and trust in his divine purpose (compare Exodus 20:5 on Jehovah/Jesus possessing sensitive and deep feelings). Jesus used forceful words in turning the rebuke back on Peter: "Get thee behind me, Satan." Jesus was not, of course, referring to Satan as in Lucifer. The Hebrew word *satan* means "adversary or tempter," and Jesus used the generic term because Peter had put himself in an offensive adversarial role by suggesting that the Savior must not give in to such a notion as serving the role of suffering Servant and sacrificing himself to provide life to all the Father's children—his most difficult but most sacred duty. At the moment Peter was not promoting the long-established plan of God but subscribing to the notions of men.

TAKE UP A CROSS (AT CAESAREA PHILIPPI)

Matthew 16:24–27; Mark 8:34–38; Luke 9:23–26
After the strong rebuke of Peter, Jesus turned to the Twelve and other disciples (Mark 8:34). He explained that not only would he suffer many things and give his life for the cause but every man who would truly follow him must "deny himself, and take up his cross, and follow me" (Matthew 16:24), or as Luke puts it, "let him deny himself, and take up his cross daily, and follow me" (Luke 9:23). Note the word "daily." It is not a one-time ordeal; it is a struggle for daily diligence.

Jesus had taught before, "he that taketh not his cross, and followeth after me, is not worthy of me" (Matthew 10:38). "And now for a man to take up his cross, is to deny himself all ungodliness, and every worldly lust, and keep my commandments" (JST Matthew 16:26; see also 3 Nephi 12:30).

Jesus expects his disciples to walk in his footsteps: "Wherefore, follow me, and do the things which ye have seen me do" (2 Nephi 31:12). As he lost himself in the service of others, so true disciples go and do likewise: They willingly wear out their lives in the service of others. President Spencer W. Kimball suggested that "the more we serve our fellowmen in appropriate ways, the more substance there is to our souls. We become more significant individuals as we serve others. We become more substantive as we serve others—indeed, it is easier to 'find' ourselves because there is so much more of us to find!" (*Ensign*, December 1974, 2).

What happened to the young missionary Gordon B. Hinckley illustrates this teaching of Jesus:

"I was not well when I arrived [on my mission]. Those first few weeks, because of illness and the opposition which we felt, I was discouraged. I wrote a letter home to my good father and said that I felt I was wasting my time and his money. He was my father and my stake president, and he was a wise and inspired man. He wrote a very short letter to me which said, 'Dear Gordon, I have your recent letter. I have only one suggestion: forget yourself and go to work.' Earlier that morning in our scripture class my companion and I had read these words of the Lord: 'Whosoever will save his life shall lose it; but whosoever shall lose his life for my sake and the gospel's, the same shall save it' (Mark 8:35)" (*Teachings of Gordon B. Hinckley,* 350).

True religion requires a willingness to sacrifice all things for his cause. "Wherefore, seek not the things of this world, but seek ye first to build up the kingdom of God and to establish his righteousness" (JST Matthew 6:38).

These sayings are given more emphasis by the Savior in all four Gospels than any other specific teaching. The Prophet Joseph Smith also saw immense value in this particular doctrine of Jesus, as evidenced by alterations and additions he made in all three of the Synoptic Gospels. Each one of the three casts light on various aspects of the principles Jesus teaches (JST Matthew 16:27–29, Bible Appendix, 803; JST Mark 8:37–38, Bible Appendix, 804; and JST Luke 9:24–25, Bible Appendix, 806).

What happened to Brother Ogden one day as he served as a mission president illustrates the encouragement given to us to dedicate ourselves to selfless service on behalf of others. Brother Ogden wrote:

"At midnight tonight I had to call two missionaries and pass on sad news. It seems like every week I have to advise someone of the death of a grandparent, as was one case tonight, but the other was a terrible tragedy. One of our brand-new elders has an uncle who's been a well-known helicopter pilot with Life-Flight in Salt Lake City. Last Sunday night he was on a rescue mission in the mountains, trying to save an avalanche victim. The fierce storm slammed the helicopter into the mountainside, killing all four of the crew. The whole State of Utah is mourning the loss, with flags flying half-mast. Our elder's father, a bishop (and brother of that pilot) called and said: 'You tell my son to get out there and work hard. [Tell him:] your uncle died in service to others, trying to save someone; now you go out there and do that, too'" (Ogden, journal).

Mark 8:37–38 *"Therefore deny yourselves of these* [transitory, worldly things], *and be not ashamed of me"* (JST Mark 8:40), for anyone who feels shame for doing the Lord's work and shame for teaching his words, will find the Lord ashamed of him at the time of his glorious coming to earth.

"And they shall not have part in that resurrection when he cometh.

"For verily I say unto you, That he shall come; and he that layeth down his life for my sake and the gospel's, shall come with him, and shall be clothed with his glory in the cloud, on the right hand of the Son of Man" (JST Mark 8:42–43).

Our choice is shame or glory. We are deciding right now, every day, which we will have.

SOME NOT TO TASTE DEATH (AT CAESAREA PHILIPPI)

Matthew 16:28; Mark 9:1; Luke 9:27 After speaking of his glorious second coming (as recorded in the previous verse), Jesus prophesied that some (at least one we know of—John) would not taste of death until that earth-changing event. In other words, some would be changed, during their mortal lives, into translated beings and continue with the Lord's work for many centuries, until he comes (see further in the commentary on John 21:23; cf. 3 Nephi 28:7).

TRANSFIGURATION: SEALING KEYS COMMITTED (ON MOUNT HERMON OR MOUNT TABOR)

Mount Tabor, the traditional Mount of Transfiguration

Matthew 17:1–13; Mark 9:2–13; Luke 9:28–36 The Transfiguration of Christ was the culminating point of his public ministry, though it occurred in a private and sacred setting. The location is uncertain; the mountain is not named in scripture. Both Mount Tabor in the eastern Jezreel Valley, which is the traditional site of the Transfiguration, and Mount Hermon, the highest mountain in the country and located about forty miles north of the Sea of Galilee, fit the description of a "high mountain" (Matthew 17:1). Both sites have been endorsed by leaders and writers in the Church.

The word "apart" in Matthew 17:1 refers not to the mountain but to his apostles. Just as he seems to have set apart Peter, James, and John (the "Rock" and the "Sons of Thunder") as the presiding authorities among the Twelve, so now he took them apart—as on other particularly sacred occasions (see Mark 5:37; Matthew 26:37)—to participate in the unique purposes of this preparatory experience.

The Transfiguration occurred possibly in October, about

The Mount of Transfiguration, *by Gary Smith*

six months before Jesus' death (see Bible Dictionary, "Transfiguration, Mount of," 786). It happened "six days" (Matthew 17:1) or "about eight days" (Luke 9:28)—in other words, about a week—after the last-recorded events at Caesarea Philippi, where Peter was promised the keys of the kingdom. It may also have happened at night, because the apostles were "heavy with sleep" (Luke 9:32) and Luke's account notes that "on the next day, when they were come down from the hill, much people met him" (9:37). Luke also recorded that Jesus took his three chief apostles into a mountain "to pray" (9:28). Jesus often went into the mountains at night to pray (Luke 6:12; Matthew 14:23).

Luke described the physical change that came over Jesus: "As he prayed, the fashion of his countenance was altered, and his raiment was white and glistering" (Luke 9:29; cf. 3 Nephi 19:30). The Greek word translated here as "glistering" means "as lightning." Matthew says he was "transfigured before them: and his face did shine as the sun, and his raiment was white" (Matthew 17:2; cf. Helaman 5:36). The energy that

A fuller and his work

radiates from a heavenly being is so splendid and refulgent that mortals must use the most elevated vocabulary at their command to describe it. Writers use words such as *brilliant, exquisite, brighter than the noonday sun,* and so on. Mark adopts a brilliant image in his word picture of the transfiguration of Jesus: "His raiment became shining, exceeding white as snow; so as no fuller on earth can white them" (Mark 9:3).

Jesus' clothing was whiter than newly made wool or linen. The fuller, who usually had his workshop near a spring, the water source for a city, worked with his soap to clean cloth, ridding it of all stains to make it white. But no fuller could approach the gleaming brightness of sun-illuminated snow, and no snow could approach the splendor of a transfigured being.

The Latin *trans figura* (like the Greek *meta morpho*) means to change into another form. Peter, James, and John were transfigured, or changed, to another condition (Smith, *Teachings of the Prophet Joseph Smith,* 158). They passed into a higher state, but what is that state? The scriptures use a number of terms to describe these changed beings: *transfigured* and *translated* are two of the descriptions, both meaning the same condition, though *transfigured* is short-term and *translated* is long-term. Other words used are "renewed" and "paradisiacal" (Article of Faith 10), "caught up" (Moses 7:27; 3 Nephi 28:36; D&C 88:96), "glorified" (Moses 1:11; 7:3), "quickened" (D&C 67:11; 88:96), and "changed in the twinkling of an eye" (3 Nephi 28:8; D&C 43:32; 63:51; 101:31). Most of these descriptions refer to the shifting upward from our current telestial condition to a terrestrial condition. To be transfigured or translated, then, means to be changed to a terrestrial level, where bodies (while in that condition) are sanctified, made holy, and do not experience mortal pains or death (3 Nephi 28:7–9, 13–17, 36–40). Transfiguration, or translation, Joseph Smith taught, "is that of the terrestrial order" (*Teachings of the Prophet Joseph Smith*, 170).

While in that higher, transfigured condition, Moses and Elias (the Greek form of the Hebrew *Elijah*), two ancient worthies representing the Law and the Prophets, talked with the Savior. Joseph Smith's translation of King James Version Mark 9:4 (JST Mark 9:3) includes John the Baptist in the Transfiguration. We have no further information about why John was present (Bible Dictionary, "Elias," 663). Moses and Elijah had both been translated upon concluding their mortal ministries so they could participate on earth in this very occasion of Transfiguration. They were taken up, interestingly, in the same area east of the Jordan River opposite Jericho (Deuteronomy 34:5; Alma 45:19; 2 Kings 2:11–12) where John the Baptist and Jesus both began their mortal ministries. Moses and Elijah "appeared in glory, and spake of his *death, and also his resurrection*, which he should accomplish at Jerusalem" (JST Luke 9:31). Moses, Elijah, and John the Baptist on this occasion were only six months away from their own resurrection and would understandably have been anxiously anticipating that glorious experience.

One purpose of this sacred event was to confer the keys of

the kingdom on those who would become the "First Presidency" of the Lord's Church after his departure. "The Savior, Moses, and Elias, gave the keys to Peter, James and John, on the mount, when they were transfigured before him" (Smith, *Teachings of the Prophet Joseph Smith,* 158; see also D&C 7:7).

Two other accounts explain additional purposes of the Transfiguration. In 2 Peter 1:16–19 the prophet-president bears his testimony of one of the spiritual highlights of his life:

"For we have not followed cunningly devised fables, when we made known unto you the power and coming of our Lord Jesus Christ, but were eyewitnesses of his majesty.

"For he received from God the Father honour and glory, when there came such a voice to him from the excellent glory, This is my beloved Son, in whom I am well pleased.

"And this voice which came from heaven we heard, when we were with him in the holy mount [of Transfiguration].

"We have also a more sure word of prophecy . . ."

"The more sure word of prophecy" is another way of saying that the Savior made their calling and election sure (D&C 131:5); they were sealed up by the Holy Spirit of Promise, or guaranteed exaltation and Godhood—which is an extraordinary demonstration of the omniscience of God. He knew these three men from their pre-mortal valiance, and he knew that their commitment and dedication to the kingdom in this life would also seal their eternal reward. Having their calling and election made sure would help prepare and strengthen them for the fiery trials they would face; such an ordinance would be an anchor to their souls in the challenging years ahead. Joseph Smith explained the glorious blessing to those who receive the more sure word of prophecy: " . . . they were sealed in the heavens and had the promise of eternal life in the kingdom of God. Then, having this promise sealed unto them, it was an anchor to the soul, sure and steadfast. Though the thunders might roll and lightnings flash, and earthquakes bellow, and war gather thick around, yet this hope and knowledge would support the soul in every hour of trial, trouble and tribulation" (*History of the Church* 5:388–89).

In modern revelation another striking reference to the Transfiguration is given (D&C 63:20–21):

"He that endureth in faith and doeth my will, the same shall overcome, and shall receive an inheritance upon the earth when the day of transfiguration shall come [the glorious millennial reign of Christ];

"When the earth shall be transfigured, even according to the pattern which was shown unto mine apostles upon the mount; of which account the fulness ye have not yet received."

In summary, we understand that the three apostles experienced the following:

(1) They received the keys of the kingdom—keys to the gathering and to the sealing power (the saving work for the living and the dead);

(2) They received a sacred gift of knowledge, perhaps what we call an endowment (Smith, *Doctrines of Salvation*, 2:165);

(3) They had their calling and election made sure; and

(4) They had a vision of the earth in its millennial, paradisiacal state.

By putting the various accounts together, we have a fair understanding of what took place on the Mount of Transfiguration, although as Doctrine and Covenants 63:21 indicates, we do not yet have a full account of the sacred events on that mount.

Notice, too, that all the individuals involved at the Transfiguration were also involved in the Restoration of the gospel eighteen hundred years later (accompanying chart adapted from one by Morgan Ashton, 2003).

INDIVIDUALS INVOLVED IN THE TRANSFIGURATION AND THE RESTORATION

Person(s)	Involvement at Mount of Transfiguration (Matthew 17)	Involvement in Restoration of the Gospel
Heavenly Father	Spoke from the cloud, "This is my Beloved Son . . . hear ye him"	Appeared in the Sacred Grove and said, "This is My Beloved Son. Hear Him!" (Joseph Smith–History 1:17)
Jesus Christ	Transfigured on the Mount and spoke with all others present	Appeared with his Father in the Grove (Joseph Smith–History 1:17)
Peter, James, and John	Ascended the mountain with Christ, were transfigured, and received keys from angelic ministers	Descended as angelic ministers to Joseph Smith and Oliver Cowdery to bestow on them the Melchizedek Priesthood and all its keys (D&C 27:12–13)
John the Baptist	Appeared on the Mount (in his spirit body) for unknown reasons	Appeared to Joseph Smith and Oliver Cowdery to bestow on them the Aaronic Priesthood and all its keys (D&C 13)
Moses	Appeared as a translated being on the Mount to bestow keys	Appeared as a resurrected being in the Kirtland Temple to bestow the keys of the gathering of Israel (D&C 110:11)
Elijah	Appeared as a translated being on the Mount to bestow keys	Appeared as a resurrected being in the Kirtland Temple to bestow the keys of the sealing power (D&C 110:13–16)

Matthew 17:4; Mark 9:5; Luke 9:33 Given these spectacular circumstances, Peter felt to exclaim that it was good for them to be there and proposed that they make three tabernacles (Hebrew, *succot*, "booths"; see Appendix 6, 765) in honor of the Savior and the two prophets. At the Feast of Tabernacles, which was soon approaching, it was customary to erect little booths for individual worship; Peter may have

thought to memorialize this never-to-be-forgotten occasion by doing the same.

Matthew 17:5; Mark 9:7; Luke 9:34–35 A bright cloud overshadowed the apostles—the *Shekhinah,* the Dwelling Cloud, or Cloud of the Presence. The cloud seems to be a protective essence that shields mortals from radiance and glory beyond their capacity to withstand or changes their bodies to a higher level in order for them to endure the greater glory and see within the veil, which is to see in the spiritual realm with spiritual eyes (Moses 1:11).

The cloud of God's presence is noted in numerous episodes throughout scriptural history; for example, the following: the cloud that covered the mount where Moses was ("the glory of the Lord was like devouring fire"; Exodus 24:15–18; Moses entered into the cloud and was transfigured for five to six weeks; Exodus 24:18; Moses 1:11); the cloudy pillar at the door of the tabernacle (Exodus 33:9–11); the pillar of cloud that went before the Israelites by day, changing to a pillar of fire by night (Exodus 40:34, 38; Numbers 14:14); the cloud, the glory of the Lord, that filled Solomon's Temple (1 Kings 8:10–11; 2 Chronicles 5:13–14); the cloud that received Jesus out of the apostles' sight when he ascended after his resurrection (Acts 1:9). And in the Book of Mormon record: "The Lord came down and talked with the brother of Jared; and he was in a cloud, and the brother of Jared saw him not"; the Lord went before that people in a cloud and gave them directions (Ether 2:4–5, 14); Nephi and Lehi were "encircled about as if by fire . . . they were encircled about with a pillar of fire" and "they were overshadowed with a cloud" (Helaman 5:23–24, 28); "there came a cloud and overshadowed the multitude" as Jesus ascended (3 Nephi 18:38–39).

The Prophet Joseph Smith described a phenomenon similar to that experienced by Peter, James, and John: "I saw a pillar of light . . . above the brightness of the sun. . . . When the light rested upon me I saw two Personages" (Joseph

Smith–History 1:16–17); "a messenger from heaven descended in a cloud of light" (Joseph Smith–History 1:68). Finally, of the Second Coming, Jesus testifies: "I shall come in a cloud with power and great glory" (D&C 34:7); and "the Saints that have slept shall come forth to meet me in the cloud" (D&C 45:45); they shall be "caught up . . . and received into the cloud" (D&C 76:102). On the cloud accompanying God's presence, see further in Ogden and Skinner, *Acts through Revelation*, 383–86.

The voice of the Father was heard out of the cloud, proclaiming once again, "This is my Son, in whom I am well pleased; hear ye him" (Matthew 17:5). His testimony was of his Son, in whom only is salvation—that is his name: Yeshua means "Salvation" or "Savior" (see commentary on Matthew 3:17). The Father's commandment is always "Hear ye him"—that is, listen to and obey my Son. The apostles were not commanded to hear and obey Moses and Elijah or any other mortals but only the Father's Son; salvation comes only in and through the holy Messiah, the Son of God.

Matthew 17:6–8 The natural reaction of Peter, James, and John to these highly unusual and awesome wonders was fear. Humans are normally afraid to enter the unknown, to enter territory unfamiliar to us. (Moses reacted similarly in his first experience with God on another mountain; see Exodus 3:6; Deuteronomy 5:5; see also commentary on Luke 1:12.) Jesus calmed them and reassured them. So with us: when we are frightened and unsure of what is happening to us, the Savior comes to our rescue. He also sends the Comforter. Those challenging moments are the very moments that often expand our capacity for light, truth, strength, and understanding.

Matthew 17:9; Mark 9:9–10; Luke 9:36 Once again Jesus charged them to not talk with others about what had happened (see commentary on Matthew 8:2–4). He charges us likewise not to talk about our sacred endowment outside the Holy Place, the Temple. The apostles were not to divulge details of this experience until after Jesus rose from the dead, leaving them puzzled about what he meant by his "rising from the dead" (Mark 9:10). As yet they had no comprehension of the Anointed One actually dying nor, especially, the concept of resurrection, which had never happened in the history of the world. John would later write, "For as yet they knew not [understood not] the scripture, that he must rise again from the dead" (John 20:9).

Matthew 17:10–13; Mark 9:11–13 Having just experienced some indelible and personal moments with a prophet they called Elias, the three chief apostles now had additional matters about which they wanted to inquire of Jesus. Even the scribes note that in the scriptures there is some reference to Elias coming. What does that mean? Jesus' response as given in the Joseph Smith Translation helps explain (see also Bible Dictionary, "Elias," 663). There are actually two Eliases referred to here, one to *prepare* and one to *restore* (JST Matthew 17:10–14):

"And Jesus answered and said unto them, Elias truly shall first come, and restore all things, *as the prophets have written.*

"*And again* I say unto you that Elias has come already, *concerning whom it is written, Behold, I will send my messenger, and he shall prepare the way before me;* and they knew him not, and have done unto him, whatsoever they listed.

"Likewise shall also the Son of Man suffer of them.

"*But I say unto you, Who is Elias? Behold, this is Elias, whom I send to prepare the way before me.*

"Then the disciples understood that he spake unto them of John the Baptist, *and also of another who should come and restore all things, as it is written by the prophets.*" (Compare JST Mark 9:10–11.)

Defining who Elias is, Elder Bruce R. McConkie wrote: "Correcting the Bible by the spirit of revelation, the Prophet restored a statement of John the Baptist which says that *Christ is the Elias who was to restore all things.* ([JST] John 1:21–28.) By revelation we are also informed that *the Elias who was to restore all things is the angel Gabriel* who was known in mortality as Noah. (D. & C. 27:6–7; Luke 1:5–25; *Teachings of the Prophet Joseph Smith,* p. 157.) From the same authentic source we also learn that *the promised Elias is John the Revelator.* (D. & C. 77:9, 14.) Thus there are three different revelations which name Elias as being *three different persons.* What are we to conclude?

"By finding answer to the question, by whom has the restoration been effected, we shall find who Elias is and find there is no problem in harmonizing these apparently contradictory revelations. Who has restored all things? Was it one man? Certainly not. Many angelic ministrants have been sent from the courts of glory to confer keys and powers, to commit their dispensations and glories again to men on earth. At least the following have come: Moroni, John the Baptist, Peter, James, and John, Moses, Elijah, Elias, Gabriel, Raphael, and Michael. (D. & C. 13; 110; 128:19–21.) Since it is apparent that no one messenger has carried the whole burden of the restoration, but rather that each has come with a specific endowment from on high, it becomes clear that *Elias is a composite personage. The expression must be understood to be a name and a title for those whose mission it was to commit keys and powers to men in this final dispensation. (Doctrines of Salvation,* vol. 1, pp. 170–74.)" (*Mormon Doctrine,* 221; italics in original).

HEALS DEMONIAC CHILD: FASTING, PRAYER (IN GALILEE)

Matthew 17:14–21; Mark 9:14–29; Luke 9:37–43; cf. Luke 17:5–6 When the Savior returned from the Transfiguration, people were amazed as they looked at him (Mark 9:14). A boy was brought to him who had been distressed for years with an evil spirit, which produced the effect of dumbness (Mark 9:17), or lunacy (Matthew 17:15), and various destructive and violent tendencies. It was reported that the disciples could not cast out this evil spirit. Jesus lamented the lack of faith his priesthood leaders had shown, assuring them that if they would just exercise faith as a grain of mustard seed they could move mountains (Matthew 17:20; cf. Helaman 10:9; on mustard seed, see commentary on Matthew 13:31–32). The idea of moving mountains was a figurative expression about overcoming difficulty, and it was common among the Jews—though God can move mountains if his work calls for such miracles (see, for example, Ether 12:30).

Luke's account says that "if ye had faith as a grain of mustard seed, ye might say unto this sycamine tree, Be thou plucked up by the root, and be thou planted in the sea; and it should obey you" (Luke 17:6). There is no other mention in the Bible of a sycamine tree (which is not the same as the sycomore tree). The sycamine tree is generally believed to be the black mulberry tree. In the parallel passages, Matthew and Mark both render "mountain" in place of "sycamine tree." The intent is the same: with faith even as minute as a mustard seed, miraculous results can be achieved.

Jesus said to the boy's father, "If thou canst believe, all things are possible to him that believeth" (Mark 9:23). The father cried out with tears, "Lord, I believe; help thou mine unbelief" (v. 24). That is the humble condition all mortals must feel as we approach the Lord for help: We do have faith, up to a point. That is where we turn to him and plead, as did this father, for help to increase our faith. In the end, we are totally dependent on Him for blessings, to meet our needs, and only He can match our faith with all that is necessary for us to see the miracle. If we throw ourselves at his feet and humbly petition him for compassion, he (or we) can cast out any evil spirit, or evil character trait, or any negative circumstance in our lives.

This particular trial—possession by an evil spirit—Jesus taught, requires more than just priesthood and faith, two of the greatest powers in the universe. We have numerous examples in the scriptures of those who used their faith and priesthood power to accomplish remarkable things, for example Enoch (Moses 7:13), the brother of Jared (Ether 12:30), and Melchizedek (Alma 13:18). But casting out this kind of evil spirit requires, in addition, much prayer and fasting. Additional strength and command of the powers of heaven come through mighty prayer and through persistent and effective fasting.

PROPHECY OF DEATH AND RESURRECTION (IN GALILEE)

Matthew 17:22–23; Mark 9:30–32; Luke 9:43–45 Jesus again prophesied plainly of his coming maltreatment, betrayal, death, and resurrection. This is not the first time he had spoken openly about his foreordained destiny in Jerusalem. Early in his ministry he had actually prophesied: "Destroy this temple [his body], and in three days I will raise it up" (John 2:19). At Caesarea Philippi he had clearly detailed the dramatic events of his final mortal hours on earth (Matthew 16:21). Now he gave a third witness. "But they understood not this saying, and it was hid from them" (Luke 9:45). John later wrote, "These things understood not his disciples at the first: but when Jesus was glorified, then remembered they that these things were written of him" (John 12:16). This passage is a hint that someone was keeping a contemporary record of these prophecies; a written record was being kept.

President Wilford Woodruff drew a parallel between the perplexity of the ancient disciples and the similar situation with the approaching death of the Prophet Joseph Smith. President Woodruff said: "I remember very well the last charge that Joseph gave to the Apostles. We had as little idea that he was going from us as the Apostles of the Savior did that He was going to be taken from them. Joseph talked with us as plainly as did the Savior to His Apostles, but we did not understand that he was about to depart from us any more than the Apostles understood the Savior" (*Collected Discourses,* 5:188).

TRIBUTE COIN IN THE MOUTH OF A FISH (AT CAPERNAUM)

Matthew 17:24–27 "Tribute money" was collected as an annual half-shekel Temple tax, used for the upkeep of the Temple. Every Israelite male twenty years and older was required to pay the annual assessment (Exodus 30:13). "When they were come to Capernaum, they that received tribute money came to Peter, and said, Doth not your master pay tribute?" (v. 24). The collectors may have wondered, because priests and rabbis claimed exemption. Jesus gave instructions for finding the needed coin in the mouth of a fish, saying, "Lest we should offend them" (v. 27). Was Jesus too poor to pay the money? Could he not have earned it by

St. Peter's fish (Tilapia Galilea)

Fisherman casting a net

fishing? Considering who he was, Jesus condescended to pay the money but demonstrated his exalted status by fulfilling the law in a supernatural way, by a miracle without parallel.

"Take up the fish that first cometh up; and when thou hast opened his mouth, thou shalt find a piece of money: that take, and give unto them for me and thee" (v. 27). Some have wondered if this particular fish was what today is called "St. Peter's fish" (see Appendix 7, 774). St. Peter's fish (*Tilapia Galilea*) is a mouth-breeder (a fish that carries its eggs and young in its mouth) and has been known to carry pebbles, bottle caps, and other foreign objects in its mouth. Perhaps the conditions that came together to produce such an extraordinary incident are not so inexplicable after all, though the knowledge of the exact location of a fish *with a coin in its mouth* is most miraculous.

WHO IS THE GREATEST IN THE KINGDOM? (IN GALILEE)

Matthew 18:1–6; Mark 9:33–37; Luke 9:46–48 On the way to Capernaum some of the Twelve carried on a conversation about who would be greatest among them. When Jesus asked about it they were embarrassed to admit their topic of discussion. He taught them several lessons. First, given the weighty callings and responsibilities they had received, they needed to elevate their thoughts, perhaps as expressed on one occasion by the Prophet Joseph Smith from Liberty Jail:

"How vain and trifling have been our spirits, our conferences, our councils, our meetings, our private as well as public conversations—too low, too mean, too vulgar, too condescending for the dignified characters of the called and chosen of God" (*History of the Church*, 3:295–96).

The chosen leaders needed to elevate their thoughts above the natural man's propensity to seek position, status, dominion, and control over others.

One day in March of 1999, while presiding over the Chile Santiago East Mission, Brother Ogden wrote: "Some elders have a problem with position-seeking. One missionary wrote to me in his weekly report: 'President, I've been here a year and a half and I've never been anything. I've never trained or even been a district leader. I must be doing something wrong, but you tell me that you trust me, so I don't get it. Maybe you have an answer.' I asked the missionaries in our next zone conference how they would respond to those comments, and they were pretty astute at identifying what the real problem was. One missionary asked the others: 'When you go back home, are you going to try to become a bishop or a stake president?' Why are we here? *To serve*. What impedes our spiritual progress the most? *Pride*. We should not allow a "ladder-climbing mentality" to grow inside us. I reminded them of what one of the other mission presidents had told me: he never was an assistant to the president, or a zone leader, or even a district leader during his mission—and here he was a mission president. Elder Dallas N. Archibald, our area president, told us that he never was an assistant, or a zone leader, or even a district leader during his mission. Then recently President Robert E. Wells of the Temple told us that he had never been an assistant, or a zone leader, or even a district leader during his mission. I think there's a message coming through! I proceeded to teach them: *You can't be a good leader until you're a good follower. You'll never preside until you learn to sustain. If you're critical of any leader, you're not ready to be one (you won't be able to handle the criticism when it comes at you)*" (Ogden, journal).

Sister Ogden wrote one day in her mission journal: "One of our missionaries called me to tell me that he knew if he could get going again on a highly disciplined exercise program he could become the leader that he had been before the mission when he captained various sports teams. I could tell he was discouraged that he hadn't achieved any positions of authority or importance in the mission. I took some time later to explain this principle of service so central to the mission of Jesus. No offense to the male gender, but LDS men can struggle with the leadership problem, equating greatness with 'important' positions. I tried to convey to this elder, that those who hold important positions in the Church neither sought them nor wanted them. They have them because they always understood clearly their role as a servant, and actually preferred it, recognizing each call as an opportunity to help. You can really see this among the general authorities. When President Ogden was called to preside over this mission, I expected they would tell us what to do at every turn. It is not like that. In all of our dealings with them, whether concerning our own personal needs in the mission or those of our missionaries, they have been so kind and compassionate. There is an air of humility about them of wanting to help. They could be so proud and intimidating, but they never are. I'll never forget one occasion when we were still living in Jerusalem. Elder Faust was visiting. He told President Ogden that he missed serving at that level where the sole meets the sidewalk, meaning being involved locally with the people and serving them" (Ogden, journal).

Jesus gathered the Twelve close together and set a little child in the middle of them. Elder Bruce R. McConkie proposed that since this discussion was taking place in Capernaum in the home of Peter, it is possible that this was one of Peter's young children (*Doctrinal New Testament Commentary*, 1:415). Jesus encouraged the apostles to become not childish but childlike. And how is that? We overcome the natural man and our preoccupation with position and status by becoming submissive, meek, humble, patient, full of love, and being willing to submit to any kind of growth-producing trial the Lord might send our way (Mosiah 3:19). Those who humble themselves and focus on serving others become the greatest in the kingdom of heaven. Leaders are not set in position to lord over others but to serve them. Those called to govern, to direct, and to lead are called to serve—to be the servant of all. Jesus would remind the Twelve of this lesson again, in a dramatic way, at the Last Supper (John 13:12–16).

Another lesson: Offenses are a huge problem, even among those trying to sanctify themselves and become real Saints. Humility is a key to avoid offending and alienating other people or to becoming offended or alienated oneself. Humility is also a key to forgiving and being reconciled with any offended brother or sister and with God (forgiveness and reconciliation are the subjects of the rest of chapter 18 of Matthew). Until we acquire real lowliness of heart, we will suffer from pride. An angel taught King Benjamin the same message a century before Jesus' mortal ministry: "Men drink damnation to their own souls except they humble themselves and become as little children" (Mosiah 3:18).

We often talk about getting rid of pride, but how is that done? We usually attempt to identify negative qualities or tendencies in ourselves and go about trying to eradicate them.

The North Galilean Ministry

But let's turn it around and try a positive approach. If we focus on the Light, the Light will automatically dispel the darkness in us. Pride will disappear in us if we have charity, the pure love of Christ. The scriptures teach us that charity includes patience, kindness, meekness, gentleness, humbleness of mind, and lowliness of heart (in contrast to being "high and lifted up" in pride).

Charity also includes a quality of character the Lord refers to often: "long-suffering." That means we are slow to anger, not easily provoked; we learn to avoid becoming upset, negative, critical, sarcastic, and condemnatory; we don't make hasty, spur-of-the-moment comments (which leave us with regrets, wishing we hadn't said them). We do not envy others, and we are not selfish. Long-suffering also means that we are willing to endure all things, including an infinite variety of trials, such as deterioration of physical health. (When we're sick or in pain or extremely tired, it's harder to control our emotions, and we react negatively.) Trials may also include challenges with mental health, which are not so-called noble trials (when you have a broken bone or leukemia or diabetes or one of so many kinds of cancer, you receive the deserved sympathy, but when you suffer from any of the numerous kinds of chemical imbalances and mental ailments—such as attention deficit disorder, depression, or bi-polar condition—it is harder for others to accept and understand what you are experiencing). Trials may also include being unable to have children, or having a rebellious child, an unfaithful spouse, or a loved one with a vicious, destructive addiction, or an acquaintance who is abusive in some way. All these trials and many others require a long-suffering nature. God himself is long-suffering (Exodus 34:6), and he wants us to become as he is.

So how do we acquire all these wonderful qualities that constitute charity, the love of Christ—patience, kindness, meekness, humbleness of mind, lowliness of heart, and long-suffering? The Holy Ghost helps all these virtues to abide in us; if we have the Spirit of the Lord in us, we have charity. And how do we get the Spirit? Through obedience to God's commandments, especially through sincere daily prayer and daily searching of the scriptures. We receive the Spirit best when we are focused on others—that is why men have the priesthood and why we all have callings. Pride flees when we are full of humility; humility is not thinking less of ourselves but thinking of ourselves less.

The great Russian writer Leo Tolstoy wrote about a man who was trying to discipline himself to "sainthood." Tolstoy said that one who "trains himself to attain sainthood by grand gestures and noticeable acts of self-sacrifice" will "fail, because no matter what he does to humble his pride, he is still proud of his very humility" (quoted in Hafen, *Disciple's Life*, 546).

Matthew 18:6 It would be better to have a millstone—a heavy limestone or basalt grinding stone (basalt is a hard, black volcanic stone)—hung around one's neck and be cast into the sea to drown than to offend one of God's little children, or one of God's older children, for that matter. True humility will always drive us to seek repentance, ask forgiveness, and quickly resolve any offensive comment or behavior. Pride, humility's opposite, will get in the way and encourage us to hold out, be stubborn, cast blame on the other person, and defend our own position. If we have hardened our heart against anyone, we have hardened our heart against the Savior ("inasmuch as ye have done it unto one of the least of these my brethren, ye have done it unto me"; Matthew 25:40). We get rid of a hard heart by developing a soft heart. Again, we overcome pride, one of the greatest sins, by acquiring charity, one of the greatest virtues (a detailed study of how to have the love of Christ in us is found in the commentary on John 15:9–17).

Those who criticize and offend the Lord's chosen ones—leaders and regular Church members—have awful consequences pronounced upon them in Doctrine and Covenants 121:19–22:

"Wo unto them; because they have offended my little ones they shall be severed from the ordinances of mine house.

"Their basket shall not be full, their houses and their barns shall perish, and they themselves shall be despised by those that flattered them.

"They shall not have right to the priesthood, nor their posterity after them from generation to generation.

"It had been better for them that a millstone had been hanged about their necks, and they drowned in the depth of the sea."

Mark 9:37 The Joseph Smith Translation expands the sense and meaning of this passage from Mark; see footnote 37a.

DISCOURSE: OFFENSES AND FORGIVENESS (IN GALILEE)

Matthew 18:7–35; Mark 9:38–50; Luke 17:1–4 Offenses will certainly continue, but those who cause them bring grief upon themselves—especially if something offensive or abusive is done to a little child. Beware, Jesus says, that you do nothing to insult or harm one of these little ones.

Elder M. Russell Ballard said: "We hear disturbing reports of parents or guardians who are so far removed from the Spirit of Christ that they abuse children. Whether this abuse is physical, verbal, or the less evident but equally severe emotional abuse, it is an abomination and a serious offense to God" (*Ensign*, May 1991, 80).

In Matthew 18:10, "angels" refers to *spirits*. Elder Bruce R. McConkie wrote: "This is a clear allusion to the doctrine of pre-existence. Because of the atoning sacrifice of Christ all children are born into the world free from sin, innocent, clean, pure, without any taint whatever attaching to them. They remain in this state until they 'begin to become accountable.' (D. & C. 29:46–50; 68:25–27; 93:38–39.) Should they die before arriving at the years of accountability, their angels or spirits, being pure and clean, are qualified to return to the presence of the Father, that is, they are saved in the celestial kingdom of heaven" (*Doctrinal New Testament Commentary*, 1:421).

The Savior came "to save that which was lost *and to call sinners to repentance; but these little ones have no need of repentance, and I will save them*" (JST Matthew 18:11). That is a message of Doctrine and Covenants 137: "All children who die before they arrive at the years of accountability [years of accountability are from eight years of age onward] are saved in the celestial kingdom of heaven" (v. 10).

Mark 9:42; Luke 17:2 See commentary on Matthew 18:6.

Matthew 18:8–9; Mark 9:43–48 Concerning offending hand, foot, and eye, see commentary on Matthew 5:27–30. Note also the considerable interpretive additions in Joseph Smith Translation Mark 9:40–48 (see Bible Appendix, 804–5), explaining that if our current family or friends or even our leaders are the kind who would lead us into temptation and sin, it would be better to dissociate ourselves from them:

"*Therefore,* if thy hand offend thee, cut it off; *or if thy brother offend thee and confess not and forsake not, he shall be cut off.* It is better for thee to enter into life maimed, than having two hands, to go into hell.

"*For it is better for thee to enter into life without thy brother, than for thee and thy brother to be cast into hell.* . . .

"*And again,* if thy foot offend thee, cut it off; *for he that is thy standard* [your leader]*, by whom thou walkest, if he become a transgressor, he shall be cut off.* . . .

"*Therefore, let every man stand or fall, by himself, and not for another; or not trusting another* [each person standing on his or her own light, not relying solely on other humans]. . . .

"And if thine eye *which seeth for thee, him that is appointed to watch over thee to show thee light* [your priesthood leader]*, become a transgressor and offend thee, pluck him out.* . . .

"For it is better that thyself should be saved, than to be cast into hell with thy brother, where their worm dieth not, and where the fire is not quenched" (cf. D&C 76:44).

Joseph Smith Translation Matthew 18:9 adds:

"And a man's hand is his friend, and his foot, also; and a man's eye, are they of his own household."

President Joseph Fielding Smith explained this passage as follows:

"When the Lord spoke of parts of the body, it is evident that he had in mind close friends or relatives who endeavored to lead us from the path of rectitude and humble obedience to the divine commandments we receive from the Lord.

"If any friend or relative endeavors to lead a person away from the commandments, it is better to dispense with his friendship and association rather than to follow him in evil practices to destruction. . . . We should not . . . take such a statement as this referred to in the words of the Savior . . . in the literal interpretation. When properly understood it becomes a very impressive figure of speech.

"If you have friends or associates who endeavor to entice you to commit sin, cut them off. Withdraw from their association lest they drag you down to the committing of some sin or transgression against divine will" (*Answers to Gospel Questions*, 5:79).

PARABLE: LOST SHEEP

Matthew 18:12–14; Luke 15:1–7 It is not a wise practice in livestock management for a shepherd to leave a flock of ninety-nine sheep to search out one unless the larger flock is secured. In the pastoral culture of Jesus' day this parable was an attention-getter.

If the Good Shepherd exerts considerable effort to save any of his sheep who are lost, then the true undershepherd will do the same. Jesus saw his faithful followers as a "little

Sheep, a mainstay of the Israelites' economy, were used in the Bible as a symbol of the Israelites themselves

flock" (Luke 12:32) that needed to be fed and protected from the perils of their earthly pasture. If a sheep were to stray and be in danger, it was incumbent on the true shepherd, loving the sheep as much as his own life, to leave the secure ones and go out to rescue the one. That is the poetic yet practical message of the hymn "Dear to the Heart of the Shepherd" (*Hymns*, 1985, no. 221).

Matthew 18:13 and Luke 15:7 suggest that the Shepherd will rejoice more over the lost sheep that is found than over the ninety-nine that did not go astray. The philosophical question then arises, Is it better to wander off and sin so you can be recovered and elicit more attention and rejoicing from your Lord? The unequivocal answer, of course, is no. As President Ezra Taft Benson said, "It is better to prepare and prevent than it is to repair and repent" (*Teachings of Ezra Taft Benson*, 285). It goes without saying that the Savior highly values, appreciates, and rewards those who do not wander far off the path but hold fast to the rod and remain firm and steadfast. As the father of the prodigal said to his other son: "Thou art ever with me, and all that I have is thine" (Luke 15:31). Still, when the prodigal comes back, when the one who was lost is found again, the Father is anxious to "make merry," "kill the fatted calf," and rejoice because the one who was spiritually dead is alive again—the lost one is found. The Father is constantly rejoicing in the ninety and nine, but for the occasion of the return of the lost one, he rejoices at that moment even more for the one.

The Prophet Joseph Smith understood the Savior's teaching here in yet another, quite different perspective. Jesus chastised the self-righteous leaders of the Jews:

"The hundred sheep represent one hundred Sadducees and Pharisees, as though Jesus had said, 'If you Sadducees and Pharisees are in the sheepfold, I have no mission for you; I am sent to look up sheep that are lost; and when I have found them, I will back them up and make joy in heaven.' This represents hunting after a few individuals, or one poor publican, which the Pharisees and Sadducees despised. . . . like I say unto you, there is joy in the presence of the angels of God over one sinner that repenteth, more than over ninety-and-nine just persons that are so righteous [self-righteous]; they will be damned anyhow; you cannot save them" (*Teachings of the Prophet Joseph Smith*, 277–78).

PARABLE: LOST COIN

Luke 15:8–10 The Savior's mission was to call not the sinless but the sinners to repentance. Some Pharisees and scribes were criticizing him for associating with sinners. He gave three analogies to justify working with sinners, the lost ones, parables about a lost sheep, a lost coin, and a lost son.

Sinners, like sheep who have wandered off and are gone astray, are worth going after to bring back. And a sinner, like a coin lost by neglect or carelessness, deserves to be diligently searched for and recovered. When the lost coin is found, there is joy in the house. Just so, when the lost soul is found, there is joy in the household of God. "And how great is his joy in the soul that repenteth!" (D&C 18:13).

Some houses in Jesus' day had floors made of stones. Gaps between flooring stones would have made losing a coin quite possible. Jesus' audience understood very well from the illustration what he was saying.

PARABLE: LOST SON (THE PRODIGAL SON)

Luke 15:11–32 Remember Joseph Smith's key to understanding a parable: What was the question that drew out the response? In this case the matter Jesus addresses is why he associates with sinners, why he cares about them and desires to bring them to a righteous course of life. In the previous two brief parables he has already illustrated why the sinner is worth pursuing. If one of a hundred sheep wanders off, we will leave the ninety-nine secured and cared for while we go out to bring the wanderer back. If one of ten coins is lost, we search until it is found. If one of two sons rebels and is determined to pursue a wasteful and destructive course, we will pray mightily and fast earnestly and do all we can to bring him back. (The accompanying chart was adapted from one by Morgan Ashton.)

THE PARABLES OF LOST THINGS

That which was lost	How it was lost	How it was redeemed
Sheep	Ignorant wandering, unwise judgment	The watch-care of the Redeemer
Coin	Neglect, carelessness	Diligent effort to resolve, make up for neglect
Prodigal son	Wilful rebellion	Had to come to himself, repent, rely on the mercy of the Savior
Elder son	Pride	Had to humble himself, find joy in return of his brother

The carob, or locust, tree grows pods, which are the husks referred to in the parable of the prodigal son

The prodigal son went into a far (Gentile) country and, after wasting his substance with riotous living (Latin, *prodigere*, from which the English *prodigal* derives, means "to squander, wastefully spend"), he found himself working during a famine feeding swine, desiring to eat even the carob pods ("husks") that the swine ate. (For more about carob pods as husks, see Ogden, *Where Jesus Walked*, 99.) Jews considered any connection with swine to be the lowest, most despicable condition to which one could fall, because swine are one of the unclean animals forbidden by the law of Moses.

The prodigal's suffering brought him to his senses. He thought back on how good his life had been in his father's house, and being about to die of hunger, he decided he might as well go back to see if he could at least hire on at his father's estate as a servant. He would humbly confess, "Father, I have sinned against heaven, and before thee, and am no more worthy to be called thy son" (vv. 18–19). Is that not the way we all feel when we have grievously sinned? In fact, are we not all prodigals in some way, at some point? Do we sometimes feel

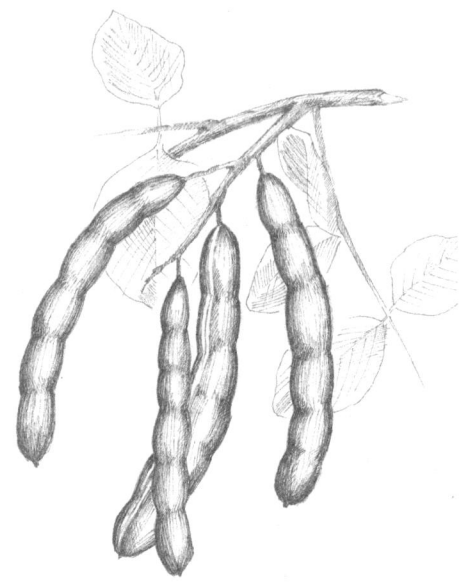

A carob pod with beanlike seeds, which are used today as a substitute for chocolate

that we are the vilest of sinners and that Heavenly Father will never accept us back? But, like the father in the parable, our Heavenly Father has compassion on us and is overjoyed at our return. And are we not all like the father in the parable at some point, forgiving and rejoicing over those who return to the family, the Church, or their own right senses? Is the father not a thinly veiled reference to our Father in Heaven, whom we should be like? And are we not commanded to look after the prodigals?

The Hebrew verb *lashuv* means "to repent"; it also means "to return." That is the whole concept of repentance: to come back and be reconciled to the loving Father. This parable of the prodigal son could also be entitled the parable of the loving father.

Gerald N. Lund wrote: "When the son finally 'came to himself,' he decided he would return home and see if his father could forgive him enough to allow him to be one of the domestic servants (15:17–18). Even that would have been an act of mercy. In strict fairness, the boy could have—perhaps even should have—been offered nothing. After all, it was his own choice that led him to this woeful state of affairs.

"But then comes the powerful lesson: 'And he arose, and came to his father. *But when he was yet a great way off,* his father saw him, and had compassion, and ran, and fell on his neck, and kissed him' (Luke 15:20, emphasis added).

"How did the father see him while he was yet a great way off? Was it because he was watching for him? Did the father, who had been deeply wronged, make the son come all the way back to where he was and fall down and grovel before him to prove his penitence? Did the father have the boy return the squandered inheritance, or at least work it off as a servant, before he could be restored to his former position in the family? No. While he was yet a great way off the father saw him, was filled with compassion, and ran to meet his son. In my mind, there is no more beautiful lesson in all of the scriptures about the grace and mercy of God" (in *Jesus Christ, Son of God, Savior,* 26).

Note that the ecstatic father called for the best robe and a ring (a mark of reinstatement) and clothing and the fatted calf (killed only for a special guest) and a gathering for celebration. "For this my son was dead, and is alive again; he was lost, and is found" (v. 24).

As mentioned before, virtually all of Jesus' parables served to illustrate one main point. This parable, however, introduces a new element in the "lost" stories: no one had complained about the lost sheep or the lost coin being found. So here is another lesson. The older son objected to all the celebrating over one who had brought so much grief, embarrassment, and shame on the family. The father went out and reasoned with him, showing tender regard for the faithful son (though he was being selfishly narrow at the moment), reassuring him that his loyalty and obedience had earned him all that the father had (v. 31).

Henry Drummond, a nineteenth-century Scottish theologian, wrote the following masterful insight:

"The peculiarity of ill temper is that it is the vice of the virtuous. It is often the one blot on an otherwise noble character. You know men who are all but perfect, and women who would be entirely perfect, but for an easily ruffled, quick-tempered, or "touchy" disposition. This compatibility of ill temper with high moral character is one of the strangest and saddest problems of ethics. The truth is there are two great classes of sins—sins of the *Body,* and sins of the *Disposition.* The Prodigal Son may be taken as a type of the first, the Elder Brother of the second. Now, society has no doubt whatever as to which of these is the worse. Its brand falls, without a challenge, upon the Prodigal. But are we right? . . . No form of vice, not worldliness, not greed of gold, not drunkenness itself, does more to un-Christianize society than evil temper. For embittering life, for breaking up communities; for destroying the most sacred relationships; for devastating homes; for withering up men and women; for taking the bloom of childhood; in short, for sheer gratuitous misery-producing power, this influence stands alone. Look at the Elder Brother, moral, hard-working, patient, dutiful—let him get all credit for his virtues—look at this man, this baby, sulking outside his own father's door. 'He was angry,' we read, 'and would not go in.' Look at the effect upon the father, upon the servants, upon the happiness of the guests. Judge of the effect upon the Prodigal—and how many prodigals are kept out of the Kingdom of God by the unlovely character of those who profess to be inside? Analyze, as a study in Temper, the thunder-cloud itself as it gathers upon the Elder Brother's brow. What is it made of? Jealousy, anger, pride, uncharity, cruelty, self-righteousness, touchiness, doggedness, sullenness—these are the ingredients of this dark and loveless soul. In varying proportions, also, these are the ingredients of all ill temper. Judge if such sins of the disposition are not worse to live in, and for others to live with, than sins of the body. Did Christ indeed not answer the question Himself when He said, 'I say unto you, that the publicans and the harlots go into the Kingdom of Heaven before you'? There is really no place in Heaven for a disposition like this. A man with such a mood could only make Heaven miserable for all the people in it. Except, therefore, such a man be born again, he cannot, he simply *cannot,* enter the Kingdom of Heaven. For it is perfectly certain—and you will not misunderstand me—that to enter Heaven a man must take it with him" (*Greatest Thing in the World,* 35–38).

Elder Jeffrey R. Holland shared the following poignant observations about the elder brother: "This son is not so much angry that the other has come home as he is angry that his parents are so happy about it. Feeling unappreciated and perhaps more than a little self-pity, this dutiful son—and he is *wonderfully* dutiful—forgets for a moment that he has never had to know filth or despair, fear or self-loathing. He forgets for a moment that every calf on the ranch is already his and so are all the robes in the closet and every ring in the drawer. He forgets for a moment that his faithfulness has been and always will be rewarded.

"No, he who has virtually everything, and who has in his hardworking, wonderful way earned it, lacks the one thing that might make him the complete man of the Lord he nearly is. He has not yet come to the compassion and mercy, the charitable breadth of vision to see that *this is not a rival returning.* It is his brother. As his father pled with him to see, it is one who was dead and now is alive. It is one who was lost and now is found" (*Ensign,* May 2002, 63).

It is wise for the faithful sons (and daughters) of the Father in Heaven to always leave the door open for the prodigals to come back. We see prodigals all around us—and some of them will come back, if we assure them that the door is always open to them. In fact, we are all prodigals, and the loving Father constantly invites us to repent and return.

Elder Orson F. Whitney explained:

"The Prophet Joseph Smith declared—and he never taught more comforting doctrine—that the eternal sealings of faithful parents and the divine promises made to them for valiant service in the Cause of Truth, would save not only themselves, but likewise their posterity. Though some of the sheep may wander, the eye of the Shepherd is upon them, and sooner or later they will feel the tentacles of Divine Providence reaching out after them and drawing them back to the fold. Either in this life or the life to come, they will return. They will have to pay their debt to justice; they will suffer for their sins; and may tread a thorny path; but if it leads them at last, like the penitent Prodigal, to a loving and forgiving father's heart and home, the painful experience will not have been in vain. Pray for your careless and disobedient children; hold on to them with your faith. Hope on, trust on, till you see the salvation of God" (Conference Report, Apr. 1929, 110).

In general conference of April 2003, President James E. Faust commented on Elder Whitney's teachings:

"A principle in this statement that is often overlooked is that they must fully repent and 'suffer for their sins' and 'pay their debt to justice.' . . . If the repentance of the wayward children does not happen in this life, is it still possible for the cords of the sealing to be strong enough for them yet to work out their repentance? In the Doctrine and Covenants we are told, 'The dead who repent will be redeemed, through obedience to the ordinances of the house of God, and after they have paid the penalty of their transgressions, and are washed clean, shall receive a reward according to their works, for they are heirs of salvation' (D&C 138:58–59).

"We remember that the prodigal son wasted his inheritance, and when it was all gone he came back to his father's house. There he was welcomed back into the family, but his inheritance was spent. Mercy will not rob justice, and the sealing power of faithful parents will only claim wayward children upon the condition of their repentance and Christ's Atonement. Repentant wayward children will enjoy salvation and all the blessings that go with it, but exaltation is much more. It must be fully earned. The question as to who will be exalted must be left to the Lord in His mercy" (*Ensign*, May 2003, 62).

OFFENSES AND FORGIVENESS (CONTINUED)

Mark 9:38–41; Luke 9:49–50 Concerning the phrase "he followeth not us," Elder Bruce R. McConkie wrote: "He was not one of the Twelve to whom the express power had been given to cast out devils (Matthew 10:8); he was not one of the inner circle of disciples who traveled, ate, slept, and communed continually with the Master. Luke has it: 'He followeth not *with* us'; that is, he is not one of our traveling companions. But from our Lord's reply it is evident that he was a member of the kingdom, a legal administrator who was acting in the authority of the priesthood and the power of faith. Either he was unknown to John who therefore erroneously supposed him to be without authority or else John falsely supposed that the power to cast out devils was limited to the Twelve and did not extend to all faithful priesthood holders. It is quite possible that the one casting out devils was a seventy" (*Doctrinal New Testament Commentary*, 1:417).

Mark 9:41 See commentary on Matthew 10:40–42.

Mark 9:49–50 See commentary on Matthew 5:13.

Matthew 18:15–17; Luke 17:3–4 If there is some friction between you and anyone else (be it friend, family member, companion, ward member, or whoever it is), go to that person and resolve the difference between you. You know in this very moment if there is someone with whom you have a strained relationship, against whom you have hard feelings. The law of the gospel requires you to go to that person now and work things out, talk it out, and resolve it. What gets in the way of doing that? Pride, of course. But, you say, it is really *the other person's* fault. You are stubborn, and you are waiting for that person to come to you. Nevertheless, the law of the gospel requires you to humble yourself and go to that person—even if you are the party less responsible for the offense—and ask for forgiveness and resolution of the conflict. Usually (not always, of course, but usually) when a person goes meekly and sincerely to seek forgiveness of another, accepting at least part of the responsibility for the discord, the other person's heart will soften and also admit to some responsibility and will desire to work things out and get rid of the contention. And if the other person does not soften but remains hard and continues to be hostile, at least you have done your part and made things right in your own heart (see further in commentary on Matthew 5:24).

This is the law of the Church governing confession of sin and reconciliation of offenses between members (and it works for others, too). The first step is to talk things out just between the two persons involved. If that does not succeed, the second step is to take the matter before two or three witnesses, brethren who hold the priesthood—an inspired council. If the contention persists and there is no forgiveness and reconciliation, the decision of the council may be to go before the Church. "If any offend openly, he or she shall be rebuked openly, that he or she may be ashamed" (D&C 42:91). As Paul wrote to Timothy, "rebuke before all, that others also may fear" (1 Timothy 5:20). If the counsel of the Church is not accepted, the person may have to be removed from membership (see Matthew 18:17; the whole process is described in D&C 42:88–91).

The old law may have allowed an eye for an eye and a tooth for a tooth, but the higher law—the gospel of Jesus Christ—requires the citizen in the kingdom of God to rise above petty offenses and even rise above deeply damaging and painful abuses, insults, calumnies, character assassinations, or whatever the difficulty may be between two children of God.

Resolve the matter quickly and in a Christlike way. Do what he would do.

SEALING KEYS TO BE USED

Matthew 18:18–20; cf. John 20:23 Whatever decisions are made under the inspired direction of the priesthood, the decisions using priesthood keys will be sealed or bound on earth and in heaven. Compare also Matthew 16:19. Whenever things are done in the Lord's kingdom with agreement, cooperation, and common consent—in the spirit of unity—the Lord promises that he will be in our midst (D&C 29:5; 45:59; 49:27). When we are gathered in his name, under the direction of his Spirit and with his priesthood power, he will be one with us. That is one of his names, Immanuel, "God with us" (see Matthew 28:20; Hebrews 8:10; Alma 56:46; D&C 6:32; 29:5; 32:3, 9; 38:7; 50:44; 61:36; 68:6).

OFFENSES AND FORGIVENESS (CONTINUED); PARABLE: UNMERCIFUL SERVANT

Matthew 18:21–35 The ancient Saints were afflicted and sorely chastened because they did not follow the Lord's counsel to forgive one another *in their hearts* (see D&C 64:8; Mosiah 26:31). The command to forgive others—all others—is specific and unqualified (D&C 64:10). But how often? How many times? Is there a limit to our ability and obligation to forgive? The answer "seventy times seven" (a hyperbolic quantity, meaning indefinitely) is for those who sin against us but repent. And for those who sin against us and refuse to repent, the first three times we are still obligated to forgive, but the fourth time the testimonies against the sinner are to be brought before the Lord. If sincere repentance and restitution ensue, forgiveness is required; but if there is no repentance, the sinner is given over to the judgments of God. All of this additional instruction is given in Doctrine and Covenants 98:39–48, the law of forgiveness.

The story Jesus related to illustrate our responsibility to forgive others is the parable of the unmerciful or unforgiving servant. To make his point, Jesus exaggerated the sums of money involved. Ten thousand talents, which the servant owed the king, was an enormous sum—millions of dollars. "It is hardly conceivable that even a rich individual of the time could have a liquid disposability of 8 talents = 600 pounds of silver = 3.6 million dinarii (keeping in mind that a dinarius was the wage for a day's work in the fields" (Rousseau and Arav, *Jesus and His World*, 59). In comparison, Josephus notes that the entire tribute of Galilee and Perea for 4 B.C. was only two hundred talents and the entire yearly income of Herod the Great was only nine hundred talents (*Antiquities* [Loeb], XVII.318).

The hundred pence which the fellow-servant owed his friend the first servant was a small debt. The striking contrast made the lesson of the parable more impressive. Our Heavenly Father forgives us of heavy burdens of accumulated sins: "The lord of that servant was moved with compassion, and loosed him, and forgave him the debt." Do we, in turn, refuse to forgive others of relatively minor offenses? The Lord asks each of us, "Shouldest not thou also have had compassion on thy fellow-servant, even as I had pity on thee?" Heavenly Father may deliver us to the tormentors, too, and make us pay personally to the very last sin if we cannot find it in our hearts to forgive his other children, our brothers and sisters.

CHAPTER 9

THE PEREAN AND LATER JUDEAN MINISTRY

TIME OF THE FEAST OF TABERNACLES (IN GALILEE)

John 7:2–9 For a brief description of the Feast of Tabernacles, or Succot, the seven-day festival which was one of three great pilgrimage festivals, see Appendix 6, 765. The Greek term here translated "tabernacles" means literally "the pitching of tents," or tabernacles, and the festival commemorates the Israelites' wilderness wanderings in Sinai.

Some of Jesus' siblings (half brothers and sisters who were children of Joseph and Mary) urged him to go into Judea so he could gain wider exposure by displaying his miraculous powers. After all, they said, no miracle-worker who wants to become publicly known does things in secret. Those siblings, John notes, did not believe in him at that time (see also Luke 4:16–30). For all intents and purposes, Jesus belonged to a "part-member family." Jesus responded that the timing was not right for him to go up to Jerusalem—it was not yet time for a "triumphal entry." The world did not hate his siblings, but the world hated him. He remained behind in Galilee while they went up to Jerusalem.

LEAVES GALILEE (LUKE'S "TRAVEL NARRATIVE")

Matthew 19:1; Luke 9:51 Jesus would be leaving Galilee soon, perhaps with some nostalgia. He had resolved to complete his appointed mission, as Luke emphasized. Subsequent verses in the various Gospels report final incidents in Galilee, further experiences in Samaria, and finally arriving in the borders of Perea ("beyond Jordan")—all before actually arriving at the Feast of Tabernacles in Jerusalem.

The "farther side of Jordan" (Mark 10:1) is the same phrase rendered seven other times as "beyond Jordan," meaning "across the Jordan" (*peran tou Jordanou*). The word *peran* is an adverb of place, and its cognate noun *Perea* is known to stand by itself as a regional name, especially in the writings of Josephus. All directions given by Hebrew peoples are given as if they are facing east. Beyond Jordan, then, would be on the eastern side of the river.

MESSENGERS SENT INTO SAMARIA

Luke 9:52–53 Jesus' journey southward could follow one of two routes: down the Jordan Valley and then up through the Judean Desert to Jerusalem, or straight south through the hill-country of Samaria. For his final journey to the Jews' capital city, he chose to go through Samaria.

Earlier in his ministry some Samaritans had happily received Jesus as their Messiah, though then he was journeying away from Jerusalem, northward toward Galilee. Now he was going to conclude his life's mission in Jerusalem, which was a rival religious center to the Samaritans. Because he honored the Jews' holy mountain, Moriah, and not the Samaritans' holy mountain, Gerizim, they resented Jesus and rejected him.

"Because his face was as though he would go to Jerusalem,"

Edersheim noted, "the political enmity and religious separation between the Jews and Samaritans account for their mutual jealousy. On all public occasions the Samaritans took the part hostile to the Jews, while they seized every opportunity of injuring and insulting them . . . they sought to . . . desecrate the Temple on the eve of the Passover; and . . . they waylaid and killed pilgrims on their road to Jerusalem. The Jews retaliated by treating the Samaritans with every mark of contempt; by accusing them of falsehood, folly, and irreligion; and, what they felt most keenly, by disowning them as of the same race or religion, and this in the most offensive terms of assumed superiority and self-righteous fanaticism" (*Jesus the Messiah*, 1:399).

SAMARITAN VILLAGE REJECTS THE APOSTLES (IN SAMARIA)

Luke 9:54–56 Finding among these Samaritans only uninterest and rejection, James and John wanted to call down fire from heaven and consume them, as Elijah had once done (2 Kings 1:9–12). No wonder Jesus had named these two apostles *Boanerges*, "sons of thunder" (Mark 3:17). The Savior's approach was not to react with vengeance but instead try to patiently work with the rebellious and hesitant. These great leaders were still learning the gospel essentials of tolerance, forbearance, and long-suffering. Every effort should be made to save rather than destroy.

THE SEVENTY APPOINTED (LOCATION UNCERTAIN)

Luke 10:1 Elders are standing ministers to the Church; the Seventy are traveling ministers, or missionaries. More missionaries were needed to prepare the way, to lay the groundwork before Jesus' coming to the people. He appointed or set apart, besides the original Twelve, seventy others to go two by two into every town and village. (The number seventy apparently originated with the seventy elders of Israel who ascended Mount Sinai with Moses [Exodus 24:1, 9–10] and who presided over Israel with Moses [Numbers 11:16].) The Seventy are also special witnesses in all the world, commissioned to build up the Church and administer its affairs worldwide (D&C 107:25, 34, 38, 93–96). After the Twelve and the Seventy were called, Jesus spent considerable time and effort to train those who would preside in his Church.

THE SEVENTY CHARGED, SENT (LOCATION UNCERTAIN)

Luke 10:2–12 Because the fields are ripe and the harvest bountiful, many laborers besides the Twelve and the Seventy are needed; see Matthew 9:37–38. The Seventy, just like the Twelve and others, are sent out as lambs among wolves (cf. Matthew 10:16). They did not take purse, nor scrip, nor shoes; see commentary on Matthew 10:8–10. They were not to salute anyone by the way, or in other words, they were not to get sidetracked or distracted by other matters; they were to stay focused on this one assignment and responsibility. "This one thing I do," wrote Paul (Philippians 3:13). When they entered a home, they were to say "Shalom aleichem" ("Peace be unto you"), and if the inhabitants of the home were inclined to accept the Prince of Peace, even greater peace would come to that house. In such a house they could accept food and drink, "for the labourer is worthy of his hire"; see commentary on Matthew 10:8–10. On shaking off the dust of the feet as a witness against those who reject the message, see commentary on Matthew 10:11–15. On the instruction "go not from house to house," note that Joseph Smith's translation of Matthew 6:26 says just the opposite: "*Ye shall* *go forth from house to house, teaching the people; and I will go before you."*

JESUS UPBRAIDS CAPERNAUM, BETHSAIDA, AND CHORAZIN

Matthew 11:20–24; Luke 10:13–16 Chorazin was situated in the hills two miles north of Capernaum in an area covered with black basalt. Bethsaida was near the entrance of the Jordan River to the Sea of Galilee at the northeast corner of the lake. Those two towns and Capernaum were included in the curses pronounced by Jesus. Jesus must have spent enough time in the three towns to feel that the inhabitants had been warned of impending judgments if they did not believe in him and repent of their sins.

We may take the curse of Jesus at face value. Today nothing but piles of rocks and partially restored ruins may be seen at the sites of Chorazin, Bethsaida, and Capernaum. Tiberias, which was not mentioned in the curse, is still a thriving city

Ruins of an ancient Chorazin synagogue, showing black basalt building stone

Ruins of Capernaum, 1893

today. It was in large part a Gentile town; strictly observant Jews did not go there, and there is no indication Jesus taught there.

The unbelief of Chorazin and Bethsaida was compared to that of Tyre and Sidon, where Jesus had also taught. It would be more tolerable for those Gentile cities on the Phoenician coast on Judgment Day than for the Galilean towns that had received the greater witness—more instruction, more miracles, more testimony by far than most other places. And, as Doctrine and Covenants 82:3 warns, "For of him unto whom much is given much is required; and he who sins against the greater light shall receive the greater condemnation."

When condemning his own town of Capernaum, Jesus intensified the curse by comparing it with Sodom. Had the depraved people of Sodom heard and seen the same teachings and miracles that the people of Capernaum heard and saw, they would have repented sufficiently to avert the destruction that engulfed them. It would be less tolerable for the people of Capernaum in the Day of Judgment because they had greater witness of divine things, yet most still rejected Jesus.

The curses pronounced on the ancient Galilean towns may be compared to those pronounced upon cities in the eastern United States in the prophetic future if they rejected the gospel (see D&C 84:114). It is always "more tolerable for the heathen in the day of judgment" (D&C 75:22)—those without the law—than for those to whom the Lord and his servants offer the good news of the kingdom and the blessings of eternity—and they reject them (cf. Alma 9:15).

Luke 10:13 "Sitting in sackcloth and ashes" was a way of showing deep penitence and mourning. Sackcloth was a coarse garment made of gunnysack-like material that was often irritating to the skin and would cause its wearer to experience physical discomfort. Ashes, symbolizing devastation, could be applied to the head to further the scene of lamentation.

Luke 10:16 Jesus said to his disciples that whoever accepted them, accepted him, and whoever rejected them, rejected him. "Whether by mine own voice or by the voice of my servants, it is the same" (D&C 1:38; see also Matthew 10:40; 3 Nephi 28:34).

THE SEVENTY RETURN; AUTHORITY CONFIRMED (LOCATION UNCERTAIN)

Luke 10:17–20 Weeks, even months, may have elapsed since the Seventy were sent out. Their experience taught them, and they were amazed, that with the commission, the authority, and the use of the sacred name of Jesus Christ, they were empowered to hold the minions of Satan in check. Jesus recalled that moment in the great Council in Heaven when Lucifer fell from his honorable place, and now, on earth, the true servants of the Lord Jesus Christ are given power over "serpents and scorpions," the poisonous and dangerous enemies of Christ. As long as the Lord's servants are faithful and worthy, none of the powers of evil can permanently harm them.

Nevertheless, Jesus encouraged them not to get excited about power over the devil (note the counsel in D&C 50:32–33); it is even more important that our names be written in heaven—in the Lamb's Book of Life.

JESUS' PRAYER AND GRATITUDE (IN JUDEA)

Matthew 11:25–26; Luke 10:21 Jesus, always our perfect Exemplar, paused to give thanks and praise to the Father for blessing his servants, holding back glorious truths and experiences from those who thought they were smart and sophisticated and instead giving such knowledge and experience to the weak, simple, and innocent (cf. 2 Nephi 9:42; Alma 32:23; 3 Nephi 26:14, 16). Joseph Smith Translation Luke 10:22 notes that Jesus was grateful that his Father withheld eternal verities "from *them who think they are* wise and prudent" and instead revealed them to humble members of his kingdom.

JESUS' PROMISE OF REST (IN JUDEA)

Matthew 11:27–30; Luke 10:22 The only way to know the Father is to know the Son, and vice versa. Philip asked Jesus to show them the Father, and Jesus said to him, "Have I been so long time with you, and yet hast thou not known me, Philip? He that hath seen me hath seen the Father" (John 14:8–9). Joseph Smith reported after his First Vision that the Father and the Son are "two glorious personages, who exactly resembled each other in features and likeness" (*History of the Church*, 4:536). The Father reveals the Son, and the Son reveals the Father. In character and mission, the Father and the Son are one; they are the same. "And *they* to *whom* the Son will reveal *himself; they shall see the Father also*" (JST Matthew 11:28).

As the Father is approachable, so is the Savior; he is personable. He gently invites: "Come unto me, all ye that labour and are heavy laden [burdened, whether spiritually, physically, mentally, or emotionally] . . . and I will give you rest" (Matthew 11:28; cf. Alma 37:34). His desire and purpose is to save, to rescue, and to relieve. He will relieve us of our heavy burdens. His rest is not merely pause or cessation from work, for his work is eternal, and it will always require effort and labor—but it will not be burdensome or painful or uncomfortable. When we become one with him, of one heart and one mind, his work becomes delightsome, even joyful. His rest is the fulness of his glory (D&C 84:24). With that kind of rest we are lifted up above the cares and burdens of this world to enjoy heavenly views, even while here in mortality. All this happens through our Savior. As Alma exclaimed, "May God grant unto you that your burdens may be light, through the joy of his Son" (Alma 33:23).

"Take my yoke upon you," Jesus said (Matthew 11:29). A yoke was a wooden beam laid across the top of animals'

A yoke

necks and fastened with straps of leather, rope, or iron under their necks. The animals were yoked together to harness their energy and strength and increase their productivity. Though a yoke was, in a sense, a weight or a burden, it was a useful, positive, desirable thing—as is the yoke of submission and obedience to God and its consequent freedom from the burden of sin. "My yoke is easy." The Savior's burden, carrying the responsibility of a covenant person, is certainly easier than carrying the heavy burden of the sinner. "My burden is light." "Light" is the opposite of heavy, and it is the opposite of dark. Those who emulate Christ, who are meek and lowly of heart, discover that the work of God is not so much wearisome as it is joyous to the soul, and their reward is "peace in this life, and eternal life in the world to come" (D&C 59:23). For an example of burdens being lightened, see the account of Alma and his people in Mosiah 24:12–17.

President Gordon B. Hinckley encouraged us:

"We are prone to complain, frequently at home, often in public. Turn your thinking around. The gospel is good news. Man is that he might have joy. Be happy! Let that happiness shine through your faces and speak through your testimonies. You can expect problems. There may be occasional tragedies. But shining through all of this is the plea of the Lord: [Matthew 11:28–30].

"I enjoy these words of Jenkins Lloyd Jones which I clipped from a column in the *Deseret News* some years ago. . . . Said he:

"'Anyone who imagines that bliss is normal is going to waste a lot of time running around shouting that he's been robbed.

"'Most putts don't drop. Most beef is tough. Most children grow up to be just people. Most successful marriages require a high degree of mutual toleration. Most jobs are more often dull than otherwise.

"'Life is like an old time rail journey—delays, sidetracks, smoke, dust, cinders, and jolts, interspersed only occasionally by beautiful vistas and thrilling bursts of speed.

"'The trick is to thank the Lord for letting you have the ride' (*Deseret News,* 12 June 1973)" (*Teachings of Gordon B. Hinckley,* 254).

PARABLE: THE GOOD SAMARITAN (AT JERUSALEM)

Luke 10:25-37 To more fully understand this story of the lawyer, meaning a student of the law (of Moses; see Appendix 4, 746), who tried to embarrass Jesus, we should consider the key Joseph Smith gave to understanding a parable: What was the question that drew out the answer?

The lawyer asked, "Master, what shall I do to inherit eternal life?" (This is the same question that a rich, young ruler later asked him; Luke 18:18.) Jesus answered with another question: "What is written in the law?" The lawyer answered properly, citing the commands to love God and love one's neighbor. Jesus responded that the lawyer's answer was correct and that if the lawyer did all that, he would have eternal life. (Could Jesus' response have been a rebuke?)

Pursuing his argument, the lawyer then asked, "And who is my neighbour?" The ensuing parable answers both questions: "What shall I do to inherit eternal life?" and "Who is my neighbour?"

The parable of the good Samaritan is a story of pride and prejudice, of losing sight of the principles of compassion and charity. One thing it accomplishes is reminding the Jews—who had the law and the commandments—that all are children of the same Heavenly Father and all deserve respect and loving effort to help them back to their heavenly home. Many Judean Jews felt resentment and disdain for Samaritans (John 4:9; 8:48; see Appendix 4, 753). "Samaritan" was a term of derision; in the Jewish mentality of the time, there was no such thing as a *good* Samaritan.

We will examine the parable itself and then the implications and applications.

"A certain man went down from Jerusalem to Jericho" (v. 30).

Without pausing to reflect on the physical setting, many teachers and students of the Bible immediately launch into a philosophical or didactic analysis of the text. In this case, however, as in most of the writings contained in the Bible, an understood geographical setting underlies the story and events in it. This account is true to all social, historical, and geographical details from the beginning. Note that the man had to walk "*down* from Jerusalem to Jericho." Jerusalem is about two thousand five hundred feet above sea level, and Jericho, at 825 feet below sea level, is the lowest town on the earth (see Bible Map 14).

The road from Jerusalem to Jericho traverses wadis (dry river beds) and hills that served as hideouts for those who preyed on solitary travelers. Thus, the road was referred to as "Ma'ale Adumim" (the "bloody path," or the "red way").

The story refers to Levites and priests along the Jericho Road. Excavators of Roman-period Jericho have uncovered many houses belonging to priests who would have worked in the Jerusalem Temple. "Jericho, the garden city, which during the days of the Second Temple extended over thousands of dunams [hundreds of acres] and was inhabited by tens of thousands of Jews, many of them priests, probably shrank after

BYU–Jerusalem Center students walk the route of the Roman road from Jerusalem down to Jericho

[the year A.D.] 70" (Netzer, *Bulletin of the American Schools of Oriental Research*, 228 [1977]:12).

Did the Levite and the priest never hear about mercy, compassion, and caring as part of their learning of the law? Indeed, wasn't "love thy neighbour as thyself" part of the old law? (Leviticus 19:18). What's more, Levites were charged specifically to help sojourners along their way financially (Leviticus 25:35–36). The Joseph Smith Translation gives us an insight into the behavior of the priest and the Levite: both "passed by on the other side *of the way; for they desired in their hearts that it might not be known that they had seen him*" (JST Luke 10:33). It is a rebuke of Jesus' own people that the one who sees the half-dead Jew and does all he can to save him is a man raised outside the covenant, whereas the priest and Levite were going to or from the Temple. The Samaritan bound up the wounds of the assaulted Jew, "pouring in oil and wine" (v. 34), which were believed to have curative and antiseptic properties. The Samaritan set the Jew "on his own beast, and brought him to an inn, and took care of him" (v. 34). He didn't just give him a ride and drop him off to someone else's care; he stayed and cared for him. When he had to continue his journey, he paid for ongoing care.

The answer to the question of who was the loving neighbor was obvious, and the injunction was plain and simple: "Go, and do thou likewise" (v. 37). Jesus is our Exemplar. He said, "I have given you an example, that ye should do as I have done to you" (John 13:15). And he said, "Love your neighbor." Who were *Jesus'* neighbors? A woman at a well in Samaria, a crippled man at the Pool of Bethesda, a blind man at the Pool of Siloam, Peter's mother-in-law, a widow in Nain, a Greek woman in Tyre or Sidon, ten lepers in Samaria, a tax collector in Jericho, a man with a withered hand in Capernaum, and a friend in Bethany who died but was raised again.

In contrast, one school of rabbinic thought believed that the term "neighbor" applied only to Jews. "We are not to contrive the death of Gentiles, but if they are in any danger of death we are not bound to deliver them, e.g. if any of them fall into the sea you need not take him out, for such a one is not thy neighbour" (Dummelow, *Commentary*, 751). Jesus answered this question and gave the guideline or standard for true Christian behavior.

And to us in modern times? We may follow his instruction and example to inherit eternal life. Latter-day Saints are committed to stop and help in the same circumstances, but the circumstances are never exactly the same. We are never on our way down from Jerusalem to Jericho and see a wounded, half-dead Jew beaten up alongside the road. We do see bruised and wounded souls all around us, however. Opportunities to stop and help persons who are afflicted in not only physical but also spiritual and emotional ways are numerous. The problem is, it is never convenient. And when we do take the time to stop and help, there is no guarantee of a positive experience. It may be very unpleasant and even risky to get involved with those around us who are beaten up. Our excuses? We are in a hurry; we are scared; we are tired. Like the Levite or priest in the parable, we are on our way home from the Temple. At times some Latter-day Saints, like some Levites and priests of old, may be too busy to live the law of God. Excuses are plentiful. What if Jesus had made excuses? What if he had said that for some reason he was really tired, so he wouldn't give the Sermon on the Mount? Or too busy to restore the blind man's sight? Or late for the next speaking appointment, so he couldn't stop to heal someone right then?

The fact of modern life is that we are all busy. The need to stop and serve another person seldom fits our schedule; it is hardly ever convenient to set aside our own concerns and pay attention to the needs of a wounded person. But if we open up our heart and our schedule to love our neighbor—even those who are lost, hurt, angry, pessimistic, or discouraged—we are on our way to inheriting eternal life, which is all about serving and saving souls, forever.

Mary and Martha, *by Del Parson*

MARY, MARTHA: ONE THING NEEDFUL (IN BETHANY)

Luke 10:38–42 This passage points to the fact that Luke, the writer, is recalling an incident in Jesus' life from a distance. "A certain village," "a certain woman named Martha," who "had a sister called Mary," all indicate that Luke was looking back on a place and a people with whom he, unlike Matthew and John (and possibly Mark), was not personally acquainted.

The incident in the sisters' home in Bethany teaches a lesson. Jesus did not criticize or condemn Martha's concerns about physical comfort and food preparations. Such efforts are always appreciated. (Martha apparently owned the home and felt more urgency in providing the accustomed hospitality for their Guest; see v. 38 and JST John 11:2, 17.) Nevertheless, Jesus did not desire to interrupt Mary's rapt attention to his teachings. Both women were demonstrating their devotion to Jesus in the way perhaps most natural to them. However, note Jesus' instructive comment: "One thing is needful: and Mary hath chosen that good part." Sometimes it is important to be less preoccupied with temporal things and more concerned about spiritual things.

Gerald Lund, in his trilogy, *The Kingdom and the Crown* (2:397–409), powerfully illustrates through his characterization of the scriptural personalities that day in Bethany, that of the two great commandments, Mary was showing her love for God and Martha was showing her love for neighbor.

FRIEND AT MIDNIGHT (IN JUDEA)

Luke 11:1, 5–8 The disciples asked Jesus how to pray. He not only gave them a model prayer but taught them through a parable to seek God—as the friend at midnight—with "importunity." The active verb *importune* means "to request with urgency; to press with solicitation; to urge with frequent or unceasing application" (*1828 Webster's Dictionary*). Jesus' story relates how a guest dropped in on a man in the middle of the night, and the man, realizing he had no food to offer his guest at that hour, attempted to wake up his sleeping neighbor to borrow three loaves of bread. The neighbor, though a friend, was reluctant to arise at that hour but finally—because of persistent knocking—got up to answer the need. (All parables have their limitations; it is not wise to push the analogy too far—God is not a sleepy neighbor who is hesitant to answer our petitions at certain hours.) The point of the parable is the importance of importuning—persisting in imploring for what we want from God. The parable is followed by the frequent injunction: "Knock, and it shall be opened unto you . . . ; and to him that knocketh it shall be opened" (vv. 9–10). God wants us to pray, plead, implore, and *importune*—specifically, frequently, and sincerely. He wants us to ask, to plead with him in humility for what we need.

The parable of the friend at midnight actually begins, in the Joseph Smith Translation, with a simple but powerful promise: "*Your heavenly Father will not fail to give unto you whatsoever ye ask of him*" (JST Luke 11:5). The message is, Don't give up or despair; keep asking. In this case the repetition is not "vain repetition." As the Prophet Joseph Smith said, "Come to God [and] weary him until he blesses you" (*Words of Joseph Smith*, 15).

HEAR, KEEP THE WORD (IN JUDEA)

Luke 11:27–28 While Jesus was teaching, a woman cried out, in essence, Blessed is the womb from which you came, and blessed are the breasts from which you fed! Jesus turned the exclamation into a teaching moment: more "blessed are they that hear the word of God, and keep it." Our focus must always be on God, our Eternal Father, and his Son, our Savior, and not on any human being—which constitutes pointed counsel not to worship Mary.

COVETOUSNESS (IN JUDEA)

Luke 12:13–21 A man apparently wanted Jesus to get involved in some dispute between him and his brother over their inheritance. Though Jesus reminded the man that he was not in a legal position to advise him on the matter, He used the situation to teach against covetousness, excessive desire for temporal possessions, having our hearts set so much on the things of this world, "for a man's life consisteth not in the abundance of the things which he possesseth" (v. 15). A story illustrates the teaching. A rich man had productive land, so he concluded that he needed bigger barns for the plentiful fruits and produce. Then feeling secure in his prosperity and self-sufficiency, he decided to relax, take it easy, celebrate, and throw a party. But God dropped a most thought-provoking question on the foolish rich man: What if you were to die this very night, "then whose shall those things be, which thou hast provided?" (v. 20). Then the point of the parable: "So is he that layeth up treasure for himself, and is not rich toward God" (v. 21). Temporal things are temporary and transitory. As the psalmist wrote, "When he dieth he shall carry nothing away: [the riches] shall not descend after him" (Psalm 49:16–17)—note the word *descend*. Jesus had earlier counseled:

"Lay not up for yourselves treasures upon earth, where moth and rust doth corrupt, and where thieves break through and steal:

"But lay up for yourselves treasures in heaven, where neither moth nor rust doth corrupt, and where thieves do not break through nor steal:

"For where your treasure is, there will your heart be also" (Matthew 6:19–21).

A penetrating modern story told by President Spencer W. Kimball is quite parallel to Jesus' parable:

"One day a friend wanted me to go with him to his ranch. He opened the door of a new automobile, slid under the wheel, and said, 'How do you like my new car?' We rode in luxurious air-conditioned comfort out through the countryside to an elegant landscaped home, and he said with no little pride, 'This is my home.'

"He drove on to a grassy knoll. The sun was setting behind the distant hills. Pointing to the north, he asked, 'Do you see that clump of trees?' I could plainly discern them in the fading day.

"He pointed to the east, 'Do you see the lake?' It too was visible shimmering in the sunset.

"'Now, the bluff that's on the south.' We turned about to scan the distance southward. Then he pointed out the barns, silos, the ranch house to the west. With a wide sweeping gesture, he boasted, 'From the clump of trees, to the lake, to the bluff, and to the ranch buildings and all in between—all this is mine. And the herd of cattle in the meadow—those are mine, too.'

"I knew this was a man with great ability as an organizer, intelligent and resourceful, yet he lived in many ways a narrow life. His possessions seemed to own him. He turned away opportunities to serve in the Church because his ranch kept him 'too busy,' and he contributed little financially because he was always 'short of cash because everything is tied up in the ranch.'

"I could not help thinking of one of the parables of Christ: . . . (Luke 12:16–21). . . .

"My friend was proud that he had developed his ranch from the desert with his own strength and toil, but where had he obtained that strength and where had he obtained the land and the water with which to make it productive, if not from the Lord? . . .

"If the earth is the Lord's, then we are merely tenants and owe our landlord an accounting. . . .

"There is no place in holy writ where God has said, 'I give you title to this land unconditionally.' It is not ours to give, to have, to hold, to sell, despoil, exploit as we see fit.

"Modern scripture says that if you live the commandments, *'the fulness of the earth is yours, the beasts of the field and the fowls of the air* . . .

"'*Yea, all things which come of the earth . . . are made for the benefit and the use of man. . . .*' (D&C 59:16, 18.)

"This promise does not seem to convey the earth but only the use and contents that are given to men on condition that they live all of the commandments of God.

"That was long years ago. I later saw my friend lying in death among luxurious furnishings in his palatial home. And I folded his arms upon his breast and drew down the little curtains over his eyes. I spoke at his funeral, and I followed the cortege from the good piece of earth he had claimed to his grave, a tiny, oblong area the length of a tall man, the width of a heavy one.

"Recently I saw that same estate, yellow in grain, green in lucerne, white in cotton, seemingly unmindful of him who had claimed it.

"Oh, puny man, thou art the busy ant moving the sands of the sea" (*Faith Precedes the Miracle*, 281–84).

REPENTANCE (IN JUDEA)

Luke 13:1–5 Jesus used current events to teach that calamities were not necessarily a sign of sin (cf. Alma 60:12). Some Galileans had been killed, apparently during riots on the Temple Mount (v. 1), and eighteen Jerusalemites had been killed in an accident at Siloam (v. 4; in the southern part of the original, Old Testament-period Jerusalem, the City of David). Were they particularly evil people or the vilest sinners among their peers? Is that why they suffered such a fate, because they deserved it above all others? No, Jesus advised them. All are sinners, and all must repent or perish. God is no respecter of persons; all are accountable before him and must resolve unrighteousness and evil inclination or suffer the awful consequences. "Every man must repent or suffer" (D&C 19:4).

WOMAN HEALED ON THE SABBATH (IN PEREA)

Luke 13:10–17 A woman endured some kind of crippling deformity for eighteen years, partly because of a physiological ailment but also, as Luke (a physician; Colossians 4:14) reports, because she was bound by Satan. Jesus loosed her from that bondage, but because he did it on the Sabbath day, he was chastised by the ruler of the synagogue where the miracle was done. The ruler cited the fourth of the Ten Commandments—that there were six other days to do such things but that the work of healing was certainly inappropriate for the holy Sabbath. Jesus, who knew perfectly well the old laws (which he had given), reminded the hypocritical religious leader that the law also provided for the needs of the ox and ass to be loosed from their stalls and led to the watering trough, even on the Sabbath. Was this daughter of Abraham not more important than an ox or an ass, deserving that her dire need be met, even on the Sabbath—or especially on the Sabbath, a time to do good, relieving the burden of one of God's children? Jesus' adversaries slunk away, ashamed because of the narrowness of their legalistic view of the old law, which law also encouraged works of compassion and charity—anytime.

TOWARD JERUSALEM (IN PEREA)

Luke 13:22 Jesus continued inexorably toward his place of sacrifice but did not disregard the spiritual needs of the people en route. He stopped and taught in the towns, great and small.

"TELL THAT FOX" (IN PEREA)

Luke 13:31–33 It is rare in the recorded words of Jesus that he ever applied an epithet, a negative label, to any individual. According to this passage in Luke, he called Herod Antipas, the tetrarch of Galilee and Perea, the one who beheaded John the Baptist, "that fox." Later, Herod would be the only person in Jesus' recorded life to speak directly to the Master but hear nothing in reply. Jesus showed real and deep contempt for Herod. (The fox in Old Testament and

Greek literature represented cunning, craftiness, and destructiveness. In rabbinic literature, the fox stood for the ignominious or contemptuous.) In the Joseph Smith Translation of the same passage, however, the epithet was omitted.

Certain Pharisees had come warning Jesus to leave Antipas's territory because Herod would try to kill him. Jesus' response to the Pharisees clearly signaled his unconcern for Herod's intentions, because Herod could not interrupt his work. He would finish his work in Perea and then journey on to Jerusalem, "for it cannot be that a prophet perish out of Jerusalem."

The Joseph Smith Translation adds: "*This he spake, signifying of his death. And in this very hour he began to weep over Jerusalem*" (JST Luke 13:34). The phrase "and the third day I shall be perfected" (v. 32) foreshadows Jesus' resurrection after his death.

COUNTING THE COST (IN PEREA)

Luke 14:28–33 If someone is going to build something, it is always wise to sit down and calculate the cost and make plans and preparations for successful completion of the work. If someone is going to build his or her life on Christ, there is a price to pay. True discipleship does not consist of merely being baptized—laying the foundation—but building up a holy temple unto the Lord, living the consecrated life, and enduring to the end. It is not enough to begin the journey; one must keep going. "*And this he said,*" the Joseph Smith Translation adds, "*signifying there should not any man follow him, unless he was able to continue*" (JST Luke 14:31). President John Taylor said, "When I first entered upon Mormonism, I did it with my eyes open. I counted the cost. I looked upon it as a life-long labor, and I considered that I was not only enlisted for time, but for eternity also, and did not wish to shrink now, although I felt my incompetency" (Roberts, *Life of John Taylor*, 48).

Jesus' other example was counting the cost of going to war. The new convert does well to consider seriously, before his or her baptism and committing to the kingdom, what it is going to cost to fight the good fight, to take on the forces of evil and do battle for the souls of men—before making the decision. Before making the commitment (or using the more sacred term, before making the *covenant*), the true disciple will determine to be willing to forsake or sacrifice all for the greatest cause on earth. Our English word *sacrifice* derives from a combination of two Latin words, *sacer* ("sacred") and *facere* ("to make"), thus meaning "to make sacred."

Joseph Smith taught: "A religion that does not require the sacrifice of all things never has power sufficient to produce the faith necessary unto life and salvation. . . . The faith necessary unto the enjoyment of life and salvation never could be obtained without the sacrifice of all earthly things" (*Lectures on Faith*, 6:7). The Prophet spoke of the need to sacrifice all earthly things, which produces in us power or faith that carries us on toward exaltation. Abraham did that. He left everything he had ever known and journeyed to an unknown land because he wanted more happiness, peace, rest, and blessings. He tells us that he had been a follower of righteousness and had gained knowledge, but he wanted to be a *greater* follower of righteousness and he wanted to gain *greater* knowledge—Temple knowledge (Abraham 1:1–2).

Abraham was an example of counting the cost and making the sacrifice. So were the apostles: "They forsook all, and followed him" (Luke 5:11; see also 5:28). One Book of Mormon writer counseled: "I would that ye should come unto Christ . . . and partake of his salvation, and the power of his redemption. Yea, come unto him, and *offer your whole souls as an offering unto him,* and continue in fasting and praying, and endure to the end; and as the Lord liveth ye will be saved" (Omni 1:26; emphasis added). The Savior teaches the same principle in modern revelation, in Doctrine and Covenants 103:27–28.

President Gordon B. Hinckley illustrated the Savior's teaching:

"I think of a friend whom I knew when I was a missionary in London many years ago. He came to our door through the rain one night. I answered his knock and invited him in.

"He said, as I remember, 'I have to talk to someone. I'm all alone.'

"I asked what the problem was.

"He said, 'When I joined the Church, my father told me to get out of his house and never come back. A few months later my athletic club dropped me from membership. Last month my boss fired me because I am a member of this Church. And last night the girl I love said she would never marry me because I'm a Mormon.'

"I said, 'If this has cost you so much, why don't you leave the Church and go back to your father's home, to your club, to the job that meant so much to you, and marry the girl you think you love?'

"He said nothing for what seemed a long time. Then, putting his head in his hands, he sobbed as if his heart would break. Finally he looked up through his tears and said, 'I couldn't do that. I know this is true, and if it were to cost me my life, I could not give it up'" (*Ensign*, September 2001, 4).

PARABLE: THE UNJUST STEWARD (IN PEREA)

Luke 16:1–8 A certain rich man had a steward, one who was accountable to care for the rich man's properties and possessions. Accused of squandering the owner's goods, the steward could see that his stewardship was in jeopardy, so he prudently went about recovering whatever he could from his master's debtors. The lord of the steward commended him for at least partly redeeming himself, and the Lord of us all concluded, for our profit and learning, that "the children of this world [those who are not members of the kingdom of God] are in their generation wiser than the children of light [members of the kingdom]" (v. 8). In some ways, we can take a lesson even from business practices of the worldly. In the first place, all of us as children of God will be held responsible for the stewardships we are given in this life. Second, the Lord expects us not to waste the goods we are given and for which we are responsible, although we are all sinners and we are all wasteful to some degree with our stewardship. We must be prudent and zealous about doing whatever we can to recover or preserve the goods with which we have been entrusted.

Elder James E. Talmage described how the Lord used this parable "to show the contrast between the care, thoughtfulness, and devotion of men engaged in the money-making affairs of earth, and the half hearted ways of many who are professedly striving after spiritual riches." The Lord was not encouraging the righteous to emulate any wicked practices of the unjust steward but urging us to go after our spiritual goals with the same enthusiasm and effort that the steward showed in pursuing his monetary goals.

Elder Talmage observed that "worldly-minded men do not neglect provision for their future years, and often are sinfully eager to amass plenty; while the 'children of light,' or those who believe spiritual wealth to be above all earthly possessions, are less energetic, prudent, or wise" (*Jesus the Christ*, 431).

PARABLE: LAZARUS AND THE RICH MAN (IN PEREA)

Luke 16:14–31 Jesus had taught that it is not possible to serve God and mammon (worldly interests, particularly money; Luke 16:13). The Pharisees, ever ready to illuminate their own righteousness, were among those Jesus addressed, and they were guilty of coveting mammon. Being guilt-ridden, they began deriding the Lord. But he exposed them directly: "Ye are they which justify yourselves before men; but God knoweth your hearts: for that which is highly esteemed among men is abomination in the sight of God." The Pharisees continued to justify themselves:

"*We have the law, and the prophets; but as for this man we will not receive him to be our ruler; for he maketh himself to be a judge over us.*

"*Then said Jesus unto them,* The law and the prophets *testify of me; yea, and all the prophets who have written, even* until John, *have foretold of these days.*

"Since that time, the kingdom of God is preached, and every man *who seeketh truth* presseth into it.

"And it is easier for heaven and earth to pass, than for one tittle of the law to fail.

"*And why teach ye the law, and deny that which is written; and condemn him whom the Father hath sent to fulfil the law, that ye might all be redeemed?*

"*O fools! for you have said in your hearts, There is no God. And you pervert the right way; and the kingdom of heaven suffereth violence of you; and you persecute the meek; and in your violence you seek to destroy the kingdom; and ye take the children of the kingdom by force. Woe unto you, ye adulterers!*

"*And they reviled him again, being angry for the saying, that they were adulterers.*

"*But he continued, saying,* Whosoever putteth away his wife, and marrieth another, committeth adultery; and whosoever marrieth her who is put away from her husband, committeth adultery. *Verily I say unto you, I will liken you unto the rich man*" (JST Luke 16:16–23).

So the Pharisees were now implicated and indicted—and became subjects of the parable that followed.

A certain rich man was clothed in purple and fine linen, "and fared sumptuously" (v. 19). Israelites, as well as other societies of the ancient Near East, prized the color dyes—blue, scarlet, and purple in particular. As with other elements and composites in nature that are comparatively rare, such as gold

The Perean and Later Judean Ministry

and diamonds, the dyes were treasured because of their limited quantity. Purple was extracted by the Phoenicians, especially Tyrians, from the Murex snails that thrive along the northeastern Mediterranean coast, and was used in dyeing textiles.

Compared to the rich man who lived sumptuously, a certain beggar lived in the extreme opposite conditions: he was laid at the rich man's gate, hoping to be fed with the crumbs that fell from the rich man's table. He was full of open sores, and the dogs came and licked them. The beggar's name was Lazarus. (*Lazarus* is the Greek form of Hebrew *Eleazer* or *Elazar*, "God is my help.") This is the only parable Jesus gave with a named character—for what reason we are not explicitly told. It is possible, however, that both the name of the protagonist and the circumstances of the parable were suggested by Jesus' real-life friend Lazarus (John 11:1–5). In fact, it is also quite possible that the story line of the parable itself was suggested by Jesus' foreknowledge of Lazarus's illness and how that illness would result in Lazarus's death and return to mortal life (John 11:6–46).

Reasons for believing that the parable and the episode of Lazarus being raised from the dead are connected center on several factors: the similarity between the story line and actual events; the unique usage of a named character in this parable, which happens to be Lazarus (too close for coincidence); the righteousness of Lazarus in the parable compared to the implied righteousness of Lazarus in real life; and geographical location. This parable was given in Perea, where Jesus was when he first learned of Lazarus' illness. Jesus waited two days before returning to Judea to perform the miracle of bringing his close friend back to mortality. It makes sense that Jesus would take time to teach his disciples about conditions in the spirit world because Lazarus had just gone there. It is also interesting to note that after Jesus raised Lazarus, the Pharisees (whom Jesus had rebuked before giving the parable) started then to plot Jesus' demise as well as Lazarus's murder (John 11:46–12:11).

Jesus continued on to the point of the story. The beggar

died and was carried by angels, or messengers, into Abraham's bosom—meaning paradise in the spirit world. The rich man also died. In hell—the spirit prison—the formerly rich man was tormented by the perfect recollection of all his actions and attitudes during mortality. Meanwhile he saw Abraham and Lazarus in paradise and cried out to Father Abraham to send Lazarus to cool the burning torment he was feeling. Abraham reminded the man who had luxuriated for a time in the good things of the former world that he would now have to suffer for a time in consequence of that behavior and those decisions.

All the inequities and unfairness of this life will be made up to the righteous in the next life. Justice actually becomes the friend of those who rely on the Atonement. As Abraham says to the rich man in the parable, the injustices of mortality are overturned: "Remember that thou in thy lifetime receivedst *thy* good things [not God's good things] and likewise Lazarus evil things: but *now* he is comforted, and thou are tormented" (Luke 16:25; emphasis added).

Abraham further explained that there is a "great gulf" (Greek, *chasma;* English, *chasm*)—some kind of physical or spiritual barrier—that separates residents of paradise and prison (cf. 1 Nephi 12:18; 15:28–30; 2 Nephi 1:13; Alma 26:20; Helaman 3:29). Passage back and forth was not possible.

The formerly rich man asked that some messenger be sent to his relatives still in mortality and warn them of what awaits them. Abraham reminded him that they had been warned, for they had had a host of messengers who gave clear warnings— from Moses to Malachi and now John the Baptist and Jesus and the apostles and the seventy—all sent out to warn mortals of impending rewards for righteousness and torments for wickedness.

But the once rich man argued that certainly his family would be convinced and repent if someone appeared to them from among the dead, from the spirit world.

Again his request was denied. Father Abraham replied, "If they hear not Moses and the prophets, neither will they be persuaded, though one rose from the dead" (v. 31). Contrary to popular belief, seeing is not necessarily believing. Laman and Lemuel are a classic example of that truth. Angels appeared to them, corrected them, and exhorted them, but such appearances did not change their hearts, and they did not change their attitudes and behavior.

Actually, the man in the parable who was now suffering the torments of hell was asking for a sign for his relatives. But faith, and corresponding changes in behavior, do not come from signs (D&C 63:9–11). People who refuse to hear and follow the words of the Lord are not going to be persuaded (v. 31; cf. Helaman 13:26), even if someone appeared to them from beyond the veil. They might be impressed, yes, but persuaded to change and repent and reform, no (D&C 133:71–72).

PARABLE: UNPROFITABLE SERVANTS (LOCATION UNCERTAIN)

Luke 17:7–10 Jesus spoke of servants out in the fields "plowing or feeding cattle." In this phrase, we have reference once again to the two main occupations of ancient Israel: agriculture and herding, or shepherding. The "cattle" spoken of in this passage are "small cattle," or domesticated animals— that is, sheep and goats. The Greek verb *poimaino* means "to herd, tend, or lead sheep and goats to pasture." The servant, when he has finished tending the flock, as is expected of him, does not immediately come in, relax, and anticipate expressions of gratitude and praise for having done his regular duty; he is still in his master's debt. So we, servants of our Heavenly Father and our Savior, should not perform our expected duties and anticipate applause and commendation to be heaped upon us; we are still unprofitable servants. We can never put the Father and the Son in our debt. That is the basic message of one part of King Benjamin's discourse:

"I say unto you that if ye should serve him who has

created you from the beginning, and is preserving you from day to day, by lending you breath, that ye may live and move and do according to your own will, and even supporting you from one moment to another—I say, if ye should serve him with all your whole souls yet ye would be unprofitable servants" (Mosiah 2:21).

When we are obedient to God's commandments we are inevitably rewarded, but even doing all we can do, we are still eternally indebted to him.

TEN LEPERS HEALED (LOCATION UNCERTAIN)

Luke 17:11–19 Journeying toward Jerusalem in Judea, a hundred miles to the south, Jesus could walk through Samaria and Galilee—but not in that order. The Joseph Smith Translation changes verse 11 to read, properly, that he passed through Galilee and Samaria. Apparently in or near one village of Samaria he encountered ten lepers, who cried out for divine help. The Savior instructed them simply to show themselves to the priests, a requirement in the process of discerning and controlling leprosy under the old Mosaic law (Leviticus 13:49).

Sometimes miraculous blessings come to those who simply follow instructions and keep a commandment. As they were obedient they were healed. One of the ten returned to give thanks, and he was a Samaritan. By speaking to a Samaritan woman at Jacob's Well, relating a story about a good Samaritan man who helped a Jewish man attacked and left for dead, and now identifying as a Samaritan the one of ten who returned to express gratitude for the dramatic healing on his behalf, Jesus once again signaled his refusal to succumb to local prejudice, showing acceptance of all people as children of the Father in Heaven. The *Samaritan* came back to Jesus to pour out his soul in gratitude to him who made his decaying flesh whole. All ten were obedient, and all ten received an immediate and extraordinary blessing for their obedience, but one wanted both to obey and to give thanks. This one leper was reminded that Jesus Christ had indeed cleansed him, but it was also the Samaritan's faith in Jesus Christ that made him whole.

PARABLE: THE UNJUST JUDGE (LOCATION UNCERTAIN)

Luke 18:1–8 The issue that drew this parable from the Lord is stated in verse 1: "that men ought always to pray, and not to faint" (not to faint means not to give up, not to despair). The story is sometimes entitled the parable of the importunate widow. The parable teaches the same lesson as the parable of the friend at midnight: perseverance and persistence in prayer (see commentary on Luke 11:1, 5–8). Keep on imploring and importuning the throne of God, and he will eventually answer. Sometimes God insists that we keep importuning because he knows we are not ready for the requested answer or blessing—at least, *not yet*. We keep asking not until he is ready but until we are ready.

God does hear the cries of his disciples, and he does eventually avenge the wrongs committed against them. The Joseph Smith Translation of Luke 18:8 begins: "I tell you that *he will come, and when he does come,* he will avenge *his Saints speedily.*"

A modern application of this parable is given by the Lord in Doctrine and Covenants 101:81–92.

JESUS ATTENDS FEAST OF TABERNACLES (IN JERUSALEM)

John 7:10–13 From the verses immediately preceding John 7:10, one might suppose that Jesus' family members went up to Jerusalem to the great pilgrimage festival in the fall, the Feast of Tabernacles (see Appendix 6, 765) and that

Jesus went up soon thereafter. But if our harmonized chronology is correct, as evidenced by the many events detailed in this commentary since John 7:8–9, he did considerable traveling, teaching, and healing before actually going up to the feast in Jerusalem (see commentary on Matthew 19:1; Luke 9:51).

Jesus deemed it wise to arrive quietly, even secretly, in Jerusalem, but when the crowds learned of his coming, intense discussion arose amid a polarization of opinions—some defending him and others opposing. No one among the Jews wanted to speak openly of him for fear of their leaders.

THE DOCTRINE OF THE FATHER (AT THE TEMPLE IN JERUSALEM)

John 7:14–36 Jesus went up to his House to teach. He went *up*, literally. From any direction one would go up to the Temple Mount, and from anywhere on the Mount one would go up into the Temple (see Appendix 3, 744).

The Jews who heard him marveled at his teaching and wondered where he had received his training; he had not learned under their curriculum; he was not a graduate of their academies; he did not cite rabbinic precedent.

The conversation between the Master and his antagonists might be paraphrased as follows:

Jesus: My doctrine is not mine; it is the doctrine of the Father—the One who sent me. And if any one of you will live this doctrine you will know if it is just I who is talking or if it really comes from God. Do it, and you will know. Whoever speaks of himself is trying to build up himself, but the true teacher is one who builds up the Father, to give him the credit and glorify him. There is no unrighteousness in that teacher. Moses gave you the law, but none of you is living it.

Abruptly, he asked the startling question: Why are you trying to kill me?

Antagonist: You must be possessed by an evil spirit; who is trying to kill you?

Jesus: I did one work (healing a man on the Sabbath), and you accuse me of breaking the Law. Moses gave circumcision as part of the Law [circumcision was instituted as a sign of the covenant long before Moses; see Appendix 7, 773], and you allow a man to be circumcised even on the Sabbath. Are you angry at me, then, because I completely healed a man on the Sabbath? Do not judge according to your traditions [JST John 7:24] but judge righteously.

Rabbinic sources themselves paralleled and wholeheartedly supported Jesus' actions and teachings about the Sabbath. Certain righteous actions superseded the prescriptions of the Sabbath (as attested in the Mishnah, Yoma 85b).

Some in the crowds were confused: Isn't this the man the rulers wanted? He is speaking boldly, and no one is saying anything. Do the rulers believe he is the Messiah now? We know where this man is from, but no one will know where the Messiah comes from. [They had been wrongly taught.]

Jesus: You know me, and you know where I am from. I know the Father in Heaven, and he sent me to you.

Considering that kind of talk blasphemous, some wanted to take him, but no one dared touch him. The time for his death was not yet.

But many who heard Jesus believed in him: When the Messiah comes, is he going to do any more miracles than this man is doing?

Pharisees got word of what was happening and sent Temple police to take Jesus (see Appendix 4, 756), who explained that he would be there a little longer with them and then was going back to his Father—the One who sent him—and where he would be, they could not come.

They reacted: Where is he going that we will not find him? Is he going to teach the Jews out in the Diaspora, or teach the Gentiles themselves? Why would he say, You will seek me but not find me, and where I will be you cannot come?

Jesus said (in modern revelation): "Where I am they [meaning those who reject their Savior] cannot come, for they have no power" (D&C 29:29)—no saving knowledge and ordinances, no righteousness, no worthiness.

THE SPIRIT PROMISED AFTER JESUS' MINISTRY (AT THE TEMPLE IN JERUSALEM)

John 7:37–53 At the Feast of Tabernacles, after half a year with no rain, the Jews would pray for moisture. It was customary to make a procession with a golden pitcher of water from the Pool of Siloam to pour onto the Temple altar, in direct fulfillment of Isaiah 12:3: "Therefore with joy shall ye draw water out of the wells of salvation" (see Talmage, *Jesus the Christ*, 403). Pouring out the water in the holy place was "symbolical of the outpouring of the Holy Spirit" (Edersheim, *Jesus the Messiah*, 2:150). This ritual, the "Drawing of the Water Ceremony," was performed each day of the feast except the last day, the great day of the feast (Bruce, *New Testament History*, 140). At that point Jesus stood forth and, carrying on the symbolism, invited all who were thirsty to come unto him and drink and enjoy living water. Now he taught his own people the same truths he had previously taught a Samaritan woman at Jacob's Well (see commentary on John 4:5–6 and John 4:13–15).

One can imagine the surprise on the part of some as Jesus not only broke with tradition in continuing this ceremony on the last and greatest day of the feast but as he also made himself the center and object of the ceremony and said, in this new and shocking way, that he was God! "He that believeth on *me*, as the scripture hath said, out of his belly shall flow rivers of *living water*" (John 7:38; emphasis added).

Water is life in that part of the world, and Jesus is the source of life to all parts of the world (see commentary on Matthew 15:39–16:4). Living or flowing water was available to all who would hear and hearken, but when he left the earth, the gift of the Holy Ghost would be available to all who would continue in him, "for the Holy Ghost *was promised unto them who believe, after that Jesus was* glorified" (JST John 7:39).

John 7:40–44 Many of the people were impressed, but there was quite a difference of opinion as to the identity of Jesus. Some concluded that he was the prophet of whom Moses had prophesied (Deuteronomy 18:15, 18; 1 Nephi 22:20; John 1:19–28); others, that he was the Christ, the Messiah. But some raised the question, Can the Messiah come out of Galilee when his prophesied birthplace is Bethlehem of Judah? (They were apparently unaware that he had been born in Bethlehem of Judah/Judea.) And were they overlooking the prophecy that he would also be called a Nazarene? (cf. Matthew 2:23).

From this point on, the divisions (v. 43) would intensify, and John records many of them (see 7:12, 43; 8:33–59; 9:16; 10:19).

John 7:45–49 Temple police or officials (see Appendix 4, 756) had been sent to apprehend Jesus, but on listening to him teach they were enthralled and overwhelmed by his manner of speaking and his message—and apparently touched by the Spirit.

A modern parallel to this episode is recorded about the missionary efforts of Elder Wilford Woodruff in England:

"When I arose to speak at Brother Benbow's house, a man entered the door and informed me that he was a constable, and had been sent by the rector of the parish with a warrant to arrest me. I asked him, 'For what crime?' He said, 'For preaching to the people.' I told him that I, as well as the rector, had a license for preaching the gospel to the people, and that if he would take a chair I would wait upon him after meeting. He took my chair and sat beside me. For an hour and a quarter I preached the first principles of the everlasting gospel. The power of God rested upon me, the spirit filled the house, and the people were convinced. At the close of the meeting I opened the door for baptism, and seven offered themselves. Among the number were four preachers and the constable. The latter arose and said, 'Mr. Woodruff, I would like to be baptized.' I told him I would like to baptize him. I went down into the pool and baptized the seven. We then came together. I confirmed thirteen, administered the Sacrament, and we all rejoiced together.

"The constable went to the rector and told him that if he wanted Mr. Woodruff taken for preaching the gospel, he must go himself and serve the writ; for he had heard him preach the only true gospel sermon he had ever listened to in his life. The rector did not know what to make of it, so he sent two clerks of the Church of England as spies, to attend our meeting, and find out what we did preach. They both were pricked in their hearts, received the word of the Lord gladly, and were baptized and confirmed members of the Church of Jesus Christ of Latter-day Saints. The rector became alarmed, and did not venture to send anybody else" (Cowley, *Wilford Woodruff,* 118).

John 7:50–53 Nicodemus, the Jewish leader in the Sanhedrin who had come to converse with Jesus at night, now defended His innocence before the law until a proper and legitimate hearing could be convened. Others objected to Nicodemus's defense on the grounds that a hearing was not needed, because prophets and messiahs do not come out of Galilee. Certainly, most of the revered prophets had come from the south—from the land of Judah—but at least one of the renowned prophets, Jonah, had indeed risen out of Galilee (from Gath-hepher, near Nazareth; 2 Kings 14:25). And the Messiah himself would be a Nazarene, and he would be the great light seen in Zebulun (Nazareth and vicinity) and Naphtali (the region around the Sea of Galilee) (Isaiah 9:1–2).

THE ADULTEROUS WOMAN
(IN THE TEMPLE OF JERUSALEM)

John 8:1–11 The mile-long Mount of Olives range lies to the east of the most ancient parts of Jerusalem. Its distance from the city is given in the New Testament: "The mount called Olivet . . . is from Jerusalem a sabbath day's journey," that is, about three thousand feet (Acts 1:12; Bible Dictionary, "Sabbath Day's Journey," 765).

The Mount of Olives may be divided into three sections. The northernmost section was called by Josephus and is still called today Mount Scopus (Greek, *scopos,* "lookout point"), where Babylonian and Roman armies camped and watched the city they were besieging. The Hebrew name of Mount Scopus is *Har HaTsofim,* meaning "mount of watchmen." The whole of the Mount of Olives is certainly a watchtower over Jerusalem, a guardian especially of the holy Temple Mount below.

Today the mid-southern portion of the Mount of Olives is a cemetery, one of the oldest continuously used cemeteries

More than seventy thousand graves are visible on the Mount of Olives

in the world. Already by Jesus' day, thousands of tombs had been cut in the soft chalky limestone, and many hundreds of ossuaries (small stone boxes for reburial of bones) have been uncovered from the New Testament period. More than seventy thousand graves are presently visible on the Mount of Olives.

The Mount of Olives is mentioned frequently in the Gospels in connection with the towns of Bethany and Bethphage on its eastern slopes and because of places on the mount where Jesus taught and prayed. "As he sat upon the mount of Olives over against the temple, Peter and James and John and Andrew asked him privately, Tell us, when shall these things be?" (Mark 13:3–4). "He came out, and went, as he was wont [accustomed], to the mount of Olives; and his disciples also followed him" (Luke 22:39). "Jesus ofttimes resorted thither with his disciples" (John 18:2). The Mount of Olives is where Jesus descended below all men (the Atonement) and where he ascended above all men (the Ascension).

Jesus probably spent the night at the home of his friends Lazarus and Martha and Mary in Bethany—on the southeastern slope of the Mount of Olives.

John 8:2 The Gospels note Jesus' activity in the Temple courts when he was in Jerusalem during his three-year ministry. Jesus declared, "I spake openly to the world; I ever taught in the synagogue, and in the temple, whither the Jews always resort; and in secret have I said nothing" (John 18:20).

Other references include the following: "The blind and the lame came to him in the temple; and he healed them" (Matthew 21:14). "Now about the midst of the feast Jesus went up into the temple, and taught" (John 7:14). "He taught daily in the temple" (Luke 19:47). "All the people came early in the morning to him in the temple, for to hear him" (Luke 21:38).

Jesus sat down and taught the people in the treasury,

within the Court of the Women, a place of public gatherings for the Jews in their Holy Temple (John 8:20; see also Appendix 1, 719; Appendix 3, 740). Later, Jesus mentioned again that he taught daily in the Temple (Matthew 26:55).

John 8:3–11 While he was teaching, scribes and Pharisees brought to him a woman taken in the very act of adultery and tried to entrap him by getting him to say something contrary to their revered law, something with which they could accuse and condemn him. (If they were so concerned about the law, what about her partner in sin? Where was he?)

Moses, in the Law, stipulated that those guilty of adultery be stoned to death—"the adulterer and the adulteress shall surely be put to death" (Leviticus 20:10; see also Deuteronomy 22:22). It was not the Roman law but the Jewish law that invoked the death penalty for such a grievous sin, though the death penalty had not been applied for centuries—because some leaders, even in the religious establishment, were likely guilty of committing adultery.

As his questioners waited for Jesus' response, he stooped down and wrote something with his finger—probably in the accumulated dust on the stone pavement. What he wrote is left to our imagination—perhaps a word about mercy, or love, or compassion.

The phrase *"as though he heard them not"* is in italics in the King James Version because those words were added by the translators (or are words attested only in later manuscripts of the Gospel of John).

Jesus' disputants pressed him for a reaction to the confrontation they had set up. The Savior finally stood up and uttered: "He that is without sin among you, let him first cast a stone at her." The perfect response! He was not contradicting the Mosaic law. This, too, was the law: The accusers were obligated to cast the first stones (Deuteronomy 17:7).

Jesus again stooped down and wrote on the ground, giving the accusers time to let his words sink into their conscience. They would all slink away, one by one, "beginning at the eldest, even unto the last" (v. 9), convicted by their own conscience. Some of those agitators may have been guilty of the same sin for which they were accusing another. They left Jesus, still stooped down, to arise and see only the woman standing there.

"Woman, where are thine accusers? Hath no man condemned thee?"

"No man, Lord."

"Neither do I condemn thee: go, and sin no more" (vv. 10–11).

Clearly Jesus was not condoning the sin, but neither was he condemning the woman. In this fragmentary account we lack the full sense of his instruction, but he certainly must have counseled her to go and complete her repentance—a difficult and painful task for such a sin.

Elder Spencer W. Kimball explained:

"In my childhood, Sunday School lessons were given to us on the 8th chapter of John wherein we learned of the woman thrown at the feet of the Redeemer for judgment. My sweet Sunday School teacher lauded the Lord for having forgiven the woman. She did not understand the impossibility of such an act. In my years since then I have repeatedly heard people praise the Lord for his mercy in having forgiven the adulteress. This example has been used numerous times to show how easily one can be forgiven for gross sin.

"But did the Lord forgive the woman? Could he forgive her? There seems to be no evidence of forgiveness. His command to her was, 'Go, and sin no more.' He was directing the sinful woman to go her way, *abandon her evil life, commit no more sin, transform her life*. He was saying, Go, woman, and start your repentance; and he was indicating to her the beginning step—to *abandon her transgressions*" (*Miracle of Forgiveness*, 165; italics in original).

Because of an inspired addition to the text given through the Prophet Joseph Smith, we assume that this woman did indeed follow the Savior's counsel and proceed to cleanse and reform her life: "*And the woman glorified God from that hour, and believed on his name*" (JST John 8:11).

In the latter days Jesus has instructed his disciples:

"Thou shalt not speak evil of thy neighbor, nor do him any harm . . . and he that committeth adultery, and repenteth not, shall be cast out. But he that has committed adultery and repents with all his heart, and forsaketh it, and doeth it no more, thou shalt forgive" (D&C 42:27, 24–25).

THE LIGHT OF THE WORLD (IN THE TEMPLE OF JERUSALEM)

John 8:12–59 Jesus proclaimed himself the light of the world. He is the light in a metaphorical sense—the light that shines through the darkness of this telestial world—but he is also the light in a literal sense (cf. Helaman 5:41). He is the source of light for the luminaries in our heavens; they receive

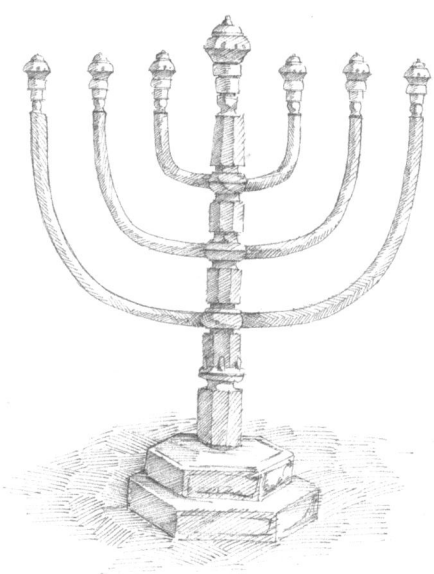

A menorah

their power, energy, and luminescence from his presence (all of that is taught in D&C 88:7–13).

Again we see how Jesus used something in his immediate surroundings, something of the present occasion, to teach that he was the Messiah. The Feast of Tabernacles continued day and night, and in the darkness after sunset, seventy-five-foot-high menorahs set up in the Temple courtyard provided light for the ongoing ritual celebrations. Both the feast itself and the giant menorahs symbolized Israel's role to be a light to the Gentiles, to send light and truth to those in the world who walk in darkness (see Isaiah 9:2; 42:6; 49:6). But even with the luminescence from the towering lampstands, the people still walked in partial darkness. Jesus invited the people to follow the greatest Light: "He that followeth me shall not walk in darkness, but shall have the light of life" (v. 12).

Some Pharisees objected that Jesus was bearing witness of himself, and according to Mosaic law there must be other witnesses. "Though I bear record of myself, yet my record is true," Jesus assured them (v. 14). "It is also written in your law, that the testimony of two men is true" (v. 17; cf. Deuteronomy 19:15). The Father and the Son are two witnesses—that satisfies the law. But "where is the Father?" the Jewish leaders persisted. "If ye had known me, ye should have known my Father also" (v. 19).

No one moved to accost or apprehend Jesus, because, as John frequently reminds his readers, "his hour was not yet come" (v. 20). He had to teach and testify and fulfill all that was written; then it would be time for the Sacrifice.

The exchange between the Savior and the Jewish leaders in the shadow of the Temple was strongly worded. Jesus told them he was going away soon and they would die in their sins (see v. 21). They asked where he was going and why they couldn't go there as well. He replied that he was from above and they were from below; moreover, if they refused to believe that he was their Savior, they would die in their sins (see v. 24).

Again they asked Jesus who he was. He answered that he had been telling them from the beginning (from the beginning of this world, certainly, and also from the beginning of his ministry).

He continued teaching and testifying of his Father, telling his questioners that he was speaking the things of his Father, the things he taught him and instructed him to speak to them, for he always did the things that would please the Father (see vv. 26–29).

Jesus' earnestness and profound conviction were felt by some of his listeners, and they believed him.

John 8:31–34 Jesus urged them to continue in his word—to obey and endure—so that they would be true disciples (as Nicodemus and Joseph of Arimathea apparently became; John 19:38–39; Matthew 27:57). The Savior testified, "And ye shall know the truth, and the truth shall make you free."

The Jewish leaders challenged him, saying in essence, Why are you telling us about freedom? We are Abraham's seed; we have never been in bondage to any man.

What? Had they forgotten the Egyptians, Assyrians, Babylonians, Greeks, and now the Romans? But that was not really what Jesus was referring to. Whoever sins is the servant of sin. Many of these Jewish leaders were in bondage. Sin is oppressive.

John 8:35–36 Jesus reminded his listeners that the servant remains in a house only if the owner so desires, but a son, especially *the* Son, has a rightful place. The Son could make them free indeed.

John 8:37–40 Genealogically, of course, they were Abraham's seed, but they were certainly not children of Abraham in a spiritual or covenant sense. If they were, they would do the works of Abraham. Because Jesus was telling them the truth, they were trying to kill him; Abraham would not do that.

John 8:41–45 Jesus declared that the leaders of the Jews were doing the works of their father the devil (Greek, *diabolos*).

They replied that they were not born of immorality or fornication or adultery (Greek, *porneia*); they were not born illegitimately, outside the covenant. (Was this a direct reference to rumors about Jesus being illegitimate? Perhaps.) Ironically, they declared that God was *their* Father.

Jesus responded that if God were their Father, they would love him because the Father had sent him. Moreover, he told them, they could not understand his speech because they could not bear his word (JST John 8:43). They could not stand his word because they were true disciples of their father the devil, and they were caught up in the lusts of the devil: murdering, lying, and all dishonesty.

John 8:46–55 Jesus asked the leaders of the Jews if they were accusing him of sin. "And if I say the truth, why do ye not believe me?" (v. 46). "He that is of God *receiveth* God's words; ye therefore *receive* them not, because ye are not of God" (JST John 8:47).

At first some Judean Jews had derided Jesus by calling him a Galilean. Now they turned hateful and verbally abusive by saying he was possessed by a devil and was a Samaritan, thereby disowning him as a Jew. Having no good answers for Jesus' questions, they resorted to name-calling.

He declared that there was no devil in him, for he was honoring the Father, not seeking his own glory. If they would live his teachings, they would never see death.

The Jewish leaders answered that now they knew he was possessed with a devil. Abraham was dead; all the prophets were dead; and Jesus was saying that if they would live his teachings they would never taste of death? Was he claiming to be greater than Abraham and the prophets? Who did he think he was?

Jesus testified that the Father honored him—the One they said was their God. Yet they had not known the Father. Jesus knew him, and if he were to deny that he knew the Father, he would be a liar—like those he was speaking with. But Jesus said again that he knew the Father and obeyed him.

John 8:56–59 Continuing, Jesus told the leaders of the Jews that their father Abraham had rejoiced to see Jesus' day. Helaman 8:17 teaches the same thing, and Joseph Smith Translation Genesis 15:12 also notes that "*Abram looked forth and saw the days of the Son of Man, and was glad.*"

Some Jews retorted, in effect, You're not even fifty years old, and you claim to have seen Abraham?

Then came Jesus' dramatic announcement, which for those Jews was shocking: "Verily, verily, I say unto you, Before Abraham was, I am." In other words, before Abraham was I Jehovah—I am Abraham's God!

Considering those words blasphemous they wanted to stone him, but Jesus had some way of making himself unseen (cf. Luke 4:30), and he passed through the midst of them.

Thus the God of Abraham bore testimony to the descendants of Abraham, in his holy House on Mount Moriah—Jerusalem's Temple Mount—where Abraham himself had gained his most indelible witness of the Lamb who would be sacrificed on the northern extension of that very mountain to bring light and life to those who would hear and obey (Genesis 22:8–14).

Why was Jesus so combative, so confrontational, with these Jewish leaders? The Prophet Joseph Smith explained the powers and purposes of the Melchizedek Priesthood (the Priesthood after the Order of *the Son of God*): "It is also the privilege of the Melchizedek Priesthood, to reprove, rebuke, and admonish, as well as to receive revelation. . . . I frequently rebuke and admonish my brethren. . . . Such a course of conduct is not calculated to gain the good will of all, but rather the ill will of many. . . . the higher the authority, the greater the difficulty of the station; but these rebukes and admonitions become necessary, from the perverseness of the brethren, for their temporal as well as spiritual welfare. They actually constitute a part of the duties of my station and calling" (*Teachings of the Prophet Joseph Smith*, 112–13).

This was part of Jesus' mission also, to testify directly against their sin and hypocrisy and to call them to repentance.

Robert J. Matthews cautions holders of this priesthood in the latter days: "Rebuking others is a prerogative of those holding the priesthood keys. The rest of us had best not use this method so directly" (*Behold the Messiah*, 233).

BLIND MAN HEALED ON THE SABBATH (IN JERUSALEM)

John 9:1–41 In Jesus' day, Jerusalem enjoyed highly developed water resources. Wells, springs, cisterns, aqueducts, and pools all served the need for water in one of the greatest walled cities in the Near East. Moving water—that is, groundwater and water transported via aqueduct—was the best quality water, because open pools have the natural disadvantages of heavy evaporation, silting, and exposure to sewage and

The Pool of Siloam (left, with colonnades on four sides), as seen in the Model City, Jerusalem

The Perean and Later Judean Ministry

other pollutants. Notwithstanding the disadvantages, Jerusalem had at least ten large pools in this period. Two are mentioned in the New Testament (see Appendix 1, 716).

The Pool of Siloam stands at the south end of the ancient city's unique hydrotechnical project: Hezekiah's Tunnel. In 701 B.C., King Hezekiah, encouraged by the lone voice of the prophet Isaiah, prepared for the attack of the Assyrian king Sennacherib's forces by repairing the city walls and carving out of solid limestone an underground water channel nearly eighteen hundred feet long to camouflage the Gihon Spring, the city's main water source, and bring its waters inside the city for safe access. By Jesus' day, the Pool of Siloam had provided water storage for seven centuries.

Jesus one day sent a man blind from birth to the Pool of Siloam. He answered the man's plea for sight by making a clay paste, applying it to his eyes, and instructing him to go to the pool and wash it off. The blind man obeyed and was healed.

John 9:1 Continuing a theme he had just spoken of in the Temple, Jesus approached the man blind from birth—a man who had been in physical darkness throughout his life. Jesus had just said: "I am the light of the world: he that followeth me shall not walk in darkness but shall have the light of life" (John 8:12). The blind man would shortly have opportunity to see the light of day and see all things around him, especially to see the Light of the world. It was a prophesied part of the ministry of the Messiah, the Savior, the Lord Omnipotent, that he would come to give sight to the blind (see, for example, Mosiah 3:5).

John 9:2–3 Some disciples raised a philosophical question: "Who did sin, this man, or his parents, that he was born blind?" The question itself implies belief in a premortal life. Jesus answered that neither the man nor his parents had sinned; his blindness was not punishment for having made some serious mistake in the premortal life. On the contrary, one purpose of his blindness was "that the works of God should be made manifest in him" (v. 3). Jesus later taught the same doctrine at the raising of his dead friend from the tomb: Lazarus's sickness and death were "for the glory of God, that the Son of God might be glorified thereby" (John 11:4). In all their omniscience the Gods had arranged these two men's maladies in order to demonstrate the Master Healer's miraculous power over the physical body, over life and death—all to reward the faith of believers and to glorify God.

John 9:4–5 The One who had originally created the greater and lesser lights in the heavens to illuminate this earth had now come to earth himself to bring more light into the world and to do the works of the Father. Jesus never missed an opportunity to testify of his Father and to praise the One who had sent him here.

The Lord's work, which is also our work, is done "while it is day: the night cometh, when no man can work" (v. 4). The Book of Mormon prophet Amulek elaborates: "After this day of life, which is given us to prepare for eternity, behold, if we do not improve our time while in this life, then cometh the night of darkness wherein there can be no labor performed" (Alma 34:33). Amulek warned against procrastinating the day of our repentance; otherwise we might be subjected to the spirit of the devil in the next world, overpowered by him, and sealed as his, to stay with him forever (Alma 34:34–35).

John 9:6–7 Jesus prepared some clay with spittle and anointed (not smeared but anointed) the blind man's eyes with the clay, probably to involve the man, who could not see what Jesus was doing, in the miracle. All ordinances are physical; they all involve touch. Touch can provide a tangible transmission of power and love.

Jesus sent him to the pool named Siloam, which means "Sent" (v. 7). Hebrew *Shiloah*, Greek *Siloam* (and today, Arabic *Silwan*), all mean "sent." The Lord had sent Naaman, the Syrian army officer who had contracted leprosy, to the Jordan River (2 Kings 5:10); he sent the ten lepers to show themselves to the priests (Luke 17:14); and now he sent the

The Perean and Later Judean Ministry

blind man to the pool—all with the promise that through obedience they would be healed of their respective afflictions. All they had to do was "go and do." Simple faith and obedience brought miraculous blessings in all three cases.

John 9:8–12 Some neighbors wondered if the seeing man was indeed the former blind man who had sat and begged. Some said yes, others affirmed that he looked like the same man, but he said himself that he was the man. He testified, further, that a man named Jesus (Christ—the Anointed One) had anointed him and told him to wash in the Pool of Siloam and he would be healed. He did so, and he was healed.

John 9:13–34 John preserved the highlights of a hearing between the formerly blind man, some Pharisees, and the man's parents.

The Pharisees interrogated the man, but the resulting testimony only caused divisiveness among them: How could this miracle-worker be a man of God if he did such things on the holy Sabbath? But then again, how could a sinner do such miraculous things?

They asked the blind man what he thought of the man who had given him his sight.

The man answered that he thought the man was a prophet.

Then the Pharisees called the parents, asking, essentially, Are you sure this is your son who was born blind? How can he see now?

They answered that this man was their son, that he had indeed been born blind, but that they did not know exactly how he could now see. They said, "He is of age; ask him." The parents knew they faced excommunication from the synagogue if they supported Jesus in any way.

Then the Pharisees called the blind man back in, telling him to give God the praise for what had happened to him, but they declared that Jesus was a sinner.

The man replied that whether or not Jesus was a sinner, he did not know. All he knew was that he had been blind, and now he could see. (They could not very well argue with the facts.)

When they asked the man what Jesus had done to restore his sight, the man responded that he had already told them and they had not really listened. Did they want to hear the story again? Did they want to become his disciples, too?

The Pharisees answered that the man was Jesus' disciple but they were Moses' disciples. They declared that God spoke to Moses, but this Jesus—they did not know where he was coming from.

The man said that it was interesting that the Pharisees did not know about Jesus, and yet He had opened the man's eyes. God in heaven certainly does not bless sinners to do this kind of marvel. In fact, since the world began, it was unheard of that any man could open the eyes of one born blind—*except he be of God* (JST John 9:32). The man asserted that if Jesus were not of God, he could not have done such a thing.

That last testimonial, convincing and true, angered the Pharisees. They scoffed that he was born a sinner and yet he pretended to teach them? Foiled in their effort to indict Jesus, they used their so-called authority to excommunicate the formerly blind man from their synagogues.

John 9:35–38 Jesus heard what had happened, and when He found the man, He gave him an opportunity to express his faith in the Savior: "Dost thou believe on the Son of God?"

The man asked, "Who is he, Lord, that I might believe on him?"

Jesus answered that not only had the man seen the Son of God but he was talking with him (the same direct testimony he bore to the Samaritan woman at Jacob's well; John 4:26).

The man exclaimed, "Lord, I believe," and worshipped him.

John 9:39–41 One of the reasons Jesus came into the world was, in a sense, to give sight to those who are blind (to help sincere seekers see the light), and to blind those who mistakenly think they already have a vision of the things of God (but are actually in the dark).

Some of the Pharisees asked Jesus if he was saying they were blind, too.

Jesus answered that if they were truly blind, doing what they were doing in ignorance, they would not be responsible—and would be guiltless—but they claimed to see (to have knowledge and be very aware of what they were doing), so they were indicting and condemning themselves.

ALLEGORY: THE GOOD SHEPHERD (AT JERUSALEM)

John 10:1–21 Shepherding stands with farming as one of the two great biblical occupations. Sheep have been inextricably tied to the pastoral economy and theology of the people of Israel since their beginning. In the biblical books of law and history, sheep are frequently mentioned in connection with their vital domestic role in the household and community ecosystem and in sacrificial practices. Sheep were vital to the

A sheepfold in the Judean desert

Jews because of the products derived from them: meat, wool, skins (Hebrews 11:37), and milk (1 Corinthians 9:7).

One of the longest, most sustained and poignant allegorics in the Bible, another of the classic and timeless illustrations of comparing something in nature to the human experience, is the detailed exposition of Jesus regarding his people as sheep and himself as Shepherd. In it we find much instructive detail about the work of the shepherd and characteristics of the sheep.

There is only one way to enter the sheepfold, the kingdom of God, and that is through the door, or gate. Jesus is the door. The porter (gatekeeper) opens it only to the true shepherd. The shepherd knows his sheep, and when he calls them, they follow him. Unlike in the West, the Near Eastern shepherd does not get out the dogs, the whips, or the horses or trucks, to drive the sheep—he just calls, and because he knows his sheep and they recognize his voice, they follow where he leads. They will not follow a stranger whose voice they do not recognize.

One Church leader describes a modern experience in the old world that illustrates the Savior's personal knowledge of each of his sheep:

"Some years ago, it was my privilege to visit the country of Morocco as part of an official United States government delegation. . . . As we topped the brow of a hill, we noticed that the limousine in front of us had pulled off to the side of the road. . . . An old shepherd, in the long, flowing robes of the Savior's day, was standing near the limousine in conversation with the driver. . . . The king's vehicle had struck and injured one of the sheep belonging to the old shepherd. The driver of the vehicle was explaining to him the law of the land. Because the king's vehicle had injured one of the sheep belonging to the old shepherd, he was now entitled to one hundred times its value at maturity. However, under the same law, the injured sheep must be slain and the meat divided among the people. My interpreter hastily added, 'But the old shepherd will not accept the money. They never do.'

"Startled, I asked him why. And he added, 'Because of the love he has for each of his sheep.' It was then that I noticed the old shepherd reach down, lift the injured lamb in his arms, and place it in a large pouch on the front of his robe. He kept stroking its head, repeating the same word over and over again. When I asked the meaning of the word, I was informed, 'Oh, he is calling it by name. All of his sheep have a name, for he is their shepherd, and the good shepherds know each of their sheep by name.'

"It was as my driver predicted. The money was refused, and the old shepherd with his small flock of sheep, with the injured one tucked safely in the pouch on his robe, disappeared into the beautiful deserts of Morocco" (Lasater, *Ensign,* May 1988, 74).

Jesus told this beautiful allegory to some of the religious leaders in Jerusalem, but they failed to understand.

So he repeated that he is the door of the sheepfold. All

A modern shepherd leading his flock through a lane on the Mount of Olives

those who came before me, *who testified not of me* (JST John 10:8), pretending to occupy that position, were thieves and robbers, and his true sheep would not listen to them. He declared that he is the door; anyone entering by him will be saved and will go in and out to find pasture. The thief comes to steal, kill, and destroy; Jesus was come that they might have life and have it more abundantly.

John 10:11–15 "I am the good Shepherd." The religious leaders among the Jews were regarded as, and were supposed to be, the shepherds of the people. They undoubtedly understood the rebuke in the adjective Jesus used: "I am the *good* shepherd" (emphasis added).

"The good Shepherd giveth his life for the sheep" is a true assessment of the dedicated shepherd out in the pastures but is also a poignant foreshadowing of the good Shepherd giving his life for his sheep.

The hireling sheepherder lacks the personal interest and sincere concern for the sheep and at any sign of trouble may flee rather than risk his own life.

Stephen R. Covey wrote: "When the hired sheepherder fails or is criticized, he leaves his sheep: 'The hireling fleeth, because he is an hireling, and careth not for the sheep' (John 10:13). He leaves by giving excuses, by asking for other jobs, or by indifference and complacency. Sheepherder officers and teachers should not wonder why their attendance is low, why so many sheep are lost. If they're honest, they'll examine their own hearts and make changes" ("The Abundant Life in Christ," in *Redeemer*, 110).

Jesus knows those who are his; he knows who his true sheep, or followers, are, and they are numbered (see commentary on John 6:37).

John 10:16 The God of all creation has other sheep, in other pastures, in this and in other worlds. To his disciples among the Nephites and Lamanites in the western hemisphere, in Book of Mormon lands, he announced: "Ye are they of whom I said: Other sheep I have which are not of this

The Perean and Later Judean Ministry

fold; them also I must bring, and they shall hear my voice; and there shall be one fold, and one shepherd" (3 Nephi 15:21).

The Jerusalemites who originally heard this teaching thought Jesus might be referring to the Gentiles, but he clarified that the Gentiles in general would not hear his voice but would receive the gospel through his disciples and through the Holy Ghost. A partial record of the Gentiles' being taught the gospel is preserved in the New Testament books of Acts through Revelation (see 3 Nephi 15:22–23).

Jesus continued, explaining that his disciples in the western hemisphere were not the only "other sheep" who would hear his voice:

"And verily, verily, I say unto you that I have other sheep, which are not of this land, neither of the land of Jerusalem, neither in any parts of that land round about whither I have been to minister.

"For they of whom I speak are they who have not as yet heard my voice; neither have I at any time manifested myself unto them.

"But I have received a commandment of the Father that I shall go unto them, and that they shall hear my voice, and shall be numbered among my sheep, that there may be one fold and one shepherd; therefore I go to show myself unto them" (3 Nephi 16:1–3).

All of God's numerous flocks of sheep will be gradually, continuously, and eventually gathered in to their eternal fold to enjoy celestial pastures.

John 10:17–18 The Father of the good Shepherd sent him to earth to lay down his life and take it up again—to die and resurrect. The Savior dramatically taught that no people and no power on earth could take his life from him—no one could kill him—only as he willingly gave his life. By virtue of his parentage, having an immortal Father and a mortal mother, he had power over life and death: "I have power to lay [my body] down, and I have power to take it again" (v. 18). His manner of birth was directly related to his manner of death; he was born in a unique way so he could die in a unique way. He could not be sacrificed by anyone else; he would willingly offer himself as a sacrifice for all (as an angel put it, he "yieldeth himself . . . into the hands of wicked men"; 1 Nephi 19:10). And after he sacrificed himself, he would (again because of his unique Parentage, having power over life and death) raise his body back up from the grave. The Father had given him power and a commandment to do that (cf. Mosiah 15:8).

John 10:19–21 Upon seeing the miracles and hearing the teachings, the crowd was confused and perplexed, some claiming that Jesus was possessed of a devil, that he was crazy. Others remonstrated: "These are not the words of him that hath a devil. Can a devil open the eyes of the blind?" (v. 21).

PHARISEES ASK ABOUT DIVORCE (IN PEREA?)

Matthew 19:3–12; Mark 10:2–12 (cf. John 8:6) When Jesus left Galilee and entered Judea toward the end of his ministry, some Pharisees tested his position on divorce, attempting to see, among other things, with whom he sided in the theological and legal dispute between two prominent rabbis and their respective schools of thought in Jesus' day. Hillel and Shammai, two contemporaries (60 B.C.–A.D. 20), disagreed over the interpretation of Deuteronomy 24:1–4. Hillel took a liberal view toward divorce and thus emphasized, as legitimate grounds, the clause "that she find no favor in his eyes" (Deuteronomy 24:1). He allowed that a man could divorce his wife if she did anything he did not like, even so minor a thing as burning his food. Shammai, on the other hand, was much more strict in his interpretation of legitimate reasons for divorce, emphasizing the subsequent clause in Deuteronomy 24:1: "Because he hath found some uncleanness in her," which he interpreted as marital unfaithfulness, the only allowable grounds for divorce.

Jesus' response may have sounded like the position of the school of Shammai, but in fact he was providing divine counsel in regard to divorce.

So the issue was: Is divorce acceptable?

Mark 10:12 notes that a woman who divorces her husband to marry another man commits adultery. The New International Version (NIV) Bible says: "In this historical and geographical context, Jesus' pronouncements confirm the bold denunciation by John the Baptist and equally condemn Herod Antipas and Herodias," for she had done what Jesus here condemns.

In his perfect response, Jesus turned immediately back to the written law. What do the scriptures say? God's children were male and female from the beginning (cf. Genesis 1:27; 2:24; 5:2), so naturally they would leave their homes and pair off, and the two would become one. Therefore, the law says, what God has joined together, man must not separate.

Why then did Moses command to give a certification and allow divorce? (Deuteronomy 24:1). Moses, of course, did not command or even recommend divorce but "because of the hardness of your hearts [he] suffered you to put away your wives: but from the beginning it was not so" (Matthew 19:8).

In the celestial realms there is no such thing as making an eternal covenant and then breaking it. Remarriage after divorce is now permitted because the higher law is still not functional in the Lord's kingdom. Marrying a divorced person is currently not considered committing adultery.

Matthew 19:10–11 Some disciples concluded that if the law is so strict, maybe it is better not to marry. Jesus' reply? All people will not be capable of living the higher law. For now, there are some exceptions, but generally it is not only vital to marry but mandated by heaven.

Matthew 19:12 A eunuch is a man who has been castrated. Elder McConkie wrote: "Some added background and additional information is needed to understand fully what is meant by this teaching about eunuchs. In the true Church and among normal people, there is no place for the practice of celibacy [intentionally remaining single; avoiding marriage]. 'Apparently those who made themselves eunuchs were men who in false pagan worship had deliberately mutilated themselves in the apostate notion that such would further their salvation. It is clear that such was not a true gospel requirement of any sort. There is no such thing in the gospel as wilful emasculation; such a notion violates every true principle of procreation and celestial marriage'"(*Doctrinal New Testament Commentary*, 1:549).

SUFFER LITTLE CHILDREN (IN PEREA?)

Matthew 19:13–15; Mark 10:13–16; Luke 18:15–17 After teaching about the need for marriage, Jesus turned to children. Little children were brought to him, and his disciples chastised those who brought them. The King James Version does not give a reason why the disciples rebuked those who brought the children, but the Joseph Smith Translation does: "The disciples rebuked them, *saying, There is no need, for Jesus hath said, Such shall be saved*" (JST Matthew 19:13). Since the children will be saved, perhaps the disciples felt the little ones were an unnecessary imposition on Jesus' time. Jesus was "much displeased" and said, "Suffer the little children to come unto me, and forbid them not: for of such is the kingdom of God" (Mark 10:14; cf. 3 Nephi 9:22; 17:11–12, 21–23). And he put his hands on them and blessed them. Then Jesus taught the universal lesson: those who want to be part of the eternal kingdom of God must become like a little child (Mark 10:15; cf. Mosiah 15:25; 3 Nephi 11:37–38).

Brother Ogden wrote the following several years ago after one of many walks with students in the Holy Land:

"When we returned home after an all-day hike from the Judean ridge down into and across the Elah Valley (where

Israelite and Philistine armies confronted each other and David squared off against the giant bully), I was excited more than anything else about a happy stir our group of thirty had caused as we marched through a little Arab village. That's one corner of the country tourists never see, and I guess the villagers thought this was the parade of the year. As we walked through, the whole village started gathering around; from out of the streets going off in all directions children came swarming out to investigate and to practice the little English dialogues they'd been taught. Every simple thing we would do, they would mimic—dance, giggle, sing—all the while their mothers and fathers would wave at us from their windows or from the flat roofs of their limestone houses. The whole scene made me reflect on similar circumstances of Jesus' entrance into this same kind of village in this same land. As he and his apostles were wending their way up to visit, certainly the villagers would spot the little caravan on their approach, and as they entered, I can visualize how all the people would gather around him, especially if he healed someone—how many more would be brought. And as the children, 75 or 100 of them, excitedly followed us out of the village, even for a mile or two, we began to sense that they were a little pesky. Then it came to mind that maybe the apostles felt the same way when surrounded by a lot of little children and they wanted to send them away, but the Savior gathered them around in his loving arms and blessed them, and he said we should become like them" (Ogden, journal).

RICH YOUNG RULER (IN PEREA?)

Matthew 19:16–26; Mark 10:17–27; Luke 18:18–27
One young, wealthy, religiously observant leader among the Jews came to Jesus inquiring what he needed to do to have eternal life. (A certain lawyer had previously asked the same question; Luke 10:25.) He called Jesus good, and Jesus, as is

typical of him, immediately turned the compliment to the Father, accepting no adulation for himself but always giving honor to the Father. Now, replying to the young man's question, He told him to keep the commandments. When asked which ones, Jesus reviewed with him the basic Ten Commandments. "All these things have I kept from my youth up: what lack I yet?" (Matthew 19:20). All of us find it fairly easy to live most of the commandments; the test is in the ones that are more difficult, that require us to change and sacrifice, to give up something that we really like, that our hearts are set on. That to which we are most attached, where our hearts are (our "treasure"), that is exactly what the all-wise God might ask us to give up, to determine our commitment and thus go on to perfection.

Brother Ogden recorded in his journal something a missionary wrote to him in 1999: "One of my professors at the university said that each of us had something precious that we'd never want to give up (for him it was his library of books in his home). He told us that the time would come when we would have to give our whole heart to the Lord, including giving up that one thing that we would never want to give up. The time has come in my life and my mission that I have chosen to give my all to the Lord. It doesn't matter where that decision leads me. I feel that this is a crucial point in my life."

Jesus gave the rich young man specific instructions to follow if he truly wanted eternal life: "If thou wilt be perfect, go and sell that thou hast, and give to the poor, and thou shalt have treasure in heaven: and come and follow me" (Matthew 19:21; cf. Mosiah 4:26; Alma 1:27). That is the same message as the brief parables of the treasure hidden in a field and the pearl of great price (Matthew 13:44, 46)—willingness to give up all else to obtain the greatest treasure, which is eternal life.

Mark 10:21 notes that "Jesus beholding him loved him." Looking into the young man's soul, Jesus saw a lot of good there and added, with the admonition to sell all he had and give it away, "Come, *take up the cross,* and follow me" (Mark

10:21; emphasis added). The cross symbolizes sacrifice, even suffering. Joseph Smith taught: "A religion that does not require the sacrifice of all things never has power sufficient to produce the faith necessary unto life and salvation. . . . The faith necessary unto the enjoyment of life and salvation never could be obtained without the sacrifice of all earthly things" (*Lectures on Faith*, 6:7).

The great religious hymn writer Isaac Watts (who also wrote "Sweet Is the Work," "He Died! The Great Redeemer Died," and "Joy to the World") penned these profound words:

> When I survey the wondrous cross
>   On which the Prince of Glory died,
> My richest gain I count but loss,
>   And pour contempt on all my pride.
>
> Forbid it, Lord, that I should boast,
>   Save in the death of Christ, my God:
> All the vain things that charm me most,
>   I sacrifice them to His blood.
>
> See, from His head, His hands, His feet,
>   Sorrow and love flow mingled down:
> Did e'er such love and sorrow meet,
>   Or thorns compose so rich a crown?
>
> Were the whole realm of nature mine,
>   That were an offering far too small;
> Love so amazing, so divine,
>   Demands my soul, my life, my all.

The sad result of the conversation was that the young man grieved and went away sorrowful, for he had many possessions. We do not know if he ever gave them up.

Matthew 19:23–24; Mark 10:23–25; Luke 18:24–25 The camel going through the eye of a needle does not refer to some hypothetical little gate in or alongside a main city gate

*In the Gospels, Jesus twice used camels in hyperboles:
a camel going through a needle's eye and swallowing a camel*

through which a camel is supposed to edge its way on its knees after being stripped of its burden. We have seen the remnants of numerous ancient cities and gates throughout the Near East, and our conclusion is that such a little gate did not exist. This notion is a figment of the imagination of someone who was probably trying to explain the image without understanding an important figure of speech that Jesus used.

The Greek word for needle, *raphis,* means "a sewing needle." In the Hebrew translation of this passage, the word *hamakhat* is used, which is also the ordinary word for a sewing needle. To make his point, Jesus was using a purposefully extreme exaggeration, a literary device common to Hebrew tradition called *hyperbole.*

Following are other examples of hyperbole, marked by italics:

Deuteronomy 1:28 (of the Israelites' fear of the Amorites): "The people is greater and taller than we; the cities are great and *walled up to heaven.*"

The Perean and Later Judean Ministry

Judges 20:16 (of the combat expertise of warriors of Benjamin): "Every one could sling stones *at an hair breadth, and not miss*" (the word "breadth" does not appear in the original; the Hebrew text says the warriors could sling stones *at a hair* and not miss).

2 Samuel 1:23 (in David's lament over the deaths of Saul and Jonathan): "They were *swifter than eagles*, they were *stronger than lions*."

Lamentations 2:11 (the depth of grief and sorrow at the loss of the Holy City): "Mine eyes do fail with tears, my bowels are troubled, *my liver is poured upon the earth.*"

Lamentations 3:48: "*Mine eye runneth down with rivers of water* for the destruction . . . of my people."

Matthew 5:29: "If thy right eye offend thee, *pluck it out, and cast it from thee:* for it is profitable for thee that one of thy members should perish, and not that thy whole body should be cast into hell."

John 12:19 (perplexity of the Pharisees after the raising of Lazarus): "Perceive ye how ye prevail nothing? Behold, *the world is gone after him.*"

John 21:25: "There are also many other things which Jesus did, the which, if they should be written every one, I suppose that *even the world itself could not contain the books* that should be written."

Jesus did not really mean, of course, that if your right eye is offensive in some way, to dig into the socket and pluck it out. The use of hyperbole makes the spiritual message more impressive and vividly engraves the meaning on the memory of receptive listeners: If there is some fault of character or sin destructive to the soul, get rid of that fault lest it destroy the whole soul.

In similar fashion, Jesus, in his scathing rebukes of the hypocritical religious leaders and the rich, used strong metaphors: swallowing a camel (Matthew 23:24) and going through the eye of a needle. When he illustrated the difficulty for rich men to earn the blessing of celestial glory, Jesus adopted a common literary device of his time to stress the hazards and challenges of having great riches. Knowing how wealth and prosperity generally work on the human personality, Jesus could appropriately and perceptively say that it is easier for a camel to go through the eye of a needle than for a rich man to enter into the kingdom of God. Riches often engender a sense of self-sufficiency and pride. The rich generally think they have no need for God, because money can buy them all they want. The more one accumulates the things of this temporal world, the less inclined one is to pursue the things of the eternal world.

"It is . . . the *natural* course of things for the rich, or perhaps for their children or grandchildren, to become first proud and then unfaithful. If the rich take no measures to keep this from happening, or if they just don't give it much thought, it *will* happen, just as surely as an untended garden will become overgrown with weeds. Therefore, wealthy Saints must be aware of the natural effect wealth has on people and must work actively and creatively to keep those weeds from their gardens. The natural progression, whether in one generation or the next, is to pride, then to unfaithfulness, and thence to wickedness and destruction" (Robinson and Garrett, *Commentary on the Doctrine and Covenants,* 1:267).

Hardly anything good or positive is said about riches or wealth in all of scripture. Jacob warned:

"But wo unto the rich, who are rich as to the things of the world. For because they are rich they despise the poor, and they persecute the meek, and their hearts are upon their treasures; wherefore, their treasure is their god. And behold, their treasure shall perish with them also" (2 Nephi 9:30).

And in modern times prophets have also warned of the dangers of lusting after worldly wealth, with its attendant luxury and ease and customary disregard for things of everlasting value. President Ezra Taft Benson declared: "Every generation has its tests and its chance to stand and prove itself. Would you like to know of one of our toughest tests? Hear the warning words of President Brigham Young, 'The worst fear I have about this people is that they will get rich in this country, forget God and His people, wax fat, and kick themselves out of the Church and go to hell. This people will stand mobbing, robbing, poverty and all manner of persecution and be true. But my greatest fear is that they cannot stand wealth'" (quoted in Larry E. Dahl, "The Abrahamic Test," in *Witness of Jesus Christ*, 59).

President Harold B. Lee said: "We are tested and we are tried, we are going through some of the severest tests today and we don't realize perhaps the severity of the tests that we're going through. . . . Today we are basking in the lap of luxury, the like of which we've never seen before in the history of the world. It would seem that probably this is the most severe test of any test that we've ever had in the history of this Church" (quoted in Dahl, "Abrahamic Test," in *Witness of Jesus Christ*, 60).

Jacob, the great Book of Mormon prophet and theologian, powerfully expressed what our attitude about riches should be:

"But before ye seek for riches, seek ye for the kingdom of God.

"And after ye have obtained a hope in Christ ye shall obtain riches, if ye seek them; and ye will seek them for the intent to do good—to clothe the naked, and to feed the hungry, and to liberate the captive, and administer relief to the sick and the afflicted" (Jacob 2:18–19).

Matthew 19:25–26; Mark 10:26–27; Luke 18:26–27 While his disciples raised the question about who can be saved, given the hazards of setting our hearts on worldly things, Jesus understood their thoughts and explained, "With men this is impossible; but *if they will forsake all things for my sake*, with God *whatsoever things I speak* are possible" (JST Matthew 19:26).

The impossibility of salvation refers not to those who *have* riches but to those who *trust in* riches:

"With men *that trust in riches*, it is impossible; but not *impossible with men who trust in God and leave all for my sake*, for with *such* all *these* things are possible" (JST Mark 10:26); or as phrased in Joseph Smith's translation of Luke: "*It is impossible for them who trust in riches, to enter into the kingdom of God; but he who forsaketh the things which are of this world, it is* possible with God, *that he should enter in*" (JST Luke 18:27).

THE TWELVE TO JUDGE THE TRIBES OF ISRAEL (IN PEREA?)

Matthew 19:27–30; Mark 10:28–31; Luke 18:28–30; 22:28–30 Having just heard Jesus' emphasis on willingness to forsake all things for his cause, Peter pointed out that he and the Twelve had forsaken all to follow the Lord—what will their reward be? Jesus described the scene in the regeneration (JST: *resurrection*) when he would sit on his throne of glory and his chosen Twelve would likewise sit on twelve thrones with crowns of glory judging the twelve tribes of Israel (see also 1 Nephi 12:9; Mormon 3:18; D&C 29:12; Judas Iscariot was later replaced by Matthias; Acts 1:26). And anyone else who has sacrificed homes or lands or family relationships for the sake of the Savior and his mission, will be compensated a hundred times over, culminating in everlasting life. "I will bless him and multiply him and give unto him an hundred fold in this world, of fathers and mothers, brothers and sisters, houses and lands, wives and children, and crowns of eternal lives in the eternal worlds" (D&C 132:55).

But another word of counsel to Peter and to all the rest of us: "*There are* many *who make themselves* first, *that* shall be last, and the last first. *This he said, rebuking Peter*" (JST Mark

10:30–31). Yes, the rewards are forthcoming for all sacrifices and faithful service, but do not forget the requisite humility.

PARABLE: LABORERS IN THE VINEYARD (IN PEREA?)

Matthew 20:1–16 (cf. Mark 10:31) The owner, or "lord of the vineyard," employed several types of workers: the steward, or manager (Matthew 20:8), the vinedresser (Luke 13:7) or husbandman (Greek, *georgos*, "farmer" or "worker of the land"; Matthew 21:33), the laborer, or temporary worker, hired from the marketplace (Matthew 20:1–16), and the watchman (Matthew 21:33). Laborers in the vineyard earned a denarius (KJV, "penny"; plural, "pence"), which was a day's wage for the common laborer. The employer hired workers at the third hour (9 A.M.; v. 3), at the sixth and ninth hours (noon and 3 P.M.; v. 5), and again at the eleventh hour (5 P.M.; v. 6).

Labor in the vineyard was physically taxing under the summer sun (v. 12). Those who were hired early in the morning complained about equal pay being given to those who had hired on late in the day.

Some are called early to labor in the Lord's vineyard; some are found and called later. The Lord taught that the exact timing does not matter nor does the amount of time we labor. The reward for hard work, for dedicated service, is the same, regardless of when we were called to serve. Each will receive his or her just due. "All that the Father has" is the ultimate reward for all faithful servants (D&C 84:38). Those who are pure in heart will not feel resentful toward others who discovered the truth later and were therefore called to labor in the vineyard at a later hour, meaning that they did not have to endure as long the burdens and the "heat of the day" (v. 12). We rejoice that they were found, were willing to work, and

A modern vineyard in Judea

dedicated themselves to the labor of love that is serving and saving souls.

Matthew 20:15–16 For more on the "evil eye," see Mark 7:17–23; Matthew 15:14; and Luke 6:39–40. As in the parable, so in life: the last and the first, the first and the last—chronology of service is not as important as becoming grafted into (or adopted into) the great tree of life, the family of God (Jacob 5:63). More essential than being called and the timing of the call are the ultimate chosen status we may enjoy, the bringing forth of fruit, and having our fruit remain forever.

FEAST OF DEDICATION (AT JERUSALEM)

John 10:22–39 Most of the pilgrimage festivals of the Jews were in spring and in autumn, during the transitional periods between the two seasons, when it was neither too wet and cold nor too dry and hot for travel. One of the feasts, however, was held in the wintertime. Jesus was teaching in the Temple, "and it was at Jerusalem the feast of the dedication, and it was winter" (v. 22). The Feast of Dedication (Hebrew,

The Perean and Later Judean Ministry

A portico (or colonnade, cloister, or porch) visible behind the Temple, as seen in the Model City, Jerusalem

Hanukkah) celebrates the rededication of the Temple under Judah the Maccabee (see Appendix 6, 763). The feast began on the twenty-fifth of Chislev, roughly our month of December, during which time the weather can still be mild, just before the heavy winter rains begin (normally in January).

As on other festive occasions in Jerusalem, Jesus went up to teach in the holy mount, where his House was. At the Feast of Dedication he was walking in Solomon's porch, the eastern portico or colonnade of the outer courtyard (see Appendix 1, 718). Herod the Great had extended the Temple area and built up the northern, western, and southern porches or porticoes, but the eastern one was refurbished in the same position it had always been in since the days of Solomon (Galbraith, Ogden, and Skinner, *Jerusalem, the Eternal City*, 188).

There, on the Temple Mount, in front of his House, the following conversation ensued:

"How long dost thou make us to doubt? If thou be the Christ, tell us plainly.

"Jesus answered them, I told you, and ye believed not: the works that I do in my Father's name, they bear witness of me. But ye believe not, because ye are not of my sheep, as I said unto you. My sheep hear my voice, and I know them, and they follow me: And I give unto them eternal life; and they shall never perish, neither shall any man pluck them out of my hand. My Father . . . gave them me" (John 10:24–29; see commentary on John 6:37).

John 10:30 "I and my Father are one." In the original Greek "one" is neuter, indicating attributes, power, and purpose. Oneness of person would require the masculine form. The meaning and intent of the expression is therefore the oneness of the Father and the Son in their design and objective with the children of God. They are one in mind and heart—as they want us to be (see commentary on John 17:21).

John 10:31–39 Considering the foregoing remark blasphemous, some of the Jews took up stones to kill Jesus.

The conversation continued:

"Many good works have I shewed [pronounced showed] you from my Father; for which of those works do ye stone me?

"The Jews answered him, saying, For a good work we stone thee not; but for blasphemy; and because that thou, being a man, makest thyself God. [See commentary on John 5:18; 19:7.]

"Jesus answered them, Is it not written in your law, I said, Ye are gods?" (That is a direct statement of our potential to become like Heavenly Father. Compare Psalm 82:6: "Ye are gods; and all of you are children of the most High.")

Then Jesus asked, in effect, Now if you believe the scriptures, are you accusing me, whom the Father sanctified and sent into the world, of blasphemy because I said I am the Son of God? (It is clear what he taught.) If I don't do the works of God, our Father, then do not believe me. But if I do, even though you do not believe me, believe the works, and then you will know that the Father is in me, and I in him.

The rabble then tried to accost Jesus once again, but he passed through them and escaped.

ADMIRERS OF THE BAPTIST BELIEVE
(AT BETHABARA, IN PEREA)

John 10:40–42 Jesus journeyed eastward to the Jordan Valley, crossed the river, and remained for a time where John at first baptized, at Bethabara (John 1:28), in the region called Perea (KJV, "beyond Jordan"). Many flocked to him there, and some commented about John's not having performed miracles; regardless, what the prophet spoke about Jesus had certainly proved true. Many at that place believed on Jesus.

SUMMONED TO LAZARUS
(IN PEREA)

John 11:1–7 When Jesus went to Jerusalem, he usually stayed in Bethany, situated on the eastern side of the Mount of Olives range. The fifteen furlongs, or stadia (mentioned in John 11:18), are just under two miles.

Today, the name of the town of Bethany is called in Arabic *el-Azariyeh*, preserving the name of Lazarus, its famous former citizen. Jesus lodged with his friend Lazarus and Lazarus's two sisters, Martha and Mary, or with "Simon the leper," a man named Simon who had been a leper but was healed (Matthew 26:6).

Lazarus and his two sisters were close friends of Jesus and may have lived together in a home in Bethany. No mention is made of their parents, so it is assumed that they had died by the time of Jesus' ministry. We have been introduced to Martha and Mary already, as recorded in Luke 10:38–42.

Verse 2 is an editorial insert advising the reader that this Mary is the one who anointed Jesus with costly ointment and wiped his feet with her hair (John 12:3; Matthew 26:7). At least five Marys are mentioned in the New Testament Gospels, all among Jesus' disciples: Mary, Jesus' mother; Mary, the mother of James (Jacob) and Joses (Joseph) (Matthew 27:56; Mark 15:40); Mary of Magdala; Mary of Bethany, sister of Martha and Lazarus; and Mary of Cleophas (John 19:25). See further in Van Dyke and Huntington, "Sorting Out the Seven Marys in the New Testament," 53–84.

The Joseph Smith Translation rewords verse 2 just enough to give the impression that Martha and Mary lived together in Bethany in a home that Martha owned and that Lazarus was also with them because he was critically ill:

"*And Mary, his* [that is, Lazarus's] *sister, who* anointed the Lord with ointment and wiped his feet with her hair, *lived with her sister Martha, in whose house her* brother Lazarus was sick" (JST John 11:2).

The sisters sent word to Jesus, who was across the Jordan in Perea, that the friend whom he loved was very sick. Upon hearing of Lazarus's illness Jesus intentionally remained where he was for two days, explaining prophetically that the sickness was "not unto death, but for the glory of God, that the Son of God might be glorified thereby" (v. 4). Already, at his earliest reaction in the recorded story, it is clear that Jesus knew what was happening and what he was going to do (compare John 9:3; see commentary on Luke 16:20).

John is the only one of the four Gospel writers who gave us a written account of the raising of Lazarus in Bethany. (At least, it is the only account that has come down to us.) Perhaps only John recorded the miracle because he wrote in the late first century after Christ; the Synoptic Gospels, which we suppose appeared earlier, may have been trying to protect a still-living Lazarus by not writing about him (we remember that the leaders of the Jews conspired to kill him; see Farrar, *Life of Christ*, 511).

PROPHECY OF DEATH AND RESURRECTION (LEAVING PEREA)

Matthew 20:17–19; Mark 10:32–34; Luke 18:31–34
On the way up to Jerusalem, Jesus taught the Twelve, for at least the third time, what would happen to him there. All the prophecies must be fulfilled: he would be betrayed to the chief priests and scribes; they would condemn him to death; he would be delivered to the Gentiles (the Romans), and they would mock him, scourge him, spit on him, and crucify him; and then on the third day he would rise again. That is such plain language that we wonder how the Twelve could not have understood, but Luke adds, "They understood none of these things: and this saying was hid from them" (Luke 18:34). John explained further: "These things understood not his disciples at the first: but when Jesus was glorified, then remembered they that these things were written of him" (John 12:16).

THE GREATEST IS TO MINISTER (AT JERICHO)

Matthew 20:20–28; Mark 10:35–45; Luke 22:24–27
Matthew and Mark record Jesus leaving Perea, passing through Jericho, enroute to Jerusalem, when he taught the following truths and lessons. Luke, on the other hand, records these teachings as part of the events at Jesus' last supper in the Upper Room. The great truths could have been taught, of course, on both occasions.

Zebedee's sons, James and John, along with their mother (who was apparently Salome; Talmage, *Jesus the Christ*, 484), approached Jesus with a question. Could they, James and John, sit in the honored positions at Jesus' right hand and left hand in the eternal kingdom? (Such questions of precedence, rank, and honor had arisen before; see commentary on

Matthew 18:1–6.) Jesus was now preparing to endure the cross, and the two apostles wanted to talk about their crown. The Lord issued an impressive rebuke to the mother and her sons: "Ye know not what ye ask. Are ye able to drink of the cup [a symbol of suffering; cf. Isaiah 51:17; Ezekiel 23:33] that I shall drink of, and to be baptized with the baptism that I am baptized with? They say unto him, We are able. And he saith unto them, Ye shall drink indeed of my cup, and be baptized with the baptism that I am baptized with: but to sit on my right hand, and on my left, is not mine to give" (Matthew 20:22–23). The Father would decide that.

The other ten apostles, on hearing about the request of James and John, were indignant, likely in the mood to rebuke them also.

Jesus called the Twelve around him to instruct them further and help them understand that they must not be like the Gentiles, exercising control and dominion over others. The greatest in his kingdom are not to be lording over everyone else as their subjects but are to serve—they are called to be the servants of all.

Service is part of being meek and humble, and only meek and humble persons will inherit the eternal kingdom. The Savior put himself forth as the supreme example, saying essentially that he did not come to be ministered to but to minister; he did not come to be served but to serve. He asked, Who is greater, the one who sits at the head of the table or the one who is serving the table? Most would say it is the one who sits at the head of the table, of course. But in truth, he taught, "*I am among you as he that serveth*" (Luke 22:27; emphasis added; cf. Mosiah 2:18).

Matthew 20:28 refers to Jesus as the "Son of man." This is Jesus' most common title for himself, used eighty-one times in the Gospels and never by anyone except himself. Jesus was *not* born into this world as the son of a man, meaning a mortal man. The more accurate or more complete title for Jesus Christ is the Son of Man of Holiness, Man of Holiness being a name-title for the Eternal Father in Heaven (Moses 6:57; 7:35).

TWO BLIND MEN HEALED (BARTIMAEUS) (LEAVING JERICHO)

Matthew 20:29–34; Mark 10:46–52; Luke 18:35–43
Old Testament Jericho, conquered and destroyed by Joshua and abandoned through most of the Israelite period, had lain in ruins for many centuries by Jesus' day. Hasmonean kings had begun a new Jericho along the north bank of Wadi Qelt, more than a mile south of the former site of Jericho. Herod the Great spread magnificent palaces, pavilions, a bathhouse, a swimming pool, a reception hall, and gardens along both banks of the *wadi* (Arabic, "streambed"). It was an inviting oasis surrounded by stark wilderness, with the Dead Sea just five miles away.

Roman-period Jericho served as a rest station for weary travelers between Galilee and Judea (Luke 19:1) and as an

Site of Roman-era Jericho, halfway between the hikers and the oasis of modern-day Jericho in the background

entry point near the border between Perea and Judea. When Jesus left Jericho with a great number of people accompanying him, about to hike up the Roman road to Jerusalem through the Judean Desert, he stopped and healed two blind men, including one named Bartimaeus, the son of Timaeus (Mark 10:46; *Bar* is Aramaic for "son of").

Jesus had taught his disciples to minister to the needs of others, to serve them and help relieve their burdens. Now he stopped and showed them an example of what he taught. He stopped what he was doing and practiced what he preached.

The blind men, including Bartimaeus, heard the commotion of the multitude passing by, asked what was happening, and upon learning it was the renowned Jesus and his followers, cried out for Jesus' attention. Others tried to silence them, but the blind men had undoubtedly heard about this Galilean worker of miracles (they knew of his royal provenance, calling him the messianic title, "Son of David"), and cried out all the louder for his mercy and compassion.

Jesus tested them with a question:

"What will ye that I shall do unto you?"

"They say unto him, Lord, that our eyes may be opened" to receive sight (Matthew 20:32–33).

They had faith in his power. Their faith would not only give them physical sight but would save them. Faith allows all people to be healed, both body and soul, if it is the will of God that it be so. And when that faith is exercised and healing is accomplished, the natural inclination of the beneficiary is to praise God and glorify him (Luke 18:43).

SALVATION COMES TO HOUSE OF ZACCHAEUS (AT JERICHO)

Luke 19:1–10 In his narrative of events at Jericho, Luke adds one more episode, involving a man named Zacchaeus.

Figs on the trunk and branches of a sycomore tree

He was a chief tax collector, a publican, in Jericho and rich (v. 2). Apparently a sincere and honest man (v. 8), Zacchaeus was also small of stature, for when he heard that Jesus was approaching, he climbed a sycomore tree to see him. Jesus invited him down so the publican could host Him at his home.

The biblical sycomore tree (not the English or American tree called the sycamore) is known scientifically as *Ficus sycomorus* (thus the spelling in the New Testament) and is not found in the Near East above one thousand feet above sea level.

Ficus sycomorus is a species of fig, or fig-mulberry, the fruit being like a fig and the leaf like the mulberry. The tree is known to grow to great size, sometimes attaining more than fifty feet in circumference, and is an evergreen. The fruit shoots forth on all parts of the stem, several figs on each leafless twig. The fruit is smaller than the regular fig and, though edible, is tasteless. In the land of Jesus, the sycomore tree grew in the mild coastal plains and in the Jordan Valley, where Jericho is situated and where Zacchaeus climbed one to see Jesus.

Antagonists and complainers objected to Jesus' association with the publican. The frequent combination of "publican" and "sinner" in the same sentence illustrates the attitude of most Jews about those who worked for the Roman government, though Zacchaeus's defense of his on-the-job integrity (v. 8) speaks highly of his concern for the law of the Jews. If there were found any irregularities in his financial dealings with his fellowman, he would restore him fourfold, which was more than the Mosaic law usually required (see, for example, Exodus 22:1–9).

Jesus had taught that he came to bring not saints but sinners to repentance (see commentary on Matthew 9:9–13). This Jewish publican was a son of Abraham and merited rescuing, for the Savior came to seek out and save anyone who was lost. "This day is salvation come to this house," Jesus announced to Zacchaeus. Jesus was using a word-play, a familiar oratorical and literary device among the Jews, with his name, which in Hebrew or Aramaic is *Yeshua*, literally meaning "salvation." Thus Jesus' words had double meaning. Salvation had indeed come to the publican's house.

PARABLE OF THE POUNDS (AT JERICHO)

Luke 19:11–27 As Jesus approached Jerusalem, some people supposed that he was about to announce and set up the much-anticipated kingdom of God, which meant to them overthrowing the Romans and displacing any such political organization with a theocracy, having God himself to rule and reign.

Jesus interrupted their suppositions with a story. His custom was to employ something in their immediate environment to teach them, usually something from nature or something from their historical memory.

"A certain nobleman went into a far country to receive for himself a kingdom, and to return" (v. 12). These circumstances were fairly fresh in the minds of the Jews because several times in the previous decades more than one generation of Herods had had to go to Rome for confirmation of a political appointment. "But his citizens hated him, and sent a message after him, saying, We will not have this man to reign over us" (v. 14). More than once deputations of Jews had followed these Herodian rulers to the capital of the empire to protest cruelties and improprieties in their rule. The Jews resisted and rejected those Herods.

Based on that historical context, which his people would definitely relate to, Jesus proceeded with the story that was really about him. He was the nobleman. He came and was rejected by the masses. They would not have him, but he will return and take an accounting of their stewardships.

He had given them pounds (or, in Matthew's version, talents; Matthew 25:14–30), some ten, some five, some one, and he would hold each accountable for proper use and development of that stewardship. To those who are faithful and productive he will give more; to those who are wasteful and unproductive he will take away even that which was originally given.

LAZARUS RESTORED (IN BETHANY)

John 11:8–53 (cf. Luke 19:28) When Jesus announced that it was time to return to Judea, his disciples were startled and reminded him that his enemies were trying to kill him there.

Jesus returned for a moment to the theme that threads its way all through the testimony of John: the motif of light and darkness. The Savior was still walking in the light of day; his night of darkness was afar off as yet.

John 11:11–15 Still speaking metaphorically, Jesus told his disciples that their friend Lazarus was "sleeping," and he was going to awake him out of sleep.

The disciples thought it good for a very sick man to sleep, getting as much rest as possible.

"Then said Jesus unto them plainly, Lazarus is dead. And I am glad for your sakes that I was not there, to the intent ye may believe" (vv. 14–15). He had already decided he was going to raise Lazarus, and such a miracle would strengthen the testimony of the faithful.

John 11:16 Then Thomas (the "doubter," some have mistakenly called him) said to the rest of the Twelve, "Let us also go, that we may die with him." If Jesus was indeed going to venture into hostile territory once again, even at the peril of his life, then Thomas was going to stay at his side and suffer with him. That is no testimony of a doubter.

The Joseph Smith Translation adds that *"they feared lest the Jews should take Jesus and put him to death, for as yet they did not understand the power of God"* (JST John 11:16). The disciples could only see Jesus' potential death as a threat of doom hanging over them; as yet they could not understand the glorious sequel—his rising from the dead, to a condition far beyond what he was about to give his dead friend.

John 11:17 Lazarus's body had now lain in the grave four days. The custom of the Jews in those days was to bury the deceased on the day of death. It was also a popular belief that the spirit remained near the body up to three days, but by the fourth day the spirit was irretrievably gone (see Ginzberg, *Legends of the Jews,* 5:78; Edersheim, *Jesus the Messiah,* 2:324–25; Farrar, *Life of Christ,* 510). Thus Jesus waited four full days to perform a miracle, the result of which would be impossible to misinterpret or ignore. This was a profound miracle, one of three recorded times the Savior raised someone from death to life (Mark 5:41–42; Luke 7:12–15). It demonstrated Jesus' absolute power over death and foreshadowed the resurrection.

John 11:20–27 Martha, learning of Jesus' coming, ran eastward, down the Roman road that comes up from the Jordan Valley, and upon meeting him, threw herself down at his feet and exclaimed, "Lord, if thou hadst been here, my brother had not died" (v. 21).

Such was Martha's faith that she felt if Jesus had only been present, Lazarus would not have died. But the second half of her anguished cry revealed her trusting nature: "But I know, that even now, whatsoever thou wilt ask of God, God will give it thee" (v. 22).

Then the following remarkable interchange ensued:

Jesus: "Thy brother shall rise again" (v. 23).

Martha: "I know that he shall rise again in the resurrection at the last day" (v. 24; this statement echoes Job's witness anciently; Job 19:26).

Jesus: "*I am the resurrection, and the life:* he that believeth in me, though he were dead, yet shall he live: and whosoever liveth and believeth in me shall never die. Believest thou this?" (vv. 25–26; emphasis added). It is not obvious that Jesus is God's Son and possesses such eternal powers, unless one has the faith to believe.

Martha: "Yea, Lord: I believe that thou art the Christ, the Son of God, which should come into the world" (v. 27).

John 11:28–37 Martha went to tell Mary that the Master was coming. The conversation was secretive because enemies were near. Mary met Jesus at the same place, at the eastward approaches to the town, and the conversation was repeated. Jesus was moved, seeing the tears of the sisters and the mourners. "Where have ye laid him?" They answered, "Lord, come and see."

Jesus wept. This is the shortest verse in the King James Bible, but it is the longest in compassion. Even though he knew he was about to raise his dead friend from the tomb, yet he felt sympathy for the people because he has a tender heart (cf. 3 Nephi 17:21–22).

Some Jews exclaimed, "Behold, how he loved him!" In fact, the Lord commands each of us: "Thou shalt live together in love, insomuch that thou shalt weep for the loss of them that die" (D&C 42:45). "You have probably experienced the pain that comes at the death of a family member or friend. It is natural to feel sorrow at such times. In fact, mourning is one of the deepest expressions of love. . . . The only way to take sorrow out of death is to take love out of life" (*True to the Faith*, 47).

Other Jews argued, "Could not this man, which opened the eyes of the blind, have caused that even this man should not have died?"

John 11:38–40 Jesus must have been dismayed at times with the incredible disbelief and hardness of heart of some people—how they shut themselves off from light and truth, from seeing and believing. No wonder he groaned in himself.

Jesus went to the burial cave, where a stone (usually square in that era) was set into place at the entrance of the sepulchre.

He instructed those standing by to take away the stone. Moments before he had asked "Where have ye laid him?" Now he has them take away the stone, and soon he will instruct them to loose Lazarus and let him go. There is no waste of divine energy; all that mortals can do, mortals do. That which only he can do, things that require uniquely divine power, he does.

Martha raised a practical objection to opening the sepulchre: there would be a terrible smell coming from inside, where serious decomposition had already begun in Lazarus's body, "for he hath been dead four days" (v. 39). Recall once again the Jewish tradition that the spirit was now irretrievably gone from the body.

In the emotional moment Jesus reminded her, "Said I not unto thee, that, if thou wouldest believe, thou shouldest see the glory of God?" (v. 40).

John 11:41–42 Everything Jesus did and said was a lesson, a message to all mortals. Before the miracle, Jesus paused to talk with his Father, to give him thanks. He intentionally did that to remind those listening to him that he was in

The Perean and Later Judean Ministry

constant touch with the One who sent him here (as we also should be with the same One who sent us here).

What Jesus was saying and doing was to teach and strengthen his faithful disciples, his closest associates. They were the ones who would record in their minds and hearts these sayings and events and believe them and be changed by them. As he had taught before, in a parable about the rich man and a beggar named Lazarus, those who would not believe Moses and the prophets would not be persuaded though one *rose from the dead* (Luke 16:19–31).

John 11:43–46 Jesus called forth his dead friend Lazarus from the burial cave with a loud voice. Why with a loud voice? Either because Lazarus's now nonfunctional ears would hear again and it was a long way down in the ground, or because he must symbolically speak loudly to call one back from the world of spirits, or because the scene would be indelibly engraved in the ears and eyes of all persons present in Bethany that day. Onlookers would not wonder, because of the softness or quietness of his voice, what exactly he had said; there would be no mistaking what words he had uttered. They all

BYU–Jerusalem Center student portraying the raising of Lazarus from an ancient tomb in Bethany

heard, and they knew what they heard. Then they saw, and they knew what they saw. The dead man, bound head and foot, even over the face, in burial wrappings, arose and came up and stood before the awestruck mourners.

Many who saw all this believed. How could they not believe? Here was not only unusual, but irrefutable evidence of Jesus' divine power.

All hearts were not changed by the miracle, however. Some who had seen it rushed to the Pharisees to report what Jesus had done.

John 11:47–53 A council gathered together to deal with the escalating threats some Jewish leaders felt against their power, position, and influence with the people. The "council" consisted of at least Pharisees and high priests (see Appendix 4, 748). Rather than exercising true priesthood, they were employing priestcraft (see 2 Nephi 26:29). "Because of priestcrafts and iniquities," the great Book of Mormon teacher Jacob prophesied, "they at Jerusalem will stiffen their necks against him, that he be crucified" (2 Nephi 10:5).

These Jewish leaders were worried about what they should do. Jesus was doing many impressive miracles too close to their domain, the Holy City. If they let him continue, all men would end up following him and the Romans would come and take away both the leaders' place and their nation (v. 48).

One of that council, the high priest Caiaphas (for more on him, see commentary on Matthew 26:3–5), stood up and said, in essence, that they did not know anything. Nor were they remembering the prophetic teaching that one man should die for the people, that the whole nation should not perish (v. 50). Either Caiaphas made that prediction in relation to their fear that the Romans would come in, remove them from their positions, and maybe reorder or even destroy the nation, or, as John explains, by virtue of his office Caiaphas was ironically prophesying that Jesus would die for the nation—which, of course, was true, but not in the way Caiaphas meant it. Jesus would be sacrificed to provide redemption not only for the

Jewish nation but for all nations of people, to gather all the children of God who would come to him. Caiaphas's prophecy of Jesus dying for the nation would conveniently fit into the high priest's own perverse intentions of destroying Jesus, whom he saw as a troublemaker and a usurper of his authority and leadership.

From that day forth (v. 53) they "took counsel together"; they fed on each other's fears, inciting, agitating, and fomenting hatred, determined to rid themselves of this holy Man whom they saw as a threat to their power and influence with the people.

Specific plans were now laid for taking Jesus' life, though the Jews in Judea had long been seeking Jesus to put him to death (John 7:1).

RETIRES TO EPHRAIM

John 11:54 After raising Lazarus in Bethany, Jesus found that walking openly among the Jews was dangerous, so he journeyed about fifteen miles northeast of Jerusalem out of the tribal inheritance of Judah into the land of Ephraim (though it was in the Roman province of Judea during Jesus' day) to a small town known by the same name, Ephraim. The place had been called Ophrah in the Old Testament (Joshua 18:23; 1 Samuel 13:17). Today the Arab village of et-Taiyibe features several ancient and modern Christian churches that Arab Christian villagers attend. There, "near to the wilderness," Jesus found respite before the final journey to Jerusalem.

CHAPTER 10

THE ATONEMENT AND THE RESURRECTION

TO JERUSALEM FOR PASSOVER

John 11:55–57 It was now Passover time, thirty-three years after the Savior's coming into the world and three years after the beginning of his ministry. People were gathering from all parts of the country and from all countries of the Mediterranean and Near Eastern world to participate in the high holy week at Jerusalem. The conspiracy to apprehend Jesus continued to unfold; there was a standing order, whenever and wherever he appeared, to arrest him.

A SUPPER AT MARTHA AND MARY'S; JESUS ANOINTED BY MARY (IN BETHANY)

John 12:1–3 John indicates this supper was held at the home of Martha and Mary. Their brother, the same Lazarus who had been restored to life, was also there. The spiritually minded Mary broke open a costly imported ointment called spikenard (see commentary on Matthew 26:7–13). A pound of pure spikenard could sell for more than three hundred pence or denarii, the better part of a year's wages. Mary anointed Jesus' feet and wiped them with her hair, and the pleasant fragrance of the ointment filled the house. This was homage rarely rendered even to a king.

JUDAS'S PROTEST (IN BETHANY)

John 12:4–8 Judas Iscariot, who had totally lost the Spirit or was fast losing it, criticized what he considered Mary's wasteful use of a precious commodity that could have been sold to relieve the suffering of the poor, as if he sincerely cared for the poor. John has nothing good to say about the hypocritical response of Judas; in fact, John calls him a thief. Apparently Judas was the treasurer of the traveling group—he carried the bag.

Leave her alone, Jesus interjected, "*For she hath preserved this ointment until now, that she might anoint me in token of my burial*" (JST John 12:7), another plain foreshadowing of his imminent fate. Mary may have understood what was coming. Faithful women usually seem to understand first. And this particular act would be a memorial to Mary whenever the gospel is preached (see commentary on Mark 14:3–9).

PEOPLE GATHER TO JESUS, LAZARUS; CONSPIRACY AGAINST LAZARUS (AT JERUSALEM)

John 12:9–12 Many people were not only anxious to see Jesus but curious also to see Lazarus, the man whose raising from the dead had been reported far and wide. The religious leaders of the Jews, especially the chief priests, were losing some of their popularity with the crowds not only because of Jesus but also because of Lazarus, who was the embodiment of and undeniable proof of Jesus' divine power. The jealous leaders wanted to see Lazarus dead again and buried to stay.

PROPHECY FULFILLED (AT BETHPHAGE, ON THE MOUNT OF OLIVES)

Matthew 21:1–5; Mark 11:1–6; Luke 19:28–34 Two of the three passages referring to Bethphage mention it side by side with Bethany; the two towns were adjacent to each other, both on the eastern slope of the Mount of Olives. Bethphage means house of figs, and many fig trees grow in the vicinity.

Rabbinic literature cites Bethphage as the eastern limit to the city of Jerusalem (*Mishnah*, 500, n. 11). Jesus' first coming to Jerusalem as king was from the east, as his second coming is prophesied to be (Joseph Smith–Matthew 1:26).

The lowly but useful and respected ass

The ass was a utilitarian and appreciated animal in the ancient Near East. The number of asses a man possessed was a measure of his wealth. Asses were associated with royalty, even with the Messiah. Zechariah had heralded the glad tidings of the messianic era with the following prophecy: "Rejoice greatly, O daughter of Zion; shout, O daughter of Jerusalem: behold, thy King cometh unto thee: he is just, and having

The Atonement and the Resurrection

BYU students portraying Palm Sunday procession of Jesus over the Mount of Olives and his triumphal entry into the Holy City

salvation; lowly, and riding upon an ass, and upon a colt the foal of an ass" (Zechariah 9:9). We learn from the prophet that the royal entry into Jerusalem on an ass was a symbol of humility, a token of peace appropriate for the Prince of Peace. Expanding on Jesus' humble act as something for his followers to emulate, Elder Spencer W. Kimball wrote:

> Humility is royalty without a crown,
> Greatness in plain clothes,
> Erudition without decoration,
> Wealth without display,
> Power without scepter or force,
> Position demanding no preferential rights,
> Greatness sitting in the congregation,
> Prayer in closets and not in corners of the street,
> Fasting in secret without publication,
> Stalwartness without a label,
> Supplication upon its knees,
> Divinity riding an ass.
> (*Humility*, 13–14)

Riding a horse would have symbolized war and fighting strength, but the Messiah was coming not to conquer but to save. It might have made the Romans smile to see this acclaimed Deliverer approaching on an ass, and it might have confused and angered the Jews who anticipated an armed confrontation and overthrow of the Romans. But this triumphal entry was no meaningless pageantry or seditious demonstration; it was an open acknowledgment by Jesus, the Prince of Peace, of his kingly and messianic titles.

Mark, Luke, and John mention a colt only, whereas the text of Matthew indicates that the disciples brought an ass and a colt (the colt being the male foal, or offspring, of an ass). Matthew, or a later editor, seems to have sought meticulous fulfillment of the prophecy of Zechariah by specifying two animals, although Zechariah's prophetic preview of the Messiah is couched in the poetic structure called parallelism, which presents an image or subject in two parallel phrases. There was actually only one animal intended—Jesus, of course, could ride only one animal. The discrepancy in the number of animals is resolved by a simple correction that the Prophet Joseph Smith made: Matthew 21:2 and 5 in the Joseph Smith Translation indicate that only one animal was involved.

TRIUMPHAL ENTRY (INTO JERUSALEM)

Matthew 21:6–11; Mark 11:7–11; Luke 19:35–38; John 12:12–18 All of the Gospel writers recorded Jesus' triumphal entry into the city of Jerusalem at the beginning of the last week of his mortal life, and all of them mention that people spread items of clothing and branches in front of him in his honor. John, however, is the only writer who specifies that the branches were from palm trees.

Palm trees do not generally grow on the slopes of the Mount of Olives, where the people had gathered to acclaim Jesus their king. The natural habitat of the palm is a more

THE LAST WEEK OF THE SAVIOR'S MORTAL LIFE

1st Day	2d Day	3d Day	4th Day	5th Day	6th Day	7th Day	1st Day
Triumphal Entry into Jerusalem	Cleansing of Temple	Parables in response	Unrecorded	Passover, Atonement	Crucifixion, Atonement	The Sabbath	Resurrection
Greeted by a very great multitude shouting "Hosanna!"	Christ cleanses the Temple, accusing those who have made it "a den of thieves"; later, heals those who come to him in the Temple.	Christ responds to questions of his authority with parables; openly condemns the scribes and Pharisees as hypocrites.	Plot to kill Christ continues to grow; Judas has agreed to deliver Christ for 30 pieces of silver, and now seeks to betray him.	Christ celebrates Passover with his disciples; completes first portion of the Atonement (Gethsemane); is betrayed by Judas; taken and illegally condemned to death.	Conspirators incite crowd against Jesus; Pilate allows death sentence to go forward; Christ is scourged, humiliated, crucified, and willingly gives up his life.	Christ ministers in world of spirits; guards placed outside the tomb.	Early in the morning, disciples find empty tomb with angels present; Mary stays, weeping; Christ, now resurrected, appears to her, and later to his disciples and many others.

Palm branches were a symbol of Jewish independence

moderate and tropical climate such as that of the Jordan Valley. Palm branches could have been transported up from Jericho for the Passover celebration, as is done to this day. The use of palm branches for Jesus' entry was not coincidental. Since the Hasmonean period, palm branches had been a symbol of Jewish patriotism, independence, and triumph over enemies (see Appendix 6, 767).

There was tremendous messianic fervor in Jerusalem at this time. Many Jews were anticipating a messiah, though he was expected to be a military and political conqueror-deliverer.

The people cried out hosanna to the Son of David (Matthew 21:9), Son of David being a royal and messianic title. "Blessed is he that cometh in the name of the Lord" is an exclamation from a messianic psalm (118:26). John's text is even more explicit: "Blessed is the King of Israel that cometh in the name of the Lord" (John 12:13). Their identifying Jesus as the Messiah and the King, combined with their plea "save us" or "deliver us, we beseech thee" (the meaning of the Hebrew *hosanna*), unmistakably reveals who they supposed he was and what they expected him to do.

The atmosphere of messianic fervor in the Holy Land during the years of the meridian dispensation helps to explain the appearance of false messiahs (see, for example, Acts 5:36–37). Satan always has a counterfeit to righteousness.

Jesus' entrance into Jerusalem created quite a stir, many citizens and pilgrims wondering who he was. The crowds kept saying, "This is Jesus the prophet of Nazareth of Galilee" (Matthew 21:11).

Some of those present when Jesus raised Lazarus from the grave now testified, and they convinced others of who He was (John 12:17–18).

"And Jesus entered into Jerusalem, and into the temple. *And* when he had looked round about upon all things, *and blessed the disciples,* the eventide was come" (JST Mark 11:13).

At Passover time, a time of independence, of victory over oppressors, of messianic expectation, Jesus accepted the acclamation of King and triumphantly proceeded into the city. He likely entered the Temple Mount where today's Golden Gate is located, and he turned into the Temple instead of into the Antonia Fortress to take on the Romans. That made all the difference—it showed what kind of Messiah he was. Yes, he had come to deliver the people from their enemies, but not from the Romans. He had come to free the people of all the earth from their greatest enemies, death and hell. The greatest Independence Day in the universe was the twenty-four-hour period that included Gethsemane, Golgotha, and the Garden of the Resurrection.

PHARISEES DISAPPROVE (IN JERUSALEM)

Luke 19:39–40; John 12:19 Some of the Pharisees, in their hyperbolic fear that "the world has gone after him" (John 12:19), told the Master to rebuke his followers. Their feeling was that this is seditious behavior, calling him a king and stirring up the crowds with this messianic fervor. This was dangerous, and they urged Jesus to tell his followers to be quiet.

Jesus replied that if he told them to stop praising and glorying in their Deliverer, the stones would immediately cry out.

It was time to publicly proclaim the truth.

JESUS WEEPS OVER JERUSALEM (NEAR JERUSALEM)

Luke 19:41–44 (cf. Matthew 23:37–39) The traditional place where Jesus stopped and looked out over Jerusalem, lamented its past and present, and forewarned of its future is partway down the western slope of the Mount of Olives, looking straight over at the Temple Mount, at a place now called *Dominus Flevit,* meaning "the Lord wept." It is likely that this episode occurred just before Jesus entered Jerusalem as he made his way to the city during the Triumphal Entry.

The Savior spoke to the city and its inhabitants, saying in effect, If you had only understood the things that were needed for you to have peace! But those things seemed to be hidden from them. The days were coming when their enemies (this time, the Romans) would set up siege machines and fortifications and surround them and seal them up within their walls. Then they would kill them and their children and level the city, not leaving one stone of the temple upon another (Joseph Smith–Matthew 1:3), all because they failed to recognize the time of their visitation (or punishment; Isaiah 10:3), and the coming of their Savior, their Deliverer.

Should this message of consequence and retribution have surprised the Jews? No. Moses had pronounced similar dire predictions upon Israelite people who deviated and apostatized from the way of the Lord. The Jews knew well these words recorded in Deuteronomy:

The Atonement and the Resurrection

"It shall come to pass, if thou wilt not hearken unto the voice of the Lord thy God, to observe to do all his commandments and his statutes which I command thee this day; that all these curses shall come upon thee, and overtake thee: . . .

"The Lord shall send upon thee cursing, vexation, and rebuke, in all that thou settest thine hand unto. . . .

"The Lord shall smite thee with a consumption, and . . . with the sword, . . . and they shall pursue thee until thou perish. . . .

"The fruit of thy land, and all thy labours, shall a nation which thou knowest not eat up; and thou shalt be only oppressed and crushed alway: . . .

"Moreover all these curses shall come upon thee, and shall pursue thee, and overtake thee, till thou be destroyed; because thou hearkenedst not unto the voice of the Lord thy God, to keep his commandments and his statutes which he commanded thee: . . .

"The Lord shall bring a nation against thee from far, from the end of the earth, as swift as the eagle flieth [the eagle was the symbol of Rome]; a nation whose tongue thou shalt not understand;

"A nation of fierce countenance, which shall not regard the person of the old, nor shew favour to the young:

"And he shall besiege thee in all thy gates, until thy high and fenced walls come down, wherein thou trustedst, throughout all thy land" (Deuteronomy 28:15, 20, 22, 33, 45, 49–52).

The greater part of a millennium after Moses, the prophet Nephi elaborated on the crushing consequences of the Jerusalemites' rejecting their true Messiah:

"And as for those who are at Jerusalem, saith the prophet, they shall be scourged by all people, because they crucify the God of Israel, and turn their hearts aside, rejecting signs and wonders, and the power and glory of the God of Israel.

"And because they turn their hearts aside, saith the prophet, and have despised the Holy One of Israel, they shall wander in the flesh, and perish, and become a hiss and a byword, and be hated among all nations" (1 Nephi 19:13–14).

Nephi further clarified the ongoing, dire results of the Jews' rejecting their Messiah: "And as one generation hath been destroyed among the Jews because of iniquity, even so have they been destroyed from generation to generation according to their iniquities" (2 Nephi 25:9). Their greatest, most tragic iniquity has been the denial and scorning of their Messiah.

The generation of Jewish leaders in the days of Jesus rejected him and suffered for it. Jews for many generations afterward continued to reject him as the Messiah, and so they continued to suffer for it. Such consequences are not exclusively the Jews', however. The truth is that *anyone* who rejects their God will experience the consequent suffering for that rejection.

GREEKS WISH TO SEE JESUS (IN JERUSALEM)

John 12:20–22 Much of the Roman world was really a Greek or Hellenized world, especially the eastern Mediterranean coastal lands, and Jews were scattered in all parts of the world (the Diaspora, or the "dispersion"; see Ogden and Skinner, *Acts through Revelation*, 387–94). The Greeks referred to in these verses of John 12 were possibly Gentile proselytes to Judaism who had journeyed to Jerusalem for the great pilgrimage festival of Passover. These Jews from Gentile lands inquired of Philip, he in turn told Andrew, and the two apostles told Jesus that these "Greeks" wanted to meet him.

DISCOURSE: JESUS SENT BY THE FATHER (IN JERUSALEM)

John 12:23–50 Jesus announced that his hour had come (enemies had been unable to take him before that time, because "his hour was not yet come"; John 7:30). Now, however, it was time to conclude his mortal mission, to climax his ministry with the ultimate sacrifice, but it is interesting that he spoke of the conclusion not as a time to suffer but as a time to be glorified.

A word about the agricultural context of the ensuing teachings: To Americans, corn is a specific crop with a cob that grows on a stalk, a plant that is elsewhere called maize. The King James Bible uses the British *corn* generally for grain of all kinds. The reason that *corn* and *wheat* are both used in this passage from John is that *corn* can mean the head of grain, whichever grain it may be.

The scripture indicates that a grain of wheat must be planted in the ground and "die"; that is, it must change from its present structure to become something bigger and better, to become fruitful. Jesus used this analogy from nature to foreshadow his own death: "The hour is come, that the Son of man should be glorified. . . . If it [a corn of wheat] die, it bringeth forth much fruit" (John 12:23–24). Sacrifice is what engenders the blessings of eternal life. Burying the physical man is necessary in order to give birth to the spiritual and eternal man.

Anyone who loves his life in this world (that is, the worldly life), Jesus taught, will lose it for eternity, and whoever "hates" his life in this world (meaning, he who is not caught up with the worldly life or focused on ephemeral things) is on course to attain life eternal. Any person who truly serves Jesus will be honored by the Father: Where He is, there his servant will be also.

Jesus turned to the Father, not for relief but for strength to endure. "Father, save me from this hour [help me get through this time of trial]: but for this cause came I unto this hour [to experience these very sufferings]" (v. 27). The New International Version of the Bible (NIV) rendering of this verse is significant: "Now my heart is troubled, and what shall

I say? 'Father, save me from this hour'? No, it was for this very reason I came to this hour. Father, glorify your name!"

As in the Council in Heaven, Jesus continues to speak and do all things to glorify not himself but his Father. The Father spoke: "I have glorified it, and will glorify it again."

Some of the people in the vicinity thought they heard thunderings; others supposed an angel was speaking to Jesus, but he explained that the voice was not for his benefit but for theirs—as always, to the intent that they believe the Father sent him.

John 12:31 "Now is the judgment of this world: now shall the prince of this world be cast out." Now, with world-changing events about to transpire, the Atonement and the Resurrection, the world will be prepared for judgment and the devil can ultimately be expelled forever, having no contact with the upgraded earth.

John 12:32–34 Jesus had already prophesied, just as Moses lifted up the serpent in the wilderness, that He would be lifted up on the cross (see commentary on John 3:14–15). Now he described the kind of death he would experience: He would be "lifted up from the earth" in his crucifixion (1 Nephi 19:10), and then he would be "lifted up from the earth" in his resurrection and ascension—and in doing that he had power to draw all men to him, "that all men might repent and come unto him" (D&C 18:11). Nephi adds: "He doeth not anything save it be for the benefit of the world; for he loveth the world [that is, the Father's children who live in this world], even that he layeth down his own life that he may draw all men unto him" (2 Nephi 26:24).

The people understood Jesus' symbolic language, but they argued that in the law, the scriptural instruction, "Christ abideth for ever" (v. 34; cf. 2 Samuel 7:16), so why was Jesus saying that "the Son of man must be lifted up?" They wanted to know who was the "Son of man" he was talking about.

John 12:35–36 The Savior referred to his teaching about himself as the Light of the world: "Yet a little while is the light with you. Walk while ye have the light, lest darkness come upon you: for he that walketh in darkness knoweth not whither he goeth. While ye have light, believe in the light, that ye may be the children of light."

Jesus taught these symbolic but deeply meaningful teachings, and then he disappeared, "hiding" himself from them (cf. Luke 4:30; John 8:59).

The light of Christ is always shining into this world, but some fail to see it and continue walking in darkness because their eyes are not opened to the Light—possibly on account of some defect or flaw in themselves that needs to be corrected. Elder Joseph B. Wirthlin related the following:

"A few years ago, I began to notice that things around me were beginning to darken. It troubled me because simple things like reading the print in my scriptures were becoming more difficult. I wondered what had happened to the quality of the light bulbs and wondered why manufacturers today couldn't make things like they had in years past.

"I replaced the bulbs with brighter ones. They, too, became dim. I blamed the poor design of the lamps and bulbs. I even questioned whether the brightness of the sun was fading before the thought occurred to me that the problem might not be with the amount of light in the room—the problem might be with my own eyes.

"Shortly thereafter, I went to an ophthalmologist who assured me that the world was not going dark at all. A cataract on my eye was the reason the light seemed to be fading. . . . I placed my faith in the capable hands of this trained specialist, the cataract was removed, and behold, light again flooded my life! The light had never diminished; only my capacity to see the light had been lessened" (*Ensign,* November 2002, 85).

John 12:37–41 Though the Lord taught such elevating doctrines and performed so many miracles, "yet they believed not on him" (v. 37), fulfilling the words of Isaiah ("Esaias" is the spelling through the Greek):

"Who hath believed our report [our witness]? And to

whom is the arm of the Lord revealed?" or, to whom has the Lord given a testimony of these things? (Isaiah 53:1).

Actually they could not believe, for the very reason Isaiah explained: "He hath blinded their eyes, and hardened their heart; that they should not see with their eyes, nor understand with their heart, and be converted, and I should heal them" (v. 40, referring to Isaiah 6:9–10). This wording assigns responsibility for the people's spiritual blindness and their hardness of heart to the Lord, but the rendering of this same passage in the Book of Mormon has the prophet teaching in such a way that only the spiritually receptive among the people would be prepared to accept the Lord's message. The Lord said to Isaiah:

"Go and tell this people—Hear ye indeed, but they understood not; and see ye indeed, but they perceived not. Make the heart of this people fat, and make their ears heavy, and shut their eyes—lest they see with their eyes, and hear with their ears, and understand with their heart, and be converted and be healed" (2 Nephi 16:9–10). This means that the effect of teaching the Lord's words would be people closing their hearts, ears, and eyes, with the resulting disinclination to be converted and healed.

These things Isaiah wrote when he saw the Lord's glory and taught about him, as recorded in Isaiah 6 and in 2 Nephi 16.

John 12:42–43 The Gospels contain numerous negative assessments of the religious establishment among the Jews, but now and then we are reminded that some did believe in Jesus. John 12:42 and Acts 6:7 report that many leaders believed on him. They were convinced but not converted. They were fearful of losing their social status among the people and their ecclesiastical standing among their fellow leaders (see, for example, Joseph of Arimathea; John 19:38). "They loved the praise of men more than the praise of God" (v. 43; see, for example, Mark 12:38–40).

John 12:44–50 Once again Jesus taught that he was the

Light that came into the world to dispel darkness. If anyone hears his words and refuses to obey them, Jesus says, "I judge him not" (v. 47), and he explains: "I came not to judge the world but to save the world." Saving the world was the main purpose of his first coming. His judgment is reserved for the time when he comes to rule and reign and prepare this sphere for his celestial home.

He said that whoever rejects him and refuses to receive his words would not need him to judge them, because his words would judge them in the end (v. 48).

Verses 44–45 and 49–50 reemphasize a truth that Jesus constantly and consistently puts before us. As much as any other teaching, he wants us to internalize and never forget that the Father sent him to earth (see, for example, commentary on Matthew 3:8–9; 10:1–4; John 5:17–47; 7:14–36; 9:4–5). For all he said and did, he gave credit and honor to the Father. The Son's words are the words of the Father, and the Son's works are the works of the Father. All of this is repeatedly reflected in 3 Nephi, beginning in chapter 11, the account of Jesus' ministry on the western hemisphere.

The Son testifies of the Father, and when the Father comes to earth, the Father testifies of the Son. The testimony of John, especially, is the testimony of a Father and a Son for each other. They have the most perfect, loving relationship of any two people we know in the universe. They are of one mind and one heart. They are the supreme example for all children of God to emulate.

MONEYCHANGERS CAST OUT (ON THE TEMPLE MOUNT, JERUSALEM)

Matthew 21:12–16; Mark 11:15–19; Luke 19:45–48
The most famous New Testament users of money were the moneychangers. Both Roman and Greek coins were legal tender for secular purposes, but the rabbis and Temple

administrators had declared only Jewish and Tyrian coinage appropriate for sacred functions, thereby setting themselves up for financial profit through the transactions of the moneychangers (Tyrian shekels were apparently preferred because of their higher silver content). According to the law of Moses, every Israelite male over twenty years of age owed annually a half shekel to the Temple treasury as an offering to Jehovah (Exodus 30:12–14). This amount had to be changed from the usual foreign currency into currency appropriate for keeping in the Temple, which also served as the economic center of the Jewish people. The Jews determined that the didrachma, or two denarii, was equivalent to the half shekel (see Appendix 7, 777; Rousseau and Arav, *Jesus and His World*, 57–58).

Though upholding the sanctity and legitimacy of the Temple proper, Jesus lashed out against the ill-motivated merchandising and fraudulent profiteering of the moneychangers and the authorities responsible for the moneychanging. At the Passover three years earlier, at the beginning of his ministry, he had cast out the moneychangers, chastising them for making "my Father's house" a "house of merchandise" (John 2:16), a strong rebuke, to be sure; but now, approaching the time when they would take his life, he became more vehement and rebuked them for making "my house" a "den of thieves" (Matthew 21:13). A modern scholar on the ancient Temple, Rabbi Leibel Reznick, explains that "the halacha (Jewish law) states that . . . the Temple is a place of holy worship and should not appear to be an area of commerce (Tosfos, Pesachim 7a). Now, if merely giving the appearance of commerce is forbidden, how much more so is the actual location of stores and shops atop the Mount" (*Holy Temple Revisited*, 69).

No improper activity was allowed in the sacred precinct, and no unclean thing was to be taken there. The Lord taught similarly regarding a latter-day Temple:

"And ye shall not suffer any unclean thing to come in

unto it; and my glory shall be there, and my presence shall be there.

"But if there shall come into it any unclean thing, my glory shall not be there; and my presence shall not come into it" (D&C 94:8–9).

The chief priests and scribes took note of the impressive things Jesus did, and they grew more and more jealous and afraid of him. This Galilean was gathering too large a following, and the crowds were hailing him with messianic titles.

Matthew 21:15–16 The "children" crying in the Temple were really the "children *of the kingdom*" (JST Matthew 21:13), those born again into the kingdom of God who recognized with spiritual eyes their Deliverer, who cried out, exulting and praising their covenant father who had come to save his "babes and sucklings," the weak and simple ones who acknowledged and adored him.

On verse 16 compare Psalm 8:2.

Matthew 21:17–18; Mark 11:11–12 When at Jerusalem Jesus usually lodged overnight with his friend Lazarus and Lazarus's sisters, Martha and Mary, in Bethany, just east of Jerusalem, on the eastern side of the Mount of Olives. Mark notes that the Twelve stayed there, too. All during this last week, after spending the day in Jerusalem, Jesus and the Twelve would walk back to their lodgings up over the Mount of Olives. Anyone who has made this trek even once knows how physically fit these Brethren were.

FIG TREE CURSED, WITHERS (BETWEEN BETHANY AND JERUSALEM)

Matthew 21:18–22; Mark 11:12–14, 20–26; Luke 13:6–9 The most memorable encounter with a fig tree in the New Testament occurred during the last week of Jesus' life on earth, while Jesus was walking one morning from Bethany over the Mount of Olives to Jerusalem. As he walked, he became hungry, "and when he saw a fig tree in the way, he came to it, and found nothing thereon, but leaves only, and said unto it, Let no fruit grow on thee henceforward for ever. And presently the fig tree withered away" (Matthew 21:18–19). Mark added, after Jesus came and found nothing but leaves, "for the time of figs was not yet" (Mark 11:13).

Insight and interpretation may be gleaned from a parable taught earlier by Jesus: "A certain man had a fig tree planted in his vineyard; and he came and sought fruit thereon, and found none. Then said he unto the dresser of his vineyard, Behold, these three years I come seeking fruit on this fig tree, and find none: cut it down; why cumbereth it the ground? And he answering said unto him, Lord, let it alone this year also, till I shall dig about it, and dung it: And if it bear fruit, well: and if not, then after that thou shalt cut it down" (Luke 13:6–9).

The fig tree was common in rabbinical lore as a symbol or type of the nation of Israel. Jesus, too, adopted the symbolism in this incident and in the parable. We have no other example of the mortal Jesus using his divine power to destroy, but he deemed the life of this one fig tree a necessary teaching tool, to illustrate in an unforgettable way the religious history of Israel. Moses 3:9 teaches us that trees are living entities; they have spirits, and can hear, understand, and obey. Jacob also advises us that "we truly can command in the name of Jesus and the very trees obey us" (Jacob 4:6).

The fig tree, or the people of Israel, had been planted in the part of God's vineyard that was the land of Israel. The tree had been watered and nourished by the Lord of the vineyard through his earthly husbandmen. It had been pruned by centuries of adversity and was expected to bear fruit. Because it was Passover time in Jerusalem, half a year before figs would normally ripen, a fig tree at this time of year would not be expected to have edible fruit on it. Jesus may have been referring to previous years' unfruitfulness. From Jesus' point of view, this tree had produced a showy flush of leaves but was perennially barren and fruitless—"these three years I come seeking fruit on this fig tree, and find none" (Luke 13:7). In a sense, the tree was a hypocrite, trying to show itself to be something it wasn't.

Judaism at the time of Jesus was ripe in ritualism and regimentation. It had been aggressive in maintaining the finer points of the law of Moses and the traditions, but it had neglected the weightier matters of justice, mercy, and faith. The fig tree representing Israel was fruitless, and although it was not cut down in that generation, because it still bore no fruit after another season, or generation, of growth, history soberly teaches us that it was cut down and removed, and pieces of it were scattered to other parts of the vineyard.

PRIESTS CHALLENGE JESUS' AUTHORITY (AT THE TEMPLE IN JERUSALEM)

Matthew 21:23–27; Mark 11:27–33; Luke 20:1–8
While Jesus was teaching in his House, the Temple, some chief priests, scribes, elders, and Pharisees approached once again trying to embarrass, argue, provoke, and antagonize: "By what authority doest thou these things? and who gave thee this authority?"

Jesus countered with his own question, with a promise that if they would answer his, he would answer theirs: "The baptism of John—whence was it? from heaven, or of men?"

It did not take the Jewish leaders long to realize they had been asked another perfectly indicting question. They reasoned: "If we shall say, From heaven; he will say unto us, Why did ye not then believe him? But if we shall say, Of men; we fear the people; for all hold John as a prophet."

They came to entrap Jesus, but they themselves were trapped: "We cannot tell."

"Neither tell I you by what authority I do these things." They were outwitted.

PARABLE: TWO SONS (AT THE TEMPLE IN JERUSALEM)

Matthew 21:28–32 Jesus answered his challengers anyway, with a story, a parable of two sons. A father asked the first son to go to work in his vineyard. The son refused but afterward repented and went. The father asked the second son to go to work in the vineyard, and this son agreed to go but did not. Which of the two sons did the will of his father?

The questioners answered correctly, The first.

Jesus responded to the leaders of the people: "The publicans and the harlots go into the kingdom of God before you. For John came unto you in the way of righteousness, and bore record of me, and ye believed him not; but the publicans and the harlots believed him; and ye, *afterward,* when ye had seen *me,* repented not, that ye might believe him. *For he that believed not John concerning me, cannot believe me, except he first repent. And except ye repent, the preaching of John shall condemn you in the day of judgment*" (JST Matthew 21:31–34).

PARABLE: WICKED HUSBANDMEN (AT THE TEMPLE IN JERUSALEM)

Matthew 21:33–46; Mark 12:1–12; Luke 20:9–20 "*And, again,* hear another parable; *for unto you that believe not, I speak in parables; that your unrighteousness may be rewarded unto you,*" that is, so that you suffer the penalty for your wrongdoing (JST Matthew 21:34).

A certain householder (God) planted a vineyard (the covenant people in the land of Israel). He put a hedge around it, a fence or enclosure, prepared a winepress, or winevat, and built a tower not only to reclaim the rocky soil by using the

The Atonement and the Resurrection

A stone tower to watch over the vineyard

stones but also to guard and protect the vineyard—the tower offered an elevated position from which the watchmen could see approaching dangers. The householder leased his vineyard to husbandmen or farmers (the watchmen on the tower were the priests, teachers, and leaders of Israel) and went away for a time.

Harvest time came, when the householder could expect produce, the fruit of the vineyard. He sent his servants (the prophets) to receive the fruits, but by this time the husbandmen had come to feel the vineyard was theirs; they had built up their own fences around the land (not only God's laws but their own traditions) and planted it with their own trees to produce what they wanted. They were annoyed when the householder, the true owner, sent servants to receive the fruit of the land, and they rejected those prophets, beating some and killing others. The householder sent more servants, or prophets; they were treated the same.

Finally, he sent his beloved son (the Son of God), saying, "They will reverence my son." But when the husbandmen saw the son, they knew he was the heir and plotted to take over his inheritance. They had him arrested and killed.

A cornerstone

Jesus asked the Jewish leaders the indicting question: When the lord of the vineyard comes, what will he do to those husbandmen?

They replied: "He will miserably destroy those wicked men, and will let out his vineyard unto other husbandmen, which shall render him the fruits in their seasons" (v. 41).

Condemned by their own mouths! But before the verdict and the sentencing, one more question: Did you never read in the scriptures, "The stone which the builders rejected, the same is become the head of the corner"? (v. 42; see Psalm 118:22).

The cornerstone (Hebrew, *rosh pinna,* "head of the corner") was a large stone placed in the corner of a building's foundation to provide stability and strength for the structure (at least symbolically), and to serve as a guide for all the other foundation stones. New Testament writers saw in Jesus (as the Messiah) the fulfillment of this prophetic analogy: "This is the stone which was set at nought of you builders, which is become the head of the corner" (Acts 4:11). Jesus Christ is the "chief corner stone" and the apostles and prophets the rest of the foundation upon which the Church is established (Ephesians 2:19–20).

These leaders among the Jews had themselves concluded that the wicked husbandmen should be destroyed and the vineyard let out to other husbandmen, who would bring forth its fruits. Thus Jesus' pointed pronouncement upon them: "The kingdom of God shall be taken from you, and given to a nation bringing forth the fruits thereof" (v. 43), a foreshadowing of what would happen in the next generation: the Jewish kingdom would be destroyed and the work of the vineyard of the Lord offered to Gentile husbandmen. The vineyard would be let out to Gentile husbandmen for many generations, until about the time the Lord of the vineyard would come again (Acts 13:46; Jacob 5:61–63, 70–76).

The Lord, through the Prophet Joseph Smith, made significant explanatory and prophetic additions to these parables and pronouncements, with a broad sweep of fulfillment from the time of Jesus' mortal ministry through the Millennium (see JST Matthew 21:47–56, Bible Appendix, 804).

PARABLE: WEDDING OF A KING'S SON (AT THE TEMPLE IN JERUSALEM)

Matthew 22:1–14; cf. Luke 14:1–24 This parable could also be entitled the "parable of the invited guests" or the "parable of the guests who refuse to attend" or even the "parable of the wedding garment," depending on what teaching or lesson one wants to emphasize (see Wayment, "Names of the Parables").

While teaching his last public parable to a mixed audience, Jesus referred to a theme that was a favorite in the synagogues and academies: the great marriage feast. A certain king (God the Father) prepared a wedding celebration for his son (Jesus Christ) and sent servants to give out invitations to the people (God's covenant people), but the people did not want to come. An invitation from a king was, of course, equivalent to a command, but the king had to send additional servants to invite his people once again.

"Tell them which are bidden, Behold, I have prepared my dinner: my oxen and my fatlings are killed, and all things are ready: come unto the marriage" (Matthew 22:4).

But the people really did not want to attend. Some made light of the occasion and the invitation (Matthew 22:5), and others made excuses for not being able to be there, putting their personal interests and pleasures above the king's call. Luke has the invited guests excusing themselves to check on a real estate deal (Luke 14:18), or a purchase of livestock (14:19), or for having just married (14:20). A few of the invited ones even killed the servants who were out delivering the invitations to be with the son, the bridegroom, at this most glorious and happy occasion.

Receiving word of the slaying of his servants, the king became angry and sent armies to destroy the people who had killed them and proved themselves unworthy of the invitations.

The king then sent out into the highways to invite others (the Gentiles) to the marriage feast, "both bad and good: and the wedding was furnished with guests" (Matthew 22:10).

But when the king arrived and started examining the guests, he saw a man who "had not on a wedding garment" (Matthew 22:11). The king demanded of the man, in effect, How did you get in here, not properly clothed for the marriage?

The man was speechless.

"Bind him hand and foot, and take him away, and cast him into outer darkness" (Matthew 22:13).

"For many are called, but few are chosen; *wherefore all do not have on the wedding garment*" (JST Matthew 22:14).

Something sacred is suggested here. To be present with God and his Son at the great wedding feast, the Second Coming, and the marriage of the Lamb with his bride (the Saints of his Church), those prepared to attend and receive further blessings must be clothed in the garment of righteousness, the garment of the holy priesthood, presenting themselves before God with the necessary covenants and ordinances (see Smith, *Teachings of the Prophet Joseph Smith*, 63).

Luke's account of the great feast, or the great supper (Luke 14:16–24), is preceded by two other episodes, or parables, involving the "eating of bread," meaning partaking of a meal, or making a dinner or supper (Luke 14:1–15).

Luke 14:1–6 Jesus went to the home of one of the Pharisees for a Sabbath meal. Luke says "they watched him" (v. 1), to see what he might do on the holy day. One of the men present suffered from dropsy (a disease in which limbs and abdomen are overly filled with fluid, often the result of a liver infection or heart disease), and perhaps he was present at the meal as a setup for the host and other guests to find something for which they could accuse Jesus. But the Savior preempted their trickery by asking them, "Is it lawful to heal on the sabbath day?" How could they answer yes? On the other hand, how could they answer no? That was certainly not the attitude of their revered law, either. So they kept quiet, and Jesus proceeded to heal the man. Then he answered his own question with another question: "Which of you shall have an ass or an ox fallen into a pit, and will not straightway pull him out on the sabbath day?" (v. 5). Of course they would pull the animal out; being humane to animals was part of the law of Moses. The unspoken lesson or understood conclusion was how much greater is a human soul than an animal (cf. Matthew 12:10–13).

Luke 14:7–11 Jesus then turned to those present in the Pharisee's home, having observed their attention to the seating order. They needed to learn some basic manners of etiquette but more important, some basic principles of humility and lowliness.

Jesus suggests that when a wise person is invited to a wedding, he would not seek out the highest positions—so he would not be embarrassed if a more renowned person came in later. In his rebuke of hypocrites, as recorded in Matthew 23, Jesus pointed to the same vice: loving "the uppermost rooms at feasts, and the chief seats in the synagogues" (Matthew 23:6).

It is better to maintain a low profile, as we would say, and sit with the rest of the congregation. Then, if we are invited to sit up front in a place of honor and respect, so be it.

"For whosoever exalteth himself [in a temporal sense and in an eternal sense] shall be abased; and he that humbleth himself shall be exalted" (v. 11; see also D&C 101:42).

Luke 14:12–15 Jesus gives another caution: Do not make a big meal and invite only friends, relatives, and rich neighbors, whom you know could reciprocate by inviting you to their home for a similarly elaborate meal. Rather, invite the poor and those who are otherwise struggling, whom you know could never afford to reciprocate. Treat the lowly ones especially well and you will be blessed and rewarded in the resurrection of the just.

TRIBUTE TO CAESAR: PHARISEES AND HERODIANS (AT THE TEMPLE IN JERUSALEM)

Matthew 22:15–22; Mark 12:13–17; Luke 20:21–26 The Pharisees counseled among themselves how to catch Jesus in his words, how to entrap and accuse him. On this occasion they collaborated with the Herodians (see Appendix 4, 746) to ask him about a sensitive political issue. First, they flattered him (with a nasty touch of sarcasm and hypocrisy): "Master, we know that thou art true, and teachest the way of God in truth, neither carest thou for any man: for thou regardest not the person of men" (Matthew 22:16); in other words, Jesus would never stoop to do exactly what they were then doing: trying to win someone's favor with flattery.

"What thinkest thou? Is it lawful to give tribute unto Caesar, or not?"

A trick question! They were cleverly trying, as someone has suggested, to gore Jesus on whichever horn of the dilemma he chose. The second commandment (which he had given centuries before) had already made the Israelite people averse to images. If Jesus answered yes, it is all right to give tribute to Caesar, he would be considered by many Jews as a disloyal son of Abraham; if he answered no, they could then accuse him of sedition or resistance against Rome.

Clever indeed, but there is no cleverness that can stand up to pure honesty and truth. The Lord of truth saw right through their wicked designs, saying in effect, Show me the tribute money (a Roman denarius, with the image of Tiberius Caesar).

"Whose is this image and superscription?"

"Caesar's."

"Render therefore unto Caesar the things which are Caesar's; and unto God the things that are God's" (Matthew 22:21). Again, the perfect response: Give whatever belongs to Caesar to him, but whatever belongs to God (and every human being comes into this world stamped with the image and inscription of his or her Father) give that back to the Father.

The Saints of God in any age submit to the laws and demands of earthly magistrates. This same Jesus has said: "Let no man break the laws of the land, for he that keepeth the laws of God hath no need to break the laws of the land. Wherefore, be subject to the powers that be, until he reigns whose right it is to reign" (D&C 58:21–22). Submission to secular government is taught in Article of Faith 12. Submission to Nebuchadnezzar in Babylon was taught by the prophet Jeremiah (Jeremiah 27:4–8); Paul taught the same principle in his day (Romans 13:1–7; Titus 3:1; 1 Timothy 2:1–3); and in the latter days we have been given the same instruction (D&C 98:4–6; 134).

We will later see that some of these Jewish leaders lied to Pilate about what Jesus taught: "We found this fellow perverting the nation, and forbidding to give tribute to Caesar" (Luke 23:2).

MARRIAGE, SEVEN HUSBANDS: SADDUCEES (AT THE TEMPLE IN JERUSALEM)

Matthew 22:23–33; Mark 12:18–27; Luke 20:27–38
The Sadducees took their turn once again in attempting to embarrass and find fault with Jesus. They were the Jewish sect who denied the resurrection (Acts 23:8), so their barbed question related to that issue. The Mosaic law included the Levirate law (Latin, *levir,* "brother-in-law") that stipulated that when a man died, his brother should marry his wife to raise up children for the deceased man (see Deuteronomy 25:5; the biblical story of Ruth also includes an example of the application of this law).

Now the hypothetical situation: There were seven brothers; each, in turn, married the widow but had no children. Then the woman herself died. So the question: In the resurrection whose wife will she be, because all seven were married to her?

To understand this question and these passages of the New Testament, additional revelation given in the latter days is required. Jesus replied: "*Ye do err therefore,* because ye know not, *and understand not* the scriptures, neither the power of God" (JST Mark 12:28). The answer was that the first brother had married for eternity; the others had married the woman for this life only, to raise up seed to their brother.

President Joseph F. Smith explained: "They did not understand the principle of sealing for time and for all eternity; that what God hath joined together neither man nor death can put asunder (Matthew 19:6); they had wandered from that principle. It had fallen into disuse among them; they had ceased to understand it; and consequently they did not comprehend the truth; but Christ did. She could only be the wife in eternity of the man to whom she was united by the power of God for eternity, as well as for time; and Christ understood the principle, but he did not cast his pearls before the swine that tempted him" (*Gospel Doctrine,* 280).

Jesus explained further that when the time of resurrection comes, they (who have chosen not to accept and abide by the law of eternal marriage) neither marry nor are given in marriage but remain separate and single forever, as ministering angels in heaven, that is, in God's celestial kingdom (D&C 131:1–4; 132:15–17). Those who accept and abide by the celestial law of marriage (including those who would have faithfully kept the eternal law if they had had opportunity in life to do so; D&C 137:8) and become exalted will be able to marry and be given in marriage in that eternal world. Elder McConkie emphasized that "there is no revelation, either ancient or modern, which says there is neither marrying nor giving in marriage in heaven itself for righteous people" (*Doctrinal New Testament Commentary,* 1:607).

But marriage was not the number one item on the Sadducees' agenda. Jesus quickly turned to the real issue about which they had come to argue, "as touching the resurrection of the dead" (Matthew 22:31).

"Have ye not read that which was spoken [by God to Moses out of the burning bush; Exodus 3:6; see also Genesis 32:9; Exodus 4:5], saying, I am the God of Abraham, and the God of Isaac, and the God of Jacob?" (Matthew 22:32).

And "as touching the dead, that they rise" (Mark 12:26), "he is not *therefore* the God of the dead, but the God of the living; *for he raiseth them up out of their graves*" (JST Mark 12:32). The great patriarchs were yet alive, in the spirit world, awaiting Jesus' own resurrection. He would raise those ancients to immortality.

The people who heard the conversation were amazed at

Jesus' perfect doctrine. Because he is the God of truth, he can see through all misinterpretation, all falsification, and all adulteration of the truth. He (as well as all his true disciples) has simply to announce in plain and simple language what was, what is, and what shall be (D&C 93:24).

GREAT COMMANDMENT: PHARISEES (AT THE TEMPLE IN JERUSALEM)

Matthew 22:34–40; Mark 12:28–34; cf. Luke 10:25–37; 20:39–40 Seeing the Sadducees silenced by Jesus, the Pharisees rejoined the parade of antagonists and prepared another attack. A lawyer (who was also a scribe; Mark 12:28) asked which was the greatest of all the commandments. Humans, by nature, seem to be curious about superlatives, but this curiosity can also engender argument. Jesus answered that the first and great commandment was the one they wore in front of their mind and next to their heart, in the frontlet or phylactery: "Hear, O Israel; the Lord our God is one Lord." This is the Shema, the Jews' chief article of faith to this day. Jesus continued: "And thou shalt love the Lord thy God with all thy heart, and with all thy soul, and with all thy mind, and with all thy strength" (Mark 12:29–30, from Deuteronomy 6:4–5). "And the second is like, namely this, Thou shalt love thy neighbour as thyself" (Mark 12:31, from Leviticus 19:18). "On these two commandments hang all the law [the Torah] and the prophets [the Nevi'im—the prophets' writings]" (Matthew 22:40).

The representative of the Pharisees, this lawyer-scribe, appeared quite satisfied with Jesus' answer: "Well, Master, thou hast said the truth: for there is one God; and there is none other but he," meaning there is only one Creator, Lawgiver, Messiah, and Savior—the great Jehovah, who is Jesus Christ (Mark 12:32).

"And to love him with all the heart, and with all the understanding, and with all the soul, and with all the strength, and to love his neighbour as himself, is more than all whole burnt offerings and sacrifices" (Mark 12:33).

Jesus felt the man was sincere and expressed hope for him: "Thou art not far from the kingdom of God" (Mark 12:34).

At that point no one dared pursue the questioning further.

PHARISEES PUT TO SILENCE (AT THE TEMPLE IN JERUSALEM)

Matthew 22:41–46; Mark 12:35–37; Luke 20:41–44
Jesus now became the interrogator: "What think ye of Christ? whose son is he?" (Matthew 22:42). Pharisees replied that the Messiah is "ben David," that is, the son of, or descendant of, David. If he is the son, or descendant, of David, "how then doth David . . . call him Lord?" in a messianic psalm, uttered by the power of the Holy Ghost.

Elder McConkie explained: "David's Messianic utterance, 'The Lord said unto my Lord' (Psalm 110:1), is here interpreted by Jesus to mean: One God said to another, that is, the Father said to the Son, that, as Paul was later to express it, the 'Son' should sit 'down on the right hand of the Majesty on high'" (*Doctrinal New Testament Commentary,* 1:612).

The lesson Jesus wanted the people to understand was that he was Jehovah, their God, before David (or Abraham or Adam) ever came to earth. Jesus the Messiah was both Lord of David and descendant of David.

The Pharisees had no answer to Jesus' question. They had attempted to confound him, but he had properly and effectively answered their questions—and then confounded them in front of their constituents. All this must have heightened their fear of him, and their jealousy and envy of him. They felt increasingly threatened by Jesus and accelerated their efforts to remove him from their lives. They dared not ask any more questions; instead they laid plans to have him killed.

Leptons ("mites")

WIDOW'S MITE
(AT THE TEMPLE IN JERUSALEM)

Mark 12:41–44; Luke 21:1–4 Against the walls of the porticoes around the Court of the Women of the Temple were chests for charitable contributions, the "treasury," where the widow cast in her smallest of Greek coins, the leptons, or "mites" (see Appendix 7, 777). Jesus sat nearby, watching the contributors. He called his disciples over to watch and learn. The rich gave large amounts, but by comparison to the widow's total sacrifice, theirs was a meager offering. All people, rich and poor, receive blessings commensurate with their willingness to sacrifice (cf. Mosiah 4:24–26).

DENUNCIATION OF HYPOCRISY
(AT THE TEMPLE IN JERUSALEM)

Matthew 23:1–36; Mark 12:38–40; Luke 11:37–54; 18:9–14; 20:45–47 Robert J. Matthews observed: "There is not a single case in the four Testimonies that ever presents

Jesus as impatient, critical, or unkind to people who were humble, teachable, and willing to change their lives. He forgave transgressions and he mingled with publicans and sinners on condition of their repentance. He cast out devils, healed the lame, raised the dead, fed the hungry, opened the eyes of the blind, gave hearing to the deaf, and restored the sick to health, if they only had the faith that he could do it. But he was a terror to the workers of iniquity and to the deceptive, the self-righteous, the hypocritical. In dealing with the repentant he was the gentle yet firm Messiah. To the proud, the haughty, and the arrogant, he was absolutely indomitable and irrepressible, and a constant threat to their craftiness" (*Behold the Messiah*, 226).

Jesus' time had come, and his words reflect it. In Matthew 23 is some of the strongest language of condemnation in all of scripture. The Lord hates hypocrisy, especially in those with positions of authority among the people—the leaders, teachers, shepherds, should-be exemplars of the laws of God. One principal reason he hates hypocrisy is that it originates in pride,

"Moses' seat" in the synagogue of Chorazin

Orthodox Jew wearing prayer shawl and phylactery

and he hates pride. The Lord not only condemns hypocrisy but gives specific illustrations of it.

Matthew 23:2 Scribes and Pharisees sit in Moses' seat (Matthew 23:2), a chair of judgment and instruction in the synagogue (one was discovered, for example, in the ruins of the synagogue of Chorazin just north of the Sea of Galilee), to expound the law and the duty of followers of the laws of God. Jesus suggested that if what they instruct you to do is good, do it, but do not follow their example; they say but they do not do.

Matthew 23:4; Luke 11:46 Some leaders, especially lawyers, place on the shoulders of their disciples the heavy burdens of all the minute demands of the law, along with even greater demands of their own traditions, and they themselves will not lift a finger to help carry those burdens.

"All their works they do for to be seen of men"; therefore, they have their reward (Matthew 22:5; cf. Matthew 6:2, 5, 16). They want the glory of men, and that is what they get—but no more. The warning is to all: Do not do things just "to be seen of men" (Matthew 23:5) or "for a pretence"

(Matthew 23:14) or because you love the praise of men more than the praise of God (John 12:43).

Matthew 23:5 They made their phylacteries bigger—for show. Centuries earlier the Lord had commanded his people to keep his words in their hearts, teach them to their children, and bind them for a sign on their hand and as "frontlets" between their eyes. Frontlets (Aramaic, *tefillin*) by Jesus' day were also known (through the Greek) as phylacteries. They were little boxes with small parchment scrolls inscribed with four passages of the Mosaic law sealed inside: Exodus 13:1–10, 11–16, and Deuteronomy 6:4–9; 11:13–21 (the passages that spoke of making the phylacteries). The Jews wore the phylacteries between their eyes (before their minds) and on their left arms (next to their hearts) to help them remember the law of the Lord. The physical objects could be powerful reminders of their duty to God, but in the case of certain hypocrites they were enlarged for ostentatious display of their religiosity, becoming what we in the latter-day Church might call "Pharisaints."

The Lord had also commanded the children of Israel to

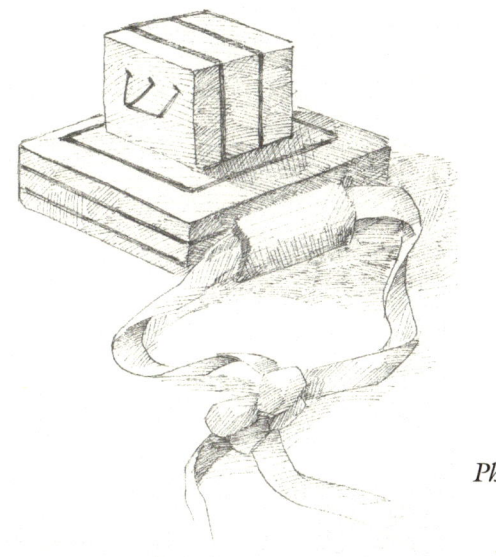

Phylactery

Hems, or fringes

"make them fringes [Hebrew, *tzitzit*] in the borders of their garments . . . that ye may look upon [them], and remember all the commandments of the Lord, and do them" (Numbers 15:38–39). Latter-day Saints have a parallel: our sacred Temple garments remind us of certain commandments and covenants. There was nothing improper in the Jews' making fringes or tassels in their garments, except that now some leaders were enlarging them, as with the phylacteries, to make a more conspicuous show of their piety.

Matthew 23:6; Mark 12:39; Luke 11:43; 20:46 Another example of hypocrisy was loving the uppermost rooms at feasts and the chief seats in the synagogues. This was not in accordance with their calling as leaders to be the servants of all. On the contrary, they wanted to be served and noticed and recognized, all in the spirit of vanity. They had a problem with gratifying their pride and aspiring to the honors of men. It was part of the human (most often male) dilemma of getting a little authority and exercising unrighteous dominion. Power or influence with the people is best maintained, as we learn through modern revelation, with humility, gentleness, meekness, kindness, and love unfeigned, "which shall greatly enlarge the soul [rather than enlarging the phylacteries and fringes] without hypocrisy, and without guile" (D&C 121:41–42). See also commentary on Luke 14:7–11.

Elder Bruce C. Hafen wrote in his biography of Elder Neal A. Maxwell: "Neal found that the show horse mentality among United States Congressmen was widespread. He eventually concluded that many of them were, 'by and large, driven by [a desire for] power and perpetuation in office' more than by a genuine commitment to the public interest. 'Power is so attractive [that] only a few people can handle it. . . . Meekness is not a common virtue.' He often noted that his impression bore out Joseph Smith's words: 'We have learned by sad experience that it is the nature and disposition of almost all men, as soon as they get a little authority,' to 'exercise unrighteous dominion' (D&C 121:39). . . . He would talk about the 'incessant strivings for glory . . . among the talented' and the 'addicting nectar of recognition.' At times he'd quote Abraham Lincoln about the way 'towering genius . . . thirsts and burns for distinction'" (*Disciple's Life*, 211).

"Hearts 'set so much upon the things of this world' are hearts so set they must first be broken" (Hafen, *Disciple's Life*, 406).

Matthew 23:7–12; Mark 12:38; Luke 11:43; 20:46
Other examples of hypocrisy Jesus saw among the leaders of his people were titles and names to distinguish themselves above others. The market was the place where scribes, Pharisees, and others were particularly greeted as "Rabbi *(which is master)*" (JST Matthew 23:4; see Appendix 4, 751) and where they would parade their fine clothing. "Beware of the scribes, which love to go in long clothing, and love

salutations in the marketplaces" (Mark 12:38). "For they loved the praise of men more than the praise of God" (John 12:43). Titles of offices in the true priesthood are too sacred to be used as marks of distinction to set one man above another. To be sure, today we use the titles "elder," "bishop," and "president" to give due respect to the position of those who preside over and serve us. But other titles we use very selectively, such as "apostle," "patriarch," and "sealer," out of deference to those sacred callings. Jesus pointed out certain titles that should not be used for men in ecclesiastical positions: "Be not ye called Rabbi [meaning "my master"]: for one is your Master, even Christ . . . and call no man your father upon the earth: for one is your Father, which is in heaven" (Matthew 23:8–9).

Regarding the relationship between leaders and followers, Jesus taught the people then and now a universal lesson: "He that is greatest among you shall be your servant. And whosoever shall exalt himself shall be abased; and he that shall humble himself shall be exalted" (Matthew 23:11–12; see also commentary on Luke 18:9–14; Luke 22:24–27). In modern revelation the Lord says: "If any man shall seek to build up himself . . . he shall have no power, and his folly shall be made manifest" (D&C 136:19). Humility is the quintessential quality of every great leader, and a sincere and selfless desire to serve others is evident in every great soul.

Matthew 23:13–15 Woes are pronounced on hypocrites (Greek, "actors"), those who are not heading in the direction of heaven themselves and, by their example, are obstructing others from getting there also. In fact, "ye compass sea and land to make one proselyte [convert], and when he is made, ye make him twofold more the child of hell than *he was before, like unto* yourselves" (JST Matthew 23:12).

"Ye devour widows' houses," Jesus continued, for these leaders unjustly extorted from widows in their poverty, and for a pretence (*acting* the part, pretending) made long prayers (cf. Matthew 6:5). In other words, they were pretending to do some right things but for the wrong reasons. That is falsification of pure religion, and it is hypocritical. For all of that they would receive the greater damnation.

Matthew 23:16–22 Jesus cited instances of hypocrisy in worship practices involving the Holy Temple and the perverted reverence with which some regarded the gold and silver there, the warped deference to metal objects instead of sacred symbols. He noted that the hypocrites, in their spiritual blindness (cf. Helaman 13:29), were condemned for adoring certain less important objects and persons instead of the more important things and persons.

Matthew 23:23–24; Luke 11:42 The scribes, Pharisees, and other hypocrites were doing well with outward ceremonialism, but something was wrong with the inner heart. Inner motives are more important than outer motions.

Elder McConkie wrote: "There is so much to learn about the great eternal verities which shape our destiny that it seems a shame to turn our attention everlastingly to the minutiae and insignificant things. So often questions like this are asked: 'I know it is not essential to my salvation, but I would really like to know how many angels can dance on the head of a pin and if it makes any difference whether the pin is made of brass or bronze?' There is such a thing as getting so tied up with little fly specks on the great canvas which depicts the whole plan of salvation that we lose sight of what the life and the light and the glory of eternal reward are all about. (See, e.g., Matthew 23:23–25.) There is such a thing as virtually useless knowledge, the acquisition of which won't make one iota of difference to the destiny of the kingdom or the salvation of its subjects" (*Doctrines of the Restoration,* 232).

Herbs are plants used for flavoring, for fragrance, or for medicine. Paul identified in his writings one of those values: "One believeth that he may eat all things: another, who is weak, eateth herbs" (Romans 14:2). Mustard, mint, and rue are specifically noted as garden herbs.

Clockwise from top left: The herbs rue, mint, anise, and cumin

Mint, rue, anise or dill, and cumin were all pungent or aromatic garden herbs with culinary and medicinal value. The Pharisaic tithe on these insignificant and inexpensive plants symbolized painstaking adherence to fine points of the law, at the same time omitting "the weightier matters of the law, judgment, mercy, and faith." Jesus told the Pharisees, "These ought ye to have done, and not to leave the other undone" (Matthew 23:23). Jesus observed that the Pharisees tithed "all manner of herbs" while passing over "judgment and the love of God" (Luke 11:42).

The Greek term translated as "gnat" may also mean mosquito or, more generally, any blood-sucking insect. This is one of many uses of *paronomasia*, a play on words, in Jesus' teaching: The Aramaic text may be rendered, "You strain out a *qalma*, but swallow a *gamla*" (Black, *Aramaic Approach to the Gospels and Acts*, 175). This hyperbolic language spoken by Jesus denounced scribes and Pharisees, the would-be guides of their people's spiritual lives. They gave too much attention to minutia, to the details of ritual and ceremony (comparable to pesky gnats or mosquitoes), and at the same time they attempted to incorporate a huge mass of accumulated rabbinic tradition and interpretation (comparable to an entire camel), neglecting the more important basic laws of justice, mercy, and faith.

The Prophet Joseph Smith explained this hyperbole of extremes by comparing it to extremes in conduct. He added this phrase to the verse: "*who make yourselves appear unto men that ye would not commit the least sin, and yet ye yourselves, transgress the whole law*" (JST Matthew 23:21).

Matthew 23:25–28; Luke 11:37–41 Two examples of outward cleanliness but inward filthiness: Polishing the outside of cups, platters, and sepulchres, so that they appear pure and spotless, but inside, like the washed cups and whitewashed tombs, is still putrefying matter that stinks and corrupts. The cups and platters need to be cleansed on the inside: "God has said that the inward vessel shall be cleansed first, and then shall the outer vessel be cleansed also" (Alma 60:23). Did not the God who established the outward ordinances also provide for the inward spiritual requirements of the gospel law? (see Luke 11:40). "But *if ye would* rather give alms of such things as ye have; and *observe to do all things which I have commanded you, then would your inward parts be clean also*" (JST Luke 11:42).

If Jesus was pronouncing all these scathing rebukes on the Temple Mount or on the monumental staircase leading to the Temple from the south (where rabbis often taught), he could have gestured to the east where only a five minutes' walk away was an already well-used burial ground on the Mount of Olives. And he said that hypocrites are like the whited sepulchres: they look good on the outside, but inside there is much rottenness (see Matthew 23:27–28).

Matthew 23:29–32; Luke 11:44–45, 47–48 Jesus said that hypocrites are like open graves in the night, and those who take shortcuts through cemeteries are not aware of them and how dangerous they are if stumbled upon (see Luke 11:44).

A nineteenth-century photograph showing impressive burial monuments on the lower slope of the Mount of Olives from the Hellenistic and early Roman periods

He said that his listeners erected beautiful monuments to the prophets that their fathers killed, and they claimed that if they had lived in the prophets' days, they would not have been accomplices in their deaths (see Matthew 23:29–30). "Truly ye bear witness that ye [agree with] the deeds of your fathers: for they indeed killed them, and ye build their sepulchres" (Luke 11:48). At the same time these descendants claimed that they would not have been co-conspirators against the prophets, they admitted they were the children of them who killed the prophets, so they should go ahead and fill the measure of their fathers: *"For ye, yourselves, kill the prophets like unto your fathers"* (JST Matthew 23:29). Not only that, they were the only people in the world blinded enough and wicked enough to kill their own God! (see 2 Nephi 10:3).

Matthew 23:33 On Jesus' epithets for some Jewish leaders as "serpents" and "vipers," see commentary on Matthew 3:7. The usage here highlights the fact that the serpent was a symbol for good or bad, for Deity or the devil (compare Moses 4:6–20 with Helaman 8:13–15).

Matthew 23:34–36; Luke 11:49–51 Amos recorded God's promise of revelation that spans the whole of human existence: All peoples will receive adequate and pointed warning to change before bringing catastrophic results upon themselves.

"Surely the Lord God will do nothing, but he revealeth his secret unto his servants the prophets" (Amos 3:7). God's servants, those who raised the warning voice, were prophets (such as Moses, Elijah, Isaiah, Lehi, and others), and wise men and scribes (such as Nehemiah, Ezra, and others).

"And the Lord God of their fathers sent to them by his messengers, rising up betimes, and sending; because he had compassion on his people, and on his dwelling place [the Temple at Jerusalem]:

"But they mocked the messengers of God and despised his words, and misused his prophets, until the wrath of the Lord arose against his people, till there was no remedy" (2 Chronicles 36:15–16).

This passage demonstrates that Jesus' words to the hypocritical leaders of his people near the end of his ministry at Jerusalem were nothing new. For centuries his people and their "shepherds" had been mistreating and abusing the messengers sent to them. Now upon this generation, having the greater witness of the King's Son himself (Matthew 22:1–7), was heaped all the culpability for the righteous blood shed from Abel to Zacharias (Matthew 23:35; Luke 11:51).

Richard Lloyd Anderson, Brigham Young University emeritus professor of ancient scripture, commented on the Zacharias of whom Jesus spoke:

"The New Testament Zacharias is the same name as the Old Testament Zechariah. Jesus refers to 'Zacharias, son of Barachias, whom ye slew between the temple and the altar.' Some envision John the Baptist's father here, but this tradition of his death comes from a late Christian apocryphal book; it came into the *Teachings of the Prophet Joseph Smith* by the mistake of thinking that the Prophet had written a Nauvoo editorial printed when he was in exile, one clearly not by him. Another possibility for the martyr is the prophet Zechariah, whose father was Berechiah (Zech. 1:1). But since there is no recorded martyrdom of this Zechariah, most scholars think that he would not be named by Jesus as a well-known case. They therefore think that 'Barachias' of Matt. 23:35 is probably a scribal mistake. However, there was a Zechariah familiar to Jesus' audience; the son of Jehoiada rebuked Israel, and he was stoned 'in the court of the house of the Lord' (2 Chron. 24:20–22), which is basically what Jesus said. The Hebrew Bible arranged Genesis first and Chronicles last, so Jesus probably gave the first and last martyrs of Jewish scripture in his testimony" (*Guide to the Life of Christ*, 94; also Brown, *Mary and Elisabeth*, 94–95).

To pronounce that the blood of all the prophets (Luke 11:50) and all the righteous blood shed upon the earth from Abel to Zacharias would come upon "this generation" (Matthew 23:36) is an extraordinary curse and condemnation. According to the Joseph Smith Translation Jesus further declared: "*Ye bear testimony against your fathers, when ye, yourselves, are partakers of the same wickedness. Behold your fathers did it through ignorance, but ye do not; wherefore, their sins shall be upon your heads*" (JST Matthew 23:34–35). A stronger denunciation can hardly be imagined than the combination of having to bear the burden of all the righteous blood shed plus the accumulated sins of their fathers. Joseph Smith commented: "As they possessed greater privileges than any other generation, not only pertaining to themselves, but to their dead, their sin was greater, as they not only neglected their own salvation but that of their progenitors, and hence their blood [the blood of their progenitors] was required at their hands" (*Teachings of the Prophet Joseph Smith*, 222–23).

Thousands of years before Jesus came into this world, Enoch asked, "When shall the blood of the Righteous be shed, that all they that mourn may be sanctified and have eternal life?" And the Lord answered him, "It shall be in the meridian of time, in the days of wickedness and vengeance" (Moses 7:45–46). The hypocrites among the Jewish leadership personified the wickedness, and their God would soon pour out the corresponding vengeance.

Luke 11:52–54 Jesus issued a specific condemnation directed at the lawyers, those who studied and taught the Law (see Appendix 4, 746)—Jehovah's law, authored by the same Person who was presently rebuking them for misusing and corrupting his words given centuries before. The lawyers and scribes were responsible for esteeming his words as naught (Moses 1:41) and actually taking away some of the plain and precious truths he wanted his people to have and use (1 Nephi 13:26). And with malice aforethought, they had done it "that they might pervert the right ways of the Lord, that they might blind the eyes and harden the hearts of the children of men" (1 Nephi 13:27).

"Woe unto you, lawyers!" Jesus denounced, "for ye have taken away the key of knowledge, *the fulness of the scriptures;* ye *enter* not in yourselves *into the kingdom;* and *those who* were entering in, ye hindered" (JST Luke 11:53; for hindering or obstructing others trying to enter the kingdom, see also the commentary on Matthew 23:13).

While Jesus forthrightly reprimanded these Jewish teachers and leaders, some of them grew more and more angry at Jesus and watched more passionately than ever how they could catch him in his words. He had vehemently accused them; now they sought desperately to find something for which they could accuse him. "When men's hearts become hardened and corrupt," wrote the Prophet Joseph Smith, "they will more readily swear to lies than speak the truth" (*History of the Church*, 3:61).

Luke 18:9–14 Now a brief parable for the self-righteous, those who admired themselves and despised others:

A Pharisee and a publican (employed in two dramatically contrasting roles in Jewish society) went up into the Temple to pray. The Pharisee prayed "with himself," saying, "I thank thee, that I am not as other men are, extortioners, unjust, adulterers, or even as this publican" (v. 11).

The Pharisee's prayer starkly manifested a "holier than thou" (Isaiah 65:5) attitude, the same self-inflated conceit that the Zoramites expressed in their prayers a century earlier on the other side of the world: "We believe that thou hast separated us from our brethren . . . that thou hast elected us to be thy holy children" (Alma 31:16), which attitude Alma later warned his son to scrupulously avoid: "Do not say: O God, I thank thee that we are better than our brethren; but rather say: O Lord, forgive my unworthiness, and remember my brethren in mercy—yea, acknowledge your unworthiness before God at all times" (Alma 38:14).

The Pharisee continued: "I fast twice in the week, I give tithes of all that I possess" (v. 12).

But the publican stood "afar off" and "would not lift up so much as his eyes unto heaven, but smote upon his breast [a sign of self-abasement and humility], saying, God be merciful to me a sinner" (v. 13).

The Savior repeated what is recorded at least twice before, that "everyone that exalteth himself shall be abased; and he that humbleth himself shall be exalted" (v. 14; see also Luke 14:7–11; Matthew 23:7–12).

JESUS' LAMENT OVER JERUSALEM (NEAR JERUSALEM)

Matthew 23:37–39; Luke 13:34–35; cf. 3 Nephi 10:4–6 Jesus was finished talking to the scribes, Pharisees, and hypocrites. He would utter one final lamentation and one final malediction.

Jesus tenderly but fiercely lamented the Holy City and the obstinance and recalcitrance of its citizens: "O Jerusalem, Jerusalem, thou that killest the prophets, and stonest them which are sent unto thee, how often would I have gathered thy children together, even as a hen gathereth her chickens under her wings, and ye would not!" (Matthew 23:37; cf. 3 Nephi 10:4–6).

The hen is one of the edible fowls mentioned in the Bible. The Greek word *ornis* actually means bird or fowl, not just a hen. God used the image of a bird hovering over Jerusalem, the place that he had chosen to make his dwelling place on earth. It was a familiar image. "As birds [hovering over their young], so will the Lord of hosts defend Jerusalem; defending also he will deliver it; and passing over he will preserve it" (Isaiah 31:5).

As with most species, birds watch over and protect their young. The Lord had said that if his people were obedient, he would be their guard and protector; he would fight their battles; he would hold them close and keep them safe.

Jesus lamented that the Holy City was not the City of Holiness. Jerusalemites had killed the prophets and were about to kill him. The deepest pathos surrounds Jesus' sigh of desire to gather his brood protectively under his wing. The same God who had sat under the wings of the cherubim could "arise with healing in his wings" (Malachi 4:2) and could keep his people from groaning under the wings of the Roman eagle, but "ye would not!"

And then the strongest of condemnations: "Behold, your house is left unto you desolate." Their house was two things: the Holy Temple, which would certainly be left desolate (cf. Jeremiah 22:5; Matthew 24:2), and their house, meaning their posterity. The whole house of Israel, to be sure, would be desolated by the ensuing worldwide scattering, but their individual houses—especially those of the hypocritical leaders he addressed—would also be left with neither root nor branch, having no eternal family connections, no ancestry nor posterity, forever.

And they, meaning the Jewish people, would not see him again until after the discipline of centuries of trials and suffering: "Ye shall not *know me,* until *ye have received from the hand of the Lord a just recompense for all your sins;* until the time come when ye shall say, Blessed is he that cometh in the name of the Lord" (JST Luke 13:36; cf. Psalm 118:26)—the day, at his second coming, when the Messiah will come in the name of the Lord, because he is the Lord.

DISCOURSE: SIGNS OF THE SECOND COMING (ON THE MOUNT OF OLIVES)

Because this profound sermon occurred on the Mount of Olives, it is often referred to as the Olivet Discourse (see Matthew 24:1–51; Mark 13:1–37; Luke 12:37–48; 17:20–37; 21:5–38; cf. D&C 45:16–45).

For commentary on Matthew 24 we follow the inspired revision made by the Prophet Joseph Smith, called Joseph Smith–Matthew, as recorded in the Pearl of Great Price, or Joseph Smith Translation Matthew 24. This portion of the Prophet's work on the biblical text was translated by the gift and power of God, not by mastery of ancient Greek. Matthew 24 was emphasized by the Prophet more than any other chapter in the New Testament, and he made more changes in its text than in any other—some of the most significant changes being the reordering of verses. His revision contains 33 percent more material than does Matthew 24 in the King James Version of the Bible (see also D&C 45:16–45 for a parallel account of much of what appears in Matthew 24, given in first person, with the Lord speaking; D&C 29:9–27 and 88:87–97 provide additional details).

Why were these instructions and prophecies given? They are given to the true believers in the Lord Jesus Christ to *prepare* us, not to *scare* us. Panic is not part of the gospel. We have his assurance that if we are prepared, we have no need to fear (D&C 38:30).

We are actually commanded to study and learn the signs of his coming: "He that feareth [respects or reverences] me shall be looking forth for the great day of the Lord to come, even for the signs of the coming of the Son of Man . . . and he that watches not for me shall be cut off" (D&C 45:39, 44). It was prophesied, of course, that the Messiah would show great signs—indications, or evidences, that he was literally the fulfillment of all that was foreshadowed of him. Many of these prophecies have dual meanings: they apply to ancient times and modern times—conditions in the world and among God's people after his first coming and before his second coming.

The Prophet's rearrangement of the verses of Matthew 24 helps immensely in understanding the proper sequence of events in the meridian of time and later in the fulness of times. The chapter called Joseph Smith–Matthew can be divided as follows:

Verses 1–11	A.D. 33–70
Verses 12–20	A.D. 70
Verses 21–55	the Restoration to the Second Coming

Joseph Smith–Matthew 1:1 The first half of this verse comes from Matthew 23:39, with the Prophet Joseph Smith's addition. The second half of the verse, beginning with the words *in the clouds of heaven,* is new material. "Blessed is he that cometh in the name of the Lord" refers to the Savior's coming in glory at the end of the world—in the clouds of heaven, with all the holy ones (the Saints) accompanying him (see also D&C 45:16).

Joseph Smith–Matthew 1:2–3 (cf. Matthew 24:1–2; Mark 13:1–2; Luke 19:43–44; 21:5–6; D&C 45:18–20) Mark 13:1 notes that the disciples were impressed with the grandeur of the Jerusalem Temple. Of all the many building enterprises of Herod the Great, none was greater than in the capital, Jerusalem. He rebuilt the former Hasmonean fortress and named it the Antonia Fortress in honor of his Roman friend, Mark Antony. He constructed his royal palace and towers, a theater, an amphitheater, a stadium, and monumental gates and staircases to the Temple Mount. His grandest edifice of all was the Temple in Jerusalem.

The Temple of Herod was constructed beginning in 20 B.C. with the help of ten thousand workmen. One of Herod's main purposes was to provide greater space for the hundreds of thousands of worshippers who came to the Temple during the pilgrimage festivals and high holy days. One thousand priests who had been trained as masons and carpenters helped to build the holiest parts, and a thousand wagons transported materials. The Temple proper was under construction for a year and a half, and the courtyards and porticoes for eight years (though embellishment of the outer courts actually continued for more than eighty years). It was said that whoever had not seen the Temple of Herod had never seen a beautiful building in his life (Talmud, *Succah* 51b; *Baba Bathra* 3b, 4a). No other temple complex in the Graeco-Roman world compared with it in expansiveness and magnificence.

Jesus prophesied that not one stone of the Temple would be left standing on another (Mark 13:1–2; Luke 21:6; D&C 45:20). The magnificent Temple, the House of the Lord, to which many Jerusalemites must have looked with a confident sense of inviolability, would be leveled to the ground and the Temple Mount plowed as a field. Isaiah had once assured the Lord's people that as birds protectively hovered over their young, so the Lord of hosts would defend and preserve Jerusalem (Isaiah 31:4–5). But with no allegiance and devotion to their God, the leaders of the Jews and many of their followers had abandoned the Hope of Israel. Without faith and faithfulness, the Lord's hand would not be stretched out to protect them or the Holy Temple. The Lord's hand, like his word, could be a sharp two-edged sword, providing either protection or destruction. In this case, the Temple would be destroyed, as foreseen by Daniel, the prophet: "[Then] shall Messiah be cut off . . . and the people of the prince [Latin, *princeps*, as the Roman general Titus] that shall come *shall destroy the city and the sanctuary*" (Daniel 9:26; emphasis added). The largest and grandest of the Temples in Jerusalem would also be the shortest lived. (See also Galbraith, Ogden, and Skinner, *Jerusalem, the Eternal City,* 154, 186–88.)

Jesus' prophecy was that not one stone would be left standing on another *upon this temple.* The last phrase was added by the Prophet Joseph Smith. The Lord was not referring to the massive retaining walls around the Temple Mount—eastern, southern, and western portions of which are still standing—but to the Temple proper. That prophecy was literally fulfilled within a generation or so after his departure.

The prophecy of the Jerusalem Temple's destruction must have been as shocking to the Lord's disciples then as it would be to us if the Lord in our time were to reveal that not many years hence the unique and beautiful Salt Lake Temple, which was forty years under construction, would be destroyed and leveled and that the authority to administer in the sacred ordinances of the House of the Lord would be taken from the earth. That will not happen in this dispensation of the fulness of times, but such would be the horrifying, comparative situation.

Joseph Smith–Matthew 1:4 (cf. Matthew 24:3; Mark 13:3–4; Luke 21:7; D&C 45:16) Upon leaving the Temple Mount, Jesus walked downward and eastward, crossed the Kidron, and then hiked up onto the Mount of Olives to some point overlooking the Temple. The apostles went to him privately and asked three questions involving two different dispensations: "[1] Tell us when shall these things be which thou hast said concerning the destruction of the temple, and the Jews; and [2] what is the sign of thy coming, and [3] of the end of the world?" Of all the question words—what, how, when, who, where, and why, etc.—the Savior's apostles, some of the greatest men on earth at the time, wanted first to know *when.* The Old Testament prophet Daniel also wanted to know *when* (Daniel 12:6). So did Joseph Smith (D&C 130:14). That seems to be the first question we all have. Our natural human curiosity wants to know when pivotal events will occur, either because of our fear of being caught unprepared or because of a righteous desire to be ready ourselves and to help others be ready.

A significant part of their questions is available in this dispensation for the first time, added into the scriptural record by the Prophet Joseph Smith: "Tell us when shall these things be *which thou hast said concerning the destruction of the temple, and the Jews* [in A.D. 70]; and what is the sign of thy coming, and of the end of the world, *or the destruction of the wicked, which is the end of the world?* [yet future]" (JST Mark 13:8). The apostles asked when, and Jesus responded with details about events.

In Doctrine and Covenants 101 the Lord gave a parable concerning the redemption of Zion, which is one of the signs of the end of the world. In verse 59 the question is asked, "When shall these things be?" The answer given in the next verse is "When I will." Verse 62 notes that "*after many days* all things were fulfilled" (emphasis added). The cross-reference on that verse is Doctrine and Covenants 105:37, which reveals the same message: all things pertaining to Zion will be accomplished "*after many days*" (emphasis added). Earlier, the Saints in Zion, Jackson County, Missouri, were advised by the Lord that they were honored in *laying the foundation* of the land upon which the Zion of God shall stand (D&C 58:7; emphasis added). The Lord continued to explain that "the time has not yet come, *for many years,* for them to receive their inheritance in this land" (D&C 58:44; emphasis added).

Luke 17:20–22 On one occasion, as the Pharisees demanded to know when the kingdom of God would come, Jesus replied that it "cometh not with observation" (v. 20). "Prophecies foretelling the events incident to the first and second comings of the Messiah were confused in the minds of the Jews," wrote Elder McConkie. "They falsely assumed that at his first coming he would come with an outward display of power which would overthrow and destroy all earthly kingdoms. Accordingly, basing their inquiry on a false premise, and with some apparent sarcasm, they demand an answer to this mocking question: 'If thou art the promised Messiah, as you have repeatedly claimed to be, when will thy power be manifest, when will the Roman yoke be broken, when will the kingdom of God actually come?'" (*Doctrinal New Testament Commentary*, 1:539).

"The kingdom of God *has already come unto you*" (JST Luke 17:21). Our Bible Dictionary helps us understand the first phrase: "Kingdom of Heaven or Kingdom of God. These terms are used in various combinations and with varying meanings. Generally speaking, the kingdom of God on the earth is the Church. It is a preparation for the greater kingdom—the celestial or kingdom of heaven. This is the manner in which these terms are used in D&C 65. However, kingdom of heaven is sometimes used in scripture to mean the Church (as in Matt. 3:2; 4:17; 13; and 25:1–13), meaning that the true church on the earth is the path to heaven, and is the kingdom of heaven on earth" (Bible Dictionary, "Kingdom of Heaven or Kingdom of God," 721).

The people need not look any more for the kingdom to arrive; their King had come, in their generation, and the kingdom was therefore present among them. "And he said unto the disciples, The days will come, when *they* [the Pharisees and others] shall desire to see one of the days of the Son of Man, and *they* shall not see it" (JST Luke 17:22).

Joseph Smith–Matthew 1:5–11 These verses describe conditions between the conclusion of the Savior's ministry (A.D. 33) and the destruction of Jerusalem and the Temple, not even forty years later. The order of the verses in Matthew 24 was appropriately changed by the Prophet Joseph Smith in his inspired revision.

Joseph Smith–Matthew 1:5–7 (cf. Matthew 24:4–5, 9; Mark 13:5–6, 9, 13; Luke 21:12–19) The disciples could expect to see false Christs or false Messiahs, who would deceive many people. They could also expect to be afflicted, hated, and killed for the cause of Christ (Luke 21:8, 12, 22).

Peter and John were delivered up to the Jerusalem Sanhedrin. Paul was delivered up to Gallio, Felix, Festus, and Agrippa. Stephen, James, Peter, Paul, and others were killed. All these things would be evidence and witness of fulfillment of prophecy: "It shall turn to you for a testimony" (Luke 21:13).

Luke adds:

"Settle it therefore in your hearts, not to meditate before what ye shall answer:

"For I will give you a mouth and wisdom, which all your adversaries shall not be able to gainsay [oppose or contradict] nor resist.

"And ye shall be betrayed both by parents, and brethren, and kinsfolks, and friends; and some of you shall they cause to be put to death.

"And ye shall be hated of all men for my name's sake [D&C 101:35].

"But there shall not an hair of your head perish [Alma 40:23].

"In your patience possess ye your souls" (Luke 21:14–19).

The secret of survival or the key quality to possess—in those days and in the last days—is *patience*.

Joseph Smith–Matthew 1:8–11 (cf. Matthew 24:10–13) In ancient days (as in modern times, too) many, even in the Church, would be offended, betray one another, hate one another, be deceived by false prophets, and because of sin lose their natural human affection. Violence, irreverence, coarseness, and crudity all cause abandonment of normal human sensitivities. Would anyone be safe and be saved during the treacherous times? Yes, *he that remaineth steadfast and is not overcome.*

Joseph Smith–Matthew 1:12–20 These verses describe conditions and events in the fateful year of A.D. 70. "These things I have spoken unto you concerning the Jews" (v. 21) and their city of Jerusalem in A.D. 70 (v. 18).

Joseph Smith–Matthew 1:12 (cf. Matthew 24:15; Mark 13:14; Luke 21:20) For many centuries scholars and lay readers alike have wondered about the meaning of Daniel's phrase "the abomination of desolation" (Daniel 9:27). The Prophet Joseph Smith added a defining statement into the verse: the abomination of desolation refers to the destruction of Jerusalem (see also Bible Dictionary, "Abomination of Desolation," 601). When the destruction comes upon Jerusalem, it is well to be found standing "in the holy place[s]," that is, among the Saints, among the pure in heart, or Zion (D&C 45:32; 87:8; 101:22–23). Any additional meaning is left to the reader: "Whoso readeth let him understand."

Luke adds: "And when ye shall see Jerusalem compassed with armies, then know that the desolation thereof is nigh" (Luke 21:20; see also 19:43–44).

Joseph Smith–Matthew 1:13–17 (cf. Matthew 24:16–20; Mark 13:14–18; Luke 21:21–24) How to survive the desolation in those days? Stand in holy places and flee the city. According to Eusebius, the members of the Church of Jesus Christ fled Jerusalem before its destruction in A.D. 70 and settled in Pella, about twenty miles southeast of the Sea of Galilee (*Ecclesiastical History*, 3.5). Survival instructions are urgent and decisive: do not even go back home to retrieve coveted items; leave, get out quickly. The escape would be particularly hard on women who are pregnant and breast-feeding their infants in those days. Pray that your flight is not on the Sabbath, the holy day of rest, nor in wintertime. Being cast out into the blustery elements in winter, to be subject to the cold blasts of wind and rain whipping over the tops of the Judean hills, could be miserable and tragic indeed.

Jesus prophesied of war that would involve Jerusalem not long after he left the earth. Among other things he warned, "Let them which are in Judea flee to the mountains; and let them which are in the midst of it depart out" (Luke 21:21). At first glance, the reference to the inhabitants of Judea fleeing to the mountains may be puzzling, since those in Jerusalem already live in the tops of the mountains. But the other side of the parallelism may help: "Let them which are in the midst of it depart out."

Jesus may have been suggesting that Judeans flee eastward through the wilderness, the usual course of flight, and find safety in the mountain refuges on the edge of the wilderness, such as Masada or En-gedi, where David had hidden from the armies of Saul a millennium before.

"There shall be great distress in the land, and wrath upon this people," wrote Luke, "and they shall fall by the edge of the sword, and shall be led away captive into all nations" (Luke 21:23–24; see also D&C 45:19).

All of this was pointedly prophesied by the prophets. The Jewish nation had adequate forewarning. As a consequence of their sin and rebellion over the centuries, and particularly as a result of their continuing rejection of their true Messiah, the Jews as a people would experience destruction, desolation, and dispersement to all parts of the earth (see commentary on Luke 19:41–44). They would be trodden down by the Gentiles (Romans, Byzantines, Muslim Umayyads, Abbasids, Fatimids, Crusaders, Muslim Ayubbids, Mamluks, Ottoman Turks, and others worldwide) until the times of the Gentiles are fulfilled. *"Now these things he spake unto them, concerning the destruction of Jerusalem"* (JST Luke 21:24; cf. 2 Nephi 25:14) and concerning subsequent centuries of suffering and exile, until the sovereignty of the Gentiles is completed (D&C 45:25, 28–30) and the Jews are once again offered the role of covenant people of the Savior with their ancient land inheritance.

Joseph Smith–Matthew 1:18–21a (cf. Matthew 24:8, 21–23; Mark 13:19–20) Much in these verses is new material. The tribulation upon the Jews and Jerusalem in A.D. 70 was the worst since the establishment of their kingdom (in the days of David, ca. 1000 B.C., or upon the death of Solomon, ca. 935 B.C.), and the worst that would ever be sent by God upon them. Other tragic tribulation would later come (such as the twentieth-century Holocaust), but it would not be sent "of God."

All that happened to the Jewish people in A.D. 70 was only the beginning of the sorrows that would come upon them (v. 19). When the Savior spoke that idea it was prophecy; now as we look back over the centuries it is history.

Had the sufferings involved in that destruction in the first century after Christ not been cut short, the Lord says (v. 20), the Jewish people might have been made extinct, but because of the covenant (the prophetic promises made to them), he would step in and stop the destruction. The remnants must be scattered to the far-flung reaches of the world, until the gathering at the end of days.

Joseph Smith–Matthew 1:21–55 (cf. Matthew 24:24) In the middle of verse 21 ("after the tribulation of those days"), the scene shifts to the latter days. Warnings are repeated (v. 22; cf. Matthew 24:24; Mark 13:21–22; Luke 17:23; 21:8): for example, we can anticipate and expect to see false Christs and false prophets, who will show great signs and wonders. The "miraculous" powers of Satan are quite visible in our modern world; spiritualistic phenomena are plentiful. "And he that seeketh signs shall see signs, but not unto salvation" (D&C 63:7). Not all supernatural manifestations are from God. "Ask of God . . . that ye may not be seduced by evil spirits, or doctrines of devils, or the commandments of men; for some are of men, and other of devils" (D&C 46:7). Even the elect have to be careful, so as not to be deceived (cf. D&C 29:7). Each must have his own light and knowledge, his own faith and testimony. Elder Harold B. Lee warned, "Unless every member of this church gains for himself an unshakable testimony of the divinity of this church, he will be among those who will be deceived" (*Teachings of Harold B. Lee*, 132). The remarkable promise is that "whoso treasureth up my word, shall not be deceived" (v. 37).

Joseph Smith–Matthew 1:23–24 (cf. Matthew 24:6, 25; Mormon 8:30; D&C 45:34–35) Jesus taught all these things for the sake of his Saints, the elect, the covenant people. There would be many wars (unceasing since the American civil war; D&C 87:1–2) and rumors of wars (meaning that which happens for some time before a war actually breaks out). Luke 21:9 adds that there would be commotions but we should "be not terrified." These are no surprises, because he has explained clearly beforehand what is to happen (cf. Mark 13:23). "See that ye be not troubled, for all I have told you must come to pass."

Joseph Smith–Matthew 1:25–26 (cf. Matthew 24:26–27) If some were to claim that the Messiah is out in the desert or in the secret chambers, do not believe them, for his coming will be open, conspicuous, and grand.

According to the King James Version, Matthew used *lightning* to describe the second coming of the Savior: "For as the lightning cometh out of the east, and shineth even unto the west; so shall also the coming of the Son of man be" (Matthew 24:27; cf. Luke 17:24). That analogy from nature—Jesus coming as lightning from the east—is a brilliant and powerful image but meteorologically incorrect. In the Holy Land, lightning does not come from the east. Lightning, as with all storm clouds and precipitation, originates in the *west*, from over the Mediterranean. The Prophet Joseph Smith (who, of course, had no training in Near Eastern weather patterns) corrected the prophecy to read: "For as the *light of the morning* cometh out of the east, and shineth even unto the west, and covereth the whole earth, so shall also the coming of the Son of Man be" (Joseph Smith–Matthew 1:26; emphasis added). In other words, as the sun comes out of the east, so the Son will come out of the east.

Joseph Smith–Matthew 1:27 (cf. Matthew 24:28; Luke 17:37) Jesus' parable indicates that wherever the carcass is, eagles will be gathered together. The King James text leaves readers to surmise for themselves what the lesson of this analogy might be, but Joseph Smith–Matthew includes a simple explanation: "so likewise shall mine elect be gathered from the four quarters of the earth." The Joseph Smith Translation of Luke 17:37–38 gives additional insight: "Wheresoever the body is *gathered; or, in other words, whithersoever the saints are gathered*, thither will the eagles be gathered together; *or, thither will the remainder be gathered together. This he spake, signifying the gathering of his saints; and of angels descending and gathering the remainder unto them.*"

Joseph Smith–Matthew 1:28–29 (cf. Matthew 24:6–7; Mark 13:7–8; Luke 21:9–11) Foreshadowing of wars and rumors of wars is repeated. So also is the Lord's declaration that he is speaking for the elect's sake. Natural disasters will also occur: famines, pestilences, and earthquakes (and we might add floods, hurricanes, tsunamis, typhoons, volcanic eruptions, tornadoes, and fires). These catastrophes seem to be increasing as we approach the time of the end. "And they that believe not in him shall be destroyed, both by fire, and by tempest, and by earthquakes, and by bloodsheds, and by pestilence, and by famine. And they shall know that the Lord is God, the Holy One of Israel" (2 Nephi 6:15; see also D&C 45:33).

Joseph Smith–Matthew 1:30 (cf. Matthew 24:12–13; D&C 45:27) And again, in the last days, the love of men shall wax cold—one of the most frightening of all conditions among those who live without God in the world. And why does this happen, this lack of natural human affection? "Because iniquity shall abound." Sin breeds more sin; satisfying the lusts of the flesh foments abortion, abuse, and other forms of violence.

Joseph Smith–Matthew 1:31 (cf. Matthew 24:14; Mark 13:10) And again, in the last days, the gospel will be carried by the missionaries and members of the kingdom to all parts of the world. The end of the world, the destruction of the wicked, will not come until the witness has penetrated all nations. "The time shall come when the knowledge of a Savior shall spread throughout every nation, kindred, tongue, and people" (Mosiah 3:20). The Lord's hand is clearly evidenced in the recognition of the Church in numerous nations and the opening of the way for the preaching of the message of salvation. Of approximately 200 nations in the world, the Church is currently represented in more than 160, but a very large portion of the earth's population is without any direct contact with the Lord's representatives.

Joseph Smith–Matthew 1:32 (cf. Matthew 24:15) And again, in the last days, the abomination of desolation, spoken of by Daniel the prophet, will be fulfilled. That is, as in the first century after Christ (v. 12), so in the last century before his second coming: Jerusalem will be besieged and suffer much destruction.

Joseph Smith–Matthew 1:33 (cf. Matthew 24:29; Mark 13:24–25; Luke 21:25–26) Immediately after the tribulation of those days (such as were enumerated in the previous verses), the sun shall be darkened, and the moon shall not give her light, and the stars shall fall from heaven. Many passages of scripture foreshadow these ominous irregularities in the celestial orbs (Isaiah 13:10; Ezekiel 32:7; Joel 2:10; 3:15; Revelation 6:12–13; D&C 29:14; 45:42; 88:87). What is the cause of this strange behavior of all the heavenly luminaries? The answer is found in Doctrine and Covenants 133:49: "So great shall be the glory of his [the Lord's] presence that the sun shall hide his face in shame, and the moon shall withhold its light, and the stars shall be hurled from their places." Doctrine and Covenants 133 details several effects of the Savior's coming in glory: (1) The sun, moon, and stars will hide or withhold their light, being insignificant compared to the brilliance of him who is literally the light of the world (D&C 88:7–13); recall that Joseph Smith described Jesus Christ and his Father as "above the brightness of the sun . . . and [their] brightness and glory defy all description" (Joseph Smith–History 1:16–17; cf. vv. 30–31); (2) Mountains will flow down at his presence (vv. 40, 44); (3) Waters on the earth will boil (v. 41); (4) All nations will tremble at his presence

(v. 42); (5) Wicked people and things will be burned and destroyed by the brightness of his glory (D&C 5:19; Malachi 4:1–3; 2 Thessalonians 2:8; Joseph Smith–History 1:37; D&C 29:9, 12; 64:24; 101:23–25; see further on Joseph Smith–Matthew 1:36).

John the Revelator wrote in his description of the celestial city of God, the New Jerusalem: "The city had no need of the sun, neither of the moon, to shine in it: for the glory of God did lighten it, and the Lamb is the light thereof" (Revelation 21:23).

Joseph Smith Translation Luke 21:25 adds other examples of the agitation of earthly elements:

"*And he answered them, and said, In the generation in which the times of the Gentiles shall be fulfilled,* there shall be signs in the sun, and in the moon, and in the stars; and upon the earth distress of nations with perplexity, *like* the sea and the waves roaring. *The earth also shall be troubled, and the waters of the great deep.*"

A frequently mentioned consequence of the catastrophes and commotions engulfing the earth will be men's hearts failing them for fear (Luke 21:26; D&C 45:26; 88:91).

Joseph Smith–Matthew 1:34 (cf. Matthew 24:34; Mark 13:30; Luke 21:32) "This generation ['of Jews'; D&C 45:21; or, '*the generation in which the times of the Gentiles shall be fulfilled*'; JST Luke 21:32], in which these things [all these signs of the Lord's coming] shall be shown forth, shall not pass away until all I have told you shall be fulfilled." The term "generation" may mean race, kind, or class of people. The Jewish people ("this generation") will still be a distinct people at the Second Coming.

Joseph Smith–Matthew 1:35 (cf. Matthew 24:35; Mark 13:31; Luke 21:33) Heaven (the atmosphere around our earth) and the earth itself will pass away; that is, they will be changed from a telestial to a terrestrial order (for the Millennium) and then from a terrestrial to a celestial order for eternity (Revelation 21:1; D&C 29:23). The word of God, however, as the prophets have testified, will not pass away; his words are unchanging and will all be fulfilled (see also D&C 1:38). "The word of our God shall stand forever" (Isaiah 40:8). "The word of the Lord endureth for ever" (1 Peter 1:25).

Joseph Smith–Matthew 1:36 (cf. Matthew 24:30; 25:31; Mark 13:26; Luke 21:27; D&C 45:16, 44–45; Daniel 7:13) The Savior repeats: after the tribulation of those days, and the powers of the heavens are shaken (v. 33), then there will appear in heaven "the sign of the Son of Man." Exactly what this one grand sign consists of has been the topic of innumerable discussions and suppositions, but the verse itself as expanded by the Lord through the Prophet Joseph Smith, defines and clarifies the subject of the sign: "They shall see the Son of Man coming in the clouds of heaven, with power and great glory." The one grand sign, Joseph Smith taught, is the Lord himself (*Teachings of the Prophet Joseph Smith*, 287).

Jesus Christ will come with power and great glory, and with tens of thousands of his holy ones (Saints) accompanying him. Who are they who accompany the Savior at his coming? They are the inheritors of his celestial kingdom: "These are they whom he shall bring with him, when he shall come in the clouds of heaven" (D&C 76:63).

The power and the glory of the Lord at his coming, when all the world will see and know that he has come, is variously described in superlative terms in the scriptures. His aura or dwelling cloud or Shekhinah is depicted as "glory," "fire," "like lightning," "light," "exquisite whiteness," "brightness," "brilliance," and "radiance" (perhaps radiation? For more details, see Ogden and Skinner, *Acts through Revelation*, 383–86). The fire, or glory, of the Lord will burn, destroy, and remove all telestial people and things from this sphere. "What power, what source of energy, will ignite the world on the last day and burn away anything that cannot abide at least a terrestrial glory? It will be the glory of the Son of Man

The Second Coming, *by Harry Anderson*

himself as he descends openly and in full view upon the world" (Robinson and Garrett, *Commentary on the Doctrine and Covenants,* 2:224). Will a literal fire or burning sweep over the earth? Elder Spencer W. Kimball answered, "As it [the Flood] was a real drowning, there will be a real burning at this next great event when the end of the world comes, and the wicked will be burned" (*Teachings of Spencer W. Kimball*, 441).

The covenant with God that we may contract and honor is the payment of tithing: "Behold, now it is called today until the coming of the Son of Man, and verily it is . . . a day for the tithing of my people; for he that is tithed shall not be burned at his coming. . . . For verily I say, tomorrow all the proud and they that do wickedly shall be as stubble; and I will burn them up, for I am the Lord" (D&C 64:23–24).

Where will the Lord come in his glory? "The Lord whom ye seek shall suddenly come to his temple" (Malachi 3:1; 3 Nephi 24:1). Here is another unequivocal sign of the Lord's coming—he will come to his Temple (see also D&C 36:8; 42:36; 133:2). But what Temple? To the house of the Lord in the New Jerusalem and in the Old Jerusalem. "This great prophecy [Isaiah 2:2–4], as is often the case, is subject to the law of multiple fulfillment. 1. In Salt Lake City and other mountain locations temples, in the full and true sense of the word, have been erected, and representatives of all nations are flowing unto them to learn of God and his ways. . . . 2. But the day is yet future when the Lord's house is to be built on that 'Mount Zion' which is 'the city of New Jerusalem' in Jackson County, Missouri. (D. & C. 84:2–4.) Mount Zion, itself, will be the mountain of the Lord's house in the day when that glorious temple is erected. 3. When the Jews flee unto Jerusalem, it will be 'unto the mountains of the Lord's house' (D. & C. 133:13), for a holy temple is to be built there also as part of the work of the great era of restoration. (Ezekiel 37:24–28.)" (McConkie, *Mormon Doctrine*, 518).

Joseph Smith–Matthew 1:37 (cf. Matthew 24:31) If we do not want to be caught up in the deceptions of the world, the Lord counsels us to treasure up his word. In fact, he puts it in the form of a promise: "Whoso treasureth up [not just reads, or even studies, but *treasures up;* cf. Ether 3:21] my word, shall not be deceived." If we are not caught up in the deceptions of the world, we may be caught up to come with the Lord in glory (vv. 44–45).

At this point Luke adds another remarkably positive promise: "When these things begin to come to pass, then look up, and lift up your heads; for your redemption draweth nigh" (Luke 21:28). Five thousand years ago, when Enoch was embittered with the vision of destruction of hundreds of millions of Heavenly Father's children and refused to be comforted, the Lord told him: "Lift up your heart, and be glad; and look"; Enoch saw the day of the coming of the Son of Man, and his soul rejoiced (Moses 7:44–47). When we have a chance to look at all of earth's history from the perspective of eternity, we will see that this mortal existence, at least for the righteous, has a happy ending. Knowing what the positive outcome of the Lord's redemption will be, we can, even now, lift up our heads and our hearts and rejoice.

Joseph Smith–Matthew 1:38–39, 47 (cf. Matthew 24:32–33, 43; Mark 13:28–29, 34–37; Luke 12:39; 21:29–31; D&C 45:37–38) We can and should become acquainted with the signs of the Lord's second coming and be prepared for all these events and phenomena. We can and should know the general timing of his coming. Jesus gave three simple illustrations to enable us to judge the proximity of his arrival: (1) the fig tree, (2) a thief in the night, and (3) a woman in travail.

The Holy Land where Jesus lived has only two seasons: the hot, dry season (summer) and the cold, wet season (winter). The New Testament mentions these two seasons only. During late winter (usually in March) the fig tree issues its first tiny leaves, signaling the beginning of the warm season. "Now learn a parable of the fig tree—when its branches are yet tender, and it begins to put forth leaves, you know that summer is nigh at hand; so likewise, mine elect, when they shall see all these things, they shall know that he is near, even at the doors" (Joseph Smith–Matthew 1:38–39).

Jesus also made the curious parallel between his return to

The Four Gospels

When the fig tree first puts forth its leaves

earth and the coming of a thief in the night (1 Thessalonians 5:2; D&C 45:19; 106:4–5). "If the good man of the house had known in what watch the thief would come, he would have watched, and . . . been ready" (Joseph Smith–Matthew 1:47). If a homeowner knows exactly when a thief is going to attempt to break into his home, he will be up and ready; likewise if Jesus told everyone exactly when he is coming, we would be up and ready. He does not want us to be prepared for a certain date; he wants us to be prepared always. Every generation needs to prepare for the Savior's coming as if it will happen in their lifetime.

Jesus also drew a parallel between his return to earth and a woman in travail (1 Thessalonians 5:3; D&C 136:35). Even though doctors can give a fairly accurate forecast of when a baby is due, even marking a certain date on the calendar, there is no way to know exactly what day or hour the baby will come. When a woman is about to deliver, the physical signs of the imminent arrival are evident. So a true disciple of Jesus will know and recognize the signs of his imminent coming.

Joseph Smith–Matthew 1:40 (cf. Matthew 24:36;

Mark 13:32) No one knows the day nor the hour of Jesus' coming again to the earth, not even the angels of God in heaven. Only the Father and the Son know when the time will be. Some have noticed the words "neither the Son" in Mark 13:32, but that phrase was deleted in the Joseph Smith Translation. Of course the Son knows when he is returning to the earth; "he knoweth all things, and there is not anything save he knows it" (2 Nephi 9:20; see also Mormon 8:17; Moroni 7:22; D&C 38:2; 130:7; Abraham 2:8).

Many over the ages, especially in modern times, have calculated and even published a date for the Second Coming, only to reap disappointment and lose faith. Our natural propensity to want to know *when* is in this case perilous and fruitless, given the explicit declaration of the Lord himself that no man would know that particular detail of the plan (or if it were at some time revealed to a prophet, he would seal it up and not reveal it to others). The Jews as a people have been disillusioned numerous times over the centuries by those who claimed to know the coming of the Messiah, to the point that one sage published a terse warning to all who think they know: "Blasted be the bones of those who calculate the end" (Talmud, Sanhedrin 97b).

Of the time of the Savior's coming, Elder Boyd K. Packer taught:

"Teenagers . . . sometimes think, 'What's the use? The world will soon be blown all apart and come to an end.' That feeling comes from fear, not from faith. No one knows the hour or the day (D&C 49:7), but the end cannot come until all of the purposes of the Lord are fulfilled. Everything that I have learned from the revelations and from life convinces me that there is time and to spare for you to carefully prepare for a long life.

"One day you will cope with teenage children of your own. That will serve you right. Later, you will spoil your grandchildren, and they in turn spoil theirs. If an earlier end should happen to come to one, that is more reason to do things right" (*Ensign*, May 1989, 59).

Elder Packer also said: "You young people, move ahead in your lives. It is a marvelous time to be alive. The world is not going to come to an end. You are going to have time to stand, as I stand now, talking about your children and your grandchildren and your great-grandchildren" (CES Fireside for Young Adults at Brigham Young University, February 2, 2003).

How grateful we are to have living prophets to help us discern the signs of the times. President Gordon B. Hinckley, in his Sunday morning address in the October 2001 general conference of the Church, said the following:

"I do not wish to sound negative, but I wish to remind you of the warnings of scripture and the teachings of the prophets which we have had constantly before us. . . . I cannot dismiss from my mind the grim warnings of the Lord as set forth in the 24th chapter of Matthew. . . .

"Now, I do not wish to be an alarmist. I do not wish to be a prophet of doom. I am optimistic. I do not believe the time is here when an all-consuming calamity will overtake us. I earnestly pray that it may not. There is so much of the Lord's work yet to be done. We, and our children after us, must do it" (*Ensign*, November 2001, 73–74).

Joseph Smith–Matthew 1:41–43 (cf. Matthew 24:37–39; Luke 17:26–27) President Lorenzo Snow reported that on one occasion the Prophet Joseph Smith was asked who he was. The Prophet smiled kindly and replied, "Noah came before the flood; I have come before the fire" (Cannon, Journal, 30).

The comparison of the last days to the time of Noah is most appropriate: a time of gross wickedness before the world is cleansed, then by water (the earth's baptism by water) and at the Second Coming by fire (the earth's "confirmation" by fire, a symbol of the Holy Ghost; cf. Helaman 5:45). Illicit social intercourse will continue until the people are caught as it were suddenly, with catastrophic destruction.

Of the conditions at his second coming, Jesus said: "As it was in the days of Noah, so it shall be also at the coming of the Son of Man." And how was that? "The earth was corrupt before God, and it was *filled with violence*. And God looked upon the earth, and, behold, it was corrupt, for all flesh had corrupted its way upon the earth. And God said unto Noah: The end of all flesh is come before me, for the earth is *filled with violence,* and behold I will destroy all flesh from off the earth" (Moses 8:28–30; emphasis added). Does that mean it will be impossible for us to live a good, wholesome life during the era just before the Second Coming? We do not know how difficult life will be for the Saints during those years, but we do know that it will be possible to remain faithful. Moses 8:27 says, "Noah found grace in the eyes of the Lord; for Noah was a just man, and perfect in his generation; and he walked with God, as did also his three sons."

The text of Luke adds another comparison to the time of the Lord's second coming:

"Likewise also as it was in the days of Lot; they did eat, they drank, they bought, they sold, they planted, they builded;

"But the same day that Lot went out of Sodom it rained fire and brimstone from heaven, and destroyed them all" (Luke 17:28–29; cf. Genesis 19:16).

Throughout biblical writings, the cities of Sodom and Gomorrah epitomized the most despicable living conditions. In the New Testament, Sodom and Gomorrah are always mentioned in connection with cursing, evil living, and destruction. Because of their iniquities, the Lord obliterated them with fire and brimstone from heaven. The sin centers of Sodom and Gomorrah were physically situated at the lowest point on earth, and the immoral behavior of their inhabitants is typically described as the lowest and most degrading on earth.

"Even thus shall it be in the day when the Son of man is

revealed" (Luke 17:31). The comparisons to the people in Noah's day and the people of Sodom in Lot's day foreshadow a latter-day destruction that is sudden and cataclysmic.

Luke adds another warning for the time of the Second Coming (parallel to Joseph Smith–Matthew 1:14–15, in the first century after Christ):

"In that day, he which shall be upon the housetop, and his stuff in the house, let him not come down to take it away: and he that is in the field, let him likewise not return back. Remember Lot's wife" (Luke 17:31–32; see also D&C 133:14–15). Luke's words plainly suggest that the fate of Lot's wife was not merely the result of *looking* back, as Genesis 19:26 indicates, but *returning* back and consequently being caught up in the total destruction of Sodom. Interestingly, the Qur'an, the holy book of Islam, also mentions this same detail; it speaks of delivering Lot "and his household, all save *his wife, who is of those who stay behind*" (Sura XXIX:32; emphasis added; see also XXVII:57; XXVI:171, from *Meaning of the Glorious Koran*, 286).

The message is that when called out of Sodom, or out of Babylon (the wicked world), or out of Jerusalem (as were Lehi and also the Saints a generation after Jesus), or out of any place—flee! Get out immediately. Do not look back wistfully on things you must now leave behind. Do not return for any reason: "Whosoever shall seek to save his life [by going back] shall lose it; and whosoever shall lose his life [sacrificing, leaving behind the old life] shall preserve it" (Luke 17:33).

Joseph Smith–Matthew 1:44–45 (cf. Matthew 24:40–41; Luke 17:34–36) At the Lord's coming there will be a selective destruction: two will be working in the field: One will be taken; the other left. Two will be grinding at the mill: One will be taken; the other left. Luke 17:34 also mentions that there will be two men in one bed: one will be taken; the other left. The original text does not say that two *men* were in the same bed, however. The word *men* is italicized in the King James text, which means it was not there in the original. The Greek text allows for two *persons* or two brothers.

When the scripture says that one will be taken and the other left, which is preferable—to be taken from the earth or to be left on the earth? Would it be preferable to remain on the earth to be with the Savior and not taken away and destroyed? Or would it be preferable to be taken up to come with him in his glory and not remain on the earth to be consumed in the inevitable mass destruction? Fortunately there is a clear and specific answer. Doctrine and Covenants 88:96 indicates that "the Saints that are upon the earth, who are alive, shall be quickened and be caught up to meet him" (see also D&C 27:18; 76:102; 109:75).

Joseph Smith–Matthew 1:46, 48 (cf. Matthew 24:42, 44; Mark 13:33; Luke 12:40; D&C 45:2) Again, the divine injunction and warning to watch and be ready at all times, because we do not know the hour of his coming. In fact, it appears that he will come when we least expect him.

The text of Luke 21:34–36 encourages us not to get carried away with the lusts, pleasures, and cares of this life, lest we be caught unawares. We are to watch and pray always and keep the commandments that we may be worthy to escape the calamities that will come and then to stand before the Son of Man *"when he shall come clothed in the glory of his Father"* (JST Luke 21:36).

Joseph Smith–Matthew 1:49–50 (cf. Matthew 24:45–47; Luke 12:37–38, 41–44) While making the "new translation" of Luke 12, the Prophet Joseph Smith added a considerable amount of new material about Jesus Christ's comings to earth, how his servants will be watching for him, and how the faithful and wise servants will be rewarded (see JST Luke 12:41–57, Bible Appendix, 806–7).

Who are the servants that are firm and steadfast? They are the chosen servant-leaders who are feeding the flock, nurturing the sheep of the good Shepherd. Those whom he finds valiantly fulfilling their callings to feed his sheep he will make rulers over all his goods; all that the Father has shall be theirs ("therefore all that my Father hath shall be given unto [them]"; D&C 84:38; see also Luke 12:44; 15:31; Romans 8:32; Revelation 21:7; D&C 50:27; 76:55, 59). The magnitude of the promise is incomprehensible and the unevenness of the offer staggering: everything we possess in exchange for everything God possesses.

Joseph Smith–Matthew 1:51–54 (cf. Matthew 24:48–51; Luke 12:45–48) Many in the second half of the twentieth century grew up thinking that the Savior's coming in glory would usher in the seventh thousand-year period of this world's temporal existence—the Millennium—but a careful examination of Revelation 8 and 9 (see chapter headnotes) and Doctrine and Covenants 77:12–13 shows that when the seventh seal, the seventh thousand-year period, opens, plagues will be poured out, signs fulfilled, Temples built, a great final war fought, and so on. All these things "are to be accomplished *after* the opening of the seventh seal, *before* the coming of Christ" (D&C 77:13; emphasis added).

It appears that, as the servant clearly hints, "my lord delayeth his coming." Matthew 25:5 notes that "the bridegroom tarried," and Doctrine and Covenants 45:26 says "Christ delayeth his coming" (cf. 3 Nephi 29:2). These combined passages teach that the Savior will intentionally delay his glorious coming until some time into the seventh thousand-year period, "in an hour that [we are] not aware of" (v. 53). Thus, the beginning of the seventh thousand-year period and the actual coming of the Lord are not the same occasion, although the era of peace, tranquillity, righteousness, and terrestrial (or transfigured/renewed/paradisiacal) glory will definitely commence when he appears and reigns as King of kings and Lord of lords.

When the Savior does come, we might wonder whether his reign on the earth will endure for a full thousand years after that moment or just finish out the thousand-year period (millennium) already begun? Scripture gives us no specific answer.

Joseph Smith–Matthew 1:55 This new verse added by the Prophet Joseph Smith includes a prophecy of Moses. The end of the wicked—that is, those who will be cut off from among the people—is the end of the world, this telestial world (see Joseph Smith–Matthew 1:4). The end of the earth itself is a different matter. The earth will be changed at the Lord's coming into a terrestrial sphere, and then, some time after the end of the Millennium, after men become evil again for a short season, the earth will be changed again, this time into a celestial sphere (see Joseph Smith–Matthew 1:35).

Following Jesus' extraordinary instruction to his disciples about the near and distant future, Luke notes that "in the day time he was teaching in the temple; and at night he went out, and abode in the mount that is called the mount of Olives [perhaps at Bethany, with his friends Martha, Mary, and Lazarus?]. And all the people came early in the morning to him in the temple, for to hear him" (Luke 21:37–38).

PARABLE: TEN VIRGINS (ON THE MOUNT OF OLIVES)

Matthew 25:1–13 (cf. Luke 12:35–36; D&C 45:56–59) Olive oil was used anciently for culinary, cosmetic, funerary, medicinal, and ritual purposes. Its most important use, though, was to provide light. It provides the clearest, brightest, and steadiest flame of all the vegetable oils. In one of Jesus' last recorded parables, he described a procession of young women (symbolizing members of God's kingdom) going out to meet the bridegroom (the Messiah; see D&C 33:17–18; 88:92; 133:10). Because Jewish weddings were celebrated at night (the beginning of a new day in their tradition), those joining the procession carried large lamps or torches for practical reasons and for brilliancy and beauty. The

Ancient olive oil lamp

oil for the lamps or torches symbolized spiritual preparation on the part of the members of his kingdom, those who desire to participate in the marriage feast, which represents his coming in glory (D&C 45:56).

"*And then, at that day, before the Son of Man comes* [JST Matthew 25:1], the kingdom of heaven [is] likened unto ten virgins, which took their lamps, and went forth to meet the bridegroom. And five of them were wise, and five were foolish. They that were foolish took their lamps, and took no oil with them: but the wise took oil in their vessels with their lamps. . . . [When the bridegroom came,] all those virgins arose, and trimmed [prepared] their lamps. And the foolish said unto the wise, Give us of your oil; for our lamps are gone out. But the wise answered, saying, Not so; lest there be not enough for us and you: but go ye rather to them that sell, and buy for yourselves. And while they went to buy, the bridegroom came; and they that were ready went in with him to the marriage: and the door was shut [Greek, 'locked']" (Matthew 25:1–10).

Those who go in to the great wedding feast, who will be

with the Bridegroom during his millennial reign, are those who receive the truth, take the Holy Spirit to be their guide, and are neither deceived by the vain things of the world nor spiritually sleeping (Matthew 25:5; D&C 35:21; Helaman 12:4). The earth will be given to them for an inheritance, and they will raise up children "without sin unto salvation" (D&C 45:57–58).

Elder Wilford Woodruff declared: "The parable of the ten virgins is intended to represent the second coming of the Son of Man, the coming of the Bridegroom to meet the bride, the Church . . . ; and I expect that the Savior was about right when he said, in reference to the members of the Church, that five of them were wise and five were foolish; . . . if he finds one-half of those professing to be members of his Church prepared for salvation, it will be as many as can be expected, judging by the course that many are pursuing" (*Journal of Discourses,* 18:110).

When the Bridegroom arrives, some will not be admitted into his presence to remain with him. They will be locked out because they did not pay the price to get acquainted with him. *They* will not know *him* (JST), and he will say he does not know them, either (v. 12).

Elder Spencer W. Kimball wrote a masterful essay about the significance of this parable to us today:

"I believe that the Ten Virgins represent the people of the Church of Jesus Christ and not the rank and file of the world. All of the virgins, wise and foolish, had accepted the invitation to the wedding supper; they had knowledge of the program and had been warned of the important day to come. They were not the Gentiles or the heathens or the pagans, nor were they necessarily corrupt and reprobate, but they were knowing people who were foolishly unprepared for the vital happenings that were to affect their eternal lives.

"They had the saving, exalting gospel, but it had not been made the center of their lives. They knew the way but gave only a small measure of loyalty and devotion. I ask you: What value is a car without an engine, a cup without water, a table without food, a lamp without oil?

"Rushing for their lamps to light their way through the blackness, half of them found them empty. They had cheated themselves. They were fools, these five unprepared virgins. Apparently, the bridegroom had tarried for reasons that were sufficient and good. Time had passed, and he had not come. They had heard of his coming for so long, so many times, that the statement seemingly became meaningless to them. Would he ever come? So long had it been since they began expecting him that they were rationalizing that he would never appear. Perhaps it was a myth.

"Hundreds of thousands of us today are in this position. Confidence has been dulled and patience worn thin. It is so hard to wait and be prepared always. But we cannot allow ourselves to slumber. The Lord has given us this parable as a special warning.

"At midnight, the vital cry was made. 'Behold, the bridegroom cometh; go ye out to meet him.' Then all the virgins arose and trimmed their lamps.

"Even the foolish ones trimmed their lamps, but their oil was used up and they had none to refill the lamps. They hastened to make up for lost time. Now, too late, they were becoming conscious of the tragedy of unpreparedness. They had been taught. They had been warned all their lives. . . .

"The foolish asked the others to share their oil, but spiritual preparedness cannot be shared in an instant. The wise had to go, else the bridegroom would have gone unwelcomed. They needed all their oil for themselves; they could not save the foolish. The responsibility was each for himself.

"This was not selfishness or unkindness. The kind of oil that is needed to illuminate the way and light up the darkness is not shareable. How can one share obedience to the principle of tithing; a mind at peace from righteous living; an accumulation of knowledge? How can one share faith or testimony? How can one share attitudes or chastity, or the experience of a mission? How can one share temple privileges? Each must obtain that kind of oil for himself.

"The foolish virgins were not averse to buying oil. They knew they should have oil. They merely procrastinated, not knowing when the bridegroom would come.

"In the parable, oil can be purchased at the market. In our lives the oil of preparedness is accumulated drop by drop in righteous living. Attendance at sacrament meetings adds oil to our lamps, drop by drop, over the years. Fasting, family prayer, home teaching, control of bodily appetites, preaching the gospel, studying the scriptures—each act of dedication and obedience is a drop added to our store. Deeds of kindness, payment of offerings and tithes, chaste thoughts and actions, marriage in the covenant for eternity—these, too, contribute importantly to the oil with which we can at midnight refuel our exhausted lamps" (*Faith Precedes the Miracle*, 253–56).

PARABLE: TALENTS (ON THE MOUNT OF OLIVES)

Matthew 25:14–30 (cf. Parable of the Pounds—Luke 19:11–27) A talent was a monetary weight, a sum with financial value (75 pounds or 34 kilograms of silver; see also Appendix 7, 779). The concept of a talent as an ability, an aptitude, skill, or strength came later. In a symbolic sense, though, both definitions could be applied to the message of this parable. God has given talents "to every man according to his several ability" (v. 15), "according to his circumstances and his wants and needs" (D&C 51:3). Each is expected to improve on what has been given by development or trading (v. 16) or deposit for interest (v. 27).

The Prophet Joseph Smith interpreted the parable in this fashion:

"Men not unfrequently forget that they are dependent upon heaven for every blessing which they are permitted to enjoy, and that for every opportunity granted them they are to give an account. You know, brethren, that when the Master in the Savior's parable of the stewards called his servants before him he gave them several talents to improve on while he should tarry abroad for a little season, and when he returned he called for an accounting. So it is now. Our Master is absent only for a little season, and at the end of it He will call each to render an account [D&C 72:3]; and where the five talents were bestowed, ten will be required; and he that has made no improvement will be cast out as an unprofitable servant, while the faithful will enjoy everlasting honors" (*Teachings of the Prophet Joseph Smith*, 68).

The parable is not about three levels of goodness but about doing the best we can with what we've been given. (As our leaders have often counseled us, it is not *where* we serve but *how* we serve that matters.) The servant who doubled his two talents earned the same reward as he who doubled the five talents. They were both faithful, and the faithful, in the end, will be given all that the Father has (see commentary on Joseph Smith–Matthew 1:49–50; Matthew 24:45–47).

For those who do not make any effort to improve their God-given talents or abilities, they "shall be taken away even that which he hath" (Matthew 25:29; cf. Ether 12:35). Alma explains, "They that will harden their hearts, to them is given the lesser portion of the word until they know nothing concerning his mysteries; and then they are taken captive by the devil" (Alma 12:11).

PARABLE: SHEEP, GOATS (ON THE MOUNT OF OLIVES)

Matthew 25:31–46 There seems to have been, even in antiquity, a symbolic dichotomy between sheep and goats. The people of God were often identified as the sheep of his fold but never as goats. Heightening the contrast, Jesus

Separating the sheep from the goats at a water source

proclaimed that after his coming in glory and in the day of judgment, "before him shall be gathered all nations: and he shall separate them one from another, as a shepherd divideth his sheep from the goats: and he shall set the sheep on his right hand, but the goats on the left" (vv. 32–33).

Both sheep and goats were essential in the pastoral economy of Israel, yet for the purpose of illustrating a doctrinal point, the two animals were called on to represent opposites, those worthy and those unworthy to enter God's kingdom. Those who are full of light will be set on the right hand, the place of honor and blessing (D&C 29:27; Moses 7:56). Those who are dark in spirit will be set on the left, the place of condemnation and punishment. President Joseph Fielding Smith wrote: "Showing favor to the right hand or side is not something invented by man but was revealed from the heavens in the beginning. . . . There are numerous passages in the scriptures referring to the right hand, indicating that it is a symbol of righteousness and was used in the making of covenants" (*Answers to Gospel Questions,* 1:156–57; cf. Mosiah 5:9–12; 26:23–24; Alma 5:58; Helaman 3:30).

Dark-haired goats and light-haired sheep are frequently found together

Matthew 25:34–46 Characteristics are given of the "sheep," those who will be forever at the right hand of God, and of the "goats," those who will remain forever at the left hand of God. The sheep exercise faith; the goats doubt and complain. Sheep learn to love; goats remain indifferent and selfish. Sheep show concern for the temporal welfare of others; goats are self-centered, concerned only about personal rewards and benefits. Sheep care about the downtrodden, unfortunate, and distressed; goats seek comfortable relationships with the wealthy, the renowned, and the stable and secure.

Jesus mentioned specific examples of the good deeds of those who would be at his right hand: feeding the hungry, giving drink to the thirsty, caring for the stranger, clothing the naked, and visiting the sick and the imprisoned (see also Jacob 2:19). We might add talking with and encouraging the depressed, checking on someone who is absent from church or family home evening, giving a blessing to the ailing, strengthening the morally weak, assisting the financially stressed, helping someone who is failing in school, and giving service in a multitude of other situations surrounding us.

If we help in any way to meet the needs of the discouraged, the deprived, and the desperate, doing good to any of Heavenly Father's children, it is the same as doing good for God himself. That was King Benjamin's message also: As we serve any other human being, we also serve the Supreme Being (Mosiah 2:17). God is love, so to become like God, we will work on that most desirable quality and learn to love others, even the seemingly unlovable. God is the personification of selfless character, so to become as he is, we will put the well-being of others as our highest priority. Everything we do for the benefit of our companion and of our family, for example, is helping build the kingdom of God—and our own eternal kingdom. Everything we do to help and lift others of the Father's children is promoting the Father's plan and purpose. Bringing to pass the immortality and eternal life of others becomes our plan and purpose, too.

It is best to serve as Jesus did—without expecting publicity, recognition, and rewards. Elder William R. Bradford of the Seventy once spoke with the bishop of a ward whose youth had worked to earn money for an activity. The bishop asked Elder Bradford if he would help the youth get some recognition for what they had done. To the bishop's surprise, Elder Bradford said he would not. He said that he was glad that the young people had worked hard but that it was not important that they receive public recognition for that work. When the youth decided to donate their money to the Church's general missionary fund instead of using it for the activity, they asked if they could have their picture taken with Elder Bradford as they made the donation, so that the picture and an article could be put into the newspaper. Again Elder Bradford surprised them by saying no. He told the bishop: "You might consider helping your young people learn a higher law of recognition. Recognition from on high is silent. It is carefully and quietly recorded there. Let them feel the joy and gain the treasure in their heart and soul that come from silent, selfless service" (*Ensign,* November 1987, 75).

THE SECOND DAY BEFORE PASSOVER

Matthew 26:1–2; Mark 14:1 Matthew reports that with just two days before Passover, the beginning of the Feast of Unleavened Bread, Jesus announced that he was about to be betrayed and crucified. Mark reports that at the same time the chief priests and scribes were plotting how they could have him killed.

JESUS' PROPHECY OF CRUCIFIXION AT PASSOVER (NEAR JERUSALEM)

Matthew 26:2 Jesus knew all things in advance; thus he could reveal the manner of his death many centuries before its occurrence (see, for example, Moses 7:55; Psalm 22:16; 2 Nephi 10:3, 5). And now, just before the event itself, Jesus explained plainly to his inner circle of leaders that he would suffer the horrors of execution by crucifixion and that his death would be arranged through betrayal by one of them. This was not a prediction (something that could happen) but a prophecy (something that would happen).

CONSPIRACY AT CAIAPHAS'S PALACE (IN JERUSALEM)

Matthew 26:3–5; Mark 14:1–2 Quirinius, the legate of Syria who had conducted a census at the establishment of Judea as a province, also established Annas as the high priest in Jerusalem. The influential family of Annas virtually monopolized that office for the succeeding thirty-five years. The high priests were drawn from the narrow Sadducean circle and were regarded by Roman governors as their immediate intermediaries in dealing with the Jewish subjects (see Appendix 4, 748).

The first Roman prefect, or governor, nominated by the

Emperor Tiberius was Valerius Gratus. Gratus was the ruler who appointed Joseph Caiaphas to the priestly hierarchy; and Caiaphas, who was a son-in-law of Annas (John 18:13), cooperated with Annas in laying down religious policy. Caiaphas remained in office through the long terms of both Valerius Gratus and Pontius Pilate (thus A.D. 18–36) and was therefore involved in the Sanhedrin's investigation of Jesus.

In November 1990, while preparing a water facility in the Peace Forest at the southern boundary of Jerusalem City, archaeologists discovered in a collapsed burial cave twelve ossuaries (secondary burial boxes for bones), one of which contained inscriptions with the name Caiaphas, evidently the same as the high priest of Jesus' day (see "Burial Cave of the Caiaphas Family," 29–44). "The Joseph Caiaphas tomb and the stone of Pilate from Caesarea Maritima . . . provide archaeological evidence relating to the two individuals most directly involved in the arrest and crucifixion of Jesus" (Rousseau and Arav, *Jesus and His World*, 140).

The palace of Caiaphas was situated either on the summit of today's Mount Zion, just outside the Zion Gate in the Armenian cemetery, or down the slope a hundred meters on the grounds of St. Peter in Gallicantu (Latin, "cockcrow"). At the latter site, excavations uncovered a complete set of Jewish weights and measures, possibly indicating judicial purposes. Also, a large lintel inscription was found featuring the Hebrew word *corban* (offering), suggesting that the residents served in priestly functions.

The plotting just before Passover was not the first time the chief priests, scribes, and elders had worked to treacherously apprehend Jesus and have him executed (John 11:49). Now, however, they were concerned about a potential riot if his arrest occurred on the feast day itself. In addition, there were increased numbers of Roman soldiers during the days of Passover.

FEAST WITH SIMON THE PHARISEE (THE FORMER LEPER?) (IN BETHANY)

Matthew 26:6; Mark 14:3; cf. Luke 7:36; John 12:1–2 Jesus joined others for a supper in the house of Simon "the leper;" that is, a man named Simon who was at one time a leper but who had been healed by Jesus. In Luke's account (if this is the same story), this Simon is identified as a Pharisee.

JESUS ANOINTED BY A WOMAN (IN BETHANY)

Matthew 26:7–13; Mark 14:3–9; cf. Luke 7:37–50; John 12:3–8 A woman came with an alabaster box containing costly ointment or perfume, and "she brake the box and poured it on his head" (Mark 14:3). Alabaster was a translucent stone, well known to the ancient Egyptians (Tutankhamen's tomb, for instance, contained many beautifully carved alabaster boxes) and was available throughout the Near East, though at some expense. The vessel in question was used as a perfume flask (Luke 7:37, footnote b). The long, narrow neck or the seal placed on it had to be broken before the perfume could be poured out.

Mark notes that the liquid was spikenard, a costly, scented ointment imported from the Himalayas. A pound of pure spikenard could be sold for more than three hundred denarii, the better part of a year's wages. Its costliness is emphasized by the petulance of those present when the woman anointed Jesus: "Why was this waste of ointment made? For it might have been sold for more than three hundred pence [denarii], and have been given to the poor. And they murmured against her" (Mark 14:4–5).

This may be one episode, with different details emphasized by the various Gospel writers, or perhaps there were two separate incidents. The latter seems possible because John identifies the woman who anointed Jesus as Mary of Bethany, sister of Lazarus (John 11:2; 12:3), whereas Luke indicates that the unnamed woman was "a sinner" (Luke 7:37).

Matthew and Mark note that Jesus' head was anointed, whereas Luke and John record that Jesus' feet were anointed. The holy anointing of the head and of the feet were both sacred and significant, sometimes depending on the ordinance and its purpose.

Matthew and Luke mention that Jesus "sat" at meat, though the Greek verb means "recline." It is much easier to visualize Jesus and other guests reclining at a low table with their feet extended away from the table when the woman "stood at his feet behind him" (Luke 7:38) to anoint and kiss and wipe his feet (cf. 3 Nephi 17:10).

Jesus kindly rebuked those who complained about this anointing, reminding them that it was a good work, an honorable act, to prepare him for his burial (Matthew 26:12). In fact, this sacred deed would be a memorial to Mary throughout gospel history (Matthew 26:13).

"*And this which she has done unto me, shall be had in remembrance in generations to come, wheresoever my gospel shall be preached; for verily* she *has* come *beforehand* to anoint my body to the burying" (JST Mark 14:8)—another clear foreshadowing of his imminent death and burial.

The accounts of Matthew and Mark end at this point, but Luke continues to describe a beautiful and moving lesson.

Luke 7:39–50 When the Pharisee who had invited Jesus to the dinner saw the woman giving such heartfelt attention to Jesus, he wondered to himself that if this man were a prophet, he would know what kind of sinful woman was touching him and be embarrassed and repulsed by her doing so.

Jesus cut short the Pharisee's condemnatory thoughts by relating a story. "There was a certain creditor which had two debtors: the one owed five hundred pence [denarii], and the other fifty. And when they had nothing to pay, he frankly forgave them both. Tell me therefore, which of them will love him most?" Simon the Pharisee replied, "I suppose that he, to whom he forgave most" (vv. 41–43). That was the correct answer, but notice how it applied to the current situation.

Extending certain courtesies to an honored guest, such as washing the feet, giving a kiss of greeting, and anointing the head with oil, was customary among the Jews in New Testament times. Jesus chastised the host of this dinner by contrasting Simon's lack of courtesies with the courtesies given him by a sinful woman:

"And he turned to the woman, and said unto Simon, Seest thou this woman? I entered into thine house, thou gavest me no water for my feet: but she hath washed my feet with tears. . . .

"Thou gavest me no kiss: but this woman since the time I came in hath not ceased to kiss my feet. My head with oil thou didst not anoint: but this woman hath anointed my feet with ointment" (vv. 44–46).

Jesus continued teaching Simon: "Her sins, which are many, are forgiven" (v. 47). Why? Because she loved much, and she loved so much because of her faith in divine forgiveness. Anyone who has the stains and pains of many sins taken away by the only Person in all the universe who can take them away is going to love that kind and merciful God. And how are the sins forgiven? Through faith in the Lord Jesus Christ. Faith in him saves us, makes us whole, and brings us peace. Faith drives us to follow through with the other steps: We trust that the Savior can and will take away our sins, so we repent of them, and then we experience the baptism of water and the baptism of fire—to wash away and burn out all uncleanliness in us and strengthen us to avoid such sin in the future, which gives us peace.

THE ATONEMENT AND THE RESURRECTION

JUDAS'S CONSPIRACY TO BETRAY JESUS (IN JERUSALEM)

Matthew 26:14–16; Mark 14:10–11; Luke 22:1–6 In one of the most chilling passages in scripture, Luke notes that Satan entered into Judas, possibly meaning that Satan, who has a spirit body, had entered into the physical body of Judas. Were this the only reference to such a matter, we might be tempted to ascribe it to symbolism or rhetorical device (Satan entering Judas in the same way he influences all of us). But John, as a second witness, also refers to this situation as a literal occurrence (see John 13:27).

Could Satan have literally entered into Judas's mortal body? Elder McConkie wrote: "Perhaps, for Satan is a spirit man, a being who was born the offspring of God in preexistence, and who was cast out of heaven for rebellion. He and his followers have power in some cases to enter the [physical] bodies of men" (*Doctrinal New Testament Commentary*, 1:701–2). Judas had so totally submitted himself to the will of his new master, Satan, that he was completely controlled by the archenemy of all righteousness.

Judas Iscariot agreed to lead some Jewish leaders to Jesus for thirty pieces of silver, which, according to Exodus 21:32, was the compensation paid for a slave who was inadvertently killed. The chief priests were glad for the help of an accomplice in apprehending Jesus, and they covenanted with Judas to pay him the blood money ("the price of blood"; Matthew 27:6). Note the terms used in these verses: these "priests" made a "covenant" with the betrayer—those who supposedly held the power of God were making a covenant to pervert the truth and betray innocent blood (which is what Jacob taught were the reasons behind Jesus' crucifixion: "priestcrafts and iniquities" among those at Jerusalem; 2 Nephi 10:5).

If the pieces of silver were Tyrian shekels, as is generally believed, then the total sum may be calculated in the following fashion: a shekel at the time of Jesus weighed slightly less than half an ounce. If today's silver is valued at $10 an ounce, for example, then one shekel (or tetradrachma) would be worth nearly $5, and thirty pieces of silver would total no more than $150 in today's money.

Judas thus sold Jesus to the leaders of the Jews and himself to the devil. And he watched for the right moment when he might "conveniently betray him" (Mark 14:11). He sought opportunity to betray him "in the absence of the multitude" (Luke 22:6).

THE FIRST DAY OF UNLEAVENED BREAD (IN JERUSALEM)

Matthew 26:17–19; Mark 14:12–16; Luke 22:7–13; John 13:1 In Jesus' day, Passover and Unleavened Bread were one celebration.

The English word *Passover* is a translation of the Hebrew *pesach*, which means "to skip over," and carries the connotation of "protecting." *Passover* can be used to mean either the sacrificial ceremony or the actual lamb itself, as in Luke 22:7: "Then came the day of unleavened bread, when *the passover* must be killed" (emphasis added).

The Greek equivalent of *pesach* is *pascha*, hence the term "paschal lamb," which was sacrificed as part of the annual Passover ceremony so that Israel would always remember the Lord's power and protection. The meaning of the practice has been summarized in the following way: "The slain lamb, the sheltering behind its blood and the eating of its flesh, constituted the *pesach*, the protection of God's chosen people beneath the sheltering wings of the Almighty. . . . It was not merely that the Lord passed by the houses of the Israelites, but that He stood on guard, *protecting* each blood-sprinkled door! ['The Lord . . . will not suffer the destroyer to come in' (Exodus 12:23*b*)]" (Rosen and Rosen, *Christ in the Passover*, 22–23).

The Atonement and the Resurrection

During Jesus' time, the Passover lambs used in the feast were killed on the fourteenth day of the month of Nisan, and the meal was eaten between sundown and midnight, in conformity with Exodus 12:6. Because the Jewish day began at sundown, the Passover feast itself took place on the fifteenth of Nisan. The Feast of Unleavened Bread followed the Passover feast and lasted seven more days (Exodus 12:15–20; 23:15; 34:18; Deuteronomy 16:1–8).

The question of Peter and John to the Savior, "Where wilt thou that we prepare [for this dinner]?" (Luke 22:9) bespeaks the prearranged nature of the traditional Passover meal. Special foods were prepared and eaten, and the special prayers, scriptures, and narrative of the Exodus were all recited in their proper order or arrangement. In fact, the Passover meal is also known as the *Seder*, a Hebrew word meaning order or arrangement.

The special foods and other items of the first Passover, as well as their arrangement, were highly symbolic, although most Jewish people today do not recognize or acknowledge the Messiah-centered symbolism of those elements. Following is a summary of the most important elements of the Passover:

1. Just as "the firstborn in the land of Egypt [would] die" (Exodus 11:5), so Jesus, the Firstborn of the Father (D&C 93:21), would die.

2. Just as the Passover sacrifice was a male lamb "without blemish" (Exodus 12:5), so Jesus was "as of a lamb without blemish" (1 Peter 1:19) and was called the Lamb of God (1 Nephi 11:21).

3. Just as no bone of the Passover lamb was to be broken (Exodus 12:46), so no bone of Jesus was broken during his atoning sacrifice (John 19:36).

4. Just as no stranger was to eat of the Passover lamb (Exodus 12:43), so, too, no stranger (one who is estranged from God through unworthiness) is to eat of the emblems of the sacrifice of the Lamb of God, the sacrament (3 Nephi 18:28–30).

5. Just as hyssop was associated with the Passover sacrifice (Exodus 12:22), so hyssop was associated with the crucifixion, the sacrifice of the Lamb of God (John 19:29; for more on hyssop, see commentary on Matthew 27:46–50).

6. Just as the blood of the Passover lamb caused death to pass by the believers (Exodus 12:13), so the blood of the Lamb of God causes the effects of sin or spiritual death to pass by the believers (John 1:29; Alma 7:14; 11:40–43).

The special foods to be prepared and eaten for the Passover meal had changed over the more than twelve hundred years between the original Passover in Moses' day (Exodus 12–13) and the Passover meal at the time of Jesus. Nevertheless, the three most important elements in Jesus' day continued to be the unleavened bread, the wine, and the male lamb without blemish.

This valuable information helps us understand the unstated historical and cultural background that Jesus and his apostles, all of them observant Jews, brought to the last Passover of Jesus' mortal life. The Jewish people generally lacked knowledge of their Redeemer, the Messiah who had come. This knowledge helps us recognize a connection between the Passover meal and the sacrament of the Lord's Supper. We see what elements of the Passover meal Jesus emphasized in order to help us remember him, particularly the bread and the wine (water).

The longest and strongest traditions indicate that the house containing the Upper Room was located on the hill today called Mount Zion. That room was where Jesus celebrated the Passover meal with his apostles, where he revealed who would betray him (Matthew 26:20–25; John 13:18–30), where he instituted the sacrament (Matthew 26:26–29; Luke 22:15–20), and where he gave special meaning to the washing of feet (John 13:2–17).

There is a fascinating parallel between Jesus' instigation of sacred events in an "upper room" and similar sacred events in upper rooms of structures in the early history of the restored

The Atonement and the Resurrection

Church. Moroni appeared to young Joseph Smith in the upper level of the Smith family log house in Palmyra, New York. The Prophet usually had a translation or revelation room (what we might even call a "visitation room") in the upper levels of various homes where he lived and worked: in the Peter Whitmer home in Fayette; in the Newel K. Whitney store in Kirtland; in the Kirtland Temple; in the John Johnson home in Hiram, Ohio; and in his Red Brick Store in Nauvoo. He sealed his testimony with his blood in an upper room of a jail in Carthage, Illinois. Upper rooms, mountaintops, Temples, meetinghouse spires—an abundance of symbols point us upward and help us elevate our minds and spirits.

In finding the guest chamber for the Passover meal, Jesus instructed Peter and John to follow a man bearing a pitcher of water from the Gihon Spring, or the Pool of Siloam. Because women usually carried the water, some scholars suppose that this man may have been part of the semimonastic Essene community known to have resided in that part of the Upper City. The apostles proceeded as Jesus had directed and made final preparations for celebrating the Passover—according to John, a day earlier than the community at large, because by sundown on Friday evening Jesus, as the Passover Lamb, would have been sacrificed at the same time as the Passover lamb on the Temple altar, and his body would be in the tomb (John 13:1; 18:28; 19:14).

The Upper Room may have been arranged by Jesus, or he may have known the place by visionary power. In any case, it was a furnished room (Greek, *estromenon,* specifically referring to a feast or festival setting); that is, it contained rugs and pillows to recline on for the meal. "The rabbis explained that this pose represented the fact that Israel had been delivered from bondage and could now eat in a relaxed, reclined position as was the custom of all freemen in ancient times" (in Holzapfel and Wayment, *From the Last Supper through the Resurrection,*

89). The room likely included a *triclinium:* a low-lying table around which persons reclined with their feet toward the outside (see also Bible Dictionary, "Furniture," 676).

If this Upper Room is the same chamber where the resurrected Jesus later appeared to many disciples (Luke 24:36–49) or where the apostles and a hundred others met to fill the vacancy in the Quorum of the Twelve Apostles (Acts 1:13–26), then it may be the home of John Mark's mother, which served as a meeting place for the followers of Jesus after the Crucifixion (Acts 12:12).

EVE OF THE PASSOVER (IN THE UPPER ROOM, IN JERUSALEM)

Matthew 26:20; Mark 14:17; Luke 22:14 In the evening Jesus arrived with all of the Twelve Apostles to observe the Passover. Whether any others were present, we are not told. Our English translation of Matthew and Luke indicates that the Savior and the Twelve "sat down," although the Greek verb means they "reclined" (see commentary on Matthew 26:7–13; 26:17–19).

"ONE OF YOU SHALL BETRAY ME" (IN THE UPPER ROOM, IN JERUSALEM)

Matthew 26:21–24; Mark 14:18–21; Luke 22:21–23; John 13:18–22 Jesus' announcement that "one of you shall betray me" was deeply troublesome to him (John 13:21), but it must have startled and shocked these close friends of his, these specially trained leaders, the apostles. They all began asking the soul-searching question, "Lord, is it I?"

Jesus gave the first signal or indicator of who the betrayer would be: "He that dippeth his hand with me in the dish, the same shall betray me" (Matthew 26:23). John adds Jesus' words: "He it is, to whom I shall give a sop, when I have dipped it" (John 13:26). A sop was a piece of bread used, like an eating utensil, to raise something from bowl to mouth. Breaking bread together and eating from the same bowl together in this case symbolized a close relationship between friends, which made this betraying moment of Judas particularly grievous.

The Son of Man would go from the world in the treacherous and violent way prophesied, as foreordained, but woe to that man by whom he was betrayed. Better for him that he had not been born.

John 13:18–22 "I know whom I have chosen." Twelve were called, but in the end only eleven would be chosen. One of the original Twelve would fulfill the scriptural prophecy, "He that eateth bread with me hath lifted up his heel against me" (cf. Psalm 41:9). Jesus was advising the apostles before it even happened, so that when it did happen, it would serve as another witness of his perfect foreknowledge—that he is indeed *the Christ* (JST John 13:19).

What was Judas's motive for perpetrating such an unspeakable injustice against such a pure soul? The Prophet Joseph Smith offered these poignant observations:

"From apostates the faithful have received the severest persecutions. Judas was rebuked and immediately betrayed his Lord into the hands of His enemies, because Satan entered into him. There is a superior intelligence bestowed upon such as obey the Gospel with full purpose of heart, which, if sinned against, the apostate is left naked and destitute of the Spirit of God, and he is, in truth, nigh unto cursing. . . . When once that light which was in them is taken from them, they become as much darkened as they were previously enlightened, and then . . . Judas like, seek the destruction of those who were their greatest benefactors. What nearer friend on earth, or in heaven, had Judas than the Savior? And his first object was to destroy Him. Who, among all the Saints in these last days can consider himself as good as our Lord? Who is as perfect? Who is as pure? Who is as holy as He was? Are they to be found?

Jesus and his apostles in the Upper Room

He never transgressed or broke a commandment or law of heaven—no deceit was in His mouth, neither was guile found in His heart. And yet one that ate with Him, who had often drunk of the same cup, was the first to lift up his heel against Him" (*Teachings of the Prophet Joseph Smith*, 67).

BETRAYER IDENTIFIED (IN THE UPPER ROOM, IN JERUSALEM)

Matthew 26:25; John 13:23–30 Positioned at the table right next to Jesus was "the disciple whom Jesus loved." By examining a number of passages in the New Testament and modern revelation, it becomes apparent that that disciple was John himself (John 19:25–27; 20:2; 21:20–24; 3 Nephi 28:6; D&C 7:1, 5). One of the name-titles by which he would be known in scriptural history is John the Beloved. (Regarding the correct conclusion that John is the disciple whom Jesus loved, see Bruce, *New Testament Documents*, 47–51.)

Peter motioned to John to ask Jesus which one of them was the betrayer. The beloved disciple was situated so he could

around a table at the Last Supper

lean back and rest his head against the chest of Jesus. The betrayer was he to whom Jesus gave a sop after he had dipped it (see commentary on John 13:18–22), and he gave it to Judas Iscariot, the son of a man named Simon.

At that point, Satan really got hold of Judas—that same Satan who is the ultimate betrayer, who despised the Savior more than any other man.

Jesus bade Judas do quickly what he was determined to do. The other apostles did not understand the conversation; some supposed that since Judas "had the bag" that he was being told to purchase something needed for the Passover feast or that he should give something to the poor (he was the treasurer of the group; see commentary on John 12:6).

Upon receiving the sop, Judas got up and went immediately out; "and it was night" (John 13:30)—especially for Iscariot. President J. Reuben Clark concluded, "The institution of the Sacrament . . . occurred, I feel, after Judas had left the chamber to arrange to betray the Master" (*Behold the Lamb of God*, 342).

Joseph Smith Translation Mark 14:30–31 explains a motive for Judas's betraying Jesus:

"And he said unto Judas Iscariot, What thou doest, do quickly; but beware of innocent blood.

"*Nevertheless,* Judas Iscariot, *even* one of the twelve, went unto the chief priests to betray *Jesus* unto them; *for he turned away from him, and was offended because of his words.*"

SACRAMENT INSTITUTED (IN THE UPPER ROOM, IN JERUSALEM)

Matthew 26:26–29; Mark 14:22–25; Luke 22:15–20; cf. 3 Nephi 18:1–11 Now that the darkness (Judas) was gone, Jesus turned back to the light. He began: "With desire I have desired to eat this Passover with you before I suffer" (Luke 22:15). He intensely wanted to celebrate this particular Passover because of what was about to happen that night. Once again he plainly foreshadowed what was immediately ahead for him. "I will not any more eat thereof, until it be fulfilled *which is written in the prophets concerning me. Then I will partake with you* in the kingdom of God" (JST Luke 22:16). He would shortly elaborate on the meaning of that statement.

"Jesus' mortal ministry," wrote David R. Seely, "was framed between two essential ordinances. He began His ministry with the ordinance of baptism by water, by which His followers enter into a covenant with God. He ended His ministry with the ordinance of the sacrament, the bread and the wine, by which members of the covenant can renew their baptismal covenant" (in Holzapfel and Wayment, *From the Last Supper through the Resurrection,* 94).

"As they were eating the Passover meal, Jesus took bread, and *brake it, and blessed it,* and gave to *his* disciples, and said, Take, eat; this is *in remembrance of* my body *which I give a ransom for you*" (JST Matthew 26:22). Instead of the King James English translation "this is my body," a metaphor that would later be distorted into a grotesque literalization among some churches, the Joseph Smith Translation simplifies and clarifies the meaning of the figure of speech: the bread *represents* his body (and the cup of wine or water *represents* his blood). The bread and the wine/water are not changed; *we* are changed as we contemplate the sacrifice of his body and blood for us personally.

The Savior asked the eleven apostles to drink of the cup of wine: "For this is *in remembrance of* my blood of the new testament, which is shed for *as many as shall believe on my name*, for the remission of *their* sins. *And I give unto you a commandment, that ye shall observe to do the things which ye have seen me do, and bear record of me even unto the end*" (JST Matthew 26:24–25; cf. Moroni 4:3; D&C 20:77). He had initiated an ordinance that we now call the sacrament of the Lord's Supper, which his true disciples are to observe through the end of mortal time (*sacrament* comes from Latin *sacrare*, "to consecrate, to make holy," signifying a sacred act or ceremony that involves symbols with deeper meaning). He would drink again with them in the distant future, at a glorious occasion "when I *shall come and* drink it new with you in my Father's kingdom" (JST Matthew 26:26). "For the hour cometh that I will drink of the fruit of the vine with you on the earth" (D&C 27:5), along with Moroni, Elias, John the Baptist, Elijah, Joseph, Jacob, Isaac, Abraham, Michael (Adam), Peter, James, John, and "also with all those whom my Father hath given me out of the world" (D&C 27:5–14).

Of this wondrous occasion, Elder McConkie wrote: "The sacrament is to be administered in a future day, on this earth, when the Lord Jesus is present, and when all the righteous of all ages are present. This, of course, will be a part of the grand council at Adam-ondi-Ahman" (*Millennial Messiah*, 587), the sacrament meeting of all sacrament meetings with the Savior of the world, Adam the first man, all the prophets, and all righteous Saints—and an invitation is already extended for each of us to be present (D&C 27:14). Some five thousand years ago Adam's righteous posterity gathered in the valley of Adam-ondi-Ahman, and just before the second coming of the

Savior, another great gathering will occur at the same place to make final preparations for his coming in glory. At that grand council all priesthood keys will be accounted for and then returned to Christ, whose right it is to rule and reign over the sanctified earth (see D&C 107:53–56 and 116, along with cross-references).

What Jesus had initiated in the Upper Room in Old Jerusalem was a new testament, a new covenant, replacing or fulfilling the old covenant. Many centuries earlier Moses had written down the Lord's words and read the words to all Israel, then "Moses took the blood and sprinkled it on the people, and said, Behold the blood of the covenant, which the Lord hath made with you" (Exodus 24:8). Now a new covenant was made, with the purest sacrificial blood, the blood of Christ, which cleanses and sanctifies the souls of all those who believe and follow him.

The Joseph Smith Translation of Mark's account of the sacrament further explains the purpose of the ordinance: to remember the Savior and bear record of him (JST Mark 14:20–25, Bible Appendix, 805).

Many gospel principles, ordinances, practices, emblems, and symbols are to remind us of our Lord and Savior. We do not define charity simply as "love" but as the love of *Christ*. We are expected not just to have faith but to have faith in *Jesus Christ*. Repentance means not just to return but to return to *Christ*. The ordinance of baptism is not merely immersion in water but immersion for the remission of sins—and who remits sins? "We preach of *Christ* . . . that our children may know to what source they may look for a remission of their sins" (2 Nephi 25:26; emphasis added). The gift of the Holy Ghost is given to bring all things to our remembrance. All what things? Things *Jesus* said. The spirit of prophecy is the testimony of *Jesus*. The priesthood is of the *Son of God*. Truly, all things remind us of him. The Savior, not we, must be center stage in the drama of life, else we will miss our most

The Atonement and the Resurrection

important cues, and when the final curtain is lifted, there will be no ovation of any eternal consequence.

The great I AM employed powerful metaphors as he taught, "I am the living bread" (John 6:51) and I am the "living water" (John 4:10), and "except ye eat the flesh of the Son of man, and drink his blood, ye have no life in you. [But on the other hand,] Whoso eateth my flesh, and drinketh my blood, hath eternal life; and I will raise him up at the last day" (John 6:53–54).

Once the betrayer had departed, the Savior initiated the sacrament, a new ordinance using the old emblems of the Passover—the bread and the wine—to signify something higher, far surpassing their use in the Passover service. Now the bread is not hastily made and left unleavened to remember the speed of their deliverance from Egypt; now the bread may be fully leavened to help us rise in deliverance from this wicked world. Now the cup of wine is drunk in sacred delight and remembrance of the blood of the Passover Lamb, which was shed to redeem us from the hard bondage of sin. (The Greek word represented by the English *redeem* means "to buy back, to liberate, to release from blame or debt," and in a spiritual sense to reclaim or absolve from the bondage of sin, to atone for or cleanse.)

JESUS WASHES DISCIPLES' FEET (IN THE UPPER ROOM, IN JERUSALEM)

John 13:2–5 Following the initiation of one holy ordinance, Jesus introduced yet another. John is the only one of the four Gospel writers who recorded the most sacred event that took place in the Upper Room. The Savior was in control of these accelerating events; he knew where he was from and where he was going—about to return to his Father, and he knew that the Father had given all things into his hands.

Jesus arose from supper and laid aside some of his outer

garments, which were not needed for the physical act he was about to perform. He took a towel and "girded himself," wrapping the towel around his waist or tucking the towel into his sash, ready for use in the humble service in which he was about to employ himself.

In ancient times, as a courtesy to guests, a servant was usually stationed at the doorway of the houses of the wealthy to wash the dusty feet of those invited to special feasts and other occasions. Jesus had said to Simon, "Seest thou this woman? I entered into thine house, thou gavest me no water for my feet: but she hath washed my feet with tears, and wiped them with the hairs of her head" (Luke 7:44).

Dr. Edward Robinson, a professor-theologian from New York City, journeyed to the Holy Land for months of exploration in 1838 (just before Elder Orson Hyde's dedicatory assignment there), and he reported in his travel journal the following memorable incident:

"Our youthful host now proposed, in the genuine style of ancient oriental hospitality, that a servant should wash our feet. This took me by surprise; for I was not aware that the custom still existed here. Nor does it, indeed, towards foreigners; though it is quite common among the natives. We gladly accepted the proposal, both for the sake of the refreshment and of the scriptural illustration. A female Nubian slave accordingly brought water, which she poured upon our feet over a large shallow basin of tinned copper; kneeling before us, and rubbing our feet with her hands, and wiping them with a napkin. It was one of the most gratifying minor incidents of our whole journey" (*Biblical Researches*, 3:26).

Now Jesus put himself in the place of the foot-washing servant to fulfill the ancient custom of the Israelites and the law of Moses, but he was also giving higher meaning to the washing of feet when "he poureth water into a bason, and began to wash the disciples' feet" (John 13:5; see also JST John 13:10, discussed below).

PETER'S PROTEST
(IN THE UPPER ROOM, IN JERUSALEM)

John 13:6–12 As Jesus came to Peter, the apostle questioned, "Lord, dost thou wash my feet?"

Jesus answered, "What I do thou knowest not now; but thou shalt know hereafter."

Peter objected, "Thou shalt never wash my feet."

Jesus responded, "If I wash thee not, thou hast no part with me."

To that Peter replied, "Lord, not my feet only, but also my hands and my head."

Jesus said, "He that *has* washed *his hands and his head*, needeth not save to wash his feet, but is clean every whit; and ye are clean, but not all. *Now this was the custom of the Jews under their law; wherefore, Jesus did this that the law might be fulfilled*" (JST John 13:10). Elder McConkie commented, "The full significance of this [the italicized JST addition] is not apparent to the casual reader, nor should it be, for the washing of feet is a sacred ordinance reserved to be done in holy places for those who make themselves worthy. It is evident, however, that the Jews also had sacred ordinances performed in their temple, a knowledge of which has not been preserved, nor could it be, in any literature that has come down to us" (*Mortal Messiah,* 4:38–39).

Jesus said that the apostles were clean, all except one—for he knew from the beginning who would betray him (John 6:64). Then the Master's question, "Know ye what I have done to you?" The instruction immediately followed.

JESUS' EXAMPLE OF WASHING FEET
(IN THE UPPER ROOM, IN JERUSALEM)

John 13:13–17 "Ye call me Master and Lord: and ye say well; for so I am. If I then, your Lord and Master, have washed your feet; ye also ought to wash one another's feet. For I have given you an example, that ye should do as I have done to you.... The servant is not greater than his lord; neither he that is sent [Greek, *apostolos*] greater than he that sent him" (John 13:12–16). In one respect, the washing with water was symbolic of the service that the leaders were to render to those under their stewardship; the greatest were really the servants of all.

Joseph Smith restored the sacred ordinance of washing of feet in the latter days, at first using it for admittance into the School of the Prophets in Kirtland, Ohio, at the end of 1832 and beginning of 1833 (D&C 88:139–41).

The Prophet further explained the purpose of this priesthood ordinance:

"The item to which I wish the more particularly to call your attention to-night, is the ordinance of washing of feet. This we have not done as yet, but it is necessary now, as much as it was in the days of the Savior; and we must have a place prepared, that we may attend to this ordinance aside from the world.... The house of the Lord must be prepared, and the solemn assembly called and organized in it, according to the order of the house of God; and in it we must attend to the ordinance of washing of feet. It was never intended for any but official members. It is calculated to unite our hearts, that we may be one in feeling and sentiment, and that our faith may be strong, so that Satan cannot overthrow us, nor have any power over us here" (*Teachings of the Prophet Joseph Smith*, 90–91; see also D&C 88:74–75, 137–41).

A NEW COMMANDMENT (IN THE UPPER ROOM, IN JERUSALEM)

John 13:31–35 Jesus was about to glorify himself and the Father through his atoning sacrifice. The time was short. The apostles would not be able to follow him (yet) to the eternal world, but first they needed some essential instruction.

Most important of all commandments was to love, for God is love, and to be like him we, too, must be full of love. In a sense, this commandment was not new, as this commandment had been given from the beginning. But Jesus was renewing it now with special emphasis: "As I have loved you [so you must] love one another." In fact, this is the way others will recognize the true Church and gospel of Jesus Christ: if we have love for one another. This is not just "tolerating" or "getting along" but learning to love people truly and purely—blemishes and all (see further in commentary on John 15:9–17).

JESUS COMFORTS THE DISCIPLES (IN THE UPPER ROOM, IN JERUSALEM)

John 14:1–15 Fear is not part of the gospel. The same John who was recording these teachings later wrote in a letter: "There is no fear in love; but perfect love casteth out fear" (1 John 4:18). Jesus had just reminded his disciples of the great commandment to love one another, and if true disciples do love one another, in addition to loving the Father, the Son, and the Holy Ghost, then there is no need for our hearts to be troubled. We just hold on to firm belief in God, and God (any and all of the Three) will see us through. We must not take counsel from our fears.

The statement "in my Father's house are many mansions" (cf. Enos 1:27; Ether 12:32) indicates gradations, levels, or degrees. The Savior prepares a place for each, according to his or her valiance. He is returning to earth to receive each one who is his at his coming (1 Thessalonians 4:17; see also commentary on John 6:37). He and the Father will dwell on this celestialized earth; then where he is, here upon this glorified sphere, we may be also (D&C 59:2; 72:4; 81:6; 98:18; 132:23).

Of this passage the Prophet Joseph Smith taught, "'In my Father's house are many mansions.' It should be—'In my Father's kingdom are many kingdoms,' in order that ye may be heirs of God and joint-heirs with me. . . . There are mansions for those who obey a celestial law, and there are other mansions for those who come short of the law[,] every man in his own order" (*Teachings of the Prophet Joseph Smith,* 366).

"Whither I go ye know," Jesus said (for he had taught them), "and the way ye know" (for he had shown them); but Thomas wondered aloud, "Lord, we know not whither thou goest; and how can we know the way?" (vv. 4–5).

"I am the way, the truth, and the life: no man cometh unto the Father, but by me" (v. 6)—that is, by my hand, by my power. "If ye had known me, ye should have known my Father also: and from henceforth ye know him, and have seen him" (v. 7; see also John 8:19).

Philip exclaimed: "Lord, [show] us the Father, and it sufficeth us"—that is all the testimony we will need (v. 8).

Jesus responded, "Have I been so long time with you, and yet hast thou not known me, Philip? He that hath seen me hath seen the Father" (v. 9)—why would you then request to see the Father?

The Father and the Son are one (see John 10:30 and commentary on John 17:21). If you come to know one, you know the other. What one would say, the other would say. What one would do, the other would do.

John 14:12–14 "He that believeth on me," Jesus taught the apostles, "the works that I do shall he do also" (such as compassionate teaching, nurturing, and healing, showing power over the elements and casting out evil spirits, even raising the dead; cf. Acts 9:36–41; 4 Nephi 1:5). "And greater works than these shall he do; because I go unto my Father. And whatsoever ye shall ask in my name, that will I do" (see also D&C 6:5, 8, 14, 15, and 20). That is a remarkable promise, to receive anything we ask for. There are conditions, of course. We must ask in faith (James 1:6), we must seek persistently (Luke 11:5–10; 18:1–5), and we must knock with rigor. We must also ask, seek, and knock obediently and not improperly ("ask not amiss"; 2 Nephi 4:35; Helaman 10:5), else we have no promise from the great Benefactor (D&C 82:10). Even so, the answer may not be exactly what we expect, but it will always be what is best for us.

Joseph Smith commented on the greater works that the apostles would perform: "He does not say that they should do these works in time [during mortality]; but they should do greater works . . . the greater works which those that believed on his name were to do were to be done in eternity, where he was going and where they should behold his glory" (*Lectures on Faith,* 7:12).

John 14:15 This is the simplest sentence, containing the powerful principle "If ye love me, keep my commandments." Loving means obeying.

ANOTHER COMFORTER (IN THE UPPER ROOM, IN JERUSALEM)

John 14:16–31 Following Jesus' departure, the Father would send "the Comforter, which is the Holy Ghost" (v. 26). His role is to comfort, teach, testify, confirm, and "bring all things to your remembrance, whatsoever I have said unto you."

There are answers to all problems and questions in the scriptures: "The words of Christ will tell you all things what ye should do" (2 Nephi 32:3). The answers come when we treasure up the Savior's words, and in the moment they are needed they will come. "The Holy Ghost . . . will show unto you all things what ye should do" (2 Nephi 32:5)—bringing to mind the words of Christ, the perfect instruction, just when they are needed.

John 14:22 Judas "not Iscariot" (possibly Judas Lebbaeus or Thaddaeus; see chart, "The Original Twelve Apostles," 156) wondered: "Lord, how is it that thou wilt manifest thyself unto us, and not unto the world?" (v. 22). The idea of the Messiah showing himself just to some and not to all, openly and dramatically, was an unconventional, non-Jewish thought in those days.

The great Prophet of the fulness of times explained in glorious detail how the Savior would come personally to the few, serving as a Second Comforter:

"There are two Comforters spoken of. One is the Holy Ghost, the same as given on the day of Pentecost, and that all Saints receive after faith, repentance, and baptism. . . . The other Comforter spoken of is a subject of great interest, and perhaps understood by few of this generation. After a person has faith in Christ, repents of his sins, and is baptized for the remission of his sins and receives the Holy Ghost, (by the laying on of hands), which is the first Comforter, then let him continue to humble himself before God, hungering and thirsting after righteousness, and living by every word of God, and the Lord will soon say unto him, Son, thou shalt be exalted. When the Lord has thoroughly proved him, and finds that the man is determined to serve Him at all hazards, then the man will find his calling and his election made sure, then it will be his privilege to receive the other Comforter, which the Lord hath promised the Saints, as is recorded in the testimony of St. John, in the 14th chapter, from the 12th to the 27th verses.

"Note the 16, 17, 18, 21, 23 verses:

"16. And I will pray the Father, and He shall give you another Comforter, that he may abide with you forever;

"17. Even the Spirit of Truth; whom the world cannot receive, because it seeth him not, neither knoweth him; but ye know him; for he dwelleth with you, and shall be in you.

"18. I will not leave you comfortless: I will come to you.

"21. He that hath my commandments, and keepeth them,

he it is that loveth me: and he that loveth me shall be loved of my Father, and I will love him, and will manifest myself to him.

"23. If a man love me, he will keep my words: and my Father will love him, and we will come unto him, and make our abode with him.

"Now what is this other Comforter? It is no more nor less than the Lord Jesus Christ Himself; and this is the sum and substance of the whole matter; that when any man obtains this last Comforter, he will have the personage of Jesus Christ to attend him, or appear unto him from time to time, and even He will manifest the Father unto him, and they will take up their abode with him, and the visions of the heavens will be opened unto him, and the Lord will teach him face to face, and he may have a perfect knowledge of the mysteries of the Kingdom of God; and this is the state and place the ancient Saints arrived at when they had such glorious visions—Isaiah, Ezekiel, John upon the Isle of Patmos, St. Paul in the three heavens, and all the Saints who held communion with the general assembly and Church of the First Born" (Smith, *History of the Church,* 3:380–81; for a detailed treatise on one's calling and election being made sure, also identified as receiving the more sure word of prophecy or being sealed by the Holy Spirit of Promise—that is, being sealed up to eternal life, guaranteed Godhood—see McConkie, *Doctrinal New Testament Commentary,* 3:325–50).

John 14:23 The Father and the Son can come unto the righteous and "make their abode," or abide, in them. Joseph Smith explained what this verse means: "The appearing of the Father and the Son, in that verse, is a personal appearance; and the idea that the Father and the Son dwell in a man's heart is an old sectarian notion, and is false" (D&C 130:3).

The Father and the Son "dwell" or "abide" in the pure and faithful (Alma 34:36) in the same sense that the Holy Ghost can dwell in us (D&C 130:22). "The Holy Ghost is a Spirit Man, an individual, an entity, who because of his spirit state has power to speak to the spirit of man, thus dwelling in man in the sense of conveying truth to the human heart" (*Doctrinal New Testament Commentary,* 3:102).

When we are living right, our thoughts become what the Holy Ghost places in our heart and in our mind. Our consuming desire is to have the constant companionship of the Holy Ghost and eventually attain the companionship of the Second Comforter, the Son of God himself, and even the Father.

John 14:27 The land where Jesus lived is often called the Holy Land, but today it is not so holy. Jerusalem is called the City of Peace, but there is little peace in that place. Some years ago, on a BBC television program with famous Christian theologians, Elie Wiesel, award-winning Jewish author, commented: "One thing we know. We know when Messiah comes there will be peace; Jesus came, and there is no peace" (Harvey, "Jesus in Medieval and Modern Jewish Thought"). But what did Jesus say? "Peace I leave with you, *my* peace I give unto you: *not as the world giveth,* give I unto you" (emphasis added).

The Savior promises peace in our lives but not the kind of peace the world is desperate for, not the kind of peace that is won at the negotiation table or with heavy weapons and armaments on the battlefield. Scientists inform us that if we could position ourselves right in the center (the "eye") of a hurricane, with fierce turbulence all around us, we could sit quietly reading the day's newspaper. It is perfectly calm at the center. So with the life of the true disciple: though the evils of the world, and even our own saintly trials, rage around us, if we keep the Savior at the center of our lives, we can feel perfect serenity, *his* kind of peace, immediately around us. Peace is not freedom from conflict, being trouble-free, but a calm assurance of our good standing before God. The wicked are always agitated, casting up mire and dirt like the troubled sea (the image described in Isaiah 57:20–21), but the righteous can enjoy serenity, peace, joy, love, and spirituality and all the other coveted virtues, even in the midst of the telestial turmoil that seeks to overwhelm us here.

Do not worry. Do not be troubled. Do not be afraid, the Savior keeps telling us (John 14:1; Joseph Smith–Matthew 1:23; 1 Peter 3:14; D&C 98:18). In him we can have peace no matter what comes. By trusting in him, we are supported and delivered out of all our troubles and fears (Alma 36:3; 38:5). As a bumper sticker reads: "No Jesus, No Peace. Know Jesus, Know Peace."

John 14:29 "And now I have told you before it come to pass, that, when it is come to pass, ye might believe." He told his disciples beforehand about the signs of the times so they need not be afraid (Joseph Smith–Matthew 1:23–24). There would be no surprises for them. He told them in advance about his death and resurrection so that when those frightening and astounding events occurred they could be at peace, recollecting and at last comprehending his foreshadowing instruction.

John 14:30 The time was short—there was not much time left to talk. "For the prince *of darkness, who is* of this world, cometh, *but* hath *no power over me, but he hath power over you*" (JST John 14:30), which is why they needed the message of peace and assurance through the Comforters. (Compare the use of this passage by Joseph Smith in D&C 127:11.)

John 14:31 The Son loves the Father, and it shows. The Father commands, and the Son obeys, "the will of the Son being swallowed up in the will of the Father" (Mosiah 15:7). Even so should we do: the Father commands, and our love for him causes us to obey.

Following all these consoling teachings Jesus said, "Arise, let us go hence." We suppose, then, that the remainder of the mortal Savior's final discourse to the eleven apostles was given somewhere on the way across the city to a favorite garden refuge: Gethsemane.

A vineyard with piles of branches cut off and ready to be burned

THE TRUE VINE (IN JERUSALEM)

John 15:1–8 One of the most brilliant and profound outpourings of imagery in all the world's literature is that recorded by John, where Jesus called himself metaphorically the "true vine." The analogy manifests perfect knowledge of the details of viticulture and of the spiritual life. We note the implication that there might be other vines to which men would look for sustenance, but Jesus is the only true vine.

As Nephi (who grew up at Jerusalem) noted, we gain strength and nourishment from the true vine (1 Nephi 15:15). Only the branch that stays firmly connected to the Vine can drink deeply of the Water of Life and absorb the Sun of Righteousness and all other necessary nutrients to assure growth leading to fruitfulness. Despite the prunings (v. 2; the purging or purifying, meaning the trials of life) when the branch is cut down (or humbled), or actually *because* of such prunings, the branch can be made more fruitful. Those who remain unproductive will in the end be cut off and burned in the fire (cf. Matthew 7:19; Luke 3:9).

The Atonement and the Resurrection

John 15:4–5 Elder Jeffrey R. Holland taught: "'Abide in me' is an understandable and beautiful enough concept in the elegant English of the King James Bible, but 'abide' is not a word we use much anymore. So I gained even more appreciation for this admonition from the Lord when I was introduced to the translation of this passage in another language. In Spanish that familiar phrase is rendered *'permaneced en mi.'* Like the English verb 'abide,' *permanecer* means 'to remain, to stay,' but even gringos like me can hear the root cognate there of 'permanence.' The sense of this then is 'stay—but stay *forever.*' That is the call of the gospel message to Chileans and everyone else in the world. Come, but come to remain. Come with conviction and endurance. Come permanently" (*Ensign,* May 2004, 32).

"Abide in the vine" means to remain connected; persist, endure, continue, persevere: all of these action verbs suggest our need to stay close to the Savior. We are totally dependent on him, as sheep are dependent on their shepherd (see commentary on Matthew 5:3).

Some years ago Brother Ogden took his children a number of times to help a woman operate a petting farm for children in Mapleton, Utah. He wrote about one of those visits: "One day the owner told me that if she ever had to get rid of her animals, she would keep her horses and her sheep. I could see why the horses, but I asked her why she would want to keep the dirty, smelly, noisy sheep. She said something I will never forget: 'Sheep have a willingness to be dependent.' It took me a while to realize the profound significance of her remark. And I learned why the good Shepherd has often referred to us as his sheep. He wants us to be dependent upon him. Although there is something to say about the virtue of exercising our independence and agency to do a lot of good, of our own free will, since the power is in us, yet in another sense, we must be dependent on him, for we have, in the end, absolutely no power whatever to save ourselves. We need his grace and his merits, his atoning sacrifice, to change our present fallen condition to something more heavenly. We will never make it without him. Actually, we *cannot* change without him. We are dependent on him" (Ogden, journal).

So it is with this image of the vine. The only way we will be productive or fruitful is to stay attached to our Source of strength and nourishment. "For without me," Jesus warned, "ye can do nothing." Whether back then as a fisherman, a publican, a political zealot, or today as a teacher, a government worker, or a computer consultant, in the end we will all be undistinguished nobodies if we fail to abide in Him. We will produce nothing of real, lasting value.

John 15:8, 11 True disciples bring forth much fruit, and thereby they glorify the Father and the Son. (The Lord does not necessarily require huge, earth-shaking, world-changing accomplishments, but he does expect of us many quiet, unpublicized acts of kindness and beneficence.) Why had Jesus taught all these beautiful metaphorical truths? "These things have I spoken unto you, that my joy might remain in you, and that your joy might be full" (v. 11). He is talking to us: If we want to be happy, we must stay close to him and be fruitful, doing all we can to work out our own salvation and helping as many others as possible to do the same.

LOVE ONE ANOTHER (IN JERUSALEM)

John 15:9–17 Jesus spoke once again of the most vital quality of character anyone could possess: the love of God (see commentary on John 13:31–35).

Faith in the Lord Jesus Christ is the first principle of the gospel. Repentance is the first doctrine of the kingdom. Obedience is the first law of heaven. And happiness is the object of our existence. But of all things in the gospel, in the scriptures, and in the plan of salvation, that which is *most important is the love of God*.

Love is charity, and charity is the pure love of Christ

The Atonement and the Resurrection

(Moroni 7:44–48). "Charity suffereth long, and is kind, and envieth not [there is no resentment or discontent over the good fortune of others], and is not puffed up [there is no contention for superiority; those converted to Christ are not threatened by others' talents, abilities, and successes], seeketh not her own, is not easily provoked, thinketh no evil, and rejoiceth not in iniquity. Charity is everlasting love" (Moroni 8:17).

We want the love of Christ because it is a commandment to love God and our neighbor, and we want to keep all commandments. And it is the number one commandment. Paul said, "Above all these things put on charity" (Colossians 3:14); Peter said, "Above all things have fervent charity among yourselves" (1 Peter 4:8); and the Savior said, "Above all things, clothe yourselves with the bond of charity" (D&C 88:125).

We want more love because it is a test we are interested in passing. "The Lord your God proveth you," Moses wrote, "to know whether ye love the Lord your God with all your heart" (Deuteronomy 13:3). The Lord is testing our discipleship: "By this shall all men know that ye are my disciples, if ye have love one to another" (John 13:35).

We want more love because it is the best quality we could possess: "The love of God . . . is the most desirable above all things . . . and the most joyous to the soul" (1 Nephi 11:22–23).

We want an increase in love because it brings us the greatest happiness: "There was no contention in the land, because of the love of God . . . in the hearts of the people" (they did not have a mind to injure one another; Mosiah 4:13) and "surely there could not be a happier people" (4 Nephi 1:15–16).

We want the love of Christ because we cannot accomplish our purposes on earth without it, and we cannot enter heaven without it. "No one can assist in this work except he shall be humble and full of love" (D&C 12:8), and "except men shall have charity they cannot inherit that place . . . prepared in the mansions of thy Father" (Ether 12:34).

How do we get the love of God? Jesus said, "If ye keep my commandments, ye shall abide in my love" (John 14:15). "Keep the commandments of God, that [ye] might . . . be filled with love towards God and all men" (Mosiah 2:4). King Benjamin taught us "to love one another, and [that means] to serve one another" (Mosiah 4:15). Alma and Moroni advised of another necessity to secure the love of God: "Pray continually, that ye may . . . [be] full of love" (Alma 13:28); "pray . . . with all the energy of heart, that ye may be filled with this love" (Moroni 7:48). Moroni also explained that the "Comforter filleth with . . . perfect love, which love endureth by diligence unto prayer" (Moroni 8:26). Alma mentioned yet another requirement to qualify for this precious character trait; we must be virtuous: "Bridle all your passions, that ye may be filled with love" (Alma 38:12).

Even doing all of the above, love is not something we can work on, checking off each qualification on our checklist, then we get it because we earned it; it is a gift. It is *the* gift of the Holy Ghost.

And what are the blessings of having the love of God in our life? "All things work together for good to them that love God," wrote Paul (Romans 8:28). That great apostle added, "Eye hath not seen, nor ear heard, neither have entered into the heart of man, the things which God hath prepared for them that love him" (1 Corinthians 2:9). And ultimately, "sanctification through the grace of our Lord . . . [is given] to all those who love and serve God" (D&C 20:31).

And what kind of influence does the love of God have in our life? Experiencing the pure love of Christ means we are praying fervently every day. We are studying and treasuring up the scriptures. We are losing ourselves in the service of others. Having the love of God, we keep his commandments, and we are obedient and happy. We are constant, or, as the Book of Mormon says, "firm and steadfast." We can be trusted. We do things for the right reasons. We are becoming more and more like the Father and like his beloved Son.

Having examined these superlative teachings of the Savior and the prophets about love, we consider one more element that should be emphasized: obedience. That truth is illustrated in the following experience that Brother Ogden had near the end of his service as a mission president in Chile:

"One of the missionaries who was departing for the USA stood to bear his final testimony in our home. He testified, 'I learned to love here in Chile. I love the people. I love God.' Then he went on to explain that he had talked in recent weeks with all the people he had baptized (which is against the rules, to go back or call back to former areas of labor), and he had given little kisses and hugs to the grandmas (also against the rules). It is interesting how people rationalize and justify their behavior. He may have testified that he learned to love, but he had not learned obedience. Jesus said, 'If ye love me, keep my commandments.' It is true, love is the highest quality, but *it's not all*. The elder I admired most during my own mission in Argentina years ago, my ideal, my model among missionaries, knew how to love people into the Church. He was incredibly successful in bringing people to the waters of baptism. But years after the mission he was excommunicated from the Church for disobedience to the laws of the land and the laws of God. Love and obedience are an indispensable combination" (Ogden, journal).

John 15:9–10, 12 The Father loved the Son, the Son loved all of us, and we are commanded to continue in that pattern; it is our turn to keep the love of God in us by loving one another. As the Savior keeps the Father's love flowing to him by keeping his commandments, so we keep the love of the Savior flowing into our lives by keeping his commandments. The Book of Mormon teaches that the manifestation of the love of God the Father is Jesus Christ and his Atonement (1 Nephi 11:18–27). The *abiding* love of God equates to exaltation and eternal life. Understood in this light, the love of God is not unconditional (see Nelson, *Ensign*, February 2003, 20–25). God himself has placed conditions on his abiding love; for example: "If ye keep my commandments, ye shall abide in my love" (v. 10). Again, the Book of Mormon provides our clearest explanation: "Behold, the Lord esteemeth all flesh in one; he that is righteous is favored of God" (1 Nephi 17:35). The opposite is also true. If we ignore or violate his commandments, we cannot be favored and abide in his love. His love includes intelligence, virtue, light, and truth. If we reject his commandments, we expel from our lives the accompanying intelligence, virtue, light, and truth.

John 15:14–15 "Ye are my friends," Jesus said, "*if* ye do whatsoever I command you" (v. 14; emphasis added). The opposite is also true. If we reject his commands, we consciously decide to preclude the privilege of being his friends, with the accompanying knowledge and blessings that the Savior learned from the Father and desires to teach us (v. 15; for example, higher knowledge available only in the Holy Place, which is accessible only to those who love and keep his commandments). Friendship is not just an honorable step up from being mere servants but the highest relationship we can enjoy with Jesus Christ.

The love of God is not unconditional. There are conditions we must meet to perpetuate the love of God in our lives. "He that is righteous is favored of God. . . . And he loveth those who will have him to be their God" (1 Nephi 17:35, 40). He has taught us to "keep the commandments of God, that [we] might be filled with love towards God and all men" (Mosiah 2:4). There is no ambiguity in his pointed warning: "If you keep not my commandments, the love of the Father shall not continue with you" (D&C 95:12). On the other hand, the Savior tenderly admonishes us: "Be faithful and diligent in keeping the commandments of God, and I will encircle thee in the arms of my love" (D&C 6:20).

We do not control God's feelings toward us, but we can control our feelings toward him. We children of God would do well to make our love for God unconditional. No matter what happens, we can be determined to show our love for him by serving him and obeying all his commandments. He will then reward us with exaltation and eternal life (see *Teachings of the Prophet Joseph Smith,* 150).

Elder Neal A. Maxwell gave the following encouragement:

"God loves us all—saint and sinner alike—with a perfect and everlasting love. We have His love, if not His approval. It is our love for Him that remains to be developed. When we come to be genuinely concerned with pleasing God—more than with pleasing any in the world, even ourselves—then our behavior improves and His blessings can engulf us. This sublime feeling can be experienced only if we come to know enough about Him so that our awe melts into adoration, and our respect into utter reverence. . . .

"To those who mean well but thoughtlessly speak of 'building a better relationship' with God (which sounds like a transaction between mortals desiring reciprocity), it needs to be said that our relationship with God is already established, in a genealogical sense. Perhaps what such individuals intend to say is that we must draw closer to God. But we are to worship, to adore, and to obey God, not build a better relationship with Him!" (*All These Things Shall Give Thee Experience,* 3).

John 15:13; cf. 1 John 3:11, 16–18 There is no greater way to show pure love than being willing to lay down our life for our friends. Jesus did that. And he expects us to follow his example, in laying down our lives for others. That consists not only in giving up our life for someone (as in dying) but in literally giving our life for others—our time, energies, talents, resources, and efforts—sacrificing or giving up our own pleasures to serve and save others, especially in our families. Elder Harold B. Lee taught, "Great love is built on great sacrifice, and that home where the principle of sacrifice for the welfare of each other is daily expressed is that home where there abides a great love" (Conference Report, April 1947, 49).

John 15:16 Our relationship with the Savior is based not so much on our having chosen him, not on our having elected to follow him, but on his having chosen us and authorized us and ordained us to teach and minister and heal and encourage and lead—all in his behalf. Our chosenness is not founded on mere belief in the Bible or on years of study and training in theology with the consequent academic degrees; our chosenness is not conferred on us at graduation ceremonies with human certificates, nor does it come simply by our saying a few prayers and feeling moved to inspired decisions. Our chosenness comes from God, through his loving kindness and grace.

He has chosen us and charged us to "go and bring forth fruit" and that our "fruit should remain"; that is *retention*. We help bring people to Christ, and we help them stay with him (the branches stay attached to the true Vine). We help our fruits remain by remembering them and nourishing them "by the good word of God, to keep them in the right way, to keep them continually watchful unto prayer, relying alone upon the merits of Christ" (Moroni 6:4).

John 15:17 One more time, for emphasis, Jesus says: "These things I command you, that ye love one another." Not a suggestion but a commandment—we must learn to love all those who come into our life.

HATRED OF THE WORLD (IN JERUSALEM)

John 15:18–25 Jesus teaches, in essence, that we should not be surprised if wicked people in the world hate us. They hated him; they will hate his followers. If we were worldly, they would embrace us; but because we care about heavenly things, they will hate us. The servant is not greater than his lord. They persecuted him; they will persecute us. We should not take it personally—it is not us; it is Jesus and his name that the world despises. If he had not come and taught the truth and done mighty works, they might be sinning in ignorance, but "now they have no cloke for their sin" (v. 22)—there is no rationalization or justification for their brash sinning. They cannot hide it, nor can they plead ignorance. They know the law (John 9:41). They are responsible.

THE SPIRIT OF TRUTH TESTIFIES (IN JERUSALEM)

John 15:26–27 Though hated by the world, the apostles would be able to endure the coming years of their ministries because of the gift that he was giving them—the Comforter who would confirm their witness of the truth and strengthen them. As the Spirit testified to them, they who had been eyewitnesses from the beginning (Acts 1:21–22) would in turn testify with courage and boldness to others (Acts 4:18–20, 29, 31; 5:29, 32, 40–42; 9:27, 29; 13:46; 14:3).

We may experience the same witness of the Spirit in our day, according to Elder Henry B. Eyring: "You could, this moment, begin to think of those for whom you bear responsibility. If you do, and do it with the intent to serve them, a face or a name will come to you. If you do something today and make some attempt to help that person come unto Christ, I cannot promise you a miracle, but I can promise you this: you will feel the influence of the Holy Ghost helping you, and you will feel approval. You will know that, for at least those minutes, the power of the Holy Ghost was with you" (*To Draw Closer to God*, 50).

WARNINGS TO THE APOSTLES (IN JERUSALEM)

John 16:1–6 In order that these Church leaders not be surprised, misled, offended, or prone to doubt and stumble,

Jesus explained beforehand what lay ahead for them (see commentary on John 14:29). "These things have I told you, that when the time shall come, ye may remember that I told you of them" (v. 4). He did not explain everything earlier because he was present with them, but now he would be leaving and returning to the Father who had sent him, and this foreknowledge would be comforting and reassuring in the times of trouble that would come. For example, in the future they would be excommunicated from the congregations of Israel (expelled from the synagogues) and threatened and killed (v. 2). The time would come when those who martyred the apostles would consider it a great service to God and his people to rid the Church of these holy men. They would do it because they did not know the God they professed to worship (v. 3).

THE COMFORTER (IN JERUSALEM)

John 16:7–16 "For some reason not fully explained in the scriptures, the Holy Ghost did not operate in the fulness among the Jews during the years of Jesus' mortal sojourn (John 7:39; 16:7). Statements to the effect that the Holy Ghost did not come until after Jesus was resurrected must of necessity refer to that particular dispensation only, for it is abundantly clear that the Holy Ghost was operative in earlier dispensations. Furthermore, it has reference only to the *gift* of the Holy Ghost not being present, since the *power* of the Holy Ghost was operative during the ministries of John the Baptist and Jesus; otherwise no one would have received a testimony of the truths that these men taught" (Bible Dictionary, "Holy Ghost," 704).

John 16:8–11 When the Comforter comes he will convict the world of sin, or expose the world's sin, because they refused to believe in their true Messiah; he will convict the world of not following righteousness. He was returning to the Father and would be seen here no more for a while; he would convict the world of judgment because the prince of this world, the devil, whom they insist on following instead of Him, is judged and found everlastingly wanting.

John 16:12–16 Jesus had yet many things to say to his apostles, but they could not bear them now, though when the Holy Ghost would come over them, they would be enlightened and empowered to comprehend greater truths and even all truths. The Holy Ghost would show them things to come. He would glorify the Savior by receiving truths from the Father and him and passing those truths on to them. For a time Jesus would not be there, but he would come back and they would see him (see also D&C 35:21; 38:8).

When Jesus visited the righteous Nephite and Lamanite disciples in the Western Hemisphere he said something similar to them: "I perceive that ye are weak, that ye cannot understand all my words which I am commanded of the Father to speak unto you at this time" (3 Nephi 17:2), so he encouraged them to take time to ponder what he had taught and ask the Father for specific understanding. Later he added, "If it shall so be that [ye] shall believe these things then shall the greater things be made manifest unto [you]" (3 Nephi 26:9; see also Mormon 8:12; Ether 4:13). The Holy Ghost would help facilitate that understanding: He helps us to "know the truth of all things" (Moroni 10:5) and show us "all things what [we] should do" (2 Nephi 32:5). In our modern day the Lord has repeated the same concept: "Ye are little children and ye cannot bear all things now; ye must grow in grace and in the knowledge of the truth" (D&C 50:40), which, again, is the providential role of the Holy Ghost. "Ye cannot bear all things now; nevertheless, be of good cheer, for I will lead you along" (D&C 78:18).

OPPOSITION: JOY AND SORROW (IN JERUSALEM)

John 16:17–30 The apostles were perplexed at what Jesus had just told them about "a little while" not seeing him and then seeing him again. That prophecy would be fulfilled in two senses: He would die, resurrect, and reappear; also, at the end of time, after the "little while" of mortality, they would see him again in a glorious reappearance.

He continued to teach them that during their mortal ministry, they would weep and lament over all they saw happening around them, while at the same time the wicked world rejoiced. They would be sorrowful, "but [their] sorrow shall be turned into joy" (v. 20; cf. 3 Nephi 10:10). To illustrate, he says that when a woman is in the process of giving birth, it is a painful and trying time, but as soon as the child is born, the anguish is no longer remembered as it is superseded by the joy of the child's birth (v. 21). "And ye now therefore have sorrow: but I will see you again, and your heart shall rejoice, and your joy no man taketh from you" (v. 22).

John 16:23–28 "And in that day ye shall ask me nothing but it shall be done unto you" (JST John 16:23; cf. Mormon 9:21). Jesus was saying in effect that they had not been asking enough; they should *ask* the Father in his name, and they would receive. Even more than ask, *importune* the Father and he will respond (see commentary on Luke 11:1, 5–8). Jesus had been using parables and figurative language, but the time was soon coming when he would speak very plainly. In addition, though they asked the Father in his name, the time was coming when they would not need him as their intermediary in addressing the Father—they would have direct access to him, in Christ's name, for the Father loves them. He loves them because they loved his Son, and they had a testimony that he had sent him. Jesus came from him and was going back to him.

John 16:29–30 The disciples testified that now Jesus was speaking plainly, not with figurative language, and they had a sure witness of his omniscience and divine provenance.

PROPHECY: FLOCK TO BE SCATTERED (IN JERUSALEM)

Matthew 26:31–32; Mark 14:27–28; John 16:31–33 The apostles had loyal testimonies, yet that very night they would be scattered in all directions. Another prophecy would be fulfilled: "Smite the shepherd, and the sheep of the flock shall be scattered abroad" (Matthew 26:31; Zechariah 13:7). Then, after his resurrection—in fulfillment of another clear prophecy—all those Galilean apostles would see him again in Galilee (the only Judean, Judas Iscariot, would be dead).

John 16:31–33 Could the eleven apostles have been overconfident in their conviction? Or were they commanded to abandon him, out of his concern for their safety? (see commentary on John 18:4–9). Jesus told them abruptly that they would all abandon him that very night and leave him alone, though he was never totally alone because the Father was always with him.

"These things I have spoken unto you, that in me ye might have peace. In the world ye shall have tribulation: but be of good cheer; I have overcome the world" (v. 33). Jesus could say he had overcome the world, even in that society, "among those who are the more wicked part of the world," among the only "nation on earth that would crucify their God" (2 Nephi 10:3).

So be happy. Though we will certainly have tribulation in this world, the Savior has come to show us the way to overcome—and we shall overcome by the blood of the Lamb and by the word of our testimony (Revelation 12:11).

Elder Neal A. Maxwell asked: "How was it possible for the Twelve to be of good cheer? The unimaginable agony of Gethsemane was about to descend upon Jesus; Judas's betrayal was imminent. Then would come Jesus' arrest and arraignment; the scattering of the Twelve like sheep; the awful scourging of the Savior; the unjust trial; the mob's shrill cry for Barabbas instead of Jesus; and then the awful crucifixion on Calvary. What was there to be cheerful about? Just what Jesus said: He had overcome the world! The atonement was about to be a reality. The resurrection of all mankind was assured. Death was to be done away with—Satan had failed to stop the atonement" ("But a Few Days," 4).

JESUS' ADVOCATORY PRAYER (IN JERUSALEM)

John 17:1–26 Jesus concluded the teaching part of his mortal mission by offering a profound, deeply doctrinal prayer. President David O. McKay exclaimed, "The greatest, most impressive prayer ever uttered in this world is found in John 17" (*Pathways to Happiness,* 345). It is often called the high priestly or great intercessory prayer, because he as our great high priest now interceded before the Father on our behalf, just as ancient Israel's high priest interceded or mediated before the Lord for the people. The Savior's prayer may be divided into three parts:

Verses 1–3 Jesus offers himself to provide eternal life.

Verses 4–19 Jesus presents a final report to the Father of his redemptive mission.

Verses 20–26 Jesus intercedes for the apostles and for all those who would believe in him through their preaching, that they would demonstrate their discipleship through their unity—becoming one with God and one with each other.

John 17:1–3 Jesus' purpose was to glorify his Father, but at the same time the Father would glorify his Son. The Father gave the Son power over all humankind, especially granting eternal life to all those whom the Father had given him. The

Father and the Son know them who are theirs (see commentary on John 6:37). And eternal life comes by knowing the Father and the Son. The word "life" in verse 3 is a plural noun in Hebrew (*khayim*). Unlike the Greek text, which renders the word "life" in the singular, the Hebrew rendering of this passage necessitates making the whole sentence plural; that is, "these are eternal lives," which well accords with the Lord's wording in modern revelation: "This is eternal lives—to know the only wise and true God, and Jesus Christ, whom he hath sent" (D&C 132:24). Life, in an eternal sense, exists only in plurality. Perpetual procreation, "a continuation of the seeds forever and ever" (D&C 132:19), is available only to those exalted in the highest degree of the celestial kingdom, the heavenly home of the Father and the Son, where all enjoy life in perpetuity—that is, eternal life.

John 17:4–19 Jesus concluded his mortal mission with the happy and successful report to his Father: "I have finished the work which thou gavest me to do" (v. 4). Paul also reported: "I have finished my course, I have kept the faith" (2 Timothy 4:7). When each of us stands before the Father on the final report day, there could be no more satisfying and gratifying report of our mortal stewardship than to be able to say, I have finished the work thou hast sent me here to do, and I was faithful.

Jesus looked forward to returning to the premortal glory that he enjoyed with the Father (v. 5). He assured the Father that he had repeatedly testified of him and ascribed credit and glory to him as he trained the apostles (v. 6). Those Church leaders were well aware that all they heard and learned from the Son really came from the Father (vv. 7–8). Jesus attested once more, as he had often done, that he came out from the Father (v. 8).

"The crowning revelation of the New Testament is the Fatherhood of God. In every recorded instance in which Christ addressed the God of heaven, he called him 'Father.' He used such expressions as 'my Father,' 'our Father,' and 'the Father,' but it was always the 'Father' that he addressed" (McConkie and Ostler, *Revelations of the Restoration*, 1050).

Jesus prayed specifically for his disciples, for those the Father had given him out of the world (v. 9; see commentary on John 6:37; 10:11–15; see also 3 Nephi 19:20, 29). Now whatever is the Father's is also the Son's, as he is heir of all the Father has (v. 10). The Savior's friends, the ones he was leaving behind in the world, were the object of his next request: "That they may be one, as we are" (v. 11).

In reporting his mission Jesus assured the Father that he had retained all his fruits: "None of them is lost, but the son of perdition" (v. 12). Only Judas was forever lost (the basic meaning of *perdition*), and that had been foreshadowed, prophesied, and recorded long in advance. Perdition is a name for Satan, and anyone who chooses to follow the evil one "becometh a child of the devil" (Alma 5:41).

C. Wilfred Griggs cautioned: "The reference in John 17:12 to the fulfillment of scripture in Judas's betrayal (Psalm 41:9, quoted in John 13:18) shows that even that act was within the divine plan of the Father. One should not, however, assume that Judas acted without volition. God's knowledge was not a causative agent depriving Judas of the responsibility to choose freely, act accordingly, and suffer the consequences of his actions" (in Holzapfel and Wayment, *From the Last Supper through the Resurrection*, 136).

On the question of whether Judas became a son of perdition, thought-provoking commentary comes from a modern prophet, President Joseph F. Smith: "If Judas really had known God's power, and had partaken thereof, and did actually 'deny the truth' and 'defy' that power, 'having denied the Holy Spirit after he had received it,' and also 'denied the Only Begotten,' after God had 'revealed him' unto him, then there can be no doubt that he 'will die the second death.' That Judas did partake of all this knowledge—that these great truths had been revealed to him—that he had received the Holy Spirit by the gift of God, and was therefore qualified to commit the unpardonable sin, is not at all clear to me. To my mind it strongly appears that not one of the disciples possessed sufficient light, knowledge nor wisdom, at the time of the crucifixion, for either exaltation or condemnation; for it was afterward that their minds were opened to understand the scriptures, and that they were endowed with power from on high; without which they were only children in knowledge, in comparison to what they afterwards become under the influence of the Spirit" (*Gospel Doctrine,* 433).

In the end, none of those who are called and elected, are faithful to all their covenants, and persevere to the end will be lost: "None of them that my Father hath given me shall be lost" (D&C 50:42).

Jesus prayed that those faithful ones would continue in his joy (v. 13), even though the world hated them because they were not worldly (v. 14). He was not asking that they be taken out of the world, just that they be kept away from worldliness (v. 15). Elder M. Russell Ballard said: "We should strive to change the corrupt and immoral tendencies in television and in society by keeping things that offend and debase *out* of our homes. In spite of all of the wickedness in the world, and in spite of all the opposition to good that we find on every hand, we should *not* try to take ourselves or our children *out* of the world. Jesus said, 'The kingdom of heaven is like unto leaven,' or yeast (Matthew 13:33). We are to lift the world and help all to rise above the wickedness that surrounds us. The Savior prayed to the Father: 'I pray not that thou shouldest take them out of the world, but that thou shouldest keep them from the evil' (John 17:15)" (*Ensign,* May 1989, 80).

Jesus said that his faithful disciples were not of the world, just as he was not (v. 16). He prayed the Father to sanctify them and make them holy through knowledge and use of the truth, the word of God (v. 17).

As the Father sent the Son into the world, now the Son sent his servants, his friends, into the world (v. 18). For the sake of those disciple-friends the Savior sanctified himself (by offering himself as a sacrifice for all); now the disciples could assist in sanctifying themselves by following the example of him who is the truth and the way (v. 19).

John 17:20–26 Jesus prayed for the apostles and for all those who believe in him through their teaching—that they may be one, that they may be united. Why? So "the world may believe that thou hast sent me" (v. 21; see also v. 23).

The concept of oneness is important and urgent in the gospel of Jesus Christ. It is the quintessential message inherent in the otherwise abstract English word *atonement,* "at-one-ment," the idea of becoming one, the same message suggested by the Latin words inscribed on United States currency: *E pluribus unum,* "out of many, one."

Note how the Lord uses various parts of the Father's crowning creation, the physical body of each of his children, to illustrate the desirability of oneness: the children of God lived "with *one eye* . . . having their *hearts knit together* in unity" (Mosiah 18:21; emphasis added here and in citations immediately following); "them that believed were of *one heart* and of *one soul*" (Acts 4:32); "his people ZION . . . were of *one heart* and *one mind*" (Moses 7:18); "we, being many, are *one body* in Christ" (Romans 12:5); "stand fast in *one spirit,* with *one mind*" (Philippians 1:27). One eye, one mind, one heart, one body, one spirit, and one soul. Every member of the body is needed; all members must unite together for the body of Christ to function perfectly. "There is neither Jew nor Greek," Paul wrote, [and we might add, there is neither European, nor Asian, nor North American, nor Latin American in the kingdom of God] "for ye are *all one* in Christ" (Galatians 3:28).

To establish Zion, then, we must become of one heart and one mind. God seems to be celebrating not diversity but unity. That may not be too popular a notion in the world, but the Godhead is encouraging us to become as they are—to feel and to think as they do.

And where are we more united, as one, than any other

place? In the House of God. In his Holy Temple we present ourselves equally before the Lord, all dressed in the same white clothing symbolic of cleanliness and purity, no one better than anyone else (no matter how much money we possess, what executive position we have, or what Church position we serve in)—all are alike before God. As we learned from Joseph Smith about the washing of feet, that ordinance and all ordinances of the Temple unite us, helping us to become one.

"I and my father are one," Jesus proclaimed (John 10:30; see also D&C 50:43; 93:3). And John testified that "there are three that bear record in heaven, the Father, the Word, and the Holy Ghost: and *these three are one*" (1 John 5:7). So much alike are they that if we know one, we know the others. The Father, the Son, and the Holy Ghost are *one God* (2 Nephi 31:21; Alma 11:44; 3 Nephi 11:36; D&C 20:28). Of us the Savior said, "They may become the sons of God, even one in me as I am one in the Father, as the Father is one in me, that *we may be one*" (D&C 35:2; emphasis added).

Is all this "three are one" merely theological doubletalk, or is there something profoundly significant and sacred in this doctrine?

Surely the three Gods are teaching us mortals the fundamental and indispensable principle that will lead us to become as they are. In this great intercessory prayer, our Advocate with the Father is pleading: "Holy Father, keep . . . those whom thou hast given me, that they may be one, as we are" (John 17:11).

"That they *all may be one;* as thou, Father, art in me, and I in thee, that they also may *be one in us.* . . .

"And the glory which thou gavest me I have given them; *that they may be one, even as we are one:*

"I in them, and thou in me, that they may be *made perfect in one*" (vv. 21–23; emphasis added).

There is the foundational reason for us to be united as one: to become perfect. That is the preparation required for our great *re-union,* becoming one again.

"I say unto you, *be one;* and if ye are not one ye are not mine" (D&C 38:27; emphasis added). In all these passages we see the basic meaning of that otherwise abstract word *atonement:* The great sacrificial offering of the Lamb is meant to help us become as one with him and the Father and as one with each other.

John 17:24–26 The Savior loves us; he wants us in his heavenly home with him. And he wants us to fully experience the Father's love as he has.

RETIREMENT TO GETHSEMANE (ON THE WESTERN SLOPE OF THE MOUNT OF OLIVES)

Matthew 26:30; Mark 14:26; Luke 22:39; John 18:1 Somewhere between the Upper Room and the Kidron (a small streambed or seasonal river that runs north-south immediately east of Jerusalem and its Temple Mount), the preceding teachings were given (John 15–17; see Appendix 1, 716).

Before leaving the Upper Room, Jesus and the eleven apostles sang a hymn. Their ancient hymnbook was the Psalms, and Psalms 113–18 (the "Hallel Psalms," collectively called "the Great Hallel") were usually sung at the Passover service, as indicated in the Mishnah, *Pesachim* 5:7 (see Farrar, *Life of Christ,* 418, 606; see also Bible Dictionary, "Hallel," 698).

Jesus had prepared and fortified his apostles against the spiritual tribulation that was to come (Gethsemane and Golgotha) by instituting the ordinances of sacrament and washing of feet. The finale of that strengthening preparation was the singing of the Hallel hymn. Elder Boyd K. Packer said: "There are many references in the scriptures, both ancient and modern, that attest to the influence of righteous music. The Lord, Himself, was prepared for His greatest test through its influence, for the scripture records: 'And when they had sung an hymn, they went out into the mount of Olives.' (Mark 14:26.)" (*Ensign,* January 1974, 28).

Now the time had come, and Jesus led his closest associates across the Kidron to a garden area called Gethsemane. On this Passover night, with a full moon lighting their way across the Kidron and past numerous tombs, Jesus and his apostles might have reflected on the words of the psalmist: "Yea, though I walk through the valley of the shadow of death, I will fear no evil" (Psalm 23:4). The Savior resolutely faced his imminent suffering and sacrifice in order to conquer the enemies of all humankind: death and hell.

PETER: "WHEN THOU ART CONVERTED" (IN OR NEAR JERUSALEM)

Luke 22:31–32 After three years of preparation and training, Peter was scheduled for more than three decades of mortal leadership in the Lord's kingdom. Satan knew that, and he wanted to destroy the future presiding officer. The devil would thrust at Peter every possible sword of doubt, indecision, discouragement, and disability in order to get the apostle to fail and fall. The Lord would allow the adversary to test, try, and prove Peter to refine him and remove all impurities. The Lord allows the same sifting process for all of us; in fact, Joseph Smith Translation Luke 22:31 indicates that Satan's effort is to sift all "*the children of the kingdom* as wheat" (cf. 3 Nephi 18:15, 18).

Jesus said that he prayed specifically for Peter, to buoy up his faith, and he admonished Peter that when he was converted, to strengthen his brethren. But wasn't Peter already converted? We have seen frequent evidence of his strong testimony and his commitment all through Jesus' ministry, but there would yet come to the chief apostle a witness from the Holy Ghost of greater force and magnitude than anything he had yet known. When that occurred (as it dramatically did, at Pentecost; see Appendix 6, 765), Peter's calling was to strengthen his brethren and strengthen the whole Church.

"The apostle Peter is the classical illustration of a convert. After he accepted Jesus as the Messiah, after he was baptized, after he spent three full years in almost constant companionship with the Son of God, after he was ordained an elder and an apostle, after he went forth on a mission healing the sick and performing other miracles, after he walked on the water amid the tempestuous waves of the Galilean sea, after he bore a fervent witness of the Savior's divinity, after all this and more, Jesus said to him: 'When thou art converted, strengthen thy brethren' (Luke 22:32). It was only then that Peter was reconciled to God and became a new creature by the power of the Holy Ghost. Peter's conversion was manifest in his valiant actions from the time of the first Pentecost after the death of Christ until he, too, died upon a Roman cross (John 21:18)" (McConkie and Ostler, *Revelations of the Restoration*, 903).

Scripture records that Peter took correction well. He responded positively to reproof and counsel, and he allowed the humbling experiences to polish off the rough edges of his personality and convert him into a spiritual giant.

PROPHECY: "BEFORE THE COCK CROW" (IN OR NEAR JERUSALEM)

Matthew 26:33–35; Mark 14:29–31; Luke 22:33–34; John 13:36–38 As the foreshadowings became darker and the omens more ominous, the apostles grew more desperate to affirm their allegiance and assert their loyalty. Peter and his companions of the Quorum boldly announced that although others might be offended and turn away from their Lord, yet they would not. They were willing to go with him to prison and even to death (Luke 22:33).

Jesus turned to Peter and told him "that this day, even in this night, before the cock [rooster] crow twice, thou shalt deny me thrice" (Mark 14:30), or as Luke recorded it, "thou shalt thrice deny that thou knowest me" (Luke 22:34).

"RECKONED AMONG THE TRANSGRESSORS" (IN OR NEAR JERUSALEM)

Luke 22:35–38 Jesus asked the apostles to reflect on their missionary labors, when he sent them forth without purse, scrip, or shoes, so they could exercise faith and allow him to provide for them. Now the policy is reversed: Take provisions and equipment so as not to be a burden to anyone. Be prepared for all temporal exigencies.

One specific prophecy regarding Jesus was about to be fulfilled—Isaiah's prophecy that he would be "numbered with the transgressors" (Isaiah 53:12; Mosiah 14:12) would be fulfilled as they crucified him between two thieves (Matthew 27:38). All prophetic utterances regarding him would "have an end" (Luke 22:37), or a fulfillment.

His disciples said, "Lord, behold, here are two swords" (v. 38). Jesus responded essentially that there should be no more talk of swords. As the apostles would soon understand, his time had come—it was now time for him to die.

JESUS' SUFFERING AND PRAYERS (IN GETHSEMANE)

Matthew 26:36–46; Mark 14:32–42; Luke 22:40–46; John 18:2 On the slope of the Mount of Olives was an orchard and garden area to which Jesus liked to retire for meditation and prayer. "Jesus ofttimes resorted thither with

An ancient olive tree in the Garden of Gethsemane on the Mount of Olives

his disciples" (John 18:2). Because Jesus and his disciples had often gone to this garden, "Judas, also, which betrayed him, knew the place" (John 18:2) and thus knew where to lead the band of Roman soldiers and Temple police officers to arrest Jesus (see Appendix 4, 756).

The garden was appropriately named *Gat Shemen*, which in Hebrew means "oil press." Just as the grape or olive is pressed and crushed by the heavy stone in the press, so the heavy burden of the sins of the world that Jesus had to carry would press the blood out of the body of this Anointed One.

As a student of the Savior's experience in Gethsemane, Brother Skinner had a profound experience that will forever remain etched in his memory. Brigham Young University maintains a study center on the Mount of Olives, overlooking the very places of our Lord's ministry. Three olive presses are situated on the grounds, where they are used both for object lessons and as invitations to explore ancient olive culture. One fall semester he supervised the students at the BYU Jerusalem Center as they participated in their own olive harvest and pressing activity. The olives were placed in the *yam*, or rock basin, and the crushing stone was pushed around and around the basin until the olives began to ooze their oil. When the oil began to run down the lip of the limestone basin, it had the distinctive red color characteristic of the first moments of the new pressing each year. At that instant an audible gasp came from the 170 students who surrounded the olive press to witness the re-creation of the ancient pressing process. It was a stunning, even chilling, minute until the oil turned back to its usual golden color. Everyone in that group seemed to have the same thought as they watched this transformation happen. It was more than just an amazing confirmation of the symbolism we had discussed. This was, right before their very eyes, a real-life reflection of Gethsemane. In Gethsemane Jesus became, as it were, the olive—bruised, broken, and crushed for each one of them (for more on the symbolism of the olive and the Atonement, see Skinner, *Gethsemane*, 77–91).

In Gethsemane, among the olive trees that were themselves symbolic of the people of Israel, was accomplished—along with its consummation at Golgotha—the most selfless suffering in the history of humankind. He who had committed no sin suffered for all sin.

Jesus suffered for *all* sin, for the wickedest actions of the vilest sinners as well as the unwitting transgressions of the meekest of souls. The spiritual and physical feelings brought about by these transgressions, as well as the full effects of all sins and violent acts ever committed, were placed upon the Savior and suffered by him on behalf of those who would repent and allow the Savior to be the proxy, or substitute, sufferer for their misdeeds.

In other words, in Gethsemane Jesus became *us*, each one of us, and we became him. Our sins were transferred to Jesus. His perfection was transferred to us. He was a substitute recipient for our pain and punishment. He acted in our place to take the consequences and sorrows of wicked behavior, which each of us deserves, so that we could be free from the devastating effects of sin. The scriptures of the Restoration teach that the Savior took to himself the full force of the punishment deserved by each of us. He suffered God's wrath in our place. Elder Neal A. Maxwell observed that "Jesus always deserved and always had the Father's full approval. But when He took our sins upon Him, of divine necessity required by justice He experienced instead 'the fierceness of the wrath of Almighty God' (D&C 76:107; 88:106)" (*Lord, Increase Our Faith,* 13).

The fierceness of the wrath of Almighty God is a terrifying thing to contemplate. In Gethsemane Jesus took the full force of God's overwhelming punishment. Justice demanded it, and we, who are sinners, deserve it. According to the rules framing the universe, the full consequences of transgressed laws cannot be dismissed or overlooked. They must be borne by someone—the sinner or the substitute. Jesus was that substitute for all of us who will allow him to be so. Elder Boyd K. Packer testified that "upon Him was the burden of all human transgression, all human guilt. . . . By choice, [Christ] accepted the penalty . . . for brutality, immorality, perversion, and corruption; for addiction; for the killings and torture and terror—for all of it that ever had been or all that ever would be enacted upon this earth" (*Ensign,* May 1988, 69). In Gethsemane Jesus suffered for us, vicariously, spiritual death.

This act of pure grace gave our Savior the right to act as our advocate with the Father and to invoke the law of mercy on our behalf.

"Listen to him who is the advocate with the Father, who is pleading your cause before him—

"Saying: Father, behold the sufferings and death of him who did no sin, in whom thou wast well pleased; behold the blood of thy Son which was shed, the blood of him whom thou gavest that thyself might be glorified;

"Wherefore, Father, spare these my brethren that believe on my name, that they may come unto me and have everlasting life" (D&C 45:3–5).

Rather than the small area now enclosed by the walls that

The Atonement and the Resurrection

Sign at the entrance to the Garden of Gethsemane

surround the Franciscan property that includes the Basilica of the Agony, the Garden of Gethsemane must have extended a considerable distance up the slope of the Mount of Olives. Upon entering the garden, Jesus left eight of his apostles to watch and pray, and he continued farther inside—meaning up the slope—with Peter, James, and John. He then left those three to watch and pray, while he hiked "a stone's cast" (Matthew 26:36–39; Luke 22:41) beyond them.

A most beautiful and moving description of the Savior in Gethsemane was penned by Elder Orson F. Whitney:

"Then came a marvelous manifestation, an admonition from a higher Source, one impossible to ignore. It was a dream, or a vision in a dream, as I lay upon my bed in the little town of Columbia, Lancaster County, Pennsylvania. I seemed to be in the Garden of Gethsemane, a witness of the Savior's agony. I saw Him as plainly as I have seen anyone. Standing behind a tree in the foreground, I beheld Jesus, with Peter, James and John, as they came through a little wicket gate at my right. Leaving the three apostles there, after telling them to kneel and pray, the Son of God passed over to the other

The Garden of Gethsemane, 1870

side, where He also knelt and prayed. It was the same prayer with which all Bible readers are familiar: 'Oh my Father, if it be possible, let this cup pass from me; nevertheless not as I will, but as Thou wilt.'

"As He prayed the tears streamed down His face, which was toward me. I was so moved at the sight that I also wept, out of pure sympathy. My whole heart went out to Him; I loved Him with all my soul, and longed to be with Him as I longed for nothing else.

"Presently He arose and walked to where those apostles were kneeling—fast asleep! He shook them gently, awoke them, and in tone of tender reproach, untinctured by the least show of anger or impatience, asked them plaintively if they could not watch with Him one hour. There He was, with the awful weight of the world's sins upon His shoulders, with the pangs of every man, woman and child shooting through His sensitive soul—and they could not watch with Him one poor hour!

"Returning to His place, He offered up the same prayer as before; then went back and again found them sleeping.

The Atonement and the Resurrection

Again He awoke them, readmonished them, and once more returned and prayed. Three times this occurred, until I was perfectly familiar with His appearance—face, form and movements. He was of noble stature and majestic mien—not at all the weak, effeminate being that some painters have portrayed; but the very God that He was and is, as meek and humble as a little child.

"All at once the circumstances seemed to change, the scene remaining just the same. Instead of before, it was now after the crucifixion, and the Savior, with the three apostles, now stood together in a group at my left. They were about to depart and ascend to Heaven. I could endure it no longer. I ran from behind the tree, fell at His feet, clasped Him around the knees, and begged Him to take me with Him.

"I shall never forget the kind and gentle manner in which He stooped, raised me up, and embraced me. It was so vivid, so real. I felt the very warmth of His body, as He held me in His arms and said in tenderest tones: 'No, my son; these have finished their work; they can go with me; but you must stay and finish yours.' Still I clung to Him. Gazing up into His face—for He was taller than I—I besought Him fervently: 'Well, promise me that I will come to you at the last.' Smiling sweetly, He said: 'That will depend entirely upon yourself.' I awoke with a sob in my throat, and it was morning" (*Through Memory's Halls,* 82–83; see also in Whitney, "Vision of Gethsemane").

Mark 14:33–36 Upon entering Gethsemane, Jesus began to be "sore amazed" and to be "very heavy," so much that he exclaimed his soul was filled with such sorrow that he felt death's grip. The Greek word translated as "sore amazed" means "terrified surprise or astonishment."

To be sure, the feelings of surprise and awful, anguished sorrow were the result of many things.

He suffered not only for the *sins* of all creation but for the sorrows, sufferings, tribulations, and injustices of the individuals of those multiple earths. Our finite mortal minds cannot grasp the tremendous load borne by the Savior in Gethsemane. But we begin to comprehend what this means in practical terms by remembering that this earth alone has had possibly a hundred billion people live upon it during its temporal history. Multiply the sins, sorrows, heartaches, and injustices of these hundred billion souls by the millions of earths that the Savior created and redeemed, and we may begin to view the term "infinite atonement" in a different light. Gethsemane paid for all these things plus an infinitely possible combination of these things—even before they happened to us who live in modern times. But even that is not all.

Another reason for the surprise has to do with the Savior's very nature. The scriptures declare with absolute certainty that Jesus was perfect, without sin. Paul testified, "For we have not an high priest which cannot be touched with the feeling of our infirmities; but was in all points tempted like as we are, yet without sin" (Hebrews 4:15).

Being perfect, Jesus did not and could not know what sin felt like. He did not have the experience of feeling the effects of sin—neither physically, spiritually, mentally, nor emotionally. Not until Gethsemane, that is. Now, in an instant, he began to feel all the sensations and effects of sin, all the guilt, anguish, darkness, turmoil, depression, anger, and physical sickness that sin brings. All of this the Savior felt and much, much more.

The shock to the Savior at this moment must have been overwhelming. Because he was perfect, he was also perfectly sensitive to all the effects and ramifications of sin on our mental, emotional, and physical makeup. His makeup was such that it could not tolerate sin or its effects, just as our systems cannot tolerate poison, disease, extreme heat, cold, dehydration, or a hundred other harmful substances and conditions. More significantly, as Mark describes for us, the experience Jesus had of finally comprehending sin as well as the feelings that issue from sin were absolutely surprising to him. He had never before experienced these sensations. Not only did it surprise him but it terrified him. For the first time in his eternal existence, the God of heaven and earth was experiencing the terrifying feelings associated with sin. Jesus felt something in Gethsemane he had never known before. Perhaps that is the full meaning of Alma's words that the Son of God, the Messiah, would be born as a mortal so that "he may know *according to the flesh* how to succor his people" (Alma 7:12; emphasis added). Elder Neal A. Maxwell wrote: "Imagine, Jehovah, the Creator of this and other worlds, 'astonished'! Jesus knew cognitively what He must do, but not experientially. He had never personally known the exquisite and exacting process of an atonement before. Thus, when the agony came in its fulness, it was so much, much worse than even He with his unique intellect had ever imagined!" (*Ensign,* May 1985, 72–73).

Under the crushing weight of sin, sorrow, and suffering—all of which were originally ours but now had become his—and in shock and terrified surprise, the Savior cried out in distress to his Father, just as a child might cry out for the comfort offered by a loving parent. The only relief the Savior could hope for might be found in prayer "that, if it were possible, the hour might pass from him" (Mark 14:35). Thus, in the most anguished cry of his life, the Savior pleaded, "Abba [Father] . . . all things are possible unto thee; take away this cup from me" (Mark 14:36).

In Gethsemane, on that terrible but glorious night, in a scene so personal as almost to dissuade us from listening in, Jesus cried out in shockingly familiar tones, Please take this experience away—it is worse than even I thought it would be. Nevertheless, I will do what thou desirest and not what I desire. This plea was not theatrics. This petition really happened between a Son and his Father.

Matthew 26:39 "If it be possible, let this cup pass from me." The cup was sometimes symbolic of experiences of suffering. Elder James E. Talmage wrote: "Our Lord's frequent mention of His foreseen sufferings as the cup of which the

The Four Gospels

Jesus Praying in Gethsemane, *by Harry Anderson*

Father would have Him drink (Matt. 26:39, 42; Mark 14:36; Luke 22:42; John 18:11; compare Matt. 20:22; Mark 10:38; 1 Cor. 10:21) is in line with Old Testament usage of the term 'cup' as a symbolic expression for a bitter or poisonous potion typifying experiences of suffering. See Psa. 11:6; 75:8; Isa. 51:17, 22; Jer. 25:15, 17; 49:12" (*Jesus the Christ*, 575; cf. 3 Nephi 11:11).

Gethsemane was the bitterest anguish, the greatest contradiction, the gravest injustice. Irony and contradiction are two of the best descriptors of Gethsemane's bitter cup, causing thoughtful disciples to reflect on the nature of tests and trials in mortality. By studying the bitter cup, we can see how the bitterest agony for One opened the door to the sweetest ecstasy for all. The Prophet Joseph Smith taught that the Savior "descended in suffering below that which man can suffer; or, in other words, suffered greater sufferings, and was exposed to more powerful contradictions than any man can be" (*Lectures on Faith*, 5:2). Perhaps the greatest trials are those that seem the most unfair, but the faithful may take comfort in knowing that there is One who understands with perfect empathy. Elder Neal A. Maxwell said of the Savior: "At the end, meek and lowly Jesus partook of the most bitter cup without becoming the least bitter" (*Ensign*, May 1989, 63).

Perhaps it was a night of infinite suffering *because* of infinite contradiction. Though Jesus was the Son of the Highest, in Gethsemane he descended below all things. Though he was sent out of love (John 3:16) and though he was characterized as the embodiment of love (1 John 4:8), in Gethsemane he was surrounded by hate and betrayal. Though he was the light and life of the world, in Gethsemane he was subjected to darkness and spiritual death. Though he was sinless, in Gethsemane he was weighed down by monumental sin and iniquity. Though he gave no offense in anything (2 Corinthians 6:3), in Gethsemane he suffered for the offenses of all. In Gethsemane, the sinless One became the great sinner (2 Corinthians 5:21), that is, he experienced fully the plight of sinners. Though he was fully deserving of the Father's love and the Father's glory, in Gethsemane he suffered the wrath of Almighty God.

Because the Savior endured perfectly his staggering contradictions, we will be recompensed for our own faithful endurance of life's contradictions, injustices, and flat-out unfair circumstances. That is, through the Atonement, all of life's contradictions, all injustices, and all unfair circumstances will be made up to us; they will all be put right—if we remain faithful to the Savior.

We, like Jesus, suffer contradictions as part of our probation on this earth. It is what we do in the face of those contradictions, how we react, that demonstrates our commitment to God and thus determines our place in eternity. The greater the contradiction, faithfully endured, the greater the blessing enjoyed afterward.

Jesus' suffering in the Garden of Gethsemane was beyond human comprehension, as King Benjamin described: "And lo, he shall suffer . . . even more than man can suffer, except it be unto death; for behold, blood cometh from every pore, so great shall be his anguish for the wickedness and the abominations of his people" (Mosiah 3:7). And Jesus Christ himself described:

"For behold, I, God, have suffered these things for all, that they might not suffer if they would repent;

"But if they would not repent they must suffer even as I;

"Which suffering caused myself, even God, the greatest of all, to tremble because of pain, and to bleed at every pore, and to suffer both body and spirit—and would that I might not drink the bitter cup and shrink" (D&C 19:16–18).

Stephen E. Robinson, our colleague in the Department of Ancient Scripture at Brigham Young University, wrote this poignant description of the Savior's sufferings for us:

"*All* the negative aspects of human existence brought about by the Fall, Jesus Christ absorbed into himself. He experienced vicariously in Gethsemane all the private griefs and heartaches, all the physical pains and handicaps, all the emotional burdens and depressions of the human family. He knows the loneliness of those who don't fit in or who aren't handsome or pretty. He knows what it's like to choose up teams and be the last one chosen. He knows the anguish of parents whose children go wrong. He knows the private hell of the abused child or spouse. He knows all these things personally and intimately because he lived them in the Gethsemane experience. Having personally lived a perfect life, he then chose to experience our imperfect lives. In that infinite Gethsemane experience, the meridian of time, the center of eternity, he lived a billion billion lifetimes of sin, pain, disease, and sorrow.

"God uses no magic wand to simply wave bad things into

nonexistence. The sins that he remits, he remits by making them his own and suffering them. The pain and heartaches that he relieves, he relieves by suffering them himself. These things can be shared and absorbed, but they cannot be simply wished or waved away. They must be suffered. Thus we owe him not only for our spiritual cleansing from sin, but for our physical, mental, and emotional healings as well, for he has borne these infirmities for us also. All that the Fall put wrong, the Savior in his atonement puts right. It is all part of his infinite sacrifice—of his infinite gift" (*Believing Christ*, 122–23).

The Savior himself testified: "I have overcome and have trodden the wine-press alone, even the wine-press of the fierceness of the wrath of Almighty God" (D&C 76:107). Treading and trampling in a winepress and staining all his raiment is symbolic of what he did in Gethsemane; the redness of the grapes in the winepress was now compared to the redness of his blood pressed from every pore, symbolic of his torturous suffering for the pains of all others. He exclaims that the exquisite pain was caused by "the fierceness of the wrath of Almighty God"; that is, the ferocity and the wrath of the justice that must come down on all sins; justice demanding payment for all sins is now satisfied by the merciful Savior himself who was willing, out of love, to personally suffer the "fierceness of the wrath of Almighty God" in place of all those penitent souls who would otherwise have to suffer the same (Mosiah 15:9).

"The Son of Man hath descended below them all" (D&C 122:8); he was willing to drink the bitterest cup to answer the ends of all the laws of eternity. And he was willing to do it because it was the Father's will, and he loved and always obeyed his Father: "Not as I will, but as thou wilt" (Matthew 26:39). Jesus used, according to Mark's account, the most endearing title for him who sent him: "Abba, Father" (Mark 14:36; *Abba* being the most intimate Aramaic title, "Father").

Luke 22:43–44 Satan himself came to Jerusalem. In this pivotal moment of eternity, where would the greatest adversary of the Gods have been except right there in Gethsemane to smile upon the divine anguish?

Elder James E. Talmage says of Satan's presence in Gethsemane: "Christ's agony in the garden is unfathomable by the finite mind, both as to intensity and cause. . . . He struggled and groaned under a burden such as no other being who has lived on earth might even conceive as possible. It was not physical pain, nor mental anguish alone, that caused Him to suffer such torture as to produce an extrusion of blood from every pore; but a spiritual agony of soul such as only God was capable of experiencing. . . . In that hour of anguish Christ met and overcame all the horrors that Satan, 'the prince of this world' could inflict" (*Jesus the Christ,* 568–69). If Satan could get the Savior to retreat from his atoning sacrifice, all would be lost.

But in this most terrible moment of the Savior's eternal existence, the Father of this suffering Son would undoubtedly have also been near by. Perhaps many of the noble and great ones were present, watching and hurting for God's Son but also rejoicing for what it all meant. At least one angel from heaven passed into the mortal sphere to strengthen Jesus. Some have understandably wondered if this messenger could be Adam, thus involving the two key men in two gardens who initiated the two pillars of the Plan: the Fall and the Atonement.

"Being in an agony he prayed more earnestly" (v. 44). What an example to his followers in all ages. We are taught to pray, to plead, to implore, even importune, and our Exemplar not only prayed but prayed *more earnestly.* Even more than at his birth thirty-three years earlier, "the hopes and fears of all the years are met in thee tonight" (*Hymns,* 1985, no. 208). This was the hardest thing the Creator and Redeemer had ever done. By the immensity of all the pains and sins he covered (the meaning of the Hebrew word translated "atonement," *kippur,* means "to cover")—he everlastingly covered from view the sins of all repentant sinners.

Because of the incredible burden of those sins, "*he sweat as it were* great drops of blood" (JST Luke 22:44; see also Mosiah 3:7). Gerald Lund expounded on this remarkable detail: "Because of the words, '*as it were*,' some commentators have tried to explain this away as a mere simile, saying that the agony he was enduring caused him to perspire copiously, and in the moonlight the drops of sweat appeared to be drops of blood. Many others [including Lund] strongly disagree with this suggestion, seeing it as an attempt to dilute and weaken the significance of the atoning sacrifice. In the first place, 'bloody sweat,' or perspiration mingled with blood, is not an unknown phenomenon. There are recorded cases where, under severe stress, the vessels inside the body rupture and blood oozes from the body like beads of sweat (for examples, see Clarke, 3:257; Edersheim, *Life and Times*, pp. 846–47; Farrar, p. 577). More to the point, the Greek word which Luke uses and which is translated as 'drops' is *thrombos*. It was an ancient medical term and means 'a large, thick drop of clotted blood' (Vine, p. 341). It was not used to describe normal perspiration. Even today, *thrombosis* is the condition where there are blood clots within the veins" (*Kingdom and the Crown*, 3:490–91). Therefore, though Luke used the phrase "as it were," there were literally great drops of blood issuing from every pore of Jesus' body during his atoning agony, as attested by the words of the Savior himself: "[these] sufferings caused myself, even God, the greatest of all, to tremble because of pain, and to bleed at every pore" (D&C 19:18).

Did Jesus suffer for all sins ever committed or did he suffer only for those repented of? Actually, the Savior's redemption was a qualitative rather than a quantitative sacrifice, having the capacity to cover all sin, whenever and wherever. Elder Neal A. Maxwell wrote: "The cumulative weight of all mortal sins—past, present, and future—pressed upon that perfect, sinless, and sensitive Soul! All our infirmities and sicknesses were somehow, too, a part of the awful arithmetic of the

Atonement.... His suffering—as it were, *enormity* multiplied by *infinity*—evoked His later soul-cry on the cross, and it was a cry of forsakenness" (*Ensign*, May 1985, 73).

When the Savior instituted the sacrament ordinance, he said, "This is in remembrance of my blood of the new testament, which is shed for *as many as shall believe on my name*, for the remission of *their* sins" (JST Matthew 26:24). Alma adds, "It is he that cometh to take away the sins of the world, yea, the sins of every man who steadfastly believeth on his name" (Alma 5:48; see also Alma 19:13). His suffering pays for the sins of "all those who have a broken heart and a contrite spirit and unto none else can the ends of the law be answered" (2 Nephi 2:7). "Whoso repenteth and cometh unto me ... him will I receive ... for such I have laid down my life" (3 Nephi 9:22). And he warns: "If they would not repent they must suffer even as I" (D&C 19:17).

Luke 22:45 Jesus found his friends "sleeping for sorrow." Frederic W. Farrar eloquently described, in part, how the apostles must have been feeling at this point: "We may not intrude too closely into this scene. It is shrouded in a halo and a mystery into which no footstep may penetrate. We, as we contemplate it, are like those disciples—our senses are confused, our perceptions are not clear. We can but enter into their amazement and sore distress. Half waking, half oppressed with an irresistible weight of troubled slumber ... they were dim witnesses of an unutterable agony, far deeper than anything which they could fathom" (*Life of Christ*, 624).

JST Mark 14:36–38 Joseph Smith added to the text of Mark a whole new dimension to the relationship between Jesus and his apostles in Gethsemane. When they entered the garden, "*the disciples began to be sore amazed, and to be very heavy, and to complain in their hearts, wondering if this be the Messiah. And Jesus knowing their hearts, said* to his disciples, Sit ye here, while I shall pray. And he taketh with him, Peter, and James, and John, *and rebuked them.*"

In the middle of all these rapidly unfolding events, the

apostles were apparently bewildered and confused, even depressed, not yet comprehending what kind of Messiah he was. The triumphal entry they could relate to, but now this talk of betrayal and crucifixion? Did they not understand the concept of a suffering Messiah? Were they still operating under the notion of a political deliverer? They were worn out—physically and spiritually drained. And they slept. How could they sleep during this night of torturous suffering of their beloved Leader? Terry B. Ball noted: "During times of great emotional distress and grief, the human body often copes by retreating to sleep. Understanding the disciples' surrender to sleep as the natural reaction of the body to intense sorrow helps us understand the Savior's observation as He roused the sleeping disciples: 'The spirit indeed is willing, but the flesh is weak' (Matthew 26:41; see also Mark 14:38)" (in Holzapfel and Wayment, *From the Last Supper through the Resurrection*, 154).

Even though we are made aware of the apostles' weaknesses, we are nonetheless wise to regard them with the highest respect and deference. These were great men, among the very best on the earth at that or any other time in history. They were *special* witnesses. They had given up everything in pursuit of their Master's call to follow him. In some cases, they had consecrated significantly—their time, talents, and possessions. By the time they reached Gethsemane that awful night, they had been awake for many hours straight, and above all, they were mortals subject to all the influences and frailties of mortality brought on by the Fall.

These apostles were also leaders in transition. Nothing like the events they were witnessing and participating in had ever happened before, nor would the events of Jesus' final days find any precedent in the history of our universe. We ought therefore to increase our gratitude for the strength and power demonstrated by Jesus' original Quorum of the Twelve rather than seek to multiply their shortcomings.

JUDAS'S BETRAYAL (IN GETHSEMANE)

Matthew 26:47–50; Mark 14:43–46; Luke 22:47–48; John 18:2–3 After Jesus' agony in Gethsemane, a multitude consisting of representatives and officers from the chief priests (Temple police or Levites; see Appendix 4, 756), elders, "captains of the temple" (Luke 22:52), and soldiers arrived seeking his arrest. The word "band" in John 18:3 is translated from the Greek word for "cohort," a subdivision of the Roman army (see Appendix 5, 759). Presumably, Roman leadership at some level was pressed into service to help with the arrest, though they probably were not involved in the actual conspiracy to take Jesus' life. Having Roman soldiers in the group would have given Jewish leaders and conspirators the cloak of "official business" and governmental power to hide behind.

At the head of the arresting party was Judas, who kissed Jesus profusely (according to the emphatic form of the Greek verb used in Mark 14:45), greatly confusing the emotions of the moment with a false display of affection. H. Curtis Wright explained: "The feeling of deep love in the traitor's kiss is inherent in the preposition *kata,* which is compounded with the verb meaning 'kiss.' This compound form is found in both Matthew and Mark. . . . the resultant form means 'kiss passionately, with warmth and tenderness.' The use of the aorist tense by both Matthew and Mark also leaves open the possibility that the kissing was done more than once" (*Thing of Naught,* 40).

The kiss of betrayal by Judas that awful Thursday night evokes an irony matched by few other episodes in scripture. By New Testament times, a kiss in public was a symbol both of distinction and of elevation. It was a token of respect with which pupils or disciples greeted their great rabbis or teachers. Among Christians, a kiss was a demonstration of fellowship and brotherhood.

How the kiss from Judas must have stung the Savior. And how Judas must have been taken aback by the Savior's rejoinder: "*Friend*, wherefore art thou come?" (Matthew 26:50; emphasis added). The next question emphasizes the irony of the episode: "Betrayest thou the Son of man with a kiss?" (Luke 22:48). Could a greater indictment of guilt have been leveled at Judas than with the single word *friend*? Or could there have been a greater expression of devastated disappointment than the Savior's asking, You are betraying me with a *kiss*?

ARRESTING OFFICERS FALL (IN GETHSEMANE)

John 18:4–9 John is the only Gospel writer who recorded a curious detail involving the cohort and the captain or tribune who came to arrest Jesus (John 18:12). The Savior asked them directly: "Whom seek ye?" They answered, "Jesus of Nazareth." He told them, "I am he," and instead of apprehending him they retreated slightly and fell to the ground. The reason for such strange behavior—fear, awe, respect, or suspicion of treachery—is not given. A second time the interchange occurred: "Whom seek ye?" "Jesus of Nazareth." "I have told you that I am he." Then, out of concern for the safety of his apostle-friends, he declared that the others with him should be allowed to "go their way." Thus, in another sense, the scripture was fulfilled: "Of them which thou gavest me have I lost none" (v. 9; see also John 17:12; cf. 3 Nephi 27:30).

PETER DEFENDS JESUS WITH A SWORD (IN GETHSEMANE)

Matthew 26:51–54; Mark 14:47; Luke 22:49–51; John 18:10–11 When the mob's intention was known, Peter stepped forward, swung his sword, and cut off the ear of the high priest's servant (which directly implicates the high priest in the arrest). What was Peter doing with a sword? At Passover time, many tens of thousands of people flocked to Jerusalem, more than could be housed inside the walls. Crowds of pilgrims would have camped as close outside the city as possible. In the darkness of the night, a sword might offer some security. When the arresting party arrived with "lanterns and torches and weapons" (John 18:3), some disciples ventured, "Shall we smite with the sword?" (Luke 22:49), possibly intending to defend themselves or still expecting Jesus to assume the popular role of the Messiah as the one who would overthrow his adversaries and establish a glorious new Jewish kingdom (cf. Luke 24:21; Acts 1:6).

Jesus responded, "Suffer ye thus far" (Luke 22:51)—saying, in effect, That's far enough. Let us not resist any further. Let us not obstruct what must now happen. "The cup which my Father hath given me, shall I not drink it?" (John 18:11). When Jesus introduced himself to his disciples in ancient America a short time later, he proclaimed, "I have drunk out of that bitter cup which the Father hath given me, and have glorified the Father in taking upon me the sins of the world, in the which I have suffered the will of the Father in all things from the beginning." Upon hearing that testimony, the scripture says, "the whole multitude fell to the earth" out of reverence and awe for their Savior (3 Nephi 11:11–12).

Peter having sliced off the ear of the high priest's servant, whose name was Malchus, Jesus healed him. Possibly John knew the man, as John was acquainted with the high priest himself (John 18:15). It is amazing that such a miraculous demonstration did not cause people to interrupt the arrest and find out more about the Man who was regarded by some as the Messiah.

Jesus told Peter to put away his sword, emphasizing Jesus' voluntary submission to what was to come, "for all they that take the sword shall perish with the sword" (Matthew 26:52). Jesus would have learned that truth from growing up in Nazareth, overlooking the Jezreel Valley, one of the greatest battlefields in history. If it were necessary to resist this travesty of justice, Jesus could have requested of the Father more than twelve legions of angels (Matthew 26:53). Considering that in those days a legion was six thousand (see Appendix 5, 760), then more than seventy-two thousand angels of the hosts of heaven could have been called up to halt the advance of this band of enemies. But, as Jesus frequently pointed out, the scriptures must be fulfilled. He had known from the beginning what must be, and he had covenanted with the Father to carry through the whole of it. "It behooveth the great Creator that he suffereth himself to become subject unto man in the flesh, and die for all men, that all men might become subject unto him" (2 Nephi 9:5).

DISCIPLES FLEE (FROM GETHSEMANE)

Matthew 26:56; Mark 14:50 The disciples forsook Jesus and fled, but not all, for as we shall see (in Matthew 26:58), Peter and John stayed close by to witness the final hours—as close as possible without also being apprehended.

JESUS ARRESTED (IN GETHSEMANE)

Matthew 26:55–57; Mark 14:46–52; Luke 22:52–54; John 18:12 Though Jesus was voluntarily submitting to the injustices and indignities, he did express a sharp reminder of his rights under the law: "Are ye come out as against a thief with swords and staves [plural of staff] for to take me?" (Matthew 26:55). One of the many illegalities in the treatment of Jesus, according to Jewish law, was his arrest at night. "I sat daily with you teaching in the temple, and ye laid no hold on me" (Matthew 26:56). But again, all the prophecies must be fulfilled. It was known well in advance that the Jews' own laws, the laws that Jehovah (this same Jesus) had given centuries before, would be ignored and violated. For, Luke adds, "this is your hour, and the power of darkness" (Luke 22:53).

Mark 14:51–52 Only Mark records a curious incident at Jesus' arrest: the arresting party seized a young *disciple* (JST Mark 14:57) wrapped only in a linen sheet, and the young man dropped the sheet and fled away naked—demonstrating that Jesus' disciples were also in jeopardy of their lives. Some scholars of the New Testament text believe that the young man of whom the Gospel writer wrote was Mark himself.

William Lane noted: "Ordinarily the outer garment was made of wool. The fine linen garment left behind in the hands of a guard indicate that the youth was from a wealthy family, while the absence of an undergarment suggests that he had dressed hastily in order to accompany Jesus. Several Fathers of the Church conjectured that the young man was Mark himself, who is known to have been a resident in Jerusalem (Acts 12:12) and in whose house, it was held by tradition, Jesus celebrated the paschal meal" (*Gospel According to Mark*, 527).

HEARING BEFORE CHIEF PRIESTS (AT CAIAPHAS'S PALACE)

Matthew 26:57–68; Mark 14:53–65; Luke 22:54; John 18:13–14, 19–24 Jesus was first taken to Annas, father-in-law of Caiaphas. Annas had served as high priest of the orthodox Jewish establishment, and Caiaphas now served in that position (see commentary on Matthew 26:3–5). (We do not know exactly where the former high priest or the current high priest lived in the city, though we have a general idea.) Thus, the plural wording of the heading of this present section: "Hearing before chief priests." Jesus would suffer through a hearing, or trial of sorts, at the hands of at least these two of the chief priests. There was actually only one

The Atonement and the Resurrection

Probable sites of the Last Supper and the palace of Caiaphas (palace complex, left of the pyramidal structure) were in the southwest section of Jerusalem, as seen in the Model City, Jerusalem

official high priest, but though the Romans had dismissed several previous ones, the predecessors of Caiaphas were, by courtesy of the Roman government, allowed to retain the title, so there were now several chief high priests (see Appendix 4, 745).

Standing before the chief priests, Jesus was in dreadful physical condition. By this time the Savior had already been awake for an entire day and night. He had experienced the bloody agony in Gethsemane and been forced to cross the Kidron Valley, marching up its steep western slope to the residence of the high priest on the western hill of Jerusalem where the wealthy and powerful lived. Ancient stone steps still mark the likely path. Jesus stood before the Jewish leaders in bloody garments. He was suffering from severe emotional and mental trauma, loss of blood, shock brought on by loss of fluids from his body, and chills from the cold night air passing over his damp body (blood mixed with sweat). Such physiological distress would have caused collapse in most mortals, but the Savior's physical ordeal was far from over in those early morning hours of what the Christian world calls Good Friday.

At the palace of the high priest, certain scribes and elders, members of the "council" (Matthew 26:59), the Sanhedrin (Greek, *synedrion*, literally "sitting together"; see Appendix 4, 753), were assembled at night—which was illegal according to their own law. Nicodemus, Joseph of Arimathea, and any others who had the slightest spiritual leanings toward Jesus, were undoubtedly not invited to participate in the ensuing mockery of justice.

These leaders of the Jews had already tried, convicted, and sentenced Jesus to death in their minds. To have some "evidence" for their verdict, they actually sought, says the scripture, "false witnesses" (Matthew 26:59). Though they brought in "many false witnesses" (v. 60), there was no consistency in their testimony. At last came two false witnesses who could agree on something. They claimed that Jesus had declared, "I am able to destroy the temple of God, and to build it in three days" (Matthew 26:61). Of course, Jesus had not said that at all. He had prophesied (as recorded in John 2:19) that they, certain Jews, would destroy his temple (his body), and then he would raise it up again, on the third day. They were the destroyers; he was the restorer.

The high priest, with increasing ire and disgust, demanded, "Answerest thou nothing? what is it which these witnesseth against thee?" (Matthew 26:62).

To be sure, there was nothing to answer. No consistent or valid testimony had been presented against him. Jesus remained silent (see Isaiah 53:7; Mosiah 14:7; 15:6).

Then Caiaphas vehemently ordered him, or charged him, under oath (which, once again, was improper according to Jewish tradition; a prisoner was to testify only voluntarily): "I adjure thee by the living God, that thou tell us whether thou be the Christ, the Son of God" (Matthew 26:63). Now the real accusations came out. These Jewish leaders wanted to hear

The Atonement and the Resurrection

from his own lips whether or not he claimed to be the Anointed One (the Messiah) and the Son of God.

Caiaphas's adjuration was in the name of the living God, so it should not have been too difficult for Jesus to respond, because he was himself that very God, the great Jehovah. Mark recorded Jesus' affirmative answer: "I am" (Mark 14:62), an unequivocal testimonial not only to the Sanhedrists then but also to some scholars and doubters today: Jesus was and is the Christ, the Messiah, and he is—by his own acclamation—literally the Son of God.

To emphasize his position, Jesus added: "And ye shall see the Son of man sitting on the right hand of power, and coming in the clouds of heaven" (Mark 14:62).

Hearing that, Caiaphas rent (tore) his clothes as a sign of his utter disgust and fury (something else that was strictly forbidden by Mosaic law: "the high priest . . . shall not uncover his head, nor rend his clothes"; Leviticus 21:10).

Caiaphas accused Jesus of blasphemy. These leaders were attempting to convict Jehovah of blasphemy against Jehovah—they who claimed to worship and adore him. So the judges in Zion concluded that he was worthy of death, and the only evidence they had was his own acknowledgment— also illegal before the eyes of their law. The high priest's companions all concurred that Jesus was guilty as accused (a unanimous decision was also illegal), and they commenced their disgraceful spitting, hitting (buffeting), slapping, and mocking of the gentlest, kindest, and holiest Man who had ever walked their land and graced their chambers.

John's account adds a few more details of the interchange between Jesus and Caiaphas. Caiaphas is he who had counseled that it was necessary for one man to die for the people (see commentary on John 11:47–53). Being interrogated about his disciples and his doctrine, the great High Priest responded to this temporary high priest: "I spake openly to the world; I ever taught in the synagogue, and in the temple, whither the Jews always resort; and in secret have I said nothing [certainly nothing seditious or criminal]. Why askest thou me? Ask them which heard me, what I have said unto them: behold, they know what I said" (John 18:20–21). When Jesus was struck by one of the Sanhedrin, he once again reiterated his rights under the law: "If I have spoken evil, bear witness of the evil: but if well, why smitest thou me?" (John 18:22–23). Jesus lived the principles he taught; here we see his gentleness under provocation. He surely had overcome the world.

Gerald N. Lund summarizes the indignities and outrages that Jesus patiently endured: "How easy it would have been for the one who cast out devils to banish the arrogant high priest. How elementary for one who loosed the tongues of the dumb to stop the tongues of false witnesses. Yet he who brought worlds and galaxies into being stood mute before his mortal accusers. He who stilled the rushing winds and pounding waves of the Sea of Galilee stilled not the stormy cries of 'Crucify him! Crucify him!' He who had escaped unharmed from the angry mob at Nazareth (Luke 4:29–30) faced the small band of arresting soldiers with a simple 'I am he.' (John 18:5.) The awesome, infinite power at his command was not unleashed to spare himself the least pain, the smallest discomfort" (*Ensign*, July 1975, 31).

It would be well at this point to identify the religious conspirators against Jesus for who they really were. H. Curtis Wright explains that "we must disagree . . . with the bulk of Christian writers who have described the leaders of the Jews as hoodlums and outlaws, rascals and ruffians, rogues and scoundrels, knaves and villains, and blackguards and highwaymen of the deepest, darkest hue. That, I'm afraid, really is . . . a gross distortion of the truth. They were criminals all right, but of a vastly different piece. They had no use for the seamy side of crime, and they campaigned relentlessly against it. . . . they didn't like darkness—or dirt! They moved in the upper strata of Jewish high society and lived in the better sections of Jerusalem. And they bathed every day. They inhabited the country club ionosphere of the city's 'velvet alleys' where they breathed the rarified air of religious piety and unimpeachable integrity. . . . They wore . . . the cloak of respectability and public trust, and the mantle of high official office. And in addition to that, they were exceptionally well educated. They were full of high-minded talk about the search for truth and the evils of ignorance. But meanwhile they went efficiently about their business unnoticed by the public at large. They operated in broad daylight, too, in full view of the law. . . . They attempted to interpret and control the legal code, but they always stayed within its boundaries, for they were above all else respectable and irreproachable citizens.

"Spiritual wickedness has always had a way of ending up in high places. . . . The plot against Jesus . . . was instigated by the calm and reasoned planning of men with cool heads, who convened in secret and covenanted with one another to form a pact, and 'took counsel together for to put him to death.' They gathered at the swank city estate of Caiaphas, the high priest, and sat down together in the palatial mansion where they 'consulted that they might take Jesus by subtlety, and kill him.' It was a conspiracy in the worst sense of the term, and the perpetrators were the elite of Jerusalem, the impeccably reputable 'men of affairs,' the 'solid citizens,' the 'chief priests, and the scribes, and the elders of the people.' . . . During that meeting the world's very finest criminal minds were at work. . . . In a few days [Jesus] would be dead, legally and lawfully executed. He would be the victim, not of hoods and con men, but of professional conspirators, and their skirts would be 'clean,' for they were only irate citizens, campaigning in the name of justice and civic virtue and insisting upon the protection of their rights!" (*Thing of Naught*, 9–10, 12–13).

PETER'S DENIAL (AT CAIAPHAS'S PALACE)

Matthew 26:69–75; Mark 14:66–72; Luke 22:55–62; John 18:15–18, 25–27 Passover is celebrated each year at

The Four Gospels

Peter's Denial, *by Carl Heinrich Bloch*

the end of the winter, at the time of resurrection of all the floral world, the season of renewal we call spring. Passover days can be lovely and warm, but the nights can still be chilling. This last mortal week of Jesus in Jerusalem was during the Passover. It was cool at night in the Garden of Gethsemane; Caiaphas's palace was cold. "The servants and officers stood there, who had made a fire of coals; for it was cold: and they warmed themselves: and Peter stood with them, and warmed himself" (John 18:18).

At the palace, some of the Sanhedrin convened illegally for Jesus' "trial." Jewish law forbade a court to sit at night and before the preparation day of the high Holy Day. In the porch, or colonnaded courtyard, of this palace (Matthew 26:71), Peter denied knowing Jesus as he warmed himself at a fire during the early morning hours.

The speech of Galileans was apparently distinct from that of their fellow countrymen. The young girl accused Peter, "Surely thou art one of them: for thou art a Galilean, and thy speech agreeth thereto" (Mark 14:70). Matthew adds, "Surely thou also art one of them; for thy speech bewrayeth thee [Greek, 'reveals you']" (Matthew 26:73).

Matthew recorded that when Peter was identified as a disciple, "then began he to curse and to swear, saying, I know not the man. And immediately the cock crew. And Peter remembered the word of Jesus, which said unto him, Before the cock crow, thou shalt deny me thrice. And he went out, and wept bitterly" (Matthew 26:74–75).

During the terrifying darkness of that tragic night, before the earliest call of morning, Peter the Rock would be crushed bitterly by the suffering of Jesus that he could not help relieve. There are at least two different perspectives we may use to view Peter's denial of Jesus.

One possibility is that Peter disclaimed his acquaintance with Jesus because Jesus instructed him to do exactly that. To suppose that such a denial was based on cowardice or weakness is contrary to every other example of Peter's personality and motives reported in the scriptures. In every other instance, Peter acted courageously, even impetuously, in his endorsement and protection of Christ. In fact, he was ready to kill to ensure his Master's safety a short time earlier in Gethsemane.

It is possible to read the text of the Savior's declaration to Peter about the latter's forthcoming denial as an instructional command rather than as a prediction. In other words, Peter may have been told to deny being associated with the Savior. That seems to be the line of reasoning followed by Elder Spencer W. Kimball in a magnificent address at Brigham

Young University entitled *Peter, My Brother.* Elder Bruce C. Hafen has written: "Consider . . . the case of Peter on the night he denied any knowledge of his Master three times in succession. We typically regard Peter as something of a weakling whose commitment was not strong enough to make him rise to the Savior's defense. But I once heard President Spencer W. Kimball offer an alternative interpretation of Peter's behavior. In a talk to a BYU audience in 1971 President Kimball, then a member of the Council of the Twelve, said the Savior's statement that Peter would deny him three times before the cock crowed just might have been a request to Peter, not a prediction. Jesus might have been instructing his chief apostle to deny any association with him in order to ensure strong leadership for the Church after the Crucifixion.

"As President Kimball asked in his talk, who could doubt Peter's willingness to stand up and be counted? Think of his boldness in striking off the guard's ear with his sword when the Savior was arrested in Gethsemane. President Kimball did not offer his view as the only interpretation, but he did suggest there is enough justification for it that it should be considered. So what is the answer—was Peter a coward, or was he so crucial to the survival of the Church that he was prohibited from risking his life? We are not sure. The scriptures don't give us enough information about Peter's motivation to clarify the ambiguity" (*Believing Heart,* 57–58).

Luke 22:61 records that "the Lord turned, and looked upon Peter," and Peter remembered what Jesus had prophesied or commanded him to do. Then the scripture notes that "Peter went out, and wept bitterly" (v. 62). Why would the chief apostle go out and weep bitterly if he was obeying an instruction from the Lord? The answer is—because it was simply not in Peter's constitution, as we read everywhere else in the Gospels, to shy away from anything, in fear or cowardice. It is understandable that he would go out and weep bitter tears at being powerless to help his dearest Friend.

Another view of Peter's denial of Jesus is that Peter did indeed succumb to weakness and failed to acknowledge his acquaintance with Jesus. Elder Kimball explained: "If we admit that he was cowardly and denied the Lord through timidity, we can still find a great lesson. Has anyone more completely overcome mortal selfishness and weakness? Has anyone repented more sincerely? Peter has been accused of being harsh, indiscreet, impetuous, and fearful. If all these were true, then we still ask, Has any man ever more completely triumphed over his weaknesses?" (*Teachings of Spencer W. Kimball,* 471).

During the course of his ministry the Savior had to rebuke Peter several times for his lack of understanding and vision. Despite Peter's strong commitment (having sacrificed all to follow his Lord) and his emphatic testimony expressed on several occasions, Peter had not yet received the gift of the Holy Ghost, which would strengthen and give depth and boldness to that testimony in months and years to come. Can we allow Peter, like Moses, Joseph Smith, and many other noble and great ones, *room to grow* in faith and conviction? Joseph Smith made a serious mistake, for example, in his handling of the 116 manuscript pages, but he overcame that mistake, was forgiven, and moved on. And can we not learn from this great leader, Peter, and profit from his splendid example of rising above his human flaws and shortcomings?

President Gordon B. Hinckley pursued this view of Peter's denial of Jesus and his subsequent rise to greatness:

"My heart goes out to Peter. So many of us are so much like him. We pledge our loyalty; we affirm our determination to be of good courage; we declare, sometimes even publicly, that come what may we will do the right thing, that we will stand for the right cause, that we will be true to ourselves and to others.

"Then the pressures begin to build. Sometimes these are social pressures. Sometimes they are personal appetites. Sometimes they are false ambitions. There is a weakening of the will. There is a softening of discipline. There is capitulation. And then there is remorse, followed by self-accusation and bitter tears of regret. . . .

"If there be those throughout the Church who by word or act have denied the faith, I pray that you may draw comfort and resolution from the example of Peter, who, though he had walked daily with Jesus, in an hour of extremity momentarily denied the Lord. . . . But he rose above this and became a mighty defender and a powerful advocate. So, too, there is a way for any person to turn about and add his or her strength and faith to the strength and faith of others in building the kingdom of God" (*Ensign,* March 1995, 2–4, 6).

John adds a curious note to his account of Jesus' arraignment before the Sanhedrin, that he himself "was known unto the high priest, and went in with Jesus into the palace" (John 18:15). Peter, who was also following Jesus, was left standing outside the door. "Then went out that other disciple, which was known unto the high priest, and spake unto her that kept the door, and brought in Peter" (John 18:16)—leaving us to wonder still what kind of relationship or acquaintance Caiaphas and John had. Someday we will know more.

SOLDIERS MOCK JESUS (IN CAIAPHAS'S PALACE)

Luke 22:63–65 Some of the arresting officers blindfolded Jesus and made sport of him and mocked him, challenging him to identify which of them had struck him. While Jesus himself stood accused of blasphemy, Luke points out that the crass things that the officers in the palace were saying were the real blasphemous expressions.

THE ATONEMENT AND THE RESURRECTION

THE NEXT MORNING (IN JERUSALEM, AT CAIAPHAS'S PALACE?)

Matthew 27:1; Mark 15:1; Luke 22:66; John 18:28 Chief priests, elders, and scribes—members of the council, the Sanhedrin—gathered together in the early morning hours to consult with each other about how they would turn Jesus over to the Roman authorities for capital punishment.

HEARING BEFORE CAIAPHAS (IN JERUSALEM, AT CAIAPHAS'S PALACE?)

Matthew 27:1; Mark 15:1; Luke 22:66–71; John 18:24, 28 Now we witness a repeat performance of the drama acted out with Jesus at center stage and the hypocritical leaders of the Jews prosecuting and persecuting. (For the previous scene, see commentary on Matthew 26:57–68.) In Luke's account the dialogue unfolds as follows:

"Art thou the Christ? tell us."

"If I tell you, ye will not believe . . . nor let me go. Hereafter shall the Son of man sit on the right hand of the power of God [the Father]."

"Art thou then the Son of God?"

"Ye say that I am." In other words, Yes, I am.

"What need we any further witness? for we ourselves have heard of his own mouth."

HEARING BEFORE PILATE (IN JERUSALEM, AT THE ANTONIA FORTRESS?)

Matthew 27:2, 11–14; Mark 15:1–5; Luke 23:1–6; John 18:28–38 At the northwestern corner of the Temple Mount stood the massive governmental and military headquarters called the Antonia Fortress, constructed by the

Hasmoneans and reconstructed and fortified by Herod the Great and named after Mark Antony. The fortress was called in the New Testament the *Praetorium* (Mark 15:16), which is a Latin term for the palace with its hearing room to which the Roman governor came to transact public business. It was also called the "hall of judgment." "It was early; and they themselves [Jesus' accusers] went not into the judgment hall, lest they should be defiled; but that they might eat the Passover." The Jewish leaders did not want to defile themselves by being in the presence of pagans (Romans) just before the Passover, yet they thirsted for innocent blood (even Jewish blood) (John 18:28; see also 18:33; 19:9; Acts 23:35).

Jesus' hearing before the Roman governor Pontius Pilate perhaps took place in the Antonia Fortress, in the hall of judgment, on what John called "the Pavement, but in the Hebrew, Gabbatha" (John 19:13). The Hebrew (or Aramaic) *Gabbatha* is equivalent to the Greek *lithostroton*, meaning the stone courtyard of the judgment hall. Under today's Sisters of Zion Convent may be seen some large Roman flagstones from the time of Hadrian's Aelia Capitolina, nearly a century

Antonia Fortress, as seen in the Model City, Jerusalem

The Atonement and the Resurrection

Inscription mentioning Tiberius and Pontius Pilate found in the ruins of the theater of Caesarea

after Jesus but similar to what likely existed in Herod's former fortress. In the same hall of judgment was Pilate's judgment seat (Greek, *bema*), a raised platform resembling a throne where the governor sat in judgment. "When Pilate therefore heard that saying, he brought Jesus forth, and sat down in the judgment seat" (John 19:13; for further information on Pontius Pilate, see Appendix 2, 731; see also Galbraith, Ogden, and Skinner, *Jerusalem, the Eternal City*, 156–57).

Though it has been proposed that the Roman governor would have been housed at Herod's palace on the west side of the city, a substantial contingent of soldiers was stationed at the Antonia, the largest fortress in Jerusalem, to keep watch over the Temple Mount, which was the soldiers' main reason for being in Jerusalem (in Holzapfel and Wayment,

From the Last Supper through the Resurrection, 278). Rousseau and Arav note that "the normal prefectoral residence in Jerusalem was the former palace of Herod; but Pilate possibly preferred to lodge in the Antonia with the cohort in times of unrest. There, he would immediately know of any disturbance and could quickly give orders accordingly" (*Jesus and His World*, 164). Years later, we find Roman soldiers and then Temple guards taking Paul down to the Sanhedrin at their meeting hall in the Temple and returning with him back up into the fortress, also called "the castle" (Acts 21:34, 37; 22:24; 23:10; see Appendix 1, 716).

The accusation brought against Jesus when arraigned before some of the Sanhedrin was blasphemy—claiming to be God or insulting or violating the sanctity of God, the greatest crime in Jewish law. Romans cared little about the God of the Jews; they themselves had numerous gods whom they cursed at will. Yet there was one accusation that was serious enough to cause the governor to arise very early in the morning to hear: sedition against the Roman government. In fact, the chief reason Pilate had come up to Jerusalem from his usual residence in Caesarea on the coast was to keep his Roman eyes on the Temple Mount, the traditional focus of insurrection and initiatives to independence. Pilate had already viciously dealt with several messianic revolutionary movements (see Galbraith, Ogden, and Skinner, *Jerusalem, the Eternal City*, 156–57). Jewish leaders were anxious to see the popular preacher, Jesus, disposed of and were interested in passing the responsibility for his elimination onto the Romans, so they sought a Roman sentence to inflict the death penalty. The charge was shifted from blasphemy to sedition (Luke 23:1–2).

Though Jews would normally not resent active hostility against the Romans, in this case they pressed the charge that Jesus was conspiring to become king of the Jews and was, therefore, a threat to Caesar (as well as to the comfortable position of the Sadducees and high priests who held their positions by the good grace of the Romans). Jewish accusers even went so far as to charge Pilate with being no friend of Caesar if he allowed the charges against Jesus to be dismissed (John 19:12).

John 18:31–32 Pilate wanted the local leaders to take Jesus and judge him according to Jewish law. The Jewish leaders quickly replied, "It is not lawful for us to put any man to death."

According to New Testament scholar F. F. Bruce, "the right of jurisdiction in capital cases was most jealously reserved by provincial governors; permission to provincials to exercise it was a very rare concession, conceded only to such privileged communities as free cities within the empire. Jerusalem was no free city, and a turbulent province like Judea was most unlikely to be granted such a concession" (*New Testament History*, 200). Stephen's later murder was apparently mob action, because the Romans did reserve the right to capital punishment.

All this, John notes, was to help fulfill a prophecy "signifying what death he should die" (v. 32). If the Jews had put Jesus to death they would have stoned him, but the Romans would crucify him, which would shed his blood. His blood had already been shed for sin in the garden, but his blood would also be shed for sin on the cross (D&C 27:2; 35:2; 46:13; 53:2; 54:1; 138:35).

Mark 15:2–5; Luke 23:2–4 Pilate interrogated Jesus directly. "Art thou the King of the Jews?" Jesus answered him, "*I am, even as* thou sayest" (JST Mark 15:4). When the chief priests interjected their accusations, Jesus refused even to respond to them (see Isaiah 53:7; Mosiah 14:7). Said they, "We found this fellow perverting the nation, and forbidding to give tribute to Caesar [that was a lie], saying that he himself is Christ a King [that was the truth]" (Luke 23:2). From what he had heard thus far, Pilate found no fault in Jesus.

John 18:33–38 A remarkable conversation then ensued between an impulsive, temporary ruler over men and a strong, eternal Ruler over all the hosts of heaven:

"Art thou the King of the Jews?"

"Sayest thou this thing of thyself, or did others tell it thee of me?"

"Am I a Jew? Thine own nation and the chief priests have delivered thee unto me: what hast thou done?"

"My kingdom is not of this world: if my kingdom were of this world, then would my servants fight, that I should not be delivered to the Jews." Notice that Jesus said not that his kingdom was not of this *earth* but that it was not of this world, for his kingdom could not be established based on worldly systems and motives; but his kingdom, in the form of his Church, had definitely seen its foundation laid on planet Earth.

"Art thou a king then?"

"Thou sayest that I am a king [meaning, You are right, or As you say; Jesus was not only the king of the Jews, or even the king of this world, but—as the Jews still refer to their God—he is literally the King of the universe]. To this end was I born, and for this cause came I into the world, that I should bear witness unto the truth. Everyone that is of the truth heareth my voice."

"What is truth?"

The governor then went out to report his verdict to the gathered Jews: "I find in him no fault at all." Jesus was obviously not a political insurrectionist, nor was he in any way a menace to Rome.

Luke 23:5–6 When the Jews heard Pilate's assessment of Jesus' case, they spoke up more fiercely, accusing Jesus of inciting and agitating the Jews in all the land, from Galilee to Judea. When Pilate heard that Jesus was a Galilean, he had an idea. Why not send him to Herod for judgment? (Luke 23:7–10).

Pilate came close to helping the Savior by defending him to his accusers, but in the end, Pilate chose a way out. Personal preservation took precedence over principle. He sought to transfer responsibility to someone else—he sought a scapegoat.

Though Pilate did not like Herod Antipas, it is easy to see how political circumstances would have dictated to Pilate the prudence of involving Herod at this point. The case of the Jewish leaders versus Jesus of Nazareth was a potential political fiasco, or worse, for Pontius Pilate. He could not simply dismiss it, for fear of provoking the Jews again and lending credibility to mounting doubts about his ability and fitness to rule Judea. Philo tells that "this last remark exasperated Pilate most of all, for he was afraid that if they really sent an embassy, they would bring accusations against the rest of his administration as well, specifying in detail his venality, his violence, his thefts, his assaults, his abusive behaviour, his frequent executions of untried prisoners, and his endless savage ferocity" (*Legatio ad Gaium*, 302).

Pilate had already provoked his subjects as well as Rome over several offenses that demonstrated his insensitivity and poor judgment. He was known to be ruthless and cruel. Luke mentions an incident involving "Galilaeans, whose blood Pilate had mingled with their sacrifices" (Luke 13:1), indicating perhaps that the governor had some Jews from Jesus' home region killed on the Temple Mount as they participated in one of the feasts. We know nothing else about this, except that Galilee was a noted hotbed of insurrectionists, zealots, and terrorist activity against Rome. Perhaps Pilate took extraordinary measures over some threat, perceived or real.

JUDAS'S REMORSE AND DEATH (AT THE TEMPLE AND AT ACELDAMA)

Matthew 27:3–10 Judas "repented himself" (v. 3), that is, he felt remorseful at all that was happening and took the betrayal money back to the Sanhedrin: "I have sinned in that I have betrayed innocent blood." The Jewish leaders' calloused reaction was, in essense, What is that to us? That is your problem. "See thou *to it: thy sins be upon thee*" (JST Matthew 27:5). Indeed, judging from scriptural epithets, Judas was one of the greatest of all sinners: According to John, he was a thief (John 12:6), and according to Jesus, he was a devil (John 6:70), even a son of perdition (John 17:12).

A certain burial place in the southern slopes of the Hinnom Valley has been associated with Judas since the early centuries after Christ: "It was known unto all the dwellers at Jerusalem; insomuch as that field is called in their proper tongue, Aceldama, that is to say, The field of blood" (Acts 1:19).

According to Acts 1:18, Judas Iscariot purchased with his betrayal money a field that was to be the scene of his suicide. Matthew 27:5–7 preserves the account of Judas casting down the coins in the Temple and going out and hanging himself. Joseph Smith Translation Matthew 27:6 adds that Judas "hanged himself *on a tree. And straightway he fell down, and his bowels gushed out, and he died.*" The chief priests bought with the money "the potter's field, to bury strangers in. Wherefore that field was called, The field of blood." Greek *Akeldama* is transliterated from the Aramaic *khakel dema* ("field of blood"). According to the New Testament record, then, the renaming of this burial ground in Jerusalem had its origin in the betrayal of Jesus and the death of Judas Iscariot (though, as we see, there are conflicting reports about who purchased the field).

Another prophecy was thus fulfilled, one spoken by Jeremiah (although it is not written in his book in our present Old Testament; compare Zechariah 11:12–13): they took the thirty pieces of silver, the price of a slave, and purchased the potter's field.

HEARING BEFORE HEROD
(IN JERUSALEM)

Luke 23:7–10 Herod Antipas, son of Herod the Great, and tetrarch of Galilee and Perea, was also in Jerusalem for the Passover. When Pilate heard that Jesus was a Galilean, he thought to rid himself of the responsibility of dealing with him by sending him to the governor of Galilee.

Herod was glad for the opportunity to see Jesus, hoping to be entertained with an example of his miraculous power. Though perhaps not as bloodthirsty a man as his father, Antipas was despicable in his own right. Thus, though Antipas talked to Jesus at length, Jesus had no desire whatever to speak to the murderer of his relative and friend, John the Baptist. In fact, Herod Antipas is the only significant person in the New Testament who saw and spoke to Jesus but never heard his voice. Antipas was totally unworthy for Jesus even to speak to.

HEROD AND SOLDIERS MOCK JESUS
(IN JERUSALEM)

Luke 23:11–12 Antipas proved his unworthiness for any attention from Jesus by joining his troops in scoffing and insulting the greatest Man of peace and refinement they would ever meet. After their disrespectful play, they sent Jesus back to Pilate, and, the record notes, the two formerly hostile rulers "were made friends together" and the suffering Jesus was the catalyst.

SECOND HEARING BEFORE PILATE
(IN JERUSALEM, AT THE ANTONIA FORTRESS?)

Luke 23:13–17 Pilate's attempt to rid himself gracefully of Jesus' case had failed. He now had to deal squarely with the God of the universe. It was, in its own way, a burden no other ruler has ever had to face. Pilate called the Jewish rulers and chief priests together once again to disclaim any guilt in Jesus; neither he nor Herod had found anything worthy of death in him. He did acquiesce to the pressure of his constituents, however, in agreeing to "chastise" him (v. 16), that is, to scourge him, even though he had done no wrong.

A MURDERER RELEASED (IN JERUSALEM, AT THE ANTONIA FORTRESS?)

Matthew 27:15–23, 26; Mark 15:6–15; Luke 23:17–25; John 18:39–40 Matthew records that the Roman governor was "wont" or accustomed to release a prisoner; Luke notes that Pilate, "of necessity" (23:17), had to release some prisoner at the great feast. Though we have no specific evidence outside the New Testament of such a practice of appeasement to the Jews, the report of the Gospel writers is accepted, along with all their other reports of contemporary customs and practices, as reliable and trustworthy. The Jews wanted Pilate to do, again, "as he had ever done unto them" (Mark 15:8).

One notable prisoner was called Barabbas. F. F. Bruce wrote: "When Barabbas, and the two men crucified along with Jesus, are called *lēstai* in the Gospels (John 18:40; Mark 15:27), we understand by the term not ordinary robbers but insurgents against the occupying power; this, indeed, is expressly indicated in the case of Barabbas when Mark tells us that he was 'among the rebels in prison, who had committed murder in the insurrection' (Mark 15:7)" (*New Testament History*, 98).

The great irony of Barabbas's release, allowing a truly guilty man to go free while condemning the Innocent One, is further compounded by the following:

1. The given name of Barabbas was Yehoshua, or Yeshua, the same as the Savior's name: Jesus. An ancient variant reading of the text of Matthew 27:16–17 preserves the full name, "Jesus Barabbas," and the early church theologian Origen (died A.D. 254) implies that the full name appeared in most of the manuscripts of his day. Scholars point out that under these circumstances a much more dramatic reading of Matthew 27:17 may have been originally intended: "Which Jesus do you want; the son of Abba, or the self-styled Messiah?" (*Anchor Bible Dictionary*, s.v. "Barabbas," 1:607).

2. The term *Barabbas* means, literally, "son of [Aramaic, *bar*] the father [Aramaic, *abba*]." Jesus *was* the true and literal Son of the Father. The angry, stirred-up mob chose to release one Jesus, son of the father, rather than the other Jesus, Son of the Father.

3. Barabbas was guilty of sedition (Luke 23:19, 25) but was freed; Jesus was falsely accused of sedition (Luke 23:2) but was sentenced to death.

4. Barabbas was the fulfillment of the ritual scapegoat of the sacrificial rites performed on the Day of Atonement—the animal led to the wilderness and released; Jesus was the fulfillment of the goat sacrificed on the Temple altar as the sin offering representing the guilt of the people (Leviticus 16:7–22).

5. The Greek word used in Mark 15:13 to denote the cry of the crowd for innocent Jesus' execution in preference to that of the guilty Barabbas is the same word used when the crowd greeted Jesus in messianic tones (Mark 11:9) less than a week before, during his triumphal entry into Jerusalem (Brown, *Death of the Messiah*, 1:824; that Greek word is translated as "cried out" in Mark 15:13 and as "cried" in Mark 11:9).

Jesus was the embodiment of everything that is good and right and just and pure, while Barabbas seems to have been the embodiment of the opposite of everything good, right, just, and pure. And yet, the bloodthirsty crowd called for the release of Barabbas. They would have nothing less than the destruction of righteousness in the person of Jesus Christ.

The multitude "began to desire him to deliver *Jesus* unto them," according to Joseph Smith's translation of Mark 15:10, "but the chief priests moved the people that [Pilate] should rather release Barabbas unto them (JST Mark 15:13). It could surprise us that some of the rabble desired Pilate to release Jesus, but the following verse (15) explains why they were clamoring for Jesus' release: "they cried out again, *Deliver him unto us to be crucified*" (JST Mark 15:15; emphasis added).

Even Pilate's wife had suffered some agitation because of impressions that came to her in a dream. She called Jesus "a just man" and warned her husband not to get involved with the unjust prosecution (Matthew 27:19).

Pilate knew the mentality of these Jewish leaders; he knew that it was for fear, envy, and jealousy that they had delivered Jesus (Matthew 27:18; Mark 15:10). Caiaphas, other Sanhedrin members, Pilate, and Herod all knew that Jesus was innocent, "but because of priestcrafts and iniquities, they at Jerusalem [did] stiffen their necks against him, that he be crucified" (2 Nephi 10:5).

With no reliable witnesses and on the testimony of the accused alone, despite Pilate's inclination to acquit Jesus due to lack of evidence (Luke 23:4, 15, 22; John 18:38; 19:4, 6), and despite Pilate's own suspicion of the motives of the Jewish accusers, Jesus was ordered to be executed by crucifixion, the usual method of execution for someone who was not a Roman citizen. Tradition claims that Peter later was crucified and that Paul, a Roman citizen, was beheaded. One of the few references to Christ in ancient state historical records is a critical aside during a description of the burning of Rome, written by Roman historian Tacitus (A.D. 55–117). It mentions both Jesus Christ and Pontius Pilate: "To suppress this rumour, Nero fabricated scapegoats—and punished with every refinement the notoriously depraved Christians (as they were popularly called). Their originator, Christ, had been executed in Tiberius's reign by the governor of Judea, Pontius Pilatus. But in spite of this temporary setback the deadly superstition had broken out afresh, not only in Judea (where the mischief had started) but even in Rome. All degraded and shameful practices collect and flourish in the capital" (*Annals of Imperial Rome*, 354).

Walter M. Chandler, a member of the New York Bar, in his two-volume treatise, *The Trial of Jesus from a Lawyer's Standpoint*, wrote: "The pages of human history present no stronger case of judicial murder than the trial and crucifixion of Jesus of Nazareth, for the simple reason that all forms of law were outraged and trampled under foot in the proceedings instituted against Him" (1:216). There was actually no trial in the case of Jesus; and if Jesus had no trial, then he was murdered.

Matthew 27:22 All real disciples of the Lord Jesus Christ must answer Pilate's question in their own lives: "What shall I do then with Jesus which is called Christ?"

BLOOD GUILTINESS (IN JERUSALEM)

Matthew 27:24–25; cf. Luke 23:4, 14, 22; John 19:4 When Pilate saw that he "could prevail nothing" (Matthew 27:24), that he would not succeed, and that he needed to placate the tumultuous crowd to prevent a riot, he gave in to their demands, released Barabbas, scourged Jesus as the official prelude to his crucifixion, and then delivered him up to his sentence of death. But first Pilate acted out his most famous gesture. He "took water, and washed his hands before the multitude, saying, I am innocent of the blood of this just person: see ye to it. Then answered all the people, and said, His blood be on us, and on our children" (Matthew 27:24–25). The ritual of hand washing was known in Mosaic times as well as from ancient Greek and Roman texts (see Deuteronomy 21:1–9; Skinner, *Golgotha*, 94–95).

The question of responsibility for Jesus' death is an

extremely sensitive issue. For example, an Israeli Jew from Kiryat Arba (Hebron) wrote to the *Jerusalem Post:*

"The fact that Jesus was crucified by the Romans is clearly reported in the Gospels. He was sentenced to death by the Roman Pontius Pilatus. Crucifixion was a *Roman* death penalty. Roman soldiers scourged him, put a crown of thorns on his head, spat upon him, smote him on his head, mocked him, nailed him on the cross and finally cast lots to share his garments among themselves.

" . . . the Jews 'were around.' But at most their guilt (supposing that there was any guilt at all) was indirect; they had delivered Jesus into Roman hands, chosen that Barabbas should live rather than Jesus, [and] castigated him for blasphemy. However harsh[ly] one judges this Jewish 'guilt,' the clear and direct criminal responsibility of the Romans is indisputable. Yet, to this very day the descendants of the Romans consider the Jews guilty of the crucifixion. It would never occur to them to find any guilt in their own people" (January 14, 1983).

Historically, the cry of the Jewish gathering as reported in Matthew 27:25 has been the source of much horrible treatment of the Jewish people. They have suffered enormously over the centuries because of their supposed guiltiness for the execution of Jesus. During the Crusades, for instance, tens of thousands of peasants swept across Europe, and upon finding large colonies of Jews in various cities they massacred them, crying, "These are the people who killed our Lord!"

Neither this passage in Matthew nor any other justifies unrighteous treatment of any member of our Heavenly Father's family. The Jewish *people* did not crucify the Savior. Jesus was a Jew, and so were the apostles and almost every other member of the early Church up to the time of the first mission to the Gentiles during the ministry of Paul of Tarsus.

Who, then, according to the scriptures, is responsible for Jesus having been put to death? Many bore responsibility for the Crucifixion, as the scriptures teach, including Herod,

The Atonement and the Resurrection

Pontius Pilate, and certain other Gentiles, members of the Jerusalem community, and, above all, the Jewish rulers and chief priests of the people. As the early apostles Peter and John said: "The kings of the earth stood up, and the rulers were gathered together against the Lord, and against his Christ. For of a truth against thy holy child Jesus, whom thou hast anointed, both Herod, and Pontius Pilate, with the Gentiles, and the people of Israel, were gathered together" (Acts 4:26–27).

No amount of hand washing could absolve Pilate of responsibility for Jesus' execution; he had the power and the opportunity to stop the illegal and immoral proceedings, but he did not. Elder Neal A. Maxwell declared: "Pilate sought to refuse responsibility for deciding about Christ, but Pilate's hands were never dirtier than just after he had washed them" (*Ensign,* November 1974, 13). In a perceptive comment about Pilate that teaches us the most important lesson of this episode for our own lives, President Spencer W. Kimball asked: "Could the Lord forgive Pilate? Certainly he could not without Pilate's repentance. Did Pilate repent? We do not know what Pilate did after the scripture drops him. He had a desire to favor the Savior. He did not display full courage in resisting the pressures of the people. . . . We leave Pilate to the Lord as we do all other sinners, but remember that 'to know and not to do' is sin" (*Miracle of Forgiveness,* 167).

Is there yet anyone more responsible for Jesus' death? John recorded Jesus' comment to Pilate: "He that delivered me unto thee hath the greater sin" (John 19:11). Did that mean *all* the Jews? Of course not. There were hundreds, maybe even thousands, of Jews in Jerusalem and vicinity at the time who loved and adored Jesus, who believed in his every word, obeyed him, and in no situation would raise a hand to harm him. Mary Magdalene, Lazarus, Martha, Mary, John Mark, the apostles, and many others were all Jews, and they were devoted followers of Jesus. But certain Jewish leaders were indeed hostile to the Savior and wanted to see him dead, and they, in that awful moment, pronounced the most horrible of curses upon themselves: "His blood be on us, and on our children" (Matthew 27:25). History records—in that generation and the next—the appalling literal fulfillment of those words of admission of blood guiltiness (for further on the tragic results of this self-pronounced curse, see Galbraith, Ogden, and Skinner, *Jerusalem, the Eternal City,* 209–20).

Let us, for a moment, pursue an even broader view of the responsibility for Jesus' sufferings and death. Nephi, son of Lehi, seeing all this in advance, described the purpose in these poignant words: "The Son of the everlasting God was judged of the world; and I saw and bear record . . . that he was lifted up upon the cross and slain for the sins of the world" (1 Nephi 11:32–33). And what preceded that slaying? Nephi continues: "And *the world,* because of their iniquity, *shall judge him to be a thing of naught;* wherefore they scourge him, and he suffereth it; and they smite him, and he suffereth it. Yea, they spit upon him, and he suffereth it, because of his loving kindness and his long-suffering towards the children of men" (1 Nephi 19:9; emphasis added).

A century before Nephi, Isaiah made the same point, writing that "he hath borne *our* griefs, and carried *our* sorrows . . . he was wounded for *our* transgressions, he was bruised for *our* iniquities" (Isaiah 53:4–5; emphasis added)—not for anything he did wrong, but to cover our sins. The seventeenth-century Dutch writer Jacobus Revius described our involvement in Jesus' sufferings and death in the following powerful lines, under the title, "He Bore Our Anguish" (translated from the Dutch by Charles D. Tate Jr., associate professor of English at Brigham Young University; in *BYU Studies* 15, no. 1, Autumn 1974, 103):

> It was not the Jews, Lord Jesus, who crucified you,
> Nor the traitors who dragged you to the law,
> Nor the contemptuous who spit in your face,

Nor those who bound you, and hit you full of
    wounds,
And it was not the soldiers who with evil hands
Lifted up the reed or the hammer,
Or set that cursed wood on Golgotha,
Or cast lots and gambled for your robe;
It is I, O Lord, it is I who have done it,
I am the heavy tree that overburdened you,
I am the rough bands that bound you,
The nail, the spear, and the cords that whipped
    you,
The bloodied crown that tore your head:
All this happened, alas! for my sins.

JESUS SCOURGED AND MOCKED (IN JERUSALEM, AT THE ANTONIA FORTRESS?)

Matthew 27:27–31; Mark 15:15–20; John 19:1–12
Pilate ordered that Jesus be scourged—flogged with a leather whip containing jagged pieces of stone, metal, or bone—thus hoping to satisfy the accusers (Luke 23:16; John 19:1–5).

We are not told how many stripes Jesus was given by the Roman soldiers. Jewish law stipulated a limit of forty stripes, and just in case of miscount, they would stop at thirty-nine (Deuteronomy 25:1–3; cf. 2 Corinthians 11:24; "How many stripes do they inflict on a man? Forty save one"; *Mishnah*, Makkoth 3:10). The Romans, however, had no such restriction and could give as many lashes as they wanted.

Jesus' skin would have been extremely fragile and sensitive, even before the flogging, because of the sweating of blood from every pore he had already experienced. Then he was brutalized further with the deep bruises or contusions and the strips of quivering and bleeding flesh that the whipping tore off his back.

Thorns like these may have been woven together for Jesus' crown of thorns

While mocking Jesus, Roman soldiers wove thorns together in the shape of a crown and placed them on his head (Matthew 27:29; Mark 15:17; John 19:2). Though only adding pain and insult to the already awful scene, yet in the eternal perspective of the early Christians, Jesus' crown of thorns was regarded as a necessary antecedent to his crown of glory. The thorn gave way to the Throne.

The thorns or thorn-branches constituting the "crown" placed on Jesus' head could have been woven together only if they were flexible. The traditional candidate is *Ziziphus spina-christi,* the Christ-thorn. The etrog tree is also a producer of stout thorns that could have been used.

Matthew noted that a "scarlet robe" was placed on Jesus when Roman soldiers mocked him (Matthew 27:26–28). The red color is derived from the eggs of an insect that lives in oak trees in the Holy Land. The red derivative is used to dye cloth. The Arabs call it *kirmiz,* which is the source of our English word *crimson.* Mark and John, on the other hand, wrote that Jesus was clothed with purple (John 19:2). Joseph Smith Translation Matthew 27:30 changes Matthew's text also to "purple," to agree with the other Gospels. Either color served the purpose of ridiculing the Lord. "When they [the Roman soldiers] had mocked him, they took off the purple from him, and put his own clothes on him, and led him out to crucify him" (Mark 15:20). What was this "purple" spoken of? It was a dye created from the Murex snail (see commentary on Luke 16:14–16, 19–31).

John 19:6–7 The awful fact was that a heathen, a pagan, was pleading with the leaders of the Jews on behalf of their own Lord and King (Talmage, *Jesus the Christ*, 593). When Jesus was finally sentenced, the Jewish leaders boldly declared the real accusation they had against him—blasphemy. "We have a law," they said (Leviticus 24:16), "and by our law he ought to die, because he made himself the Son of God." There is no doubt what Jesus had taught: he plainly taught the truth, and some of his people plainly rebelled against it (see also commentary on John 5:17–47; 10:31–39).

John 19:8–12 When the Jewish leaders openly admitted the real accusation against Jesus, Pilate's worst fears were realized. As the Gospel writers recorded, the Roman ruler suspected all along that it was a matter of their own law for which they had apprehended Jesus (John 18:31), and now the truth came out: the real charge was blasphemy.

Pilate asked Jesus again: "Whence art thou?"

Jesus did not answer him.

Pilate: "Speakest thou not unto me? knowest thou not that I have power to crucify thee, and have power to release thee?"

Now Jesus answered: "Thou couldest have no power at all against me, except it were given thee from above."

At this point Jesus placed more responsibility for this legal fiasco squarely on those who were guilty: "He that delivered me unto thee hath the greater sin" (v. 11). Pilate was still partly responsible for not standing up to the mockery of justice taking place under his rulership, and therefore he was participating in the crime and sin, but those who had delivered Jesus—Annas, Caiaphas, and other corrupt Jewish leaders—had the greater sin.

And they accepted the dreadful responsibility: "His blood be on us and on our children" (Matthew 27:25).

The more Pilate endeavored to acquit Jesus, the more his opponents cried out for the death sentence, even so far as to defend the Roman government and its emperor, whom they despised: "If thou let this man go, thou art not Caesar's friend: whosoever maketh himself a king [back to the other accusation] speaketh against Caesar" (v. 12). In a sense, we could conclude that these Jewish leaders hated Jesus Christ more than they hated the Roman oppression.

JESUS TAKEN TO GOLGOTHA (NEAR JERUSALEM)

Matthew 27:32–34; Mark 15:20–23; Luke 23:26–31; John 19:13–17 On the preparation day of the Passover (Jesus had already eaten the Passover with the apostles a day early; see commentary on Matthew 26:17–19), about the sixth hour—therefore, Friday about 6 A.M. (see Appendix 7, 778)—Pilate, with consternation and bewilderment, declared to the assembled Jewish rabble: "Behold your King!" (John 19:14).

Chief priests: "Away with him, away with him, crucify him."

Pilate: "Shall I crucify your King?"

Chief priests: "We have no king but Caesar" (John 19:15).

"With this cry," wrote the eminent Jewish-Christian theologian, Alfred Edersheim, "Judaism was, in the person of its representatives, guilty of denial of God, of blasphemy, of apostasy. It committed suicide; and, ever since, has its dead body been carried in show from land to land, and from century to century: to be dead, and to remain dead, till He come a second time, Who is the Resurrection and the Life!" (*Jesus the Messiah*, 2:581).

Jacob, brother of Nephi, recorded the words of Jesus about his Kingship, a pointed rebuttal to those who would have Caesar or any other mortal to be their king: "He that raiseth up a king against me shall perish, for I, the Lord, the king of heaven, will be their king, and I will be a light unto them forever, *that hear my words*" (2 Nephi 10:14; emphasis added).

The New Testament contains a number of allusions to Cyrenian Jews and Christians: "As they led him away, they laid hold upon one Simon, a Cyrenian, coming out of the country, and on him they laid the cross, that he might bear it after Jesus" (Luke 23:26). Mark adds that this Simon was the father of Alexander and Rufus, apparently two young members of the Church (Mark 15:21).

Cyrene was a Mediterranean port on the northern coast of Africa and the chief city of the Roman province Cyrenaica (or western Libya). Cyrene had been settled as a Greek city, but by Jesus' day it had a large colony of Jews.

Luke 23:27–31 As the procession was moving toward the place of execution, a great company, especially women, gathered, and the people were bewailing and lamenting him. Jesus turned and lamented back to them: "Daughters of Jerusalem, weep not for me, but weep for yourselves, and for your children [given what their leaders had recently taken upon themselves: 'His blood be on us, and on our children'; Matthew 27:25].

"For behold, the days are coming, in the which they shall say, Blessed are the barren, and the wombs that never bare, and the paps [breasts] that never gave suck" (see also Joseph Smith–Matthew 1:16).

Portending ominous consequences for the future of his people, Jesus queried, "If they do these things in a green tree, what shall be done in the dry?" (v. 31). Elder John Taylor used the same image in his description of the martyrdom of the Prophet Joseph and Hyrum Smith: "If the fire can scathe a green tree for the glory of God, how easy it will burn up the dry trees to purify the vineyard of corruption" (D&C 135:6). Such was the contemporary proverb, meaning in this ancient context that if such an outrage could be perpetrated in a time of relative tranquillity (*pax Romana*), what terrifying and foreboding judgments would be meted out when the calm is dried up and destruction and desolation would be unleashed on the Holy City?

Joseph Smith's translation of Luke 23:32 adds: "*This he spake, signifying the scattering of Israel, and the desolation of the heathen, or in other words, the Gentiles,*" meaning that in coming years a bleak future awaited both the Jews and the Romans.

This warning was of impending disaster of the greatest proportions. In Jewish society the birth of a child was understood to be among the highest blessings that God could bestow upon a woman and a people. It was a tangible symbol of hope in the future. The Savior was prophesying that things in the future would get so ugly, so terrible, for the Jewish nation and the people in Jerusalem that women would not want to bring children into the world to experience such horrors. Rather, they would wish for themselves to be annihilated without the blessing of motherhood.

In the last part of his warning, Jesus explicitly tied the disasters of the future to the Jewish leaders' treatment of himself. He himself is the Green Tree referred to in the warning; he is the Life and the Light, the giver of enlightenment and all good things, and provider of the very environment in which righteousness could most easily flourish. Jesus was saying, in essence, that if the Jewish nation could carry out such wickedness (as the Crucifixion) when the very Son of God was among them *and* at a time when they could have flourished religiously, what would happen to them after the Green Tree was killed and gone and only "the withered branches and dried trunk of apostate Judaism" remained? (Talmage, *Jesus the Christ*, 607). What would happen to Judaism after disaster overtook the Jews?

Little did the Jewish people of the Savior's day realize that in only forty short years their world would be devastated—changed forever. By A.D. 70 the Romans would lay siege to Jerusalem and ultimately obliterate the Temple. Things would indeed get so bad, as the Jewish historian Josephus later reported, that the besieged inhabitants of Jerusalem, even the women, would one day resort to cannibalism.

The Savior foresaw impending doom for his people as he himself approached his own death at Golgotha. Ironically, the Jewish inhabitants of Jerusalem that Friday morning had as much regard for the possibility that their great city could be destroyed as had Laman and Lemuel six hundred years before (1 Nephi 2:13). To them it was impossible. But obliviousness did not forestall the destruction, either in Lehi's time or a few decades after the Savior's.

The King James Version of Luke 23:33 identifies the place of Jesus' execution as Calvary, whereas the other three Gospel writers call the place Golgotha: "He bearing his cross went forth into a place called the place of a skull, which is called in the Hebrew Golgotha" (John 19:17). All four writers associated the execution site with a skull. Hebrew *gulgoleth* and Aramaic *gulgutha* mean "skull." Luke's term *Calvary* is actually not a place-name; it is the Latin translation of the Greek *kranion*, which also means "skull" (Luke 23:33 reads from the Greek: "When they were come to the place, which is called *kranion*, there they crucified him").

To what does the skull refer? The site could have had the physical appearance of a skull, or the name could have been derived from the long-standing use of the place for executions. It probably involves the fact that it was also a place of burial. John 19:17 in the Joseph Smith Translation indicates that Jesus was taken "into a place called the *place of a burial;* which is called in the Hebrew Golgotha."

On the cross Jesus thirsted, and, according to Matthew's report, soldiers offered him cheap wine mixed with gall, thus fulfilling another prophecy (Psalm 69:21). Gall is a substance that is bitter, even poisonous. Some believe it to be the juice of the opium poppy, which causes heavy sleep and insensibility.

Gall was used in the Old Testament for a parallel with wormwood, a repulsive plant always used metaphorically for something that is bitter or cruel. Its poisonous nature gave rise to the idiomatic expression, "the gall of bitterness" (Acts 8:23). The gall in the cheap wine offered to Jesus was presumably to act as a painkilling narcotic in order to prolong the suffering.

According to Mark's account, wine "mingled [mixed or flavored] with myrrh" was offered to Jesus on the cross, but "he received it not" (Mark 15:23). Jesus may have refused the drink because he was intent on being fully conscious to the moment of death.

THE CRUCIFIXION (AT GOLGOTHA/CALVARY, NEAR JERUSALEM)

Matthew 27:35–44; Mark 15:24–33; Luke 23:32–43; John 19:18–22 Despite many paintings over the centuries showing Jesus crucified on a hill, and despite some of our hymns referring to the "hill" of Calvary, there is nothing in all of scripture that indicates that the Crucifixion occurred on a hill. It could have taken place alongside the main road just outside Jerusalem's walls, to show that the Romans were in charge and anyone who defied their authority and their laws could meet an ignominious death on a cross so that everyone could pass by and revile. Quintilian (ca. A.D. 35–95) wrote: "Whenever we crucify the guilty, the most crowded roads are chosen, where the most people can see and be moved by this fear. For penalties relate not so much to retribution as to their exemplary effect" (*Declamations*, 274, as quoted in *Anchor Bible Dictionary*, 1:1208).

"The evidence from antiquity is overwhelming that crucifixion meant being *nailed* to the cross, not tied, as is sometimes depicted in art and claimed by modern commentators" (in Holzapfel and Wayment, *From the Last Supper through the Resurrection*, 320; see also Talmage, *Jesus the Christ*, 655).

It is well known that spikes were driven through the

The Atonement and the Resurrection

Skull Hill, possible site of Golgotha where Jesus was crucified. Some see the semblance of a face in the hillside

Savior's wrists in addition to the palms of his hands for fear that the weight of his body would cause it to tear away from the cross. Medical authorities attest that it "has been shown that the ligaments and bones of the wrist can support the weight of a body hanging from them, but the palms cannot" (Edwards et al., "On the Physical Death of Jesus Christ," 1460).

Two thieves were crucified with Jesus, one on each side. They were *lêstai*, which means more than thieves; they were likely revolutionaries and insurrectionists. Thus were fulfilled the words of Isaiah, that the Messiah would be numbered with the transgressors (Isaiah 53:12/Mosiah 14:12; cf. Isaiah 53:9/Mosiah 14:9).

The question is sometimes asked, "Why don't the Latter-day Saints use the cross in their worship?" The Church answers that question in the following way:

"The cross is used in many Christian churches as a symbol of the Savior's death and Resurrection and as a sincere expression of faith. As members of The Church of Jesus Christ of Latter-day Saints, we also remember with reverence the suffering of the Savior. But because the Savior lives, we do not use the symbol of His death as the symbol of our faith" (*True to the Faith*, 45–46).

SOLDIERS CAST LOTS FOR JESUS' ROBE (AT GOLGOTHA/CALVARY, NEAR JERUSALEM)

Matthew 27:35; Mark 15:24; Luke 23:34; John 19:23–24 The crucifiers divided Jesus' garments among them and cast lots for his vesture, or his robe, unwittingly fulfilling another prophetic utterance of a psalmist: "They part my garments among them, and cast lots upon my vesture" (Psalm 22:18).

DERISION OF JESUS ON THE CROSS (AT GOLGOTHA/CALVARY, NEAR JERUSALEM)

Matthew 27:39–44; Mark 15:29–32; Luke 23:34–37, 39–43 The soldiers and others in the crowd mocked and ridiculed the Savior in various ways, some of them deriding Jesus' kingship: "If thou be the king of the Jews, save thyself" (Luke 23:37). Jesus displayed only mercy to the Romans carrying out their orders: "Father, forgive them; for they know not what they do *(Meaning the soldiers who crucified him)*" (JST Luke 23:35).

The chief priests, scribes, and elders took up the same insults: "He saved others; himself he cannot save. If he be the King of Israel, let him now come down from the cross, and we will believe him. He trusted in God; let him deliver him now, if he will have him: for he said, I am the Son of God" (Matthew 27:42–43).

The truth is, Jesus could have come down from the cross—instantly, and with a vengeance—but he showed divine restraint and perfect submission to the will of the Father. Despite the taunting and scoffing, Jesus knew that this was his paramount purpose in coming to earth, to shed his blood in infinite sacrifice. As he said, "I lay down my life, that I might take it again. No man taketh it from me, but I lay it down of myself" (John 10:17–18).

Another way the mockers cast doubt on his divine Sonship was by falsifying and distorting a prophecy he had uttered early in his ministry: "Thou that destroyest the temple, and buildest it in three days, save thyself. If thou be the Son of God, come down from the cross" (Matthew 27:40; see also Matthew 26:61 and commentary on John 2:18–22).

"The thieves also, which were crucified with him, cast the same in his teeth" (Matthew 27:44), meaning that the two criminals joined in the scornful refrain. One malefactor ("evil-doer," especially one who has committed an offense against the law) suggested to Jesus, Save yourself and us.

The second malefactor spoke to the first, saying essentially, Don't you have any respect for God, seeing that you are a condemned man? We are getting our just reward, but this man has done nothing wrong. Then, turning to Jesus, the second malefactor said, "Lord, remember me when thou comest into thy kingdom" (Luke 23:42).

Jesus replied to the second, "To day shalt thou be with me in paradise." That is, that very day the malefactor would be with Jesus in the spirit world—and given the criminal's behavior, he was likely going to that part of the spirit world called the spirit prison, awaiting the opportunity to hear, accept, and live the gospel. "'To day shalt thou be with me in paradise' (Luke 23:43) . . . is incorrect. The statement would more accurately read, 'Today shalt thou be with me in the world of spirits' since the thief was not ready for paradise (HC 5:424–25)" (Bible Dictionary, "Paradise," 742). Joseph Smith further explained, "Hades, Sheol, paradise, spirits in prison, are all one: it is a world of spirits. The righteous and the wicked all go to the same world of spirits" (*Teachings of the Prophet Joseph Smith,* 310).

Any doctrinal confusion over Jesus' statement to the second malefactor has been further clarified by President Spencer W. Kimball:

"Another mistaken idea is that the thief on the cross was forgiven of his sins when the dying Christ answered: 'Today shalt thou be with me in paradise.' (Luke 23:43.) These men on the cross were thieves. How could the Lord forgive a malefactor? They had broken laws. There was no doubt of the guilt of the two men, for the one voluntarily confessed their guilt.

"The Lord cannot save men *in* their sins but only *from* their sins, and that only when they have shown true repentance. The one thief did show some compassion, whether selfishly with hope we are not sure. He was confessing, but how could he abandon his evil practices when dungeon walls made evil deeds impossible? How could he restore the stolen goods when hanging on the cross? How could he, as John the Baptist required, 'bring forth fruits meet for repentance'? How could he live the Lord's commands, attend his meetings, pay his tithing, serve his fellowmen? All these take time. Time was the one thing he was running out of very rapidly. 'No unclean thing can enter the kingdom of heaven.' This thought has been repeated throughout the scriptures numerous times and is a basic truth. We may be sure that the Savior's instructions to the thief on the cross were comparable to his instructions to the woman caught in adultery: 'Go your way and transform yourself and repent.'

"As the hours passed, the thief's life would ebb out and his spirit would abandon the lifeless body and go into the spirit world, where Christ was going to organize his missionary program. (See 1 Peter 3:18–20; 4–6.) There he would live along with . . . all others who had died in their sins. All the Lord's statement promised the thief was that both of them would soon be in the spirit world. The thief's show of repentance on the cross was all to his advantage, but his few words did not nullify a life of sin. The world should know that since the Lord himself cannot save men *in* their sins, no man on earth can administer any sacrament which will do that impossible thing. Hence the mere display of death-bed faith or repentance is not sufficient" (*Miracle of Forgiveness,* 166–67).

We must keep in mind that repentance after this life is a doctrinal reality. Otherwise, why preach to those spirits in prison who have never heard of Christ nor been converted to him? (1 Peter 3:18–19; 4:6; D&C 138:30–37). Furthermore, we believe that repentance in the spirit world is possible for those of us who knew the truth while in mortality but were not always valiant. We also believe, however, that such repentance is not without additional challenges, as Elder Melvin J. Ballard of the Quorum of the Twelve Apostles declared:

"It is my judgment that any man or woman can do more to conform to the laws of God in one year in this life than they could in ten years when they are dead. The spirit only can repent and change, and then the battle has to go forward with the flesh afterwards. It is much easier to overcome and serve the Lord when both flesh and spirit are combined as one. This is the time when men are more pliable and susceptible. When clay is pliable, it is much easier to change than when it gets hard and sets.

"This life is the time to repent. That is why I presume it will take a thousand years after the first resurrection until the last group will be prepared to come forth. It will take them a thousand years to do what it would have taken but three score years and ten to accomplish in this life" (*Sermons and Missionary Services,* 241).

The Savior's gracious plea on behalf of the Roman soldiers was the first of seven recorded utterances from the cross; his declaration to the malefactor was the second. It is instructive to view these seven statements together, for they teach much about Jesus' last thoughts and feelings. They could each be considered a sermon in its own right. Even today we tend to regard a person's dying declarations with an extra measure of respect, credibility, and significance.

Jesus uttered the following seven sentences from the cross:

1. "Father, forgive them; for they know not what they do" (Luke 23:34).

2. "To day shalt thou be with me in paradise" (Luke 23:43).

3. "Woman, behold thy son! . . . Behold thy mother!" (John 19:26–27).

4. "My God, my God, why hast thou forsaken me?" (Matthew 27:46).

5. "I thirst" (John 19:28).

6. "It is finished" (John 19:30). Joseph Smith Translation Matthew 27:54 adds: "*Father, it is finished, thy will is done.*"

7. "Father, into thy hands I commend my spirit" (Luke 23:46).

In his dying breaths, Jesus taught about the spirit world, forgiveness, obedience, submissiveness, and love.

THE SIGN: KING OF THE JEWS (AT GOLGOTHA/CALVARY, NEAR JERUSALEM)

Matthew 27:37; Mark 15:26; Luke 23:38; John 19:19–22 Pilate ordered a sign placed above the head of Jesus on the cross with an inscription identifying who Jesus was. The sign told the truth.

Matthew: THIS IS JESUS THE KING OF THE JEWS
Mark: THE KING OF THE JEWS
Luke: THIS IS THE KING OF THE JEWS
John: JESUS OF NAZARETH THE KING OF THE JEWS

The title-plate was written in the three languages used in

The Atonement and the Resurrection

"Jesus of Nazareth, King of the Jews" in Aramaic, Latin, and Greek

the land—Hebrew/Aramaic, Greek, and Latin—so that everyone passing by could read and understand.

The four slightly different translations of the same inscription may indicate that the wording was slightly different in the three languages, and subsequent translations would also differ.

Note that Pilate focused on Jesus' political title, King, rather than his spiritual title, Messiah—*melech, basileus,* and *rex* instead of *mashiah, christos,* and *christus.*

The chief priests of the Jews still did not like what Pilate wrote: "Write not, The King of the Jews; but that *he said,* I am King of the Jews" (emphasis added). By this time Pilate was exasperated with the Jewish leaders and answered them abruptly: "What I have written I have written" (John 19:21–22). So, in the end, the truth stood.

DARKNESS: SIXTH TO NINTH HOUR (AT JERUSALEM)

Matthew 27:45; Mark 15:33; Luke 23:44 Mark tells us that the Crucifixion began at the third hour (Mark 15:25), which would be 9 A.M. So Jesus endured a total of six hours on the cross. A few minutes can feel like a much longer time when we humans are in extreme pain, but try to imagine *six* *hours* in the unspeakable physical and spiritual pain and agony that the Savior was experiencing!

"Now from the sixth hour [noon] there was darkness over all the land unto the ninth hour [3 P.M.]" (Matthew 27:45). In the western world instead of three hours there were three days of darkness (1 Nephi 19:10; Helaman 14:20, 27). When the Light came into the world, at his birth, Book of Mormon peoples experienced more light; when he departed from the world, at his death, they experienced more darkness.

JESUS' MOTHER PUT IN JOHN'S CARE (AT GOLGOTHA/CALVARY, NEAR JERUSALEM)

John 19:25–27 Among Jesus' faithful followers were four women who remained close by in his final hours. They were as follows:

1. His mother, Mary.
2. His mother's sister.
3. Mary, the wife of Cleophas. Some believe Cleophas or Clopas to be the same person as Alphaeus, the father of Matthew and James the younger—making this Mary the mother of two apostles (see further in Van Dyke and Huntington, "Sorting Out the Seven Marys in the New Testament," 53–84).
4. Mary Magdalene.

All together, there were three Marys and an unnamed sister (Salome). The text is not clear whether three or four women are meant (that is, whether or not his mother's sister and Mary, the wife of Cleophas, are the same person). We suppose there are four because Mary, Jesus' mother, and her sister probably did not bear the same name, being from the same family. Mary's sister is usually identified as Salome (cf. Mark 15:40; Matthew 27:56), the mother of James and John—which would make those two apostles Jesus' cousins, and she,

Salome, would be Jesus' aunt (see *Encyclopedia of Mormonism*, 2:717).

With her Son dying a brutal death, Mary's own soul was wounded, as Simeon had prophesied thirty-three years before (Luke 2:34–35).

Despite his excruciating physical, mental, emotional, and spiritual agony—still suffering for the sins of the world (D&C 35:2; 46:13; 53:2; 54:1; 138:35)—he was concerned for his beloved mother, that she be cared for now that he was leaving. Jesus turned to his mother, Mary, and said, "Woman, behold thy son!" indicating that John, who would outlive all the other disciples (see commentary on John 21:23), would care for her until her mortal life was finished. He then turned to John, the disciple "whom he loved" (John 20:2; 21:20–24), and gave him to understand that his was the sacred responsibility of taking care of the mother of the Son of God.

DEATH OF JESUS CHRIST (AT GOLGOTHA/CALVARY, NEAR JERUSALEM)

Matthew 27:46–50; Mark 15:34–37; Luke 23:46; John 19:28–30 Two great Latter-day Saint authorities on the life of Christ, Elders James E. Talmage and Bruce R. McConkie, have pointed out that the agonies of Gethsemane came back to Jesus on the cross. "It seems, that in addition to the fearful suffering incident to crucifixion, the agony of Gethsemane had recurred, intensified beyond human power to endure" (Talmage, *Jesus the Christ*, 661). "All of the anguish, all of the sorrow, and all of the suffering of Gethsemane recurred during the final three hours on the cross" (McConkie, *Mortal Messiah*, 4:232); "while he was hanging on the cross . . . all the infinite agonies and merciless pains of Gethsemane recurred" (McConkie, *Ensign*, May 1985, 10).

About the ninth hour (3 P.M.) Jesus cried with a loud voice, "*Eli, Eli, lama sabachthani?*" (Matthew 27:46). The Hebrew words mean as follows: *Eli* is "my God" (Mark recorded the Aramaic form "Eloi" in Mark 15:34, meaning exactly the same); *lama* is Hebrew/Aramaic for "why"; the Aramaic verb *shavak* means to "leave," "leave alone," or "abandon." Thus *sabachthani* is "left me" or "forsaken me." Once again Jesus uttered a scriptural phrase he had inspired a psalmist to record a thousand years earlier. One reason he chose the phrase was to fulfill another messianic prophecy (Psalm 22:1). But why would he fill the air with such a heart-rending question?

President Brigham Young explained: "God never bestows upon His people, or upon an individual, superior blessings without a severe trial to prove them, to prove that individual, or that people, to see whether they will keep their covenants with Him, and keep in remembrance what He has shown them. Then the greater the vision, the greater the display of the power of the enemy. And when such individuals are off their guard they are left to themselves, as Jesus was. For this express purpose the Father withdrew His spirit from His Son, at the time he was to be crucified. . . . The light, knowledge, power, and glory with which [Jesus] was clothed were far above, or exceeded that of all others who had been upon the earth after the fall, consequently at the very moment, at the hour when the crisis came for him to offer up his life, the Father withdrew Himself, withdrew His Spirit, and cast a [veil] over him. That is what made him sweat blood. If he had had the power of God upon him, he would not have sweat blood; but all was withdrawn from him and a veil was cast over him, and he then pled with the Father not to forsake him. 'No,' says the Father, 'you must have your trials, as well as others.'

"So when individuals are blessed with visions, revelations,

The Atonement and the Resurrection

The humble hyssop bush with the mighty cedar behind it

and great manifestations, look out, then the devil is nigh you, and you will be tempted in proportion to the vision, revelation, or manifestation you have received" (*Journal of Discourses,* 3:205–6).

The Father had withdrawn his immediate presence for a moment so his Son would know what it is like when we (other children of the Father) are alone, without the Spirit. We believe this to be true in Gethsemane and on the cross. The Savior would be able to relate to any mortal circumstance. None of us could ever say, "But you don't understand!" He not only descended *to* our condition but descended *below* all things.

Upon hearing Jesus' soul-stirring cry, some misunderstood, supposing that he was calling for Elijah. Others wanted to see if Elijah would indeed come and rescue Jesus (Matthew 27:47, 49).

John 19:29 recalls the scene of Jesus crying out that he was thirsty, his only spoken expression of physical suffering while on the cross. Some soldiers attending him lifted a vinegar-filled sponge to his lips on a hyssop branch. The vinegar was a kind of cheap, sour wine commonly drunk by poorer people and soldiers (see commentary on Luke 23:27–31).

The hyssop is a small tree, though we might call it a shrub or a bush. It is used as a food, spice, and medicine, and the woody stem and branches are often used for kindling. Its appearance is unimposing and unpretentious, in contrast to the lofty and mighty cedar. Use of the hyssop branch may have some symbolic relation to the saving blood spread on the houses of Israel during the first Passover night (Exodus 12:21–23) or to the blood of remission that Moses applied to the people (Exodus 24:6–8; Hebrews 9:19–20). Paul noted that the Mosaic practices were "patterns," "figures," "shadows," and "images" of things to come (Hebrews 9–10). Or it may have been a symbol of humility involved in the fulfillment of a messianic prophecy: "In my thirst they gave me vinegar to drink" (Psalm 69:21).

From first to last, the Savior was exactly obedient to the Father's will. In the premortal Council in Heaven, he had said, "Father, thy will be done" (Moses 4:2). Now, at the end of his mortal mission, Jesus cried with a loud voice, "*Father, it is finished, thy will is done*" (JST Matthew 27:54). Luke records other words at this point, fulfilling another inspired declaration of the psalmist: "Father, into thy hands I commend [commit] my spirit" (Luke 23:46; cf. Psalm 31:5).

Having spoken his last mortal words, Jesus "gave up the ghost." The English word "ghost" derives from the German *geist*, which means "spirit" (for example, "the Holy Ghost" in German is *der Heilige Geist*, or "the Holy Spirit"). In other words, Jesus' spirit left his body, and he died as to the mortal body.

At this point in our examination of the scriptural text it may be appropriate to pause and reflect on the sacrifice the Father made in giving his Beloved Son for the salvation of his children and on the willingness of the Beloved Son to make that sacrifice.

The Atonement and the Resurrection

Brother Ogden recalls a scene described by his daughter Sara as she prepared in the Missionary Training Center in January 1998 for her missionary service. She wrote about sitting on the front row of the MTC choir while singing a special arrangement of "How Great Thou Art": "The place was quiet and we sang that song with all our hearts. The choir director just had two daughters killed in a car accident, and his other two children are critically injured in the hospital. He left the MTC for a month, and he chose this song when he came back this week. He bore his testimony of the incredible love he has for his Lord and Savior, and through this song we joined with him. After the elders softly ended with 'How great thou art,' the tears were streaming down his face. The choir felt the Spirit, and the audience, and together the tears were flowing. I've never felt so strongly about something in my life. This gospel is true, and the Lord loves us more than we can know. This sweet, humble, and heartbroken man was standing before us and leading the choir with all the faith that he has, just after he lost his dear children. He still followed the Lord, and he wanted the audience to feel the truth by the Spirit. . . . 'And when I think that God, his Son not sparing, Sent him to die, I scarce can take it in, That on the cross, my burden gladly bearing, He bled and died to take away my sin, Then sings my soul, my Savior God, to thee, How great thou art! How great thou art!'" (Ogden, letter).

Elder Melvin J. Ballard wrote one of the most stirring testimonies ever recorded of the Father's sacrifice of his Beloved Son:

"I think as I read the story of Abraham's sacrifice of his son Isaac that our Father is trying to tell us what it cost Him to give His Son as a gift to the world. You remember the story of how Abraham's son came after long years of waiting and was looked upon by his worthy sire, Abraham, as more precious than all his other possessions; yet, in the midst of his rejoicing, Abraham was told to take this only son and offer him as a sacrifice to the Lord. He responded. Can you feel what was in the heart of Abraham on that occasion? You love your son just as Abraham did; perhaps not quite so much, because of the peculiar circumstances, but what do you think was in his heart when he started away from Mother Sarah and they bade her goodbye? What do you think was in his heart when he saw Isaac bidding farewell to his mother to take that three days' journey to the appointed place where the sacrifice was to be made? I imagine it was about all Father Abraham could do to keep from showing his great grief and sorrow at that parting, but he and his son trudged along three days toward the appointed place, Isaac carrying the fagots that were to consume the sacrifice. The two travelers rested, finally, at the mountainside, and the men who had accompanied them were told to remain while Abraham and his son started up the hill.

"The boy then said to his father: 'Why, Father . . . we have the fire to burn the sacrifice; but where is the sacrifice?'

"It must have pierced the heart of Father Abraham to hear the trusting and confiding son say: 'You have forgotten the sacrifice.' Looking at the youth, his son of promise, the poor father could only say: 'The Lord will provide.'

"They ascended the mountain, gathered the stones together, and placed the fagots upon them. Then Isaac was bound, hand and foot, kneeling upon the altar. I presume Abraham, like a true father, must have given his son his farewell kiss, his blessing, his love, and his soul must have been drawn out in that hour of agony toward his son who was to die by the hand of his own father. Every step proceeded until the cold steel was drawn and the hand raised that was to strike the blow to let out the life's blood, when the angel of the Lord said: 'It is enough.'

"Our Father in heaven went through all that and more, for in his case the hand was not stayed. He loved his Son, Jesus Christ, better than Abraham ever loved Isaac, for our Father had with him his Son, our Redeemer, in the eternal worlds, faithful and true for ages, standing in a place of trust

The Atonement and the Resurrection

and honor, and the Father loved him dearly, and yet he allowed this well-beloved Son, to descend from his place of glory and honor, where millions did him homage, down to the earth, a condescension that is not within the power of man to conceive. He came to receive the insult, the abuse, and the crown of thorns. God heard the cry of his Son in that moment of great grief and agony, in the garden when, it is said, the pores of his body opened and drops of blood stood upon him, and he cried out: 'Father, if thou be willing, remove this cup from me.'

"I ask you, what father and mother could stand by and listen to the cry of their children in distress, in this world, and not render aid and assistance? I have heard of mothers throwing themselves into raging streams when they could not swim a stroke to save their drowning children, rushing into burning buildings to rescue those whom they loved.

"We cannot stand by and listen to those cries without its touching our hearts. The Lord has not given us the power to save our own. He has given us faith, and we submit to the inevitable, but he had the power to save, and he loved his Son, and he could have saved him. He might have rescued him from the insult of the crowds. He might have rescued him when the crown of thorns was placed upon his head. He might have rescued him when the Son, hanging between the two thieves, was mocked with, 'Save thyself, and come down from the cross. He saved others; himself he cannot save.' He listened to all this. He saw that Son condemned; he saw him drag the cross through the streets of Jerusalem and faint under its load. He saw that Son finally upon Calvary; he saw his body stretched out upon the wooden cross; he saw the cruel nails driven through hands and feet, and the blows that broke the skin, tore the flesh, and let out the life's blood of his Son. He looked upon that.

"In the case of our Father, the knife was not stayed, but it fell, and the life's blood of his Beloved Son went out. His

Father looked on with great grief and agony over his Beloved Son, until there seems to have come a moment when even our Savior cried out in despair: 'My God, my God, why hast thou forsaken me?'

"In that hour I think I can see our dear Father behind the veil looking upon these dying struggles until even he could not endure it any longer; and, like the mother who bids farewell to her dying child, has to be taken out of the room, so as not to look upon the last struggles, so he bowed his head and hid in some part of his universe, his great heart almost breaking for the love that he had for his Son. Oh, in that moment when he might have saved his Son, I thank him and praise him that he did not fail us, for he had not only the love of his son in mind, but he also had love for us. I rejoice that he did not interfere, and that his love for us made it possible for him to endure to look upon the sufferings of his Son and give him finally to us, our Savior and our Redeemer. Without him, without his sacrifice, we would have remained, and we would never have come glorified into his presence. And so this is what it cost, in part, for our Father in Heaven to give the gift of his Son unto men." (*Sermons and Missionary Services*, 152–55.)

EARTHQUAKE: VEIL OF TEMPLE RENT (IN JERUSALEM)

Matthew 27:51–53; Mark 15:38; Luke 23:45 Just as earthquakes convulsed the lands in the western world at the time of Jesus' death (Helaman 14:21–24; 2 Nephi 8:6), so upheavals occurred in the land of Jerusalem. Not only did Matthew and other contemporaries report the physical effects when the sun hid its face in shame (Luke 23:45; cf. Joseph Smith–Matthew 1:33; D&C 133:49), and the earth itself groaned at the Crucifixion, but the Lord had shown various

The Atonement and the Resurrection

prophets hundreds and even thousands of years in advance what physical catastrophes would transpire at his mortal death. For example, the Lord said to Enoch: "Look, and he looked and beheld the Son of Man lifted up on the cross, after the manner of men; and he heard a loud voice; and the heavens were veiled; and all the creations of God mourned; and the earth groaned; and the rocks were rent" (Moses 7:55–56; see also 1 Nephi 19:12).

The veil of the Temple was rent in twain (torn in two) from top to bottom, symbolizing the rending of the veil of the Mosaic dispensation—the great High Priest, Israel's God himself, now opening the way for all who are willing and worthy to enter the divine Presence. We have a hope set before us, Paul later wrote, "which hope we have as an anchor of the soul, both sure and steadfast, and which entereth into that within the veil; whither the forerunner is for us entered, even Jesus, made an high priest for ever after the order of Melchisedec" (Hebrews 6:19–20).

The symbolism of the old law was now complete in the sacrifice of the Lamb. He had removed all obstacles for us to be redeemed from the Fall and to be able to enter fully into the eternal presence of God, which was symbolized by going through the veil into the Holy of Holies (we would say into the celestial room) of the Temple.

The veil of the Temple was rent; the Lord himself symbolically went in, and he opened the way for us to enter also.

Matthew 27:52–53 As Matthew prepared his account of Jesus' ministry years after the Lord's departure, he recalled that the graves (on the Mount of Olives, overlooking the Temple Mount and the Holy City) were opened and many righteous Saints who had died arose out of their sepulchres *after his resurrection*. They went into the Holy City and appeared to many people, so there were numerous witnesses to the first resurrections ever to occur in the history of the world (cf. Helaman 14:25; 3 Nephi 23:11). Doctrine and Covenants 133:54–55 specifically identifies some of those "who were with Christ in his resurrection": Enoch and his people, Noah, Abraham, Isaac, Jacob, Moses, Elijah, and John the Baptist (cf. Alma 40:18; see McConkie, *Mormon Doctrine*, 136).

Matthew's two verses testifying of the many eyewitnesses of the earliest resurrections are slightly out of order chronologically as they appear in the book of Matthew that we have. These stunning appearances actually occurred on the third day after Jesus' death, for there was no resurrection of anyone until the Savior himself rose from the tomb. He was the firstfruits of the resurrection (1 Corinthians 15:20).

PIERCED BY A SPEAR (AT GOLGOTHA/CALVARY, NEAR JERUSALEM)

John 19:31–34 The last week of Jesus' mortal life culminated in a holy Sabbath day (Saturday) that was apparently the high day, the culminating point, of the Passover also. The day before this double holy day was "the preparation" day (Mark 15:42 and Luke 23:54, 56), and the three crucified bodies had to be removed and buried by the beginning of the holy day (Deuteronomy 21:22–23 and footnote 23a), which began at sundown on Friday. The Jewish leaders, always conscientious with the law, sought the Roman governor's permission to break the legs of the crucified individuals in order to hasten their death and thus expedite their burial. Not only would breaking leg bones cause shock but the victims could no longer use their legs to periodically stand and relieve the pressure in their lungs caused by hanging from their arms. While they were hanging by their arms, their diaphragms could not move up and down properly and the victims would suffocate.

Nonetheless, there was a prophecy that not one of the Savior's bones would be broken (Psalm 34:20). The soldiers broke the bones of the two thieves, but they saw that Jesus was already dead, so the brutal act was unnecessary. One of the soldiers did thrust a spear through his side, and blood and water came out.

Thus, Jesus received seven wounds during the Crucifixion: two in his hands, two in his wrists, two in his feet, and one in his side.

PASSOVER SCRIPTURE FULFILLED (AT GOLGOTHA/CALVARY, NEAR JERUSALEM)

John 19:35–37 All of the incidents of the Crucifixion were readily regarded by the early Christian Saints as fulfillment of centuries-old prophecies. John the Beloved bore testimony that he was an eyewitness of these sacred events and that his written testimony of them is true. And all the prophetic utterances of the past were literally fulfilled to every detail in the Lord Jesus Christ. Not a bone of the Lamb (as with the Passover lamb; Exodus 12:46; Numbers 9:12) was broken, and the people did "look on him whom they pierced" (v. 37; Zechariah 12:10). Prophecy indicated that "they pierced my hands and my feet" (Psalm 22:16). That would happen, even though when the psalmist wrote, the cruel method of killing by crucifixion had not yet been invented.

WATCHERS NEAR THE CROSS (AT GOLGOTHA/CALVARY, NEAR JERUSALEM)

Matthew 27:54–56; Mark 15:39–41; Luke 23:47–49 A Roman centurion and his associates, while watching Jesus and listening to his utterances (the Lord was still teaching right to the end) and observing all the unusual commotions, were moved by the Spirit to proclaim, "Truly this was the Son of God" (Matthew 27:54).

Many disciples who came up with Jesus from Galilee, especially a large group of women, helped minister to the needs of the Savior and his whole company (Luke 8:1–3). These loyal followers "stood afar off," observing all that was transpiring, and "smiting their breasts," an ancient mode of mourning the death of loved ones by expressing their grief physically.

Matthew, Mark, and John identified certain of the devoted women:

1. Mary, the mother of Jesus (John 19:25).
2. Mary Magdalene.
3. Mary, the mother of James (Jacob) and Joses (Joseph).
4. Mary of Cleophas (John 19:25).
5. "The mother of Zebedee's children" (Matthew 27:56), whom Mark identified as Salome (Mark 15:40), who was the mother of apostles James and John (see also commentary on John 19:25–27).

Thus, there were four Marys and Salome plus "many other women" (Mark 15:41), including Joanna (Luke 24:10) and possibly Martha and Mary of Bethany (for more on the relationship between the women at the cross, see Skinner, *Golgotha*, 138–40).

JESUS' BURIAL (NEAR JERUSALEM)

Matthew 27:57–61; Mark 15:42–47; Luke 23:50–56; John 19:38–42 All four Gospel writers mention a man named Joseph who was "of Arimathaea, a city of the Jews" (Luke 23:51), who petitioned the Roman governor, Pilate, for Jesus' body in order to give it a proper burial. Matthew tells us that he was a rich man and Jesus' disciple (27:57), and Luke describes him as "a good man, and a just" (23:50). Mark relates that he was an "honourable counselor," meaning a member of the Sanhedrin, who "waited for the kingdom of God" (15:43). Luke adds that he had "not consented to the

The Atonement and the Resurrection

The Burial, *by Carl Heinrich Bloch*

counsel and deed" of the other Sanhedrin members (23:51). John describes him as "a disciple of Jesus, but secretly for fear of the Jews" (19:38; see also 12:42).

Arimathea is a Greek form of the Hebrew *Ramah*. Eusebius was the first to associate Arimathea with Rentis, in the coastal district of Diospolis-Lod. Josephus and 1 Maccabees both suggest a location to the east of Lod (Lydda). Rentis was located in the hills of New Testament period Judea, about thirty miles via Roman roads northwest of Jerusalem (see Appendix 1, 713).

Joseph was joined by Nicodemus, also a ruler of the Jews, who was a secret believer in Jesus (see commentary on John 3:1–10), and the two of them prepared Jesus' body for burial.

The spices used for Jesus' body were a mixture of myrrh and aloes, "about an hundred pound weight" (John 19:39).

"Pound" is the translation of Greek *litra,* which was actually twelve ounces by United States standards. Still, the total mixture amounted to a hefty seventy-five pounds.

Myrrh is said to come from an odorous gum that grew in Arabia, Ethiopia, India, and the Rift Valley of the Holy Land. It is mentioned three times in the New Testament. Myrrh first appears as one of the gifts of the wise men from the east to the child Jesus and is mentioned among two other costly gifts, gold and frankincense (Matthew 2:11).

There is a variety of plants in the *aloe* family. Some are used for medicinal purposes, and others for fragrant perfumes. We do not know which specific aloes were brought for Jesus' burial, but those used for his embalmment may have come from the oil extracted from the aloe vera plant, which was used in ancient Egypt and elsewhere in the Old World for embalming.

The New Testament speaks of "clean linen cloth" (Matthew 27:59), "fine linen" (Mark 15:46; Luke 16:19), and "pure and white linen" (Revelation 15:6). Linen was used as burial cloth for the dead; most New Testament references to linen refer to the shroud or burial cloth of Jesus: "When Joseph had taken the body, he wrapped it in a clean linen cloth" (Matthew 27:59). "Then took they the body of Jesus, and wound it in linen clothes with the spices, as the manner of the Jews is to bury" (John 19:40). Joseph of Arimathea owned some land just outside the walled city of Jerusalem. It was a garden area, and in the garden was a tomb newly cut out of the native stone. The Testimony of John contains two key verses describing the place of Jesus' burial:

"Now in the place where he was crucified there was a garden; and in the garden a new sepulchre, wherein was never man yet laid.

"There laid they Jesus therefore because of the Jews' preparation day; for the sepulchre was nigh at hand" (John 19:41–42).

As with other events during the last days of Jesus' mortal

The Atonement and the Resurrection

life, there are two major candidates for the location of the crucifixion, burial, and resurrection, all of which occurred at the same place just outside the walled city. According to scripture and Jewish customs, the site must meet certain conditions:

1. It must be outside the city walls (John 19:20).
2. It must be near a main thoroughfare (Matthew 27:39; Mark 15:29; John 19:20).
3. It must be a place of execution (Mark 15:27; Luke 23:33).
4. There must be a garden nearby (John 19:41; 20:15).
5. The garden must contain at least one tomb (the tomb was therefore near the place of crucifixion) (John 19:41–42).
6. The rock tomb must be newly cut (Matthew 27:60; Luke 23:53; John 19:41).
7. The tomb apparently had an anteroom (mourning chamber) and several places for burial; the tomb must be large enough to walk into (Mark 16:5; Luke 24:3; John 20:8).
8. The tomb must have a large, heavy stone to seal the entrance (Matthew 27:60; Mark 15:46; 16:4; Luke 24:2).
9. The tomb entrance must be small, so that one has to stoop to look inside; a person looking in from the outside could see the place where the body was laid (Luke 24:12; John 20:5, 11–12).
10. The tomb must have some place where linen burial cloths could lie and where a "young man" could sit (Mark 16:5), or where two angels could sit, one at the head and one at the foot of where Jesus' body had lain (John 20:6–7, 12).

Considering all of these conditions, we examine the two traditional options for the site of the crucifixion, burial, and resurrection.

Site 1. The Church of the Holy Sepulchre has long been the traditional site of these venerated events. In the fourth century after Christ, Emperor Constantine's mother, Helena, made her pilgrimage to the Holy Land and identified the spot, over which a pagan temple had been built. Some believe that recent excavations show that the site, though now within the

The Church of the Holy Sepulchre

walls of the Old City of Jerusalem, was outside the walls in Jesus' day. Its location just outside the western city wall could have provided a busy thoroughfare for travelers. There is no evidence, however, that it was a place of execution, nor is there evidence of a garden in the vicinity. A stone quarry existed at the Holy Sepulchre site in the first century after Christ.

Tombs (likely from the Hellenistic period) have been discovered in the bedrock below the church. They are *kokhim*, the typical style of sepulchre from that period, which are burial niches cut into the rock large enough for only a single body. There would be room for someone to walk into the entry chamber of the tomb, but there is no evidence that large stones could be positioned to seal the entrance. The condition that most precludes the Holy Sepulchre site is the lack of a bench or shelf on which a body could be placed or on which someone could sit inside the sepulchre. Two angels could in no way situate themselves inside a *kokh*, where Jesus' body would have lain.

The Atonement and the Resurrection

Kokhim *(burial niches) in the Church of the Holy Sepulchre*

Scholars have recently pointed to another complication: "Burial sites are found everywhere around Jerusalem except west of the Temple, which is the direction from which the prevailing winds blow . . . so that the sacred place would not be defiled by impurities the western wind might carry. . . . no tombs were within 2,000 cubits (about 1,100 yards) west of the Temple. . . . If burial customs in the first half of the first century C.E. [unlike what may have been done in earlier periods] preclude burials and their attendant impurities west (windward) of the Temple, then the crucifixion and burial of Jesus could not have taken place at the site of the Church of the Holy Sepulchre, which is almost exactly due west of the Holy of Holies. . . . This is a most important argument against the authenticity of the site" (Rousseau and Arav, *Jesus and His World*, 164, 114, 169, 115; see also Chadwick, *Revisiting Golgotha*, 16–17).

Site 2. The other site hallowed as a possibility is the Garden Tomb, just north of the Damascus Gate of today's Old City of Jerusalem. This tomb, discovered in the late nineteenth century, is a place of pilgrimage for many thousands of Christians,

The Garden Tomb, another possibility for Jesus' burial place

including some Catholics who would like to see "how it might have been." This site was outside the walls of the city in Jesus' day. It was definitely alongside a main thoroughfare. It appears to have been a place of execution, because today's Damascus Gate was often called "St. Stephen's Gate" during the first millennium after Christ, suggesting that Stephen was killed in this same area. St. Stephen's Church, from the fifth century after Christ, is immediately north of this site.

Many tombs have been discovered in the vicinity, most of them dating to the seventh and eighth centuries before Christ. The Garden Tomb itself appears to be part of a complex of earlier Judean tombs, and most of the complex lies to the north of the Garden Tomb in the property of the École Biblique, the French School of Archaeology. These tombs, unlike the later *kokhim*, are chambers with side rooms branching off in several directions, each containing usually three benches on which bodies were placed and featuring repositories for bones underneath one of the benches in each room, suggesting perpetual use of the tombs over many generations, as was customary in antiquity.

A "new tomb" could also mean a newly remodeled tomb, not yet used in the newly cut form. The Garden Tomb is nearly identical in style to these older tombs but has some features of later styles. There is no repository for bones, and no evidence that it was used many times. It does have more than one room and is large enough to walk into. There is presently no stone at its entrance, but there could have been in that day. The original entrance was short enough to require stooping to enter. And there was a bench or shelf (before Byzantine architects or others later carved out a sarcophagus) on which angels could have sat, even on the *right side* upon entering (Mark 16:5).

Some have objected to the Garden Tomb as the burial place of Jesus because, by its structural design, it appears strictly related to the style used seven or eight centuries earlier. There are tombs from the early Roman period, however, that combine both old Judean and Roman styles. At Khirbet Midras, twenty miles southwest of Jerusalem, for example, is a tomb complex dating to the first century before Christ that has the older style chambers containing benches but also features the later *kokhim*, or niches, and sarcophagi and ossuaries. Even the St. Etienne tomb complex, of which the Garden Tomb seems to be a part, has a chamber with sarcophagi—quite distinct from the other chambers.

Of these two candidates, the enduring reverence of tradition favors the Holy Sepulchre site, but the Garden Tomb fulfills more of the scriptural conditions. Rousseau and Arav, citing the work of a Roman Catholic archaeologist who served as codirector of the restoration of the Church of the Holy Sepulchre, concluded that "the most likely site [of the Crucifixion] was beyond the northern wall, because the Gate of Ephraim was in the north, most likely on the site of today's Damascus Gate" (*Jesus and His World*, 115).

Still, we do not dogmatically acclaim the one over the other. There is presently no way to know if one of these two sites or yet another site was used for Jesus' burial. Regardless of investigations and evidences and surmises and conclusions, affixing faith to a particular site is not wise. Belief is beyond physical territory. To the Christian the most important message is, "He is risen; he is not here" (Mark 16:6).

Matthew 27:61; Mark 15:47 Observing the work of Joseph and Nicodemus were eminent women—Mary, his mother, and Mary Magdalene, his closest female associate (see commentary on John 20:14–17).

CHIEF PRIESTS AND PHARISEES SEAL THE TOMB (NEAR JERUSALEM)

Matthew 27:62–66 On Saturday, the Sabbath, while Jesus' body was in the tomb and his spirit was in the spirit world, some chief priests and Pharisees continued their agitation by approaching Pilate and insisting that he set a more secure guard around Jesus' tomb: "We remember that that deceiver said, while he was yet alive, After three days I will rise again" (v. 63). So they had understood the Savior's prophetic foreshadowing after all! (see commentary on John 2:18–22). Jesus did indeed declare on more than one occasion that he would be crucified but then rise again on the third day. Of course, no number of additional guards around the tomb would prevent the miracle from taking place.

The Jewish leaders, not believing in this man Jesus of Nazareth as the first person who would be resurrected on this earth, reasoned that his disciples would steal the body and claim he had risen from the dead—and that the final deception would prove worse than all the previous deceptions.

By this time the Roman governor was exasperated with the paranoid local leaders and brushed off their request with "you have your watch; make it as sure as you can" (v. 65). So they sealed the stone and secured the guard. Sealing the stone may mean placing it firmly at the opening of the sepulchre, or possibly using some substance such as wax or other sealant.

FIRST DAY: WOMEN COME; EARTHQUAKE; ANGELS OPEN TOMB (NEAR JERUSALEM)

Matthew 28:1–2; Mark 16:1–4; Luke 24:1–3; John 20:1–2 "In the end of the Sabbath, as it began to dawn toward the first day of the week" (Matthew), or "very early in the morning the first day of the week . . . at the rising of the sun" (Mark), or "upon the first day of the week, very early in the morning" (Luke), or "the first day of the week . . . when it was yet dark" (John), women disciples were making their way toward the tomb when an aftershock of the earthquake of the previous Friday struck Jerusalem again, as angels came down from heaven to open the tomb of God's Son. No heavy stone seal nor secure guard of the Sanhedrin would stand up to nature's convulsive powers directed by the God of the universe, nor could they withstand angelic messengers sent by that very God to open the tomb. It may have seemed that Jesus' mortal life was terminated at the hands of men, but his postmortal life, again in the mortal sphere, commenced at the hands of the Father and his messengers. The *two angels* (JST Matthew 28:2) removed the stone at the entrance of the sepulchre and sat on it (JST John 20:1).

Jesus did not need angels to roll away the great stone from the door of the sepulchre so that he could leave. Resurrected beings have power to pass through the elements and objects of the earth. In the resurrection we shall become acquainted with a whole new dimension of the laws of physics. President Joseph Fielding Smith taught:

"Resurrected bodies pass through solid objects. Resurrected bodies have control over the elements. How do you think the bodies will get out of the graves at the resurrection? When the Angel Moroni appeared to the Prophet Joseph Smith, the Prophet saw him apparently come down and ascend through the solid walls, or ceiling of the building. If the Prophet's account had been a fraud, he never would have stated such a story . . . but would have had the angel come in through the door. Why should it appear any more impossible for a resurrected being to pass through solid objects than for a spirit, for a spirit is also matter?

"It was just as easy for the Angel Moroni to come to the Prophet Joseph Smith down through the building as it was for our Savior to appear to his disciples after his resurrection in the room where they were assembled when the door was closed. . . .

"How could he do it? He had power over the elements" (*Doctrines of Salvation,* 2:288).

Why, then, did the angels roll the stone away and open the tomb?

First, there was important symbolic meaning in this act. Just as the door of the tomb of the resurrection was now open, signaling its Occupant was no longer there, so too the door of spirit prison was now open, signaling that its righteous inhabitants were free from the bondage of death and would no longer be confined there. This symbolism is not unlike the tearing of the veil of the Jerusalem Temple at the final moment of the Crucifixion. The exposed Holy of Holies symbolized, among other things, a new order or dispensation that allowed, through the atonement of Christ, all the righteous to enter the presence of God—which the Holy of Holies represents (Hebrews 9:19–24; 10:19–20).

Second, with the opening of the tomb, the disciples could look inside as well as enter the sepulchre and know for themselves that the tomb was empty, that Jesus had returned to life, that he really was the Savior, with power to raise his own physical body back to life.

Others would likewise visit the tomb, and out of their initial experience with its emptiness would blossom the witness that Jesus was who he said he was, that he had told the truth, that he was the Savior, Messiah, and Son of God alive again.

Among the women who approached the tomb that

glorious morning were Mary Magdalene; Mary, the mother of James the younger and Joses (Joseph); Salome, the mother of apostles James and John (see commentary on John 19:25–27 and Matthew 27:54–56); and Joanna, wife of Chuza, steward of Herod Antipas (Luke 8:3 and 24:10). We wonder if the two beloved sisters from Bethany, Martha and Mary, along with some of the apostles' wives, were not also present.

Among the women disciples who followed Jesus, Mary Magdalene seems to have served in a leadership capacity. She is mentioned first in several listings of female followers (see, for example, Matthew 27:56; Luke 24:10), and she was first to see the resurrected Lord (John 20:1–18). Mary of Magdala appears to have had a preeminent relationship with Jesus of Nazareth.

On Friday the women had prepared spices and ointments and then on Saturday, the Sabbath, they rested, "according to the commandment" (Luke 23:56). Now on Sunday morning they brought "the spices which they had prepared" (Luke 24:1). The Greek word for *spice* is *aroma*. Spices and ointments were usually scented and were used for funerary, cosmetic, and medicinal purposes. Every time the word *spice* appears in the New Testament, it refers in some way to Jesus' embalming and burial. The women arrived at the tomb with their spices and found the stone removed.

ANGELS: "HE IS RISEN" (NEAR JERUSALEM)

Matthew 28:2–8; Mark 16:5–8; Luke 24:4–8 Angelic visitors came at the Savior's birth, during his ministry (for example, at the Transfiguration), in Gethsemane, and now at his tomb. There was frequent contact between heaven and earth while the great Creator sojourned here for a brief time

BYU–Jerusalem Center student approaches a first-century burial tomb at Khirbet Midras, with a large stone to seal the entrance. This tomb is similar in some respects to the tomb owned by Joseph of Arimathea in Jerusalem

(see Matthew 1:20; 2:13, 19; 4:11; 28:2–8; Luke 1:11–20, 26–30; 2:9–15; 22:43).

When the angels appeared, the guards were scared to death (Matthew 28:4), but the heavenly messengers calmed the women's fears, assuring them that the Man they were seeking was "not here: for he is risen, as he said" (Matthew 28:6). Then they invited the women to "come, see the place where the Lord lay."

"But when they looked, they saw that the stone was rolled away, (for it was very great,) *and two angels sitting thereon,* clothed in long white *garments;* and they were affrighted.

"*But the angels said* unto them, Be not affrighted; ye seek Jesus of Nazareth, *who* was crucified; he is risen; he is not here; behold the place where they laid him;

"*And* go your way, tell his disciples and Peter, that he goeth before you into Galilee; there shall ye see him as he said unto you.

"*And they, entering into the sepulcher, saw the place where they laid Jesus*" (JST Mark 16:3–6).

Joseph Smith's translation of Luke 24:2–4 describes the same scene with slightly variant details:

"And they found the stone rolled away from the sepulcher, *and two angels standing by it in shining garments.*

"And they entered *into the sepulcher,* and *not finding* the body of the Lord Jesus, they were much perplexed thereabout;

"And were *affrighted,* and bowed down their faces to the earth. *But behold the angels* said unto them, Why seek ye the living among the dead?" (JST Luke 24:2–4; incidentally, the word "sepulcher" in the JST is the American English spelling, whereas the KJV uses the British English spelling).

Seeing and hearing all these astonishing things, Mary Magdalene ran to tell Peter and John (we are not told where James was). Representing all the women, Mary exclaimed to the two leading apostles: "They have taken away the Lord out of the sepulchre, and we know not where they have laid him" (John 20:2). If, by mentioning "they" who took away the body, Mary meant the Romans or the Jewish leaders or even the angels, she had not quite comprehended the divine message the women had heard from those angels: "He is risen; he is not here." It would yet require some personal experience, seeing, hearing, and touching for Mary and for all others to comprehend the glorious fact of resurrection.

The angels had instructed the women to go quickly and tell the apostles and other disciples that Jesus was risen from the dead and that the apostles had an appointment with Jesus in Galilee: "He goeth before you into Galilee; there shall ye see him" (Matthew 28:7). The sisters "departed quickly from the sepulchre with fear and great joy; and did run to bring his disciples word" (v. 8). They were experiencing, understandably, a dramatic mix of feelings—fright, perplexity, amazement, respect, excitement, joy—over what was happening, and their minds were beginning from these very moments to piece together the doctrines Jesus had taught that only now, as they actually occurred, could be fully comprehended by mortals.

PETER AND JOHN RUN TO THE TOMB (NEAR JERUSALEM)

Luke 24:12, 24; John 20:3–10 Luke, who likely learned what happened next from Peter himself (years later) and from John, recorded that the two apostles, hearing these extraordinary, unbelievable reports, ran together to the sepulchre, John outrunning Peter (John was apparently one of the youngest of the apostles).

John arrived, stooped down, and looked in, and then Peter arrived and immediately entered. Respectfully giving way to the chief apostle, John followed Peter inside. They both saw the burial cloths where Jesus' body had been. According to his own written report, John "saw and believed" (John 20:8). He saw what? And believed what? That a dead mortal being was alive again. But both Peter and John sensed that there was something very different about this Being. He was not just brought back to life temporarily to eventually die again; raising of the dead was a miracle they knew not only from scripture, the Old Testament, but from personal experience, having seen Jesus do it at least three times: the son of the widow of Nain (Luke 7:11–17); the daughter of Jairus (Matthew 9:18–26; Mark 5:22–43; Luke 8:41–56); and Lazarus (John 11:1–46). This was different. The apostles were coming to understand that their Savior had been raised by the power of the Father into immortality. As the next verse (John 20:9) explains, up to this point "they knew [comprehended] not the scripture, that he must rise again from the dead."

We raise the question again: how *could* they comprehend such a thing? For four thousand years mortals had been dying and were buried, their physical bodies remaining dead, having no spirit, no life. Resurrection had never happened in this world. But now the apostles were fitting together the current facts and the teachings and the prophecies (they had been pondering this doctrine of resurrection for some time, at least since the occasion of the Transfiguration; see Mark 9:10). They had weighty matters to reflect on as they returned home, wherever "their own home" (John 20:10) was at Jerusalem.

It seems significant that no scriptural records discuss the details of the actual resurrection process or what went on inside the tomb immediately after the resurrection. We do not know how long Jesus was there. We *do* know that Jesus passed through his burial cloths, leaving them lying in place, in the outline and form of the body around which they had been wrapped. Resurrected bodies have the power to move through solid objects. John recorded in his own Gospel that when he came to the tomb and looked inside, and when Peter entered it shortly thereafter, they both saw the strips of burial linen lying in place in the burial chamber as well as the burial cloth that had been wrapped around Jesus' head (John 20:4–7). The strips of cloth "were left in such a way as to show that his resurrected body had passed through their folds and strands without the need of unwinding the strips or untying the napkin" (McConkie, *Mortal Messiah*, 4:268).

This was explicit evidence of Jesus' resurrection. No mortal man had disturbed his body. The cloth that had been wrapped about Jesus' head ("napkin" in the King James Version) was still by itself, separate from the linen.

Jesus, then, left his burial cloths in place as one more witness of the greatest of the miraculous acts that compose the Atonement. The scriptures make no mention of Jesus donning postresurrection robes or clothing, but such was surely the case.

"WOMAN, WHY WEEPEST THOU?" (NEAR JERUSALEM)

John 20:11–13; cf. Mark 16:9 One woman, alone, remained at the sepulchre, crying. Of all the Marys who had

BYU–Jerusalem Center student portraying Mary looking into Jesus' tomb at a first-century tomb at Khirbet Midras, twenty miles southwest of Jerusalem

been attending to the body, the one from Magdala stooped down and looked into the burial chamber and saw two angels arrayed in brilliant white "sitting the one at the head, and the other at the feet, where the body of Jesus had lain."

The angels asked: "Woman, why weepest thou?"

Mary responded: "Because they have taken away my Lord, and I know not where they have laid him."

Mark 16:9 Proving to be one of the most powerful female instruments of the Lord in the meridian of time, Mary Magdalene had been assailed by seven evil spirits or devils (see also Luke 8:2).

Joseph Smith once commented on encounters he had experienced with evil spirits and said: "The nearer a person approaches the Lord, a greater power will be manifested by the adversary to prevent the accomplishment of His purposes" (Whitney, *Life of Heber C. Kimball,* 132). Frightful evidence of that truth occurred eighteen hundred years after the time of Mary Magdalene when two members of the Quorum of the

Twelve Apostles, Heber C. Kimball and Orson Hyde, were laboring in Preston, England. About to initiate tremendous success in that land, they were attacked by a host of devils (see account in commentary on Matthew 8:28–34).

"TOUCH ME NOT" (NEAR JERUSALEM)

John 20:14–17 Mary turned around and saw Jesus, but through her tears she did not recognize him, and when asked who she was looking for, she replied to that man she supposed was the gardener:

"Sir, if thou have borne him hence, tell me where thou hast laid him, and I will take him away."

Jesus spoke her name: "Mary."

Then she recognized him: "Rabboni" (Master).

Mary instantly desired to embrace him, but his first embrace was reserved for his Father—then mortals.

"*Hold* me not," he gently explained to her, "for I am not yet ascended to my Father: but go to my brethren, and say unto them, I ascend unto my Father, and your Father; and to my God, and your God" (JST John 20:17).

There would now be a respectful separation between immortals and mortals. Jesus taught: He is first my Father and God, then your Father and God. And Jesus himself was now more than mortal friend and associate in the divine work; he was Savior, Lord, and God to those brethren and sisters and to all humankind.

If, as the Savior indicated, he had not yet ascended to his Father, where had he been? The answer is more gloriously and plainly presented in Doctrine and Covenants 138 than anywhere else in scripture. The Lord Jesus Christ had not yet ascended to the home of his Father but had gone only to the spirit world, which is the place of all spirit beings and living things occupying the very same space as this physical Earth. He had organized in the world of spirits, among the billions of the Father's children who had lived from the days of Adam and Eve until his own day, that same missionary effort that he had organized on earth during his mortal ministry. "And there he preached to them the everlasting gospel, the doctrine of the resurrection and the redemption of mankind from the fall, and from individual sins on condition of repentance" (D&C 138:19).

Jesus taught those in the spirit world that all the consequences of the fall of Adam and Eve were now resolved through His great atonement, or redemption. Adam's fall had brought all children of the Father into a fallen condition that could be remedied only by yielding to the enticings of the Holy Spirit and putting off the natural man and becoming a Saint through the atonement of Christ, by submitting humbly and patiently to all trials and ordeals which the Lord would see fit to inflict upon them (Mosiah 3:19).

Jesus further taught those in the spirit world, just as he taught in the mortal world, that the eternal law of justice could be satisfied by the law of mercy, put into effect by God himself—taking upon himself all of our sins on condition of sincere repentance.

Jesus described how two deaths, physical and spiritual, both dire consequences of the Fall, were now overcome through his atonement: physical death (separation of the spirit from the body, which would have been forever) was now resolved completely for all of the Father's children who come to this and all other earths through the resurrection provided by the Savior. Someone might ask: "'Did Jesus have to suffer and die on any other worlds to redeem them, as he did on this earth?' The answer, based on the provisions of Alma 11 . . . can only be 'No.' The fact that he was born, died and resurrected on this earth—these being one-time events—demonstrates that he had never done these things elsewhere, or he would not have been able to do them here. And having done them on this earth, he cannot repeat them anywhere else. We see how unique our own world is in the universe.

The Atonement and the Resurrection

This earth is called God's footstool (D&C 38:17). On this earth Jesus Christ obtained his only physical body, and on this earth he was resurrected with that same body, and on this earth he will stand again and reign in his body throughout eternity (see D&C 130:9)" (Matthews, *Behold the Messiah*, 283).

The great monster, death, has no more effect on us. "There is a resurrection, therefore the grave hath no victory, and the sting of death is swallowed up in Christ" (Mosiah 16:8). In the end, only death will die. All living things (things with a spirit) will live forever. Why is the resurrection of the body so important to each of us? The Prophet Joseph Smith taught: "We came to this earth that we might have a body and present it pure before God in the celestial kingdom. The great principle of happiness consists in having a body" (*Teachings of the Prophet Joseph Smith*, 181). Robert J. Matthews adds: "The resurrection of our individual bodies is important because our Heavenly Father has a resurrected body of flesh and bone (see D&C 130:22), as has our Heavenly Mother. It would be possible to continue in eternity as spirit bodies without the physical body, but as such we could not reach the fulness of salvation. A spirit body without a resurrected physical body cannot obtain a fulness of joy (see D&C 93:33–34)" (*Behold the Messiah*, 280).

The other consequence of the Fall, spiritual death (separation of every child of God from his presence), has likewise been totally overcome by taking every soul back into God's presence. Since by the fall of Adam every child of the Father is taken out of his presence for a time of trial and testing, the atonement of Christ completely resolves that consequence by taking everyone back into his presence (2 Nephi 2:10; 9:22, 38; Alma 11:41, 44; 42:23; Mormon 9:12–14; Helaman 14:15–17). At that point the Savior will have done his part; then it will be up to each of us whether we are privileged to remain with the Father and the Son or if we will have to be escorted out of their presence, for "no unclean thing can dwell with God" (1 Nephi 10:21). If we have not cleansed ourselves through continuous repentance, strengthened ourselves through obedience to all commandments and ordinances and consecration to all celestial laws, and filled ourselves with light and truth in order to dwell in everlasting glory, we will not be able to (and will not even want to) remain and live with the Gods and with the millions in process of becoming Gods.

The Savior has done everything necessary to reverse the otherwise negative effects of the Fall, and through the Atonement he has made it possible for all who will to return and resume life with our Father, enjoying his style of life, eternal life, forever. They have done their part; now it is up to us. We are determining our eternal destiny by how we are living each day on earth. Jesus made it possible for us to live forever. All of us, without exception, will live forever. We are currently in the process of determining *where* and *with whom* we will live forever.

WOMEN MEET JESUS (NEAR JERUSALEM)

Matthew 28:9–10 The elect women, chosen to be the first to see the miracle of the Savior's resurrection, even before the priesthood leaders, rushed to tell the Brethren that they had personally met and talked with him, and touched his feet (the same feet showing the wounds of crucifixion), and worshipped him.

"One may wonder," Elder James E. Talmage wrote, "why Jesus had forbidden Mary Magdalene to touch Him, and then, so soon after, had permitted other women to hold Him by the feet as they bowed in reverence. We may assume that Mary's emotional approach had been prompted more by a feeling of personal yet holy affection than by an impulse of devotional worship such as the other women evinced. Though the resurrected Christ manifested the same friendly and intimate regard as He had shown in the mortal state toward those with whom He had been closely associated, He was no longer one of them in the literal sense. There was about Him a divine dignity that forbade close personal familiarity" (*Jesus the Christ*, 633–34).

One of the main messages for the Brethren was to leave Jerusalem, journey the hundred miles down to Galilee, and there, in that less threatening, more peaceful setting, they would see him and receive further instructions.

DISCIPLES TOLD BUT DISBELIEVE (NEAR JERUSALEM)

Mark 16:10-11; Luke 24:9-11; John 20:18 Mary Magdalene told the eleven apostles and other disciples what she had seen and heard, testifying that she had seen the Lord. Jesus' mother, Mary, and Joanna, and the other women likewise described the visitation of the angels and their witness that the Lord had risen from the dead and that they, the women, had seen Jesus and touched his resurrected body. The words of the women "seemed to them as idle tales, and they believed them not" (Luke 24:11).

OFFICIALS BRIBE SOLDIERS (NEAR JERUSALEM)

Matthew 28:11-15 Some of the Roman soldiers fled their guard duty at the now empty tomb and hurried to the chief priests (to whom the soldiers had apparently been made responsible by Roman authorities) to relate all that had happened. The Jewish leaders gave them considerable bribe money to report that Jesus' followers had come by night, while the guards slept, and stolen the body. That was a particularly bad lie, for if they were asleep (which was a capital offense for a Roman soldier), how would they know that it was his disciples who came and stole the body?

The Jewish leaders assured the soldiers that if this matter came to the attention of the governor Pilate, they would stand up for them and secure them.

The Roman soldiers took the money and did as they were told. Matthew reported years later that this was one of the most common explanations for the end of Jesus still in circulation.

JESUS APPEARS TO TWO DISCIPLES (ON THE ROAD TO AND AT EMMAUS)

Mark 16:12; Luke 24:13–32 Only Luke narrates and Mark briefly mentions a postresurrection appearance of Jesus to two disciples walking along the road from Jerusalem down to Emmaus. There are three possible locations of this Judean village: Emmaus Colonia, about three and a half miles northwest of Jerusalem; Qubeiba, about three miles northwest of Colonia; and Emmaus Nicopolis, about twenty miles northwest of Jerusalem at the edge of the Aijalon Valley.

Three score furlongs, or sixty stadia, is what Luke 24:13 says, although some early manuscripts indicate the distance was one hundred sixty stadia. If the figure of one hundred sixty stadia is correct, then Emmaus Nicopolis could be the site intended. It is the only one of the three candidates attested in historical records; many references to it are preserved through apocryphal writings and the works of Flavius Josephus during the Hellenistic and Roman periods.

On the other hand, twenty miles is a considerable distance for the two disciples to walk to Emmaus and return to Jerusalem all in one afternoon and evening. That memorable resurrection day had already been full of events: Early in the morning, women had discovered that Jesus' tomb was empty and had circulated the shocking news. Other disciples had

The Atonement and the Resurrection

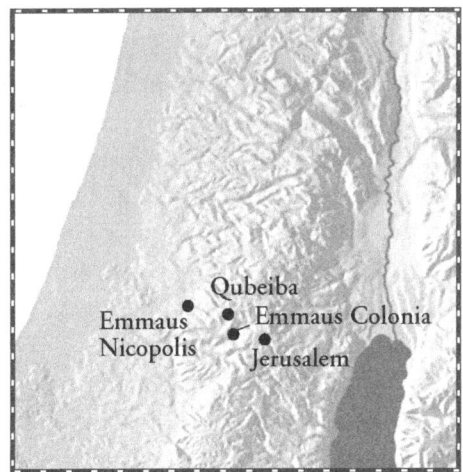

Possible locations of Emmaus

gone to verify the report. Later that day these two disciples had begun their walk to Emmaus and encountered Jesus along the way, who apparently talked with them at length: "Beginning at Moses and all the prophets, he expounded unto them in all the scriptures the things concerning himself" (Luke 24:27).

They approached the village in the evening when the "day [was] far spent" (v. 29). They prepared a meal and sat down to eat, and as he broke bread, they recognized who he was. He disappeared when they recognized him, and they "rose up the same hour, and returned to Jerusalem, and found the eleven gathered together, and them that were with them" (v. 33).

With the day "far spent," it is unlikely that the disciples, as excited as they would have been, would rush out the door to begin a twenty-mile, six- to seven-hour return trip up to Jerusalem and at the end of the journey still find disciples gathered in a meeting. A more likely candidate for New Testament Emmaus may be Emmaus Colonia, situated one to two hours' walking distance west of Jerusalem, at today's suburb of Motza.

Why would the two disciples not have recognized Jesus

right from the beginning of their walk together? They would have been quite familiar with his appearance, his mannerisms, and his way of teaching. But Mark notes that "he appeared in another form" (16:12). As a resurrected being Jesus was certainly in "another form," a condition with which no one on earth (except the women that morning) was yet acquainted. Besides that, Luke points out that "their eyes were holden that they should not know him" (v. 16)—the recognition was withheld for a time so that the resurrected Lord could teach them and help them come to an understanding.

We also learn from this experience that the resurrected Savior has the ability to appear as a normal man (or at least to cause others to see him that way). The disciples saw no radiance or brilliance about his person that would indicate someone other than a mortal.

Luke 24:19–24 The two disciples rehearsed the events of the previous three days with this "stranger in Jerusalem," who surprisingly seemed to know nothing of these momentous events (v. 18). They testified of their belief that Jesus of Nazareth was a mighty prophet, but "we trusted that it had been he which should have redeemed Israel" (v. 21). They did not yet understand. (Whether their reference to Israel's redemption was in a political or a spiritual sense is not clear; compare Acts 1:6.)

The two disciples explained what the women had earlier reported about seeing angels and hearing those angels declare that Jesus was alive.

Luke 24:25–26 Jesus then chastised these disciples, as he would chastise the apostles and others later (Mark 16:14), for being hard of heart and slow to believe the eyewitness testimony of their peers and all that the prophets and he himself had taught them about the Messiah and his mission.

"Ought not Christ to have suffered these things, and to enter into his glory?" (v. 26). Was it so difficult to comprehend that Jesus' crown of thorns had to come before his crown of glory? The prophets—the Messiah's forerunners—

The Atonement and the Resurrection

had plainly testified over the course of four millennia that the Messiah (who would eventually rule and reign at his second coming to earth) would come first to suffer, bleed, and die.

Luke 24:27 "And beginning at Moses and *all the prophets,* he expounded unto them *in all the scriptures* the things concerning himself" (v. 27; emphasis added; cf. 3 Nephi 23:14). Moses was assigned to write about the Creator, the same who would be the Redeemer, and his work from the very beginning of this earth, so while the three were walking along for miles, Jesus laid out in plainness the many foreshadowings and direct prophecies of his life, ministry, and atoning sacrifice, right from the beginning: "And many signs, and wonders, and types, and shadows showed he unto them, concerning his coming; and also holy prophets spake unto them concerning his coming" (Mosiah 3:15). "Yea, and even all the prophets who have prophesied ever since the world began—have they not spoken more or less concerning these things?" (Mosiah 13:33). As Peter later declared on the Jerusalem Temple grounds: "These things, which God before had shewed by the mouth of all his prophets, that Christ should suffer, he hath so fulfilled" (Acts 3:18).

Jesus may have reminded the disciples, for example, of Lehi's teaching that Adam and Eve "fell that men might be . . . and the Messiah cometh in the fulness of time, that he may redeem the children of men from the fall" (2 Nephi 2:25–26). He may have recalled for them the testimony of Enoch: "Behold, Enoch saw the day of the coming of the Son of Man, even in the flesh; and his soul rejoiced, saying: The Righteous is lifted up, and the Lamb is slain from the foundation of the world" (Moses 7:47). Jesus may have described Abraham's heart-wrenching test, how he showed obedience in being willing to sacrifice his beloved son Isaac, "which is a similitude of God and his Only Begotten Son" (Jacob 4:5).

Jesus undoubtedly cited the teachings of the Jews' great mentor, Moses, showing how the great deliverer and lawgiver was a type of the greatest Deliverer and Lawgiver: "Did he

[Moses] not bear record that the Son of God should come? And as he lifted up the brazen serpent in the wilderness, even so shall he be lifted up who should come" (Helaman 8:14). Besides the serpent raised on a pole, Moses taught Israel about the Passover lamb, the manna from heaven, water from the rock, blood of the covenant, atonement sacrifices for the people, sacrificial offerings of blemishless animals, and firstborn who were hallowed for divine service—all of which were types and shadows of the coming Suffering Servant, the Messiah.

Jesus may have reviewed with the disciples during their scripture study while walking together that Sunday afternoon the inspired, prophetic declarations of the psalmists: "My God, my God, why hast thou forsaken me?" (Psalm 22:1); "they pierced my hands and my feet" (Psalm 22:16); "he keepeth all his bones: not one of them is broken" (Psalm 34:20); "in my thirst they gave me vinegar to drink" (Psalm 69:21); and "the stone which the builders refused is become the head stone of the corner" (Psalm 118:22).

Jesus may have helped them recollect the words of the great messianic prophet Isaiah: "I gave my back to the smiters" (Isaiah 50:6); "he hath borne our griefs, and carried our sorrows" (Isaiah 53:4; Mosiah 14:4); "he was wounded for our transgressions, he was bruised for our iniquities" (Isaiah 53:5; Mosiah 14:5); "he was oppressed and he was afflicted, . . . he was cut off out of the land of the living: for the transgression of my people was he stricken" (Isaiah 53:7–8; Mosiah 14:7–8); "and he bore the sin of many, and made intercession for the transgressors" (Isaiah 53:12; Mosiah 14:12).

Jesus may have called up a host of prophets to witness of every detail of his life: that the Messiah would come forth out of Bethlehem (Micah 5:2); that the Son would be called back up out of Egypt (Hosea 11:1); that the King of the Jews would come to them in a lowly way, riding upon an ass (Zechariah 9:9); that he would be sold for thirty pieces of silver (Zechariah 11:13); that he would be wounded in the house of his friends (Zechariah 13:6); and that the Messiah would be cut off (Daniel 9:26).

The Savior might even have taught them from the powerful teachings of prophets on the other side of the world, of whom they had no record. Lehi had helped those who looked forward to the Redeemer to understand that "redemption cometh in and through the Holy Messiah" and he helped them comprehend "the merits, and mercy, and grace of the Holy Messiah, who layeth down his life according to the flesh, and taketh it again by the power of the Spirit" (2 Nephi 2:6, 8). Lehi's son, Nephi, gave one of the strongest and plainest testimonies ever: "My soul delighteth in proving unto my people the truth of the coming of Christ; . . . all things which have been given of God from the beginning of the world, unto man, are the typifying of him. . . . and my soul delighteth in proving unto my people that save Christ should come all men must perish. . . . the Messiah cometh in six hundred years from the time that my father left Jerusalem; and . . . his name shall be Jesus Christ, the Son of God. . . . we talk of Christ, we rejoice in Christ, we preach of Christ, we prophesy of Christ . . . that our children may know to what source they may look for a remission of their sins" (2 Nephi 11:4, 6; 25:19, 26).

So on and on, mile after mile, the minds of the two disciples were opened to understand the foreshadowings and prophecies concerning Jesus Christ—what he would say and what he would do. Why was it so important to understand all that? Why such emphasis on one Person's words and works? The latter-day prophet Joseph Smith was once asked, "What are the fundamental principles of your religion?" He answered: "The fundamental principles of our religion are the testimony of the Apostles and Prophets, concerning Jesus Christ, that He died, was buried, and rose again the third day, and ascended into heaven; and all other things which pertain to our religion are only appendages to it" (*Teachings of the Prophet Joseph Smith,* 121).

There is no knowledge in all the world as important as knowledge of the Savior and his Father and the Spirit and their plan of happiness, which is the plan of salvation, for salvation comes only in and through the Holy Messiah (2 Nephi 2:6–8).

Luke 24:28–32 As they approached Emmaus it looked as though Jesus would continue on the road, but the disciples pleaded with him, because it was getting late in the afternoon, to come in and eat with them. As they were eating, Jesus took some unleavened bread (it was still Passover week) and broke it, blessed it, and handed them some. Their spiritual eyes were opened, and they realized who he was. He disappeared in that instant, leaving them reflecting on the singularity of their feelings: "Did not our heart burn within us, while he talked with us by the way, and while he opened to us the scriptures?" (v. 32; cf. 3 Nephi 11:3) Perhaps they saw the wounded hands as he handed them the unleavened bread. They knew! The Spirit of God, the Holy Ghost, burns like a fire within all spiritually minded disciples, especially while the scriptures are opened to their understanding.

This appearance of the risen Lord is the subject of one of our great latter-day hymns, "Abide with Me; 'Tis Eventide" (*Hymns,* 1985, no. 165):

> Abide with me; 'tis eventide.
> The day is past and gone;
> The shadows of the evening fall;
> The night is coming on.
> Within my heart a welcome guest,
> Within my home abide.
>
> *Chorus:*
> O Savior, stay this night with me.
> Behold, 'tis eventide.
> O Savior, stay this night with me.
> Behold, 'tis eventide.
>
> Abide with me; 'tis eventide.
> Thy walk today with me

Has made my heart within me burn,
As I communed with thee.
Thy earnest words have filled my soul
And kept me near thy side.

Many are the lessons to be gleaned from the experience of the disciples on the road to Emmaus. First, sadness, when wallowed in, can sometimes prevent even good people from seeing the obvious. Second, like the ancient disciples, when we modern disciples are "slow of heart to believe all that the prophets have spoken," we, too, are foolish. Third, Moses and all the prophets in the Old Testament had the witness of the Messiah as their ultimate message. In fact, as Jesus shows us by his method of scriptural explanation to the two disciples, the Old Testament truly was and is the human family's first witness of Jesus Christ. Fourth, just as the Savior used the scriptures to teach of his divinity, so should we. Fifth, Jesus used just the right teaching method that fit the circumstances and created the setting that suited his instructive purposes. He did not attempt to deceive the disciples, but he did use their lack of recognition to draw out of them the information he needed to best teach them. This approach serves as an example for all teachers. Sixth, Jesus kept his identity hidden from the disciples in order to demonstrate the nature of a resurrected body.

TWO TELL OTHERS, WHO DISBELIEVE (AT JERUSALEM)

Mark 16:13; Luke 24:33–35 Cleopas and his companion rushed back up to Jerusalem to report to the eleven apostles and others gathered together (Luke 24:33; although Luke mentions "the eleven," we learn later, in John 20:19–29, that only ten of the apostles were there; Thomas, for some reason, was absent on that occasion). They excitedly described what had just happened to them in the preceding hours—how Jesus had walked and talked with them, opening the scriptures to their understanding, and how they realized who he was. Meanwhile the apostles and others confirmed to the two the report of Jesus' appearance to Peter (Luke 24:34; see also 1 Corinthians 15:5).

EVENING: JESUS APPEARS TO DISCIPLES (AT JERUSALEM)

Mark 16:14; Luke 24:36–49; John 20:19-23 Sometime later that same evening (on that first day of the week, Sunday, Resurrection day) the group of ten apostles and other disciples were gathered behind locked doors, fearful of what had already happened, and of what they knew the Jewish leaders could still attempt to do. If this is the same gathering noted in Mark 16:14, they were eating a late evening meal. Jesus suddenly appeared in the room (not coming in through the door, showing that physical walls are no obstacle for a resurrected being). The Savior greeted them with *shalom aleichem*, which is Hebrew/Aramaic: "Peace be unto you."

The disciples were startled and afraid, supposing that some spirit had joined them, but Jesus calmed their anxiety and satisfied their curiosity by inviting them to become acquainted with a resurrected body: "Behold my hands and my feet, that it is I myself: handle me, and see; for a spirit hath not flesh and bones, as ye see me have" (Luke 24:39). He extended his hands and his feet for them to touch, just as he would do for his disciples in the western hemisphere: "Come forth unto me, that ye may thrust your hands into my side, and also that ye may feel the prints of the nails in my hands and in my feet" (3 Nephi 11:14).

Tad R. Callister explained about the effects of Jesus' physical wounds: "In his resurrected state, Jesus retained the prints of nails in his hands and feet as a special manifestation to the world. Such marks, however, are only temporary. After all have confessed that he is the Christ, his resurrected body will, like

The Atonement and the Resurrection

those of all mankind, be restored to its 'proper and perfect frame' (Alma 40:23)" (*Encyclopedia of Mormonism*, 2:734; see also Smith, *Gospel Doctrine*, 23).

The Lord wanted his still-mortal friends to know that an immortal body is corporeal; the flesh is real and physical—though now in a more refined and perfected condition. It was important for them to see and feel, to be eyewitnesses with an unequivocal testimony of the nature of the body of the resurrected Lord, because for many generations thereafter—from ancient through modern times—some would corrupt and distort the reality of physical resurrection and question the corporeality of Jesus' postmortal body.

The disciples "yet believed not for joy" (Luke 24:41). They were so happy they could hardly believe what was happening, and they continued marveling, trying to figure out how a resurrected body works.

Jesus offered a practical illustration: they brought food, a piece of broiled fish and a honeycomb, and he ate before them. They learned that a resurrected body can still consume and digest mortal food. (Fish, interestingly, became a symbol later of Christianity and is still commonly used as a Christian symbol. The symbolism derives, in part, from the first letters of the Greek words *Iesous Christos, theou hyios soter* [Jesus Christ, Son of God, Savior], which form the acronym ICHTHYS, which means "fish" in Greek.)

As he satisfied their curiosity and fascination with his immortal body, he also chastised the apostles for their hardness of heart in refusing to believe the women who had already seen him earlier in the day (Mark 16:14). Then he taught the whole group, as he had taught the two on the road to Emmaus, how all the foreshadowings and prophecies concerning him must be fulfilled, those from the Torah (the law of Moses), from the prophets' writings, and from the Psalms (the Old Testament book most often quoted in the New Testament). (See examples in commentary on Luke 24:27.) They knew the scriptures, but this time it was different. This time "opened he their understanding, that they might understand the scriptures" (Luke 24:45). Again he testified to them that as it was written, so it was necessary for the Messiah "to suffer, and to rise from the dead the third day" (v. 46; cf. Isaiah 53:5; Mosiah 3:10). Now they would realize how often he had taught them those very truths (Matthew 16:21; 20:17–19; Mark 8:31; 10:32–34; Luke 9:22; 18:31–34).

Why was all this teaching, suffering, dying, and rising from the dead necessary? "That repentance and remission of sins should be preached in his name among all nations [in all this mortal world and in all the spirit world], beginning at Jerusalem" (Luke 24:47). At Jerusalem the suffering, dying, and rising were consummated, and from Jerusalem the glad tidings of repentance and remission of sins—the most basic and essential message of the gospel of Jesus Christ—would go forth to the Father's children in all the world.

As the climax to this unforgettable scene, Jesus declared to the group of Saints that they now had a weighty responsibility: "Ye are witnesses of these things" (Luke 24:48). He admonished them, in essence, that through them as eyewitnesses, they who had a solid, incontrovertible knowledge of those truths, through them the glorious message must go out to all, beginning at Jerusalem, then through Judea, Samaria, and to the uttermost part of the earth (see Acts 1:8).

John 20:21–22 Having been commissioned to carry their knowledge and testimonies from Jerusalem to the uttermost part of the earth, Jesus knew these leaders in the kingdom needed a gift and power to accompany them, to be their constant companion. "As my Father hath sent me, even so send I you. And when he had said this, he breathed on them, and saith unto them, Receive ye the Holy Ghost." So they had the gift of the Holy Ghost bestowed on them under Jesus' hands, though the enjoyment of the gift was delayed until the day of Pentecost, some seven weeks later (Acts 2; see Appendix 6, 765). They had the immediate companionship of one member of the Godhead, the Son of God himself, during his postresurrection ministry of forty days (five to six weeks). When the resurrected Savior finally departed after his forty-day ministry, then, on the tenth day (fifty days after Passover, on the day of Pentecost) that empowering gift of the Spirit would come over them in an extraordinary way.

Luke 24:49 Again, Jesus assured his disciples that the "promise of the Father," the gift of the Holy Ghost, would come upon them, but they were to remain in the city of Jerusalem until they were endowed with that heavenly power (Acts 1:4–5, 8; cf. D&C 38:32). A holy endowment was to come to them with and through the gift of the Holy Ghost. "The endowment was to prepare the disciples for their missions unto the world" (Smith, *Teachings of the Prophet Joseph Smith,* 274). Similarly, in the latter days the Lord commanded the Saints to "build a house, in the which house I design to endow those whom I have chosen with power from on high; for this is the promise of the Father unto you; therefore I command you to tarry, even as mine apostles at Jerusalem" (D&C 95:8–9).

THOMAS, ABSENT, DOES NOT BELIEVE (AT JERUSALEM)

John 20:24–25 Thomas was also called Didymus, but to refer to the apostle as "Thomas Didymus" is redundant, as the two names mean exactly the same thing, "twin," in Aramaic and Greek. He was not present when the Lord appeared to the other ten, and when he heard their exclamation that they had seen the Lord, he insisted: "Except I shall see in his hands the print of the nails, and put my finger into the print of the nails, and thrust my hand into his side, I will not believe." Thomas desired the same privilege that the other Brethren and the women had received; and an eyewitness he, too, had to be.

EIGHT DAYS LATER: WITH THOMAS (AT JERUSALEM)

John 20:26–29 A week later, on Sunday (which was now the new Sabbath, the day of worship, "the Lord's day"; Revelation 1:10), the Church leaders were meeting again, and Thomas was also present. The Savior appeared and invited him to do exactly as he had desired: to touch with his finger the prints of the nails and thrust his hand into Jesus' side (cf. 3 Nephi 11:14) and not to doubt but to believe. He told Thomas, "Because thou hast seen me, thou hast believed: blessed are they that have not seen, and yet have believed." Being convinced by eyesight is good, but better and more lasting is to be convinced by the Spirit through faith. In worldly matters, as we say, seeing is believing, but in the realm of sacred, spiritual truth, the opposite is true: believing is seeing. "Faith is not to have a perfect knowledge of things; therefore if ye have faith ye hope for things which are not seen, which are true" (Alma 32:21). Then, upon showing our faith for a time, eventually we will see how true all these things are with our very own eyes.

PURPOSE OF JOHN'S GOSPEL

John 20:30–31 John pauses to explain that the resurrected Lord said and did many other things beyond what is written in this record of John's testimony (see John 21:25; D&C 93:6), but what is written has been preserved to witness that Jesus is truly the promised Messiah, the Son of God, and that our having faith in him can lead us to eternal life (see also 1 John 5:13; Mormon 5:14).

At this point we likewise pause to ponder the unprecedented nature and meaning of these three days of the greatest week in the history of the world. Nothing had ever happened, or ever would happen, that could compare in grandeur and scope with the events between the Garden of Gethsemane and the Garden of the Resurrection, events that affect the mortal and immortal life of every soul to come to this world and all the other worlds of our Father in Heaven.

This is not a "womb to tomb" story. "[Jesus'] Death on Calvary was no more the ending, than the Birth in Bethlehem was the beginning, of that Divine Career" (Whitney, *Saturday Night Thoughts,* 152).

Elder Howard W. Hunter proclaimed that "the doctrine of the Resurrection is the single most fundamental and crucial doctrine in the Christian religion. It cannot be overemphasized, nor can it be disregarded. Without the Resurrection, the gospel of Jesus Christ becomes a litany of wise sayings and seemingly unexplainable miracles—but sayings and miracles with no ultimate triumph. No, the ultimate triumph is in the ultimate miracle: for the first time in the history of mankind, one who was dead raised himself into living immortality" (Conference Report, April 1986, 18).

Thanks to Jesus, who died and raised his body to immortality, we can die and be raised to live forever also. One of our colleagues at Brigham Young University had a little daughter who died at age thirteen. When she was seven, already struggling with the disease that would eventually take her life, she stood one day in testimony meeting to bear witness to these beautiful truths: "I love Jesus Christ. Because of him, I only have to die once. I'll never have to die again."

Bible scholars recognize the pivotal importance and far-reaching consequences of the resurrection of the Lord Jesus Christ. "Were it not for the resurrection event," wrote F. F. Bruce, "there would have been no resurrection faith" (*New Testament History,* 206). The followers of Jesus would not live and die for a lie. Something dramatic and true had changed their lives forever. The truth is, none of the early leaders and preachers in the first-century Church could say enough about the resurrection. It was on the lips of Peter, Stephen, Paul, and all others everywhere they went and with everyone they taught.

Another prominent scholar declared: "Whether we are comfortable with it or not, Christianity does indeed stand or fall on certain historical facts—not merely historical claims, but historical facts. Among these facts that are most crucial to Christian faith is that of Jesus' resurrection from the dead. The Christian faith is not mere faith in faith—ours or someone else's—but rather, a belief about the significance of certain historical events" (Witherington, *New Testament History*, 166).

"We have to ask, Why is there no other first-century Jew who has millions of followers today? Why isn't there a John the Baptist movement? Why, of all first-century figures, including the Roman emperors, is Jesus still worshipped today, while the others have crumbled into the dust of history?

"It's because this Jesus—the historical Jesus—is also the living Lord. That's why. It's because he's still around, while the others are long gone" (Ben Witherington, as quoted in Strobel, *Case for Christ*, 141).

The resurrection transformed the lives of the early Saints and the lives of all true Saints since that day. The day following the Crucifixion and burial of Jesus was the holy Sabbath, the day the Saints met to worship. But that Saturday must have been a Saturday of deepest depression. Who would have wanted to hold a meeting? And who would have been willing to give a talk? And talk about what? It must have been a most oppressive time for the spirit of those early members of the Church. But that depressing day was followed, the very next morning, by a Sunday of most brilliant joy.

This single historical fact and doctrine forever changed the course of the ancient Church and the course of the world. There is no fact in history that is so widely attested and confirmed by credible witnesses. Besides the appearances already recounted, the scriptures relate the visits of the risen Lord with members of the Twelve in Galilee (John 21) and with more than five hundred brethren (1 Corinthians 15:6), as well as with James (1 Corinthians 15:7). For five to six weeks (forty days) after the Resurrection, Jesus met with and taught the apostles and others and then said farewell from the Mount of Olives, near Bethany (Luke 24:50–51; Acts 1:3–11). He appeared to Paul (1 Corinthians 9:1; 15:8) and again to John (Revelation 1:9–18). He also visited personally with thousands of righteous descendants of Lehi (3 Nephi 11:1–18:39), including choosing another Quorum of Twelve Apostles in the western hemisphere (3 Nephi 27:1–28:12), and went on to the lost tribes of Israel (3 Nephi 16:1–4; 17:4).

Centuries later the resurrected Christ appeared to Mormon and to Moroni (Mormon 1:15; Ether 12:39). In the last days he has appeared to Joseph Smith (Joseph Smith–History 1:14–20) and to others. Following is a list of latter-day witnesses of the resurrected Christ, along with the documentation of their accounts of seeing the Savior: Martin Harris (1827), *Personal Writings of Joseph Smith*, 13; Oliver Cowdery (1829), *Personal Writings of Joseph Smith*, 14; Newel Knight (1830), *History of the Church*, 1:85; Lyman Wight (1831), *Church History in the Fulness of Times*, 100; Orson F. Whitney (1876), *Best Loved Stories of the LDS People*, 216–17; Heber J. Grant (1883), *Best Loved Stories of the LDS People*, 261; John Taylor (before 1888), *Ensign*, May 1978, 48; Lorenzo Snow (1898), *Best Loved Stories of the LDS People*, 239–40; George Q. Cannon (before 1902), Flake, *Prophets and Apostles of the Last Dispensation*, 184; George F. Richards (1906), Tate, *LeGrand Richards: Beloved Apostle*, 47; Joseph F. Smith (1918), Doctrine and Covenants 138:18; David O. McKay (1921), McKay, *Cherished Experiences*, 102; LeGrand Richards (1926), Tate, *LeGrand Richards: Beloved Apostle*, 137; David B. Haight (1989), *Ensign*, November 1989, 60. (We thank Gary Ford for helping to prepare this list.)

Elder Melvin J. Ballard had the following remarkable experience with the Savior:

"Away on the Fort Peck Reservation where I was doing missionary work with some of our brethren, . . . I found myself one evening in the dreams of the night in that sacred building, the temple. After a season of prayer and rejoicing I was informed that I should have the privilege of entering into one of those rooms, to meet a glorious Personage, and, as I entered the door, I saw, seated on a raised platform, the most glorious Being my eyes have ever beheld or that I ever conceived existed in all the eternal worlds. As I approached to be introduced, he arose and stepped toward me with extended arms, and he smiled as he softly spoke my name. If I shall live to be a million years old, I shall never forget that smile. He took me into his arms and kissed me, pressed me to his bosom, and blessed me, until the marrow of my bones seemed to melt! When he had finished, I fell at his feet, and, as I bathed them with my tears and kisses, I saw the prints of the nails in the feet of the Redeemer of the world. The feeling that I had in the presence of him who hath all things in his hands, to have his love, his affection, and his blessing was such that if I ever can receive that of which I had but a foretaste, I would give all that I am, all that I ever hope to be, to feel what I then felt! . . . I see Jesus now not upon the cross. I do not see his brow pierced with thorns nor his hands torn with the nails, but I see him smiling, with extended arms, saying to us all: 'Come unto me!'" (*Sermons and Missionary Services*, 156–57).

PETER: "I GO A FISHING" (AT THE SEA OF GALILEE)

John 21:1–19 One of the resurrected Lord's first instructions had been for the Brethren to gather in Galilee, there to receive further direction about how to carry forth the kingdom in succeeding generations. The leaders gathered probably somewhere on the north or northwest shore of the Sea of Tiberias (see commentary on John 6:1), which was the location of Jesus' home during much of his mortal ministry.

Seven of the apostles were there awaiting the Savior's arrival: Simon Peter, Thomas called Didymus, Nathanael of Cana, the sons of Zebedee (James and John; Matthew 4:21), and two others. They followed Peter, James, and John, who were skilled fishermen, and launched out onto the lake. During the night of fishing they caught nothing.

The Atonement and the Resurrection

The next morning they saw a man on the shore who called out to them, asking if they had any food. When they replied no, he told them to cast the net on the right side of the ship. They did so and found that they could not draw the net back in because it was so heavy with fish. That aroused memories in the apostles. This same scene had been played out before (Luke 5:4–11). John said to Peter, "It is the Lord," and Peter, who was half naked, impulsively threw on his fisher's coat and dived into the water, heading for shore. Norbert Duckwitz explains that the Greek term translated "naked" means "without an outer garment; the adjective traditionally means *lightly clad* and Peter would be wearing a loincloth as the modesty of Jewish sensibilities demands" (*Reading the Gospel of St John in Greek,* 176; cf. Isaiah 20:2, where that prophet is instructed by the Lord to walk naked and barefoot for three years as a sign to the people. "It is probable that Isaiah removed only his upper garment, which would have made only the upper portion of his body bare"; Parry, Parry, and Peterson, citing Keil and Delitzsch, *Understanding Isaiah,* 185).

The other disciples, working about three hundred feet off shore, dragged the net full of fish to the shore. Peter helped them draw it in, and upon count they discovered the net contained a total of 153 big fish, and the net was surprisingly unbroken.

As the disciples in the boat approached shore they noticed a fire of coals and fish cooking, along with some bread. Jesus invited them to come and eat. He prepared and gave them food to eat. Meanwhile, John notes, no one dared ask Jesus who he was, for they knew him (though they were still marveling over this Man they were well acquainted with who was now resurrected). John also notes that this was the third time Jesus had shown himself to the apostles (v. 14), giving them time and experience to come to an understanding of resurrection and to put all his teachings in a much wider and eternal perspective (especially the ordinance work for the dead that they would now begin, after Jesus' recent organization of the work in the spirit world; D&C 138).

John 21:15–17 Apparently right in front of the other apostles Jesus asked Peter a direct and personal question: "Simon, son of Jonas, lovest thou me more than these?" We understand the question, though we wonder what "these" represents. Was the Savior asking Peter if he loved him more than these other Brethren? or more than the fish they had been catching? ("these" perhaps standing for temporal occupations and things). In a sense the Lord is asking each of us the same question: Do we love him more than "these"? Each of us has to define what "these" represents in our lives.

Peter had said, "Though all men shall be offended because of thee, yet will I never be offended" (Matthew 26:33), but then he had denied his acquaintance with Jesus three times. Once again he had opportunity to recommit himself—after three denials, three avowals.

Three times Jesus asked Peter if he loved him, and with the apostle's insistent "yea, Lord; thou knowest that I love thee," came the pointed directive, "Feed my lambs"; "Feed my sheep." The Greek verb translated in English as "feed" actually means "to shepherd, to tend, to take care of." In the Hebrew translation the verb means "to lead." The great Shepherd was calling on the chief apostle to serve as the shepherd of the Lord's sheep through the tribulations of the coming decades. The fisherman was now to be a shepherd; his presidency and responsibility mandated a permanent refocus of his life's work.

And so with all of us. We have the same mandate: Go out and shepherd (tend, take care of) the sheep. And those who have wandered off—help bring them back. President Ezra Taft Benson testified: "We realize, as in times past, that some of the sheep will rebel and are 'as a wild flock which fleeth from the shepherd.' (Book of Mormon, Mosiah 8:21.) But most of our problems stem from lack of loving and attentive shepherding. . . .

"With a shepherd's loving care, many of our young people, our young lambs, would not be wandering. And if they were, the crook of the shepherd's staff, a loving arm, would retrieve them.

"With a shepherd's care, many of those who are now independent of the flock can still be reclaimed" (*Come unto Christ*, 65).

John 21:18–19 The Savior continued his personal instructions to Peter. The apostle's death by crucifixion was prefigured, as the Savior in essence said to Peter, When you were young, you prepared yourself and went wherever you wanted, but when you are old, your arms will be stretched out and someone else will prepare you and carry you to a place you will not want to go. Nevertheless, Jesus charged his close associate and friend, "Follow me." Indeed, Peter would follow Jesus; in his ministry during the next three decades, Peter would follow his Master's example in teaching, leading, healing, even raising the dead, and then eventually he would follow Him in the manner of his death (see Peter's witness of what lay ahead for him; 2 Peter 1:14).

PETER INQUIRES ABOUT JOHN (AT THE SEA OF GALILEE)

John 21:20–22 Peter asked Jesus what was to become of "the disciple whom Jesus loved" (see commentary on John 13:23–30). That "the disciple whom Jesus loved" is John himself is more obvious in this passage than possibly any other, not only because he is described as the one who leaned on Jesus' breast at the sacred supper and asked who would betray him but because Jesus went on to identify the beloved disciple as the one who would tarry (that is, be translated) and continue living until the Second Coming (D&C 7:1, 3). He is the one who wrote this testimony, the Gospel of John (John 21:24).

THE FOUR GOSPELS

TESTIMONY ABOUT JOHN (AT THE SEA OF GALILEE)

John 21:23–25 The word spread: John the Beloved was not going to die a mortal death but would continue to live as a translated being in the mortal sphere until the Lord returned to reign during the Millennium (Matthew 16:28). The condition of translated beings, not merely transfigured for a specific occasion, but changed to live on with the mortal body for an indefinite period, is described further in 3 Nephi 28:6–9ff.; see also commentary on Matthew 17:1–13. Doctrine and Covenants 7 contains our most detailed account of the conversation between the Savior and John and Peter (a "record made on parchment by John and hidden up by himself"; D&C 7 headnote).

This same John prepared this account of Jesus' ministry, his testimony of these world-changing events, and some later writer(s) editorialized, "We know that his testimony is true" (v. 24).

"And," added John or the compiler/editor, "there are also many other things which Jesus did, the which, if they should be written every one, I suppose that even the world itself could not contain the books that should be written" (v. 25; cf. John 20:30). That is a hyperbolic way of saying that the Gospel writers did not or could not include the hundredth part (cf. 3 Nephi 26:6), or even the thousandth part, of all that the mortal Messiah said and did during his three-year ministry.

THE GREAT COMMISSION TO THE TWELVE (ON A MOUNTAIN OF GALILEE)

Matthew 28:16–20; Mark 16:15–18; cf. Mormon 9:22–24 Another postresurrection appearance of Jesus may have occurred on Mount Arbel, a high point overlooking the whole Sea of Galilee region where much of his teaching ministry had been accomplished. Mount Arbel, rising up dramatically immediately west of Magdala, has a grand panorama from Mount Hermon in the northeast to the volcanic cones of the Golan, to the canyon cutting through the Decapolis, around to Mount Tabor in the southwest, and directly behind to the Horns of Hittin, an extinct volcano looming up on the west. There, on the secluded edge of the twelve-hundred-foot precipice, Jesus could have inspired his leading disciples with their commission to take the gospel to all the world.

When Jesus' apostles saw him, they worshipped him, Matthew reported (28:17), "but some doubted," otherwise meaning that some *hesitated;* they were still piecing together this wonderful mystery of the resurrected Lord.

The Savior reminded them that all power had been given him in heaven and in earth (cf. 1 Nephi 19:6); therefore, they could go forth teaching the pure gospel, making real Christians of people, and baptizing them in the names of all three members of the Godhead: Father, Son, and Holy Ghost. Believing and being baptized meant they were on the way to salvation; refusing to believe and be baptized meant they were promoting their own damnation (Mark 16:16). Subsequent

The Sea of Galilee from Mount Arbel, showing the Plain of Gennesaret along the northwestern shore of the lake

to becoming members of the kingdom of God, they must be nourished by the good word of God (Moroni 6:4) and taught to keep all the commandments (Matthew 28:20). If they did that, the Lord promised, he would be with his faithful disciples always (cf. D&C 62:9), even unto the end of the world (on the Lord being with us, see commentary on Matthew 18:18–20).

By being faithful and having the Lord with us, certain signs or evidences of the divinity of the work would automatically follow.

Mark 16:17–18; cf. Mormon 9:22–25 In all dispensations of the gospel the promise of certain confirmatory proofs has been given, evidence that the name and true power of Jesus Christ are being used: casting out devils, speaking with new tongues (meaning miraculous ability to speak otherwise unknown languages), taking up serpents (being unaffected by the poisons of venomous snakes/serpents), drinking lethal liquids but not being harmed, and laying hands on the sick, administering to them, and healing them.

The Lord in our day adds: "In my name they shall open the eyes of the blind, and unstop the ears of the deaf; and the tongue of the dumb shall speak" (D&C 84:69–70). These miraculous signs, gifts, and powers are given by the Lord with a caution: Disciples who use them "shall not boast themselves of these things, neither speak them before the world; for these things are given unto you for your profit and for salvation" (D&C 84:73). These powers are not to be used for ostentatious harnessing of the wonders of heaven; they are private and sacred.

ASCENSION, PROCLAMATION (NEAR JERUSALEM, ON THE MOUNT OF OLIVES)

Mark 16:19–20; Luke 24:50–53 Back in the southern part of the land, Jesus led his closest followers out as far as to

The Atonement and the Resurrection

The Russian Orthodox Tower of Ascension marks the traditional site where Jesus ascended into heaven from the Mount of Olives

Bethany (Luke 24:50), on the eastern slope of the Mount of Olives (Acts 1:9–12), and there he blessed them. Afterward he ascended to heaven, to sit "on the right hand of God" (Mark 16:19; for discussion of the symbolic use of right and left, see commentary on Matthew 25:31–46), and the disciples returned with joy to Jerusalem to continue praising God in the Temple precincts. Luke's Testimony begins and ends at the Temple—with Zacharias and Elisabeth in the Temple, then Mary and Joseph in the Temple, and now in the end, the apostles and other disciples were continually in the Temple (Luke 24:53; Acts 2:46) and preaching about Jesus Christ everywhere they went, "the Lord working with them" (Mark 16:20). The Savior promised that he would not leave them helpless; he would not leave them comfortless: "I will come to you" (John 14:18). Indeed, he proclaimed, *"I will go before you"* (JST Matthew 6:26), and signs and evidences would confirm the authenticity and veracity that their words and their works were of Christ. His name in days of old was Immanuel, meaning "God with us." He is still the same God, and he is still working with his loyal disciples.

CONCLUSION

As we end this study of these four Testimonies of the Savior's life and mission, we also testify that he lived on earth two thousand years ago and performed the most difficult and selfless labor for all humankind. We also know that he lives today and forever, continuing his work on behalf of the Father's children everywhere, especially for those who love and live the commandments and spiritually become the children of Christ, his sons and daughters (Mosiah 5:7; D&C 25:1).

When all is said and done, there has never been nor ever will be anything so powerful, so majestic, so wondrous, so merciful as the atonement of Jesus Christ. There are no words capable of describing the infinite goodness and omnipotence of the Savior. As the apostle John testified, the time is coming for the followers of the Lord when "God shall wipe away all tears from their eyes; and there shall be no more death, neither sorrow, nor crying, neither shall there be any more pain: for the former things are passed away" (Revelation 21:4). The power by which all this is accomplished is the infinite atonement of Jesus Christ. The grace he extends to us is freely given, but it did not come free. Its cost was infinite, and yet he asks no price. All he wants from us is our loyalty, love, gratitude, and repentance.

The crucial question is, "What shall [we] do then with Jesus [who] is called Christ?" (Matthew 27:22). Upon learning these things, we all have a serious choice to make. We must decide how we will respond to Jesus' teachings. We will either ignore them (as many have), or spurn them (as the Pharisees and other leaders did), or pervert them (as many apostate groups and individuals have done), or learn them, love them, and live them (as many of the noble and great ones have done over the millennia). One way or another, we will all make a choice.

APPENDIX 1

MAPS

The Holy Land at the time of Jesus

Appendix 1

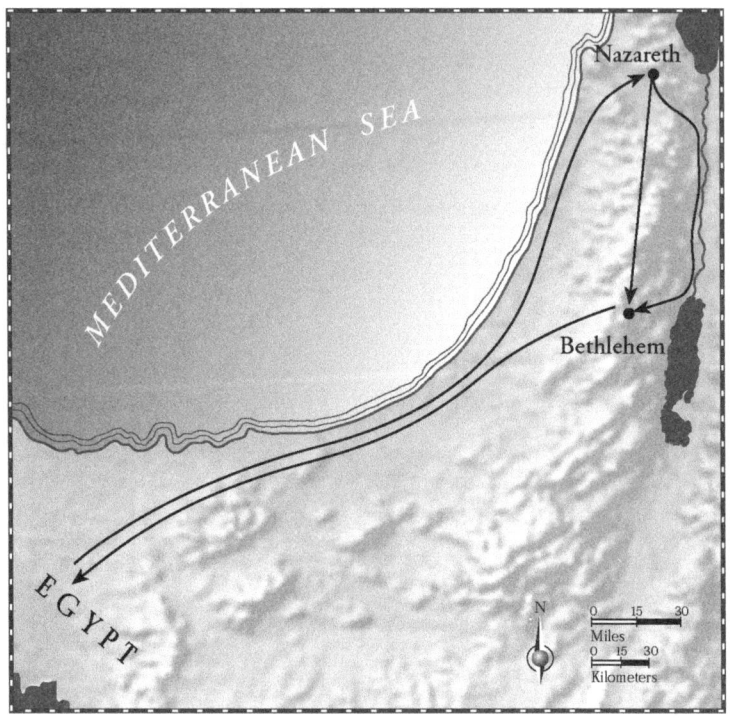

Journeys from Nazareth to Bethlehem, Bethlehem to Egypt, and Egypt to Nazareth

MAPS

The Galilean ministry

Appendix 1

New Testament Jerusalem

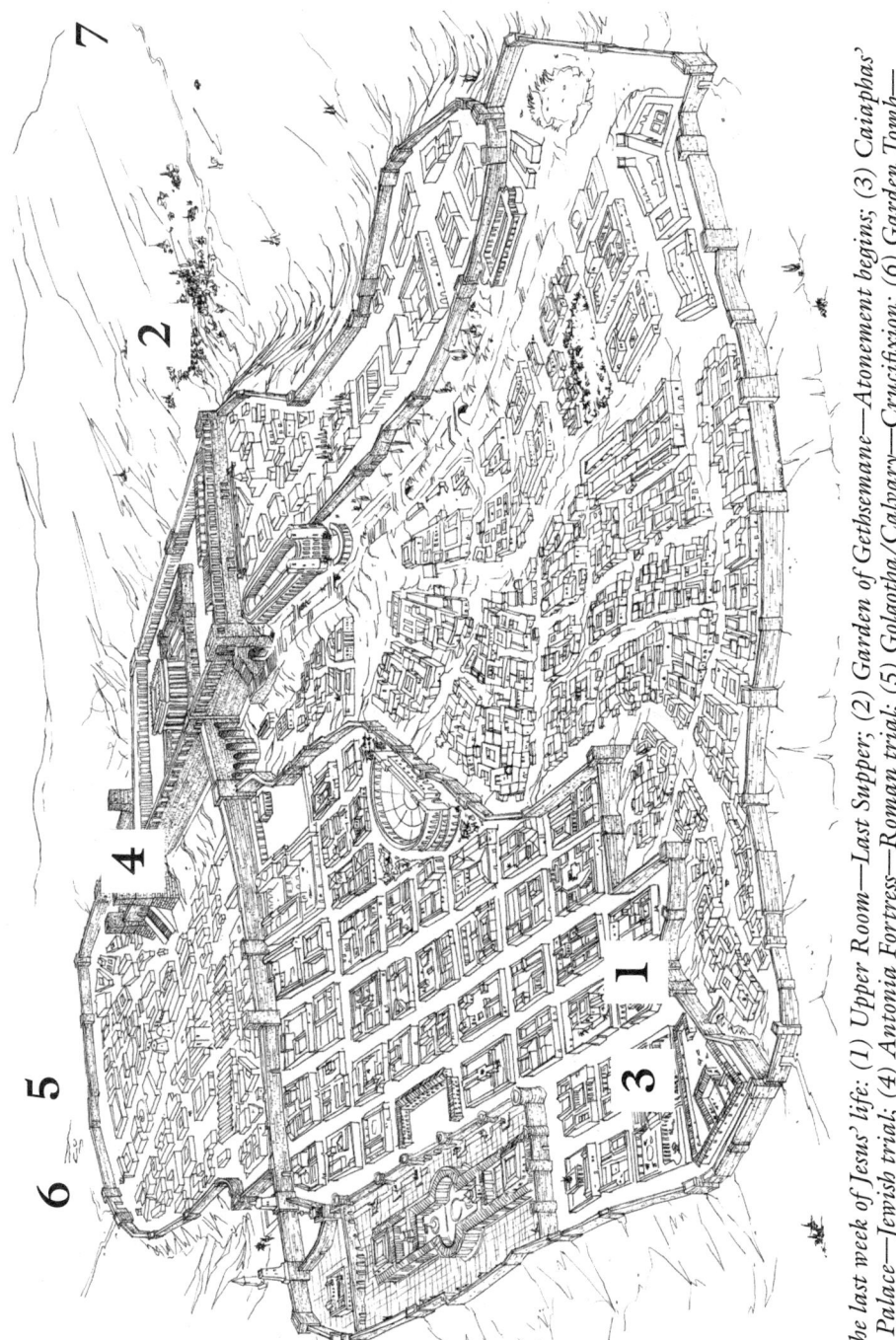

The last week of Jesus' life: (1) Upper Room—Last Supper; (2) Garden of Gethsemane—Atonement begins; (3) Caiaphas' Palace—Jewish trial; (4) Antonia Fortress—Roman trial; (5) Golgotha/Calvary—Crucifixion; (6) Garden Tomb—Resurrection; (7) Mount of Olives—Ascension

APPENDIX 1

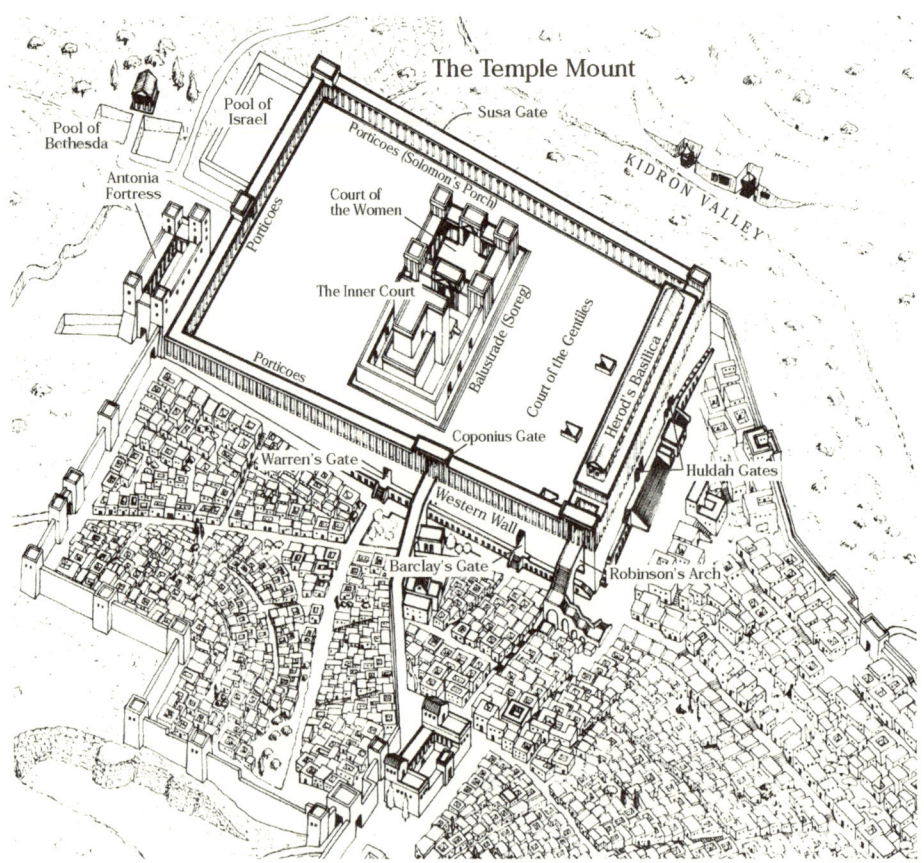

The Temple Mount

Maps

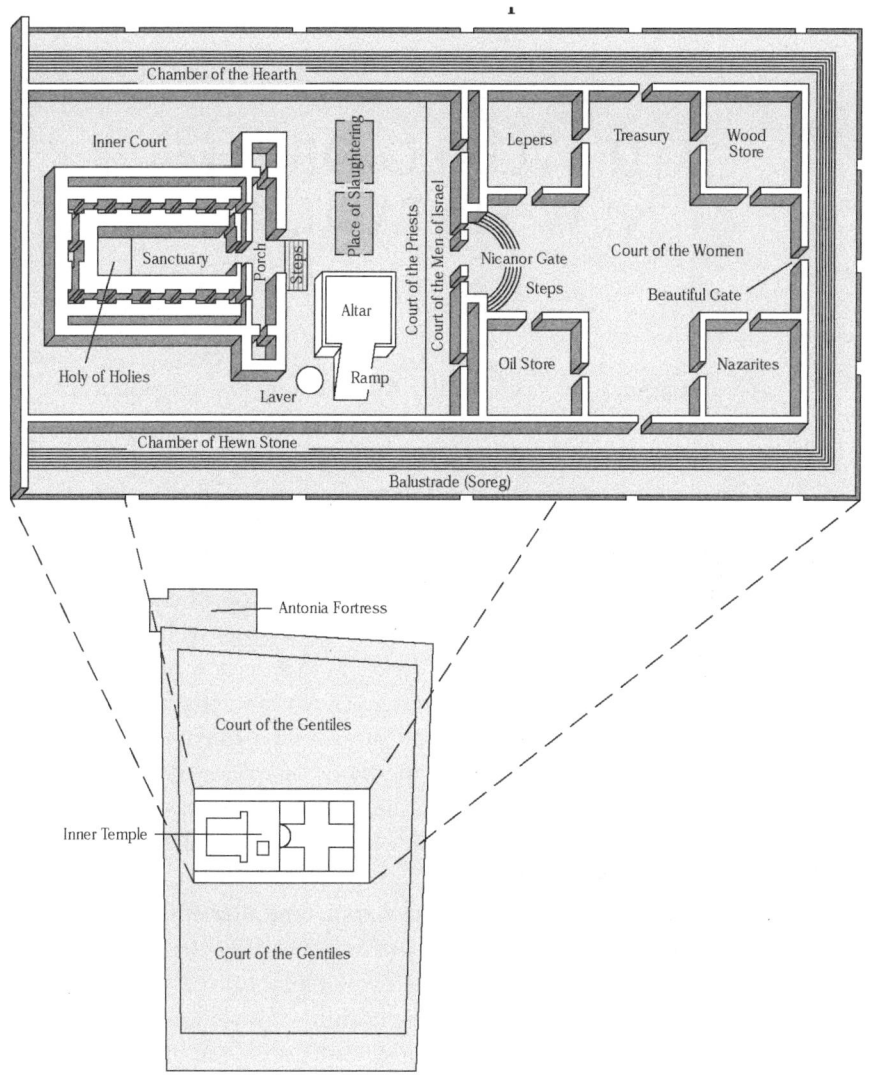

The Inner Temple

APPENDIX 2

THE WORLD OF THE NEW TESTAMENT

To understand the world of the New Testament—the political, social, and religious circumstances into which Jesus was born—we must go back several hundred years before the meridian of time. After Israel's return from the Babylonian Captivity (538 B.C.), life in the Holy Land was controlled by the Persian Empire, which allowed the inhabitants a fair degree of autonomy; however, many of the returnees and their descendants possessed a profound distrust of things Gentile. By this time, the Israelite inhabitants of Judea and Galilee were referred to as "Jews," though they were a mixture of several tribes with Judah predominating. They were obliged to obey a series of prophet-governors like Nehemiah who ruled in concert with the high priest of the Aaronic Priesthood in Jerusalem. But ultimately everyone owed allegiance to the Persian emperor.

In the fifth and fourth centuries before Christ, religious and political changes dramatically affected the course of Judaism. According to Jewish belief in Jesus' day, sometime after 400 B.C. biblical prophecy ceased. The Talmud declares that after the deaths of the last biblical prophets—Haggai, Zechariah, and Malachi—the Holy Spirit, including prophetic inspiration, departed from Israel (Sotah 48b; Sanhedrin 11a). Political authority seems to have devolved solely on the high priest; religious authority was shared between the high priest and learned men called scribes or sages. Thus, Jewish teaching advised, "From now on incline your ear and listen to the instructions of the Sages" (*Seder 'Olam Rabbah* 6, quoted in Talmon, *"Dead Sea Scrolls,"* 16). The belief in the cessation of prophets and prophecy was alive and well in Jesus' day, as attested in a comment made by the apostles to Jesus: "*And then said his disciples unto him, they* [Jewish leaders] *will say unto us, We ourselves are righteous, and need not that any man should teach us. God, we know, heard Moses and some of the prophets; but us he will not hear. And they will say, We have the law for our salvation, and that is sufficient for us*" (JST Matthew 7:14–15).

In 333 B.C., after two centuries of Persian domination, a new military power arose in the Near East. Alexander the Great, whose outnumbered troops defeated the Persians at the Battle of Issus, began creating a world empire that would stretch from Gibraltar in the west to the Punjab in India in the east. In 332 B.C. Alexander conquered Jerusalem, and Hellenistic (Greek-like) culture was brought to Judah by the very person who viewed himself as the great emissary of Greek ways. Having been tutored as a boy by Aristotle, Alexander believed his mission was to Hellenize the whole world.

Ten years later, after Alexander the Great died in 323 B.C., his empire was carved up by four of his commanders and their families, as prophesied in Daniel 7:2–7. The two most important were the Ptolemies, who ruled over Egypt-Judea, and the Seleucids, who ruled over Syria-Mesopotamia. These two dynasties fought incessantly over control of the Holy Land, though both were promoters of Hellenism. Finally in 198 B.C., at a place in the northern Galilee region called Panias, a showdown occurred. Seleucid forces under Antiochus III (the Great) soundly defeated the Ptolemaic army, and control of the Holy Land passed to the Seleucids. Panias was not only a great battlefield but was also known in New Testament times as the place where Peter made his great confession of Jesus as the Christ—called Caesarea Philippi in Matthew 16.

Antiochus III, the first Syrian ruler of Judea (the Greek rendering of *Judah*), granted the Jews many favors, and they were not slow to take advantage of them. A governing Council of Elders, called in Greek the *Gerousia* ("assembly"), was established to assume the general administrative, political, judicial, and social leadership of the Jewish community, under the direction of the high priest of the Aaronic Priesthood. This governing body later came to be known as the Sanhedrin (Greek, *synedrion*), a term translated in the King James New Testament as "the council" (Matthew 26:59; Acts 4:15); it was also referred to as the "senate of the children of Israel" (Acts 5:21). In New Testament times it was composed of seventy-one

Appendix 2

members, and, under Roman supervision, had tremendous decision-making powers. The Sanhedrin sometimes exercised those powers without balance or restraint, as in the case of the trial and execution of Jesus of Nazareth.

Under Antiochus III the pace of Hellenization was accelerated in Judea. This process brought two world views into conflict, and the battleground was Jerusalem. Jews began to coalesce into groups according to their disposition toward Greek cultural influences. As time passed the chasm widened between pro-Hellenistic Jews and anti-Hellenistic Jews. Among the members of the pro-Hellenistic party were aristocratic Jews, the Zadokim (or high priestly families, later called the Sadducees), those excited by Greek culture, and those favoring the political and economic status quo. The anti-Hellenists formed a group called the Hasidim, or Hasideans (Hebrew for "pious ones," though no relation to the modern Hasidic Jews). The ancient Hasidim seem to be the predecessors of the Pharisees; they were orthodox religionists and ardent supporters of God's laws as revealed in the Torah (1 Maccabees 2:42–43).

Points of conflict between Judaism and Hellenism were numerous and profound. Hellenism promoted art, appreciation of the human body (including sexuality), athletic competitions (performed without clothing), and philosophy. Torah-based Judaism was diametrically opposed. "To the Jews, art, in all its physical forms, was in conflict with the Second Commandment. Nude statuary as well as swimming and exercising in the nude or almost nude was offensive to the Jewish people, who in the course of several centuries, had built up rigid standards against displaying any part of the body except hands, feet, neck and head in public. . . . [Hellenistic] theatre presentations often treated sex in a mode offensive to Jewish sensitivity. Extra-marital relations were discussed or depicted on the stage without any punishment for the sin being presented; this violated the wishes of the Jews, who had insisted that punishment follow such acts. Jewish religion was based on revelation from God, through the prophets and patriarchs. Hellenistic culture substituted human reason, observation, and experience with other humans as the sources from which religion came, apart from any type of communication from divine beings" (Lyon, *Ensign*, September 1974, 20).

In 175 B.C. a new king in Syria enacted decrees that brought

Judaism to the brink of disaster. His name was Antiochus IV, and he determined not only to complete the process of Hellenization but eventually to wipe out the Jewish religion all together. A Greek-style gymnasium was constructed in Jerusalem, and Jews were encouraged to dress after the Greek fashion. An intertestamental text (part of the Apocrypha) entitled First Maccabees describes the situation:

"In those days certain renegades came out from Israel and misled many, saying, 'Let us go and make a covenant with the Gentiles around us, for since we separated from them many disasters have come upon us.' This proposal pleased them, and some of the people eagerly went to the king, who authorized them to observe the ordinances of the Gentiles. So they built a gymnasium in Jerusalem, according to Gentile custom, and removed the marks of circumcision, and abandoned the holy covenant. They joined with the Gentiles and sold themselves to do evil" (1 Maccabees 1:11–15).

The gymnasium (Greek, *gymnos,* "naked") changed the whole spiritual and social atmosphere of Jerusalem. It was a place where athletes ran around naked. Because of this, certain Jews—in their zeal to conform to Hellenism—sought to remove the marks of circumcision (the great symbol for the Jews of the Abrahamic covenant), just as the author of 1 Maccabees indicates. The gymnasium began to rival the Temple as the center of cultural activity and religious-like devotion. The gymnasium was under the patronage of the Greek gods Hermes (Mercury) and Hercules, and its Jewish patrons seem to have wanted to imitate those gods more than their own Jehovah.

Orthodox Jews, especially the Hasidim, or Pious Ones, were outraged at the spread of this virulent and aggressive Hellenism. The split between the two segments of the population widened until fighting broke out in Jerusalem between the pro-Hellenist and pro-Torah parties.

In 168 B.C. Antiochus IV set about to destroy every distinctive feature of the Jewish faith. Forbidden upon penalty of death were the offering of all Jewish sacrifices, the observance of all Sabbaths and feast days, and the practice of circumcision. Books of the Torah were desecrated or destroyed. Jews were forced to eat swine flesh and perform sacrifices at idolatrous altars set up throughout the land. To crown his despicable actions, Antiochus IV desecrated the

Appendix 2

Temple by erecting an altar to the Greek god Zeus (perhaps molded in the image of Antiochus himself) on the altar of burnt offering within the Temple court (1 Maccabees 1:41–61). Antiochus claimed that Zeus had manifested himself to the Syrian king, and thus he referred to himself as *Epiphanes,* Greek for "God manifest" (2 Maccabees 4:7). His enemies, however, now applied the epithet and pun, *Epimanes,* Greek for "madman."

Naturally, many orthodox Jews chose to die rather than be defiled by the Syrian sacrilege or forced to profane the covenant (1 Maccabees 1:62–63). Many fled Jerusalem and crowded into towns, where they were pursued by royal agents intent on erasing the Jewish faith.

Open revolt against the Syrian depredations began in Modi'in, a village about twenty miles northwest of Jerusalem where a priest named Mattathias, of the house of Hasmon (the Hasmoneans) lived with his five sons (1 Maccabees 2:1–6). They fled into the mountains, were joined by many zealous Jews, including the Hasidim (1 Maccabees 2:23–43), organized an army, "struck down [the] sinners," and "rescued the law out of the hands of the Gentiles and kings, and they never let the sinner gain the upper hand" (1 Maccabees 2:44, 48).

After the death of Mattathias, the struggle was carried on by three of his sons in turn, Judas (166–160 B.C.) surnamed Maccabeus ("the Hammerer"), Jonathan (160–143 B.C.), and Simon (142–134 B.C.). Success followed success in their campaigns against Syrian forces through guerrilla tactics. After Judas's fourth victory near Beth-Zur, south of Jerusalem, the freedom fighters occupied the Temple Mount. On the 25th of Kislev (December), 165 B.C., the very day on which it had been desecrated three years before (1 Maccabees 4:54), the Temple in Jerusalem was cleansed and rededicated under the leadership of Judas, and true worship was restored (1 Maccabees 4:36–59; 2 Maccabees 10:1–7). This event has been commemorated ever since as the wintertime "feast of the dedication" (John 10:22), the Festival of Lights, or Hanukkah.

The Hasmonean dynasty controlled political and religious life in Judea for the next one hundred years (165–63 B.C.). In 141 B.C. a bronze plaque was set up in the Temple courtyard in Jerusalem, celebrating Jerusalem's deliverance from the Syrian Greeks and conferring upon Simon the office of high priest as a hereditary possession. Under the Hasmoneans an independent Jewish state emerged in which the offices of political king and high priest were vested in a single person.

Out of the Hasmonean, or Maccabean, period also emerged the major Jewish sects that occupy so prominent a place in the New Testament. The Pharisees, as already indicated, seem to have evolved from the Hasidim. Their name, from the Hebrew *parash*, means "separatists," either in the sense of resisting Hellenism, or, more likely, in separating themselves from the people through strict adherence to a set of ritual purification observances. Hence, the Pharisees were often antagonistic toward Jesus on the basis of disagreement over such things as Sabbath observance (picking food and healing the sick on that day), cleanliness laws (eating with unwashed hands), their emphasis on the fast, lawful divorce, and on tithing little things but neglecting ethical matters. The Pharisees claimed the right to rule all the Jews by virtue of their possessing the "Oral Torah" of Moses, that is, the body of traditions revealed to Moses alongside what came to be known as the written Torah, or Pentateuch.

The Sadducees seem to have evolved from elements of the pro-Hellenists in Judea, and they identified themselves or even legitimized themselves by taking their name from Zadok, the high priest of the Temple in Jerusalem in the time of Solomon. The Zadokite family of high priests had served at the head of the priesthood throughout the First Temple period as well as during Second Temple times until the Hasmoneans took control of the high priesthood. Ezekiel 44:9–16 had assigned the priestly duties exclusively to the Zadokite clan. The Sadducees rejected the "Oral Torah," which the Pharisees considered to be law.

Another influential group encountered by Jesus and his disciples was the scribes. Though it has been argued that they came from the ranks of both the Pharisees and Sadducees, those from the Pharisees predominated. They studied, copied, and interpreted scripture. Scribes could even render authoritative judgments according to the Torah and occupied important seats in the Sanhedrin. They were not, strictly speaking, a party or sect within Judaism but, rather, legal and religious specialists. Their prominence in the New Testament

Appendix 2

narrative makes them very significant, however, and they are undoubtedly related in some way to another group encountered in first-century Judaism—the rabbis. The term *rabbi* is an honorific title (Hebrew, meaning "my master" or "my great one") and was bestowed according to one's knowledge of Jewish law and lore as well as teaching reputation. Though the term, as some modern scholars contend, may not have been applied as an official (academic) title until after the destruction of the Second Temple by the Romans in A.D. 70, it seems to have been very much used in at least unofficial ways by the time of Herod the Great. The disciples called Jesus "rabbi" (Matthew 26:25, 49; Mark 9:5; 11:21; 14:45).

Resistance to Jesus and his message may be traced in part to the beliefs and attitudes of some of the leading scribes of this period. They increasingly discounted the very principle Jesus preached and the one by which they themselves could have known that he was the Messiah—revelation. In a remarkable passage, the Babylonian Talmud (the collected wisdom of the Pharisaic scribes and sages through the centuries) illustrates the superiority of tradition over revelation in a fanciful story of an argument between two great and learned rabbis. After calling forth many impressive and unmistakable signs regarding the correctness of a particular idea, one of the rabbis was finally able to call forth a voice from heaven declaring the truth of his position (in other words, the voice of direct revelation). At this, the other rabbi arose and said, "The Torah declares concerning itself, 'It is not up in heaven'; that is to say, once the Torah was given on Mount Sinai, we pay no heed to heavenly voices but, as the Torah ordains further, we follow the opinion of the majority" (Steinberg, *Basic Judaism*, 68–69).

Though not mentioned in the Bible but certainly encountered by Jesus were the Essenes, a sect described by contemporary historians. It is probable they originated from different elements of the same Hasidim which gave rise to the Pharisees. Some of the Essenes reacted to the corrupting influences of Hellenism by withdrawing from Jerusalem in the second century before Christ and establishing a semimonastic community on the shores of the Dead Sea at a place now called Qumran. There the Essene settlement existed on and off from about 150 B.C. until A.D. 68, when the Roman armies swept through the land during the First Jewish War. Realizing that their sacred writings were endangered, they hid their scrolls in at least eleven nearby caves.

The discovery of the Dead Sea Scrolls beginning in 1947 has provided an extraordinary window of insight into the religious climate that produced both "normative," or Pharasaic, Judaism and Christianity—the only two of more than twenty Jewish groups to survive the destruction of Jerusalem and the Temple in A.D. 70. Among the hundreds of texts as well as thousands of parchment fragments and far fewer rolled-up scrolls, archaeologists have found samples of every book of the Old Testament except Esther, apocryphal and pseudepigraphical works, community rule books, scriptural commentaries, and prayer texts. The value of the Qumran finds is at least twofold: first, we now have actual scriptures dating from the time of Jesus—the kind his contemporaries actually used (whereas before 1947 the oldest Old Testament texts dated only to the ninth or tenth century after Christ); second, we now know that some of the doctrines Jesus taught were almost certainly intended as a direct counter to ideas current in Judaism of that period. For example, some of the sacred texts at Qumran teach that no one had the right to worship the Lord unless a *minyan* (quorum) of ten men was gathered in the company of a Levitical priest. Also, the Essenes at Qumran taught that they were to love their own kind but hate their enemies. Jesus unmistakably contradicted both notions with true doctrine (Matthew 18:19–20; 5:43–44).

Great changes came once again to the Holy Land in 63 B.C. when the Roman general Pompey marched his troops into Jerusalem and proclaimed the Jews subject to the authority of Rome. Though the independent Hasmonean Jewish state came to an end, Hellenism did not. It was simply adopted, adapted, and promoted by new Gentile masters of the entire Mediterranean (including Jewish) world. The Jews were allowed to retain some territories as semiautonomous political districts, including Judea, Perea, the eastern part of Idumea, and Galilee. But the Samaritans became independent. In short, Roman overlordship seemed to the Jews to be immediately very harsh on the once-autonomous Jewish state. In 52 B.C., for example, thirty thousand Jews of the district of Tarichae, on the western shore of the Sea of Galilee, were enslaved.

To give the appearance of independence, however, the Romans

Appendix 2

eventually entrusted the political administration of Jewish territory to a man named Antipater. He was the son of a rich man from Idumea, a region that had been forcibly converted to Judaism in the days of the Hasmonean ruler John Hyrcanus I (134–104 B.C.). Hyrcanus became king and high priest after his father, Simon the Hasmonean (ruled 142–134 B.C.), was murdered.

Antipater's political career began under the tutelage of his father as governor of Idumea. His own power base was greatly strengthened when he sided with Julius Caesar in the latter's struggle for control of the Roman Republic against his associate in the First Triumvirate, General Pompey. By 47 B.C. Antipater was solidly in control of Judea, and he gave his sons Phasael and Herod (the future Herod the Great) the tasks of governing Jerusalem and Galilee, respectively.

Though Caesar was assassinated at Rome in 44 B.C., Antipater and his sons held onto the reins of power for a time. But in 43 B.C. Antipater was murdered by one of his opponents, and Herod was left to avenge his father's death as well as suppress unrest in Galilee and Judea. Galilee was known for its brigands and rebels, and Herod moved against them swiftly. In 42 B.C. he, together with his brother, was appointed ruler over all the land. Unfortunately, a short time later the Parthians invaded, forcing Herod to flee south. He stopped at Masada to find security for his entourage before going on to Rome to seek help. When Herod returned to his native land in the winter of 39 B.C., he had Rome's full support, having been appointed king de jure by Mark Antony and Octavian, who eventually gained sole control of the Republic and transformed it into the Empire. Beginning in Galilee Herod consolidated his strength and in 37 B.C. became de facto king of the Jews with the capture of Jerusalem. By 20 B.C. his kingdom included all of the Holy Land west of the Jordan River and even some of Transjordan. In that year the Roman emperor Augustus met personally with Herod to transfer various areas to Herod's control. Herod continued to maintain tight control over the entire region until his death just after the birth of Jesus Christ.

Throughout his reign Herod encountered fierce opposition for several reasons. First, most Jews hated subjugation by a foreign power, and Herod personified that power. He was a Roman puppet.

The Pharisees, who wielded significant influence with the common people, had refused to swear an oath of loyalty to the Roman emperor. Hence they looked upon Herod with disdain.

Second, Herod was not just harsh in his rule but ruthless and downright cruel. The list of those he executed in order to maintain power and assuage his raging paranoia is staggering. It includes rabbinic students; two leading rabbis of Jerusalem; his sister's husband; his wife's grandfather; his Hasmonean wife, Mariamne; his mother-in-law; two sons by Mariamne; another son; and not least, the children in and around Bethlehem two years of age and under (Matthew 2:16). As his own death approached, Herod devised a monstrous outrage. He gathered the most eminent men of every town in the whole of Judea, locked them in the Hippodrome, and gave orders that as soon as he died the soldiers were to be turned loose and slaughter all. The reason? He said he knew there would be no mourning over his passing, but he could ensure there would be mourning at the time of his passing (Josephus, *War* [Loeb] I.659–60).

The third reason Herod was disliked and encountered opposition was rooted in his origins. The Pharisees and Essenes refused to recognize an Idumean as king of the Jewish people, in large measure because Idumeans had been forced to convert to Judaism by the Hasmonean John Hyrcanus (died 104 B.C.). Their "Jewishness" was questionable. Therefore many Jews suspected Herod's religious sincerity. Herod had good reason to be looking over his shoulder constantly; he prevented massive uprisings against his regime through cruelty, intimidation, and manipulation. He was especially hated in Galilee, as were the Romans.

Immediately after Herod's death, popular outbreaks occurred in virtually every quarter of the land. These included demands for tax reductions, for relief from economic and political oppression, and for religious reform. The most significant revolt came from Galilee, the longtime hotbed of revolutionary activity—where one Judas, son of Hezekiah, raised an army to attack the royal arsenal at Sepphoris and sought to become king. At this point Varus, governor of Syria, entered Judea with two Roman legions and four regiments of cavalry to crush the revolt. Galilee was the first region to be subdued

Appendix 2

as the city of Sepphoris was captured, burnt, and its people enslaved. The rest of the country was soon brought under control.

Caesar Augustus divided the country among Herod's sons; they were each to oversee much smaller districts than their father had ruled, and they "ruled" at the pleasure of an overall governor appointed by Rome in A.D. 6. Archelaus inherited Samaria, Judea, and Idumea in 4 B.C. but was deposed and banished to Gaul in the ninth year of his rule (A.D. 6) because of his tyrannical cruelty. Herod Philip inherited the northern parts of the land and stayed in power from 4 B.C. to A.D. 34. Herod Antipas governed Galilee and Perea from 4 B.C. to A.D. 39, all during the years of Jesus' life. As the Gospels indicate, Antipas remained Jesus' nemesis to the very end.

A number of Jesus' parables (see, for example, Matthew 20:1–15; Mark 12:1–11; Luke 15:11–32; 16:1–12, 19–31) give us tremendous insight into the social and economic conditions of the Holy Land during the years of his ministry. The main characters are rich men or large landowners. On the basis of evidence from the Mishnah and archaeology, it has been argued that single ownership of large tracts of land increased markedly during the first century after Christ. More and more farmers were forced to sell their land as a result of sickness, drought, and exorbitant taxes. Whole villages sometimes came to be owned by one person. Farmers and their sons became day-workers. This situation was nowhere more keenly felt than in Galilee, where agriculture was always the mainstay of existence. It seems clear from the New Testament that in this period there was tremendous debt, many beggars, and numerous slaves; the situation of the people was very bad (Josephus, *War* [Loeb], IV.508).

Jewish resistance to Roman domination was extremely complex, but it seems clear that Galilee was a critical focal point of this resistance from 4 B.C. to A.D. 66. In fact, Josephus traces the origins of the Zealot movement in A.D. 6 to Saddok the Pharisee and Judas the Galilean, a man from Gamla. They called for armed revolt, saying that the heavy tax assessments they endured amounted to slavery and that only God was master of the Jewish people (Josephus, *Antiquities* [Loeb], XVIII.4–5, 23; *War* [Loeb], II.433). Thus, Jesus was probably suspected of Zealot activity by political officials, both Roman and Jewish. He was, after all, from Galilee, spent most of his time there during the very period when the Zealot movement emerged, and associated with one known Zealot within the ranks of his closest followers (Simon Zelotes). As one scholar notes: "Jesus can hardly have been a Zealot. However, it is quite conceivable that the Roman authorities and the Sadducees, who were sympathetic to them, saw it as such, given his Galilean background, above all because in recent decades Galilee had been regarded as a cradle of rebel movements" (Jagersma, *History of Israel,* 127).

Things went from bad to worse in the first century as banditry and resistance to Roman domination spread through Galilee and Judea. A series of corrupt and incompetent Roman prefects and procurators (governors) exacerbated conditions. In 27 B.C. Caesar Augustus had divided the thirty-two provinces of the empire into two categories: senatorial and imperial. The eleven senatorial provinces were governed under the supervision of the Senate, while the twenty-one imperial provinces were under the direct control of the emperor. The senatorial provinces were, on the whole, the older, richer, and more peaceful territories where there was little danger of an uprising. Imperial provinces were usually newer frontier areas, recently added to the empire, containing many revolutionary elements, seething and ready to explode. Such territories were kept under the direct surveillance of the emperor himself.

Imperial provinces were of two types. Larger ones were governed by a legate who served as both military governor and chief magistrate. Smaller imperial provinces were ruled by a governor who bore the title of *praefectus*. From the time of Emperor Claudius (ruled A.D. 41–54) on, however, it became customary to call such a governor by the title of *procurator Augusti,* or simply procurator. Judea was such a province, and its governors resided in an official residence at Caesarea by the sea. They were accustomed to go up to Jerusalem at feasts and festival times and sometimes to winter there.

The most famous governor of Judea was Pontius Pilate (ruled A.D. 26–36), whose administration was depicted by contemporary writers as harsh and corrupt. An inscription found at Caesarea calls him "Praefect of Judea," though later Jewish and Roman historians, such as Josephus and Tacitus, refer to him as procurator since that is the designation for governor that had become current in their day.

Appendix 2

Throughout the New Testament, Pilate and his successors are designated by the general term "governor." Aside from his role in the crucifixion of the Savior, Pilate was widely disliked by his subjects, the Jews, and he was finally removed from office and sent to Rome to answer charges of brutality and incompetence.

This brief examination of the events and undercurrents in New Testament times illustrates two ironic and competing forces in Jesus' day. On the one hand, there was a manifest desire for the arrival of a foretold Messiah to deliver Israel from poverty, foreign domination, and oppression, and establish an enduring kingdom of justice under divine power. On the other hand, there was a constant movement afoot to reject the true Messiah in the person of Jesus of Nazareth because certain leaders could not, or would not, recognize Jesus' infinite messianic power. History confirms the truth of a statement by President J. Reuben Clark that the Holy Land at the time of the Savior's birth was the "habitation of some of the most terrible passions that were loose in the world" (*Behold the Lamb of God,* 18).

APPENDIX 3

THE TEMPLE AT THE TIME OF JESUS

No single place in all the world was holier to Jews and to Christians at the time of Jesus than Jerusalem's Temple Mount. It was known as *Har Habayit*, the "Mountain of the House [of God]," and no mountain on earth has such a unique history. To this most sacred parcel of ground the God of all creation came to converse with his servants, the prophets and priests. "The Temple was the approach of a Nation to their God," wrote George Adam Smith (*Jerusalem*, 2:522). And Jesus said, "In this place is one greater than the temple" (Matthew 12:6). There is evidence in word and in deed that Jesus considered the Temple to be the legitimate sanctuary of the true God. At one point he called it "my Father's house" (John 2:16); later he called it "my house" (Matthew 21:13).

Jesus' life from beginning to end was bound up with the Temple. An angel of the Lord had appeared to Zacharias in the Holy Place, announcing the birth of the prophet who would prepare the way for the Messiah (Luke 1:5–22). When Mary had fulfilled the forty-day ritual of purification after giving birth, Jesus was taken to the Temple in Jerusalem for the ceremonial redemption of the firstborn. There the aged Temple worker Simeon looked upon the promised Messiah in the flesh (Luke 2:22–32). At age twelve, Jesus was found "in the temple, sitting in the midst of the doctors, *and they were hearing him, and asking him* questions" (JST Luke 2:46).

We wonder what kinds of ordinance work were performed in Herod's Temple. We do know that although the Temple was under the control of wicked persons, there were righteous Temple workers, such as Zacharias, Simeon, and Anna. The only clarifying scriptural passage on this subject is Doctrine and Covenants 124:38–39. President Joseph Fielding Smith and Elder Bruce R. McConkie

Appendix 3

suggested that Peter, James, and John received their endowment on the Mount of Transfiguration (see commentary on Matthew 17:1–13; such sacred ordinances would not have been available in the Temple at Jerusalem, which operated without the Melchizedek Priesthood, although it may be instructive to compare Luke 24:49 with D&C 95:8–9). Baptisms for the dead, at least, could be performed after the Savior's preparation for such work in the spirit world (D&C 138) and after his resurrection. Truman Madsen wrote: "There is some evidence, in addition to the statement in 1 Corinthians 15:29, that proxy baptism for the dead was practiced among and by early Christians. Indeed, in the iconography, in the typology, and in the baptismal instruction of the early church fathers one may discern at least two different sorts of initiation: one through water baptism, and the other through certain initiatory oblations and anointings and baptism for the dead. That men and women are privileged to 'go through' each and all of the patterns and ordinances for and in behalf of their deceased families and others is unusual in contemporary religious practice. But, again, the proxy and representational ideas are not at the periphery of early Jewish and Christian practice; they are at the core" (*Temple in Antiquity,* 12; see also Adams, "Iconography of Early Christian Initiation"; Nibley, *Improvement Era,* December 1948–April 1949; Foschini, *Catholic Biblical Quarterly* 13 [1951]: 328–44; Trumbower, *Rescue for the Dead,* 4–6, 35–36).

Near the commencement of his ministry, "*Jesus was taken* up into the holy city, and *the Spirit* setteth him on *the* pinnacle of the temple" (JST Matthew 4:5), where Satan tempted him. Of the whole length of the Temple Mount retaining walls, the southeast corner is the highest point—two hundred and eleven feet above ground level. The distance from the top of Herod's Portico to the bottom of the Kidron Valley was more than four hundred feet, however. That is the traditional "pinnacle of the temple" on which Jesus stood, since it is the highest man-made height ever achieved anciently in the Holy Land, and the point of Satan's temptation was to entice Jesus into misusing his divine power by throwing himself off the dizzying height and counting on angels to rescue him from the fall (Matthew 4:6).

Some researchers consider the south*western* corner of the Mount to be a more logical location for the temptation of Jesus because that corner has a much better angle for looking out over the city and because a specially carved platform stone was discovered in the toppled ruins below. That stone indicated by a Hebrew inscription where one of the priests would blow the shofar, or ram's horn trumpet, to signal the advent and the departure of the Sabbath and other holy days. The inscription reads: "*Leveit hatekiya lehakh* . . . to the place of trumpeting to [announce?]" (see illustration in Bahat, *Illustrated Atlas of Jerusalem*, 44; see also Yadin, *Jerusalem Revealed*, 27; *New Encyclopedia of Archaeological Excavations in the Holy Land*, 2:740).

The Gospels contain frequent notices of Jesus' activity in the Temple courts and in the Temple itself when he was in Jerusalem during his three-year ministry.

"The blind and the lame came to him in the temple; and he healed them" (Matthew 21:14).

"Now about the midst of the feast Jesus went up into the temple, and taught" (John 7:14).

"And early in the morning he came again into the temple, and all the people came unto him; and he sat down, and taught them" (John 8:2).

"And he taught daily in the temple" (Luke 19:47).

"And all the people came early in the morning to him in the temple, for to hear him" (Luke 21:38).

"I spake openly to the world; I ever taught in the synagogue, and in the temple, whither the Jews always resort; and in secret have I said nothing" (John 18:20).

DESCRIPTION OF THE TEMPLE BUILT BY HEROD

The Temple of Herod was constructed beginning in 20 B.C. with the help of ten thousand workmen. One of the king's main purposes was to provide greater space for the hundreds of thousands of worshippers who came to the Temple during the pilgrimage festivals and high holy days. One thousand priests who had been trained as masons and carpenters helped to build the holiest parts and a thousand wagons transported materials.

Herod was aware of the Jews' distrust of him and their sensitivities regarding their holiest place. Before he began reconstruction of

Appendix 3

the Temple itself, he had all stone and other materials cut, prepared, and put in place. Then the demolition of the old Temple and the building of the new proceeded (see Josephus, *Antiquities* [Loeb] XV.388–90). Also, we might note that the use of priests as masons gave rise over the ages to Freemasonry—temple workers who were also builders.

The Temple proper was under construction for a year and a half and the courtyards and porticoes for eight years, though embellishment of the outer courts actually continued for more than eighty years. It was said that whoever had not seen the Temple of Herod had never seen a beautiful building in his life (Talmud, *Succah* 51b, and *Baba Bathra* 3b, 4a). No other temple complex in the Greco-Roman world compared with it in expansiveness and magnificence. According to Josephus, the polished white marble exterior of the Temple was covered with so much gold that when the sun shone on it, those who looked upon it could be blinded (*War* [Loeb] V.222). Although the architectural glories of Herod's Temple far surpassed those of Solomon's Temple, Herod's Temple had little of the former's hallowed and spiritual atmosphere. The Ark of the Covenant, mercy seat, cherubim, the Urim and Thummim, which could provide revelatory contact with God, and other holy objects were lacking. And yet it was a place of revelation to Zacharias (Luke 1), and Jesus still acknowledged it as the Father's and his own House.

Herod had nearly doubled the size of the Temple Mount from what it was during the period of the First Temple, making it in Jesus' day nearly forty acres in area (compare Salt Lake Temple Square's *ten* acres). To expand so much, he had to extend the platform of the mount, particularly to the north, west, and south. He built a massive retaining wall, trapezoidal in shape, around the entire Temple Mount. That retaining wall alone was the longest, highest, and most impressive around any shrine in the ancient world, and the artificial esplanade or enclosure inside was the largest of its kind in antiquity (see Ben-Dov, *In the Shadow of the Temple,* 78; see also Bahat, *Illustrated Atlas of Jerusalem,* 42–43; C. Meyers, "Temple, Jerusalem" in *Anchor Bible Dictionary* VI:365; Broshi, "The Role of the Temple in the Herodian Economy," 31–37).

Of the Western Wall of Herod's Temple Mount (popularly called

The Temple at the Time of Jesus

the "Wailing Wall") only a middle portion is visible today. At least fifteen courses of beautifully carved stones with Herod's characteristic marginal dressing are now underground. The top portion of the Western Wall is also not seen today. It was destroyed by the Romans, though the Ottoman Turkish ruler Suleiman in the early 1500s restored the upper courses of stone along with the ramparts. Suleiman's work is quite inferior to the work of Herod's engineers more than fifteen hundred years earlier. The original retaining wall was some 100 feet above the paved road (as high as a modern ten-story building) and the towers were nearly 113 feet high. The prodigious undertaking of bringing into position all of Herod's massive pre-cut building stones is evidenced by the finding of one stone that measures almost 46 feet long, nearly 10 feet high, and 13 feet thick, and weighs around 400 tons (Ben-Dov, *In the Shadow of the Temple*, 88; Bahat claims the largest of these stones could weigh 570 tons; see also Geva, *Ancient Jerusalem Revealed*, 181). At the southeast corner of the Temple Mount, a little more than 100 feet north of the corner, is a "seam." An obvious difference in the cut of the stone is visible: to the north, stones were left rough on the exterior; and to the south, they are very smooth. North of the seam is pre-Herodian work, but the extension south is definitely Herod's addition to the platform of the Temple Mount (see *New Encyclopedia of Archaeological Excavations in the Holy Land*, 2:743).

Below floor level to the north and west was earth-fill, but to the south Herod supported the floor with vaults—twelve rows of arched colonnades, with a total of eighty-eight pillars. The area under the floor of the southeast portion of the Temple courtyard, therefore, was hollow. A large, columned chamber occupies that space. Because it was constructed by Herod, the place did not exist in Solomon's day, though it was later used by the Crusaders for stabling horses and was erroneously called "Solomon's Stables." The chamber was converted at the turn of the twenty-first century into a mosque.

The Temple Mount was a huge space measuring more than 172,000 square yards (144,000 square meters; see Avi-Yonah, "Jerusalem in the Hellenistic and Roman Periods," 215; Yadin, *Jerusalem Revealed*, 14; *New Encyclopedia of Archaeological Excavations in the Holy Land*, 2:737; Ben-Dov, *In the Shadow of the Temple*, 77). The Forum in Rome was only half that size, the

Appendix 3

Acropolis in Athens one-fifth that size, and the largest temple complex in the world—Karnak, in Upper Egypt, which was two thousand years in the building—is only a third bigger. Above ground on all sides of the Mount were extraordinary colonnaded *porticoes* or *porches* (also called *cloisters,* that is, covered walkways with colonnades opening to the inside; see Appendix 1, 718.) Each portico had a double row of Corinthian columns, each column a monolith (cut from one block of stone), and the columns rose more than thirty-seven feet.

According to Josephus, Herod was responsible for extending the Mount northward, westward, and southward and erecting porticoes inside his newly positioned walls, but the eastern portico was built up by Herod in the same position as the previous Temple Mount. This eastern portico was called "Solomon's Porch" (1 Kings 6:3). There Jesus, having come to the Passover at age twelve, conversed with the learned rabbis; there he later walked and taught at the Feast of Dedication (Hanukkah) and testified that he was God's Son; and there the Jews tried to stone him (John 10:22–39). Also, Peter and John, after performing a miracle at the gate of the Temple, drew a large crowd in Solomon's Porch and preached and called for repentance following the denying and killing of the Holy One. They were arrested by Temple police and Sanhedrin officials (Acts 3:1–4:2).

The southern portico, grander than the others, is often called Herod's Basilica. The word *basilica* (from the Greek *basileus,* meaning "king" and therefore designating a royal portico) meant a public hall that was rectangular in shape and had colonnaded aisles (a similar ground plan was later adopted for early Christian churches). The Royal Basilica, or Portico, contained one hundred sixty-two Corinthian columns. At its foot were the ramps leading onto the Temple courtyard from the south.

The eastern gate of the Temple Mount was called the Susa Gate. It faced eastward toward Susa (*Shushan* in the Bible), which was the Persian capital where the biblical stories of Daniel, Esther, Nehemiah, and others in part unfolded (Daniel 8:2; Esther 1:2; Nehemiah 1:1). When this gate was originally built in the early Second Temple period, the memory of Shushan was fresh in the minds of the remnant newly returned from Babylon. This gate was

The Temple at the Time of Jesus

The Temple and its courts: The Court of the Gentiles is the great outer court, the Court of the Women is the enclosed area between the two gates, and the Court of the Priests is the area immediately around the Temple (center); Model City, Jerusalem

said to have been lower than the other gates so that the priests gathered across the bridge on the Mount of Olives for the sacrifice of the red heifer might still look directly into the Temple. (On the sacrifice of the red heifer, whose ashes, mixed with water, were used for purification from sin and symbolized the Savior's atoning sacrifice, see Numbers 19:1–10 and the Mishnaic tractate called *Parah*; see also Hebrews 9:11–16; McConkie, *Mortal Messiah*, 1:136, 152.)

THE COURTS OF THE TEMPLE

The outer court was called the Court of the Gentiles, where Jesus cast out the money-changers. Gentiles were allowed to enter this far onto the Temple Mount. (Similarly, those who are not Latter-day Saints are allowed onto Temple Square in Salt Lake City to within a certain proximity of the Temple.) Surrounding the Temple proper was a balustrade (Hebrew, *soreg*), an elevated stone railing about four and a half feet high with posted inscriptions in Greek and Latin warning Gentiles not to pass beyond. One of these

Appendix 3

inscriptions was found in 1935 just outside the Lion's Gate of the Old City and is now on display in the Rockefeller Archaeological Museum. It reads: "No Gentile shall enter inward of the partition and barrier surrounding the Temple, and whosoever is caught shall be responsible to himself for his subsequent death" (see Bahat, *Illustrated Atlas of Jerusalem*, 44, with photo). Another warning inscription was discovered earlier, in 1870 (see *New Encyclopedia of Archaeological Excavations in the Holy Land*, 2:744; photo in Connolly, *Living in the Time of Jesus of Nazareth*, 36). Josephus mentions the partition wall with warning inscriptions in *Antiquities* [Loeb] XV.418 and *War* [Loeb] V.193–94). Roman authorities conceded to the Jewish religious leaders control of the sacred inner area to the point of capital punishment for non-Jews who passed beyond the stone railing.

A fortified inner wall with towers and gates surrounded the Court of the Women, which both female and male Israelites were permitted to enter (in contrast to the next court, which only male officiators could enter). The main gate into the Court of the Women was called the Beautiful Gate because of its rich decoration. At this gate Peter and John, on their way to Temple worship, stopped to hear the petition of a lame man. Peter dramatically healed the man, who joined them in the Temple, "walking, and leaping, and praising God" (Acts 3:1–11).

The Court of the Women was a large space, occupying nearly forty thousand square feet (see Appendix 1, 719). In the four corners were chambers for various functions. The eastern chambers served the Nazarites, where those who had made special vows could prepare their sacrifices, and another chamber was used for storing wood. The western chambers were used for storage of olive oil and for purification of lepers, which required a private ritual bath. It was perhaps to this Court of the Women that Joseph and Mary brought the infant Jesus five to six weeks (forty days) after his birth in order for him as a firstborn to be redeemed and for Mary to be ceremonially cleansed (Luke 2:22–23).

The Court of the Women was surrounded by porticoes. Against the walls inside the porticoes were trumpet-shaped boxes for charitable contributions, the place called "the treasury," where the widow cast in her mites (Mark 12:41–44) and where Jesus taught during

The Temple at the Time of Jesus

Right to left (east to west): Court of the Women, fifteen steps, Nicanor Gate, two pillars, entry to the Holy Place; as seen in the Model City, Jerusalem

the Feast of Tabernacles (John 8:20). In this court stood giant lampstands (*menorot*), fifty cubits (seventy-five feet) in height, giving light to the Temple Mount and much of the City (Talmud, *Succah* 5:2–3). There Jesus proclaimed himself the Light of the world. There he bore witness of his own divinity, dealt mercifully with the woman taken in adultery, announced his Messiahship, and bore testimony that he was the God of Abraham. Jews tried to stone him again (John 7–8).

Authorized persons could walk up fifteen curved steps and then through the Gate of Nicanor to enter the innermost court, which was actually a double court—the Court of the Men of Israel and the Court of the Priests. (Nicanor was a wealthy Jew from Alexandria who donated the ornate doors of the gate.) Only priests and other authorized Temple officiators and participants entered this court. To the sides of its porticoes were the Chamber of the Hearth, where priests on duty could spend their nights, and the Chamber of Hewn Stone, where the Sanhedrin met. In the latter chamber, before the council, Stephen was transfigured (Acts 6:12–15) and Paul later testified (Acts 22:30–23:10).

Appendix 3

*The altar of sacrifice in the Court of the Priests,
as seen in the Model City, Jerusalem*

On the north side of this innermost court was the Place of Slaughtering. On the south side was the giant brass basin, or laver, supported on the backs of twelve lions (Edersheim, *Temple*, 55). For all the water needs of the Temple Mount, millions of gallons of water were brought in from "Solomon's Pools," south of Bethlehem, and stored in a connected series of rock-cut reservoirs, or cisterns.

Near the laver stood the great horned Altar of Sacrifice or burnt offering, measuring forty-eight feet square and fifteen feet high. Some think that the huge rock mass inside the Dome of the Rock—which now measures approximately forty feet by fifty feet by seven feet high—once formed the base of the altar of sacrifice. At least it is clear from scripture that King David purchased the rock in order to build an altar to the Lord (2 Samuel 24:18–25). The altar consisted of whitewashed unhewn stone, and it had a ramp leading up to it from the south that was forty-eight feet long and twenty-four feet wide. The altar either stood off center in the court or was low enough in the center of the court so that the priest sacrificing the red heifer on the Mount of Olives could see straight into the giant

The Temple at the Time of Jesus

The Holy Place, with one tower of the Antonia Fortress in the background, as seen in the Model City, Jerusalem

entryway of the Holy Sanctuary, which stood sixty-six feet high and thirty-three feet wide (twenty by ten meters). The Sanctuary, or Holy Place, was made of marble. Two columns in front were named *Jachin* and *Boaz* (meaning "He will establish" and "In him is strength"), after the names of the entry columns of Solomon's Temple. The Temple proper was more than one hundred fifty feet high (*Encyclopedia Judaica*, 9:1398; today's Dome of the Rock reaches a height of just over one hundred feet) and was surrounded on top by golden spikes to discourage birds from landing on and tarnishing the stone.

Inside the Holy Place was the veil leading to the most sacred chamber, the Holy of Holies. That same veil was torn from top to bottom at the death of Jesus (Matthew 27:51). Whereas only the high priest once a year could enter the symbolic presence of God, Jesus, through his death, rent that partition, signifying accessibility for all people to reach God's presence (Hebrews 9:11–14; 10:19–22 for Paul's explanation of the symbolism). The rending of the Temple veil may also denote the rending of the Judaism of the Mosaic dispensation.

Overall, the Temple area consisted of a series of rising platforms.

Appendix 3

From the Court of the Gentiles, one ascended stairs to the Court of the Women; from there, one ascended fifteen curved stairs (possibly singing fifteen Psalms of Ascent, Psalms 120–34) to the Court of the Men of Israel and the Court of the Priests; and finally an ascent was required to enter the Holy Place itself. Thus the phrase "Jesus went up into the temple" (John 7:14) is quite literal. The three courtyards surrounding the holiest place where the Divine Presence could be manifest may appropriately be compared to three degrees of glory and three settings for instruction in modern Temples: telestial, terrestrial, and celestial. It is not enough to progress into the third courtyard, or heaven; it is incumbent upon each worshipper, now that the Great High Priest has made it possible for all, to actually enter into the highest degree of that realm, to symbolically enter into the Presence of God and be exalted. (Sources for the description of the Temple during the late Second Temple Period include Josephus, *Antiquities,* book XV, and *War,* book V; the tractate of the *Mishnah* called *Middoth* ["Measurements"]. See also Bahat, *Illustrated Atlas of Jerusalem,* 42–43; N. Avigad, "The Architecture of Jerusalem in the Second Temple Period" in Yadin, *Jerusalem Revealed,* 14–20; for illustrations and reconstructions, see Ogden, *Illustrated Guide to the Model City; Model of Herod's Temple* [slide set], circulated internationally by Ritmeyer Archaeological Design, York, England; and Connolly, *Living in the Time of Jesus of Nazareth.*)

APPENDIX 4

RELIGIOUS AND POLITICAL GROUPS, OCCUPATIONS, AND INSTITUTIONS

CHIEF PRIESTS

The chief priests were the leaders (aristocracy) of the priesthood in Jerusalem. Included in their ranks were members of the high priestly families and other priests of influence. All priests were to be descendants of Aaron's sons (Exodus 28:41; Numbers 18:1) and possessed the main responsibility of presiding over the sacrificial system of the Temple at Jerusalem. King David divided the priestly families into twenty-four courses or groups, each known by the name of its head. Though only some of these returned from the exile, the priests were subdivided again into twenty-four courses (1 Chronicles 24; Nehemiah 12), with each course responsible for officiating in the Temple a week at a time, as in the case of Zacharias (Luke 1:5, 8–9).

In New Testament times, the chief priests had a role in supervising the priestly functions and, as members of the Sanhedrin, assisting the high priest in the Aaronic Priesthood in governing and regulating Jewish life (see, for example, Matthew 2:4; Mark 11:18, 27; 14:55). The chief priests are mentioned several times in the Gospels as planning and carrying out the arrest, trial, and crucifixion of the Savior (Matthew 26:3; 27:1; Mark 15:1; Luke 22:2, 52; 23:13–23; John 18:3), even though they were supposed to preserve Israel's spiritual foundation.

APPENDIX 4

ELDERS

The term *elder* originated in Old Testament times and referred to the men of authority among the tribes of Israel—hence "elders of Israel" (Exodus 3:16, 18). The Hebrew word for which the term "elder" is used (*zaqan*) meant "bearded ones," undoubtedly reflecting the wisdom and experience to guide the people which was greatly valued in ancient societies. Sometimes the elders represented all the people (Exodus 19:7–8) and sometimes individual towns or cities (Deuteronomy 21:1–3; Joshua 20:4). They served as judges, pronouncing sentences (Deuteronomy 22:13–19), and filled roles as military leaders, advisors, and counselors (1 Samuel 4:3; 2 Samuel 17:4, 15; 1 Kings 20:7–8).

During intertestamental and New Testament times, councils of elders (Greek, *presbyteros*) evolved. They possessed executive, legislative, and judicial powers in Jewish communities and even represented the Jewish people to outside authorities. The most prominent of such councils was the Great Sanhedrin in Jerusalem.

The New Testament also presents the term "elder" as a priesthood office in the Church of Jesus Christ and discusses important duties of an elder (Acts 14:23; 1 Timothy 5:17; James 5:14).

HERODIANS

The Herodians were a quasipolitical party with a religious orientation that supported the Herodian family and Herodian leadership, in particular Herod Antipas during the days of Jesus' ministry. They appear to have been in league with the Pharisees in opposing the Savior and attempting to entrap him (Matthew 22:15–16; Mark 3:6; 12:13). To what extent they were influenced by the Pharisees is not known.

LAWYERS

The term *lawyer* (Greek, *nomikos*) as used in the four Gospels denotes one who is an expert in Jewish law. The term may very well be a synonym for "scribe." In some instances, in Luke in particular,

Pharisees and lawyers are mentioned together (Luke 7:30; 14:3), though elsewhere the combination is usually Pharisees and scribes (see, for example, Matthew 23:2; Mark 2:16; Luke 6:7). Luke reports Jesus chastising one of the lawyers for ladening men "with burdens grievous to be borne" (Luke 11:46), and Matthew indicates that Jesus castigated the scribes and Pharisees because "they bind heavy burdens and grievous to be borne" as a result of their requirements, commands, and interpretations of the Law (Matthew 23:2–4). It is obvious that scribes, Pharisees, rabbis, and lawyers were all interpreting the Law through the lenses of an oral tradition, of which Jesus did not approve.

PHARISEES

The Pharisees (Greek, *Pharisaioi*) were perhaps the most prominent religious party or group in Judaism during Jesus' day (Matthew 23; Mark 3; John 3). They were a lay association (not priestly or aristocratic) who prided themselves on their expert understanding of both the written and oral Torah (Law of Moses), their strict observance of the Law (in all its ramifications), and their avoidance of contact with people and things that brought spiritual contamination or ritual impurity, especially Gentiles. Hence, the name of this group is believed to derive from the Hebrew term denoting "separatists" (*perushim*) and may also be related to their origins. Though not known with any precision, it is thought by some that the Pharisees originated during the period of the Maccabean Revolt when a group called the *Hasidim* (Hebrew, "pious ones") joined Mattathias the priest and his sons in opposing the attempted Hellenization of Judaism by the Seleucid king Antiochus IV (175–164 B.C.). The Pharisees and Essenes grew out of a split among the Hasidim during and after the Hasmonean family of priests (led by Judah Maccabee) waged their war of liberation, and the Pharisees further separated themselves owing to untenable political and religious developments (see Appendix 2, 725).

The Gospels indicate that many Pharisees obsessed over issues of ritual purity, tithing, and strict interpretation of the Law but were hypocrites when it came to true religious practice (Mark 2:1–3:6;

APPENDIX 4

Matthew 23:13–15). The Pharisees opposed the Sadducees over some fundamental doctrines; they believed in a bodily resurrection, an afterlife, angels and spirits, and the oral law or oral tradition by which the written law was to be explained (Acts 23:6–9; Mark 7:5–9). Though Jesus acknowledged the importance of living the scriptural principles taught by the Pharisees (Matthew 23:2–3), he strongly criticized their multiplication of rules and the burdensome requirements of their oral tradition (Matthew 23:3–6; 15:1–6). The Pharisees are often lumped together with the scribes in the Synoptic Gospels (Matthew 15:1; 23:2; Mark 2:16; Luke 6:7), indicating the close connection between the two groups. Both Pharisees and Sadducees held membership in the ruling legislative-judicial council of the Jews known as the Sanhedrin (Acts 23:1–6). Nicodemus is an example of a Pharisee who became loyal to Jesus (John 3:1; 7:50–51; 19:39–40). The apostle Paul is another (Acts 23:6; Philippians 3:5). A comparison of Jesus' teachings with those of the Pharisees shows certain similarities.

PRIESTS, LEVITES, AND HIGH PRIESTS

After Israel's apostasy at Mount Sinai, the Lord took away from his chosen people (as a whole) the higher law, the Melchizedek Priesthood, and the higher ordinances and endowments of the gospel of Jesus Christ (D&C 84:19–27; JST Exodus 34:1–2). Instead, a lesser priesthood and a lesser law continued. The lesser priesthood was conferred only upon men of the tribe of Levi, and even among them not all priesthood offices were of equal power and authority. Within the tribe of Levi only Aaron and his male posterity could hold the office of priest. And, furthermore, only firstborn sons of Aaronite families were eligible to become the high priest, the president or presiding officer of the Aaronic and Levitical Priesthood. Thus, Aaron and his posterity held greater offices and greater power than the other Levites, and a clear distinction between "the priests and the Levites" existed in ancient times up through the beginning of the New Testament period and was noted in scripture (1 Kings 8:4; Ezra 2:70; John 1:19). The priests officiated in the Jerusalem Temple, offered the prescribed sacrifices, burnt the Temple incense (as John the Baptist's father did; see Luke 1:8–12), and taught the law of Moses to the people. The Levites performed more menial tasks, such as keeping the Temple clean, replenishing stocks of supplies, and assisting the priests (Numbers 3:5–10; 18:1–7; 1 Chronicles 23:27–32).

The Aaronic and Levitical Priesthood was a preparatory priesthood put in place to prepare the people for the coming of the Messiah and the return of the higher law and higher priesthood. It continued as a separate power through the administration of John the Baptist. Though John the Baptist was not recognized as the high priest by the Jewish people because the nation was in the throes of apostasy, he held the keys of the Aaronic Priesthood and was the legitimate presiding priest, the last legal administrator, holding authority for and under the Mosaic dispensation (Smith, *Teachings of the Prophet Joseph Smith,* 276; McConkie, *Mormon Doctrine,* 393). After John the Baptist came Jesus Christ, who was then the legal administrator of the kingdom of God, holding all the keys for both the Melchizedek and Aaronic Priesthoods. Before the coming of Jesus, the right to possess the Aaronic Priesthood was determined by lineage. But when Jesus came and restored the Melchizedek Priesthood to the earth during his mortal ministry (JST John 1:26–28), priesthood was not restricted to one tribe of Israel. Furthermore, it was the ultimate power on earth, the overarching power and authority under which all priesthood functions and ordinances were performed.

The office of high priest in the Aaronic Priesthood was first held by Aaron, and it continued as a hereditary appointment down through Aaron's posterity. The special duties and responsibilities as well as unique garments of the high priest were outlined by the Lord early in the Mosaic dispensation (see, for example, Exodus 28:3–43; 29:6; 39:27–29; Leviticus 6:19–23; 21:10). The high priest was bound to a higher or more stringent standard of ritual purity than anyone else, even other priests and Levites. These rules applied to such things as marriage, contact with dead things, and sacrificial duties. An important function of the high priest that continued through New Testament times was the performance of the special Temple service on the Day of Atonement, the holiest day of the year for Israel (the Jews).

The office of high priest was usually held for life and originally

Appendix 4

came by divine revelation, for "no man [took] this honor unto himself, but he that [was] called of God, as was Aaron" (Hebrews 5:4). With one major exception, the high priest's office remained in the family of Aaron's third son, Eleazar, through the line of Zadok until Hasmonean times. The power, prestige, and legitimacy of the high priestly office was greatly diminished when Jason (of the Zadokite line) was able to wrest the high priest's office from his brother, Onias III, by bribing the Seleucid Gentile ruler Antiochus IV; ironically, he fell victim to the same tactic a few years later by a non-Zadokite pretender named Menelaus (2 Maccabees 4:7–27). The old, legitimate high priestly line was gone, and the office itself was increasingly questioned as the Jewish nation spiraled deeper into apostasy. During the Hasmonean (Maccabean) period, the office of high priest and the office of king were merged in the person of Simon, son of Mattathias and brother of Judah the Maccabee (ruled 143–134 B.C.).

After this family was overthrown and the Holy Land began to be ruled by the Roman-supported king, Herod the Great (37–4 B.C.), the office of high priest was greatly marginalized. Herod and the Roman procurators appointed after him deposed high priests at their pleasure (twenty-eight different men served between 37 B.C. and A.D. 68, including Annas, his son-in-law Caiaphas, and five of Annas's sons). Roman prefects and procurators after Herod allowed the high priest some extended powers with the hope of creating a pro-Roman aristocracy composed of the high priest and his family, former high priests, and members of the families closely associated with the high priests. These helped make up a group referred to in the New Testament as the chief priests, with whom Jesus had to deal. The office of high priest ceased to exist when Jerusalem and the Temple were destroyed by Titus in A.D. 70. The last high priest was a layman named Phannias, chosen by lot during the great Jewish revolt (Josephus, *War* [Loeb], I.147–57).

PUBLICANS

From the Latin *publicani*, the term *publicans* refers to tax farmers, men who were responsible to the Roman government in the land of Israel for the collection of taxes, as well as to those who worked for them and actually collected the revenue. Tax farmers were required to pay a fixed amount to the imperial treasury each year, but they were free to collect as much from the public as they could. Thus, in Jesus' day, publicans were one of the most corrupt and despised groups of people among the Jewish populace. Jews who became publicans were usually cut off from their people.

One of the Lord's original apostles, Matthew (also known as Levi before his conversion) was a publican (Matthew 9:9; Mark 2:14). He hosted a feast attended by many of his fellow publicans, whom the Pharisees labeled sinners. Jesus took the opportunity to teach a powerful lesson about pride (Luke 5:27–32). Because his headquarters were located at or near the fishing village of Capernaum, Matthew may also have collected payments on fishing leases, because fishing was contracted by lease in the Mediterranean region (including the Sea of Galilee) and tax collectors were often brokers for these leases. Apparently, tax collectors also collected fees for processing, transporting, and marketing fish.

The publicans mentioned in the New Testament seem to have been particularly ready to accept the gospel, perhaps because they were especially humble owing to their lowly social status (Matthew 9:9–11; 21:31–32; Luke 7:29; 18:13–14).

RABBIS

Rabbi was a title of respect applied to powerful teachers in first-century Judaism. It derives from the Hebrew *rab* ("big, great") and literally means "my master" or "my great one." The term is found in three of the four Gospels, usually in reference to Jesus, although John the Baptist is also called "Rabbi" (John 3:26). Matthew reports Jesus' description of the prideful scribes and Pharisees as loving to be hailed in public as "Rabbi, Rabbi." But Matthew goes on to say that Christ is the only true Rabbi or Master of men (Matthew 23:7–8).

The word *rabbi* does not appear in Luke. Scholars suppose that Luke's intended Gentile audience would not have appreciated its significance. The only one who is reported by Matthew as calling Jesus by the title Rabbi is Judas Iscariot (Matthew 26:25, 49). In Mark, only the disciples refer to Jesus as Rabbi, usually after a miraculous episode (Mark 9:5; 11:21; 14:45). John records that both followers and others referred to Jesus as Rabbi (John 1:38, 49; 3:2; 4:31; 6:25; 9:2; 11:8). In one of the greatest moments in history, when Jesus appeared for the first time as a resurrected Being, Mary Magdalene addressed him with the heightened form of the title, "Rabboni" (John 20:16).

After the destruction of the Temple (A.D. 70), the term became an official academic title applied to someone who was an ordained scholar.

SADDUCEES

The Sadducees (Greek, *Saddoukaioi*) were a principal religious party in Judaism from around the second century before Christ to the destruction of the Temple in A.D. 70. They disappeared after the first Jewish Revolt against Rome (A.D. 66–70). Their ranks derived mostly from the priestly aristocracy, though not all priests were Sadducees. Their name likely came from Zadok, the high priest in Solomon's day. They competed with the Pharisees, another religious party, for the leadership of the Jewish people in Jesus' day. Luke indicates that the high priest and Temple authorities were Sadducees (Acts 4:1; 5:17).

Mark tells us that the Sadducees taught "there is no resurrection" (Mark 12:18), and thus they opposed both the apostles and the disciples of our Lord, as well as the Pharisees (Acts 4:1–3; Mark 12:18–27). Both Sadducees and Pharisees were members of the Sanhedrin (the Jewish leadership council), and the apostle Paul used the issue of their sharp disagreement over the resurrection to further divide them and free himself from their clutches (Acts 23:6–10).

The Sadducees also rejected the Pharisaic belief in the existence of angels and spirits, an afterlife, and the oral tradition or "tradition of the fathers." The Sadducees believed only in the written laws of Moses, were staunch supporters of free will, and were more harsh than the Pharisees in administering punishment for wrongdoing (Josephus, *Antiquities* [Loeb] XIII.293–98). Josephus, himself a member of the Temple-based priestly aristocracy, appears overall not to favor the Sadducees though he admires certain of their practices. The Pharisees enjoyed more popular support in Jesus' day than the Sadducees.

SAMARITANS

In 722 B.C. the northern kingdom of Israel, made up of approximately ten tribes, fell to the Assyrian Empire after a long siege. Samaria was the capital of the Northern Kingdom and became the name of the entire geographical region inhabited by the northern tribes. In 721 B.C., King Sargon II of Assyria (722–705 B.C.; see Isaiah 20:1) made Samaria an Assyrian province and deported a significant proportion of the ten northern tribes, sometimes called the lost tribes. To replace them, the Assyrians imported a group of non-Israelites into the region (2 Kings 17:1–26).

The residue of northern Israel—those not carried away captive—and the new foreign inhabitants intermarried, producing a mixed race known as the Samaritans, who were partly Israelite and partly Gentile. Their religion also developed into a mixture of Israelite and heathen practices (2 Kings 17:27–41).

The Samaritans were regarded as "half-breeds" and were despised by the Jews of the Savior's day. Many references in the Gospels reflect this antagonism (Matthew 10:5; John 4:9). However, the Savior went to Samaria and taught the people (John 4) and later explicitly commissioned the apostles to teach and testify of him and his gospel in Samaria (Acts 1:8).

SANHEDRIN

The Greek term *synedrion* means "a council or assembly." In the New Testament the term refers to both the Great Sanhedrin, the highest legislative and judicial council or court of the Jewish people located in Jerusalem, and to local city or town councils (Matthew 10:17; Mark 13:9). The Great Sanhedrin was composed of seventy-one members and was presided over by the high priest (Matthew 26:59; Mark 14:55; Acts 5:21). One of its meeting places was the Chamber of Hewn Stone in the Temple complex (*Mishnah*, Sanhedrin, 11:2). There its members sat in a semicircle, backed by three rows of their followers. The Sanhedrin possessed an aristocratic character, its members drawn from the two main religious groups of the period, the Pharisees and Sadducees, who were deeply divided over such fundamental religious issues as the concept of resurrection

APPENDIX 4

(Acts 23:1–10). During the time of the Savior, the Pharisees seem to have wielded the predominating influence over the Jerusalem Sanhedrin (Acts 5:34, 40).

Because Rome had granted the Jews of Jesus' day considerable self-government, the Great Sanhedrin held sweeping powers, including the authority to make laws regulating Jewish life, hand down final decisions in legal disputes, judge the fitness of priests to serve in the Temple, and place individuals under arrest (Acts 4:13–17; 5:17–21; 9:2). But the Sanhedrin's power was not limitless. At the time of the Savior, the Great Sanhedrin seems to have possessed the power to try capital cases but not the power to carry out capital punishment or execution (John 18:31; see also commentary on John 18:31–32). Apparently there were certain areas where the jurisdiction of the Jerusalem Sanhedrin did not reach. In Galilee, for example, Jesus seems to have been beyond the power of the Sanhedrin (John 7:1). Galilee was a known hotbed of anti-Roman sentiment.

SCRIBES

In New Testament times, a class of influential scholars preserved and interpreted the Law. Originally, in Old Testament times, they performed record-keeping functions and secretarial duties. Baruch, Jeremiah's secretary, was this kind of scribe (Jeremiah 32:12; 36:18, 32). But after Israelites returned from exile, scribes became associated with the transmission and interpretation of the Torah to maintain its consistency with previous editions and to ensure its centrality in Judaism. Ezra the priest is portrayed as such a scribe—"a ready scribe in the law of Moses" (Ezra 7:6), who read and interpreted the law of Moses to the people (Nehemiah 8:1–9).

In the Synoptic Gospels, the scribes are most often mentioned in connection with the Pharisees (see, for example, Matthew 15:1; 23:2; Mark 2:16; Luke 6:7), indicating that the scribes of Jesus' day had a close affinity with the Pharisees and rabbis and were largely taken from the ranks of those two groups. That is the implication of Matthew 7:28–29, in which Jesus is described as teaching as one having independent authority and not as the scribes, meaning that Jesus did not cite previous rabbinic authority or traditions of the elders to establish the validity of his teachings. That the scribes and Pharisees shared the same ideology, including absolute fidelity to the Pharisaic or rabbinic oral tradition, seems certain (Matthew 15:1–2). Later rabbinic writings also equate Pharisees, rabbis, and scribes.

Numerous verses testify that the scribes not only opposed Jesus (Matthew 21:15; Luke 5:30) but were, along with other groups, directly responsible for the death of Jesus (Matthew 26:3; Mark 8:31; 11:18; 14:1).

SYNAGOGUE

A synagogue is the place of assembly and worship used by Jewish communities. The ancient Greek word *synagoge* originally referred to a "group of people," but by the Second Temple period it most frequently referred to the building itself, which is the way it is used in the New Testament.

The exact origin of the synagogue is unknown, though some scholars believe it developed during the Babylonian Exile (586–538 B.C.) as Jewish communities came together to worship in place of the destroyed Temple in Jerusalem. In the synagogue the sacrificial system of the Temple was replaced by the study of the Torah, prayer, and acts of kindness. Latter-day Saints know, however, that the Book of Mormon prophet Nephi specifically refers to the synagogue (2 Nephi 26:26), implying that it was in existence before the Exile and that the ancient American Israelites would have brought the institution with them when they left Jerusalem around 600 B.C. (1 Nephi 10:4).

In Jesus' day, each synagogue was governed by a council of elders who decided such things as who could be admitted to the assembly of worshippers (John 9:22; 12:42; 16:2). The most important official of the synagogue was the ruler of the synagogue, or *chazan* (Luke 4:20; 13:14; Mark 5:22). The Jewish historian Josephus corroborates New Testament evidence that synagogue worship on the Sabbath was well established by the first century A.D. (*War* [Loeb], II.289). It was Jesus' custom to teach in the synagogue on the Sabbath day (Matthew 4:23; Mark 1:21; Luke 4:16–30).

The best evidence suggesting what New Testament synagogues

looked like comes from four sources: the earliest known synagogue outside the Holy Land, which has been excavated on the Aegean island of Delos, dating from the first century before Christ; and three synagogues dated before A.D. 70 excavated at Gamla, Masada, and Herodium in the Holy Land. Though they resemble each other in appearance, the earliest of the three is at Gamla and was an elongated hall (66 feet x 52 feet), divided by columns and featuring a principal entrance facing toward Jerusalem.

TEMPLE POLICE

The Temple police (Greek, *hyperetai*), translated as "officers" in the King James Version, worked under the direction of the Pharisees and chief priests (John 7:32; 18:3). They were Levites of the Temple, charged with maintaining proper order and decorum within the Temple precincts and occasionally outside (in and around Jerusalem) during a crisis. The Temple police were part of the contingent sent to arrest Jesus in Gethsemane. They were also called the "officers of the Jews" in John 18:12. This was done by John to distinguish them from the "band," or part of the cohort of Roman soldiers, who also participated in the arrest of Jesus.

The Synoptic Gospels' descriptions of the force sent to arrest Jesus are more general. Mark 14:43 (see also Matthew 26:47) speaks of "a great multitude . . . from the chief priests and the scribes and the elders." Luke 22:52 describes the chief priests and elders as being right with the "captains of the temple" or Temple police (Brown, *Gospel According to John*, 314, 808).

ZEALOTS

The Zealots were a group of ardent Jewish patriots in Judea and Galilee who combined an intense love of country, a desire for independence, a hatred for the Romans (or any foreign domination for that matter), and a *zeal* for the Torah, the law of Moses. They were ready to fight and die for their beliefs. The Jewish historian Josephus calls the Zealot movement Judaism's "fourth philosophy" to distinguish it from the other three—the Pharisees, Sadducees, and Essenes (*Antiquities* [Loeb] XVIII.11–25). He traces the origins of the

Zealot sect to one Judas, son of Hezekiah, a man from Galilee, which was a region known as a hotbed of Jewish rebellion. In A.D. 6 the Romans decided to make Judea and nearby districts into a Roman province. Josephus states that the new sect was established at this point, when Judas the Galilean incited the indigenous population to revolt (*War* [Loeb] II.118).

One of the original Twelve Apostles, Simon, was called Zelotes (the Greek form of *Zealot*), presumably because of his association with the sect (Luke 6:15; Acts 1:13). Matthew and Mark refer to him as Simon the Cananean (Matthew 10:4; Mark 3:18), which is the Aramaic word for *zealot* (*qan'an*) and not related at all to the term *Canaanite*. That Jesus could be linked to the Zealots (since one of his inner circle was called Zelotes) may have contributed both to the charge that Jesus was an insurrectionist and ultimately to his death by the Roman capital punishment of crucifixion.

Significantly, Josephus indicates that the Zealot movement was responsible in some fundamental way for the downfall of the Jewish state. The Zealot sect died out after the Romans finally overran the last Zealot stronghold on Masada in A.D. 73, after the devastation of Jerusalem and the Temple.

APPENDIX 5

ROMAN GOVERNMENT AND MILITARY SYSTEM

By the first century after Christ, the Roman Empire (27 B.C.–A.D. 476) was more or less in firm control of the Mediterranean basin, of which the Holy Land was a part. Life in the empire was based on a Hellenistic cultural substratum (Greek ideas, customs, religious forms, and language) overlaid with Roman legal and governmental systems and such Roman values as military strength. Some of the tools that the Romans used to control and administer their empire included taxation, the legal system, and the military.

Rome had begun to take a serious interest in the Holy Land (the eastern part of what was then the Roman Republic) in 143 B.C., by which time Judea had voluntarily allied itself with Rome. In 63 B.C. General Pompey had conquered the independent Hasmonean Jewish state and placed the Jews under Roman rule, though the Romans continued to recognize officially the Jewish religion. After a time, Julius Caesar became sole ruler of the Roman Republic and was on his way to declaring himself king when he was murdered in 44 B.C. by Roman senators.

CAESAR

In 27 B.C. Julius Caesar's grandnephew and adopted son, Octavian, was proclaimed Augustus by the Roman senate and became the first emperor of the newly established Roman Empire, which succeeded the Republic. The emperor was the ultimate ruler and final arbiter in all areas within the empire, including the Holy Land. The term *Caesar* became a title and a synonym for the emperor. Octavian became known as Caesar Augustus and ruled from 27 B.C. to A.D. 14, the years of Jesus' youth. He was followed by Caesar Tiberius, who ruled during the years of Jesus' ministry (A.D. 14–37). Three other members of Julius Caesar's family were emperors during the later New Testament era: Caligula (A.D. 37–41), Claudius (A.D. 41–54), and Nero (A.D. 54–68). The emperor held autonomous power in all matters.

LEGATES, PREFECTS, AND PROCURATORS

Under the Roman system of government, imperial provinces were of two types. Larger provinces were governed by a legate, who served as both military governor and chief magistrate. Smaller imperial provinces were ruled by a minor official who bore the title *praefect* (or prefect), also called a governor. A legate might supervise a prefect, as was the case with the first prefects of Judea being supervised by the legate of Syria, beginning in A.D. 6. Judea was ruled by a prefect from A.D. 6–41 and was considered one of the least important provinces until revolutionary events of the late 60s riveted Roman attention on it. From the time of Emperor Claudius (A.D. 41–54) onward, it became customary to refer to the prefect or governor of Judea by the title of *procurator Augusti*, or simply procurator. The governors of Judea resided officially at Caesarea by the sea and went to Jerusalem on special occasions. Though he is arguably the most famous now, Pontius Pilate was in his day a low-ranking prefect (see Appendix 2, 731).

COHORTS, CENTURIES, AND LEGIONS

Smaller, less important imperial provinces such as Judea did not have a garrison of large Roman army units but only a small contingent of six hundred soldiers, called a cohort, which served as the governor's bodyguard. Larger provinces had two or more cohorts stationed within their territories. Each cohort of six hundred infantrymen was divided into six centuries (a century was a complement of up to one hundred men and was commanded by a centurion). A cohort was commanded by a military tribune, the

APPENDIX 5

lowest-ranking government official in the empire, who possessed limited power to protect the citizens of Rome.

The largest military unit of the Roman army was the legion, composed of six thousand legionnaires organized into ten cohorts. A legion was commanded by a legionary legate. When Jesus declared he had twelve legions of angels at his disposal (Matthew 26:53), he was referring to a staggeringly large number of warriors, seldom, if ever, seen in the Holy Land.

CLIENT KINGS, ETHNARCHS, AND TETRARCHS

Rome administered its vast empire through a system of patronage, including client kings and rulers who were allowed or delegated some autonomy in their respective areas but who depended upon and served under the sponsorship and support of Rome's highest officials. In Judea, Herod the Great was the first client king of note. He ruled (37–4 B.C.) with considerable latitude and support from Rome. He controlled his kingdom well from the Roman perspective. After his death in 4 B.C., the kingdom was divided among three of his sons.

Archelaus received Judea and Samaria, as well as cities along the Mediterranean coast. He never bore the technical title of king, only *ethnarch* (Greek, "ruler of a people"). In the tenth year of his reign (A.D. 6), charges of brutality and tyranny were brought against him by his brothers and his subjects, and he was deposed and banished by Rome to Gaul, where he died. Judea was then attached to the Roman province of Syria and governed by a Roman prefect or governor. The first five prefects of Judea were Coponius (A.D. 6–9), Ambivulus (A.D. 9–12), Rufus (A.D. 12–15), Valerius (A.D. 15–26), and Pontius Pilate (A.D. 26–36). These all governed during the lifetime of Jesus of Nazareth.

Herod Philip, son of Herod the Great by a local woman named Cleopatra, was, after his father's death, named *tetrarch* (Greek, "ruler of a part," originally a "fourth part" but more generally a part of a kingdom or province). Herod Philip was given authority to rule the area northeast of the Sea of Galilee, which he did from 4 B.C. to A.D. 34. Luke 3:1 names his territory as the region of Iturea and

ROMAN GOVERNMENT AND MILITARY SYSTEM

Trachonitis, which also included Auranitis, Gaulanitis, Batanea, and the area around Panias, or Caesarea Philippi (Matthew 16:13). His capital was Panias, rebuilt as a Hellenistic city and renamed Caesarea Philippi in honor of Caesar and himself. Philip also rebuilt the fishing village of Bethsaida (Mark 6:45; Luke 9:10) and called it Bethsaida Julias in honor of Caesar Augustus' daughter, Julia. His rule was fairly uneventful, although he minted coins bearing the images of the emperors Augustus and Tiberius, which was a sacrilege to devout Jews. When Philip died, his tetrarchy was put under the legate of Syria (Jeffers, *Greco-Roman World of the New Testament Era*, 124–25).

Another son of Herod the Great, Herod Antipas, had originally been named by his father as successor to the entire kingdom, but a last-minute change in the will of Herod the Great appointed Antipas "Tetrarch of Galilee and Perea." He ruled from 4 B.C. to A.D. 39. Some New Testament verses refer to Antipas as "king" (Mark 6:14, 22–27), following the habit of the local people, but other verses correctly indicate his position only as tetrarch (Matthew 14:1; Luke 3:19; 9:7; Acts 13:1). Antipas executed John the Baptist because he preached against the ruler's immoral life (Matthew 14:1–12; Luke 3:19–20). Antipas had discarded his first wife, the daughter of the Nabatean king, and entered into an adulterous marriage with Herodias, the wife of his half brother Philip. The king of Nabatea used this divorce as a pretext to attack and defeat the forces of Antipas. Josephus relates that the Jews believed this was a punishment of Antipas sent by God for the execution of the righteous John the Baptist (*Antiquities* [Loeb] XVIII.109–24). Because most of the subjects in his tetrarchy were Gentiles, however, Antipas was fairly popular with the people. The Gospel of Luke alone describes Antipas's role in the trial of Jesus (Luke 23:6–12).

In the end, according to Josephus, Antipas was deposed as tetrarch by the emperor Caligula in A.D. 39, ironically as a result of the goading of Antipas's wife, Herodias. She persuaded Antipas to petition the emperor for the official title and status of king. Rome refused his demand, banished him, and gave his tetrarchy to the grandson of Herod the Great, Herod Agrippa I. Agrippa I had managed to label Antipas as power-hungry and had him discredited. For a brief time, between A.D. 41 and 44, the rule of the governors was

Appendix 5

suspended, and the full powers of monarchy were restored to Herod Agrippa I. As a legitimate Jewish king, he ruled over most of the region his grandfather had held. Roman suspicions about Agrippa were aroused when he began constructing a new wall to enclose and fortify the city of Jerusalem to the north, the weakest point in the city's defenses. Agrippa responded to the suspicions by inaugurating a series of games at Caesarea to celebrate Roman victories in Britain and in honor of the emperor. On the second day of the celebrations, while he was presiding over the events in a robe made entirely of silver, Agrippa suddenly fell ill and died. He was fifty-four years of age. Luke rightly depicts this event as the king being smitten by an angel of the Lord in just recompense for his atrocities against the leaders of the early Church (Acts 12). While the Jews mourned deeply his passing, Christians and Gentiles rejoiced.

APPENDIX 6

ISRAELITE FEASTS, FESTIVALS, AND HOLY DAYS

DEDICATION

The Feast of Dedication, instituted relatively late in Israel's ritual history and thus unknown in Old Testament times, celebrated the rededication or repurification of the Jerusalem Temple and consecration of its new altar in 163 B.C. under Judah Maccabee (1 Maccabees 4:36–61). The Syrians led by Antiochus Epiphanes had desecrated the Temple in 168 B.C. and attempted to eradicate Jewish religious practices. But Jewish freedom fighters led by a Hasmonean family of priests (the most famous being Judah, who was nicknamed the Maccabee, or "hammerer") repelled the Syrians in a war of liberation.

The Hebrew name for the feast is Hanukkah, which is the Hebrew word meaning "dedication" and is associated with lights. Josephus says Hanukkah itself was known as the "festival of lights" (*Antiquities* [Loeb] XII.325). The celebration lasts eight days and is likely based on the duration of the First Temple dedication under King Solomon (1 Kings 8:66; 2 Chronicles 7:9), though the Talmud relates it to a story about the Maccabees finding a small amount of oil when they recovered the Temple, which miraculously burned for eight days (*Talmud of Babylonia*, 34; Farrar, *Life of Christ*, 490).

The Feast of Dedication begins on the 25th of Kislev of every year (November-December). Thus, John 10:22 refers to Jesus being in Jerusalem at wintertime, during the Feast of Dedication. He was crucified the following spring.

APPENDIX 6

PASSOVER

Every year since the time of Moses, during the spring, the house of Israel has celebrated Jehovah's passing over (hence "Passover") the houses of the children of Israel in Egypt when he smote the firstborn of the land of Egypt and delivered the covenant community from Egyptian bondage (Exodus 12:3–11; 13:8–9). Passover became one of the three annual pilgrimage feasts commanded by the Lord, when all males of the covenant were to appear before the Lord at the place of his choosing (Exodus 23:14–17; Deuteronomy 16:16). By New Testament times the specified place was the Jerusalem Temple.

Exodus 12 describes the first Passover observance, which was done within individual family units. A lamb was slaughtered by each family at evening on the 14th of Nisan. The blood of the lamb was placed on the side posts and lintel of the door of each house, which saved the firstborn of every participating family from destruction. No bone of the lamb was to be broken, but the lamb was roasted with fire and served to family members, along with unleavened bread (in remembrance of Israel's hasty flight from Egypt) and bitter herbs (in remembrance of the bitterness of bondage). All ritual elements of the Passover observance in Old Testament times foreshadowed the Atonement of the coming Messiah, Jesus Christ, in one way or another.

By New Testament times the Feast of Unleavened Bread had merged with, and was synonymous with, Passover (Luke 22:1, 7). Several more elements had been added to the Passover celebration. Among the more significant, four cups of wine were drunk at different stages of the feast; at least one of them—the cup of blessing—was mixed with water (Luke 22:17, 20; 1 Corinthians 10:16). The great Hallel—Psalms 113–18—was sung. This was undoubtedly the hymn spoken of by Matthew and Mark at the end of the Last Supper (Matthew 26:30; Mark 14:26). The feast was eaten reclining, not standing as in olden times, at a low table called a triclinium. Hence, during the Last Supper most of the disciples were situated in such a way that they could lean against the breast of the person behind them.

The Passover was extremely important in the life of Jesus. The years of his public ministry are measured from Passover to Passover, starting with the first mentioned in John 2:23 (John 5:1; 6:4; 13:1). All four Gospels describe Jesus' death in relation to Passover (Matthew 26:1–30; Mark 14:1–26; Luke 22:1–39; John 13:1–38). The Last Supper was a Passover observance, and Jesus' death was the culmination and fulfilment of all the lambs sacrificed in the Temple at Passover season (John 1:29; 19:36).

PENTECOST

The Greek term *Pentecost* (literally "fiftieth") is the New Testament name for the Israelite festival called the Feast of Harvest or Firstfruits (Exodus 23:16), or the Feast of Weeks (Deuteronomy 16:10). It occurred fifty days after the Feast of Passover, celebrated the spring harvest, and lasted only one day. It was one of three annual pilgrimage festivals prescribed by Mosaic law, during which all males of the covenant were required to appear before the Lord at the place he chose (Exodus 23:14–17). The specified place by New Testament times was the Jerusalem Temple, so the city was filled with Jews from many different lands on the day of Pentecost (Acts 2:9–11).

The celebration of Pentecost is not mentioned in the Gospel accounts but is featured prominently in Acts 2 when the Holy Ghost descended on the apostles and others in Jerusalem, resulting in three thousand baptisms (Acts 2:41). Thus, the celebration of the first harvest of the year symbolized the first great harvest of souls in the postresurrection Church.

TABERNACLES

The Feast of Tabernacles or Booths was the final, most joyous, and greatest of the yearly agricultural celebrations of the Israelite calendar. It was one of three annual pilgrimage festivals in which all males of the covenant were required to appear before the Lord in the place he chose (Exodus 23:14–17; Deuteronomy 16:16). The specified place by New Testament times was the Jerusalem Temple, so many travelers made their way to Jerusalem for this feast. The Feast of Tabernacles or Booths (*sukkoth* in Hebrew) was also referred to in the Old Testament as the Festival of Ingathering (Exodus 23:16); the feast of the Lord (Leviticus 23:39, 41); or simply "the feast" because of its significance (1 Kings 8:2, 65; 12:32; John 7:37).

The Feast of Tabernacles was celebrated for eight days, from the 15th through the 22d of the seventh month (September-October), with the last day being the "great day of the feast," involving special sanctity (John 7:37). Tabernacles followed two other major observances in the calendar, New Year or *Rosh Hashanah* (first day of the seventh month) and the Day of Atonement or *Yom Kippur* (tenth day of the seventh month; see Leviticus 23:23–36, 39–43).

The Feast of Tabernacles was a time of special celebration. It began and ended with a special sabbath (Leviticus 23:39). The harvest was complete and the people were to rest and rejoice, eat and drink, and tithe their crops (Leviticus 23:40; Deuteronomy 14:22–26). Participants were to construct temporary tabernacles or booths to live in during the feast to commemorate the Lord's protection of the Israelites as they sojourned in the wilderness (Leviticus 23:42–43). During the feast the priests offered special and more numerous sacrifices than for any of the other feasts (totaling seventy-one). And every seventh year the whole law of Moses was read aloud (Numbers 29:13–38; Deuteronomy 31:10–11).

After the return from the Babylonian Exile, observances and ceremonies of the Feast of Tabernacles also included the lighting of four great menorahs in the Temple courtyard to signify the covenant people's role as the light unto the nations. Jesus used this ceremony as the backdrop for his "light of the world" discourse in John 8:12–20. Also added to the observances of the feast was the drawing of the water ceremony, in which water was taken from the Pool of Siloam and poured out on the Temple altar. Of this ritual it was said that whoever had not seen the drawn water ceremony at the Feast of Tabernacles did not know the meaning of joy. Against the backdrop of this ceremony, Jesus stood and spoke about himself as the source of rivers of living water (John 7:37–38).

Other activities during the Feast of Tabernacles in New Testament times included priests marching around the altar carrying fruit and waving palm branches. Prayers were offered for rain (for the next agricultural cycle) as well as for the resurrection of the dead. In fact, the Feast of Tabernacles came to be associated by the Jews with hopes for a Messiah-Deliverer who would bring national independence. Because Jesus Christ was known by some (and believed by others) to be the fulfillment of these messianic longings and hopes, elements of the Tabernacles celebration were invoked by people at the time of Jesus' Triumphal Entry into Jerusalem when messianic fervor was running so high, even though it was Passover time and not the fall Tabernacles season. These messianic elements included the cutting down and waving of palm branches (Matthew 21:8), the Hosanna cry, and the use of the messianic title Son of David (Matthew 21:9).

Though only the Gospel of John discusses an actual Feast of Tabernacles celebration, the season of the Feast of Tabernacles was probably the backdrop for the experience of Jesus, Peter, James, and John on the Mount of Transfiguration (Matthew 17:1–9; Mark 9:2–9; Luke 9:28–36). The chief apostle, Peter, wanted to construct tabernacles for the Savior, Moses, and Elijah.

APPENDIX 7

CULTURAL AND RELIGIOUS PRACTICES

BETROTHAL

Marriage customs in New Testament times derived from Mosaic laws and practices exemplified in the Old Testament. The modern concepts of dating and marrying whomever one chooses were foreign to ancient Israelite culture. Whether in 1200 B.C. or A.D. 30, marriage between a young man and young woman was arranged and agreed to by the heads of the respective families (Miller and Miller, *Harper's Encyclopedia of Bible Life*, 98–99). These heads were usually the fathers, although notable exceptions are described in the patriarchal narratives. One such exception is Jacob, the prospective bridegroom who dealt directly with Laban, the father of the intended bride (Genesis 24:29–60). Most Israelite or Jewish families lived life in a rather constricted social circle made up of relatives and fellow townsfolk. From this small world, marriage choices were made and matches decided upon. Once a prospective wife had been identified by the groom's father or family head, negotiations were begun. These negotiations focused on, but were not limited to, the size of the *mohar*, a Hebrew word (found in Genesis 34:12; Exodus 22:17; 1 Samuel 18:25) meaning a kind of dowry in reverse. This was a "purchase price" or "bride price" paid by the groom's father or family head to the bride's family. There is some evidence to indicate that the *mohar* was to be held in trust as a kind of insurance fund for the bride that she could use in case of the death of her husband or other troubles. Rachel and Leah, for example, charged their father, Laban, with "devouring" the money initially given for them and their children and thus using up their inheritance. The *mohar* or "bride price" may also have served as remuneration to the bride's family for the loss of the bride's continuing help in running the household, because a bride left her home forever to join her husband in his father's household. Certain Old Testament episodes illustrate that occasionally a young man received the young woman he actually longed for to be his wife (see, for example, Genesis 34:4; Judges 14:2).

Once the marriage was agreed upon, the wedding consisted of two stages: betrothal (also called espousal; Matthew 1:18) and a wedding ceremony. There is little evidence in the biblical text that suggests the age at which young men and women were betrothed. Many scholars believe young men worked with their fathers in the family profession or trade for several years after puberty to earn a living, to become expert in their profession, and to save enough to pay the *mohar* as well as to make a gift of jewelry to the bride for her personal possession and to signal her betrothal (Genesis 24:22, 30). (The custom of presenting the bride with jewelry is still practiced among certain groups in the Near East.) Twenty is regarded by scholars as a likely average age for young men to have become betrothed in New Testament times, and fifteen for a young woman (Miller and Miller, *Harper's Encyclopedia of Bible Life*, 100).

Betrothal was legally and religiously more significant than the subsequent marriage ceremony, after which cohabitation actually began. Betrothal was regarded as finalization of a solemn agreement. It carried the force of a covenant to be honored between God-fearing parties (Genesis 2:24; Ezekiel 16:8; Ephesians 5:21–33). Legal action was required to dissolve a betrothal (Deuteronomy 24:1). Mosaic law also recognized the changed status of a man and woman after betrothal by excusing the man from military service until after the wedding ceremony (Deuteronomy 20:7).

Though betrothed couples were regarded as husband and wife legally (Deuteronomy 22:23–24), between the time of betrothal and the ceremony that inaugurated cohabitation, a strict code of chastity was enforced (Matthew 1:18, 25). At the time of betrothal the young man took legal possession of the young woman but not physical. Unfaithfulness during the period of betrothal (espousal) could be punished by death (Deuteronomy 22:23–24). The bride's virtue was also protected by law against rape by calling for the execution of the rapist (Deuteronomy 22:25–27). The groom could "put

APPENDIX 7

away" or quietly divorce his betrothed for unfaithfulness, if he so chose (Matthew 1:19). Various rabbinic authorities and interpreters of the Law described a whole host of justifications allowing a man to put away his wife after the marriage had been consummated. They ranged from childlessness to burning the husband's dinner. But he who gave the Law allowed only one reason: marital infidelity (Matthew 5:32; 19:3).

Once betrothed, a young woman wore a veil whenever she ventured outside her family's home, even when encountering her betrothed husband (Genesis 24:65). The bride remained heavily veiled until after the wedding ceremony. This custom helps to explain how Laban was able to substitute Leah for Rachel as Jacob's first bride (Genesis 29:23–25). There was no set period of betrothal.

On the day of the wedding ceremony and celebration the betrothed woman was typically escorted from her father's or family's house to the house of the bridegroom. The apocryphal book of 1 Maccabees presents a good description of the bridal procession, with a large escort of friends conducting the bride to a predetermined meeting point with her groom, who "came out with his friends and his brothers to meet them with tambourines and musicians" (1 Maccabees 9:37–39). Thus, the context of betrothal and the cultural practices attendant to it among the Israelites (Jews) in the ancient world not only inform our understanding of the situation of Mary and Joseph before Jesus' birth (Matthew 1:18–25) but also form the backdrop of other episodes and parables recounted in the four Gospels (see, for example, the parable of the marriage feast in Matthew 22:2–14, which tells the story after the arrival of the bride and bridegroom at the latter's home; and the parable of the ten virgins in Matthew 25:1–13).

THE CHALLENGE OF JESUS' DATE OF BIRTH

The scriptures are unequivocal that Jesus was born during the reign of Herod the king, also called Herod the Great (Matthew 2:1; Luke 1:5). Historians have set the death date of Herod the Great at 4 B.C., based on several factors. These include Josephus's discussion about Herod's death occurring shortly after a lunar eclipse and before Passover (*Antiquities* [Loeb], XVII.167, 213) and the date of the eclipse, which occurred on the night of March 12–13, 4 B.C. Though history is always subject to revision based on the recovery of data, the best historical evidence dictates that the birth of Jesus occurred in 4 B.C. or earlier. One of the premier New Testament historians has written, "A birth of Jesus dated two years (Matthew 2:16) before the death of Herod in 4 BC would be consonant with the information in Luke 3:23 that Jesus was 'about thirty years of age' in the fifteenth year of the reign of Tiberius Caesar (Luke 3:1)" (Brown, *Birth of the Messiah*, 166–67).

For Latter-day Saints, the challenge comes in attempting to reconcile available historical evidence with Doctrine and Covenants 20:1, which refers to the organization of the Church on April 6, 1830, as being "one thousand eight hundred and thirty years since the coming of our Lord . . . in the flesh." Interpretations of this verse as they relate to the Savior's birth basically fall into two groups. The first views Doctrine and Covenants 20:1 literally, and it champions the statements of Elder James E. Talmage and President Harold B. Lee. Elder Talmage, summarizing various scholarly views, compares their conclusions with modern revelation and then states: "We believe that Jesus Christ was born in Bethlehem of Judea, April 6, B.C. 1" (*Jesus the Christ*, 98). President Harold B. Lee said, "This is the annual conference of the Church. April 6, 1973, is a particularly significant date because it commemorates not only the anniversary of the organization of The Church of Jesus Christ of Latter-day Saints in this dispensation, but also the anniversary of the birth of the Savior, our Lord and Master, Jesus Christ" (Conference Report, April 1973, 4).

A second group follows the admonitions of Elder Bruce R. McConkie and President J. Reuben Clark Jr. in which they advocate suspending final judgment on the question. Elder McConkie wrote:

"We do not believe it is possible with the present state of our knowledge—including that which is known both in and out of the Church—to state with finality when the natal day of the Lord Jesus actually occurred. . . .

"Elder Hyrum M. Smith of the Council of the Twelve wrote in the *Doctrine and Covenants Commentary:* 'The organization of the Church in the year 1830 is hardly to be regarded as giving divine

Appendix 7

authority to the commonly accepted calendar. There are reasons for believing that those who, a long time after our Savior's birth, tried to ascertain the correct time, erred in their calculations, and that the Nativity occurred four years before our era, or in the year of Rome 750. All that this Revelation means to say is that the Church was organized in the year commonly accepted as 1830, A.D.' Rome 750 is equivalent, as indicated, to 4 B.C.

"President J. Reuben Clark, Jr., in *Our Lord of the Gospels*, a scholarly and thoughtful work, says in his preface that many scholars 'fix the date of the Savior's birth at the end of 5 B.C., or the beginning or early part of 4 B.C.' He then quotes the explanation of Doctrine and Covenants 20:1 as found in the *Commentary*, notes that it has been omitted in a later edition, and says: 'I am not proposing any date as the true date. But in order to be as helpful to students as I could, I have taken as the date of the Savior's birth the date now accepted by many scholars,—late 5 B.C., or early 4 B.C., because Bible Commentaries and the writings of scholars are frequently keyed upon that chronology and because I believe that so to do will facilitate and make easier the work of those studying the life and works of the Savior from sources using this accepted chronology.' This is the course being followed in this present work [Elder McConkie's *Mortal Messiah* series], which means, for instance, that Gabriel came to Zacharias in October of 6 B.C.; that he came to Mary in March or April of 5 B.C.; that John was born in June of 5 B.C.; and that Jesus was born in December 5 B.C., or from January to April in 4 B.C. . . .

"We should add that if the slaughter of the Innocents by Herod occurred not weeks but a year or so after our Lord's birth, as some have concluded from the recitation in Matthew 2, . . . Christ could have been born on April 6 of 5 B.C. We repeat, as President Clark repeated, that this is not a settled issue. Perhaps also it does not matter too much as long as we have an accepted framework of time within which to relate the actual events of his life, and one that gives us a reasonably accurate view of when those events took place" (*Mortal Messiah*, 1:349–50).

Regarding the season of the year in which the Savior's birth occurred, the Book of Mormon is extremely helpful. The Nephites inaugurated a new calendar at the time the sign of the Savior's birth was given in the western hemisphere (3 Nephi 2:8). In this new calendar system the signs of the Crucifixion came "in the thirty and fourth year, in the first month, on the fourth day of the month" (3 Nephi 8:5). Thus, the Crucifixion took place shortly after Jesus' thirty-third birthday. The Gospels make clear that the Crucifixion occurred at the time of the Jewish Passover, set by the lunar calendar in late March or early April. Therefore, we know that the birth of Jesus also occurred at this season.

CIRCUMCISION

This symbol of God's covenant with Abraham was enacted by a ceremonial procedure which cut away the foreskin on the part of the male body involved with procreation. It was to be performed on Israelite boys the eighth day after birth in order to teach that children are not accountable before the Lord until they are eight years of age (JST Genesis 17:11–12). Because the Abrahamic covenant includes the promise of eternal posterity (Abraham 2:9–11), the manner of circumcision, involving as it does the organ of procreation, seems highly symbolic—all the descendants of the great patriarch are to be separate and apart from the world, cut off from the world, dedicated to God. Others were commanded to be circumcised, including those who had not been circumcised as babies (Exodus 4:25–26); slaves of covenant households (Genesis 17:13); and strangers desiring to participate in the Lord's Passover (Exodus 12:48). Circumcision from early times came to represent one's attitude toward God and devotion to him. Deuteronomy 10:16 entreats Israel to "circumcise therefore the foreskin of your heart, and be no more stiffnecked" (see also Deuteronomy 30:6). The disobedient, stubborn, or closed-off to God are called the uncircumcised of heart or of ears (Leviticus 26:41; Romans 2:28–29; Jeremiah 6:10).

By New Testament times, the ceremony of circumcision explicitly accompanied the naming of baby boys, as the lives of John the Baptist and Jesus show (Luke 1:59; 2:21). Also by this time, circumcision itself had come to represent the law of Moses, and there was great controversy in the Church of Jesus Christ of the first century over the question of whether or not all male Church members,

Appendix 7

both Jewish and Gentile, were obliged to participate in ritual circumcision (Acts 15:1–31; Galatians 2:1–15). In fact, circumcision as an ordinance or ritual ceremony was done away in Christ (Moroni 8:8). That is, Jesus fulfilled the Law, including circumcision, and "it hath an end" (3 Nephi 15:5). Nevertheless, there was tremendous reluctance on the part of Jewish members of the Church in the meridian dispensation to cease practicing circumcision and other Mosaic rituals (Acts 21:17–25), even after visions and revelations had been received indicating that circumcision was not to be required (Acts 10); a general Church conference had resolved the matter (Acts 15), and arguments had been heard on the issue (Galatians 2:11–21).

FISHING ON THE SEA OF GALILEE

Fishing methods and equipment used at the Sea of Galilee remained about the same from Jesus' day to the 1950s, when modern mechanization and technology changed the occupation dramatically. Three types of nets were used. First, the cast net or throw net, used by a single person, was circular, approximately twenty feet in diameter, with lead or flint weights at the edges; it would trap the fish under the net, and the fisherman would dive down to secure the net and draw up the fish (Matthew 4:18–20; Mark 1:16–18). Second, there was the dragnet, or *seine* (Greek, *sagene;* see Matthew 13:47–48). Third, there was the trammel net, which consisted of multiple layers of nets (Matthew 4:21–22; Mark 1:19–20; Luke 5:1–7). Both the seine and the trammel nets required a crew of sixteen to twenty men in two boats, or were drawn in from the shore, and laid out up to a thousand feet; corks were used to raise one level of netting while weights were attached so the lower level of netting would sink. It was also possible to catch fish using hook and line, as Peter did to obtain the tribute money (Matthew 17:24–27).

Fish of the New Testament period are still represented by three surviving groups: (1) *musht* (Arabic, "comb," because the dorsal fin looks like a comb); the main fish of this group is called *Tilapia Galilea* or "Saint Peter's fish"; (2) barbels, part of the carp family; and (3) freshwater sardines (cf. "two small fishes" in John 6:9),

Cultural and Religious Practices

which still constitute more than half of the lake's annual catch, about one thousand tons.

The best fishing was between October and April, before the hot season when fish remain at greater depths, and during early morning hours (Luke 5:5; John 21:3).

Fish swarm especially to the northwest corner of the lake, between Capernaum and Gennesaret, because they are attracted to the copious warm springs there. Another highly successful fishing spot is the northeast corner, near Bethsaida, where the Jordan River enters the lake, which also features warm springs.

Simon Peter apparently owned a boat, nets, and other fishing gear. These properties, along with a home in Capernaum, made Peter's family relatively wealthy (Matthew 8:14; Luke 5:3; 18:28).

In May 2005, Brother Ogden went out on the Sea of Galilee for nearly nine hours with Ya'ir, Yo'el, and Moti, fishermen from Kibbutz Ginnosar. Following are a few notes from that experience:

"For many centuries most fishing was done at night, but in recent years the expert fishermen have proved that fishing in some parts of the year is just as successful during the daytime, so that's when much of the fishing is done now. When asked where the best

Nets used by fishermen in the Sea of Galilee today

Appendix 7

Casting the bad away (Matthew 13:48)

fishing was, Ya'ir said with a smile, 'At Capernaum—the fish go there to pray first thing in the morning.' With the help of their heavy-duty hydraulic equipment they laid the nets in a big circle, maybe 50 to 60 meters in diameter, then they started drawing them in. The nets had cork floats at the top, and heavy metal rings served as weights at the bottom. The fish caught were mostly carp, *musht* (St. Peter's fish), and small sardines. These three fishermen were quite selective; they kept the big carp and St. Peter's fish, the commercially valuable ones, then they scooped up the smaller fish (the "bad ones"; Matthew 13:48 says they "gathered the good into vessels, but cast the bad away") and threw them back into the water—to the delight of the forty to fifty egrets that fluttered around us all day just to have a tasty meal of the leftovers. Most of their fishing was done between Capernaum and Bethsaida at the north and northeast of the lake. Ya'ir responded to questions all day long: 'Why were the apostles washing their nets?' 'Because the fish don't like dirty ones,' he said. 'Why were the apostles mending their nets?' (as I saw these men do at least twice during the day). 'Because they get ripped by rocks or trees under the surface' (Ogden, journal; for further details, see Nun, "Cast Your Net upon the Waters," 46–56, 70, and *Sea of Galilee and Its Fishermen*).

MONEY

During Old Testament times silver and gold were the primary mediums of exchange and were measured or weighed by units called shekels and talents. Unless otherwise specified, a shekel referred to a quantity of silver, the most common monetary unit in ancient Israel. In the period just after the last of the Old Testament prophets, a shekel on average weighed slightly more than 11 grams, or .4 of an ounce, but it may have been less in earlier times. In New Testament times a talent weighed about 75 pounds (34.2 kilograms) and was the equivalent of 3,000 shekels. Thus, when Jesus refers to 10,000 talents in the parable of the unforgiving servant, he was speaking of an enormous sum of money (Matthew 18:24).

The first minted coins seem to have been circulated beginning in the seventh century before Christ in Lydia, a region in what is now western Turkey. Coinage did not come into use in the Holy Land until near the end of Old Testament times, during the Persian period. During the Hasmonean period, Simon the Maccabee (the first king and high priest to preside over the newly reconstituted independent nation of Israel), minted silver coins called shekels and half-shekels. On the obverse side of the shekel was engraved the figure of a cup with the inscription "shekel of Israel." On the reverse side was engraved a branch with three buds and the inscription "Jerusalem the Holy." The minting of coins is one symbol of a nation's sovereignty or a people's desire for or declaration of sovereignty.

During New Testament times Greek, Roman, and Jewish coins all circulated in the Holy Land. They are referred to by specific names in the original Greek text of the New Testament, ranging from the Greek *lepton*, or "mite," which was the smallest coin used by the Jews (Luke 12:59), to the largest, the silver *stater* (Greek), which was equal to four *drachmas* and probably is to be identified with the pieces of silver spoken of in Matthew 26:15; 27:3–6. The *stater* was the equivalent of the Jewish shekel.

Other important coins include the Greek *drachma* (Luke 15:8–9) and the *didrachmon*, which was the equivalent of the

APPENDIX 7

half-shekel or annual Temple tax owed by every adult Jewish male twenty years of age and older (Exodus 30:13; 2 Chronicles 24:9) and which was used for the upkeep of the Temple (Matthew 17:24). The Roman *denarius* is always translated as "penny" in the King James Version and is the coin mentioned in Jesus' exchange with the Pharisees and Herodians when he issued the famous statement about rendering unto Caesar the things that are Caesar's (Matthew 22:19–21). The Greek *kodrantes* (Latin, *quandrans*) is translated as "farthing" (Matthew 5:26) and is the term used in the episode involving the widow's mites (Mark 12:42). The *kodrantes* is slightly more valuable than the *lepton*. As with *talent*, a *mina* was not a coin but a sum of money (Luke 19:13) equivalent to fifty shekels.

TIME

During the New Testament era the day technically began at sundown and ran to the next sundown, following the ancient Israelite interpretation of the Hebrew text of Genesis 1:5—"the evening and the morning were the first day." The hours of the day, however, were counted from roughly sun up, about 6 A.M., onward. Thus, the first hour of the day corresponded to the period from 6 A.M. to 7 A.M., the second hour from 7 A.M. to 8 A.M., and so forth. The counting of the day ended with the twelfth hour, 5 P.M. to 6 P.M. Thus, important moments in the Savior's ministry are referenced in the Gospels by the hour of the day in which they occurred: Jesus was crucified at the third hour, or 9:00 A.M. (Mark 15:25); darkness came over the whole land during the Crucifixion from the sixth hour to the ninth hour, or from noon until 3:00 P.M. (Matthew 27:45; Mark 15:33; Luke 23:44); he expired about the ninth hour, or 3:00 P.M. (Matthew 27:46–50; Mark 15:34–37).

The night was divided into four "watches" by the Jews, based on Roman practice. The first watch ran from sunset (or 6 P.M.) to 9 P.M. (Mark 13:35). The second watch ran from 9 P.M. to midnight (Matthew 25:6; Luke 11:5). The third watch went from midnight to 3 A.M. (called the cock crowing; Matthew 26:74; Mark 14:68, 72; Luke 22:60–61; John 18:27); and the fourth watch from 3 A.M. to 6 A.M., or sunrise (Matthew 14:25; Mark 6:48).

Cultural and Religious Practices

WEIGHTS AND MEASURES

The different terms found in the King James New Testament for the many and varying weights and measures that were used in the Holy Land are only sometimes identifiable with modern equivalents. Some of the more prominent ones include the following:

Talent (Matthew 25:15) = 75 pounds
Mile (Matthew 5:41) = 4,500 feet
Furlong (Luke 24:13) = 600 feet
Cubit (Matthew 6:27) = 18 inches
Bushel (Matthew 5:15) = 7.5 dry quarts or less than half a
    U.S. bushel (8.75 liters, or one peck)
"Measure of wheat" (Luke 16:7) = 11 bushels
Firkin (John 2:6) = 9 gallons

SOURCES

Adams, Roger J. "The Iconography of Early Christian Initiation: Evidence for Baptism for the Dead." Unpublished manuscript. Brigham Young University, 1977.
Albright, W. F., and C. S. Mann. *Matthew*. A volume in *The Anchor Bible*. New York: Doubleday, 1971.
The Anchor Bible Dictionary. 6 vols. Edited by David Noel Freedman. New York: Doubleday, 1992.
Anderson, Richard Lloyd. *Guide to the Life of Christ*. Reprint. Provo, Utah: FARMS, 1999.
Arndt, William F., and F. Wilbur Gingrich. *A Greek-English Lexicon of the New Testament and Other Early Christian Literature*. 2d ed. Chicago: University of Chicago Press, 1979.
Asay, Carlos E. *Ensign*, May 1980, 42.
Ashton, Marvin J. *Ensign*, May 1992, 18.
Avi-Yonah, Michael. "Jerusalem in the Hellenistic and Roman Periods." In *The World History of the Jewish People*. 8 vols. Edited by B. Netanyahu, et al. New Brunswick, N.J.: Rutgers University Press, 1975.
Babylonian Talmud. Edited, corrected, formulated, and translated into English by Michael L. Rodkinson. Vol. 1, *Tract Sabbath*. Boston: Talmud Society, 1918.
Bahat, Dan. *The Illustrated Atlas of Jerusalem*. New York: Simon and Schuster, 1990.
Ballard, Melvin J. *Sermons and Missionary Services of Melvin Joseph Ballard*. Compiled by Bryant S. Hinckley. Salt Lake City: Deseret Book, 1949.
Ballard, M. Russell. *Ensign*, May 1989, 80.
———. *Ensign*, May 1991, 80.
Ben-Dov, Meir. *In the Shadow of the Temple: The Discovery of Ancient Jerusalem*. Jerusalem: Keter Publishing House, 1985.
Benson, Ezra Taft. *Come unto Christ*. Salt Lake City: Deseret Book, 1983.

———. *The Teachings of Ezra Taft Benson*. Salt Lake City: Bookcraft, 1988.

Best Loved Stories of the LDS People. Edited by Jack M. Lyon, Linda Ririe Gundry, and Jay A. Parry. Salt Lake City: Deseret Book, 1997.

Biblical Archaeology Review. [Periodical.] Washington, D.C.: The Biblical Archaeology Society, 1974–present.

Black, Matthew. *An Aramaic Approach to the Gospels and Acts*. Oxford: Clarendon Press, 1946.

The Book of Mormon. Salt Lake City: The Church of Jesus Christ of Latter-day Saints, 1981.

Bradford, William R. *Ensign*, November 1987, 75.

Broshi, M. "The Role of the Temple in the Herodian Economy." *Journal of Jewish Studies* 38 (Spring 1987).

Brown, Raymond E., trans. *The Gospel According to John*. Anchor Bible Series, Vols. 29 and 29A. Garden City, N.Y.: Doubleday, 1966–1970.

Brown, Raymond S. *The Birth of the Messiah—A Commentary on the Infancy Narratives in Matthew and Luke*. Garden City, N.Y.:Doubleday, Image Books, 1979.

———. *The Death of the Messiah: From Gethsemane to the Grave—A Commentary on the Passion Narratives in the Four Gospels*. New York: Doubleday, 1994.

Brown, S. Kent. *Mary and Elisabeth*. American Fork, Utah: Covenant Communications, 2002.

Bruce, F. F. *The New Testament Documents: Are They Reliable?* 5th ed. Downers Grove, Ill.: InterVarsity Press, 2001.

———. *New Testament History*. New York: Doubleday, Galilee Book, 1969.

"Burial Cave of the Caiaphas Family." *Biblical Archaeology Review*, September/October 1992.

Burton, Theodore M. *Ensign*, November 1974, 54.

The Cambridge Bible Dictionary.

Cannon, Abraham H. Private Journal of 1892. Vault Mss. 62, Box 2, Folder 4. L. Tom Perry Special Collections Library, Harold B. Lee Library, Brigham Young University, Provo, Utah.

Chadwick, Jeffrey R. "Revisiting Golgotha and the Garden Tomb." *Religious Educator* 4, no. 1 (2003).

Chandler, Walter M. *The Trial of Jesus from a Lawyer's Standpoint*. 2 vols. New York: Empire Publishing, 1908.

Children's Songbook of The Church of Jesus Christ of Latter-day Saints. Salt Lake City: The Church of Jesus Christ of Latter-day Saints, 1989.

SOURCES

Christiansen, ElRay L. *Ensign,* June 1971, 37.

Church History in the Fulness of Times. Prepared by the Church Educational System of The Church of Jesus Christ of Latter-day Saints. 2d ed. Salt Lake City: Intellectual Reserve, 2003.

Clark, J. Reuben, Jr. *Behold the Lamb of God.* Salt Lake City: Deseret Book, 1962.

———. *Our Lord of the Gospels.* Salt Lake City: Deseret Book, 1974.

Collected Discourses. Edited by Brian H. Stuy. 5 vols. Sandy, Utah: B.H.S. Publishing, 1992.

Condie, Spencer J. *Ensign,* September 1995, 16.

Conference Reports. Salt Lake City: The Church of Jesus Christ of Latter-day Saints, 1898–present.

Connolly, Peter. *Living in the Time of Jesus of Nazareth.* Oxford: Oxford University Press, 1983.

Correspondence of Palestine Tourists. Salt Lake City, Utah Territory: Deseret News Steam Printing Establishment, 1875.

Cowley, Matthias F. *Wilford Woodruff: History of His Life and Labors.* 1909. Reprint, Salt Lake City: Bookcraft, 1964.

Dahl, Larry E. *Ensign,* February 1991, 7.

Derrick, Royden G. *Temples in the Last Days.* Salt Lake City: Bookcraft, 1987.

Dew, Sheri. *No Doubt about It.* Salt Lake City: Bookcraft, 2001.

Doctrine and Covenants. Salt Lake City: The Church of Jesus Christ of Latter-day Saints, 1981.

Douglas, Colin B. *Ensign,* April 1989, 13.

Drummond, Henry. *The Greatest Thing in the World.* New York: Dodge Publishing Company, n.d.

Duckwitz, Norbert H. O. *Reading the Gospel of St. John in Greek.* New York: Aristide D. Caratzas, 2002.

Dummelow, J. R. *A Commentary on the Holy Bible.* New York: Macmillan, 1956.

Edersheim, Alfred. *The Life and Times of Jesus the Messiah.* McLean, Va.: Macdonald Publishing, n.d.

———. *The Temple: Its Ministry and Services As They Were at the Time of Jesus Christ.* 1874. Reprint, Grand Rapids, Mich.: William B. Eerdmans, 1990.

Edwards, William D., et al. "On the Physical Death of Jesus Christ." *Journal of the American Medical Association* 255, no. 11 (March 21, 1986).

Encyclopedia Judaica. Edited by Geoffrey Wigoder. 16 vols. Jerusalem: Keter, 1972.

Encyclopedia of Latter-day Saint History. Edited by Arnold K. Garr,

Donald Q. Cannon, and Richard O. Cowan. Salt Lake City: Deseret Book, 2000.

Encyclopedia of Mormonism. Edited by Daniel H. Ludlow. 5 vols. New York: Macmillan, 1992.

Eusebius. *Ecclesiastical History.* Translated by Kirsopp Lake. 2 vols. Loeb Classical Library. Cambridge: Harvard University Press, 1992.

———. *The History of the Church from Christ to Constantine.* Translated by G. A. Williamson. London: Penguin Books, 1989.

———. *Onomasticon: Latin & Greek.* Hildesheim: G. Olms, 1966.

Eyring, Henry B. *To Draw Closer to God.* Salt Lake City: Deseret Book, 1997.

Farrar, Frederic W. *The Life of Christ.* London and New York: Cassell and Company, 1898.

Faust, James E. *Ensign,* May 1993, 35.

———. *Ensign,* May 2003, 61.

Federer, William J. *America's God and Country—Encyclopedia of Quotations.* St. Louis, Mo.: Amerisearch, 2000.

Finegan, Jack. *The Archeology of the New Testament: The Life of Jesus and the Beginning of the Early Church.* Princeton, N.J.: Princeton University Press, 1992.

First Presidency Statement. *Ensign,* August 1992, 80.

Flake, Lawrence R. *Prophets and Apostles of the Last Dispensation.* Provo, Utah: Religious Studies Center, Brigham Young University, 2001.

Foschini, Bernard M. "Those Who Are Baptized for the Dead." *Catholic Biblical Quarterly* 13 (1951).

Franklin, Benjamin. "The Way to Wealth—Being the Preface to Poor Richard's Almanac for 1758." Philadelphia: Jacob Johnson, 1808.

Galbraith, David B., D. Kelly Ogden, and Andrew C. Skinner. *Jerusalem, the Eternal City.* Salt Lake City: Deseret Book, 1996.

Gaster, Theodor H. *The Dead Sea Scriptures.* 3d ed. New York: Anchor Books, 1976.

Geikie, Cunningham. *The Life and Words of Christ.* New York: Columbian Publishing, 1891.

Geva, Hillel, ed. *Ancient Jerusalem Revealed.* Jerusalem: Israel Exploration Society, 1994.

The Gift of the Atonement. Salt Lake City: Deseret Book, 2002.

Ginzberg, Louis. *The Legends of the Jews.* Philadelphia: Jewish Publication Society of America, 1906–38.

Hafen, Bruce C. *The Believing Heart.* Salt Lake City: Deseret Book, 1990.

———. *A Disciple's Life: The Biography of Neal A. Maxwell.* Salt Lake City: Deseret Book, 2002.
Hall, John F. *New Testament Witnesses of Christ: Peter, John, James, & Paul.* American Fork, Utah: Covenant Communications, 2002.
Harvey, Zeev. "Jesus in Medieval and Modern Jewish Thought." Israeli government-sponsored Seminar on Christ, Galei Zohar Hotel on the shore of the Dead Sea, March 23–25, 1990. Personal notes by author D. Kelly Ogden.
Hinckley, Gordon B. *Stand a Little Taller.* Salt Lake City: Deseret Book, 2001.
———. *Teachings of Gordon B. Hinckley.* Salt Lake City: Deseret Book, 1997.
———. *Ensign,* May 1991, 71.
———. *Ensign,* March 1995, 2.
———. *Ensign,* March 1998, 2.
———. *Ensign,* September 2001, 2.
———. *Ensign,* November 2001, 73.
———. *Ensign,* November 2002, 78.
Hite, Steven J., and Julie M. Hite, comp. *The New Testament—with the Joseph Smith Translation.* Orem, Utah: Veritas Group, 1994.
Holland, Jeffrey R. *Ensign,* May 2002, 63.
———. *Ensign,* May 2004, 32.
Holy Bible. Authorized King James Version.
Holzapfel, Richard Neitzel, and Thomas A. Wayment, eds. *From Bethlehem through the Sermon on the Mount.* Vol. 1 of *The Life and Teachings of Jesus Christ* series. Salt Lake City: Deseret Book, 2005.
———. *From the Last Supper through the Resurrection.* Vol. 3 of *The Life and Teachings of Jesus Christ* series. Salt Lake City: Deseret Book, 2003.
Hunter, Howard W. *Ensign,* November 1979, 65.
———. *Ensign,* November 1984, 33.
Hymns. Salt Lake City: The Church of Jesus Christ of Latter-day Saints, 1948.
Hymns of The Church of Jesus Christ of Latter-day Saints. Salt Lake City: The Church of Jesus Christ of Latter-day Saints, 1985.
Improvement Era. [Periodical] Salt Lake City: The Church of Jesus Christ of Latter-day Saints.
Jackson, Kent P. and Robert L. Millet, eds. *The Gospels.* Vol. 5 of *Studies in Scripture* series. Salt Lake City: Deseret Book, 1986.
Jagersma, Henk. *A History of Israel from Alexander the Great to Bar Kochba.* Translated by John Bowden. Philadelphia: Fortress Press, 1986.

Jeffers, James S. *The Greco-Roman World of the New Testament Era:exploring the background of early Christianity*. Downer's Grove, Ill.: InterVarsity Press, 1999.

Jerusalem Post. English language newspaper published in Jerusalem, Israel, 1983.

Jesus Christ, Son of God, Savior. Edited by Paul H. Peterson, Gary L. Hatch, and Laura D. Card. Provo, Utah: Religious Studies Center, Brigham Young University, 2002.

Joseph Smith's "New Translation" of the Bible [JST]. Independence, Mo.: Herald House, 1970.

Josephus, Flavius. *Complete Works*. Translated by William Whiston. Grand Rapids, Mich.: Kregel Publications, 1973.

———. *Jewish Antiquities*. Translated by Louis H. Feldman. Loeb Classical Library. Cambridge: Harvard University Press, 1965.

———. *Jewish War*. Translated by H. St. J. Thackeray. 2 vols. Loeb Classical Library. Cambridge: Harvard University Press, 1927–28.

Journal of Discourses. 26 vols. Liverpool: Latter-day Saints' Book Depot, 1854–86.

Kelly, Burton C. *Ensign*, February 1980, 9.

Kimball, Spencer W. *Faith Precedes the Miracle*. Salt Lake City: Deseret Book, 1972.

———. *The Miracle of Forgiveness*. Salt Lake City: Bookcraft, 1969.

———. *The Teachings of Spencer W. Kimball*. Edited by Edward L. Kimball. Salt Lake City: Bookcraft, 1982.

———. Munich Germany Area Conference Report 1973, 76–77.

———. *Humility*. Brigham Young University Speeches of the Year. Provo, Utah, January 16, 1963.

———. *Peter, My Brother*. Brigham Young University Speeches of the Year. Provo, Utah, July 13, 1971.

———. *Ensign*, December 1974, 2.

———. *Ensign*, October 1979, 9.

———. *Ensign*, November 1979, 104.

Kloner, Amos. "Did a Rolling Stone Close Jesus' Tomb?" in *Biblical Archaeology Review* 25, no. 5 (September/October 1999).

Lane, William L. *The Gospel According to Mark*. Grand Rapids, Mich.: William B. Eerdmans, 1974.

Lasater, John R. *Ensign*, May 1988, 74.

Lee, Harold B. *Decisions for Successful Living*. Salt Lake City: Deseret Book, 1973.

———. *The Teachings of Harold B. Lee*. Compiled by Clyde Williams. Salt Lake City: Bookcraft, 1996.

Lewis, C. S. *Mere Christianity*. New York: Simon & Schuster, Touchstone, 1996.

SOURCES

The Life and Teachings of Jesus and His Apostles. Prepared by the Church Educational System. 2d. ed., rev. Salt Lake City: The Church of Jesus Christ of Latter-day Saints, 1979.

Longden, John. Conference Report, April 1966.

Ludlow, Daniel H. *A Companion to Your Study of the New Testament—The Four Gospels.* Salt Lake City: Deseret Book, 1982.

———. *A Companion to Your Study of the Old Testament.* Salt Lake City: Deseret Book, 1981.

Lund, Gerald N. *The Kingdom and the Crown.* 3 vols. Salt Lake City: Shadow Mountain, 2000–2002.

———. *Ensign,* July 1975, 31.

Lyon, T. Edgar. *Ensign,* September 1974, 20.

Madsen, Truman G., ed. *The Temple in Antiquity: Ancient Records and Modern Perspectives.* Provo, Utah: Brigham Young University Religious Studies Center, 1984.

Martin, James C. *The Life and World of Jesus the Messiah—The Gospels in Context.* Gaithersburg, Md.: Preserving Bible Times, 2002.

Matthews, Robert J. *A Burning Light: The Life and Ministry of John the Baptist.* Reprint, Orem, Utah: Granite, 2000.

———. *Behold the Messiah.* Salt Lake City: Bookcraft, 1994.

Maxwell, Neal A. *All These Things Shall Give Thee Experience.* Salt Lake City: Deseret Book, 1980.

———. *Lord, Increase Our Faith.* Salt Lake City: Bookcraft, 1994.

———. "But a Few Days." Brigham Young University Devotional Address, February 12, 1982.

———. *Ensign,* November 1974, 13.

———. *Ensign,* May 1985, 72.

———. *Ensign,* May 1989, 63.

———. *Ensign,* May 1991, 88.

McConkie, Bruce R. *Doctrinal New Testament Commentary.* 3 vols. Salt Lake City: Bookcraft, 1976.

———. *Doctrines of the Restoration.* Edited by Mark L. McConkie. Salt Lake City: Bookcraft, 1989.

———. *The Millennial Messiah.* Salt Lake City: Deseret Book, 1982.

———. *Mormon Doctrine.* 2d. ed. Salt Lake City: Bookcraft, 1966.

———. *The Mortal Messiah.* 4 vols. Salt Lake City: Deseret Book, 1979–81.

———. *New Witness for the Articles of Faith.* Salt Lake City: Deseret Book, 1985.

———. *The Promised Messiah.* Salt Lake City: Deseret Book, 1978.

———. *Ensign,* May 1985, 9.

———. "The Probationary Test of Mortality." Address delivered at

University of Utah Institute of Religion, 10 January 1982. Typescript.

McConkie, Joseph Fielding. *The Bruce R. McConkie Story.* Salt Lake City: Deseret Book, 2003.

McConkie, Joseph Fielding, and Craig J. Ostler. *Revelations of the Restoration: A Commentary on the Doctrine and Covenants and Other Modern Revelations.* Salt Lake City: Deseret Book, 2000.

McKay, David O. *Cherished Experiences.* Compiled by Clare Middlemiss. Salt Lake City: Deseret Book, 1967.

———. *Pathways to Happiness.* Salt Lake City: Bookcraft, 1957.

The Meaning of the Glorious Koran. An explanatory translation by Marmaduke Pickthall. New York: Dorset Press, n.d.

Messages of the First Presidency of The Church of Jesus Christ of Latter-day Saints, 1833–1964. Compiled by James R. Clark. 6 vols. Salt Lake City: Bookcraft, 1971–75.

Millard, Alan. *Discoveries from the Time of Jesus.* Oxford: Lion Publishing, 1990.

Miller, Madeleine S., and J. Lane Miller. *Harper's Encyclopedia of Bible Life.* Edison, N.J.: Castle Books, 1996.

The Mishnah. Translated by Herbert Danby. London: Oxford University Press, 1933.

Monson, Thomas S. *Ensign,* October 1979, 12.

———. *Ensign,* December 1985, 48.

Mumford, Thomas M. *Horizontal Harmony of the Four Gospels in Parallel Columns.* Salt Lake City: Deseret Book, 1976.

Nelson, Russell M. *Ensign,* February 2003, 20.

Netzer, Ehud. *Bulletin of the American Schools of Oriental Research,* 228 (1977).

New Encyclopedia of Archaeological Excavations in the Holy Land. 4 vols. Edited by Ephraim Stern. London: Israel Exploration Society and Carta, 1993.

The New Oxford Annotated Apocrypha: The Apocryphal/ Deuterocanonical Books of the Old Testament (New Revised Standard Version). Edited by Bruce M. Metzger and Roland E. Murphy. New York: Oxford University Press, 1991.

The New Testament for Latter-day Saint Families. Edited by Thomas R. Valletta et al. Salt Lake City: Bookcraft, 1998.

New Testament Gospel Doctrine Teacher's Manual. Prepared by the Church Educational System. Salt Lake City: The Church of Jesus Christ of Latter-day Saints, 2002.

New Testament Student Study Guide. Prepared by the Church Educational System. Salt Lake City: The Church of Jesus Christ of Latter-day Saints, 1999.

Nibley, Hugh. "Baptism for the Dead in Ancient Times." *Improvement Era* 51–52 (December 1948–April 1949).

The New International Version Study Bible. Kenneth Barker, general ed. Grand Rapids, Mich.: Zondervan, 1985.

The New International Version Learning Bible. New York: American Bible Society, 2003.

Nun, Mendel. *The Sea of Galilee and Its Fishermen in the New Testament*. Kibbutz En Gev, Israel: Kinnereth Sailing Co., 1989.

———. "Cast Your Net upon the Waters—Fish and Fishermen in Jesus' Time." *Biblical Archaeology Review*, November-December 1993.

Oaks, Dallin H. *Ensign*, January 1995, 7.

Ogden, D. Kelly. *Illustrated Guide to the Model City and to New Testament Jerusalem*. 2d ed. Jerusalem: Jerusalem Center for Near Eastern Studies, 1990.

———. *Where Jesus Walked: The Land and Culture of New Testament Times*. Salt Lake City: Deseret Book, 1991.

———. *Pioneering the East*. Provo, Utah: n. p., 2002.

Ogden, D. Kelly, and Jeffrey R. Chadwick. *The Holy Land: A Geographical, Historical, and Archaeological Guide to the Land of the Bible*. Jerusalem: Jerusalem Center for Near Eastern Studies, 1990.

Ogden, D. Kelly, and Marcia H. Ogden. *The President and the Preacher—Memoirs of a Mission President and Companion*. Provo, Utah: n. p., 2002.

Ogden, D. Kelly, and Andrew C. Skinner. *New Testament Apostles Testify of Christ: A Guide for Acts through Revelation*. Salt Lake City: Deseret Book, 1998. Reprint, *Verse by Verse, Acts through Revelation*. Salt Lake City: Deseret Book, 2006.

Our Savior in the Gospels. [34 television programs on the New Testament Gospels] Provo, Utah: Brigham Young University: Continuing Education/BYU Television, 2002.

Packer, Boyd K. *Teach Ye Diligently*. Salt Lake City: Deseret Book, 1975.

———. CES Fireside for Young Adults at Brigham Young University, February 2, 2003.

———. *Follow the Brethren*. Brigham Young University Speeches of the Year, Provo, Utah, 1965.

———. "Teach the Scriptures." In *Charge to Religious Educators*. 3d ed. Salt Lake City: The Church of Jesus Christ of Latter-day Saints, 1994.

———. *Ensign*, January 1974, 28.

———. *Ensign*, May 1980, 62.

———. *Ensign,* November 1982, 51.
———. *Ensign,* May 1988, 69.
———. *Ensign,* May 1989, 59.
———. *Ensign,* November 2005, 70.
Parry, Donald W., Jay A. Parry, and Tina M. Peterson. *Understanding Isaiah.* Salt Lake City: Deseret Book, 1998.
Parry, Donald W., and Dana M. Pike. *LDS Perspectives on the Dead Sea Scrolls.* Provo, Utah: Foundation for Ancient Research and Mormon Studies (FARMS), 1997.
The Pearl of Great Price. Salt Lake City: The Church of Jesus Christ of Latter-day Saints, 1981.
Philo of Alexandria [Philonis Alexandrini]. *Legatio ad Gaium.* Edited and translated by E. Mary Smallwood. Leiden: E. J. Brill, 1970.
Pirke Aboth—The Ethics of the Talmud: Sayings of the Fathers. Edited by R. Travers Herford. New York: Schocken Books, 1962.
Pixner, Bargil. *With Jesus through Galilee—According to the Fifth Gospel.* Rosh Pina, Israel: Corazin Publishing, 1992.
Pratt, Orson. *The Seer* 1, no. 4 (April 1853). Reprint, Orem, Utah: Grandin, 1990.
Rector, Hartman, Jr. *Ensign,* May 1979, 29.
The Redeemer: Reflections on the Life and Teachings of Jesus the Christ. Salt Lake City: Deseret Book, 2000.
Religion 211 Independent Study Course. Provo, Utah: Brigham Young University, 2002.
The Religious Educator. Provo, Utah: Brigham Young University, Religious Education.
Revillo, Carlos C. *Ensign,* January 2004, 21.
Reznick, Leibel. *The Holy Temple Revisited.* Northvale, N. J.: Jason Aronson, 1990.
Richards, LeGrand. *A Marvelous Work and a Wonder.* Salt Lake City: Deseret Book, 1976.
Roberts, B. H. *The Life of John Taylor.* Salt Lake City: Bookcraft, 1963.
Robinson, Edward. *Biblical Researches in Palestine and the Adjacent Regions: A Journal of Travels in the Years 1838 and 1852.* 4 vols. Boston: Crocker and Brewster, 1841 and 1856.
Robinson, Stephen E. *Are Mormons Christians?* Salt Lake City: Bookcraft, 1991.
———. *Believing Christ.* Salt Lake City: Deseret Book, 1992.
Robinson, Stephen E., and H. Dean Garrett. *A Commentary on the Doctrine and Covenants.* 4 vols. Salt Lake City: Deseret Book, 2000–2006.

Rosen, Ceil, and Moishe Rosen. *Christ in the Passover.* Chicago: Moody Press, 1978.

Rousseau, John J., and Rami Arav. *Jesus and His World: An Archaeological and Cultural Dictionary.* Minneapolis: Augsburg Fortress Press, 1995.

Schurer, Emil. *The History of the Jewish People in the Age of Jesus Christ.* Edited by Geza Vermes and Fergus Millar. Edinburg: T. & T. Clark Ltd., 1973.

Scott, Richard G. *Ensign,* November 1995, 16.

Skinner, Andrew C. *The Garden Tomb.* Salt Lake City: Deseret Book, 2005.

———. *Gethsemane.* Salt Lake City: Deseret Book, 2002.

———. *Golgotha.* Salt Lake City: Deseret Book, 2004.

———. *Ensign,* June 2002, 24.

———. "Serpent Symbols and Salvation in the Ancient Near East and the Book of Mormon." *Journal of Book of Mormon Studies* 10, no. 2 (2001).

Skinner, Andrew C., and W. Jeffrey Marsh. *Scriptural Parables for the Latter Days.* Salt Lake City: Deseret Book, 2002.

Smith, Eliza R. Snow. *Biography and Family Record of Lorenzo Snow.* Salt Lake City: Deseret News Company Printers, 1884.

Smith, George Adam. *Jerusalem: The Topography, Economics and History from the Earliest Times to A.D. 70.* 2 vols. London: Hodder and Stoughton, 1907.

Smith, George Albert. *Sharing the Gospel with Others.* Salt Lake City: Deseret Book, 1950.

Smith, Hyrum M., and Janne M. Sjodahl. *Doctrine and Covenants Commentary.* Revised ed. Salt Lake City: Deseret Book, 1978.

Smith, Joseph. *History of The Church of Jesus Christ of Latter-day Saints.* Edited by B. H. Roberts. 2d ed. rev. 7 vols. Salt Lake City: Deseret Book, 1980.

———. *Lectures on Faith.* Independence, Mo.: Price Publishing, 1988.

———. *Personal Writings of Joseph Smith.* Compiled and edited by Dean C. Jessee. Salt Lake City: Deseret Book, 1984.

———. *Scriptural Teachings of the Prophet Joseph Smith.* Selected by Joseph Fielding Smith, with annotations and introduction by Richard C. Galbraith. Salt Lake City: Deseret Book, 1993.

———. *Teachings of the Prophet Joseph Smith.* Sel. Joseph Fielding Smith. Salt Lake City: Deseret Book, 1938.

———. *The Words of Joseph Smith: The Contemporary Accounts of the Nauvoo Discourses of the Prophet Joseph.* Compiled and edited by Andrew F. Ehat and Lyndon W. Cook. Orem, Utah: Grandin, 1991.

Smith, Joseph F. *Gospel Doctrine*. Salt Lake City: Deseret Book, 1939.

Smith, Joseph Fielding. *Answers to Gospel Questions*. Compiled by Joseph Fielding Smith Jr. 5 vols. Salt Lake City: Deseret Book, 1979.

———. *Church History and Modern Revelation*. 2 vols. Salt Lake City: The Church of Jesus Christ of Latter-day Saints, 1953.

———. *Doctrines of Salvation*. Compiled by Bruce R. McConkie. 3 vols. Salt Lake City: Bookcraft, 1954–56.

———. *Man: His Origin and Destiny*. Salt Lake City: Deseret Book, 1954.

Snow, Lorenzo. *Correspondence of Palestine Tourists*. Salt Lake City: Deseret News Steam Printing Establishment, 1875.

Sowell, Madison U. "Along with the Command." In *Brigham Young University Speeches of the Year, 1997*. Provo, Utah: Brigham Young University, 1997.

Stein, Robert H. *Difficult Sayings in the Gospels—Jesus' Use of Overstatement and Hyperbole*. Grand Rapids, Mich.: Baker Book House, 1985.

Steinberg, Milton. *Basic Judaism*. Northvale, N.J.: J. Aronson, 1987.

Stern, David H. *Jewish New Testament*. Jerusalem: Jewish New Testament Publications, 1989.

Strobel, Lee. *The Case for Christ*. Grand Rapids, Mich.: Zondervan, 1998.

Tacitus. *The Annals of Imperial Rome*. Translated with an introduction by Michael Grant. Baltimore: Penguin Books, 1956.

Talmage, James E. *Articles of Faith*. Salt Lake City: The Church of Jesus Christ of Latter-day Saints, 1966.

———. *Jesus the Christ*. Classics in Mormon Literature Series. Salt Lake City: Deseret Book, 1983.

Talmon, Shemaryahu. *The "Dead Sea Scrolls" or "The Commentary of the Renewed Covenant."* Tucson, Ariz.: University of Arizona, 1993.

The Talmud of Babylonia. Translated by Jacob Neusner. Chico, Calif.: Scholars Press, 1985.

Tate, Charles D. Jr., trans. In *BYU Studies* 15, no. 1 (Autumn 1974); 103.

Tate, Lucile C. *LeGrand Richards: Beloved Apostle*. Salt Lake City: Bookcraft, 1982.

Thompson, J. A. *The Bible and Archaeology*. 3d ed. Grand Rapids, Mich.: William B. Eerdmans, 1982.

True to the Faith. Salt Lake City: The Church of Jesus Christ of Latter-day Saints, 2004.

Trumbower, Jeffrey A. *Rescue for the Dead: The Posthumous Salvation of Non-Christians in Early Christianity.* New York: Oxford University Press, 2001.

Van Dyke, Blair G., and Ray L. Huntington. "Sorting Out the Seven Marys in the New Testament." *Religious Educator* 5, no. 3 (2004).

Vermes, Geza. *The Dead Sea Scrolls in English.* 3d ed. London and New York: Penguin Books, 1987.

———. *The Dead Sea Scrolls: Qumran in Perspective.* Cleveland: William Collins and World Publishing, 1978.

Watts, Isaac. "When I Survey the Wondrous Cross."

Wayment, Thomas A. "Names of the Parables." *Religious Educator* 4, no. 1 (2003).

Webster, Noah. *American Dictionary of the English Language.* 1828. Reprint, San Francisco: Foundation for American Christian Education, 1980.

Welch, John W., and John F. Hall. *Charting the New Testament.* Provo, Utah: Foundation for Ancient Research and Mormon Studies (FARMS), 2002.

Wells, Robert E. *Ensign,* November 1995, 65.

Whitney, Orson F. *Life of Heber C. Kimball.* 3d ed. Salt Lake City: Bookcraft, 1967.

———. *Through Memory's Halls: The Life Story of Orson F. Whitney.* Independence, Mo.: Zion's Printing and Publishing Co., 1930.

———. "A Vision of Gethsemane." *Instructor* 103 (February 1968).

———. *Saturday Night Thoughts: A Series of Dissertations on Spiritual, Historical and Philosophic Themes.* Salt Lake City: Deseret News, 1921.

Wiesel, Elie. In Israeli government-sponsored Seminar on Christ, Galei Zohar Hotel on the shore of the Dead Sea, March 23–25, 1990. Personal notes by D. Kelly Ogden.

Wirthlin, Joseph B. *Ensign,* November 2002, 82.

Witherington, Ben, III. *New Testament History—A Narrative Account.* Grand Rapids, Mich.: Baker Book House, 2001.

A Witness of Jesus Christ: The 1989 Sperry Symposium on the Old Testament. Edited by Richard D. Draper. Salt Lake City: Deseret Book, 1990.

Wright, H. Curtis. *A Thing of Naught: World Judgment and the Trial of Jesus Christ.* Provo: Brigham Young University Extension Publications, 1960.

Yadin, Yigael, ed. *Jerusalem Revealed: Archaeology in the Holy City, 1968–1974.* New Haven, Conn.: Yale University Press and the Israel Exploration Society, 1975.

SCRIPTURE INDEX

OLD TESTAMENT

Genesis
1:1, p. 30
1:5, p. 778
1:9–13, p. 107
1:27, p. 429
2:24, pp. 429, 769
5:2, p. 429
6:9, p. 203
7:4, 12, p. 91
11:30, p. 37
12:7, p. 99
15:8, p. 37
15:12, p. 417 (JST)
16:2, p. 37
17:1, pp. 99, 203
17:11–12, p. 773 (JST)
17:13, p. 773
18:1, p. 99
19:26, p. 528
19:16, p. 527
22:2, p. 95
22:3, p. 151
22:8–14, p. 417
24:22, 30, p. 769
24:29–60, p. 768
24:65, p. 770
25:20, p. 92
25:21, p. 37
26:34, p. 92
29:23–25, p. 770
29:31, p. 37
30:23, p. 37
32:9, p. 487
32:22–30, p. 35
32:30, p. 99
33:18, p. 125
33:18–19, p. 131
34:4, p. 769
34:12, p. 768
37:26–28, p. 160
43:11, p. 74
50:3, p. 91

Exodus
3, p. 95
3:6, pp. 345, 487
3:13–15, p. 16
3:16, 18, p. 746
4:5, p. 487
4:12, p. 165
4:25–26, p. 773
6:3, p. 30
6:23, p. 34
11:5, p. 547
12, p. 764
12:3–11, p. 764
12:5, p. 547
12:6, p. 547
12:13, p. 548
12:15–20, p. 547
12:21–23, p. 658
12:22, p. 548
12:23, p. 546
12:43, p. 547
12:46, pp. 547, 665
12:48, p. 773
12–13, p. 548
13:1–10, 11–16, p. 493
13:2, p. 59
13:8–9, p. 764
15:20, p. 60
15:26, p. 249
16:31–35, p. 315
19:7–8, p. 746
20, p. 171
20:3, p. 96
20:4, p. 168
20:5, p. 333
20:12, p. 319
20:13, p. 189
20:14, p. 195
21:24, p. 200
21:32, p. 545
22:1–9, p. 450
22:17, p. 768
23:14–17, pp. 764, 765
23:15, p. 547
23:16, pp. 765, 766
24:1, 9–10, p. 376
24:6–8, p. 658
24:8, p. 556
24:9–10, p. 99
24:15–18, p. 344
24:18, p. 344
28:3–43, p. 749
28:41, p. 745
29:6, p. 749
30:12–14, p. 474
30:13, pp. 350, 778
30:34–36, p. 63
33:9–11, p. 344
33:11, p. 99
34:1–2, p. 748 (JST)
34:4, p. 151
34:6, p. 355
34:18, p. 547
34:28, p. 92
34:29–30, p. 37
39:27–29, p. 749
40:34, 38, p. 344

Leviticus
1:2, p. 319
1:14, p. 59
2:13, p. 183

5:7, p. 59
6:19–23, p. 749
8:33, p. 37
11:21–22, p. 74
12:8, p. 59
13:49, p. 402
13–14, p. 157
16:7–22, p. 633
18:6–17, p. 302
18:16, p. 302
19:12, p. 199
19:18, pp. 385, 488
20:10, p. 411
20:21, pp. 128, 302
21:10, pp. 615, 749
23:23–36, 39–43, p. 766
23:39, 41, p. 766
23:39, p. 766
23:40, p. 766
23:42–43, p. 766
24:16, p. 641
24:20, p. 200
25:35–36, p. 385
26:3–4, p. 134
26:41, p. 773

Numbers
3:5–10, p. 749
4:3, 47, p. 33
6:2–8, p. 35
9:12, p. 665
11:16, p. 376
11:29, p. 61
13:25, p. 91
14:14, p. 344
14:33–34, p. 92
14:34, p. 91
15:38–39, p. 494
18:1, p. 745
18:1–7, p. 749
19:1–10, p. 739
24:17, pp. 24, 62
29:13–38, p. 766
30:2, p. 199
31:50, p. 319
32:13, p. 92
34:11, pp. 153, 318

Deuteronomy
5, p. 171
5:5, p. 345
6:4, p. 89
6:4–5, p. 488
6:4–9, p. 493
6:5, p. 168
6:13, p. 96
6:16, p. 95
8:2, p. 92
8:3, p. 94
9:9, 11, 18, 25, p. 92
10:10, p. 92
10:16, p. 773
11:10–17, p. 134
11:11–15, p. 325
11:13–21, p. 493
14:22–26, p. 766
16:1–8, p. 547
16:10, p. 765
16:16, pp. 764, 765
17:7, p. 411
18:13, p. 203
18:15, 18, p. 407
20:7, p. 769
21:1–3, p. 746
21:1–9, p. 635
21:22–23, p. 664
22:13–19, p. 746
22:23–24, p. 769
22:25–27, p. 769
23:21, p. 199
23:25, p. 270
24:1, pp. 198, 428, 429, 769
24:1–4, p. 428
25:1–3, p. 639
25:5, p. 486
28:15, 20, 22, 33, 45, 49–52, p. 467
29:5, p. 92
30:6, p. 773
31:10–11, p. 766
32:4, 31, p. 329
34:5, p. 340

Joshua
2:6, p. 272
5:6, p. 92
14:7, p. 92
15:8, p. 192
15:25, pp. 156, 160
18:16, p. 192
18:23, p. 457
19:10, 15, p. 53
20:4, p. 746 (JST)

Judges
3:11, p. 92
4:4, p. 60
5:31, p. 92
6:17, p. 37
8:28, p. 92
13:1, p. 92
14:2, p. 769
20:16, p. 435

1 Samuel
1:2, p. 60
2:1, p. 48
2:1–10, p. 46
2:2, p. 329
4:3, p. 746
4:18, p. 92
8:11, p. 74
13:17, p. 457
17:16, p. 91
18:25, p. 768
21:4–6, p. 270

2 Samuel
1:23, p. 435
5:2, p. 53
7:16, p. 470
17:4, 15, p. 746
22:2, p. 329
22:3, p. 48
24:18–25, p. 742

1 Kings
1:5, p. 74
2:11, p. 92
6:3, p. 738
8:2, 65, p. 766
8:4, p. 748
8:10–11, p. 344
8:61, p. 203
8:66, p. 763
11:42, p. 92
12:32, p. 766
15:14, p. 203
17:1–10, p. 141
17:21–22, p. 230
19:8, p. 92
20:7–8, p. 746

2 Kings
1:1–6, p. 166
1:9–12, p. 375
2:10, p. 92

Scripture Index

2:11–12, p. 340
4:32–35, p. 230
5:1–14, p. 142
5:10, p. 420
5:14, p. 253
12:1, p. 92
14:25, p. 408
17:1–26, p. 753
17:27–41,
  p. 753
20:3, p. 203
20:8, p. 37
22:14, p. 60
23:10, p. 192

1 Chronicles
23:27–32, p. 749
24, p. 745

2 Chronicles
5:13–14, p. 344
7:9, p. 763
24:9, p. 778
28:3, p. 192
33:6, p. 192
34:22, p. 60
36:15–16,
  p. 501

Ezra
2:70, p. 748
7:6, p. 754

Nehemiah
1:1, p. 738
6:14, p. 60
8:1–9, p. 754
12, p. 745

Esther
1:2, p. 738

Job
1:1, p. 203
1:5, p. 151
19:26, p. 453

Psalms
1:1, p. 173
2, p. 540
8:2, p. 475
18:2, p. 48
22:1, pp. 656, 692
22:16, pp. 540, 665, 692
22:18, p. 648
23:4, p. 589
31:5, p. 658
34:20, pp. 664, 692
37:11, p. 177
41:9, pp. 551, 584
48:2, p. 199
49:16–17,
  pp. 210, 390
69:9, p. 116
69:21, pp. 645, 658, 692
82:6, p. 442
91:11–12, p. 94
110:1, p. 489
113–18, pp. 588, 764
118:22, p. 692
118:26,
  pp. 464, 506
120–34, p. 744

Proverbs
20:1, p. 111
23:7, p. 195

Isaiah
2:2–4, p. 522
6, p. 472
6:1, p. 99
6:9–10, p. 472
7:14, pp. 41, 231
8:3, p. 60
8:6, p. 133
8:8, 10, p. 44
8:14, p. 258
9:1, p. 143
9:1–2, pp. 142, 408
9:2, p. 414
9:6, p. 24
9:7, p. 40
9:32, p. 40
10:3, p. 466
11:1, p. 66
12:3, p. 406
13:10, p. 518
14:12–13,
  p. 166
20:1, p. 753
20:2, p. 705
29:13, p. 318
31:4–5, p. 508
31:5, p. 505
40:3, pp. 72, 73
40:8, p. 520
42, p. 272
42:3, p. 272
42:6, p. 414
49:6, p. 414
50:6, p. 692
51:17, p. 446
51:17, 21,
  p. 600
53, p. 210
53:1, p. 472
53:4, pp. 232, 692
53:4–5, p. 638
53:5, pp. 692, 698
53:7, pp. 100, 614, 627
53:7–8, p. 692
53:8, p. 100
53:9, p. 647
53:10, p. 100
53:12, pp. 591, 647, 692
54:5, p. 249
57:20–21,
  p. 566
61:1–2, p. 140
62:10, p. 74
65:5, pp. 248, 504

Jeremiah
2:13, p. 133
3:14, p. 249
6:10, p. 773
7:31, p. 192
25:15, 17,
  p. 600
27:4–8, p. 485
31:16–17, p. 65
32:12, p. 754
36:18, 32,
  p. 754
49:12, p. 600

Lamentations
2:11, p. 435
3:48, p. 435

Ezekiel
16:8, p. 769
23:33, p. 446
27:17, p. 74
29:11–12, p. 92
32:7, p. 518
37:16, p. 47
37:24–28,
  p. 522
44:9–16, p. 725

Daniel
7:2–7, p. 721
7:13, p. 520
8:2, p. 738
9:26, pp. 100, 508, 693
9:27, p. 513
10:15, p. 37
12:6, p. 509

Hosea
5:14, p. 100
6:6, pp. 249, 271
11:1, pp. 64, 692

Scripture Index

11:10, p. 100
12:10, p. 290

Joel
2:10, p. 518
3:15, p. 518

Amos
2:9, p. 320
3:7, p. 501
9:1, p. 99

Jonah
1:17, p. 276
3:4, p. 91

Micah
3:8, p. 143
5:2, pp. 51, 62, 692
7:6, p. 168

Zechariah
1:1, p. 502
9:9, pp. 461, 692
11:12–13, p. 630
11:13, p. 693
12:10, p. 665
13:6, p. 693
13:7, p. 581

Malachi
3:1, pp. 72, 73, 74, 258, 522
4:1, p. 320
4:1–3, p. 519
4:2, p. 505
4:5, p. 82

NEW TESTAMENT

Matthew
1:1, p. 27
1:2, p. 160
1:2–17, p. 31
1:16, pp. 5, 32
1:17, p. 32
1:18, pp. 29, 769
1:18, 25, p. 769
1:18–24, p. 41
1:18–25, p. 770
1:19, p. 770
1:20, pp. 41, 678
1:21, p. 43
1:22–23, p. 44
1:23, p. 231
1:24, p. 44
1:25, p. 58
2, p. 772
2:1, pp. 61, 770
2:1–12, pp. 28, 61
2:2, p. 61
2:3, p. 62
2:4, pp. 53, 745
2:4–6, p. 62
2:6, p. 53
2:7–8, p. 63
2:9–10, p. 63
2:11, p. 668
2:11–12, p. 63
2:13, 19, p. 678
2:13–15, p. 64
2:16, pp. 54, 729, 771
2:16–18, p. 64
2:19–23, p. 66
2:23, pp. 66, 407
3:1, p. 74
3:1–3, p. 74
3:2, pp. 75, 76, 511
3:2, p. 62 (JST)
3:3, p. 72
3:4, p. 63 (JST)
3:4, pp. 73, 74
3:5–6, p. 79
3:5–6, p. 63 (JST)
3:7, pp. 80, 274
3:8–9, pp. 81, 82, 473
3:10, p. 83
3:11–12, p. 84
3:12, p. 86
3:13–17, p. 86
3:14–15, p. 86
3:16, p. 88
3:17, pp. 89, 263, 345
3:24–26, p. 70 (JST)
3:34–36, p. 82 (JST)
3:38–40, p. 84 (JST)
3:43, p. 86 (JST)
3:44, p. 86 (JST)
4:1, pp. 5, 91
4:1, p. 91 (JST)
4:1–11, p. 90
4:2, pp. 91, 92
4:2, p. 92 (JST)
4:3, p. 93
4:4, p. 94
4:5, pp. 94, 734 (JST)
4:5, p. 94
4:6, p. 734
4:6–7, p. 94
4:8–9, p. 95
4:9, p. 95
4:10, p. 96
4:11, pp. 96, 678
4:11, pp. 98, 128 (JST)
4:12, 17, p. 138
4:12, p. 129
4:13, pp. 143, 246
4:13–16, p. 142
4:15, p. 143
4:16, p. 48
4:17, pp. 75, 138, 511
4:18, p. 149 (JST)
4:18, pp. 156, 159
4:18–20, p. 774
4:18–22, pp. 148, 154
4:21, pp. 156, 704
4:21–22, pp. 149, 774
4:22, p. 149 (JST)
4:23, p. 755
4:23–24, p. 149
4:24–25, p. 172
4:25, p. 150
5, p. 172
5:1, pp. 171, 172
5:1–2, p. 172
5:3, pp. 6, 141, 175, 569
5:3–4, p. 172 (JST)
5:3–12, p. 172
5:4, p. 177
5:5, p. 177
5:5, p. 175 (JST)
5:6, p. 178
5:7, p. 179
5:8, p. 179
5:9, p. 180
5:10–12, p. 180
5:11, p. 181
5:13, pp. 182, 282, 369
5:14–16, pp. 184, 289
5:15, p. 779
5:17, p. 186
5:18–20, p. 187

798

Scripture Index

5:21, p. 188 (JST)
5:21–22, p. 189
5:22, p. 191 (JST)
5:23–24, p. 193
5:24, p. 370
5:25, p. 193
5:25–26, pp. 167, 193
5:26, p. 778
5:27–28, p. 197
5:27–30, pp. 195, 282, 358
5:29, p. 435
5:29–30, p. 197
5:31–32, p. 198
5:32, p. 770
5:33, p. 199
5:33–37, p. 199
5:34, p. 196 (JST)
5:38–42, p. 200
5:41, p. 779
5:43–44, p. 727
5:43–47, p. 201
5:45, p. 202
5:46–47, p. 202
5:48, pp. 202, 203
5–7, p. 170
6, p. 205
6:1–4, p. 204
6:1–6, p. 204
6:2, 5, 16, p. 492
6:3, p. 300
6:5, p. 496
6:5–15, p. 205
6:6, p. 204
6:9–13, p. 207
6:10, p. 207
6:11, p. 207
6:14, p. 208 (JST)

6:14–15, p. 208
6:16–18, p. 209
6:19–21, p. 390
6:19–34, p. 210
6:22, p. 211 (JST)
6:22–23, p. 211
6:24, p. 211
6:25–7:27, p. 212
6:25–27, p. 213 (JST)
6:25–34, p. 212
6:25–39, p. 172 (JST)
6:26, p. 376
6:26, p. 711 (JST)
6:27, p. 779
6:33, p. 214
6:34, p. 215
6:38, pp. 215, 335 (JST)
7:1, p. 216 (JST)
7:1–2, p. 217 (JST)
7:1–5, pp. 216, 289
7:2, p. 217
7:3, p. 300
7:6, pp. 218, 282, 322
7:6–8, p. 218 (JST)
7:6–17, p. 172 (JST)
7:7–12, p. 220
7:10–11, p. 219 (JST)
7:12, p. 221
7:13–14, p. 221
7:14–15, p. 721 (JST)
7:14–17, p. 220 (JST)

7:15, p. 164
7:15–20, pp. 222, 274, 290
7:19, p. 568
7:21–23, p. 224
7:23, p. 5
7:24, p. 225
7:24–25, p. 300
7:24–27, pp. 225, 290
7:28–29, pp. 227, 754
7:29, p. 144
7:33, p. 225 (JST)
7:33, p. 5 (JST)
7:37, p. 227 (JST)
8:1, p. 227
8:1–4, p. 147
8:2–4, pp. 155, 246, 322, 332, 345
8:5–13, pp. 147, 228
8:6, p. 229
8:10, p. 229
8:12, p. 229 (JST)
8:14, p. 775
8:14–15, pp. 147, 232
8:16–17, pp. 147, 232
8:18–22, pp. 233, 282
8:23–27, pp. 146, 234
8:24, p. 309
8:27, p. 235
8:28–34, pp. 146, 238, 269, 683

8:29, pp. 145, 245, 246
8:29, p. 238 (JST)
8:34, p. 246
9:1–8, p. 246
9:2, p. 6
9:2–8, p. 147
9:5, p. 247 (JST)
9:9, p. 751
9:9–13, pp. 248, 450
9:9–11, p. 751
9:12, p. 248
9:13, pp. 248, 249
9:14, p. 249
9:14–17, pp. 59, 249
9:15, p. 249
9:16, p. 251
9:17, p. 251
9:18–21, p. 250 (JST)
9:18–26, pp. 146, 252, 680
9:20–22, p. 147
9:23, p. 253
9:27–31, pp. 147, 256
9:30, p. 157
9:32, p. 240
9:32–34, pp. 146, 257
9:35–38, p. 268
9:36, pp. 157, 177, 268
9:37–38, p. 376
10:1–4, pp. 158, 473
10:2–4, p. 159
10:3, p. 156
10:4, pp. 156,

159, 160, 757
10:5, p. 753
10:5–42, p. 160
10:8, p. 369
10:8–10, pp. 161, 376
10:11–15, pp. 163, 376
10:14, p. 164 (JST)
10:16, pp. 164, 222, 282, 376
10:17, p. 753
10:17–18, p. 164
10:19, p. 165
10:19–20, p. 165
10:21–23, p. 165
10:24–25, p. 166
10:26–28, pp. 166, 289
10:29–31, pp. 167, 194
10:32–33, p. 167
10:34, p. 169 (JST)
10:34–36, pp. 165, 167
10:36, p. 168
10:37–39, p. 168
10:38, p. 334
10:40, p. 379
10:40–42, pp. 170, 369
10:42, p. 170
11:1, p. 257
11:2–6, p. 257
11:7, p. 258
11:7–19, p. 258
11:10, p. 73
11:11, pp. 258, 259, 271
11:13–15, p. 259
11:14, p. 36
11:16–19, p. 260
11:19, p. 271
11:20–24, p. 377
11:21–24, p. 278
11:25–26, p. 380
11:27–30, p. 380
11:28, p. 381
11:28, p. 380 (JST)
11:28–30, p. 382
11:29, p. 381
12:1–21, p. 270
12:6, 8, p. 271
12:6, pp. 271, 733
12:8, p. 271
12:9–13, p. 147
12:10–13, pp. 271, 483
12:14–21, p. 272
12:20, p. 272
12:22, p. 240
12:22–23, p. 146
12:22–37, p. 273
12:23, p. 274 (JST)
12:25–26, p. 273
12:26, p. 274 (JST)
12:29, p. 274
12:33–37, p. 274
12:34, pp. 80, 274
12:36, p. 275
12:37–38, p. 278 (JST)
12:38, p. 275
12:39–40, p. 325
12:39–45, pp. 276, 333
12:40, p. 277
12:41, pp. 271, 277
12:42, pp. 271, 277
12:43–45, p. 278
12:46, p. 113
12:46–50, p. 279
13, pp. 284, 285, 291, 298, 299, 511
13:1–53, p. 279
13:2, p. 284
13:3–9, 18–23, p. 285
13:3–23, p. 280
13:10–17, 34–35, p. 288
13:19, p. 287
13:20–21, p. 287
13:21, p. 288 (JST)
13:22, p. 287
13:24–25, p. 291
13:24–30, 36–43, pp. 280, 290
13:29, p. 292
13:29, p. 292 (JST)
13:29–30, p. 292
13:31–32, pp. 282, 293, 348
13:31-33, p. 280
13:32, p. 294
13:33, pp. 295, 326, 585
13:38, pp. 285, 291
13:39, p. 293
13:39–44, p. 293 (JST)
13:44, 46, p. 432
13:44, p. 296
13:44–47, p. 291
13:44–48, p. 280
13:45–46, p. 297
13:47–48, p. 774
13:47–50, p. 298
13:48, p. 776
13:51–52, p. 298
13:53–58, p. 300
13:55, pp. 159, 160
13:55–56, pp. 113, 279
13:57, p. 301
14:1, p. 761
14:1–2, p. 301
14:1–12, p. 761
14:3–5, pp. 127, 302

14:3–12,
   pp. 127, 301
14:13–15,
   p. 302
14:14, pp. 157,
   177
14:15–21,
   p. 146
14:16–21,
   pp. 305, 323
14:21, p. 305
14:22–33,
   p. 309
14:23, pp. 152,
   309, 338
14:23–33,
   p. 146
14:24, p. 309
14:25, p. 778
14:25–27,
   p. 310
14:28–33,
   p. 311
14:33, p. 264
14:34, p. 317
14:34–36,
   pp. 147, 317
15:1, pp. 748,
   754
15:1–2, p. 755
15:1–6, p. 748
15:1–20, p. 318
15:2, p. 318
15:3, p. 318
15:13, p. 320
15:14, pp. 320,
   440
15:21–28,
   pp. 147,
   219, 321
15:22, p. 321
15:24, p. 322
15:26, p. 219
15:29–31,
   p. 322
15:29–38,
   p. 146
15:32, p. 177
15:32–38,
   p. 323
15:38, p. 323
15:39–16:4,
   pp. 323, 406
16, p. 721
16:2–3, p. 324
16:4, p. 325
16:5–12, p. 326
16:13, pp. 329,
   761
16:13–19,
   p. 102
16:13–20,
   p. 328
16:16, pp. 264,
   329
16:17, p. 149
16:18, pp. 4,
   300, 329
16:18, 19,
   p. 331
16:19, pp. 331,
   371
16:20, pp. 157,
   332
16:21, pp. 333,
   349, 698
16:22–23,
   p. 333
16:24, pp. 169,
   334
16:24–27,
   p. 334
16:25, p. 215
16:26, pp. 169,
   197, 334
   (JST)
16:27–29,
   p. 335 (JST)
16:28, pp. 336,
   708
17, p. 343
17:1, pp. 95,
   152, 331,
   337, 338
17:1–9, p. 767
17:1–13,
   pp. 337,
   708, 734
17:2, pp. 78,
   282, 338
17:4, p. 343
17:5, pp. 89,
   263, 344,
   345
17:6–8, p. 345
17:9, pp. 157,
   345
17:10–13,
   pp. 36, 259,
   346
17:10–13, p. 83
   (JST)
17:10–14,
   p. 346 (JST)
17:14–21,
   pp. 146, 347
17:15, p. 347
17:20, pp. 294,
   348
17:21, p. 249
17:22–23,
   p. 349
17:24, pp. 350,
   778
17:24–27,
   pp. 146,
   350, 774
17:27, pp. 350,
   351
18, p. 354
18:1–6,
   pp. 352, 446
18:6, pp. 356,
   358
18:7–35, p. 357
18:8, p. 196
18:8–9,
   pp. 196, 358
18:9, p. 359
   (JST)
18:10, p. 357
18:11, p. 358
   (JST)
18:12–14,
   p. 359
18:13, p. 360
18:15, p. 193
18:15–17,
   p. 369
18:17, p. 370
18:18–20,
   pp. 371, 710
18:19–20,
   p. 727
18:21–35,
   p. 371
18:23–35,
   p. 280
18:24, p. 777
19:1, pp. 374,
   404
19:3, p. 770
19:3–12,
   pp. 199, 428
19:6, p. 486
19:8, p. 429
19:10–11,
   p. 429
19:12, p. 429
19:13, p. 430
   (JST)
19:13–15,
   p. 430
19:16–26,
   p. 431
19:20, p. 432
19:21, pp. 203,
   432
19:23–24,
   pp. 282, 433
19:25–26,
   p. 437

19:26, p. 437 (JST)
19:27–30, p. 438
20:1–15, p. 730
20:1–16, pp. 280, 439
20:3, p. 439
20:5, p. 439
20:6, p. 439
20:8, p. 439
20:12, p. 439
20:15–16, p. 440
20:17–19, pp. 445, 698
20:20–28, p. 445
20:22, p. 600
20:22–23, p. 446
20:28, p. 446
20:29–34, pp. 147, 447
20:32–33, p. 448
20:34, pp. 157, 177
21:1–5, p. 460
21:2, 5, p. 462
21:6–11, p. 462
21:8, p. 767
21:9, pp. 464, 767
21:11, p. 465
21:12–16, p. 473
21:13, pp. 474, 733
21:13, p. 475 (JST)
21:14, pp. 410, 735
21:15, p. 755
21:15–16, p. 475
21:16, p. 475
21:17–18, p. 475
21:18–19, p. 476
21:18–21, p. 146
21:18–22, pp. 240, 475
21:23–27, p. 477
21:28–32, pp. 280, 478
21:31–32, p. 751
21:31–34, p. 478 (JST)
21:33, p. 439
21:33–46, pp. 280, 478
21:34, p. 478 (JST)
21:41, p. 480
21:42, p. 480
21:43, p. 481
21:47–56, p. 481 (JST)
22, p. 4
22:1–7, p. 501
22:1–14, pp. 280, 481
22:2–14, p. 770
22:4, p. 482
22:5, pp. 482, 492
22:10, p. 482
22:11, p. 482
22:13, p. 482
22:14, p. 482 (JST)
22:14, p. 5
22:15–16, p. 746
22:15–22, p. 484
22:16, p. 484
22:19–21, p. 778
22:21, p. 485
22:23–33, p. 486
22:30, p. 5
22:31, p. 487
22:32, p. 487
22:34–40, p. 488
22:40, p. 488
22:41–46, p. 489
22:42, p. 489
23, pp. 318, 484, 491, 747
23:1–36, p. 490
23:2, pp. 492, 747, 748, 754
23:2–3, p. 748
23:2–4, p. 747
23:3–6, p. 748
23:4, p. 492
23:4, p. 495 (JST)
23:5, pp. 252, 492, 493
23:6, pp. 177, 484, 494
23:7–8, p. 751
23:7–12, pp. 495, 504
23:8–9, p. 496
23:11–12, p. 496
23:12, p. 496 (JST)
23:13, p. 503
23:13–15, pp. 496, 748
23:14, p. 493
23:16–22, p. 497
23:21, p. 499 (JST)
23:23, p. 498
23:23–24, pp. 282, 497
23:23–25, p. 497
23:24, p. 435
23:25–28, p. 499
23:27–28, p. 499
23:29, p. 500 (JST)
23:29–30, p. 500
23:29–32, p. 499
23:33, pp. 80, 500
23:34–35, p. 502 (JST)
23:34–36, p. 501
23:35, pp. 501, 502
23:36, p. 502
23:37, p. 505
23:37–39, pp. 466, 504
23:39, p. 507
24, pp. 506, 507, 511, 526
24, p. 506 (JST)
24:1–2, p. 507
24:1–51, p. 506
24:2, p. 505
24:3, p. 509
24:4–5, 9, p. 511
24:6, 25, p. 515
24:6–7, p. 517
24:8, 21–23, p. 514

Scripture Index

24:10–13, p. 512
24:12–13, p. 517
24:14, p. 517
24:15, pp. 512, 518
24:16–20, p. 513
24:24, p. 515
24:26–27, p. 516
24:27, p. 516
24:28, p. 516
24:29, p. 518
24:30, p. 520
24:31, p. 522
24:32–33, p. 523
24:34, p. 519
24:35, p. 519
24:36, p. 524
24:37–39, p. 526
24:40–41, p. 528
24:42, 44, p. 529
24:42–51, p. 280
24:45–47, pp. 529, 536
24:48–51, p. 530
25:1, p. 532 (JST)
25:1–10, p. 532
25:1–13, pp. 24, 280, 511, 531, 770
25:5, pp. 530, 533
25:6, p. 778
25:11, p. 5 (JST)
25:12, pp. 5, 533
25:12, p. 533 (JST)
25:14–30, pp. 280, 451, 535
25:15, pp. 535, 779
25:16, p. 535
25:27, p. 535
25:29, p. 536
25:31, p. 520
25:31–46, pp. 280, 536, 711
25:32–33, p. 537
25:34–46, p. 538
25:40, p. 356
26:1–2, p. 540
26:1–30, p. 765
26:2, p. 540
26:3, pp. 745, 755
26:3–5, pp. 456, 540, 612
26:6, pp. 159, 443, 542
26:7, p. 444
26:7–13, pp. 458, 542, 550
26:12, p. 543
26:13, p. 543
26:14–16, p. 545
26:15, p. 777
26:17–19, pp. 546, 550, 642
26:20, p. 550
26:20–25, p. 548

26:21–24, p. 550
26:22, p. 554 (JST)
26:23, p. 550
26:24, p. 606 (JST)
26:24–25, p. 555 (JST)
26:25, 49, pp. 726, 751
26:25, p. 552
26:26, p. 5
26:26, p. 555 (JST)
26:26, 28, p. 282
26:26–29, pp. 548, 554
26:30, pp. 588, 764
26:31, p. 581
26:31–32, p. 581
26:33, p. 706
26:33–35, p. 590
26:36, p. 152
26:36–39, p. 595
26:36–46, p. 591
26:37, p. 337
26:39, pp. 599, 603
26:39, 42, p. 600
26:41, p. 607
26:47, p. 756
26:47–50, p. 608
26:50, p. 609
26:51–54, p. 609
26:52, p. 610

26:53, pp. 611, 760
26:55, pp. 411, 611
26:55–57, p. 611
26:56, p. 611
26:57–68, pp. 612, 623
26:58, p. 611
26:59, pp. 614, 721, 753
26:60, p. 614
26:61, pp. 117, 614, 649
26:62, p. 614
26:63, p. 614
26:63–64, p. 263
26:69–75, p. 617
26:71, p. 619
26:73, p. 619
26:74, p. 778
26:74–75, p. 619
27:1, pp. 623, 745
27:2, 11–14, p. 623
27:3, p. 629
27:3, 9, p. 160
27:3–6, p. 777
27:3–10, p. 629
27:5, p. 630 (JST)
27:5–7, p. 630
27:6, pp. 545, 630
27:15–23, 26, p. 632
27:16–17, p. 633
27:17, p. 633
27:18, p. 634
27:19, p. 634

803

27:22, pp. 635, 712
27:24, p. 635
27:24–25, p. 635
27:25, pp. 636, 638, 642, 643
27:26–28, p. 640
27:27–31, p. 639
27:29, p. 640
27:30, p. 640 (JST)
27:32, p. 159
27:32–34, p. 642
27:35, p. 648
27:35–44, p. 646
27:37, p. 652
27:38, p. 591
27:39, p. 669
27:39–40, p. 117
27:39–44, p. 648
27:40, pp. 93, 649
27:42–43, p. 648
27:43, p. 263
27:44, p. 649
27:45, pp. 653, 654, 778
27:46, pp. 652, 656
27:46–50, pp. 548, 655, 778
27:47, 49, p. 657
27:51, p. 743
27:51–53, p. 662
27:52–53, p. 663
27:54, pp. 264, 665
27:54, p. 652, 658 (JST)
27:54–56, pp. 665, 677
27:56, pp. 444, 654, 666, 677
27:57, pp. 415, 666
27:57–61, pp. 63, 666
27:59, p. 668
27:60, p. 669
27:61, p. 674
27:62–64, p. 117
27:62–66, p. 674
27:63, p. 674
27:65, p. 674
27:65–66, p. 117
28:1–2, p. 675
28:2, p. 675 (JST)
28:2–8, pp. 677, 678
28:4, p. 678
28:6, p. 678
28:7, p. 679
28:8, p. 679
28:9–10, p. 686
28:11–15, p. 687
28:16–20, p. 708
28:17, p. 709
28:20, pp. 371, 710

Mark
1:1, pp. 27, 264
1:1–3, p. 73
1:4, p. 76
1:5, p. 79
1:6, p. 73
1:7, p. 84
1:8, p. 84
1:9, p. 86
1:9–11, p. 86
1:11, p. 92 (JST)
1:12–13, p. 90
1:13, p. 92
1:14, p. 129
1:14–15, p. 138
1:16–18, p. 774
1:16–20, pp. 148, 154
1:19–20, p. 774
1:21, p. 755
1:21–28, pp. 144, 146
1:24, p. 240
1:29–31, pp. 147, 232
1:32–34, pp. 147, 232
1:33, p. 233
1:34, p. 233
1:35–39, pp. 151, 309
1:40–45, pp. 147, 155
1:41, pp. 157, 177
1:45, p. 157
2:1, p. 6
2:1–3:6, p. 747
2:1–12, pp. 147, 246
2:12, p. 247
2:13–17, p. 248
2:14, pp. 156, 751
2:16, pp. 747, 748, 754
2:18–22, p. 249
2:22, p. 251
2:23–3:12, p. 270
2:26–27, p. 271 (JST)
3, p. 747
3:1–5, pp. 147, 271
3:6, p. 746
3:6–12, p. 272
3:8, p. 321
3:13–19, p. 158
3:16–19, p. 159
3:17, pp. 159, 375
3:18, pp. 156, 159, 757
3:20–30, p. 273
3:21, p. 271
3:21–25, p. 274 (JST)
3:31, p. 113
3:31–35, p. 279
4:1, p. 284
4:1–34, p. 279
4:3–9, 14–20, p. 285
4:10–13, p. 288
4:20, p. 289 (JST)
4:21–25, p. 289
4:24–25, p. 289
4:26–29, pp. 290, 293
4:30–32, pp. 280, 293
4:31, p. 293
4:35–41, pp. 146, 234
4:37, p. 309
4:41, p. 247
5:1–20, pp. 146, 238
5:7, p. 240
5:13, p. 239
5:19, pp. 157, 177

Scripture Index

5:21–43, p. 252
5:22, p. 755
5:22–43,
  pp. 146, 680
5:25–34, p. 147
5:35–43, p. 231
5:37, p. 337
5:41, p. 253
5:41–42, p. 452
5:42, p. 247
6:1–6, p. 300
6:3, p. 113
6:4, p. 141
6:6, p. 268
6:7–9, p. 161
6:10–13, p. 163
6:14, 22–27,
  p. 761
6:14–16, p. 301
6:15, p. 301
6:17–20, p. 127
6:17–29, p. 301
6:21, p. 302
  (JST)
6:30–32, p. 302
6:33–44,
  pp. 146, 305
6:34, pp. 157, 177
6:40, p. 306
6:45, p. 761
6:45–52, p. 309
6:47–48, p. 309
6:47–52, p. 146
6:48, p. 778
6:53, p. 317
6:53–56,
  pp. 147, 317
7:1–4, p. 126
7:1–23, p. 318
7:5–9, p. 748
7:6, p. 318
7:7–9, p. 319
7:10–13, p. 319
7:13, p. 319
7:14–16, p. 319

7:15, p. 319
  (JST)
7:17–23,
  pp. 319, 440
7:22–23,
  pp. 303, 321
  (JST)
7:24–30, p. 321
7:25–30, p. 147
7:26, p. 321
7:26, p. 322
  (JST)
7:28, p. 322
7:31–36, p. 157
7:31–37, p. 322
7:32–37, p. 147
7:37, p. 247
8:1–9, pp. 146, 323
8:10, p. 323
8:10–13, p. 323
8:14–21, p. 326
8:22–26,
  pp. 147, 326
8:26, p. 157
8:27–30, p. 328
8:30, p. 157
8:31, pp. 333, 698, 755
8:32–33, p. 333
8:34, p. 334
8:34–38, p. 334
8:35, p. 335
8:37–38, p. 336
8:37–38, p. 335
  (JST)
8:40, p. 336
  (JST)
8:42–43, p. 336
  (JST)
9:1, p. 336
9:2–9, p. 767
9:2–13, p. 337
9:3, p. 339
9:3, p. 340
  (JST)

9:4, p. 340
9:5, pp. 343, 726, 752
9:7, p. 344
9:9, p. 157
9:9–10, p. 345
9:10, pp. 346, 681
9:10–11, p. 346
  (JST)
9:11–13, p. 346
9:14, p. 347
9:14–29,
  pp. 146, 347
9:17, p. 347
9:23, p. 348
9:24, p. 348
9:30–32, p. 349
9:33–37, p. 352
9:37, p. 357
9:37, p. 357
  (JST)
9:38–41, p. 369
9:38–50, p. 357
9:40–48, p. 358
  (JST)
9:41, p. 369
9:42, p. 358
9:43–48,
  pp. 196, 358
9:49–50, p. 369
9:50, p. 183
10:1, p. 374
10:2–12, p. 428
10:12, p. 429
10:13–16,
  p. 430
10:14, p. 430
10:15, p. 430
10:17–27,
  p. 431
10:21, pp. 432, 433
10:23–25,
  p. 433

10:26, p. 438
  (JST)
10:26–27,
  p. 437
10:27, p. 5
10:28–31,
  p. 438
10:30–31,
  p. 439 (JST)
10:31, p. 439
10:32–34,
  pp. 445, 698
10:35–45,
  p. 445
10:38, p. 600
10:46, p. 448
10:46–52,
  pp. 147, 447
11:1–6, p. 460
11:7–11, p. 462
11:9, p. 633
11:11–12,
  p. 475
11:12–14, 20–26,
  p. 475
11:12–21,
  p. 146
11:13, p. 465
  (JST)
11:13, p. 476
11:15–19,
  p. 473
11:18, p. 755
11:18, 27,
  p. 745
11:21, pp. 726, 752
11:27–33,
  p. 477
12:1–11, p. 730
12:1–12, p. 478
12:13, p. 746
12:13–17,
  p. 484
12:18, p. 752

12:18–27, pp. 486, 752
12:26, p. 487
12:28, p. 486 (JST)
12:28, p. 488
12:28–34, p. 488
12:29–30, p. 488
12:31, p. 488
12:32, p. 488
12:32, p. 487 (JST)
12:33, p. 489
12:34, p. 489
12:35–37, p. 489
12:38, pp. 495, 496
12:38–40, pp. 472, 490
12:39, p. 494
12:41–44, pp. 490, 740
12:42, p. 778
13:1, p. 507
13:1–2, pp. 507, 508
13:1–37, p. 506
13:3–4, pp. 410, 509
13:5–6, 9, 13, p. 511
13:7–8, p. 517
13:8, p. 510 (JST)
13:9, p. 753
13:10, p. 517
13:11, p. 165
13:12–13, p. 165
13:14, p. 512
13:14–18, p. 513
13:19–20, p. 514
13:21–22, p. 515
13:23, p. 516
13:24–25, p. 518
13:26, p. 520
13:28–29, 34–37, p. 523
13:30, p. 519
13:31, p. 519
13:32, p. 525
13:33, p. 529
13:35, p. 778
14:1, pp. 540, 755
14:1–2, p. 540
14:1–26, p. 765
14:3, p. 542
14:3–9, pp. 459, 542
14:4–5, p. 542
14:8, p. 543 (JST)
14:10–11, p. 545
14:11, p. 546
14:12–16, p. 546
14:17, p. 550
14:18–21, p. 550
14:20–25, p. 556 (JST)
14:22–25, p. 554
14:26, pp. 588, 589, 764
14:27–28, p. 581
14:29–31, p. 590
14:30, p. 591
14:30–31, p. 553 (JST)
14:32–42, p. 591
14:33–36, p. 597
14:35, p. 599
14:36, pp. 599, 600, 603
14:36–38, p. 606 (JST)
14:38, p. 607
14:43, p. 756
14:43–46, p. 608
14:45, pp. 608, 726, 752
14:46–52, p. 611
14:47, p. 609
14:50, p. 611
14:51–52, pp. 28, 612
14:53–65, p. 612
14:55, pp. 745, 753
14:57, p. 612 (JST)
14:62, p. 615
14:66–72, p. 617
14:68, 72, p. 778
14:70, p. 619
15:1, pp. 623, 745
15:1–5, p. 623
15:2–5, p. 627
15:4, p. 627 (JST)
15:6–15, p. 632
15:7, p. 632
15:8, p. 632
15:10, p. 634
15:10, p. 634 (JST)
15:13, p. 633
15:13, p. 634 (JST)
15:15, p. 634
15:15, p. 634 (JST)
15:15–20, p. 639
15:16, p. 624
15:17, p. 640
15:20, p. 641
15:20–23, p. 642
15:21, p. 643
15:23, p. 646
15:24, p. 648
15:24–33, p. 646
15:25, pp. 653, 778
15:26, p. 652
15:27, pp. 632, 669
15:29, p. 669
15:29–32, p. 648
15:33, pp. 653, 778
15:34, p. 656
15:34–37, pp. 655, 778
15:38, p. 662
15:39–41, p. 665
15:40, pp. 444, 654, 666
15:41, p. 666
15:42, p. 664
15:42–47, p. 666
15:43, p. 666
15:46, pp. 668, 669
15:47, p. 674

16:1–4, p. 675
16:2, p. 151
16:3–6, p. 679 (JST)
16:4, p. 669
16:5, pp. 669, 673
16:5–8, p. 677
16:6, p. 674
16:9, pp. 269, 681, 682
16:10–11, p. 687
16:12, pp. 688, 690
16:13, p. 695
16:14, pp. 690, 696, 697
16:15–18, p. 708
16:16, p. 709
16:17–18, p. 710
16:19, p. 711
16:19–20, p. 710
16:20, p. 711

Luke
1, pp. 28, 736
1:1, p. 29 (JST)
1:1–4, p. 29
1:4, p. 30
1:5, 8–9, p. 745
1:5, p. 770
1:5–22, p. 733
1:5–25, pp. 33, 347
1:6–7, p. 34
1:8–11, p. 34
1:8–12, p. 748
1:11–20, 26–30, p. 678
1:12, pp. 35, 345
1:13, p. 35
1:14–17, p. 35
1:15, p. 45
1:18–20, p. 36
1:21–23, p. 37
1:24–25, p. 37
1:26–38, p. 37
1:27, p. 38
1:28, p. 39 (JST)
1:28–33, p. 39
1:32, 35, p. 264
1:34–35, pp. 40, 42, 123
1:36, pp. 41, 45
1:36–38, p. 40
1:39–56, p. 45
1:42–45, p. 45
1:46–55, pp. 45, 48
1:56, p. 46
1:57–58, p. 46
1:59, p. 773
1:59–66, p. 46
1:62, p. 37
1:63, p. 47
1:64–66, p. 47
1:67–80, p. 47
1:76–79, p. 48
1:80, p. 48
2:1–5, pp. 49, 51
2:2, p. 50
2:3–4, p. 51
2:6–7, p. 54
2:7, p. 55
2:7, p. 55 (JST)
2:8–18, p. 28
2:8–20, p. 55
2:9, p. 55
2:9–15, p. 678
2:10–11, p. 55
2:12, p. 56
2:13, p. 56
2:14, pp. 57, 168
2:15–18, p. 58
2:19, 51, p. 58
2:21, pp. 58, 773
2:22–23, p. 740
2:22–32, p. 733
2:22–39, p. 59
2:25, p. 160
2:25–32, p. 59
2:33, p. 60
2:34, p. 60
2:34–35, p. 655
2:35, p. 60
2:35, p. 60 (JST)
2:36–37, p. 60
2:36–38, p. 60
2:38, p. 199
2:39–40, p. 66
2:41–50, p. 67
2:41–52, p. 28
2:46, p. 5
2:46, p. 733 (JST)
2:49, p. 6
2:51–52, p. 70
3, p. 31
3:1, pp. 760, 771
3:1–3, p. 77
3:2, p. 77
3:3, p. 76
3:4–6, p. 73
3:5–9, p. 73 (JST)
3:7, p. 80
3:8, p. 81
3:9, pp. 83, 84, 568
3:10–11, p. 84
3:11, p. 84
3:12–13, p. 84
3:14, p. 84
3:15–18, p. 85
3:17, pp. 6, 86
3:19, p. 761
3:19–20, pp. 84, 127, 761
3:21–22, p. 86
3:22, p. 88
3:23, p. 771
3:23–38, p. 33
3:45, p. 33 (JST)
4, p. 138
4:1, p. 91
4:1–13, p. 90
4:2, p. 92
4:5, p. 5
4:6, p. 96
4:13, p. 96
4:14, p. 129
4:14–15, p. 138
4:16–30, pp. 139, 140, 373, 755
4:18–19, p. 141
4:20, p. 755
4:23, p. 141
4:24, p. 301
4:24–27, p. 230
4:25–26, p. 141
4:27, p. 142
4:28–30, p. 146
4:29–30, p. 616
4:30, pp. 142, 417, 471
4:31–32, p. 143
4:31–37, p. 146
4:33–37, p. 144
4:38, p. 149
4:38–39, pp. 147, 232
4:40–41, pp. 147, 232
4:41, p. 233
4:42, p. 152
4:42–44, pp. 151, 309
5:1–3, p. 153

Scripture Index

5:1–7, p. 774
5:1–11, p. 146
5:3, pp. 149, 775
5:4–11, pp. 154, 705
5:5, p. 775
5:5–6, p. 154
5:6, p. 154
5:7–9, p. 154
5:10–11, p. 154
5:11, p. 395
5:11, 28, p. 149
5:12–15, pp. 147, 155
5:16, p. 152
5:16–26, p. 246
5:17–26, p. 147
5:18–19, p. 247
5:20, p. 247
5:26, p. 247
5:27–32, pp. 248, 751
5:28, p. 395
5:30, p. 755
5:33–39, p. 249
5:39, p. 251
6:1–11, p. 270
6:6, p. 271
6:6–10, p. 147
6:7, pp. 747, 748, 754
6:9, p. 272
6:12, pp. 152, 158, 338
6:12–16, p. 158
6:14–16, p. 159
6:15, pp. 156, 159, 757
6:16, p. 160
6:17, pp. 79, 171, 172
6:17–49, p. 170
6:19, p. 253
6:20, p. 175
6:21, p. 178
6:22–23, p. 180
6:27–36, p. 201
6:29–30, p. 200 (JST)
6:37–38, 41–42, p. 216
6:38, p. 217
6:39–40, pp. 318, 320, 440
6:41, p. 300
6:43–44, p. 222
6:44, p. 222
6:45, pp. 273, 274
6:46, p. 224
6:47–49, p. 225
6:48, pp. 225, 290
7:1–10, p. 228
7:2–10, p. 147
7:5, p. 228
7:11–17, pp. 146, 229, 680
7:12–15, p. 452
7:13, pp. 157, 177
7:18–23, p. 257
7:24–35, p. 258
7:27, p. 74
7:29, p. 751
7:30, p. 747
7:34, p. 271
7:36, p. 542
7:36–50, p. 280
7:37, pp. 542, 543
7:37–50, p. 542
7:38, p. 543
7:39–50, p. 543
7:41–43, p. 544
7:44, p. 558
7:44–46, p. 544
7:47, p. 544
8:1, p. 269
8:1–3, pp. 269, 666
8:2, pp. 269, 682
8:3, p. 677
8:4–8, 11–15, p. 285
8:4–18, p. 279
8:5–15, p. 280
8:9–10, p. 288
8:11, p. 285
8:16, p. 184
8:16–18, p. 289
8:19, p. 113
8:19–21, p. 279
8:22–25, pp. 146, 234
8:23, p. 309
8:23, p. 309 (JST)
8:26–39, p. 146
8:26–40, p. 238
8:30, p. 240
8:33, p. 239
8:39, p. 246
8:41–56, pp. 146, 252, 680
8:42, p. 252
8:43–48, p. 147
8:45, p. 252
8:50, p. 253
8:56, p. 157
9:1–3, p. 161
9:4–6, p. 163
9:7, p. 761
9:7–9, p. 301
9:8, p. 301
9:9, p. 301
9:10, pp. 153, 302, 305, 761
9:10, p. 302 (JST)
9:10–17, p. 146
9:11–17, p. 305
9:18–21, p. 328
9:22, pp. 333, 698
9:23, p. 334
9:23–26, p. 334
9:24–25, p. 335 (JST)
9:27, p. 336
9:28, pp. 153, 338
9:28–36, pp. 337, 767
9:29, pp. 6, 338
9:31, p. 340 (JST)
9:32, p. 338
9:33, p. 343
9:34–35, p. 344
9:36, p. 345
9:37, p. 338
9:37–43, pp. 146, 347
9:43–45, p. 349
9:45, p. 349
9:46–48, p. 352
9:49–50, p. 369
9:51, pp. 200, 374, 404
9:51–56, p. 28
9:52–53, p. 374
9:54, p. 159
9:54–56, p. 375
9:56, p. 124
9:57–62, p. 233
10:1, pp. 161, 213, 375
10:1–24, p. 28
10:2–12, p. 376
10:3, p. 164
10:7, p. 162
10:13, p. 379
10:13–16, p. 377
10:16, p. 379

Scripture Index

10:17–20, p. 379
10:21, p. 380
10:21–22, p. 263
10:22, p. 380 (JST)
10:23–24, p. 288
10:25, p. 431
10:25–37, pp. 280, 383, 488
10:30, p. 383
10:33, p. 130
10:33, p. 385 (JST)
10:34, p. 385
10:37, p. 385
10:38, p. 388
10:38–42, pp. 387, 443
11:1, 5–8, pp. 388, 403, 580
11:2–4, p. 205
11:4, p. 208 (JST)
11:5, p. 389 (JST)
11:5, p. 778
11:5–10, pp. 220, 563
11:5–13, p. 280
11:9–10, p. 389
11:9–13, p. 220
11:14–15, p. 257
11:14–26, pp. 146, 273
11:15, p. 257 (JST)
11:16, p. 275
11:21–22, p. 274
11:24–26, pp. 275, 278
11:27–28, p. 389
11:29–32, p. 276
11:31, p. 277
11:33, p. 184
11:34–36, p. 211
11:37–41, p. 499
11:37–54, p. 490
11:40, p. 499
11:42, pp. 497, 498
11:42, p. 499 (JST)
11:43, pp. 494, 495
11:44, p. 499
11:44–45, 47–48, p. 499
11:46, pp. 492, 747
11:48, p. 500
11:49–51, p. 501
11:50, p. 502
11:51, p. 501
11:52–54, p. 503
11:53, p. 503 (JST)
12, p. 529
12:1, p. 326
12:2–5, p. 166
12:6–7, p. 167
12:7, p. 167
12:8–9, p. 167
12:10, p. 273
12:11–12, p. 165
12:12, p. 165
12:13–21, pp. 280, 389
12:15, p. 390
12:16–21, p. 391
12:20, p. 390
12:21, p. 390
12:22–32, p. 212
12:24, p. 213
12:27, p. 214
12:30, p. 214 (JST)
12:32, pp. 215, 360
12:33–34, p. 210
12:35–36, p. 531
12:35–40, p. 280
12:37–38, 41–44, p. 529
12:37–48, p. 506
12:39, p. 523
12:40, p. 529
12:41–48, p. 280
12:41–57, p. 529 (JST)
12:44, p. 530
12:45–48, p. 530
12:49–53, p. 167
12:50, p. 167
12:54, p. 325
12:54–57, p. 323
12:55, p. 325
12:58–59, p. 193
12:59, p. 777
13:1, pp. 392, 629
13:1–5, p. 392
13:4, p. 392
13:6–9, pp. 146, 280, 475, 476
13:7, pp. 439, 477
13:10–17, p. 392
13:12, p. 109
13:14, p. 755
13:18–19, p. 293
13:18–21, p. 291
13:19, pp. 223, 282, 293
13:20–21, p. 295
13:22, p. 393
13:23–24, p. 221
13:23–30, p. 280
13:25–30, p. 224
13:31–33, p. 393
13:32, p. 394
13:33, pp. 200, 333
13:34, p. 394 (JST)
13:34–35, p. 504
13:36, p. 506 (JST)
14:1, p. 483
14:1–6, p. 483
14:1–15, p. 483
14:1–24, p. 481
14:3, p. 747
14:5, p. 483

14:7–11,
pp. 280,
483, 495,
504
14:11, p. 484
14:12–15,
p. 484
14:16–24,
pp. 280, 483
14:18, p. 482
14:19, p. 482
14:20, p. 482
14:25–27,
pp. 168, 282
14:25–33,
p. 280
14:26, p. 168
14:28–30,
p. 300
14:28–33,
p. 394
14:31, p. 394
(JST)
14:34–35,
p. 182
14:35–37,
p. 184 (JST)
15:1–7, p. 359
15:3–32, p. 280
15:7, p. 360
15:8–9, p. 777
15:8–10, p. 361
15:11–32,
pp. 362, 730
15:16, p. 6
15:17–18,
p. 365
15:18–19,
p. 363
15:20, p. 365
15:24, p. 365
15:31, pp. 360,
365, 530
16:1–8, p. 396
16:8, p. 397
16:1–12,
19–31,
p. 730
16:1–13, p. 280
16:7, p. 779
16:9, p. 211
16:9–13, p. 211
16:10–12,
p. 212
16:13, p. 397
16:14–16,
19–31,
p. 641
16:14–31,
p. 397
16:16–23,
p. 398 (JST)
16:17, p. 187
16:18, p. 198
16:19, pp. 398,
668
16:19–31,
pp. 280, 455
16:20, p. 444
16:25, p. 400
16:31, p. 401
17:1–4, p. 357
17:2, p. 358
17:3–4, p. 369
17:5–6, p. 347
17:6, pp. 223,
348
17:7–10,
pp. 280, 401
17:11–19,
pp. 147, 402
17:14, p. 420
17:16, p. 130
17:20, p. 510
17:20–22,
pp. 76, 510
17:20–37,
p. 506
17:21, p. 4
17:21, p. 511
(JST)
17:22, p. 511
(JST)
17:23, p. 515
17:24, p. 516
17:26–27,
p. 526
17:28–29,
p. 527
17:31,
p. 528
17:31–32,
p. 528
17:33, p. 528
17:34, p. 528
17:34–36,
p. 528
17:37, p. 516
17:37–38,
p. 517 (JST)
18:1, p. 403
18:1–5,
pp. 220, 563
18:1–8,
pp. 280, 403
18:8, p. 403
(JST)
18:9–14,
pp. 280,
490, 496,
503
18:11, p. 503
18:12, p. 504
18:13, p. 504
18:14, p. 504
18:13–14,
p. 751
18:15–17,
p. 430
18:18, p. 383
18:18–27,
p. 431
18:24–25,
p. 433
18:26–27,
p. 437
18:27, p. 438
(JST)
18:28, pp. 149,
775
18:28–30,
p. 438
18:31–34,
pp. 445, 698
18:34, p. 445
18:35–43,
pp. 147, 447
18:43, p. 448
19:1, p. 447
19:1–10, p. 448
19:2, p. 449
19:4, p. 223
19:8, pp. 449,
450
19:11–27,
pp. 280,
450, 535
19:12, p. 450
19:13, p. 778
19:14, p. 451
19:28, p. 451
19:28–34,
p. 460
19:35–38,
p. 462
19:39–40,
p. 465
19:41–44,
pp. 466, 514
19:43–44,
pp. 507, 513
19:45–48,
p. 473
19:47, pp. 410,
735
20:1–8, p. 477
20:9–18, p. 280
20:9–20, p. 478
20:17–18,
p. 300
20:21–26,
p. 484

Scripture Index

20:27–38, p. 486
20:39–40, p. 488
20:41–44, p. 489
20:45–47, p. 490
20:46, pp. 494, 495
21:1–4, p. 490
21:5–6, p. 507
21:5–38, p. 506
21:6, p. 508
21:7, p. 509
21:8, p. 515
21:8, 12, 22, p. 511
21:9, p. 516
21:9–11, p. 517
21:12–19, p. 511
21:13, p. 512
21:14–19, p. 512
21:20, pp. 512, 513
21:21, p. 513
21:21–24, p. 513
21:23–24, p. 514
21:24, p. 200
21:24, p. 514 (JST)
21:25, p. 519 (JST)
21:25–26, p. 518
21:26, p. 519
21:27, p. 520
21:28, p. 523
21:29–31, p. 523
21:32, p. 519
21:32, p. 519 (JST)
21:33, p. 519
21:34–36, p. 529
21:36, p. 529 (JST)
21:37–38, p. 531
21:38, pp. 151, 410, 735
22:1, 7, p. 764
22:1–6, p. 545
22:1–39, p. 765
22:2, 52, p. 745
22:6, p. 546
22:7, p. 546
22:7–13, p. 546
22:9, p. 547
22:14, p. 550
22:15, p. 554
22:15–20, pp. 548, 554
22:16, p. 554 (JST)
22:17, 20, p. 764
22:21–23, p. 550
22:24–27, pp. 445, 496
22:27, p. 446
22:28–30, p. 438
22:31, pp. 85, 589
22:31–32, p. 589
22:32, p. 590
22:33, p. 591
22:33–34, p. 590
22:34, p. 591
22:35–38, p. 591
22:37, p. 591
22:38, p. 591
22:39, pp. 410, 588
22:40–46, p. 591
22:41, p. 595
22:42, p. 600
22:43, p. 678
22:43–44, p. 603
22:44, pp. 28, 604
22:44, p. 605 (JST)
22:45, p. 606
22:47–48, p. 608
22:48, p. 609
22:49, p. 610
22:49–51, p. 609
22:50–51, p. 147
22:51, p. 610
22:52, pp. 608, 756
22:52–54, p. 611
22:53, p. 612
22:54, p. 612
22:55–62, p. 617
22:60–61, p. 778
22:61, p. 620
22:62, p. 620
22:63–65, p. 622
22:66, p. 623
22:66–71, p. 623
23:1–2, p. 626
23:1–6, p. 623
23:2, pp. 271, 486, 627, 633
23:2–4, p. 627
23:4, 14, 22, p. 635
23:4, 15, 22, p. 634
23:5, p. 271
23:5–6, p. 628
23:6–12, p. 761
23:7–10, pp. 628, 631
23:11–12, p. 631
23:13–17, p. 631
23:13–23, p. 745
23:16, pp. 632, 639
23:17, p. 632
23:17–25, p. 632
23:19, 25, p. 633
23:26, p. 643
23:26–31, p. 642
23:27–31, pp. 643, 658
23:31, p. 643
23:32, p. 644
23:32–43, p. 646
23:33, pp. 645, 669
23:34, pp. 648, 652
23:34–37, 39–43, p. 648
23:35, p. 648 (JST)
23:37, p. 648
23:38, p. 652
23:39–43, p. 28

Scripture Index

23:42, p. 649
23:43, pp. 649, 650, 652
23:44, pp. 653, 778
23:45, p. 662
23:46, pp. 652, 655, 658
23:47–49, p. 665
23:50, pp. 6, 666
23:50–56, p. 666
23:51, pp. 666, 667
23:53, p. 669
23:54, 56, p. 664
23:56, p. 677
24:1, pp. 151, 677
24:1–3, p. 675
24:2, p. 669
24:2–4, p. 679 (JST)
24:3, p. 669
24:4–8, p. 677
24:9–11, p. 687
24:10, pp. 269, 666, 677
24:11, p. 687
24:12, 24, p. 680
24:12, p. 669
24:13, pp. 688, 779
24:13–32, p. 688
24:16, p. 690
24:18, p. 690
24:19–24, p. 690
24:21, pp. 610, 690

24:25–26, p. 690
24:26, p. 690
24:27, pp. 689, 691, 697
24:28–32, p. 694
24:29, p. 689
24:32, p. 694
24:33, pp. 689, 695
24:33–35, p. 695
24:34, p. 696
24:36–49, pp. 550, 696
24:39, p. 696
24:41, p. 697
24:42, p. 74
24:42–43, p. 28
24:45, p. 698
24:46, p. 698
24:47, p. 698
24:48, p. 698
24:49, pp. 143, 699, 734
24:50, p. 711
24:50–51, p. 702
24:50–53, p. 710
24:53, pp. 33, 711

John
1, pp. 78, 100
1:1, p. 30 (JST)
1:1–3, p. 12
1:1–5, p. 30
1:3, p. 30
1:4, p. 30
1:4–5, p. 30
1:6–14, p. 78
1:9, p. 281
1:9–11, p. 78
1:12–13, p. 78
1:13, p. 123

1:14, pp. 78, 264
1:15–18, p. 98
1:17, p. 98 (JST)
1:18, pp. 5, 98
1:19, pp. 99, 748
1:19–28, pp. 36, 82, 407
1:21–22, p. 82 (JST)
1:21–28, p. 346 (JST)
1:23, pp. 72, 82
1:24, p. 82
1:26–28, p. 749 (JST)
1:27, p. 84
1:28, pp. 83, 125, 443
1:29, pp. 548, 765
1:29, 36, p. 100
1:29–31, p. 99
1:30, p. 100 (JST)
1:31, p. 100
1:32, p. 88
1:32–34, p. 86
1:34, p. 264
1:35–51, p. 101
1:38, 49, p. 752
1:39–42, p. 101
1:41, 43, 45, p. 102
1:42, p. 101 (JST)
1:42, pp. 5, 156, 329
1:43–44, p. 102
1:45, p. 102
1:46, p. 102
1:47, p. 156
1:47–48, p. 102

1:49, pp. 104, 264, 311
1:50–51, p. 104
2:1, p. 107
2:1, p. 107 (JST)
2:1–11, pp. 28, 107, 111, 146
2:4, p. 109 (JST)
2:6, pp. 109, 779
2:8–9, p. 111
2:11, p. 111
2:11, p. 112 (JST)
2:12, p. 112
2:13, 23–25, p. 114
2:14–17, p. 114
2:16, pp. 474, 733
2:18–22, pp. 116, 649, 674
2:19, pp. 349, 614
2:23, p. 765
2:24, p. 114 (JST)
3, p. 747
3:1, p. 748
3:1–10, pp. 28, 117, 667
3:2, pp. 117, 752
3:3, p. 118
3:4–7, p. 118
3:8, p. 119
3:9–10, p. 119
3:11–21, p. 119
3:12, p. 119
3:13, p. 120
3:14–15, pp. 120, 470

3:16, pp. 123, 601
3:16, 35, p. 264
3:16–17, p. 123
3:18–21, p. 124
3:22, 26, p. 125
3:23–36, pp. 83, 125
3:25, p. 126
3:26, pp. 83, 126, 751
3:27, p. 126 (JST)
3:27–36, p. 126
3:30, p. 178
3:34, p. 127 (JST)
3:36, p. 127 (JST)
4, p. 753
4:1, p. 125
4:1–4, p. 129
4:1–4, p. 125 (JST)
4:1–42, p. 28
4:2–4, p. 129
4:4–42, p. 129
4:5–6, pp. 131, 406
4:7, p. 132
4:9, pp. 51, 130, 132, 383, 753
4:10, pp. 133, 313, 557
4:11–12, p. 133
4:12, p. 271
4:13–15, pp. 134, 406
4:14, pp. 134, 282
4:16–19, p. 135
4:20, p. 131
4:20–21, p. 135
4:22–23, p. 135
4:24, pp. 5, 135, 136
4:25–26, p. 136
4:26, pp. 5, 6, 422
4:27–30, p. 136
4:31, p. 752
4:31–35, p. 136
4:36, p. 137
4:37–38, p. 138
4:38, p. 138
4:39, 42, p. 131
4:39–42, p. 138
4:40, p. 138 (JST)
4:43–45, p. 138
4:44–45, p. 139
4:46–54, pp. 112, 139, 147, 229
4:47–50, p. 139
4:47–51, p. 139
4:51–53, p. 140
4:54, p. 140
5:1, pp. 260, 765
5:1–16, p. 147
5:2–16, p. 260
5:11, p. 261
5:16, pp. 262, 271
5:17–47, pp. 262, 473, 641
5:18, p. 442
5:18–27, p. 263
5:21–27, p. 265
5:24, p. 265
5:28–29, p. 265
5:29, pp. 265, 266
5:30, p. 266
5:31, p. 266
5:31–39, p. 267
5:32, p. 266 (JST)
5:32–38, p. 266
5:35, p. 266
5:35, p. 267 (JST)
5:39, p. 267
5:40–44, p. 267
5:45–47, p. 268
6, pp. 303, 317
6:1, pp. 303, 704
6:1, 23, p. 311
6:1–4, p. 302
6:1–14, p. 146
6:4, p. 765
6:5–14, pp. 305, 323
6:6, p. 306
6:9, pp. 306, 774
6:12, p. 307
6:15, p. 152
6:15–21, pp. 146, 309
6:17, p. 312
6:18, p. 309
6:22, p. 312
6:22–71, p. 311
6:24, p. 312
6:25, pp. 312, 752
6:26, p. 312 (JST)
6:27–71, p. 28
6:31, p. 315
6:35, p. 282
6:37, pp. 313, 316, 426, 442, 561, 583, 584
6:38–40, p. 314
6:39–40, 44, 54, p. 314
6:40, p. 314
6:41–44, p. 314
6:46, p. 99
6:48–58, p. 315
6:49–50, p. 315
6:51, pp. 313, 557
6:52, p. 315
6:53, p. 315
6:53–54, p. 557
6:56, p. 315
6:59, p. 315
6:60–62, p. 315
6:62, p. 316
6:63, p. 316
6:63–65, p. 316
6:64, p. 559
6:65, p. 316 (JST)
6:66–69, p. 316
6:68–69, p. 317
6:69, p. 264
6:70, p. 630
6:71, p. 160
7:1, pp. 457, 754
7:2–9, p. 373
7:5, p. 141
7:8–9, p. 404
7:10, p. 403
7:10–13, p. 403
7:12, p. 271
7:12, 43, p. 407
7:14, pp. 410, 735, 744
7:14–36, pp. 404, 473
7:24, p. 405 (JST)
7:30, p. 469
7:32, p. 756
7:37, p. 766
7:37–38, p. 766
7:37–53, p. 406
7:38, pp. 134, 406
7:39, p. 407 (JST)

7:39, p. 578
7:40–44, p. 407
7:43, p. 407
7:45–49, p. 407
7:45–53, p. 119
7:46, p. 247
7:50–51,
  pp. 117, 748
7:50–53, p. 408
7–8, p. 741
8, p. 4
8:1–11, p. 409
8:2, pp. 410,
  735
8:3–11, p. 411
8:6, p. 428
8:9, p. 412
8:10–11, p. 412
8:11, p. 413
  (JST)
8:12, pp. 124,
  283, 313,
  414, 419
8:12–20, p. 766
8:12–59, p. 413
8:13, p. 271
8:14, pp. 266,
  414
8:17, p. 414
8:19, pp. 414,
  562
8:20, pp. 411,
  414, 741
8:21, p. 414
8:24, p. 414
8:26–29, p. 415
8:31–34, p. 415
8:33–59, p. 407
8:35–36, p. 415
8:37–40, p. 415
8:41, p. 45
8:41–45, p. 415
8:43, p. 416
  (JST)
8:46, p. 416
8:46–55, p. 416

8:47, p. 416
  (JST)
8:48, pp. 130,
  271, 383
8:53, p. 271
8:56–59, p. 417
8:58, p. 136
8:59, pp. 142,
  146, 471
9, p. 124
9:1, p. 419
9:1–41,
  pp. 147, 418
9:2, p. 752
9:2–3, p. 419
9:3, pp. 111,
  420, 444
9:4, p. 420
9:4–5, pp. 420,
  473
9:6–7, pp. 253,
  420
9:7, p. 420
9:8–12, p. 421
9:13–34, p. 421
9:16, p. 407
9:22, p. 755
9:24, p. 271
9:32, p. 5
9:32, p. 422
  (JST)
9:35–37, p. 263
9:35–38, p. 422
9:39–41, p. 422
9:41, p. 577
10, 283
10:1–21, p. 423
10:8, p. 426
  (JST)
10:9, pp. 283,
  313
10:11, pp. 283,
  313
10:11–15,
  pp. 426, 584
10:12, p. 164

10:13, p. 426
10:16, p. 426
10:17–18,
  pp. 427, 649
10:18, p. 427
10:19, p. 407
10:19–21,
  p. 428
10:20, p. 271
10:21, pp. 247,
  428
10:22, pp. 440,
  724, 763
10:22–39,
  pp. 440, 738
10:24–29,
  p. 442
10:30, pp. 17,
  266, 442,
  562, 587
10:31–39,
  pp. 262,
  442, 641
10:33, p. 271
10:36, p. 263
10:40–42,
  p. 443
10:41, p. 247
11:1–5, p. 399
11:1–7, p. 443
11:1–46,
  pp. 146, 680
11:1–56, p. 28
11:2, pp. 443,
  543
11:2, p. 444
  (JST)
11:2, 17, p. 388
  (JST)
11:4, pp. 111,
  420, 444
11:6–46, p. 399
11:8, p. 752
11:8–53, p. 451
11:11–15,
  p. 451

11:14–15,
  p. 452
11:16, pp. 156,
  452
11:16, p. 452
  (JST)
11:17, p. 452
11:18, p. 443
11:20–27,
  p. 452
11:21, p. 453
11:22, p. 453
11:23, p. 453
11:24, p. 453
11:25, p. 313
11:25–26,
  p. 453
11:27, pp. 264,
  453
11:28–37,
  p. 453
11:38–40,
  p. 454
11:38–44,
  p. 231
11:39, p. 454
11:40, p. 454
11:41–42,
  p. 454
11:43–46,
  p. 455
11:46–12:11,
  p. 399
11:47–53,
  pp. 456, 615
11:48, p. 456
11:49, p. 541
11:50, p. 456
11:53, p. 457
11:54, p. 457
11:55–57,
  p. 458
12, p. 468
12:1–2, p. 542
12:1–3, p. 458

814

12:3, pp. 444, 543
12:3–8, p. 542
12:4–8, p. 459
12:6, pp. 553, 630
12:7, p. 459 (JST)
12:9–12, p. 459
12:12–18, p. 462
12:13, pp. 223, 464
12:16, pp. 349, 445
12:17–18, p. 465
12:19, pp. 435, 465
12:20–22, p. 468
12:23–24, p. 469
12:23–50, p. 468
12:27, p. 469
12:31, p. 470
12:32–34, p. 470
12:34, p. 470
12:35–36, p. 470
12:37, p. 471
12:37–41, p. 471
12:40, p. 472
12:42, pp. 472, 667, 755
12:42–43, p. 472
12:43, pp. 472, 493, 496
12:44–45, 49–50, p. 473
12:44–50, p. 472
12:47, p. 473
12:48, p. 473
13:1, pp. 546, 549, 765
13:1–16, p. 28
13:1–38, p. 765
13:2–5, p. 557
13:2–17, p. 548
13:5, p. 558
13:6–12, p. 559
13:10, p. 558 (JST)
13:10, p. 559 (JST)
13:11, p. 316
13:12–16, pp. 354, 560
13:13–17, p. 559
13:15, p. 385
13:18, p. 584
13:18–22, pp. 550, 551, 553
13:18–30, p. 548
13:19, p. 551 (JST)
13:21, p. 550
13:23–30, pp. 552, 707
13:26, p. 551
13:27, p. 545
13:30, p. 553
13:31–35, pp. 560, 570
13:35, p. 571
13:36–38, p. 590
14, p. 4
14, 15, 16, p. 28
14:1, p. 567
14:1–15, p. 561
14:4–5, p. 562
14:6, pp. 313, 562
14:7, p. 562
14:8, p. 562
14:9, p. 562
14:8–9, p. 380
14:10, p. 17
14:12–14, p. 562
14:12–27, p. 564
14:15, pp. 563, 572
14:16, p. 564
14:16–18, 26, p. 178
14:16–31, p. 563
14:17, p. 564
14:18, pp. 564, 711
14:21, p. 564
14:22, p. 564
14:23, p. 565
14:26, p. 563
14:27, pp. 168, 566
14:29, pp. 567, 578
14:30, p. 567
14:30, p. 567 (JST)
14:31, p. 567
15, p. 283
15:1, pp. 283, 313
15:1–8, p. 568
15:2, p. 568
15:4–5, p. 569
15:5, p. 282
15:8, 11, p. 570
15:9–10, 12, p. 573
15:9–17, pp. 356, 561, 570
15:10, p. 574
15:11, p. 570
15:13, p. 575
15:14, p. 574
15:14–15, p. 574
15:15, p. 574
15:16, p. 576
15:17, p. 576
15:18–19, p. 166
15:18–25, p. 576
15:22, pp. 6, 577
15:26–27, p. 577
15–17, p. 588
16:1–6, p. 577
16:2, pp. 578, 755
16:3, p. 578
16:4, p. 578
16:7, p. 578
16:7–16, p. 578
16:8–11, p. 578
16:12–16, p. 579
16:13–16, p. 179
16:17–30, p. 580
16:20, pp. 177, 580
16:21, p. 580
16:22, p. 580
16:23, p. 580 (JST)
16:23–28, p. 580
16:29–30, p. 580
16:31–33, p. 581

Scripture Index

16:33, p. 581
17, p. 582
17:1–3, p. 582
17:1–26, p. 582
17:3, p. 583
17:4, p. 583
17:4, 12, p. 314
17:4–19,
  pp. 582, 583
17:5, p. 583
17:6, p. 583
17:7–8, p. 583
17:8, p. 583
17:9, p. 584
17:10, p. 584
17:11, pp. 584,
  587
17:12, pp. 584,
  609, 630
17:13, p. 585
17:14, p. 585
17:15, p. 585
17:16, p. 585
17:17, p. 585
17:18, p. 585
17:19, p. 586
17:20–26,
  pp. 582, 586
17:21, pp. 442,
  562, 586
17:21–23, p.
  587
17:22, p. 17
17:23, p. 586
17:24–26, p.
  588
18:1, p. 588
18:2, pp. 410,
  591, 592
18:2–3, p. 608
18:3, pp. 608,
  610, 745,
  756
18:4–9,
  pp. 581, 609
18:5, p. 616

18:9, pp. 314,
  609
18:10–11,
  p. 609
18:11, pp. 600,
  610
18:12, pp. 609,
  611, 756
18:13, pp. 77,
  541
18:13–14,
  19–24,
  p. 612
18:15, pp. 610,
  622
18:15–18,
  25–27,
  p. 617
18:16, p. 622
18:18, p. 618
18:20, pp. 410,
  735
18:20–21,
  p. 616
18:22–23,
  p. 616
18:24, 28,
  p. 623
18:27, p. 778
18:28, pp. 549,
  623, 624
18:28–38,
  p. 623
18:31, pp. 641,
  754
18:31–32,
  pp. 627, 754
18:32, p. 627
18:33, p. 624
18:33–38,
  p. 627
18:38, p. 634
18:39–40,
  p. 632
18:40, p. 632
19:1–5, p. 639

19:1–12, p. 639
19:2, p. 640
19:4, 6, p. 634
19:4, p. 635
19:6–7, p. 641
19:8–12, p. 641
19:9, p. 624
19:11, pp. 637,
  641
19:12, pp. 627,
  642
19:13, pp. 624,
  625
19:13–17,
  p. 642
19:14, pp. 549,
  642
19:15, p. 642
19:17, p. 5
19:17, p. 645
  (JST)
19:18–22,
  p. 646
19:19–22,
  pp. 652, 653
19:20, p. 669
19:23–24,
  p. 648
19:25, pp. 444,
  666
19:25–27,
  pp. 552,
  654, 666,
  677
19:26, p. 109
19:26–27, p.
  652
19:28, p. 652
19:28–30,
  p. 655
19:29, pp. 548,
  657
19:30, p. 652
19:31, p. 5
19:31–34,
  p. 664

19:35–37,
  p. 665
19:36, pp. 547,
  765
19:37, p. 665
19:38, pp. 472,
  667
19:38–39,
  p. 415
19:38–40,
  p. 117
19:38–42,
  p. 666
19:39, p. 667
19:39–40,
  p. 748
19:39–42,
  p. 119
19:40, p. 668
19:41, p. 669
19:41–42,
  pp. 668, 669
20:1, p. 5
20:1, p. 675
  (JST)
20:1–2, p. 675
20:1–18, p. 677
20:2, pp. 552,
  655, 679
20:3–10, p. 680
20:4–7, p. 681
20:5, 11–12,
  p. 669
20:6–7, 12,
  p. 669
20:8, pp. 669,
  680
20:9, pp. 346,
  680
20:10, p. 681
20:11–13, p.
  681
20:13, p. 109
20:14–17,
  pp. 674, 683

Scripture Index

20:15, pp. 109, 669
20:16, p. 752
20:17, p. 5
20:17, p. 683 (JST)
20:18, p. 687
20:19–23, p. 696
20:19–29, p. 695
20:21, p. 263
20:21–22, p. 698
20:23, p. 371
20:24, p. 156
20:24–25, p. 699
20:26–29, p. 700
20:30, p. 708
20:30–31, p. 700
20:31, p. 264
21, p. 4, p. 702
21:1, p. 311
21:1–19, p. 704
21:3, p. 775
21:3–6, p. 154
21:6–14, p. 146
21:14, p. 705
21:15–17, p. 706
21:18–19, p. 707
21:18, p. 590
21:20–22, p. 707
21:20–24, pp. 28, 552, 655
21:23, pp. 336, 655
21:23–25, p. 708
21:24, pp. 707, 708
21:25, pp. 435, 700, 708
21:27, p. 100

Acts
1:1, p. 30
1:3, p. 91
1:3–11, p. 702
1:4–5, 8, p. 699
1:6, pp. 610, 690
1:8, pp. 79, 143, 698, 753
1:9, p. 344
1:9–12, p. 711
1:12, p. 409
1:13, pp. 156, 159, 160, 757
1:13–26, p. 550
1:14, p. 113
1:15, p. 331
1:18, p. 630
1:19, p. 630
1:21–22, p. 577
1:21–26, p. 156
1:26, p. 438
2, pp. 698, 765
2:9–11, p. 765
2:14, p. 331
2:22, p. 118
2:41, p. 765
2:46, pp. 33, 711
3:1, p. 33
3:1–11, p. 740
3:1–4:2, p. 738
3:13, 26, p. 264
3:18, p. 691
4:1, p. 752
4:1–3, p. 752
4:11, p. 480
4:13–17, p. 754
4:15, p. 721
4:18–20, 29, 31, p. 577
4:26–27, p. 637
4:32, p. 586
5:12, p. 33
5:17, p. 752
5:17–21, p. 754
5:21, pp. 721, 753
5:29, 32, 40–42, p. 577
5:34, 40, p. 754
5:36–37, p. 465
5:37, pp. 50, 160
6:7, p. 472
6:12–15, p. 741
7:30, p. 92
8:9, p. 160
8:23, p. 646
8:37, p. 264
9:2, p. 754
9:11, p. 160
9:15, p. 165
9:20, p. 264
9:27, 29, p. 577
9:36–41, p. 562
9:43, p. 160
10, pp. 331, 774
10:38, pp. 24, 118
12, pp. 156, 762
12:12, pp. 550, 612
13:1, pp. 160, 761
13:2, p. 249
13:21, p. 92
13:46, pp. 481, 577
14:3, p. 577
14:23, p. 746
15, p. 774
15:1–31, p. 774
15:14, p. 160
15:22, 27, 32, p. 160
19:12, p. 253
19:15, p. 240
20:29, p. 164
21:9, p. 60
21:17–25, p. 774
21:34, 37, p. 626
22:30–23:10, p. 741
22:24, p. 626
23:1–6, p. 748
23:1–10, p. 754
23:6, p. 748
23:6–9, p. 748
23:6–10, p. 752
23:8, p. 486
23:10, p. 626
23:35, p. 624
25:12, p. 50

Romans
1:4, p. 264
1:25, p. 168
2:28–29, p. 773
8:3, 32, p. 264
8:28, p. 572
8:32, p. 530
11:16, p. 83
11:17, 24, p. 223
12:5, p. 586
13:1–7, p. 485
14:2, p. 497
15:6, p. 264

1 Corinthians
2:9, p. 572
2:11, 14, p. 127
3:6, p. 138
5:6–7, p. 326
5:7, p. 100
9:1, p. 703

817

Scripture Index

9:5, p. 232
9:7, p. 424
10:4, p. 329
10:16, p. 764
10:21, p. 600
15:5, p. 696
15:6, p. 702
15:7, p. 702
15:8, p. 703
15:20, p. 664
15:29, p. 734

2 Corinthians
1:19, p. 264
3:7, p. 37
5:21, p. 601
6:3, p. 601
7:10, p. 174
11:3, p. 121
11:24, p. 639

Galatians
1:19, p. 113
2:1–15, p. 774
2:11–21, p. 774
2:20, p. 264
3:28, p. 586
4:4, p. 264

Ephesians
2:19–20, p. 480
4:13, pp. 203, 264
4:26, p. 189 (JST)
5:21–33, p. 769

Philippians
1:27, p. 586
3:5, p. 748
3:13, p. 376

Colossians
1:13, p. 264
3:14, p. 571
4:12, p. 203
4:14, pp. 28, 392

1 Thessalonians
1:10, p. 264
4:17, p. 561
5:2, p. 524
5:3, p. 524

2 Thessalonians
2:8, p. 519

1 Timothy
1:15, p. 249
2:1–3, p. 485
5:17, p. 746
5:20, p. 370
6:7, p. 211

2 Timothy
2:19, p. 314
3:12, p. 181
3:17, p. 203
4:7, p. 583
4:11, p. 28

Titus
1, p. 485
3:1, p. 485

Hebrews
1:1–3, p. 30
1:2, p. 264
1:3, p. 79
2:18, p. 90
3:1, p. 158
4:14, p. 264
4:15, pp. 90, 598
5:4, p. 750
6:19–20, p. 663
8:10, p. 371
9:11–14, p. 743
9:11–16, p. 739
9:19–20, p. 658
9:19–24, p. 676
9–10, pp. 183, 658
10:19–20, p. 676
10:19–22, p. 743

11:37, p. 424
12:22–23, p. 12

James
1:6, pp. 220, 563
3:2, p. 203
5:14, p. 746
5:15, p. 247

1 Peter
1:18–20, p. 19
1:19, p. 547
1:20, p. 30
1:25, p. 520
3:14, pp. 180, 567
3:18–19, p. 651
3:18–20, p. 650
3:19, p. 141
4:6, p. 651
4:8, p. 571
4–6, p. 650
5:13, p. 28

2 Peter
1:14, p. 707
1:16, p. 78
1:16–19, p. 341

1 John
2:21–22, p. 264
3:8, 23, p. 264
3:11, 16–18, p. 575
4:8, p. 601
4:9, p. 124
4:10, 14–15, p. 264
4:12, p. 99
4:18, p. 561
5:5, 10–13, p. 264
5:7, p. 587
5:9–11, p. 263
5:13, p. 700

Jude
1:1, p. 160

Revelation
1:9–18, p. 703
1:10, p. 700
5:8, p. 100
5:12, p. 100
6:12–13, p. 518
6:16, p. 100
7:14, p. 100
8, p. 530
9, p. 530
12:9, p. 121
12:11, p. 581
12:12, p. 246
13:8, p. 100
15:3, p. 100
15:6, p. 668
17:14, p. 100
19:7, p. 100
19:9, p. 100
19:20, p. 193
20:2, pp. 121, 274
20:10, p. 193
21:1, p. 519
21:4, p. 712
21:7, p. 530
21:8, p. 193
21:9, p. 100
21:23, pp. 100, 519
21:27, p. 100

THE BOOK OF MORMON

1 Nephi
2:13, p. 645
2:14, p. 143
8, p. 287
8:20, p. 221
8:23, 28, p. 288
8:24, 30, p. 288
8:26–27, pp. 175, 287
8:28, p. 287
10:4, p. 755
10:4–5, p. 44

Scripture Index

10:7–10,
  pp. 72, 74, 86
10:9, p. 83
10:17, p. 264
10:21, p. 686
11:1, pp. 8, 95
11:7, 18, 21, 24, p. 264
11:13, 15, p. 39
11:13–21, p. 44
11:16, p. 22
11:18–20, p. 40
11:18–27, p. 573
11:21, pp. 23, 547
11:22–23, p. 571
11:26, p. 22
11:27, pp. 72, 74, 88
11:31, p. 233
11:32–33, p. 638
12:9, p. 438
12:18, p. 400
13:24–25, p. 29
13:26, p. 503
13:27, p. 503
13:28, p. 29
13:39, p. 29
13:40, pp. 23, 44, 264
14:12, p. 221
15:9, p. 123
15:15, p. 568
15:24, p. 8
15:28–30, p. 400
16:2, p. 124
17:35, 40, p. 574
17:41, p. 122
18:3, pp. 95, 104

19:6, p. 709
19:9, p. 638
19:10, pp. 428, 470, 654
19:12, p. 663
19:13–14, p. 468
22:20, p. 407
22:26, p. 274

2 Nephi
1:13, p. 400
1:24, p. 104
2:6, 8, p. 693
2:6–8, p. 694
2:7, p. 606
2:8, p. 79
2:10, p. 685
2:25–26, p. 691
4:17–19, 27–29, p. 189
4:17–31, p. 189
4:35, pp. 220, 563
6:15, p. 517
8:6, p. 662
9:5, p. 611
9:18, p. 169
9:20, p. 525
9:22, 38, p. 685
9:30, p. 436
9:41, p. 221
9:42, p. 380
9:46, p. 275
9:51, p. 314
10:3, pp. 500, 581
10:3, 5, p. 540
10:5, pp. 456, 545, 634
10:14, p. 643
11:3, p. 296
11:4, 6, pp. 44, p. 693
16, p. 472
16:9–10, p. 472

25:1, p. 315
25:9, p. 468
25:12, 16, 19, p. 264
25:13, p. 46
25:14, p. 514
25:19, pp. 29, 40, 59
25:19, 26, p. 693
25:26, p. 556
25:29, p. 168
26:24, pp. 124, 470
26:26, p. 755
26:29, p. 456
27:11, p. 166
27:25, p. 318
28:28, p. 226
28:30, p. 289
30:17, p. 166
31:4, 8, p. 74
31:4, p. 72
31:5–12, p. 87
31:12, p. 334
31:17–20, p. 221
31:21, p. 587
32:3, p. 563
32:5, pp. 563, 579
33:1–2, p. 143

Jacob
1:8, p. 169
2:13, p. 214
2:18–19, p. 437
2:19, p. 538
4:4, p. 19
4:5, 11, p. 264
4:5, p. 691
4:6, p. 476
4:9, p. 235
5, p. 283
5:46, p. 84
5:61–63,

70–76, p. 481
5:63, p. 440
5:70, p. 268
6:11, p. 221
7:19, p. 267

Enos
1:27, p. 561

Omni
1:26, p. 395

Words of Mormon
1:17, p. 143

Mosiah
2:4, pp. 572, 574
2:17, p. 539
2:18, p. 446
2:21, p. 402
3, p. 430
3:5, p. 419
3:5–6, pp. 150, 233
3:5–8, pp. 21, 24
3:5–13, p. 19
3:7, pp. 92, 132, 167, 602, 605
3:8, pp. 14, 39, 44, 264
3:9, p. 257
3:10, p. 698
3:15, p. 691
3:18, p. 354
3:19, pp. 201, 354, 684
3:20, p. 518
3:24–25, p. 275
4, p. 210
4:2, pp. 176, 264
4:11, p. 176
4:13, p. 571

819

Scripture Index

4:15, p. 572
4:16–21, p. 84
4:24–26, p. 490
4:26, p. 432
5:5–8, p. 78
5:7, pp. 279, 712
5:9–12, p. 537
7:30, p. 86
8:21, p. 706
13, p. 171
13:5, p. 37
13:33, pp. 19, 691
14:4, pp. 232, 692
14:5, p. 692
14:7, pp. 100, 614, 627
14:7–8, p. 692
14:8, p. 100
14:9, p. 647
14:10, p. 100
14:12, pp. 591, 647, 692
15:1, p. 24
15:2, pp. 29, 264
15:4, p. 15
15:5, p. 97
15:6, p. 614
15:7, p. 567
15:8, p. 428
15:9, pp. 157, 603
15:25, p. 430
16:8, p. 685
16:9, p. 30
16:11, p. 266
18:9, p. 177
18:21, p. 586
24:12–17, p. 382
26:23, p. 15
26:23–24, p. 537

26:27, p. 225
26:31, pp. 208, 371
27:19, p. 37

Alma
1:27, p. 432
5:15, p. 15
5:33, p. 79
5:34, p. 313
5:36, p. 83
5:37, p. 268
5:41, pp. 211, 584
5:48, pp. 264, 606
5:52, p. 84
5:58, p. 537
5:59, p. 164
6:8, p. 264
7:9, p. 222
7:10, pp. 39, 40, 41, 51
7:11, pp. 97, 232
7:12, pp. 79, 90, 599
7:14, p. 548
7:19, p. 72
7:20, p. 222
9:15, p. 379
11, p. 684
11:32–35, p. 264
11:40–43, p. 548
11:41, 44, p. 685
11:43, p. 275
11:44, p. 587
12:9–10, p. 288
12:10, p. 281
12:11, p. 536
12:14–15, p. 275
12:33–34, p. 264

13:5, 16, p. 264
13:18, p. 349
13:19, p. 258
13:28, p. 572
19:13, p. 606
24:30, p. 278
26:20, p. 400
26:22, p. 288
26:28, p. 213
26:37, p. 79
30:43, p. 276
31:14–18, p. 205
31:16, p. 504
31:37–38, p. 213
31:38, p. 181
32:8, p. 177
32:21, p. 700
32:23, pp. 60, 380
32:28, p. 285
32:39, p. 285
32:42, p. 288
33:7, p. 205
33:13–17, p. 264
33:14, p. 264
33:14, 22, p. 264
33:18–19, p. 264
33:19, p. 122
33:19–20, p. 121
33:20, p. 122
33:23, p. 381
34:2, 5, p. 264
34:10, p. 21
34:26, p. 205
34:33, p. 420
34:34, p. 76
34:34–35, p. 420
34:36, p. 565
36:3, p. 567

36:17–18, p. 264
37:2, p. 29
37:12, p. 222
37:34, p. 381
38:5, p. 567
38:12, pp. 195, 572
38:14, p. 504
39:9, p. 169
39:14, p. 211
40:13, p. 229
40:18, p. 664
40:23, pp. 512, 697
41:14–15, p. 217
42:23, p. 685
42:27, p. 133
45:19, p. 340
56:46, p. 371
60:12, p. 392
60:23, p. 499

Helaman
3:28, p. 264
3:29, p. 400
3:29–30, p. 97
3:30, p. 537
3:35, p. 210
5:12, p. 226
5:23–24, 28, p. 344
5:36, pp. 37, 338
5:41, p. 413
5:45, pp. 85, 526
5:47, p. 24
8:13–15, pp. 121, 264, 500
8:14, p. 692
8:17, p. 417
8:19–20, p. 264
8:20, p. 264
8:25, p. 210

Scripture Index

10:4–10, p. 332
10:5, pp. 220, 563
10:7, p. 331
10:9, p. 348
12:4, p. 533
12:16, p. 235
13:26, pp. 257, 401
13:29, pp. 124, 320, 497
14:2, 8, 12, p. 264
14:5, p. 62
14:8, p. 123
14:15–17, p. 685
14:18, p. 196
14:20, 27, p. 654
14:21–24, p. 662
14:23, p. 73
14:25, p. 663
14:28, p. 104

3 Nephi
1:13, 21, p. 62
1:25, p. 188
2:8, p. 773
5:13, 26, p. 264
8:1, p. 118
8:5, p. 773
9:13, p. 123
9:15, pp. 17, 30, 263
9:16, p. 78
9:17, p. 78
9:18, p. 30
9:22, pp. 430, 606
10:4–6, pp. 504, 505
10:6, p. 76
10:10, p. 580
11, p. 473
11:1, p. 171

11:1–18:39, p. 703
11:3, p. 694
11:7, pp. 89, 263
11:11, pp. 30, 100, 314, 600
11:11–12, p. 610
11:14, pp. 696, 700
11:27, p. 17
11:36, p. 587
11:37–38, p. 430
11:39, p. 329
11:39–40, p. 225
12, p. 158
12:1, p. 174
12:1–12, p. 172
12:2, p. 174
12:3, pp. 141, 174, 175
12:3–10, p. 174
12:4, p. 177
12:5, p. 177
12:5–9, p. 174
12:6, p. 178
12:7, p. 179
12:8, p. 179
12:9, p. 180
12:10–12, p. 180
12:11–12, p. 175
12:13, p. 182
12:14–16, p. 184
12:17, p. 186
12:18, p. 188
12:18–20, 46–47, p. 187
12:21, p. 188

12:21–22, p. 189
12:22, pp. 191, 193
12:23–24, p. 193
12:24, p. 193
12:25–26, p. 193
12:27–30, p. 195
12:29–30, p. 196
12:30, p. 334
12:31–32, p. 198
12:33–37, p. 199
12:38–42, p. 200
12:43–45, p. 201
12:46–47, p. 202
12:48, pp. 203, 204
12–14, p. 170
13:1–4, p. 204
13:5–15, p. 205
13:9–13, p. 207
13:10, p. 207
13:14–15, p. 208
13:16–18, p. 209
13:19–34, p. 210
13:22–23, p. 211
13:24, p. 211
13:25–34, p. 212
14:1–5, p. 216
14:6, p. 218
14:7–12, p. 220

14:13–14, p. 221
14:15–20, p. 222
14:19, p. 84
14:21–23, p. 224
14:24–27, p. 225
15:1, p. 314
15:1–5, p. 30
15:4–5, p. 16
15:5, pp. 79, 774
15:9, pp. 16, 166
15:21, p. 427
15:22–23, pp. 322, 427
15:24, p. 313
16:1–3, p. 427
16:1–4, p. 703
16:13, p. 76
16:15, p. 182
17:2, p. 579
17:4, p. 703
17:6, p. 157
17:8, p. 229
17:10, p. 543
17:11–12, 21–23, p. 430
17:21–22, p. 453
18:1–11, p. 554
18:13, pp. 225, 329
18:15, 18, p. 589
18:24, p. 185
18:28–30, p. 547
18:31, p. 313
18:38–39, p. 344
19:11–12, p. 88

821

19:20, 29, p. 584
19:20, p. 313
19:23, p. 17
19:24, p. 206
19:30, p. 338
19:35, pp. 229, 301
20:3–7, p. 307
20:31, p. 263
23:11, p. 663
23:13, p. 29
23:14, p. 691
24:1, p. 522
26:6, p. 708
26:9, p. 579
26:14, 16, p. 380
27:1–28:12, p. 703
27:13, p. 314
27:21, p. 151
27:29, p. 220
27:30, p. 609
27:33, p. 221
28:6, p. 552
28:6–9, p. 708
28:7, p. 336
28:7–9, 13–17, 36–40, p. 340
28:8, p. 340
28:10, p. 17
28:34, p. 379
28:36, p. 340
29:2, p. 530

4 Nephi
1:5, p. 562
1:15–16, p. 571
1:39, p. 201

Mormon
1:15, p. 703
3:18, p. 438
5:14, pp. 264, 700
7:5–7, p. 264
8:12, p. 579
8:17, pp. 193, 525
8:19–20, p. 217
8:30, p. 515
9:12–14, p. 685
9:21, p. 580
9:22–24, p. 708
9:22–25, p. 710

Ether
2:4–5, 14, p. 344
2:23, p. 109
3:1, p. 95
3:16, p. 15
3:21, pp. 97, 522
4:1, p. 95
4:13, pp. 104, 579
12:12, p. 301
12:18, p. 264
12:23–37, p. 198
12:27, p. 176
12:28, p. 79
12:30, pp. 348, 349
12:32, p. 561
12:33, p. 123
12:34, p. 572
12:35, p. 536
12:39, p. 703

Moroni
4:3, p. 555
6:4, pp. 576, 710
7, p. 210
7:3, p. 82
7:5, p. 222
7:14–18, p. 217
7:15–18, p. 281
7:16, p. 78
7:18, p. 217
7:22, p. 525
7:37, p. 301
7:48, p. 572
8:8, pp. 248, 774
8:17, p. 571
8:26, p. 572
10:5, p. 579
10:30, 32, p. 197
10:32, p. 204

DOCTRINE AND COVENANTS

1:3, p. 166
1:10, p. 217
1:38, pp. 170, 379, 520
3:2, p. 222
4:4, p. 138
4:5, p. 211
5:19, p. 519
6:5, 8, 14, 15, 20, p. 562
6:7, p. 297
6:9, pp. 76, 282
6:20, p. 574
6:21, p. 263
6:32, p. 371
7, p. 708
7:1, 3, p. 707
7:1, 5, p. 552
7:7, pp. 332, 341
9:8, p. 109
10:52, p. 187
10:57, p. 263
11:9, p. 282
11:28, p. 263
11:30, p. 78
12:8, p. 571
13, pp. 34, 35, 74, 343, 347
13:1, p. 76
14:7, p. 170
14:9, p. 263
15:6, p. 76
16:6, p. 76
18:11, p. 470
18:10, p. 191
18:10, 15–16, p. 246
18:13, p. 362
19:4, p. 392
19:16–18, p. 602
19:17, p. 606
19:18, p. 605
20:1, pp. 55, 771, 772
20:21, p. 264
20:22, p. 97
20:28, p. 587
20:31, p. 572
20:77, p. 555
20:77, 79, p. 315
21:1, p. 29
24:15, p. 163
24:18, p. 162
25:1, pp. 78, 712
27:2, p. 627
27:5, p. 555
27:5–14, p. 555
27:6–7, p. 347
27:7, pp. 35, 38
27:9, p. 332
27:12–13, p. 343
27:14, pp. 313, 555
27:18, p. 529
29:5, pp. 215, 371
29:7, p. 515
29:9, 12, p. 519
29:9–27, p. 506
29:12, p. 438
29:14, p. 518
29:23, p. 519

SCRIPTURE INDEX

29:27, p. 537
29:28–29, p. 245
29:29, p. 406
29:42, p. 263
29:46–50, p. 357
31:5, p. 247
32:3, 9, p. 371
33:17–18, p. 531
34:7, p. 345
35:2, pp. 263, 587, 627, 655
35:21, pp. 533, 579
36:1, p. 247
36:8, pp. 263, 522
38:2, p. 525
38:7, p. 371
38:8, p. 579
38:17, p. 685
38:27, p. 588
38:30, p. 506
38:32, p. 699
38:39, p. 297
39:4, p. 78
41:6, pp. 219, 322
41:11, p. 103
42, p. 171
42:1, pp. 44, 264
42:6, p. 161
42:23, p. 197
42:27, 24–25, p. 413
42:36, p. 522
42:45, pp. 303, 453
42:88–91, p. 370
42:91, p. 370
43:32, p. 340

45:2, p. 529
45:3–5, p. 594
45:16, 44–45, p. 520
45:16, pp. 507, 509
45:16–45, p. 506
45:18–20, p. 507
45:19, pp. 514, 524
45:20, p. 508
45:21, p. 519
45:25, 28–30, p. 514
45:26, pp. 519, 530
45:27, p. 517
45:32, p. 513
45:33, p. 517
45:34–35, p. 515
45:37–38, p. 523
45:39, 44, p. 507
45:42, p. 518
45:45, p. 345
45:52, p. 263
45:56, p. 532
45:56–59, p. 531
45:57–58, p. 533
45:59, p. 371
46:7, p. 515
46:13, pp. 627, 655
46:13–14, p. 264
49:5, p. 263
49:7, p. 525
49:27, p. 371
50:24, p. 290

50:27, pp. 263, 530
50:32–33, p. 380
50:40, p. 579
50:41, p. 313
50:42, p. 585
50:43, pp. 266, 587
50:44, pp. 329, 371
51:3, p. 535
53:2, pp. 627, 655
54:1, pp. 627, 655
55:2, p. 264
56:18, p. 176
58:7, p. 510
58:21–22, p. 485
58:27–28, p. 215
58:44, p. 510
59:2, p. 562
59:16, 18, p. 391
59:23, p. 382
60:7, p. 247
60:15, p. 163
61:36, p. 371
62:3, p. 247
62:9, p. 710
63:7, p. 515
63:9–11, pp. 112, 276, 401
63:16, p. 195
63:20–21, p. 342
63:21, p. 342
63:23, p. 135
63:51, p. 340
64:8, p. 371
64:8–10, p. 208
64:10, p. 371

64:23–24, p. 522
64:24, p. 519
65, p. 511
66:12, p. 79
67:11, pp. 99, 340
68:6, p. 371
68:6, 25, p. 264
68:25–27, p. 357
72:3, p. 536
72:4, p. 562
72:6, p. 29
75:20, p. 163
75:22, p. 379
76, p. 265
76:15–19, p. 266
76:19, p. 8
76:19–20, p. 21
76:20–23, p. 263
76:20–25, p. 264
76:22–24, p. 30
76:23–24, pp. 13, 21
76:25, p. 18
76:28, p. 166
76:32–38, p. 246
76:44, p. 359
76:55, 59, p. 530
76:63, p. 520
76:69, p. 124
76:102, pp. 345, 529
76:107, pp. 594, 603
77:9, 14, p. 347
77:12–13, p. 530
77:13, p. 530
78:14, p. 214

Scripture Index

78:18, p. 579
81:6, p. 562
82:3, p. 378
82:10, pp. 220, 563
82:22, p. 212
84:2–4, p. 522
84:19–27, p. 748
84:22, p. 99
84:24, pp. 82, 381
84:27, p. 35
84:27–28, p. 47
84:36–37, p. 170
84:38, pp. 181, 439, 530
84:46, p. 78
84:61, p. 247
84:63, p. 313
84:69–70, p. 710
84:73, p. 710
84:81–82, p. 213
84:83, p. 214
84:84, p. 215
84:85, p. 165
84:89–90, p. 170
84:92, p. 163
84:114, p. 379
85:1, p. 29
86, p. 292
86:1–7, pp. 291, 293
86:2–3, p. 292
86:7, p. 292
87:1–2, p. 516
87:8, p. 513
88:6–13, p. 281
88:7–13, pp. 15, 30, 414, 518

88:17–22, p. 178
88:42, p. 16
88:67, p. 211
88:74–75, 137–41, p. 560
88:87, p. 518
88:87–97, p. 506
88:91, p. 519
88:92, p. 531
88:96, pp. 340, 529
88:106, p. 594
88:124, p. 151
88:125, p. 571
88:139–41, p. 560
90:5, p. 227
93:1, p. 179
93:3, pp. 266, 587
93:6, p. 700
93:6–18, p. 98
93:8, p. 12
93:11, p. 78
93:13, pp. 70, 79
93:14, p. 264
93:15, p. 263
93:21, pp. 11, 30, 547
93:22, p. 12
93:24, pp. 79, 488
93:33, p. 135
93:33–34, p. 685
93:38, p. 21
93:38–39, p. 357
93:51, p. 141
94:8–9, p. 475
95:8–9, pp. 699, 734

95:12, p. 574
97:7, p. 84
97:15–16, p. 180
98:4–6, p. 485
98:18, pp. 562, 567
98:39–48, p. 372
101, p. 510
101:22–23, p. 513
101:23–25, p. 519
101:31, p. 340
101:35, p. 512
101:39–40, pp. 182, 184
101:42, p. 484
101:59, p. 510
101:62, p. 510
101:64–65, p. 86
101:65–66, p. 293
101:81–92, p. 403
103:9–10, p. 184
103:27–28, p. 395
104:14, p. 96
105:37, p. 510
106:4–5, p. 524
107:3, p. 84
107:20, p. 76
107:25, 34, 38, 93–96, p. 376
107:35, p. 160
107:43, p. 203
107:53–56, p. 556
109:21, p. 76
109:53, p. 24
109:74, p. 73

109:75, p. 529
110, p. 347
110:1–4, p. 30
110:11, p. 343
110:13–16, pp. 332, 343
112:3, p. 247
112:13, p. 123
116, p. 556
121:19–22, p. 356
121:35, p. 287
121:39, p. 495
121:41–42, p. 495
122:8, pp. 102, 603
122:9, p. 167
124:38–39, p. 733
127:11, p. 567
128, p. 331
128:8–14, p. 332
128:19–21, p. 347
130:3, p. 565
130:7, p. 525
130:9, pp. 178, 685
130:14, p. 509
130:22, pp. 565, 685
131:1–4, p. 487
131:5, p. 341
131:7–8, p. 88
132:15–17, p. 487
132:19, p. 583
132:20, p. 245
132:23, p. 562
132:24, p. 583
132:25, p. 221
132:37, p. 229
132:55, p. 438
133, p. 518

133:2, p. 522
133:10, p. 531
133:10, 19, p. 24
133:13, p. 522
133:14–15, p. 528
133:49, pp. 518, 662
133:54–55, p. 663
133:71–72, p. 401
134, p. 485
135:6, p. 643
136:19, p. 496
136:35, p. 524
137, p. 358
137:8, p. 487
137:10, p. 358
138, pp. 683, 706, 734
138:1–2, p. 8
138:8, 31, p. 141
138:18, p. 703
138:19, p. 684
138:30–37, p. 651
138:31, p. 141
138:35, pp. 627, 655
138:58–59, p. 368

PEARL OF GREAT PRICE

Moses
1:1, 11, p. 92
1:2, 11, p. 37
1:11, pp. 95, 99, 340, 344
1:31–33, pp. 13, 30
1:32, p. 13
1:33, pp. 111, 263
1:35, p. 14
1:41, p. 503
1:42, p. 95
2:1, 26, p. 263
2:1, p. 29
2:27, p. 15
3:9, p. 476
4:1, p. 166
4:2, pp. 24, 263, 658
4:4, p. 245
4:6–20, p. 500
5:4–8, p. 6
5:9, p. 263
6:22, 68, p. 33
6:53, pp. 20, 86
6:54, p. 20
6:57, pp. 104, 120, 447
6:59–60, pp. 86, 118
7:2–3, p. 95
7:3, pp. 37, 340
7:13, p. 349
7:18, p. 586
7:27, p. 340
7:30, pp. 14, 30
7:35, p. 447
7:39, p. 24
7:44–47, p. 523
7:45–46, p. 503
7:47, pp. 19, 691
7:55, p. 540
7:55–56, p. 663
7:56, p. 537
8:27, p. 527
8:28–30, p. 527

Abraham
1:1–2, p. 395
2:8, p. 525
2:9–11, p. 773
3:11–12, p. 30
3:24, p. 11

Joseph Smith—Matthew
1:1, p. 507
1:1–11, p. 507
1:2–3, p. 507
1:3, p. 466
1:4, p. 509, p. 531
1:5–7, p. 511
1:5–11, p. 511
1:8–11, p. 512
1:12, pp. 512, 518
1:12–20, pp. 507, 512
1:13–17, p. 513
1:14–15, p. 528
1:16, p. 643
1:18, p. 512
1:18–21, p. 514
1:19, p. 515
1:20, p. 515
1:21, pp. 512, 515
1:21–55, pp. 507, 515
1:22, p. 515
1:23, p. 567
1:23–24, p. 515, p. 567
1:25–26, p. 516
1:26, p. 460, p. 516
1:27, p. 516
1:28–29, p. 517
1:30, p. 517
1:31, p. 517
1:32, p. 518
1:33, pp. 518, 520, 662
1:34, p. 519
1:35, p. 519, p. 531
1:36, pp. 519, 520
1:37, pp. 8, 515, 522
1:38–39, 47, p. 523
1:40, p. 524
1:41–43, p. 526
1:44–45, pp. 523, 528
1:46, 48, p. 529
1:47, p. 524
1:49–50, p. 529, p. 536
1:51–54, p. 530
1:53, p. 530
1:55, p. 531

Joseph Smith—History
1:12, p. 8
1:14–20, p. 703
1:16–17, pp. 345, 518
1:17, pp. 89, 263, 343
1:30–31, p. 518
1:37, p. 519
1:40, 44, p. 518
1:41, p. 518
1:42, p. 519
1:68, p. 345
1:69, p. 76
1:72, p. 75
1:75, p. 214

Articles of Faith
10, p. 340
12, p. 485

SUBJECT INDEX

Aaron, 748
Aaronic Priesthood: Zacharias held, 34; John the Baptist and, 36, 75; and baptism of water, 84; continued at Mount Sinai, 748; as preparatory, 749
Abba, 603
Abide, 565–66, 569
"Abide with Me; 'Tis Eventide," 694–95
Abraham: sacrifice of, 395, 659–60, 691; seed of, 415; God of, 417; resurrection of, 664; covenant of, 773
Abuse, 357, 370
Accountability, 357–58
Aceldama, 630, 716
Adam: transgression of, forgiven 20; in Christ's genealogy, 33; holds priesthood keys, 332; at Adam-ondi-Ahman, 555; as angel, 604; fall of, 684–86
Adam-ondi-Ahman, 555
Adoption, 82, 229, 440
Adultery: and lust, 195–98; of Herod, 301–2; and divorce, 398, 429, 769–70; woman caught in, 409–13, 741
Advocate, 167, 594
Aenon, 125–26
Agency, 20, 584
Agriculture, 730
Agrippa. *See* Herod Agrippa I
Alabaster, 542
Alexander the Great, 721
Allegory, 283, 423–28, 568–70

Alma, 504
Alms, 204–5
Aloes, 667–68
Altar of Sacrifice, 742
Amazed, 597–99
Ambivulus, 760
Amulek, 21
Analogy, 134
Ancestry, 31
Anderson, Harry: *John the Baptist Baptizing Jesus, 87; Calling of the Fishermen, 148; Christ Ordaining the Apostles, 159; Sermon on the Mount, 171; The Second Coming, 521; Jesus Praying in Gethsemane, 600*
Anderson, Richard Lloyd, 501–2
Andrew, 101, 148–49
Angel(s): appears to Zacharias, 35–37; appears to Mary, 37; appears to Joseph, 41, 63; appears to shepherds, 55–58; minister to John the Baptist, 97–98, 128; do not change hearts, 401; strengthens Christ, 604; legions of, 611; open tomb, 675–76; Moroni, 675–76; announce resurrection, 677–80; speak to Mary, 681–82
Anger, 188–94, 366–67
Anna, 60–61, 733
Annas: as high priest, 77, 540–41, 750; as shareholder, 115–16; Christ taken to, 612
Annunciation: to Zacharias, 33–37;

Subject Index

to Mary, 37–41; to Joseph, 41–44; to shepherds, 55–58
Anoint, 32, 458–59, 542–44
Antiochus III, 721–22
Antiochus IV, 723–24, 750, 763
Antipater, 728
Antonia Fortress, 623–26, *624,* 743, 718
Apocrypha, 723, 727
Apostates, 292, 551–52
Apostles, twelve: faith of, 111–12, 306; baptize, 129; Christ prays with, 153, 338; selection of, 154–55; chart of, *156;* called and ordained, 158–60; missions of, 161, 305, 709; as special witnesses, 161; persecuted, 165–66; Sermon on Mount given to, 172; as salt, 182; Christ teaches, how to teach, 216, 220–21; transience of, 234; and fasting, 249; fear storm, 310–11; do not understand resurrection, 346, 452; do not understand Christ's role, 349–50, 445, 470, 606–7, 690; ask who is the greatest, 352; learn to preside, 376; accepting, 379; as judges, 438–39; ask about second coming, 509; persecution of, 511–12; ask about betrayal, 550, 552–53; Christ washes feet of, 557–60; scattered, 581; Christ prays for, 584; sing hymn, 588; left to watch and pray, 595; fall asleep, 596, 606–7; weaknesses of, 606–7; strengths of, 607; flee, 611; begin to comprehend resurrection, 680–81; don't believe women, 687; see Christ behind locked doors, 696–99; receive gift of Holy Ghost, 698–99. *See also* Disciples
Archelaus, 730, 760
Arimathea, 667, *713*
Aroma, 677

Articles of Faith, 2
Ashes, 379
Ass, *460,* 460–62
Atonement: in premortality, 19–21; as infinite and eternal, 21, 43, 598, 603; works personally, 76; as pure mercy, 79; as cover, 82; meaning of word, 586, 588, 604; overcomes death, 676, 684–86; importance of, 700–704, 712
Authority: divine investiture of, 17–18; of Christ, 227, 265, 477–78; and corruption, 495
Ave Maria, 39

Babylon, 720
Baker, Mary Ann, 235–38
Ball, Terry B., 607
Ballard, Melvin J.: on divine conception, 41–42; on achieving celestial glory, 171–72; on repentance after death, 651; on Father's sacrifice, 659–62; experience of, with Savior, 703–4
Ballard, M. Russell, 357, 585
Balustrade, *718,* 739
Banquet, story of, 308–9
Baptism: by Spirit, 36, 84; in Jordan River, *75;* of repentance, 76–77; by immersion, 76, 84, 88; Christ gives example of, 86–89, *87;* Christ teaches Nicodemus about, 118–19; Christ and John the Baptist perform, 125–26; as gate, 221; Pharisees ask about, 250; of John the Baptist, 477; as remembrance, 556; brings salvation, 709; for dead, 705–6, 734
Barabbas, 632–35
Barley, 306
Bartimaeus, 448
Baruch, 754
Basilica, *718,* 738
Beam, 217–18, 300
Beasts, 92–93
Beatitudes, 173–82

Beelzebub, 166, 257
Behavior, 401
Belief, 348
Benedictus, 47–48
Be Not Afraid, 310
Benson, Ezra Taft: on divine Sonship, 40; on putting God first, 215; on not sinning, 360; on wealth, 436–37; on wandering sheep, 706–7
Bethabara, 83, *713*
Bethany, 460, *716*
Bethlehem: map of journey to, *52, 714;* location of, 53; photo of, *54;* as city of David, 56; prophecy of, as Messiah's birthplace, 62–63
Bethphage, 460, *716*
Bethsaida, *306,* 377–79, *715,* 761
Betrayal, 545–46, 550–54
Betrothal, 38, 768–70
Bible, 1–7
Bible Dictionary, 6
Bier, 230
Bird, 505
Birthright, 12
Bitter cup, 599–600, 603, 610
Blasphemy: and forgiving sins, 247; against Holy Ghost, 274, 278, 584–85; and claims of divinity, 405, 417, 442; Christ charged with, 615, 626, 641; of officers in palace, 622; of Jewish leaders, 642
Blessings, priesthood, 158, 254–56
Blindness: healing of, 124, 256, 322, 326–28, 418–23, 447–48; of Pharisees, 320; one purpose of, 419–20; spiritual, 124, 472
Bloch, Carl Heinrich: *Jesus Clears the Temple,* 115; *Jesus with the Woman at the Well, 133; Peter's Denial, 618; Burial, The, 667*
Blood: and Passover, 548; and sacrament, 555; from every pore, 602–3, 605, 656

Body: versus spirit, 94; of Christ, as temple, 116–17, 349, 614, 649; God has, 136; control over, 188–89; evil spirits desire, 240, 244–45; care of, 319; sins of, 366–67; bread in remembrance of, 554–55; as symbol of unity, 586; resurrected, 675–76, 681, 696–97
Bones, 664–65
Book of Mormon, 3, 295
Boy Jesus in the Temple, 69
Bradford, William R., 539
Bramble, 222–23
Bread: feeds thousands, 306, 323; of Life, 307, 313; unleavened, 546–48, 694, 764; of sacrament, 554–55, 557
Bridegroom, 24, 249
Brimstone, 193
Brown, Hugh B., 203
Bruce, F. F., 627, 632, 701
Burdens, 381–82
Burial, *500,* 666–74
Burial, The, 667
Burton, Theodore M., 189–90
Bushel, 779
Busyness, 386

Caesar (as title), 50–51, 627, 642, 758
Caesar, Julius, 728, 758–59
Caesar Augustus, 49, 730, 731, 758
Caesarea Philippi: photo of, *328;* history of, 328–30, 721; location of, *715;* as capital of Herod Philip, 761
Caesar Tiberius, 759
Caiaphas: as high priest, 77, 750; as shareholder, 115–16; on Christ dying, 456–57; and crucifixion, 541; Christ's hearing before, 612, 623
Caligula, 759
Calling and election, 341–42, 564–65
Calling of the Fishermen, 148

829

Subject Index

Callister, Tad R., 696–97
Calvary, 645, *717*
Camel, 433–38, *434*
Camel's hair, *73*
Cana, *107,* 108, 139, *715*
Canaan, 321
Canaanite, 159, 321–22
Candle, 289–90
Capernaum: ruins of, *112, 378;* elevation of, 139; aerial view of, *144;* as crossroads, 228, 311–12; as home of Christ's family, 246; as tax collection point, 248; synagogue in, 315; Christ upbraids, 377–79; location of, *715*
Carob tree, *363, 364*
Carpenter, 300
Catholic church, 330
Celestial kingdom: reaching, 172; Church as preparation for, 511; inheritors of, 520; and procreation, 583; symbolism of, in Temple, 744
Celibacy, 430
Cemetery, 409–10
Centuries, 759–60
Centurion, 228–29, 665
Chaff, 85–86, 270, 292
Chamber of Hewn Stone, 741, 753
Chamber of the Hearth, 741
Chandler, Walter M., 635
Charity: and sharing wealth, 84; characteristics of, 355; as love of Christ, 355, 556, 570–76; and Mosaic law, 393. *See also* Jesus Christ: Love of; Love
Chastise. *See* Rebuke
Chastity, 769–70
Cheer, 581–82
Chief priests: jealous of Christ, 475; challenge authority of Christ, 477–78; work with Judas, 545; hearing before, 612–17; history of, 745, 750. *See also* High priest; Priest
Childbirth, 580, 644
Children: slaughter of, 64–65; when to have, 213–14; needs of, 231; Joseph Smith on blessing, 254; healing of, 347–49; becoming like, 354, 430; offending, 356–57, 357–58; wayward, 368; Christ loves, 430–31; of kingdom, 475
Chorazin, 377–79, *715*
Chosen, 576
Christianity, 634–35, 701–2
Christ Ordaining the Apostles, 159
Church of the Holy Sepulchre: as traditional site of Christ's burial, 669–71, 673–74; photos of, *670, 671*
Church of the Nativity, 53
Church of Jesus Christ (ancient): and parable of tares, 292; founding of, 329–30; as kingdom of God, 511; and circumcision, 773–74
Church of Jesus Christ of Latter-day Saints, The: and parable of mustard seed, 295; and parable of leaven, 296; and parable of treasure, 296–97; and Catholicism, 330; councils in, 370; as kingdom of God, 511; missionary work of, 517–18; and parable of virgins, 533; doesn't use cross as symbol, 647–48; fundamental principles of, 693. *See also* Latter-day Saints; Mormonism
Circumcision, 58, 723, 773–74
Cisterns, 132
Clark, J. Reuben, 553, 732, 772
Claudius, 759
Clawson, Grant Romney, *69*
Cleopas, 695
Cleopatra, 760
Client kings, 760–62
Clothes, 615, 681, 705. *See also* Garment

SUBJECT INDEX

Cloud, 344–45, 507
Cohorts, 608–9, 759–60
Coin(s): Roman, 167, 194; photo of, *194;* in fish, 350–51, 774; parable of, 361–62; used in Temple, 473–74; in Bible, 777–78
Comforter. *See* Holy Ghost
Commandment(s): save us, 188; first and great, 488–89, 561, 570–71; keeping, 572
Commitment, 234
Compassion: Christ is "moved with," 157, 177, 303; meaning of word, 177; and judgment, 216; in Mosaic law, 393
Conception, divine, 42–43
Condescension, 22–23, 88, 661
Conflict, 369–70, 566
Conspiracy, 616–17
Contradictions, 600–602
Conversion, 118–19, 589–90
Converts, 395, 407–8
Coponius, 760
Corban, 319
Corn, 469
Cornerstone, 480, *480*
Council, 721–22
Countenance, 37
Courage, 619–20
Court of the Gentiles, *718, 739,* 739–40
Court of the Men of Israel, *719,* 741
Court of the Priests, *719, 739,* 741, *742*
Court of the Women, *719, 739,* 740, *741*
Covenant(s): blessings of, 82; as necessary, 483; with Judas, 545; old and new, 556; betrothal as, 769; of Abraham, 773
Covetousness, 389–92
Covey, Stephen R., 426
Creation, 13–15
Cross: Christ on, *120,* 648–52; as symbol of shame, 169; taking up, 169, 334–35, 196–97; Simon bears, 643; not used as symbol by Latter-day Saints, 647–48; sign on, 652–53
Crown, 640, 690
Crucifixion: Simeon prophesies of, 60; foreshadowing of, 60, 470; method of, 169, 470, 646–48; reasons behind, 545; fulfills prophecy of manner of death, 627; Romans and, 627; responsibility for, 635–39; prophecy of gall given at, 645–46; prophecy of casting lots at, 648; prophecy of Christ crying out at, 656; lasts six hours, 653–54; and giving up ghost, 658; earthquake at, 662–64; Temple veil rent at, 663, 676, 743; prophecy of no bones broken during, 664–65; prophecy of wounds at, 665; site of, 669–72; disciples reminded of prophecies about, 690–91; in spring, 763. *See also* Death; Guilt; Jesus Christ: prophesies of his death and resurrection
Cubit, 779
Cursing, 163–64, 475–77
Cyrene, 643
Cyrenius, 50
Cyrenian, 643

Dahl, Larry E., 195–96
Daniel, 508, 513
Darkness: spiritual, 124–25, 142, 289; Joseph B. Wirthlin's story about, 471; at time of crucifixion, 654
David: Christ as Son of, 31, 40, 489, 767; genealogy of, 33
Day, 778
Day of Atonement, 749, 766
Dead Sea Scrolls, 727
Death: shadow of, 142; some not to taste, 336, 707–8; power over, 427–28, 582; traditions

Subject Index

surrounding, 452; and mourning, 453–54; atonement overcomes, 676, 684–86; physical, 684; spiritual, 685–86. *See also* Crucifixion
Deborah, 60–61
Debt, 401
Decapolis, 150, *713*
Defilement, 319–20
Denarius, 778
Dependence, 569–70
Depression, 702
Derrick, Royden G., 180
Desert, 91, 303–5, 325
Desires, 196–97
Desolation, abomination of, 513, 518
Destruction, at end of world, 526–29
Devil(s): casting out, 232–33, 257, 273–74, 347–49; enter swine, 238–246; Christ accused of having, 257, 428; cast out of Mary Magdalene, 269, 682
Didrachmon, 777–78
Disciples: true, 314, 415; abandon Christ, 316–17; Christ's expectations for, 334; recognize signs of second coming, 524; feel peace, 566–67; see Christ on road to Emmaus, 688–95. *See also* Apostles
Discipleship, 394–95
Disposition, 366–67
Divine investiture of authority, 17–18
Divorce: ancient and modern, 198–99; and adultery, 398, 769–70; Pharisees ask about, 428–30
Doctrine and Covenants, 3
Dog, 218–19, 322
Dome of the Rock, 742–43
Dove, *88*, 88–89, 164
Drachma, 777–78
Dreams: of Joseph, 44; of Orson F. Whitney, 595–97; of Pilate's wife, 634; of Melvin J. Ballard, 703–4
Drummond, Henry, 366–67
Duckwitz, Norbert, 705
Dust, shaking off, 163, 376

Eagles, 516–17
Earth: change in topography of, 73; as living entity, 235; transfiguration of, 342, 519–20, 531, 561–62; before second coming, 519, 527; as God's footstool, 685. *See also* World(s)
Earthquake, 662–64, 675
East, 460, 516
Edersheim, Alfred, 62, 642
Egypt, 64, *714*
Elders, 746
Eleazar, 750
Elect, 314, 516–17
Elias: John the Baptist as, 35–36, 82, 259; Noah as, 38; transfiguration of, 340; identity of, 346–47
Elijah: end of ministry of, 83; in time of drought, 141–42; foreshadows ministry of Christ, 230; return of, 301; and keys of kingdom, 332; some think Christ calls for, on cross, 657; resurrection of, 664
Elisabeth: ancestry of, 34; hides herself, 37; relationship of, to Mary, 40–41; Mary visits, 45–46
Elisha, 142, 230
Elohim. *See* God the Father
Emmaus, 688–89, *689*, *713*
Emperor. *See* Caesar
Endowment, 342, 345, 699
Enemies, 181–82, 201–2, 727
Enoch: on God's creations, 14; sees coming of Christ, 19, 523; asks about meridian of time, 502–3; resurrection of, 664; testimony of, 691
Ephraim, 457, *713*

832

Subject Index

Epiphanes, 724
Essenes, 726
Ethnarchs, 760–62
Eunuch, 429–30
Eve, 20, 269
Evidence, 710
Eye: for an eye, 200, 370; single to the glory of God, 211, 320; blind, 320; of a needle, 433–38
Eyring, Henry B., 577
Ezekiel, 4
Ezra, 754

Fable, 283
Faith: brings forgiveness, 76, 247, 544; signs follow, 112, 275–76, 301, 348, 401, 710; heals, 123, 139, 149, 229, 253–56, 322, 403, 448; during trials, 236; as a grain of mustard seed, 294, 348; praying for, 348; to move mountains, 348; comes from sacrifice, 395; in Jesus Christ, 556; better than seeing, 700
Fall, of Adam, 20, 60, 684–86
Family: dividing of, 167–68; loving God more than, 168–69; eternal, of Christ, 279; in Mosaic law, 319; withdrawing from, 358–59; sacrifice in, 575
Farrar, Frederic W., 606
Farthing, 167, 778
Fasting: of Christ, 91; proper manner of, 209–10; John's disciples ask about, 249–52; and miracles, 348–49
Father, of prodigal son, 362–69
Faust, James E., 354, 368–69
Fear: of antagonists, 166–67; meaning of word, 230; of disciples in storm, 235; prayer dissolves, 308; of Peter, James, and John on Mount of Transfiguration, 345; and preparation, 506; love casts out, 561, 567; caused by sin, 598–99
Feast: at house of Matthew, 248–49;

of Tabernacles, 343, 373, 403–4, 765–67; of Dedication, 440–43, 724, 763; of Passover, 546–47; of Unleavened Bread, 546–47, 764; of Harvest (Pentecost), 765
Feet: shaking dust from, 163, 376; washing of, 544, 557–60, 587
Festival of Lights, 724, 763
Field: photos of, *137, 290;* ready to harvest, 137–38, 376; world as, 291
Fig tree: under, 102–3; leaves and fruit of, *103, 524;* number of references to, 223; Christ curses, 240, 475–77; at Bethphage, 460; as illustration of signs of times, 523
Fire, 520–22, 526
Firkin, 779
Firstborn, 11–12
First estate, 20
First Maccabees, 723
First Presidency: on King James Version, 3; on children of Deity, 11; on Jesus Christ, 11; on divine investiture of authority, 17–18; on parentage of Christ, 40
Fish: Jonah in, 276–77; feed thousands, 306, 323; St. Peter's, *350;* coin found in, 350–51, 774; as symbol of Christianity, 697; of New Testament period, 774; casting away bad, *776*
Fishermen: painting of, *148;* called to be fishers of men, 148–49; Christ helps, 154; casting a net, *351;* see resurrected Christ, 704–5
Fishing, 774–77
Five thousand, feeding of, 303, 305–9
Flattery, 484
Flax, 272–73
Fleeing, 528
Flesh, overcoming, 171–72

833

Subject Index

Food, 305–9
Foot, 358
Foreordination, 18–19
Forerunner, 46–47, 72, 74
Forgiveness: for premortal sins, 20; through faith, 76, 247, 544; of one another, 193; of enemies, 201; of former Nazi, 208–9; of Christ, 247, 544, 556, 602–603; missionary work brings, 247; service brings, 247; humility as key to, 354; asking for, 369–70; law of, 371–72; of God the Father, 372; of Roman soldiers, 648, 652; Christ teaches, 652
Forty, 91–92
Four thousand, feeding of, 323
Foxes, 233–34, 393–94
Franklin, Benjamin, 195
Freemasonry, 736
Friends, 358–59, 574
Fringes, 494, *494*
Fruits: works as, 81–82, 83; of false prophets, 222–24; from vine, 570
Fuller, *338*, 339
Furlong, 779

Gabbatha, 624
Gabriel, 37–38
Galilee: and volcanoes, 142; and Gentiles, 143; Christ leaves, 374; resurrected Christ appears in, 687; map of, *715;* as point of Zealot resistance, 730–31, 754, 757
Gall, 645–46
Gamla, 756
Garden Tomb, 671–74, *672, 717*
Garment: of camel's hair, *73;* of righteousness, 482–83; of Jews, 494; of Temple, 494; worn by disciple, 612; of high priest, 749. *See also* Clothes
Gathering, 516–17
Gazetteer, 6–7
Genealogies, 31–33

Gennesaret, 317–18, *709, 715*
Gentiles: adoption of, 82, 229; Galilee of, 143; apostles wait to go to, 160–61; healing of, 321–22; receive gospel through Holy Ghost, 427; in parables, 481, 482; Jews trodden down by, 514; distrust of, 720; Jews join with, 723; Court of, 739–40; and Temple, 739–40
Gentleness, 615–16
Gethsemane: personal, 269; Christ and apostles walk to, 567, 588–89; meaning of word, 592; tree in, *592;* size of, 594–95; sign at entrance of, *595;* photo of, *596;* as contradiction, 600–602; Satan in, 603–4; map-drawing of, *717*
Ghost, 658
Glory, 205
Gnat, 498–99
Goats, 536–39, *537, 538*
Goatskin "bottle," *251*
God, love of: for Son, 123–24, 662; for all children, 123–24; as perfect, 202, 575; not unconditional, 573–74. *See also* God the Father
God, will of: commandment to do, 224–25; Christ came to do, 314, 603; swallowed up in, 567; submission to, 649; fulfilled, 658. *See also* God the Father
Godhead, 89, 561, 587, 709
God the Father: children of, 11, 78; as creator, 13, 15; as one with Christ, 17, 266, 380, 442, 473, 562, 586–88; bears record of Son, 18, 89, 99, 263, 414, 582; plan of, 18, 293; as separate from Christ, 30; as father of Christ, 40–43, 69, 78–79, 89, 123, 262–68, 415, 583; voice of, 89, 345, 470; seeing, 99; as Man of Holiness, 104; Christ glorifies,

Subject Index

111, 262–68, 415, 431–32, 469–70, 473, 582–83; gives all to Son, 127; watches over all creations, 167, 213–14; love for, 168, 574–75; praying to, 205–9; knows those who are his, 313–14; compassion of, 364; forgives, 372; no respecter of persons, 392; indebtedness to, 401–2; doctrine of, 404–6; knowing, 416–17, 583; becoming like, 442, 539, 572–73, 686; right hand of, 537, 711; purpose of, 539; heirs of, 562; abides in faithful, 565–66; commandment to love, 570; glorifies Son, 582; as father, 583–84; wrath of, 594; withdraws from Christ, 656–57; sacrifices Son, 658–62; returning to, 686, 744. *See also* God, love of; God, will of
Gold, 63
Golden rule, 221
Golgotha, 642–46, 645, *716, 717*
Gospel(s): meaning of word, 27, 55–56; synoptic, 27; chart comparing, *28;* as light, 30–31; of repentance, 76; undefiled, 182–83; taken to all the world, 709
Governors, 731–32
Grace, 79, 576, 594, 712
Grain, 85–86, 270
Gratitude, 380, 402–3
Gratus, 541
Graves, 499
Greeks, 468, 721
Griggs, C. Wilfred, 132–33, 584
Guests, 544
Guilt: of Jews, 636–38, 641–42; of Romans, 636; of Pontius Pilate, 641–42
Gymnasium, 723

Habits, 278
Hafen, Bruce C., 495, 620
Haggai, 720
Hallel, 764
Hands, 358, 635, 637
Hannah, 45–46
Hanukkah, 724, 763
Happiness: unrighteous do not know, 96; comes from Christ, 175; gospel brings, 382; Christ teaches about, 570; and bodies, 685. *See also* Joy
Harvest: process of, 85; fields ready to, 137–38, 291, 376; law of, 179; ultimate, 293; parable about, 479; Feast of, 765
Hasidim, 722, 724, 747
Hasmoneans, 724–25
Hate, 168–69, 576–77
Healing: and serpent on pole, *120,* 121–23; by faith, 123, 139, 149, 229, 253–56, 322, 403, 448; of blind, 124, 256, 322, 326–28, 418–23, 447–48; of nobleman's son, 108, 139–40; reactions to, 141, 247–48, 273–74; King Benjamin lists, 149–50; of lepers, 155–58, 402–3; of centurion's servant, 228–29; of Peter's mother-in-law, 232; in evening, 232–33; of paralytic, 246–48; of Jairus's daughter, 252–56, *255;* of woman with issue of blood, 252–56; of demoniac, 257, 347–49; on Sabbath, 260–62, 270–73, 392–93, 405, 418–23, 483; of withered hand, 271–72; of multitude, 303; in Gennesaret, 317–18; of Canaanite daughter, 321–22; of lame, 322; of dumb, 322; not accepting, 472; emotional, 603; of servant's ear, 610; of lame man by Peter, 740
Hearings: before chief priests, 612–17; before Caiaphas, 623; before Pilate, 623–29, 631–32; before Herod, 631
Heart(s): pure in, 179–80; change

Subject Index

of, 248–49; abundance of, 274–75; hardening, 281, 356, 472; far from God, 318; as command-center of character, 320; and treasure, 390, 432, 436; set on worldly praise, 495; and motives, 497; failing, 519; lifting up, 523

Heaven, 519

Heavenly Father. *See* God the Father

Heavenly Mother, 11, 685

"He Bore Our Anguish," 638–39

Helena, 669

Hell, 192–93, 400

Hellenization, 721–23, 747

Hen, 505

Henry, Patrick, 2

Herbs, 497–98, *498*

Herod Agrippa I, 761–62

Herod Antipas: immorality of, 127–28, 301–2, 761; executes John the Baptist, 151, 301; Christ shows contempt for, 393–94; Christ's hearing before, 628–29, 631; mocks Christ, 631; as Christ's nemesis, 730; as tetrarch, 761

Herodians, 272, 484–86, 746

Herodias, 127–28, 761

Herodium, 756

Herod Philip, 730, 760–61

Herod's Basilica, *718,* 738

Herod the Great: extermination order of, 54, 64–65; jealousy of, 62–63; builds Temple, 507–8, *718,* 735–39; rise of, 728–29; cruelty of, 729; deposes high priests, 750; as client king, 760

Hiding Place, The, 208–9

High priest: Annas as, 540; hearing before, 612–17; political authority of, 720, 725; religious authority of, 720; duties of, 749–50; end of office of, 750. *See also* Chief priests; Priest

Hillel, 428

Hinckley, Gordon B.: on God as spirit, 136; on meekness, 178; on mercy, 179; on divorce, 199; on Joseph Smith, 251–52; as missionary, 334–35; on happiness, 382; on sacrifice, 396; on signs of times, 526; on Peter's denial of Christ, 621–22

Hinnom Valley, *192,* 192–93, *716*

Holland, Jeffrey R., 367, 569

Holocaust, 208–9, 514–15

Holy Ghost: and Christ's conception, 40, 41–42; and baptism of fire, 84; descended like a dove, 88–89; endows with power, 143; teaches what to say, 165, 563; filled with, 178–79; blasphemy against, 274, 278, 584–85; gives testimony, 276, 565–66; and scriptures study, 281, 694; brings charity, 355–56; Christ teaches about, 406–7; brings remembrance, 556, 563; abides, 565–66; gives love of God, 572; strengthens apostles, 577; gift of, not present during Christ's life, 578; convicts world of sin, 578–79; brings understanding, 579; disciples receive gift of, 698–99

Holy Land, *713,* 720–32

Holy of Holies: symbolism of, 663, 676, 743; drawing of, *719*

Holy Place, *719, 741, 743, 743*

Honey, 74

Horn, 48

Hosanna cry, 464, 767

House, 225, *226,* 278, 505

Householder, 298–99, 478–81

"How Great Thou Art," 659

Humility: of Savior, 19, 56; of John the Baptist, 84, 127, 178; of servants, 164, 353–56; weaknesses bring, 175–76; required, 439; of leaders, 446, 495–96; Spencer W. Kimball on,

836

Subject Index

461; Christ on, 483–84; sign of, 504; of Peter, 590
Hunter, Howard W.: on house built on rock, 227; tells story of Mary Ann Baker, 235–38; on healing power of Christ, 252; on resurrection, 701
Husbandmen, 478–81
Hyde, Orson, 242–44, 683
Hymn, 588
Hyperbole: definition of, 169, 282, 434–35; about weaknesses, 196; about missionary work, 219; about forgiveness, 371; about camel, 434–35, 498–99; about books, 708
Hypocrisy: in prayer, 205; in fasting, 209–10; of Christ's antagonists, 218, 747–48; prophecy about, 318; and traditions, 318–20, 393, 747–48; Isaiah prophesies of, 318; and inability to see signs, 324; leaven of Pharisees as, 326; indicts and condemns, 423; Christ hates, 491; in leaders, 435, 491–92, 616–17; of fig tree, 477; and vanity, 494; and titles, 495–96; of reverencing objects, 497; and filthy inner vessel, 499
Hyrcanus, 728, 729
Hyssop, 548, *657,* 657–58

I AM: as title for Jehovah, 16, 615; and declaration to woman at well, 136; as descriptive title, 313, 557; "before Abraham was," 417. *See also* Jesus Christ: Roles and titles
Idumeans, 729
Immanuel, 230–31, 371
Imperial provinces, 731
Importune, 388–89, 403, 580, 604
Incest, 301–2
Injustices, 601
Innocence, 20–21, 357–58
Intercession, 582

Invitation, 481–84
Irony, 600, 608–9, 632
Isaac, 659–60, 664
Isaiah: on names of Christ, 24; prophesies about Messiah, 142, 232; prophesies of hypocrisy, 318; on blind eyes and hard hearts, 471–72; on Jerusalem, 508; on Christ numbered with transgressors, 591, 647; on crucifixion, 638; Christ expounds words of, 692
Israel, captivity of, 720

Jacob, 131, 664, 768
Jacob (in Book of Mormon): on riches, 436, 437; on crucifixion, 545; on Christ as king, 642–43
Jacob's Well, *130, 131,* 131, 313
Jacobus Revius, 638–39
Jairus, 252–56, *255*
James: calling of, 149; as fisherman, 154; as "son of thunder," 159, 375; and Transfiguration, 337; receives keys, 341; asks about rank, 446; death of, 512; sees Christ while fishing, 704–5
Jason, 750
Jealousy, 366–67
Jehovah. *See* Jesus Christ: as Jehovah
Jeremiah, 64–65
Jericho, 53, 384, 447–48, *713*
Jerome, 66
Jerusalem: as center of early church, 79, 199–200; as Jewish capital, 150; Jesus laments over, 466–68, 504–6; prophecies of destruction of, 466–68, 513–14, 518, 643–45; lacks peace, 566; model of, *613;* map of, *716;* Hellenization of, 721–23; gymnasium in, 723; occupied by Rome, 727
Jesus Blessing Jairus's Daughter, 255
Jesus Christ:
  Roles and titles
    as Firstborn, 11–12, 123;

837

Subject Index

premortal divinity of, 12, 30; as
Creator, 13–15, 30, 78, 99,
111, 235; as Jehovah, 16, 30,
56, 79, 136, 307–8, 417, 489;
as spokesman for God the
Father, 17–18; as one with God
the Father, 17, 266, 380, 442,
473, 562, 587; foreordination
of, 18–19; God the Father bears
record of, 18, 89, 99, 263, 414,
582; as hope of Israel, 24; as
Anointed One, 24, 32; as
spiritual father, 24, 78; as
Bridegroom, 24, 249; as
separate from God the Father,
30; as Light, 30–31, 48, 55, 78,
124–25, 142, 185, 413–18,
470–71, 766; as Son of David,
31, 40, 489, 767; divine
Sonship of, 40–43, 69, 78–79,
89, 123, 262–68, 415, 583;
testifies of own divinity, 69,
262–68, 271, 741; as Lion of
Judah, 99–100; as Lamb, 100,
260, 547–48, 557; as Son of
Man, 104, 235, 446–47;
glorifies the Father, 111,
262–68, 415, 431–32, 469–70,
473, 582–83; symbolized by
serpent, *120,* 121; as Living
Water, 132–35, 313, 406–7,
568, 766; as Advocate, 167,
594; as Rock, 226, 329–30;
authority of, 227, 265, 477–78;
as Immanuel, 230–31, 371; as
Physician, 248–49; as stumbling
block, 258; as Good Shepherd,
268, 423–28; as Bread of Life,
307, 313; as judge, 473, 537; as
Messiah, 511; as Second
Comforter, 564–65; as True
Vine, 568–70; as King, 628,
642–43, 652–53; types and
shadows of, 692. *See also* I AM

Character traits
humility of, 19, 56; peace of,
57–58, 167–68, 566–67; grace
of, 79, 576, 594, 712;
understands every trial, 91;
compassion of, 157, 303;
Beatitudes show character of,
173; perfection of, 204, 598;
forgiveness of, 247, 544, 556,
602–603; virtue of, 253–56;
teaching method of, 290–91;
knows true followers, 313–14,
316, 423–28; deep feelings of,
333, 453, 466–68; gives rest,
381–82; power of, over death,
427–28, 452; judgment of,
473; kindness of, 491; firmness
of, 491; knows all things, 525;
physical stamina of, 613–14;
gentleness of, 615–16. *See also*
Charity; Jesus Christ, love of

Atonement and resurrection
Atonement of, in premortal
life, 19–21; redeemed all
creation, 21–22; condescension
of, 22–23, 88, 661; on cross,
120, 648–52; resurrection of,
120, 144, 675–81; ascension
of, 315–16, 710–11; power of,
over death, 427–28, 452;
suffered for all sin, 593–94,
597–607; is "sore amazed,"
597–99; comprehends sin,
598–99; cries out to Father,
599; and contradictions,
600–602; suffering of, in
Gethsemane, 597–606; bleeds
from every pore, 602–3, 605;
strengthened by angel, 604;
prays more earnestly, 604; gives
Mary to John's care, 654–55;
death of, 655–62; cries out to
Father, 656–57, 661–62; burial
of, 666–74, *667. See also*
Atonement; Crucifixion;
Prophecies; Resurrection

Mortality/ministry
ministry of, 27–29, *304;*

838

Subject Index

genealogy of, 31–33; Mary conceives, 39–40; birth of, 54–55; naming of, 58–59; is presented in Temple, 59–61, 733, 740; wise men visit, 61–63; goes to Egypt, 64; learns gradually, 66–67, 70–71, 98; visits Temple at Passover, 67–69, *69,* 733, 738; John the Baptist prepares the way for, 82, 85–86; baptism of, 86–89, *87;* temptation of, 90–98; on pinnacle of Temple, 94, 734–35; invites disciples to follow, 101, 102, 576; at wedding, 107–112; and ordinances, 108–9; and marriage, 108–9; siblings of, 112–13, 279, 300–301, 373; cleanses Temple, 114–16, *115,* 473–75, 739; prophesies of his death and resurrection, 116–17, 277, 333, 346, 349–50, 394, 405, 445, 459, 470, 540, 543, 614, 649; teaches Nicodemus, 117–25; performs baptisms, 125; and Samaritans, 130; and woman at well, 129–38, *133;* rejected at Nazareth, 140–43; prays, 151–53, 207–8, 338, 380, 454–55, 469–70, 582–88; teaches from a boat, 154, 284–85; gives Sermon on the Mount, 170–227, *171;* teaches about loving enemies, 201–2, 727; teaches apostles to teach, 220–21; evil spirits know of, 238–46; attends feast at publican's house, 248–49, 751; accusations against, 257, 271, 428; crowds gather to hear, 273; teaches with parables, 279–84; as carpenter, 300; tests faith of apostles, 306; goes to mountain, 309, 337; condemns hypocrisy, 318–20, 324, 326, 423, 491, 747–48; uses visual aids, 330; transfiguration of, 337–47; associates with sinners, 361; trains apostles to preside, 376; teaches about prayer, 388–89; shows contempt for Herod, 393; teaches in Temple, 404, 407, 410–11; and adulterous woman, 409–13; and Mount of Olives, 410; on divorce, 428–30; and rich young ruler, 431–38; Jews try to stone, 442, 738, 741; on ranking, 445–46; weeps, 453, 466–68; strengthens faith of disciples, 455; order to arrest, 458; triumphal entry of, 460–65, *461,* 767; last week in life of, *463, 717;* lament of, over Jerusalem, 466–68, 504–6; outwits Jewish leaders, 477–78; in home of Pharisee, 483–84; hearings of, before Pilate, 486, 623–29, 631–32; prophesies of Temple destruction, 508–9; prophesies of destruction of Jerusalem, 513–14, 518, 643–45; plots to kill, 541, 616–17; on sinners, 543–44; announces betrayal, 550–54; institutes sacrament, 553, 554–57; washes disciples' feet, 557–60; teaches new commandment, 560–61; comforts disciples, 561–63; warns apostles of future, 578; advocatory prayer of, 582–88; sings hymn, 588; prays for Peter, 589; denied by Peter, 590–91, 617–22, *618;* arrest of, 608–12; Judas kisses, 608–9; hearing of, before chief priests, 612–17; mocked by soldiers, 622, 640–41; hearing of, before Caiaphas, 623; hearing

839

of, before Herod, 631; received no trial, 635; taken to Golgotha, 642–46; warns of disaster in Jerusalem, 643–45; contradicts current ideas of Judaism, 727; as Galilean, 730–31; life of, bound with Temple, 733–35; linked to Zealots, 757; birth date of, 770–73. *See also* God, will of; Healing; Miracles; Parables; Prophecies

After resurrection
believing, 122–23, 127, 606; dependence on, 176, 569–70; seeing, 179–80; becoming one with, 204, 586–88; knowing, 225, 583; ascension of, 315–16, 710–11; in day of judgment, 472–73, 536–37; right hand of, 537–38; remembering, 556–57; remits sin, 556, 602–603; abides in faithful, 565–66; becoming like, 572–73; friendship with, 574; visits Americas, 579; latter-day visions of, 595–97, 703–4; resurrection of, announced, 677–80; leaves burial clothes behind, 681; speaks to Mary, 683; visits spirit world, 683–84; on road to Emmaus, 688–95; chastises disciples, 690; expounds words of prophets, 691–93; breaks bread, 694; knowledge about, 694; appears behind locked doors, 696–99; disciples feel wounds of, 696–97; sends disciples on missions, 698–99; appears to thousands, 702–3; latter-day witnesses of, 703–4; appears to fishing disciples, 704–7; tells Peter to feed his sheep, 706–7; choosing to follow, 712. *See also* Second coming

Jesus Christ, love of: salvation comes because of, 123–24; charity as, 355, 556, 570–76; as example, 385; for children, 430–31. *See also* Charity; Love

Jesus Clears the Temple, 115
Jesus Praying in Gethsemane, 600
Jesus with the Woman at the Well, 133

Jewelry, 769

Jews: do not believe God has son, 89; and Samaritans, 129–30, 374–75, 383–86; salvation is of, 135; criticize Christ, 260–62; suffering of, 467–68, 505–6, 514–15, 636, 638; misunderstand prophecies, 510–11; generation of, 519; guilt of, 636–38, 641–42; king of, 653; early, 720; and Greek influences, 722; Orthodox, 723–24. *See also* Judaism

Joanna, 269, 666, 677

John: testimony of, 27, 708; never refers to self by name, 78; called as fisher of men, 149, 154; as "son of thunder," 159, 375; not to taste death, 336, 707–8; and Transfiguration, 337; receives keys, 341; asks about rank, 446; delivered up to Sanhedrin, 512, 738; finds Upper Room, 549; as "disciple whom Jesus loved," 552; during Christ's final hours, 611, 622; Mary put in care of, 654–55; runs to empty tomb, 680–81; purpose of Gospel of, 700; sees Christ while fishing, 704–5

John the Baptist: angel announces coming of, 35–37; as Elias, 35–36, 82, 259; Joseph Smith on, 36; related to Jesus, 41; birth of, 46; naming of, 46–47; as

Subject Index

forerunner, 46–47, 72, 74, 478; prophecies about, 72, 258; as messenger, 73; in wilderness, 73–74; visits Joseph Smith, 74–75; explains his mission, 82, 85; at Bethabara, 83; humility of, 84, 127, 178; baptizes Christ, 86–89, *87;* imprisoned, 97–98, 127–28; testimony of, 98–100, 266–67; selflessness of, 127; disciples of, 249, 257–58, 443; as great prophet, 258–60; death of, 301–2; authority of, 477; resurrection of, 664; holds keys to Aaronic Priesthood, 749

John the Baptist Baptizing Jesus, 87
Jonah, 276–77
Jonathan, (son of Mattathias), 724
Jones, Jenkins Lloyd, 382
Jordan River, *75, 126*
Joseph (husband of Mary): genealogy of, 31; Annunciation to, 41–44; obedience of, 41; travels to Bethlehem, *49,* 51–54; owns land in Bethlehem, 50; names Jesus, 58; in Temple, 60; warned to go to Egypt, 63–64; returns to Nazareth, 66; searches for young Jesus, 68; as carpenter, 300
Joseph of Arimathea, 666–67
Joseph Smith–Matthew, 506
Joseph Smith Translation, 2, 5
Josephus: on death of John the Baptist, 128; gives name of Salome, 302; on tribute money, 372; and Zealots, 730, 756–57; on Temple, 736, 738; does not favor Sadducees, 752; on synagogue worship, 755; on Herod's death date, 770–71
Jot, 187
Joy: in finding lost souls, 361–62; and sorrow, 580; and bodies, 685; in resurrection, 702. *See also* Happiness

Judah the Maccabee, 763
Judaism, 251, 477, 723–24. *See also* Jews
Judas (son of Hezekiah), 729, 757
Judas (son of Mattathias), 724
Judas Iscariot: meaning of name, 160; Christ knows, 316; protests anointing, 459; betrays Christ, 545–46, 553–54, 608–9; Satan enters, 545, 553; fulfills prophecy, 551; motive of, 551–52, 553–54; as son of perdition, 584–85, 630; agency of, 584; feels remorse, 629–30; commits suicide, 630
Judas "not Iscariot," 564
Judea, 79, 150, *713*
Judge, 403
Judgment, 216–18, 472–73, 537
Julia, 761
Julius Caesar. *See* Caesar, Julius
Justice, 684

Kant, Immanuel, 1–2
Keys: sealing, 331–32, 371; of kingdom, 332, 340–41; to Aaronic Priesthood, 749; to Melchizedek Priesthood, 749
Kidron, 588–89, *716, 718*
Kimball, Heber C., 242–46, 682–83
Kimball, Spencer W.: on LDS edition of Bible, 3–4; on service, 96, 334; on giving blessings, 158; on anger, 189; on lust, 197; on expecting miracles, 233; on unpardonable sin, 274; on material possessions, 390–92; on adulterous woman, 412; on humility, 461; on fire at second coming, 521–22; on parable of ten virgins, 533–35; on Peter's denial of Christ, 619–20, 621; on Pontius Pilate, 637; on thieves on crosses, 650–51
King, 628, 642–43, 652–53
King Benjamin, 232, 257, 401–2, 539

Subject Index

Kingdom of God: building, 214–15, 539; and mustard seed, 294; and pearl, 297; seeking, 437; as vineyard, 478–81; Jews wait for, 510–11; Church as, 511; not of world, 628
King James Version, 2–7
Kiss, 544, 608–9
Knight, Newel, 145–48
Kodrantes, 778
Kokhim, 670–71

Laban, 768
Laborers, 439
Lamanites, 426–27
Lamb: Christ as, 100, 260, 547–48, 557; Passover, 546–48, 764
Lane, William, 612
Lasciviousness, 320
Last days, 512, 515, 527
Last Supper, 354, 445, *552–53*
Latter-day Saint edition of Bible, 3–7
Latter-day Saints, 205–6. *See also* Church of Jesus Christ of Latter-day Saints, The; Mormonism
Law: of land, 485; fine points of, 497–98; broken at Christ's arrest and crucifixion, 611, 635. *See also* Mosaic law
Lawsuits, 193–94
Lawyers, 383, 503, 746–47
Layton, Deborah, 326–28
Lazarus: Christ stays with, 410, 443, 475; glorifies God, 420, 444; Christ summoned to, 443–44; raising of, 451–57, *455;* leaders seek death of, 459
Lazarus, parable of, 397–401, 455
Leaders: laziness of, 492; use titles, 495–96; seek to kill Christ, 503; arrest Christ, 608–12; true identity of, 616–17. *See also* individual titles
Leadership: Sermon on the Mount directed at, 172; humility in, 352–54, 446

Leah, 768, 770
Leaven, 295–96, 326
Lee, Harold B.: on divine conception, 42–43; arose early, 151–52; on Sermon on the Mount, 171; on Beatitudes, 174; on wealth, 437; on testimony, 515; on sacrifice, 575; on birth date of Christ, 771
Legates, 759
Legions, 611, 759–60
Lehi, 44, 287–88, 691, 693
Lepers, *155,* 155–58, 402–3, 740
Leprosy, 155
Lepton, *490,* 778
"Let Each Man Learn to Know Himself," 217–18
Levites, 385, 748–49, 756
Lewis, C. S., 90–91
Life: losing and finding, 169–70, 334–36, 469, 528; priorities in, 215; enjoying, 382; giving up, for others, 575
Life, eternal: as gift, 123; lawyer seeks, 383; rich young ruler seeks, 431–32; gaining, 469, 575; as knowing Father and Son, 583
Light: Christ as, 30–31, 48, 55, 78, 124–25, 142, 185, 413–18, 470–71, 766; John the Baptist bears witness of, 78; of the world, 184–85; body filled with, 211; receiving greater, 289–90; pillar of, 344–45; as opposite of heavy, 381–82; at second coming, 518–19
Lightning, 516
Lilies, 214
Lineage, 82
Linen, 668
Lion, 99–100
Locust, 73–74
Longfellow, Henry Wadsworth, 57
Long-suffering, 355
Lord's Supper, 555

842

Subject Index

Lot, 527–28
Love: for God, 168, 574–75; for enemies, 181–82, 201–2; for neighbor, 385, 560; for children, 430–31; commandment to, 488–89, 561, 570–76; growing cold, 517; learning to, 539; casts out fear, 561, 567; and obedience, 563, 573; as test, 571; as quality, 571; brings happiness, 571; receiving, 572; as gift, 572; blessings of, 572; influence of, 572; service brings, 572; conditions on, 573–74; sacrifice brings, 575; Christ teaches, 652; and sacrifice, 662. *See also* Charity; God the Father: love of; Jesus Christ, love of
Lucifer. *See* Satan
Ludlow, Daniel, 60–61
Luke, 29, 50–51
Lund, Gerald N.: on prodigal son, 364–65; and Mary and Martha, 388; on sweating blood, 605; on Christ's suffering, 616
Lust, 195–98, 517

Maccabean period, 725
Machaerus, 128, *713*
Madsen, Truman, 734
"Magnificat," 45
Malachi, 258, 720
Malchus, 610
Malefactors, 649
Maltz, Maxwell, 196
Mammon, 211–12
Manna, 315
Mansions, 561–62
Maps, 6–7
Mark, 27, 612
Marriage: Christ and, 108–9; loving God in, 168; and divorce, 198–99, 429; Sadducees ask about, 486–88; customs of, 768–70; arranged, 768; parable of, 770
Martha: Luke did not know, 387–88; Christ stays in home of, 410, 475; and Lazarus, 443–44; believes Christ, 452–53; possibly at cross, 666; possibly at tomb, 677
Martyrs, 302, 578
Mary (mother of James and Joses), 666, 677
Mary (mother of Jesus): ancestry of, 31; Annunciation to, 37–41; as virgin, 38–39; and Holy Ghost, 40, 41–42; righteousness of, 41, 45, 269; visits Elisabeth, 45–46; gives song of praise, 45–46; travels to Bethlehem, *49,* 51–54; ponders sacred events, 58; purification of, 59, 733, 740; Simeon prophesies to, 60, 733; searches for young Jesus, 68; in Capernaum, 143; desires to speak with Christ, 279; not to be worshiped, 389; put in John's care, 654–55; waits at cross, 666; observes burial, 674
Mary (sister of Martha): Luke did not know, 387–88; Christ stays in home of, 410, 475; and Lazarus, 443–44; anoints Christ's feet, 443–44, 458–59, 543; believes Christ, 453; possibly at cross, 666; possibly at tomb, 677
Mary (wife of Cleophas), 654, 666
Mary and Martha, 387
Mary Magdalene: devils cast out of, 269, 682; as faithful follower, 654; at cross, 666; observes burial, 674; approaches tomb, 677, *682;* leadership of, 677; angels speak to, 678–79; sees Christ at tomb, 681–83, 686, 752
Masada, 728, 756, 757
Masters, 211
"Master, the Tempest Is Raging," 235–38

843

Subject Index

Mattathias, 724, 747
Matthew, 27, 248, 751
Matthews, Robert J.: on John the Baptist, 74; on Christ's obedience, 109; on rebuking, 418; on Christ's character, 490–91; on resurrection, 685
Maxwell, Neal A.: on suffering, 91; on corruption of power, 495; on relationship with God, 575; on atonement, 581–82, 594, 599, 601, 605–6; on Pontius Pilate, 637
McConkie, Bruce R.: wrote chapter headings, 4; on Church of the Firstborn, 12; on creation, 15; on the Father and Son as one, 18; on condescension of God, 23; on parentage of Christ, 40; on Joseph, 41; on Mary, 46; on John the Baptist, 48; on Christ's childhood, 67, 70; on John 3:16, 123; on avoiding sin, 197–98; on perfection, 204; on families of disciples, 232; on devils and swine, 239–40; and healing of woman, 254–56; on Elias, 346–47; on Peter's child, 354; on premortality, 357–58; on authority of unnamed disciple, 369; on eunuchs, 429–30; on marriage, 487; on David's psalm, 489; on insignificant details, 497; on Christ's coming, 510–11; on Satan entering Judas, 545; on future sacrament, 555–56; on washing of feet, 559; on Christ's pain on cross, 655–56; on resurrected bodies, 681; on Peter, James, and John, 733–34; on birth date of Christ, 771–72
McConkie, Joseph Fielding, 22, 89, 583–84, 589–90
McKay, David O., 582
Medical association, *122*
Mediterranean Sea, 324

Meekness, 177–78, 200–201
Melchizedek, 258
Melchizedek Priesthood: and gift of Holy Ghost, 84; keys to, 332, 749; and Temple at Jerusalem, 734; taken away, 748
Menelaus, 750
Menorahs, *413,* 414, 766
Mental health, 355
Mercy, 179, 365, 594, 684
Messiah, 511, 610, 653. *See also* Jesus Christ
Metaphor, 282–83
Micah, 53–54, 62
Michael, 15
Mikvah, *250*
Mile, 779
Milestone, *228*
Milky Way Galaxy, 14
Millennium, 530–31
Millstone, 356
Mina, 778
Minefield, 207
Miracle(s): at wedding, 107–112; purpose of, 111–12, 233, 710; wrought by faith, 112, 275–76, 301; as sign of true servant of God, 118; of casting out unclean spirit, 144–48; chart about, *146–47;* of storm calmed, 234–38; of casting devils into swine, 238–46; reactions to, 247–48, 273–74, 312–13; of feeding multitudes, 303, 305–9, 323; of walking on water, 309–11, *310;* of coin in fish, 350–51, 774; of Lazarus raised, 451–57, *455;* strengthen testimonies, 452; of fig tree cursed, 475–77. *See also* Healing
Mishnah, 33, 224
Missionaries: story about, 190–91; need for more, 268–69; seek leadership positions, 352–54; seventy as, 375–77; in last days, 517–18; choir of, 659

844

Subject Index

Missionary work: and finding, 102; pattern of, 138; and temporal needs, 162, 213; losing self in, 170; brings forgiveness, 247; includes friends and associates, 257; in spirit world, 683–84
Mite, *490,* 777
Mohar, 768
Money: in Christ's time, 194, 777–78; dangers of, 436–38; betrayal, 629–30; of Old Testament, 777. *See also* Coin(s); Wealth
Moneychangers, 114–16, 473–75, 739
Monson, Thomas S., 4
Moon, 518–19
Mormonism, 330, 394. *See also* Church of Jesus Christ of Latter-day Saints, The; Latter-day Saints
Morning, 151–52
Moroni, 675–76
Mortality, 203–4, 601–2
Mosaic law: on firstborn males, 59; came from Christ, 98, 272; Christ fulfills, 186–88, 556, 663; traditions outside of, 318; testifies of Christ, 398; and adultery, 411; and money, 474; and animals, 483; seen as sufficient, 720–21; Pharisees have oral, 725; scribes interpret, 754; read aloud at Feast of Tabernacles, 766. *See also* Law
Mosaics, *153, 307*
Moses: talks with God, 13; ministry of, 83; and serpent on pole, 121–22; and Satan, 245; writings of, 268; Jews revere, 315; transfiguration of, 340; prophesies about Jerusalem, 466–67; seat of, *491;* resurrection of, 664; Christ expounds words of, 691–92
Mosque, 737
Mote, 217–18, 300

Mountains: size of, 95; and spiritual encounters, 95; Christ prays in, 309; moving, 348; fleeing to, 513–14, 522; tremble at second coming, 518
Mount Arbel, 708–9
Mount Ebal, *130*
Mount Gerizim, *130, 713*
Mount Hermon, 328–30, 337, *715*
Mount of Olives, *409,* 409–10, *716*
Mount of Transfiguration, 337, *339,* 734, 767
Mount of Transfiguration, The, 339
Mount Tabor, 337, *337, 715*
Mount Zion, 522, 548, *716*
Mourning: with those that mourn, 177; professional, 253; as commandment, 302–3; at death of Lazarus, 453–54; and smiting breast, 666; and Herod the Great, 729
Murders, 189, 729
Music, 588–89
Muslims, 89
Mustard seed, 293–95, *294,* 348
Myrrh, 63, 667–68

Nain, *230*
Naked, 705, 723
Names, 24, 32, 101
Naphtali, *143*
Narrow, 221
Nathanael, 102–4, 704–5
Natural disasters, 517
Nazarene, 66, 102, 408
Nazareth: photos of, *38, 39;* Mary and Joseph return to, 66; as lowly place, 102; rejection at, 300–301; map of, *714*
Nazarite, 35, 740
Needle's eye, 433–38
Nehemiah, 720
Neighbor, 383–86
Nephi: angel visits, 22; sees Bible, 29; prophecy of, 44; and anger, 189; on Jerusalem, 467–68; on true vine, 568; on crucifixion,

Subject Index

638; testimony of, 693; mentions synagogue, 755; at time of Christ's birth, 772–73
Nephi (son of Helaman), 332
Nephites, 89, 173–74, 426–27
Nero, 759
Net, 298, 705, 774, *775*
New Jerusalem, 522
Nicanor Gate, 741, *741*
Nicodemus: nighttime visit of, 117–25; defends Christ, 408; not at hearings, 614; at Christ's burial, 667; as Pharisee, 748
Noah: as Gabriel, 37–38; priesthood authority of, 332; days of, 526–27; resurrection of, 664
Nobleman, 139–40
Notoriety, 204–5

Oaks, Dallin H., 65
Obedience: brings testimony, 276; brings Spirit, 356; brings blessings, 402–3; brings miracles, 420–21; and preparation, 535; and love, 563, 573; Christ teaches, 652
Offenses, 354, 357–59, 369–71
Officers, 756
Ogden, D. Kelly: walks routes to Bethlehem, 52; emotional visits to Bethlehem, 57–58; attends seminar on Christ, 62; recounts story of viper, 80–81; prayer experience of, 206–7; hikes with students, 229; witnesses Orthodox Jews, 262; on wheat, 270; experience of, with Mark E. Petersen, 317; experience of, as mission president, 335–36; on position-seeking, 352–53; experience of, with Arab children, 430–31; and letter about sacrifice, 432; experience of, with sheep, 569–70; on love and obedience, 573; daughter of, in MTC, 659; experience of, on Sea of Galilee, 775–76

Ogden, Marcia H., 190–91, 353–54
Oil lamp, *186*, 531–35, *532*
Oil press, 592
Old Testament, 120–21, 695. *See also* Prophecies
Olive oil, 531–32, 534–35
Olive tree, *592*
Olsen, Greg, *255*
Oneness: of Father and Son, 17, 266, 380, 442, 473, 562, 587; meaning of, 442; commandment to achieve, 586–88
Onias III, 750
Opposition, 580–81
Ordinance(s): Christ received, 109; of Temple, 483; and inward spirituality, 499; of sacrament, 554; of washing feet, 557–60; for the dead, 705–6, 734; in Herod's Temple, 733–34
Origen, 633
Ostler, Craig J., 22, 89, 583–84, 589–90
Outcasts, 248–49

Packer, Boyd K.: on LDS edition of Bible, 4; on rising early, 151–52; on apostolic witness, 161; quotes Marion G. Romney, 165; on scriptures, 281; on second coming, 525–26; on music, 588–89; on atonement, 594
Palm branches, 462–64, 766–67
Panias, 328, 721, 761. *See also* Caesarea Philippi
Parable(s): of good Samaritan, 130, 383–86; of house on sand, 225–27; reasons for, 279–84, 288–89; tables about, *280, 299, 362;* Joseph Smith interpreted, 284–85; of sower, 285–88, *286;* of candle, 289–90; of tares, 290–93; of mustard seed, 293–95; of leaven, 295–96; of treasure in field, 296–97; of pearl, 297; of net, 298; of householder, 298–99; of lost

sheep, 359–61; of lost coin, 361–62; of prodigal son, 362–69; of unmerciful servant, 372; of friend at midnight, 388–89; of unjust steward, 396–97; of Lazarus and rich man, 397–401; of unprofitable servants, 401–2; of unjust judge, 403; of laborers in vineyard, 439–40; of pounds, 450–51; of fig tree, 476; of two sons, 478; of wicked husbandmen, 478–81; of wedding of king's son, 481–84, 770; of Pharisee and publican, 503–4; of eagles, 516–17; of ten virgins, 531–35, 770; of talents, 535–36; of sheep and goats, 536–39; expose social and economic conditions, 730

Paradise, 649–50

Parallelism, 72, 218, 462, 514

Paronomasia, 329, 498

Parson, Del, *310, 387*

Partridge, Edward, 103

Pascha, 546

Passover: symbolism of, 67–68, 547–48, 764; in life of Christ, 114, 260, 764–65; meaning of word, 546; feast, 547–50; foods of, 548; apostles prepare for, 548–50; at end of winter, 617–18; foreshadows Atonement, 764

Path, straight and narrow, 203–4, 221–22

Patience, 512

Paul: death of, 512, 634; and Sanhedrin, 626, 752; testifies in Temple, 741; as Pharisee, 748

Peace: comes only from Christ, 57–58; Christ's form of, 57–58, 167–68, 566–67; hymn about, 236–38

Peacemakers, 180

Pearl of Great Price, 3, 297

Pearls, 218–19, 297

Penny, 778

Pentateuch, 725

Pentecost, 590, 698–99, 765

Perdition, 584–85

Perea, 150–51, 374

Perfection: through Christ, 124; as commandment, 202; and salvation, 203–4; and unity, 587

Permanence, 569

Persecution, 174–75, 180–82

Persian Empire, 720

Pesach, 546

Peter: on foreordination of Christ, 18–19; meets Christ, 101, 148–49; name of, 101; as rock, 101–2, 329–30; called to catch men, 154–55; mother-in-law of, 232; walks on water, 311; bears testimony of Christ, 317, 328–30; receives keys, 331–32, 340–41; rebuked, 333–34, 621; and Transfiguration, 337, 767; catches fish with coin, 350–51, 774; delivered to Sanhedrin, 512, 738; finds Upper Room, 549; protests washing of feet, 559; conversion of, 589–90; tribulations of, 589–90; humility of, 590; denies Christ, 590–91, 617–22, *618;* cuts off servant's ear, 609–11; during Christ's final hours, 611; courage of, 619–20; rises above weaknesses, 621; crucifixion of, 634, 707; runs to empty tomb, 680–81; sees Christ while fishing, 704–5; tells Christ he loves him, 706; follows Christ, 707; heals lame man, 740; wealth of family of, 775

Peter's Denial, 618

Petersen, Mark E., 317

Phannias, 750

Pharisees: warning to, 80–83; as vipers, 80–83; pray to be seen, 205; rigidly observe law, 249, 747–48; ask about baptism, 250;

Subject Index

seek to destroy Christ, 272; ask
for sign, 275–78, 323–25; Christ
condemns hypocrisy of, 318–20,
324, 326, 423, 491, 747–48;
and bad leaven, 326; and parable
of lost sheep, 361; covet,
397–98; and adulterous woman,
411; interrogate healed man,
421–23; ask about divorce,
428–30; and raising of Lazarus,
456–57; at triumphal entry,
465–66; Christ in home of,
483–84; ask about paying
Caesar, 484–86; ask about
greatest commandment, 488–89;
put to silence, 489; parable
about, 503–4; insist on guard for
tomb, 674; origin of, 722, 725,
747–48; meaning of name, 725,
747; despise Herod, 729; more
popular than Sadducees, 752;
and scribes, 754–55
Phasael, 728
Philip, 102, 380, 562
Phylacteries, *492*, 493, *493*
Physician, 248–49
Pigs, 219. *See also* Swine
Pilgrimages, 764–67
Place of Slaughtering, *719*, 742
Plan of salvation, 19, 22–23
Plants, 320
Pompey, 727, 758
Pondering, 7–8, 579
Pontius Pilate: Christ's hearings
before, 486, 623–29, 631–32;
seeks scapegoat, 629; cruelty of,
629; releases Barabbas, 632–35;
wife of, 634; washes hands, 635,
637; guilt of, 641–42; as
governor, 731–32, 759, 760
Pool of Bethesda, 260–62, *261*, 716
Pool of Siloam, *418*, 419, 549, *716*,
766
Poor, 484
Poor in spirit, 175–76
Portico, *441*

Position seeking, 352–54
Possessions, 389–92
Posterity, 505, 583, 773
Pots, 109–10
Potter's field, 630
Pounds, 450–51, 667–68
Power: Holy Ghost gives, 143; of
Satan, 245–46; over elements,
234–38, 676; earthly, 510–11
Praetorium, 624
Praise, 472, 493, 496
Pratt, Orson, 20
Prayer: in morning, 151–52; Christ
offers, 151–53, 207–8, 338,
380, 454–55, 469–70; in private,
204–9; and fasting, 210, 349;
Christ teaches about, 220–21,
388–89, 403; answers to,
562–63, 580; for love, 572
Prefects, 759, 760
Pregnancy, 37
Premortality: Jesus Christ in, 11–23;
and Atonement, 19–21; sins
committed in, 20
Preparation: constant, 165; for
second coming, 506, 524; olive
oil symbolizes, 532; and parable
of ten virgins, 531–35; brings
peace, 567; temporal, 591
Pride: devoid of, 175–76; and
seeking high rank, 352–56; of
prodigal son's brother, 366–67;
and asking forgiveness, 369–70;
and hypocrisy, 491–92; Christ
teaches about, 751
Priest, 33–34. *See also* Chief priests;
High priest
Priestcrafts, 545, 634
Priesthood, 332, 556. *See also*
Aaronic Priesthood; Melchizedek
Priesthood
Priorities, 214–15, 234
Procrastination, 535
Procurators, 731, 759
Prodigal son, 360–61, 362–69
Prophecies: about Christ's mission,

848

44, 53–54, 62, 65, 116, 142, 232, 665, 690–93; of Simeon, 60, 733; about Christ coming out of Egypt, 64; about John the Baptist, 72, 258; about hypocrisy, 318; of Caiaphas, 456–57; about destruction of Jerusalem, 466–68, 513–14, 518, 643–45; about second coming, 507; about destruction of Temple, 508–9; Jews misunderstand, 510–11; about Judas, 551; about silver pieces, 630; of Christ's manner of death, 627; of gall, 645–46; of casting lots, 648; of Christ crying out during crucifixion, 656; of no bones broken, 664–65; of Christ's wounds, 665; disciples reminded of, 690–91; cease before Christ's birth, 720. See also Jesus Christ: prophesies of his death and resurrection

Prophet(s): not honored in own country, 139, 140–41, 301; false, 164, 222–24; destroying, 186; blood of, 500–502; receive revelation, 501; discern signs of times, 526; Christ expounds words of, 691–93

Prophetess, 60–61
Protection, 546
Psalms, 588, 692
Ptolemies, 721
Publicans: believe John the Baptist, 84, 478; Jews' opinion of, 248–49; Feast at home of, 248–49; Zacchaeus as, 449–50; parable about, 503–4; meaning of word, 750; corruption of, 751
Purple, 640–41
Purse, *163*

Queen of Sheba, 277–78
Quetzalcoatl, 121–22, *122*
Quintilian, 646

Quirinius, 50, 540
Qumran, *250,* 726–27

Rabbis: and scripture, 267; meaning of word, 726, 751; history of, 751–52; chosen from Pharisees and scribes, 754–55
Raca, 191
Rachel, 768, 770
Rain, 324–25
Ranking, 445–46
Rebirth, 118–19
Rebuke: and storm, 234–38; of Peter, 333–34, 621; of Pharisees, 318–20, 324, 326, 423, 491, 747–48; and Melchizedek Priesthood, 417–18; of disciples on road to Emmaus, 690
Redeem, 557
Reed, 258
Rejoice, 523
Remembering, 556–57
Repentance: importance of, 75–77, 138, 392, 606, 686; true, 81–82, 650; and perfection, 124; now is time for, 275, 651; meaning of, 364, 556; of wayward children, 368; for adultery, 412; procrastinating, 420; deathbed, 651; in spirit world, 651; Christ asks for, 712
Repetition, 8, 205, 389
Restoration, 298–99, 342, *343*
Resurrection: Christ was first, 120; as Christ's greatest miracle, 144; of God the Father, 265; modern revelation about, 266; prophecies about, 333, 349–50, 445; apostles do not understand, 346, 452; Sadducees ask about, 486–88; of others after Christ, 663–64; earthquake at Christ's, 675; and laws of physics, 675–76, 681; announced by angels, 677–80; apostles begin to comprehend, 680–81; as universal, 685; as triumph, 701

Subject Index

Retention, 569, 576
Revelation: testimony gained by, 41; Joseph receives, 44; Christ receives, 67; comes line upon line, 104; rock symbolizes, 329–30; promise of, 501; scribes discount, 726
Revillo, Carlos C., 308–9
Reznick, Leibel, 474
Richards, LeGrand, 240
Riches. *See* Wealth
Rich young ruler, 431–38
Right hand, 537, 711
Righteousness, 84, 178–79, 245
Rituals: Pharisees and, 725; of Passover, 764; of Feast of Tabernacles, 766; of circumcision, 773–74
Rivers, 74–75
Robe, 640–41
Robinson, Edward, 65, 558
Robinson, Stephen E., 135–36, 602–3
Rock: Peter as, 101–2, 329–30; Christ as, 226, 329–30; of offense, 258. *See also* Stone
Romans, 636
Roman soldiers. *See* Soldiers
Rome, 727, 758–63
Romney, Marion G., 165
Roosevelt, Theodore, 2
Rooster, 590–91
Rosh Hashanah, 766
Rufus, 760

Sabbath: healing on, 260–62, 270–73, 392–93, 405, 418–23, 483; and crucifixion, 664–65; Pharisees and, 725
Sackcloth, 379
Sacrament: cleanses, 77, 262; language of, 315; symbolism of, 547; purpose of, 548, 556, 606; Christ institutes, 553, 554–57; meaning of word, 555; future, 555
Sacrifice: animal, 59, 183, 633, 692, 739; required, 201, 335, 395, 469; importance of mercy over, 271; willingness to, 297, 432, 490, 575; brings love, 575; of Father, 658–62; of Abraham, 659–60; during Feast of Tabernacles, 766
Sadducees: warning to, 80–83; ask for sign, 323–25; and parable of lost sheep, 361; do not believe in resurrection, 486–88, 752; origin of, 722, 725, 752; Pharisees more popular than, 752
Sadness, 695
Sages, 720
Saints, 520. *See also* Latter-day Saints
Salome (daughter of Herodias), 302
Salome (mother of James and John): asks Christ about rank, 445; as Christ's aunt, 654–55; devotion of, 666; approaches tomb, 677
Salt, 182–84, *183*
Salvation, 166
Samaria, 129, *130, 185,* 374–75, *713*
Samaritan(s): and Jews, 129–30, 374–75, 383–86; gives thanks to Christ, 402–3; independence of, 727; origin of, 752
Sanctification, 585–86
Sanctuary, 743
Sanhedrin: groups in, 117; apostles delivered to, 164; as council, 191–92; assemble at night, 614; beginnings of, 721–22; meeting place of, 741, 753; division of, 752, 753; meaning of term, 753; authority of, 754
Satan: arrogance of, 18; rejects atonement, 21; tempts Christ, 90–98, 734–35; takes away, 96; uses serpent image, 121; selects followers, 154–55; tries to rise above God, 166; uses anger,

SUBJECT INDEX

190–91; and divorce, 199; minions of, 238–46; power of, 245–46; will be bound, 274; strengthening ourselves against, 275; meaning of word, 333; counterfeits of, 465; in latter days, 515; enters Judas, 545, 553; judged, 579; children of, 584; attacks Peter, 589–90; in Gethsemane, 603–4; attacks good people, 682–83
Saviors, 184. *See also* Jesus Christ
Scapegoat, 629, 633
Scott, Richard G., ix, 220
Scourging, 639
Scribes: rigidity of, 249; and adulterous woman, 411; jealousy of, 475; religious authority of, 720; early, 725–26; discount revelation, 726; and Pharisees, 754–55; responsible for Christ's death, 755
Scrip, 162, *163*
Scriptures: studying, 7–8; interpreting, 65; Satan quotes, 94–95; familiarity with, 97; testify of Christ, 264, 267; pondering, 281; changing of, 503; answers in, 563; teaching with, 695; understanding, 697–98
Sealing power, 331–32, 368–69, 371
Sea of Galilee: discourse at, 153–55; photos of, *173, 305, 709;* maps of, *230, 715;* Christ calms, 234–38; size and location of, 303, 309–10; Christ walks on, 309–11, *310;* fishing on, 774–77
Second Comforter, 564–65
Second coming: glory of, 336, 516, 518, 520–22; Christ testifies of, 345; Jews at, 505–6; signs of, 506–31; no one knows date of, 509–11, 525–26; watching for, 529; parable of virgins represents, 531–35; sacrament at, 555–56
Second Coming, The, 521
Second estate, 20
Secrets, 166, 345–46
Seder, 547
Sedition, 626, 633
Seeds, 285–88, 293–95
Self-righteousness, 503–4
Seely, David R., 554
Seleucids, 721
Senate, 731
Sepphoris, 729–30
Sepulchre, 668–74, 679
Sermon on the Mount, 170–227, *171*
Sermon on the Mount, 171
Serpent: picture of, *120;* Satan as, 121; Christ as, 121, 692; cunning of, 164; Jewish leaders as, 500. *See also* Viper
Servant(s): parable of, 372, 536; voice of, 379; power of, 379; unprofitable, 401–2; leaders as, 446, 558–60; in second coming, 529–30
Service: to two masters, 211; sins forgiven through, 247; Christ as example of selfless, 303; losing self in, 334–36, 539; without pride, 352–56; inconvenience of, 386; offering, 536, 538–39; silent, 539; brings love, 572
Seven, 32–33
Seventh seal, 530
Seventy, 369, 375–77, 379–80
Shammai, 428
Sheep: humility of, 164; as symbol, 268; lost, 359–61, 706–7; photos of, *360, 537, 538;* parable of, 401, 423–28, 536–39; other, 426–27; feeding, 706–7
Sheepfold, 268, *423*
Shekels, 545–46, 777
Shepherd(s): annunciation to, 55–58; Christ as, 268, 424–28;

851

Subject Index

parable about, 359–61, 423–28; in modern times, 424–25; photo of, *425*
Shunem, *230*
Sign on cross, 652–53, *653*
Signs: follow faith, 112, 275–76, 301, 348, 401, 710; Pharisees ask for, 275–78, 323–25; and parable of Lazarus, 401; of second coming, 506–31; command to study, 506–7; seeking, 515
Silver, 545–46, 629–30
Simeon, 59–60, 655, 733
Simile, 282
Simon (son of Mattathias; the Hasmonean or the Maccabee), 724, 728, 750, 777
Simons, list of, 159–60
Simon Peter. *See* Peter
Simon the Cyrenian, 643
Simon the Leper, 443, 542
Simon Zelotes, 731, 757
Sin(s): in premortality, 20; washing away, 76–77; casting away, 196–98; unpardonable, 274, 278, 584–85; avoiding, 360; of body and disposition, 366–67; calamities not always sign of, 392; all have committed, 411–12; brings bondage, 415; blindness not caused by, 419–20; breeds more sin, 517; Christ remits, 556, 602–603; Christ suffered for all, 593–94, 597–607; of omission, 637; Christ saves men from, 650. *See also* Forgiveness
Sincerity in prayer, 206
Sinners, 361–62, 543–44
Skinner, Andrew C.: experience of, with Marjorie Hinckley, x; experience of, with children in Nain, 231–32; witnesses Orthodox Jews, 262; experience of, with Mark E. Petersen, 317; experience of, with olive presses, 592–93
Skull, 645
Skull Hill, *647*
Smith, Gary, *339*
Smith, George Adam, 733
Smith, Joseph: on Jesus Christ as creator, 13; poetry of, 21–22; on Zacharias, 35; on spirit of Elias, 36; on prophets, 61, 502; on Jesus in Temple, 69; visited by John the Baptist, 74–75; on Holy Ghost as sign of dove, 88–89; hears voice of God the Father, 89; on obedience of Christ, 109; on casting out of evil spirit, 145–48, 244–45; on meekness, 178; on restored gospel, 187; on enemies, 202, 208; youth of, 251–52; on becoming weak while giving blessings, 253–54; on John the Baptist, 259; on Christ's power, 265; has vision of kingdoms, 265–66; on unpardonable sin, 274; on seeking signs, 276; on parables, 284, 288–89, 362; interpreted parables of Matthew 13, 284–85; on parable of sower, 286–87; on parable of wheat and tares, 292; on parable of mustard seed, 294–95; on parable of leaven, 295–96; on parable of treasure in field, 296; on parable of pearl, 297; on parable of net, 298; on latter-day scripture, 298; mission of, 298–99; necessity of, 330; on calling and election made sure, 341–42, 564–65; on First Vision, 344–45, 380; predicts own death, 349–50; on elevating thoughts, 352; on Pharisees and Sadducees, 361; on wayward children, 368; on sacrifice, 395, 433; on Melchizedek Priesthood,

Subject Index

190–91; and divorce, 199; minions of, 238–46; power of, 245–46; will be bound, 274; strengthening ourselves against, 275; meaning of word, 333; counterfeits of, 465; in latter days, 515; enters Judas, 545, 553; judged, 579; children of, 584; attacks Peter, 589–90; in Gethsemane, 603–4; attacks good people, 682–83
Saviors, 184. *See also* Jesus Christ
Scapegoat, 629, 633
Scott, Richard G., ix, 220
Scourging, 639
Scribes: rigidity of, 249; and adulterous woman, 411; jealousy of, 475; religious authority of, 720; early, 725–26; discount revelation, 726; and Pharisees, 754–55; responsible for Christ's death, 755
Scrip, 162, *163*
Scriptures: studying, 7–8; interpreting, 65; Satan quotes, 94–95; familiarity with, 97; testify of Christ, 264, 267; pondering, 281; changing of, 503; answers in, 563; teaching with, 695; understanding, 697–98
Sealing power, 331–32, 368–69, 371
Sea of Galilee: discourse at, 153–55; photos of, *173, 305, 709;* maps of, *230, 715;* Christ calms, 234–38; size and location of, 303, 309–10; Christ walks on, 309–11, *310;* fishing on, 774–77
Second Comforter, 564–65
Second coming: glory of, 336, 516, 518, 520–22; Christ testifies of, 345; Jews at, 505–6; signs of, 506–31; no one knows date of, 509–11, 525–26; watching for, 529; parable of virgins

represents, 531–35; sacrament at, 555–56
Second Coming, The, 521
Second estate, 20
Secrets, 166, 345–46
Seder, 547
Sedition, 626, 633
Seeds, 285–88, 293–95
Self-righteousness, 503–4
Seely, David R., 554
Seleucids, 721
Senate, 731
Sepphoris, 729–30
Sepulchre, 668–74, 679
Sermon on the Mount, 170–227, *171*
Sermon on the Mount, 171
Serpent: picture of, *120;* Satan as, 121; Christ as, 121, 692; cunning of, 164; Jewish leaders as, 500. *See also* Viper
Servant(s): parable of, 372, 536; voice of, 379; power of, 379; unprofitable, 401–2; leaders as, 446, 558–60; in second coming, 529–30
Service: to two masters, 211; sins forgiven through, 247; Christ as example of selfless, 303; losing self in, 334–36, 539; without pride, 352–56; inconvenience of, 386; offering, 536, 538–39; silent, 539; brings love, 572
Seven, 32–33
Seventh seal, 530
Seventy, 369, 375–77, 379–80
Shammai, 428
Sheep: humility of, 164; as symbol, 268; lost, 359–61, 706–7; photos of, *360, 537, 538;* parable of, 401, 423–28, 536–39; other, 426–27; feeding, 706–7
Sheepfold, 268, *423*
Shekels, 545–46, 777
Shepherd(s): annunciation to, 55–58; Christ as, 268, 424–28;

Subject Index

parable about, 359–61, 423–28; in modern times, 424–25; photo of, *425*
Shunem, *230*
Sign on cross, 652–53, *653*
Signs: follow faith, 112, 275–76, 301, 348, 401, 710; Pharisees ask for, 275–78, 323–25; and parable of Lazarus, 401; of second coming, 506–31; command to study, 506–7; seeking, 515
Silver, 545–46, 629–30
Simeon, 59–60, 655, 733
Simile, 282
Simon (son of Mattathias; the Hasmonean or the Maccabee), 724, 728, 750, 777
Simons, list of, 159–60
Simon Peter. *See* Peter
Simon the Cyrenian, 643
Simon the Leper, 443, 542
Simon Zelotes, 731, 757
Sin(s): in premortality, 20; washing away, 76–77; casting away, 196–98; unpardonable, 274, 278, 584–85; avoiding, 360; of body and disposition, 366–67; calamities not always sign of, 392; all have committed, 411–12; brings bondage, 415; blindness not caused by, 419–20; breeds more sin, 517; Christ remits, 556, 602–603; Christ suffered for all, 593–94, 597–607; of omission, 637; Christ saves men from, 650. *See also* Forgiveness
Sincerity in prayer, 206
Sinners, 361–62, 543–44
Skinner, Andrew C.: experience of, with Marjorie Hinckley, x; experience of, with children in Nain, 231–32; witnesses Orthodox Jews, 262; experience of, with Mark E. Petersen, 317;

experience of, with olive presses, 592–93
Skull, 645
Skull Hill, *647*
Smith, Gary, *339*
Smith, George Adam, 733
Smith, Joseph: on Jesus Christ as creator, 13; poetry of, 21–22; on Zacharias, 35; on spirit of Elias, 36; on prophets, 61, 502; on Jesus in Temple, 69; visited by John the Baptist, 74–75; on Holy Ghost as sign of dove, 88–89; hears voice of God the Father, 89; on obedience of Christ, 109; on casting out of evil spirit, 145–48, 244–45; on meekness, 178; on restored gospel, 187; on enemies, 202, 208; youth of, 251–52; on becoming weak while giving blessings, 253–54; on John the Baptist, 259; on Christ's power, 265; has vision of kingdoms, 265–66; on unpardonable sin, 274; on seeking signs, 276; on parables, 284, 288–89, 362; interpreted parables of Matthew 13, 284–85; on parable of sower, 286–87; on parable of wheat and tares, 292; on parable of mustard seed, 294–95; on parable of leaven, 295–96; on parable of treasure in field, 296; on parable of pearl, 297; on parable of net, 298; on latter-day scripture, 298; mission of, 298–99; necessity of, 330; on calling and election made sure, 341–42, 564–65; on First Vision, 344–45, 380; predicts own death, 349–50; on elevating thoughts, 352; on Pharisees and Sadducees, 361; on wayward children, 368; on sacrifice, 395, 433; on Melchizedek Priesthood,

SUBJECT INDEX

417–18; on abusing authority, 495; on corrupt men, 503; on second coming, 520; compares himself to Noah, 526; on parable of talents, 535–36; receives revelation in upper rooms, 549; on Judas, 551–52; on washing of feet, 560, 587; on different kingdoms, 562; on works of apostles, 563; on Second Comforter, 564–65; on Father and Son appearing, 565; on Christ's suffering, 600–601; on spirit world, 649–50; on evil spirits, 682; on fundamental principles of religion, 693. *See also* Joseph Smith–Matthew; Joseph Smith Translation

Smith, Joseph F.: on loving enemies, 181–82; on forgiveness, 201; on seeking signs, 276; on keys of kingdom, 332; on sealing, 486–87; on Judas, 584–85

Smith, Joseph Fielding: on Christ's premortal divinity, 12; on Christ as God of Old Testament, 18; on Gabriel, 37–38; on making "friends with the mammon," 212; on evil spirits, 241–42; on resisting temptation, 359; on right hand, 537; on resurrected beings, 675–76; on Peter, James, and John, 733–34

Snake, 80–81
Snow, Lorenzo, 66–67, 98, 526
Sodom, 378, 527–28
Solar system, 14
Soldiers: and John the Baptist, 84–85; arrest Christ, 608; mock Christ, 622, 631, 640–41, 648; duties of, in Jerusalem, 625–26; scourge Christ, 639; cast lots for Christ's clothes, 648; Christ asks forgiveness for, 648, 652; give Christ vinegar, 657–58; thrust spear in Christ's side, 665; bribed by officials, 687–88

Solomon's Pools, 742
Solomon's Porch, 738
Son of Man, 104, 235, 446–47
Sop, 550–51
Sorrow, 580, 597, 607
Sower, 285–88
Sparrow, 167
Spear, 665
Spices, 677
Spikenard, 458–59, 542
Spirit(s): born of, 118–19; God as, 135–36; unclean, 144–48; evil, 238–46, 275, 682. *See also* Holy Ghost
Spirit world, 400, 649–51
Staff, 162, *163*
Star(s), 14, 62, 63, 518–19
Stater, 777
Status, social, 472
Stephen: death of, 512, 627, 672; transfiguration of, 741
Stepparent, 58
Stewardship, 396–97, 451, 583
Stone: of stumbling, 258; Christ uses, to teach, 300; killing with, 442, 738, 741. *See also* Rock
Strait, 221
Stumbling block, 258
Submission, 166, 652
Sun, 518–19
Surprise, 516, 597–99
Survival, 513
Susa Gate, *716, 718,* 738–39
Susanna, 269
Swearing an oath, 199–200
Swine: casting pearls before, 218–19; photo of, *219;* devils enter, 238–46; map of incident with, *239;* in parable of prodigal son, 363
Swords, 591, 609–10
Sychar, *130, 713*
Sycamore tree, 449, *449*
Synagogue: service held in, 140;

Subject Index

ruins of, *312, 316, 377;* history of, 755–56

Tabernacles, 343–44, 373, 765–67
Tacitus, 634
Talent: parable of, 535–36; definition of, 777, 778, 779
Talmage, James E.: on creation, 13; on Christ's ancestry, 31, 32; on priorities, 234; on spiritual wealth, 396; on bitter cup, 599–600; on Satan in Gethsemane, 604; on Christ's pain on cross, 655; on women touching Christ's feet, 686–87; on birth date of Christ, 771
Talmud, 720, 726
Tares, 290–93, *291*
Taxation, 49–50, 750–51, 758
Taylor, John, 224, 394, 643
Teaching, 220–21, 695
Tempest, 234–38, 309
Temple: and understanding scriptures, 8; Luke's account of, 33–37; Jesus presented in, 59–61, 733, 740; frankincense used in, 63; young Christ visits, 67–69; pinnacle of, *93;* Jesus on pinnacle of, 94, 734–35; cleansing of, 114–16, *115,* 473–75, 739; Christ's body as, 116–17, 349, 614, 649; keeping sacred, 219, 345; Christ teaches in, 404, 407, 410–11, 441–43; latter day, 474–75; and hypocrisy, 497; greatness of, 507–9; destruction of, 508–9, 644; in second coming, 522; ordinances of, 559–60; unity in, 587; veil of, rent, 663, 676, 743; disciples go to, after ascension, 711; inner, *719;* Antiochus IV desecrates, 723–24; retaken from Syrian Greeks, 724; description of Herod's, 735–39; Solomon's, 736; courts of, 739–44; in Salt Lake City, 739; courts of, *739;* symbolism of platforms in, 744; and tax, 778
Temple Mount, 94, *718,* 733, 736–37
Temple police, 756
Temptation: of Christ, 90–91; resisting, 97, 195–96; God does not lead us to, 208; surrounded by, 227; of friends and family, 358–59; accompanies blessings, 656–57
Ten Boom, Corrie, 208–9
Tennyson, Alfred, Lord, 2
Testimony: gained by revelation, 41, 276; as spirit of prophecy, 61; bearing, 247; of Christ's divinity, 267, 422; staying true to, 396; having own, 515; and overcoming tribulation, 581
Tetrarchs, 760–62
Theophilus, 30
Thief, 524, 630
Thieves, on crosses, 647, 649–51
Thistles, *223*
Thomas: mistakenly called "doubter," 452; asks about the way, 562; absent, 695, 699–700; sees Christ while fishing, 704–5
Thorns, 222, *223,* 640, *640*
Tiberias, 311
Time, 778
Tithing, 522
Titles, 496
Tittle, 187
Tolstoy, Leo, 356
Tomb, 668–74, *678, 682*
Topical Guide, 5
Torah: as Law, 186; photo of, *187;* Hasidim support, 722; fighting over, 723; oral, 725; esteemed over revelation, 726; Zealots and, 756
Touch, 420
Traditions: and hypocrisy, 318–20, 393, 747–48; outside of Mosaic law, 318; surrounding death,

Subject Index

452, 498–99; esteemed over revelation, 726; of weddings, 769–70
Transfiguration, 78, 89, *343*, 337–47
Translation, 336, 339–40, 707–8
Treasure: on earth and in heaven, 210–15, 390, 432; in field, 296–97, 432; hearts set on, 390, 432, 436; word as, 522
Treasury, *719*, 740–41
Trees: represent people, 83–84, 223–24; sycamine, 348; sycomore, 449; palm, 462–64; as living entities, 476; olive, *592*; imagery of, 643–44. *See also* Fig tree
Trials: and long-suffering, 355; Christ overcomes, 581, 603; and blessings, 656–57
Tribes, 438
Tribulation. *See* Trials
Triclinium, 550, 764
Truth, 503, 628
Tuesday, 107–8
Twelve. *See* Apostles, twelve

Unbelief, 348
Unity. *See* Oneness
Universe, 14, 235, 684
Unleavened bread, 546–48, 694, 764
Unpardonable sin, 274, 278, 584–85
Upper Room, 548–50

Valerius, 760
Varus, 729
Veil: of Temple, rent, 663, 676, 743; worn by betrothed women, 770
Vessel, inner, 319, 499
Vine, 568–70
Vinegar, 657–58
Vineyard: parables of, 439–40, 478–81; photo of, *440*; tower in, *479*; branches cut off in, 568

Viper, *80*, 80–81. *See also* Serpent
Virgin(s), 38–39; parable of, 531–35
Virtue, 253–56
Visions. *See* Dreams

Wailing Wall, 736–37
War, 513–14, 516
Warning: Joseph receives, 63–64; to Pharisees and Sadducees, 80–83; of crafty men, 164; about future of apostles, 578; of destruction in Jerusalem, 643–45; on partition wall, 740
Washing: ritual, 318–20; of feet, 544, 557–60, 587
Washington, George, 1
Watches, 778
Water: pot, *110*; living, 132–35, 313, 406–7, 568, 766; walking on, 309–11, *310*; in Jerusalem, 418–19; at second coming, 518, 526
Watts, Isaac, 433
Weakness, 196, 198
Wealth: as master, 211, 438; seeking, 397; in parable, 398–401; giving up, 431–36; and pride, 436; as test, 437
Weather, 323–25
Webster, Daniel, 2
Wedding: Christ attends, 107; parable about, of king's son, 481–84; parable of ten virgins at, 531–35; traditions, 769–70
Weeping, 453–54
Weights and measures, 779
Welch, John W., 116
Wells, 132
Wells, Robert E., 43
Wheat: eating, 270; pictures of, *290, 291*; parable of, and tares, 290–93; must die to change, 469; measure of, 779
"When I Survey the Wondrous Cross," 433
Whip, 639

855

Subject Index

Whitney, Orson F., 330, 368, 595–97
Widow, 229–32, 490, 740
Wiesel, Elie, 167–68, 566
Wilderness, 303–5
Wind, 119
Wine: Christ creates, 107–12; in old bottles, 251; at Passover, 548, 764; Soldiers give Christ, 645–46
Winepress, 603
Winnowing, *85*
Wirthlin, Joseph B., 471
Wise men, 61–63
Witness(es): of Father, 262–68; receiving greater, 277–78, 378; three, 296; of Christ, 414; latter-day, 595–97, 703–4; false, 614; to first resurrections, 663–64; disciples as, 698
Wolves, 164, 222
Woman: meaning of word, 109; at well, 129–38, *133;* with issue of blood, 252–56; healing of modern-day, 254–56; adulterous, 409–13, 741; in travail, 524; anoints Christ, 542–44
Women: accompany Christ, 269, 654; at the cross, 666; visit tomb, 675–77; angels announce resurrection to, 677–80; meet resurrected Christ, 686–87; Court of, *718, 719,* 740
Woodruff, Wilford, 349–50, 407–8, 533
Word(s): Christ as, 12, 13; we are accountable for, 275; portion of, 281; as seed, 285–88; judge, 473; unchanging, 519–20; treasuring up, 522–23
Work(s): as fruits, 81–82, 83; on Sabbath, 270–71; as eternal, 381; during mortality, 420; in vineyard, 439
World(s): creation of, 13–14, 21–22; judgment of, 470; Christ overcomes, 581; living in, 585; Kingdom of God not of, 628; atonement happened on our, 684. *See also* Earth
Worldliness, 585
Worship, 211
Wrath of God, 594, 603
Wright, H. Curtis, 608, 616–17
Writing table, *47*
Wycliffe, John, 41

Yeshua, 43, 58–59
Yoke, 381, *381*
Yom Kippur, 749, 766
Young, Brigham, 233, 437, 656

Zacchaeus, 448–50
Zacharias: annunciation to, 33–37; psalm of, 47–48; angel appears to, 733
Zadokim, 722, 725, 750
Zealots, 730–31, 756–57
Zebulun, *143*
Zechariah, 460–61, 501–2, 720
Zeus, 724
Zion: Jerusalem as, 79; and pearl of great price, 297; in Missouri, 510; as pure in heart, 513; and oneness, 586
Zoramites, 504